THE
SURNAMES
OF
NORTH WEST IRELAND

Concise Histories of the
Major Surnames of
Gaelic and Planter Origin

By
Brian Mitchell

CLEARFIELD

Printed for Clearfield Company by
Genealogical Publishing Company
Baltimore, Maryland
2010

ISBN 978-0-8063-5457-6

The Surnames of North West Ireland:
Concise Histories of the Major Surnames
of Gaelic and Planter Origin

North West Ireland – bounded by the Atlantic Ocean to the north and west, by the Glens of Antrim to the east and by the lakes of Fermanagh to the south – refers to Counties Derry, Donegal and Tyrone. Not only was this region the last stronghold of powerful Gaelic tribes it also became home to many settlers from England and, in particular, Scotland during the Plantation of Ulster in the 17th century. North West Ireland was home to many emigrants, of Gaelic and Planter descent, who departed, in significant numbers during the 18th, 19th and 20th centuries, for new lives in North America, Great Britain and Australasia.

The dynamic history of North West Ireland can be seen in the richness and variety of its surnames. In this book I have attempted to compile concise but informative histories of those surnames which are most closely associated, through numerical strength or uniqueness, with North West Ireland.

I have compiled over 323 histories of surnames which either originated in or became established in North West Ireland. I estimate that these histories document the surname origins of over 80% of people with roots in North West Ireland. These surname histories are also relevant to those whose ancestors originated in the northern province of Ulster (i.e. Counties Antrim, Armagh, Down, Fermanagh, Londonderry and Tyrone in Northern Ireland and Counties Cavan, Donegal and Monaghan in the Republic of Ireland) as many of the surnames in this book will be found throughout this part of Ireland. However, as particular emphasis has been given to their origins and development in North West Ireland these surname histories will be less relevant to those whose ancestors originated outside Ulster (i.e. in the provinces of Connaught, Munster and Leinster). In Gaelic Ireland it was quite common for the same surname to arise inde-

iii

pendently in different parts of the country. Hence, Kelly, derived from both Gaelic *O Ceallaigh* and *Mac Ceallaigh*, came into being independently in at least seven widely separated places in Ireland, with the most powerful sept being the O'Kellys of Ui Maine who ruled over much of Galway and Roscommon. In Ulster, however, Kellys are more likely to be descended from a Kelly sept, based in south Derry, who claim descent from Colla, the 4th century King of Ulster.

Surnames, or inherited family names, are the building blocks of genealogy; without them, it would be impossible to trace our ancestors back through the generations. Although only detailed family research will confirm the actual origins of your ancestors, surnames can provide clues and insight into your family history.

Surnames of Gaelic Irish origin frequently confirm membership of a sept. It was assumed that members of an Irish sept had a common tribal ancestor. Thus, even today, Gaelic Irish surnames are still very dominant and numerous in the very localities where their names originated. For example, the surname McCloskey both originates and predominates today in the Dungiven area of County Derry, while 80% of McLaughlins in County Donegal are still concentrated in the Inishowen peninsula, the ancestral homeland of the McLaughlin sept.

From the 17th century Gaelic surnames were translated, and in many cases mistranslated, into English; others were changed to similar-sounding English names. Family names of Gaelic origin were often disguised in the 18th century by discarding the prefix Mac, Mc and O. In many cases, anglicisation will obscure the true origin of a surname; for example, Smith may be a British surname or an anglicisation of Gaelic McGowan. The McGowan sept of County Cavan, in Gaelic *Mac an Ghabhann*, meaning 'son of the smith', was one of the principal septs of the ancient kingdom of Breffny, which included County Cavan and west Leitrim. In its homeland, i.e. County Cavan, the great majority of McGowans anglicised their name to

Smith. Today Smith is among the five most numerous names in County Cavan.

This process of anglicisation, together with illiteracy, gave rise to numerous spelling variations of the same name. Surname variants are very much a part of Irish family history research. For example, variant spellings of Doherty include Daugherty, Docherty, Dockerty, Dogerty, Dogherty, Dorrety, Dougherty, O'Doagharty, O'Dochartaigh, O'Doghartye, O'Dogherty and O'Doherty.

You will find that in the context of Irish historical records there are many spelling variations of the same name. Thus, in conducting family history research you should be aware of the possibility of different spellings of the same surname. I have, therefore, tabulated the major surnames, with associated spelling variations, of North West Ireland.

Sources

A range of primary and secondary sources were used in compiling the surname histories in this book.

The following Surname reference books were consulted:
- *Irish Families* by Edward MacLysaght
  (Irish Academic Press, Dublin, 1985)
- *More Irish Families* by Edward MacLysaght
  (Irish Academic Press, Dublin, 1996)
- *The Surnames of Ireland* by Edward MacLysaght
  (Irish Academic Press, Dublin, 1978)
- *The book of Ulster Surnames* by Robert Bell
  (Blackstaff Press, Belfast, 1988)
- *The Surnames of Scotland* by George Black
  (The New York Public Library, New York, 1986)
- *A Dictionary of Surnames* by Patrick Hanks & Flavia Hodges
  (Oxford University Press, Oxford, 1990)
- *A Dictionary of British Surnames* by P H Reaney
  (Routledge & Kegan Paul, London, 1976)
- *The Concise Oxford Dictionary of English Place-names*
  by Eilert Ekwall (Oxford University Press, Oxford, 1990)

INTRODUCTION

The Annals of The Kingdom of Ireland by the Four Masters (a chronicle of Irish history from 'the earliest period to the year 1616') which is, in effect, a comprehensive history of conflict in Gaelic Ireland from the 6th century AD were examined for any references to the Gaelic names of North West Ireland. *The Annals,* for example, contain over three hundred references to the exploits of the O'Donnells of Donegal.

William R. Young's *Fighters of Derry Their Deeds and Descendants: Being a Chronicle of Events in Ireland during the Revolutionary Period 1688-1691* (published by Eyre and Spottiswoode, London, 1932) was examined for references to Planter families. This book names and, in many cases, provides biographical detail of 1660 "Defenders" and 352 officers of the "Jacobite Army" who fought in the Williamite War in Ireland between 1689 and 1691. For example, Young's book demonstrates that the Hamiltons, of Scottish Plantation stock, fought on both sides during the Siege of Derry of 1689. Forty-three Hamiltons were recorded as 'defenders' of Derry and six Hamiltons served with the 'Jacobite Army', including Claud Hamilton, Baron Strabane and 4th Earl of Abercorn.

For more precise information as to the frequency and location of surnames within North West Ireland I examined the following record sources:

- Census of Ireland of 1659 for Counties Derry, Donegal and Tyrone
- Hearth Money Roll of 1663 for County Derry
- Protestant Householders Lists of 1740 for County Derry
- 1831 census for County Derry
- Mid-19th century Griffith's Valuation for Counties Derry, Donegal and Tyrone

Brian Mitchell
15 September 2009

The Surnames of North West Ireland

Surname	Recorded Variants of Surname in North West Ireland
Anderson	
Andrews	Andrew
Armstrong	Armestronge, Armstronge
Barr	Bar, Bare, Barre
Beattie	Batey, Baitey, Battie, Beatty
Begley	Beagley, Beglay, Bigley
Black	Blacke
Bonner	Bannar, Bonar, Boner, Bonnor
Boyd	Boid, Boide, Boyde
Boyle	Aboyl, Boil, Boile, Boyl, O'Boyle
Bradley	Braddly, Bradely, Bradly, Braidly
Breslin	Bracelan, Braceland, Braislan, Bresland
Brolly	Brally, Brauley, Brawly, Browley
Brown	Broun, Browen, **Browne**
Buchanan	Bucanan, Bucannon, Buchannan, Buckanan
Burns	Burn, Burne, Burnes
Caldwell	Callwell, Calwill, Cauldwell, Cawlwell
Campbell	Cambel, Camble, Cammel, Campble
Canning	Caning, Canninge, Channing
Carlin	Carland, Carlane, Karland, Karlin
Cassidy	Casedy, Cashady, Casiday, Kasidy
Cavan	Caven, Keevan, Kieven
Clark	Clarke, Clarks, Clerk
Clyde	Clyd, Clide
Cochrane	Caughrin, Cocharan, Cocherin, Cockerane
Colhoun	Cahoon, Colhoune, Colquhoun, Culhoon
Convery	Confery, Confrey, Convry
Conway	Cannaway, Conaway
Corr	Coor, Cor, Curr
Cowan	Cowen, Cowin, Cown
Coyle	Coil, Coile, Coyl, Koyle
Craig	Crag, Crage, Crague, Craigge
Crawford	Crafford, Crauford, Crawfort
Crilly	Chrilly, Crealy, Creilly, Crely
Crossan	Chrosson, Macrossan, McAcrossan, **McCrossan**
Crumley	Crimley, Cromly, Crumaly, Crumbley
Crumlish	Cremlish, Crimblisk, Crimlesk, Cromlish
Cunningham	Conaghan, Conahan, Coonachan, Conyingham, Cunnenghan
Curran	Corin, Corran, Curin, Currens
Darcy	D'Arcy, Darcey, Dorcey
Deeney	Deeny, Diney, Dinny
Deery	Dairy, Deary, O'Derrie
Devenney	Davenny, Devany, Devenay, Devenny
Devine	Davine, Deven, Divin, Divine, O'Devine
Devlin	Develin, Devlahan, Divelin, O'Devlin

Diamond	Diemont, Dimond, Dymond, O'Diamond
Diver	Dever, Devir, Difer, Divver
Doherty	Daugherty, Docherty, Dogherty, Dougherty, O'Dogherty, **O'Doherty**
Donaghy	Donachie, Donaghey, Donahey, McDonagh
Donnell	Donal, Donnall
Donnelly	Donaly, Donely, Donily, Donly
Downey	Donay, Douny, Downie
Duddy	Duddie, Dudey, O'Duddy
Duffy	Duffie, Dufy, O'Duffy
Dunlop	Donlop, Dunlap, Dunlope
Edwards	Edward, Edwardes
Elliott	Eliot, Ellet, Elliotte
Farren	Fairan, Faran, Fearan, Fearn
Fee	Afee, Fea, Fey, Fie, **Foy**
Feeney	Feaney, Feeny, Fieney, Finnay
Ferguson	Fargison, Fergison, Forgison
Ferry	Fairy, Fearey, Ferrie
Fleming	Flemin, Fleminge, Flemming
Friel	Freal, Freel, Freil, Friele
Gallagher	Galachar, Galaher, Golligher, Kallagher
Gallen	Galen, Gallan, Gallin, Gallon
Gillanders	
Gillen	Gilan, Magillan, McGillan, McGillen
Gillespie	Galespie, Gillaspey, Killespie
Gilligan	Gillagan, Magilligan, **McGilligan**
Gilliland	Gililan, Gillylan, Gileyland
Gormley	Gormly, Gormally, Grimbly
Graham	Gragham, Grahames
Grant	
Hamill	Hamel, Hamil, Hammill
Hamilton	Hambelton
Hampson	**Hampsey,** Hampshey, Hansey, **Hanson,** Hansen
Hanna	Hana, Hanagh, Hannay
Hargan	Horgan, O'Hargan
Harkin	Harkan, Harkins, Horkan
Harrigan	Haragan, Haraghan, Herrigan
Harrison	Hareson, Herison
Harron	Haran, Harn, **Heron,** Herron
Hassan	Hasan, Hassin, Hasson
Heaney	Hainey, Haney, Heany, Heeney
Hegarty	Hagarty, Haggarty, Heagherty
Henderson	Hendarson, Hendyson, Hinderson
Henry	Henery, **McHenry,** McKendry
Houston	Hewston, Houghston, Howston, Huston
Hughes	Hews, Hues, Hughs, Huws
Hunter	
Hutchinson	Huchinson, Hutchison, McHucheon, McHutchinson
Inch	

Irvine	Ervin, Irving
Irwin	Erewin, Errwin, Erwing, Irwing
Jackson	Jacson
Jameson	Jamieson, Jamison, Jemmison, Jemyson
Johnson	Johnsonne, Jonson
Johnston	Johnstan, **Johnstone**, Johnstoun, Johnstown
Jones	Joans, Jonnes
Kelly	Kally, Keley, Kellie, Killy
Kennedy	Kenadey, Kenedie
Kerr	Carr, Keer, Keir, Ker
Killen	McKellin, **McKillen**, McKillion
Kitson	Kitchen, Kitsen, Kittson
Lafferty	**Laverty**, Lefarty, Leverty, Liferty
Little	Lettle, Lightle, Lytle, Lyttle
Logue	Loag, Loage, Louge, Loge
Long	Longe, Longs
Lyle	Liele, Lile, Lisle
Lynch	Linch, Linsh, Lynche
Magee	McGee, McGhee, Megee
Maguire	McGuire, McGwire, McQuire
Martin	Martan, Marten, Martine
Maxwell	Maxewell, Maxwill
Mellon	Mallon, Melan, Mellian
Millar	Miller, Myler
Milligan	Melican, Melligan, **Milliken**, **Mulligan**
Mitchell	Michel, Mitchael, Mitchil
Montgomery	Magomery, McGomery, Montgumery
Moore	Moor, Moores, Mor, More, Muir
Moran	Marrin, Meran, Mirran, **Morrin**
Morrison	Moressin, Morisan
Mulholland	Macholland, McElholland, Molhollan, Mulhalan
Mullen	Mollan, Mulean, Mulin, Mullan
Murphy	Murfey, Murphay
Murray	Morey, Morrie, Murey
McAfee	Macafee, Mahaffy, McFee, **Mehaffey**
McAllister	McCallister, McClestor, McLister
McAteer	Matier, McAtyre, McEteer, McTeer
McBrearty	McBrairty, McBreirty, McBrerty, McBrirty
McBride	
McCafferty	Macaferty, McAferty, McCaverty, McKafferty
McCaffrey	McAfrey, McCaffer, McCaffray, McCawfrey
McCallion	Macallion, McAlion, McCalan
McCann	Macann, McAnn, McConn
McCarron	Macarran, McArran, McCarin, McCarn
McCartney	Macartney, McArtney, McCarteny, McKartney
McCauley	Macally, McAula, McAuley, McAwley, McKally
McCausland	McAshlin, McAsland, McCaslan
McCawell	McCawl, McCawal

McCay	**Kee, Keys, Keyes, Mackay, Mackey, Mackie, McCoy, McCue, McHugh, McKay, McKee, McKie**
McClay	McAlea, McClea, McIlee
McClean	McLain, McLane, McLean
McClelland	McClalland, McClellan, McLelan, McLelland
McClintock	McClintoch, McClintough, McLintoc
McCloskey	Macloskie, McCluskey, McLoskey
McColgan	Macolgan, McColgin
McConnell	Maconnel, McCannel, McChonell, McConal
McConnellogue	Connelogue, Maconelogue, McConalaog, McConalogue,
McConomy	McConamay, McConaway, **McConway**
McCool	Macool, McCoal, McCole, McCuil
McCorkell	McCorkill, McKorkell
McCormick	Macormac, Macormic, McCarmick, McCormack
McCourt	Macourt, McCort, McQuort
McCracken	Macrackin, McCrakin, McKracken
McCrea	Macreagh, McCrae, McCray, McRae
McCready	Macready, McAready, McCreadie
McCullagh	Macullow, **McCulloch**, McCullogh, **McCullough**, McCully
McCurdy	Macurdy, McCurdie, McMurty, **McMurtry**
McCutcheon	McCustion, McCutchen, McHutcheon, McKitchen, McQuiston
McDaid	McDade, McDeade, McDavid, McDavit, **McDevitt**
McDermott	McDermaid, McDermont, McDeyermott, McDiarmed
McDonald	MacDonald, McDonal, **McDonnell**
McDowell	Madole, McAdool, McDoal, McDowal
McEldowney	McEldony, McIldowney
McElhinney	Mackelhiney, McAlenny, McElenay, McEleney, McIlany
McElhone	Mackeloan, McElhoan, McIlhone, McKilhone
McElwee	Macelwee, **McGilloway**, McIlwee, Mucklewee
McErlean	Macarlane, McErlain, McErlane, McNerland, **McNerlin**
McFadden	McFadin, McFayden, McPhadden
McFall	Macfaul, McFaul, McPaul, McPoyle, Mulfall
McFarland	McFarlane, McParland, McPartland, McPartlin
McFeely	McFealy, McFeeley, McFehilly, McPheely
McFetridge	McFatrick, McFatridge, McFetrich, McPhetridge
McGarrigle	McGaragal, McGaragill, McGargil, McGerigal
McGarvey	Magarvey, McGarvie, McGervay
McGeady	McGaddy, McGeddie
McGeehan	Mageeghan, McGehan, McGeechen
McGettigan	McEttigan, McGatigan, McGetikin
McGinley	Maginley, McGinely, McGinnelly
McGinty	Magintey, McGenity, McGinaty
McGirr	Magerr, McGure, **McKerr**
McGlinchey	Maglinchy, McGlenchy, McGlinchy, McGlinshey
McGoldrick	Magolrick, McGoalrick
McGonagle	Magonagal, McGongal, McGonigle, McGonnigal,
McGowan	Magown, McGaun, McGoan, McGoun
McGrath	Magra, Magrath, McGraw

McGregor	Magregor, McGreggar, McGriggor
McGuigan	McGoogan, McGookin, **McGuckian**, McGuicken, McQuiggan and McWiggin
McGuinness	Maginess, McGenis, McGinnes, McGinnis, McGuiness
McGurk	Magurk, McGirk, McQuirk
McIlfatrick	McElfatrick, McElphatrick, McIlfatridge
McIntyre	McAntire, McEntire, McIntire, McIntier
McIvor	McIver, **McKeever**
McKelvey	McKelvie, McKilvy
McKenna	McCanna, McKeney, McKenny
McKinley	Makinley, McInly, McKenley
McKinney	Makinny, McKinnie
McKnight	**McNatt, McNaught, McNaughton, McNutt**
McLaughlin	Maglaghlin, McGlaghlin, McLaughlan, McLoughlin
McMahon	McMaghan, McMahan, McMaughan
McManus	McMains, McManes, McMannus
McMenamin	McManamay, McManamon, **McMenamy**
McMillan	McMillen, **McMullan**, McMullen
McMonagle	McManagle, McMongle, McMonigal, McMonigle,
McNamee	McAnamee, McNamie, McNemee
McNeill	Macneil, McNeal, McNiel
McNelis	McAneilis, **Nelis**, Neilus
McNulty	McAnulty, McEnulty, McNultie
McPeake	McPake, McPike, Peake
McRory	Macrory, **McCrory, McGrory**
McShane	McShain, McShawn
McWilliams	
Neill	Neal, Neel, Niel
Nixon	Nickson
Noble	Nobell
O'Brien	O'Brian, O'Brine, O'Bryan
O'Connor	**Connor**
O'Donnell	O'Donel
O'Hagan	Hagan, Heggan
O'Hara	O'Harah, O'Harra
O'Kane	Cain, **Kane**, O'Cahan, O'Kain
O'Neill	O'Nail, O'Neal, O'Neel
O'Reilly	O'Realey, O'Rieley, **Reilly**, Riely,
Orr	Oar, Or
Parkhill	Parkehill, Parkill
Patterson	Paterson, Pattison
Patrick	Patricke
Patton	Patan, Petton, Peyton
Peoples	Peeples, Peopels
Porter	
Quigg	Quig
Quigley	Coghley
Quinn	Quin

Rankin	Ranckin, Ranking
Roberts	Robert
Robertson	
Robinson	Robison
Ross	
Scobie	Scoby
Scott	Scot
Scroggie	Scroggy
Scullion	Scullin, Skullian
Shiels	Sheils, **Shields**
Simmons	Simans, Simmonds
Simms	Sims
Simpson	Symson
Smith	Smithe, Smyth, Smythe
Starrett	Starritt, Sterrett, Sterritt
Stevenson	**Stephenson,** Steenson, Stinson
Sterling	Stirling
Stewart	Steward, **Stuart**
Sweeney	McSwine, McSweeney, Sweeny
Taggart	McEntaggart, **McTaggart**
Taylor	Tailor
Thompson	Thomson, Tomson
Tohill	Toaghill, Tochil, Toghil, Tohal
Tolan	Toland, Toolan
Toner	Tonnar
Walker	
Ward	McAward, McWard, Warde
Watson	
White	Whight, Whyte, Wight
Williams	William
Williamson	
Wilson	Willson
Young	Younge

Note:

These surnames and linked names are recorded in the database of church and civil registers, dating from 1642 to 1922, created by Derry Genealogy Centre which is now accessible online at http://derry.brsgenealogy.com.

Surname History produced for all surnames highlighted with bold type

North West Ireland
Surname Histories

North West Ireland
Surname Histories

ANDERSON

This name is among the forty most common names in Ulster where it is most numerous in Counties Antrim, Down and Derry. This name was brought to Ulster in large numbers by settlers from Scotland in the 17th century.

Anderson, derived from the personal name Andrew, simply means 'son of Andrew'. Anderson is among the ten most common names in Scotland and the majority of these are in the Lowlands of Scotland. Andrew was a popular choice as a child's name in medieval Scotland, and at a time when fixed surnames, based on a father's first name, were being established. The popularity of the name stems from the Scottish patron saint, Andrew. Andrew was the first of Jesus Christ's disciples, and according to legend the relics of Andrew were brought to Scotland in the 4th century by St Regulus. Thus the surname Anderson sprang up in many different locations, independently of each other, throughout Scotland.

In the Highlands of Scotland, McAndrew, in Gaelic *Mac Gille Andrais*, meaning 'son of the servant of St Andrew', was later anglicised to Anderson. There were Anderson septs attached to Clans Ross and Donald. The Andersons connected to Clan Donald were numerous in the west of Scotland, particularly on Islay and Kintyre.

It is believed that the Andersons of Rathlin Island and of north Antrim are descended from the Clan Donald sept. As followers of Clan Donald they came over to Ulster to settle on their lands. Clan Donald had acquired new territories in the north of Ireland ca.1400 when John Mor MacDonald had married Margery Bissett, an heiress in the Glens of Antrim. By the mid-16th century the MacDonalds, known as the MacDonnells of the Glens, had carved out an extensive territory in County Antrim at the expense of the MacQuillans.

The Andersons were also recorded as one of the lawless riding or reiving families of the Scottish Borders who raided, on horseback, and stole each other's cattle and possessions. These Andersons lived in Redesdale on the English side of the Border. When the power of the riding clans was broken by James I in the decade after 1603 many came to Ulster, particularly County Fermanagh, to escape persecution.

Movement of Scottish settlers to Ulster began in earnest from 1605 in a private enterprise colonisation of counties Antrim and Down when Sir Hugh Montgomery and Sir James Hamilton acquired title to large estates in north Down and Sir Randall MacDonnell, 1st Earl of Antrim, to large tracts of land in north Antrim. By the mid-19th century the Andersons were concentrated in the barony of Lower Antrim in County Antrim, and in the barony of Ards in County Down.

Further impetus came in 1609 when James I adopted the policy to encourage English and Scottish settlers to settle on the forfeited estates of the Gaelic chiefs in counties Armagh, Cavan, Donegal, Fermanagh, Londonderry (then known as Coleraine) and Tyrone.

During the famous 105 day Siege of Derry, from 18 April to 31 July 1689, John Anderson of County Leitrim, James Anderson of County Cavan and Quartermaster W Anderson were recorded as 'defenders' of the city.

3

ANDREWS

This surname is found almost exclusively in Ulster where it is most common in Counties Antrim and Down. This name was brought to Ulster by settlers from Scotland in the 17th century.

Andrews, derived from the personal name Andrew, simply means 'son of Andrew'. Andrew was a popular choice as a child's name in medieval Scotland, and at a time when fixed surnames, based on a father's first name, were being established. The popularity of the name stems from the Scottish patron saint, Andrew. Andrew was the first of Jesus Christ's disciples, and according to legend the relics of Andrew were brought to Scotland in the 4th century by St Regulus. Thus the surname Andrews sprang up in many different locations, independently of each other, throughout Scotland. Most of the Ulster Andrews are of this Lowland Scottish stock.

In the Highlands of Scotland, McAndrew, in Gaelic *Mac Gille Andrais*, meaning 'son of the servant of St Andrew', was later anglicised to Anderson and Andrews. There were Anderson septs attached to Clans Ross and Donald. The Andersons connected to Clan Donald were numerous in the west of Scotland, particularly on Islay and Kintyre.

The defeat of the old Gaelic order in the Nine Years War, 1594-1603 and the escape of the most prominent Gaelic Lords of Ulster in 'the Flight of the Earls' in 1607 from Lough Swilly, County Donegal were ultimately responsible for the settlement of many Scottish families in the northern counties of Ireland.

Movement of Scottish settlers to Ulster began in earnest from 1605 in a private enterprise colonisation of counties Antrim and Down when Sir Hugh Montgomery and Sir James Hamilton acquired title to large estates in north Down and Sir Randall MacDonnell, 1st Earl of Antrim, to large tracts of land in north Antrim.

In 1609 the Earl of Salisbury, Lord High Treasurer, suggested to James I a deliberate plantation of Scottish and English colonists on the forfeited estates of the Gaelic chiefs in counties Armagh, Cavan, Donegal, Fermanagh, Londonderry (then known as Coleraine) and Tyrone.

Settlers to Ulster came, by and large, in three waves: with the granting of the initial leases in the period 1605 to 1625; after 1652 and Cromwell's crushing of the Irish rebellion; and finally in the fifteen years after 1690 and the Glorious Revolution. It is estimated by 1715, when migration to Ulster had virtually stopped, the Scottish population of Ulster stood at 200,000.

Scottish families entering Ireland through the port of Londonderry settled in the Foyle Valley which includes much of the fertile lands of counties Donegal, Londonderry and Tyrone.

During the famous 105 day Siege of Derry, from 18 April to 31 July 1689, Reverend John Andrews of Kinohir, County Fermanagh was recorded as one of the 'defenders' of the city.

ARMSTRONG

Armstrong is among the fifty most common Ulster surnames, and the third most numerous in County Fermanagh. This well-known name from the Scottish Borders came with numerous Scottish immigrants at the time of the Plantation of Ulster in the 17th century. They settled mainly in Counties Fermanagh, Tyrone and Cavan.

The Armstrongs were a border clan who trace their descent from an armour bearer to a king of Scots who rescued his monarch in the midst of battle when his horse was killed under him. From this deed, the family came to be known as 'Armstrong' and received a gift of lands in Liddesdale in the western and middle Marches of England and Scotland. The valley of the Liddel Water which rises in Scotland, close to the border with England, flows south-westwards to the border and joins the Esk before entering the Solway Firth was home to the Armstrongs. The Armstrong clan became very powerful, and at the height of their power in the 16th century they could muster an army of 3,000 men.

From the 14th to the late-17th century, the border between England and Scotland – the Debatable Lands – was a turbulent place. The Border country was ravaged by the lawless Reiver families who stole each other's cattle and possessions. They raided in large numbers, on horseback, and they killed and kidnapped without remorse. This type of life resulted in the growth of large closely-knit family groups with intense clan loyalties and fierce feuds against others.

Prior to the Union of the Crowns of England and Scotland in 1603 the Scottish Border was divided into three districts; the east, west and middle Marches. Each March was presided over by a warden who settled disputes with the warden of the appropriate March in England, as border warfare was rife at this time with frequent cattle raids.

The Armstrongs were the most feared and most dangerous of the reiving families, and one of the most infamous was William Armstrong of Kinmont, known as Kinmont Willie. Unlike other reivers he liked to ride by day rather than under cover of darkness. The year 1593 saw his biggest raid. He rode with an army of 1,000 men who stole 2,000 cattle and £300 worth of goods. Three years later he was captured and imprisoned in Carlisle Castle, only to be set free by his sons in a daring rescue.

When the power of the riding clans was broken by James I in the decade after 1603 many came to Ulster to escape persecution. This flight to Ulster also suited the needs of the king. James I, from 1610, was determined to implement a deliberate plantation of Scottish and English colonists on the forfeited estates of the Gaelic chiefs in Counties Armagh, Cavan, Donegal, Fermanagh, Londonderry (then known as Coleraine) and Tyrone. The death of the 10th chief of clan Armstrong in 1610 also encouraged clan members to scatter.

The Armstrongs settled particularly in County Fermanagh. These Border families were well suited to life in the frontier of the Plantation of Ulster. They were a resilient people who stayed in County Fermanagh throughout the upheavals of the 17th century. Scottish settlers were hardier than their English counterparts, and the Borderers were even better adapted again to life on a new, insecure frontier.

5

BARR

This name, most common in Counties Down, Antrim, Derry and Donegal, is of predominantly Scottish origin. This name was brought to Ulster in large numbers by settlers from Scotland in the 17th century.

In England the surname Barr may have a number of origins: as a name for someone who lived by a gateway or barrier; as an occupational name for a maker of bars; as a nickname for a tall, thin man; and as a place name.

In Scotland this surname, variously recorded as Bar, Barr and Barre, is derived from the placenames of Barr which are located in Ayrshire and Renfrewshire. Both placenames are derived from Gaelic *barr*, meaning 'top' or 'height'. The first recorded person of the name was Atkyn de Barr who was bailie of Ayr around 1340. In the 15th and 16th centuries references to the name can be found in both Edinburgh and Glasgow. Indeed the surname is most common today in the district around Glasgow.

Movement of Scottish settlers to Ulster began in earnest from 1605 in a private enterprise colonisation of counties Antrim and Down when Sir Hugh Montgomery and Sir James Hamilton acquired title to large estates in north Down and Sir Randall MacDonnell, 1st Earl of Antrim, to large tracts of land in north Antrim. Further impetus came in 1609 when James I adopted the policy to encourage English and Scottish settlers to settle on the forfeited estates of the Gaelic chiefs in counties Armagh, Cavan, Donegal, Fermanagh, Londonderry (then known as Coleraine) and Tyrone.

Settlers came to Ulster, by and large, in three waves: with the granting of the initial leases in the period 1605 to 1625; after 1652 and Cromwell's crushing of the Irish rebellion; and finally in the fifteen years after 1690 and the Glorious Revolution. Scottish families entering Ireland through the port of Londonderry settled in the Foyle Valley which includes much of the fertile lands of counties Donegal, Londonderry and Tyrone. The lands along the Firth of Clyde in the county of Ayrshire and the Clyde Valley were home to many of these Scottish settlers. It is estimated by 1715, when migration to Ulster had virtually stopped, the Scottish population of Ulster stood at 200,000.

English settlers, mostly drawn from the northern counties of Cheshire, Cumberland, Lancashire, Northumberland, Yorkshire and Westmorland tended to favour settlement along the Lagan Valley, in the east of the Province, on lands straddling the borders of Counties Armagh, Antrim and Down.

During the famous 105 day Siege of Derry, from 18 April to 31 July 1689, Tom Barr's exploits in the garrison's first sortie against the Jacobite besiegers on 21 April are remembered in verse:

> Tom Barr, a trooper, with one mighty blow
> Cut off the head of an opposing foe.

In County Cork, Barr, in Gaelic *O Baire*, can be of Irish origin. This rare west Cork name was also anglicised as Barry.

BEATTIE

This name is common throughout Ulster, especially in County Fermanagh where it is the fifteenth most numerous name. The Beattie spelling is most common in Counties Antrim and Down and the Beatty spelling in Counties Armagh and Tyrone. This name was brought to Ulster in large numbers by settlers from Scotland in the 17th century.

Beattie, derived from the personal name Bartholomew, simply means 'son of Baty'. The Beatties were one of the riding or reiving clans of the Scottish Borders. Beatties were numerous in Upper Eskdale, and in Ewesdale and Wauchopedale. The name was recorded at Berwick-on-Tweed as early as 1334. The name also spread further north as in 1473 a John Betty was recorded as burgess of Aberdeen, and a James Batty as an officer in Inverness in 1574.

From the 14th to the late-17th century, the border between England and Scotland – the Debatable Lands – was a turbulent place. The Border country was ravaged by the lawless Reiver families who stole each other's cattle and possessions. They raided in large numbers, on horseback, and they killed and kidnapped without remorse. This type of life resulted in the growth of large closely-knit family groups, such as the Beatties, with intense clan loyalties and fierce feuds against others.

Prior to the Union of the Crowns of England and Scotland in 1603 the Scottish Border was divided into three districts; the east, west and middle Marches. Each March was presided over by a warden who settled disputes with the warden of the appropriate March in England, as border warfare was rife at this time with frequent cattle raids.

Pacification of the riding families began in earnest from 1603 with the Union of the Crowns of England and Scotland. The Beatties suffered as King James I set about pacifying the borders in a ruthless campaign which included executions and banishment. In 1603 thirty-two Elliotts, Armstrongs, Johnstons, Beatties and others were hanged, fifteen were banished and one hundred and forty outlawed.

When the power of the riding clans was broken by James I in the decade after 1603 many came to Ulster to escape persecution. This flight to Ulster also suited the needs of the king. James I, from 1610, was determined to implement a deliberate plantation of Scottish and English colonists on the forfeited estates of the Gaelic chiefs in Counties Armagh, Cavan, Donegal, Fermanagh, Londonderry (then known as Coleraine) and Tyrone.

The Beatties settled initially in County Fermanagh. The families from the Scottish Borders were well suited to life in the frontier of the Plantation of Ulster. They were a resilient people who stayed in Fermanagh throughout the upheavals of the 17th century. Scottish settlers were hardier than their English counterparts, and the Borderers were even better adapted again to life on a new, insecure frontier. During the famous 105 day Siege of Derry, from 18 April to 31 July 1689, Captain William Beatty of Moneymore, County Derry and Claud Beatty were recorded as 'defenders' of the city.

Confusion can be caused by the fact that, in some instances, the County Fermanagh sept name of McCaffrey was anglicised to Beatty.

BEGLEY

This name is most numerous in Ireland in Counties Donegal and Kerry.

Ireland was one of the first countries to adopt a system of hereditary surnames which developed from a more ancient system of clan or sept names. From the 11th century each family began to adopt its own distinctive family name generally derived from the first name of an ancestor who lived in or about the 10th century. The surname was formed by prefixing either Mac (son of) or O (grandson or descendant of) to the ancestor's name. Surnames in Ireland, therefore, tended to identify membership of a sept.

Begley is derived from Gaelic *O Beaglaoich*, the root words being *beag*, meaning 'little' and *laoch* meaning 'hero'. This sept originated in the barony of Kilmacrenan in County Donegal. The parish name of Tullaghobegley, a stretch of rugged land between the Rosses and Bloody Foreland in west Donegal, commemorates the former association of this sept with the area.

By the time of the mid-19th century Griffith's Valuation, however, there were no Begley households recorded in the parish of Tullaghobegley. Twenty-three Begley households were recorded in County Donegal in this survey, with the biggest concentration in the Fanad Peninsula in Clondavaddog Parish which contained 8 Begley households.

The name is now common in County Kerry as a branch of the sept migrated there as galloglasses, i.e. mercenary soldiers, in the fifteenth century. Derived from Gaelic *galloglach*, galloglass refers to a paid soldier fighting on behalf of an Irish chief. The first of the O'Begleys went to County Cork with the McSweeneys as galloglasses at the end of the 15th century. They subsequently settled in County Kerry and from there spread into County Limerick.

The Annals of The Kingdom of Ireland by the Four Masters (a chronicle of Irish history from 'the earliest period to the year 1616') provide detailed and graphic descriptions of galloglasses. In one account dated 1557 the *Annals* describe the galloglass in the camp of the O'Neills who were on a raiding expedition into O'Donnell territory in Donegal. It states that 'sixty grim and redoubtable gallowglasses, with sharp, keen axes, terrible and ready for action, and sixty stern and terrific Scots, with massive, broad, and heavy-striking swords in their hands, ready to strike and parry, were watching and guarding the son of O'Neill.'

Begley is a common name in Derry city today. This name illustrates the very close links, both historic and economic, between the city of Derry and County Donegal. As Derry developed an industrial base in the 19th century in shirt making, shipbuilding and distilling it attracted much of its workforce from Donegal. In the 90-year period 1821 to 1911 the population of the city quadrupled to 40,780. In this period Derry stamped her dominance over local rivals and emerged as an important urban centre within Ireland.

For no apparent reason Begley was changed, in some instances, to Morris around Enniskillen, County Fermanagh.

BLACK

This common Ulster name is most numerous in Counties Antrim, Armagh, Tyrone and Down. The majority of Blacks in Ulster are of Scottish origin.

Black is a common name in England. In England and the Lowlands of Scotland the surname Black may have derived either as a nickname, from Middle English *blak*, meaning 'black' or as a nickname, from Old English *blac,* meaning 'fair'.

Black is one of the fifty most common names in Scotland. In the Lowlands of Scotland the surname was common in St Andrews and in Prestwick in the 15th and 16th centuries, and very common in Edinburgh in the 17th century. In the Highlands of Scotland the surname Black was connected with three clans – MacGregor, Lamont and Maclean of Duart. Black was one of the names adopted by both the McGregors and Lamonts, in the early 17th century, when they were outlawed and their names were proscribed.

Black was a particularly popular name with the Lamonts. It is claimed that a branch of Clan Lamont, under a leader called the Black Priest, adopted the surname Black. It is also claimed that the McIldowies, in Gaelic *Mac Gille Dhuibh*, meaning 'son of the black lad', who were a sept of Clan Lamont, further anglicised their name to Black. In Argyllshire, the surname Huie, also derived from *Mac Gille Dhuibh*, was further anglicised as Black.

The Lamonts were at one time very powerful in south Argyllshire. After a bitter feud with the Campbells, towards the end of the 16th century, the Lamonts lost most of their lands, scattered and adopted various aliases. Owing to the nature of the Scottish clan system once the power and influence of the chief had been weakened and the bond of tribal loyalty broken the clan tended to scatter. It is believed that many of the Blacks who settled in north Antrim were descendants of Clan Lamont.

Loss of power also encouraged clan members to hire themselves out as galloglasses, i.e. mercenary soldiers, to Irish chiefs. Followers of Clan Maclean of Duart were hired by both the O'Donnells and the O'Neills in the 16th century. It is quite possible that Blacks were among these galloglasses.

Movement of Scottish settlers to Ulster began in earnest from 1605 in a private enterprise colonisation of counties Antrim and Down when Sir Hugh Montgomery and Sir James Hamilton acquired title to large estates in north Down and Sir Randall MacDonnell, 1st Earl of Antrim, to large tracts of land in north Antrim. Further impetus came in 1609 when James I adopted the policy to encourage English and Scottish settlers to settle on the forfeited estates of the Gaelic chiefs in counties Armagh, Cavan, Donegal, Fermanagh, Londonderry and Tyrone.

During the famous 105 day Siege of Derry, from 18 April to 31 July 1689, Reverend Bartholomew Black, Curate of Aghaloo, County Tyrone and John Black of Belfast, County Antrim were recorded as 'defenders' of the city.

In some cases Irish surnames such as Duff and Kilduff that contain *dubh,* meaning 'black', were anglicised as Black.

9

BONNER

The great majority of Ulster Bonners today are still to be found in their homeland in County Donegal and, in particular, in the vicinity of Ballybofey and Stranorlar.

Ireland was one of the first countries to adopt a system of hereditary surnames which developed from a more ancient system of clan or sept names. From the 11th century each family began to adopt its own distinctive family name generally derived from the first name of an ancestor who lived in or about the 10th century. The surname was formed by prefixing either Mac (son of) or O (grandson or descendant of) to the ancestor's name. Surnames in Ireland, therefore, tended to identify membership of a sept.

Bonner is ultimately derived from Gaelic *O Cnaimhsighe*, the root word possibly being *Cnaimhseach*, a woman's personal name which may have meant 'midwife'. In this case Bonner is one of the few Irish surnames derived from the name of a female ancestor as opposed to a male one.

Bonner also has the further distinction of being one of Ireland's oldest surnames, first recorded in 1095. *The Annals of The Kingdom of Ireland by the Four Masters* record, in 1095, that 'there was a great pestilence over all Europe' which killed one quarter of the population of Ireland including one Scannlan Ua Cnaimhsighe who was confessor of Lismore.

Owing to the mistaken belief, by English administrators in the 17th century, that *O Cnaimhsighe* was derived from the root word *cnamh*, which means 'bone', the name was anglicised as Bonar or Boner. The name was also anglicised as Kneafsey and Crampsy. In the census of 1659 it was a common name in Inishowen, County Donegal where it was recorded as O'Knawsie.

By the 19th century Bonar or Boner were, by far, the most common spellings of this County Donegal sept name. The 1864 civil birth registrations for Ireland record: 43 registrations for Bonar or Boner, nearly all in County Donegal; 4 for Cramsey, all in Donegal; and 5 for Kneafsey, all in County Mayo.

Owing to the strong links between the city of Derry and County Donegal the surname Bonner is well represented in the city today. As Derry developed an industrial base in the 19th century in shirt making, shipbuilding and distilling it attracted much of its workforce from Donegal.

In England and Scotland the surname Bonar is derived from Old French *bonnaire*, meaning 'gentle' or 'courteous'. The name first appears in Scotland in 1281 when Thomas Boner witnessed a charter in Aberdeen. In George F Black's *The Surnames of Scotland* it is stated that Bonar was, at one time, such a numerous name in Scotland that thirty-seven different lines of Bonars could be identified, 'each styled by their territorial designation'.

It is quite likely, therefore, that some Bonners in Ulster will be descendants of 17th century Scottish settlers. It is estimated by 1715, when migration to Ulster had virtually stopped, the Scottish population of Ulster stood at 200,000.

BOYD

This Scottish surname, introduced by settlers in the 17th century, is among the thirty most common names in Ulster and among the fifteen most common in both Counties Antrim and Down. It is also popular in County Derry.

This surname is derived either from the Isle of Bute in Scotland or from the Gaelic *buidhe*, meaning 'yellow'. The Gaelic name for Bute is *Bod*. It is also claimed that Boyd is a sept name of the royal line of Clan Stewart, tracing their descent from a Norman family who founded the Stewart dynasty in Scotland. The family takes their surname from one Robert Buidhe, meaning 'Robert with the yellow hair'.

The Boyd family was well established in Ayrshire 'in the regality of Largs' before the reign of Robert the Bruce in the early 14th century. Robert Boyd was granted these lands after distinguishing himself at the Battle of Largs when Alexander III, King of Scotland, defeated the Norsemen in 1263. The Lordship of Boyd was created in 1454 and William, 10th Lord Boyd, was created Earl of Kilmarnock in 1661. The Boyds supported Bonnie Prince Charlie in the 1745 uprising.

Movement of Scottish settlers to Ulster began in earnest from 1605 in a private enterprise colonisation of counties Antrim and Down when Sir Hugh Montgomery and Sir James Hamilton acquired title to large estates in north Down and Sir Randall MacDonnell, 1st Earl of Antrim, to large tracts of land in north Antrim. A branch of the Boyd family was related to the Montgomerys and came to the Ards peninsula, County Down at this time. The name Boyd is still numerous there. The main County Antrim centre of the name was in the Ballycastle area.

Further impetus came in 1609 when James I adopted the policy to encourage Scottish settlers to settle on the forfeited estates of the Gaelic chiefs in counties Armagh, Cavan, Donegal, Fermanagh, Londonderry (then known as Coleraine) and Tyrone.
Settlers came to Ulster, by and large, in three waves: with the granting of the initial leases in the period 1605 to 1625; after 1652 and Cromwell's crushing of the Irish rebellion; and finally in the fifteen years after 1690 and the Glorious Revolution.

Scottish families entering Ireland through the port of Londonderry settled in the Foyle Valley which includes much of the fertile lands of counties Donegal, Londonderry and Tyrone. The lands along the Firth of Clyde in the county of Ayrshire were home to many of these Scottish settlers. It is estimated by 1715, when migration to Ulster had virtually stopped, the Scottish population of Ulster stood at 200,000.

In the initial granting of leases in Ulster in 1610/1611, Sir Thomas Boyd of Ayrshire, one of the principal Scottish planters (sixty-one in total), was granted an estate of 1,500 acres in the barony of Strabane, County Tyrone. Many of the settlers farming on this estate in Tyrone were also called Boyd as it was a feature of 17th century Scotland for tenants to take on their landlord's surname. The Boyd family also settled, at this time, in the city of Derry and at Ballymacool, near Letterkenny, County Donegal.

Seven Boyds, including Rev. Thomas Boyd, minister of Aghadowey Presbyterian Church, were recorded as 'defenders' of Derry during the famous Siege of 1689.

BOYLE

Boyle is among the fifty most common names in Ireland, among the fifteen most popular in Ulster and is the third most popular in County Donegal. Over half of all the Ulster Boyles live in County Donegal. The name is also common in Counties Antrim, Armagh and Tyrone.

Ireland was one of the first countries to adopt a system of hereditary surnames which developed from a more ancient system of clan or sept names. The surname was formed by prefixing either Mac (son of) or O (grandson or descendant of) to the ancestor's name. Boyle is derived from Gaelic *O Baoighill*, the root word *geall,* meaning 'pledge'. It is only in recent times that the discarded prefix O has been widely restored.

The O'Boyle sept shared with the O'Donnells and O'Dohertys the leadership of northwest Ireland. According to O'Dugan's topographical poem the O'Boyles of Donegal were chiefs of Cloch Chinnfhaolaidh, now Cloghineely, in the northwest barony of Kilmacrenan; of Tir Ainmire, now the barony of Boylagh or 'O'Boyle's Country'; and of Tir Boghaine, now Banagh barony.

In 1343 Aindiles O'Boyle was styled chief of Tir Ainmirech. *Tir Ainmirech,* i.e. the territory of Ainmire, was the ancient name for the present barony of Boylagh in the west of county Donegal. This was not O'Boyle's original territory as prior to the 14th century and the arrival of the MacSweeny galloglasses, i.e. mercenary soldiers, from Scotland, at the invitation of the O'Donnells, he was chief of Tri Tuatha in the northwest barony of Kilmacrenan.

In 1247 the O'Boyles were styled 'the head Chieftain of the Three Tuathas'. These were three territories, one of which was Cloghineely, in the northwest of county Donegal. They passed afterwards into the possession of a branch of the MacSweenys.

In Cork and Waterford a powerful family of Boyles were of English origin, descended from Richard Boyle, who arrived in Ireland in 1588, and acquired extensive estates in County Waterford. By the time of his death in 1643 Richard Boyle was the Earl of Cork.

In Ulster, especially outside of County Donegal, many Boyles will be descended from 17th century Scottish settlers. An Anglo-Norman family of de Boyville, derived from Beauville near Caen in France, settled in Scotland from the 12th century and became very powerful in Galloway and in Ayrshire. The Boyle family have held lands at Kelburn in Ayrshire since the 13th century, and the family seat is still Kelburn Castle at Fairlie, Ayrshire.

The lands along the Firth of Clyde in the county of Ayrshire were home to many of the Scottish settlers who were initially encouraged by James I, from 1610, to settle on the forfeited estates of the Gaelic chiefs in counties Armagh, Cavan, Donegal, Fermanagh, Londonderry (then known as Coleraine) and Tyrone. It is estimated by 1715, when migration to Ulster had virtually stopped, the Scottish population of Ulster stood at 200,000. The Boyles of Limavady, County Derry, for instance, settled in 1660.

BRADLEY

This name is most common in Ulster and, in particular, in County Derry, where it is the fourth most numerous, and in Counties Antrim, Donegal and Tyrone. The name is most concentrated in central and south Derry.

Ireland was one of the first countries to adopt a system of hereditary surnames which developed from a more ancient system of clan or sept names. From the 11th century each family began to adopt its own distinctive family name generally derived from the first name of an ancestor who lived in or about the 10th century. The surname was formed by prefixing either Mac (son of) or O (grandson or descendant of) to the ancestor's name. Surnames in Ireland, therefore, tended to identify membership of a sept.

Bradley and O'Brollaghan, an earlier anglicized form of the name, are derived from Gaelic *O Brollachain*, meaning 'descendant of Brollach'. Brollach is an old personal name, the root word being *brollach*, meaning 'breast'. The territory of this sept was the area which straddles the borders of Counties Derry, Donegal and Tyrone.

In the 12th century, in particular, *The Annals of The Kingdom of Ireland by the Four Masters* makes many references to the O'Brollaghans.

In 1158 Flahertagh O'Brollaghan was appointed as 'successor of Colum Cille', i.e. Abbot of all monasteries under the rule of Colum Cille, which included Derry and Iona in Scotland. He began preparations for the erection of a new cathedral in Derry worthy of its distinguished founder, St Colum Cille (also known as Columba). In 1164, in the space of 40 days, Templemore or 'the great church of Doire' was erected near the original *Dubh Regles* or Black Abbey church. From this cathedral, the parish of Templemore, which contains the city of Derry, derived its name.

Today O'Brollaghan has been entirely anglicised to Bradley. In some instances, notably in County Derry, the earlier version of O'Brallaghan survived into the 17th century. For example the Hearth Money Rolls of 1663 for Maghera Parish, County Derry records one Edmond O Brallaghan.

A branch of the O'Brollaghans was established, in the 12th century, in the Highlands of Scotland through their connections with the monastery on Iona. Donal O'Brollaghan, prior of Derry, who died in 1202, was Abbot of Iona in the 12th century. Here too the name was anglicised to Bradley.

Another branch of the O'Brollaghans early migrated to County Cork and the numerous Bradleys of that area descend from them.

Bradley is also an English name derived from many places of that name in northern England. Here Bradley is derived from the Old English *bradleah*, meaning 'broad wood or clearing'. Few Bradleys in Ulster, however, are of English origin.

13

BRESLIN

Breslin, originally O'Breslin, is primarily a Donegal name. The name is still most common in its homeland around Inniskeel on the Fanad peninsula, which extends from Lough Swilly to Mulroy Bay, in north Donegal.

The O'Breslin sept trace their lineage to Enda, the youngest son of the 5th century High King of Ireland, Niall of the Nine Hostages, who ruled from the Hill of Tara, County Meath. Enda and his brothers Eogan, Conall *Gulban* and Cairbre conquered northwest Ireland, ca.425 AD, capturing the great hill-fort of Grianan of Ailech in County Donegal which commanded the entrance to Inishowen between Lough Swilly and Lough Foyle.

Enda established his own kingdom in Donegal called after him Tir-Enda, i.e. the 'Land of Enda', which lay to the south of Inishowen between the present-day towns of Lifford and Letterkenny.

Ireland was one of the first countries to adopt a system of hereditary surnames which developed from a more ancient system of clan or sept names. From the 11th century each family began to adopt its own distinctive family name generally derived from the first name of an ancestor who lived in or about the 10th century. The surname was formed by prefixing either Mac (son of) or O (grandson or descendant of) to the ancestor's name. Surnames in Ireland, therefore, tended to identify membership of a sept.

Breslin, in Gaelic *O Breaslain*, is possibly derived from *bres*, meaning 'strife'. By the end of the 12th century the O'Breslin sept were rulers of Fanad, County Donegal. In 1186 *The Annals of The Kingdom of Ireland by the Four Masters* record that 'Con O'Breslen, Chief of Fanad, the lamp of the hospitality and valour of the north of Ireland, was slain by the son of Mac Loughlin and a party of the Kinel-Owen; in consequence of which Inishowen was unjustly ravaged.'

In 1261 'sixteen of the most distinguished of the clergy of Kinel-Connell were killed at Derry by Conor O'Neill and the Kinel-Owen, together with Conor O'Freel. Conor O'Neill was slain immediately afterwards by Donn O'Breslen, Chief of Fanad, through the miracles of God and St Columbkille.' Columbkille (also known as Columba) was the founder of the monastery at Derry in 546AD.

The power of the O'Breslins as chiefs of Fanad, which up to the 14th century merited frequent mention in *the Annals*, was broken by the McSweenys in the late 13th century. Although no longer rulers of their homeland their name remained prominent as O'Breslin was recorded as a 'principal name' in Fanad in the census of 1659.

With their power broken the leading families of the O'Breslins of Fanad now migrated to County Fermanagh where they distinguished themselves as brehons, i.e. judges in the Gaelic legal system, to the Maguires. They also became *erenaghs*, i.e. hereditary stewards, of the church lands of Derryvullan parish in Fermanagh.

In County Donegal some families of Breslin have changed their name to Brice or Bryce and Bryson.

BROLLY

The Brolly sept of County Derry trace their lineage to Eogan, son of the 5th century High King of Ireland, Niall of the Nine Hostages, who ruled from the Hill of Tara, County Meath. Eogan and his brother Conall *Gulban* conquered northwest Ireland, ca.425 AD, capturing the great hill-fort of Grianan of Ailech in County Donegal.

Eogan, styled 'King of Ailech', established his own kingdom in the peninsula in County Donegal still called after him Inishowen (Innis Eoghain or Eogan's Isle). His descendants, known as the Cenel Eoghain (the race of Owen), became the principal branch of the Northern Ui Neill (descendants of Niall of the Nine Hostages). The Cenel Eoghain in the next five centuries expanded to the east and south from their focal point in Inishowen.

Ireland was one of the first countries to adopt a system of hereditary surnames which developed from a more ancient system of clan or sept names. From the 11th century each family began to adopt its own distinctive family name generally derived from the first name of an ancestor who lived in or about the 10th century. The surname was formed by prefixing either Mac (son of) or O (grandson or descendant of) to the ancestor's name. Surnames in Ireland, therefore, tended to identify membership of a sept.

Brolly, sometimes anglicized as Brawley, is derived from Gaelic *O Brolaigh*, the root word possibly being *Brollach*, an old Irish personal name. In this case O'Brolly would literally mean 'descendant of Brollach'.

The O'Brollys were one of the leading septs of Clan Binny (*Eochaid Binnigh* was a son of Eogan) possessing territory on the banks of the River Foyle near Lifford in County Donegal.

The first outward thrust of the Owen clan was that of Clan Binny in the 6th century AD who thrust southeast into County Tyrone, bypassing a hard core of resistance in County Derry of the Cianachta, as far as the river Blackwater on the borders of Tyrone and Armagh. Clan Binny eventually ousted the Oriella clans from the district lying west of the river Bann from Coleraine to beside Lough Neagh, and drove them across the river.

The Annals of The Kingdom of Ireland by the Four Masters records that in 1188 'Martin O'Broly, chief Sage of the Irish, and Lector at Armagh, died.' In the course of time the O'Brollys became well established in the lands to the east of the city of Derry between the Rivers Foyle and Roe.

Brolly is also an anglicised form of the French *de Broglie* but this rarely if ever applies to Ireland.

BROWN

Brown is among the forty most common names in Ireland and among the ten most popular in Ulster. Its main centres in Ulster are County Derry, where it is one of the five most popular surnames; County Down, where it is one of the first ten; and County Antrim, where it is one of the first fifteen. The great majority of the Ulster Browns are of English and Scottish descent.

In England and Lowland Scotland the surname Brown was derived from the Old English personal name Brun, or as a nickname from Old English *brun*, meaning 'brown of hair or complexion', or from the Norman name Le Brun, meaning 'the Brown'.

In the Highlands of Scotland two Scots Gaelic septs anglicised their name to Brown: *Mac a Bhriuthainn*, meaning 'son of the judge' and *Mac Ghille Dhuinn*, meaning 'son of the brown lad'. Brown was also one of the colour names assumed by Clan Lamont after they were outlawed by the Crown in the 17th century.

In 1609 the Earl of Salisbury, Lord High Treasurer, suggested to James I a deliberate plantation of Scottish and English colonists on the forfeited estates of the Gaelic chiefs in counties Armagh, Cavan, Donegal, Fermanagh, Londonderry (then known as Coleraine) and Tyrone. Settlers to Ulster came, by and large, in three waves: with the granting of the initial leases in the period 1605 to 1625; after 1652 and Cromwell's crushing of the Irish rebellion; and finally in the fifteen years after 1690 and the Glorious Revolution. It is estimated by 1715, when migration to Ulster had virtually stopped, the Scottish population of Ulster stood at 200,000.

Scottish families entering Ireland through the port of Londonderry settled in the Foyle Valley which includes much of the fertile lands of counties Donegal, Londonderry and Tyrone. The lands along the Firth of Clyde in the county of Ayrshire, the Clyde Valley and the Border Lands consisting of the counties of Wigtown, Kirkcudbright and Dumfries were home to many of these Scottish settlers.

Browne with an 'e' is more common in the south of Ireland. The Brownes were one of the 'Tribes of Galway'. The Galway Brownes are descended from a Norman, le Brun, who came to Ireland at the time of the Anglo-Norman invasion in the 12th century. They established themselves in Galway by intermarriage with its leading family, the Lynches and by similar alliances with powerful Gaelic septs such as the O'Flahertys and O'Malleys.

The Brownes of Killarney descend from a sixteenth century English adventurer. Through intermarriage with influential Gaelic families the Brownes consolidated their position in County Kerry as the Earls of Kenmare.

Other distinguished families of Brownes established themselves in Counties Mayo and Limerick. In the 19th century in County Mayo, from their seat at Westport, the Brownes, as the Marquis of Sligo, owned an estate of 114,000 acres. The Brownes of Camus, County Limerick provided a number of famous soldiers, including George Count de Browne, who fought for thirty years, from 1730, in the Russian army.

BROWNE

Brown and Browne are among the forty most common names in Ireland and among the ten most popular in Ulster. Brown without an 'e' predominates in Ulster and Browne with an 'e' is more common in the south of Ireland.

The Brownes were one of the 'Tribes of Galway'. The Galway Brownes are descended from a Norman, le Brun, who came to Ireland at the time of the Anglo-Norman invasion in the 12th century. They established themselves in Galway by intermarriage with its leading family, the Lynches and by similar alliances with powerful Gaelic septs such as the O'Flahertys and O'Malleys.

The Brownes of Killarney descend from a sixteenth century English adventurer. Through intermarriage with influential Gaelic families the Brownes consolidated their position in County Kerry as the Earls of Kenmare.

Other distinguished families of Brownes established themselves in Counties Mayo and Limerick. In the 19th century in County Mayo, from their seat at Westport, the Brownes, as the Marquis of Sligo, owned an estate of 114,000 acres. The Brownes of Camus, County Limerick provided a number of famous soldiers, including George Count de Browne, who fought for thirty years, from 1730, in the Russian army.

The great majority of the Ulster Browns are of English and Scottish descent. Its main centres in Ulster are County Derry, where it is one of the five most popular surnames; County Down, where it is one of the first ten; and County Antrim, where it is one of the first fifteen.

In England and Lowland Scotland the surname Brown was derived from the Old English personal name Brun, or as a nickname from Old English *brun*, meaning 'brown of hair or complexion', or from the Norman name Le Brun, meaning 'the Brown'.

In the Highlands of Scotland two Scots Gaelic septs anglicised their name to Brown: *Mac a Bhriuthainn*, meaning 'son of the judge' and *Mac Ghille Dhuinn*, meaning 'son of the brown lad'. Brown was also one of the colour names assumed by Clan Lamont after they were outlawed by the Crown in the 17th century.

In 1609 the Earl of Salisbury, Lord High Treasurer, suggested to James I a deliberate plantation of Scottish and English colonists on the forfeited estates of the Gaelic chiefs in counties Armagh, Cavan, Donegal, Fermanagh, Londonderry (then known as Coleraine) and Tyrone. Settlers to Ulster came, by and large, in three waves: with the granting of the initial leases in the period 1605 to 1625; after 1652 and Cromwell's crushing of the Irish rebellion; and finally in the fifteen years after 1690 and the Glorious Revolution. It is estimated by 1715, when migration to Ulster had virtually stopped, the Scottish population of Ulster stood at 200,000.

Scottish families entering Ireland through the port of Londonderry settled in the Foyle Valley which includes much of the fertile lands of counties Derry, Donegal and Tyrone.

BUCHANAN

This surname is found almost exclusively in Ulster where it is most common in County Tyrone. This name was brought to Ulster by settlers from Scotland in the 17th century.

In Scotland, Clan Buchanan derives its name from the district of Buchanan, in Gaelic *both chanain*, meaning 'house of the canon', in Stirlingshire. The lands of Clan Buchanan were located on the east side of Loch Lomond, and the gathering place of the clan was on the island of Clarinch in Loch Lomond. Clan Buchanan prospered and a number of branches were established at Amprior, Auchamar, Carbeth, Drumakill, Leny and Spittal.

The original name of Clan Buchanan was Macauslan, or McCausland, in Gaelic *Mac Ausalain*, meaning 'son of Ausalan'. Clan Buchanan claim descent from Ausalan Buoy O'Kane, a chief of a branch of the O'Kanes of County Derry who settled in Argyll in 1016. The name was changed to Buchanan by Gilbrid MacAuslan in the 13th century.

From the 12th century until the early 17th century the O'Kanes were overlords and all-powerful in County Derry. The O'Kanes trace their lineage to Eogan, son of the 5th century High King of Ireland, Niall of the Nine Hostages, who ruled from the Hill of Tara, County Meath. Eogan and his brother Conall *Gulban* conquered northwest Ireland, ca.425 AD, capturing the great hill-fort of Grianan of Ailech in County Donegal.

There was also a Buchanan sept of Glendaruel in Cowal in Argyllshire who were followers of Clan Campbell. They had no connection with Clan Buchanan of Loch Lomond.

Movement of Scottish settlers to Ulster began in earnest from 1605 in a private enterprise colonisation of counties Antrim and Down when Sir Hugh Montgomery and Sir James Hamilton acquired title to large estates in north Down and Sir Randall MacDonnell, 1st Earl of Antrim, to large tracts of land in north Antrim. Further impetus came in 1609 when James I adopted the policy to encourage Scottish settlers to settle on the forfeited estates of the Gaelic chiefs in counties Armagh, Cavan, Donegal, Fermanagh, Londonderry (then known as Coleraine) and Tyrone.

During the famous 105 day Siege of Derry, from 18 April to 31 July 1689, John Buchanan, Deputy Mayor of Derry; James Buchanan; and George Buchanan and Marc Buchanan of Enniskillen, County Fermanagh were recorded as 'defenders' of the city. George Buchanan, tracing his descent from the Carbeth branch of Clan Buchanan, had settled at Lisnamallard near Omagh, County Tyrone in 1674.

Some Buchanans in County Antrim are Mawhinneys by origin. The surname Mawhinney is especially associated with County Antrim. In some instances Mawhinney became Mawhannon, which in turn, became Bohannon and then Buchanan. Mawhinney originated in Galloway in southwest Scotland as an anglicised form of MacKenzie, in Gaelic *Mac Coinnich*, and in Ireland as a variant of McSweeney, in Gaelic *Mac Shuibhne*.

18

BURNS

Burns is one of the seventy most common names in Ireland and among the thirty most common in Ulster. In Ulster, which claims two-thirds of the Irish total, the name is most numerous in Counties Antrim, Down and Armagh. The majority of Burns in Ulster are of Scottish origin. This name, however, was also widely adopted by descendants of several Irish septs.

Many Burns, especially outside of Ulster, will have Irish origins. Irish septs such as O'Beirne, in Gaelic *O Birn*, of Counties Mayo and Roscommon; Birrane, in Gaelic *O Biorain*, of Connaught and Munster; and Byrne, in Gaelic *O Broin*, of County Wicklow have, in many instances, been changed to Burns.

A small minority of Burns in Ulster will be of Irish origin as some of the Wicklow Byrnes, who settled in Ulster in the 17th century, anglicised their name to Burns, as did some of the County Down sept of McBrin, in Gaelic *Mac Broin*.

In Scotland Burns is believed to be derived from the place name of Burnhouse in Argyllshire. They were a sept of Clan Campbell. Until the end of the 18th century the name was usually recorded as Burness. The ancestors of Robert Burns, the poet, were known as the Campbells of Burnhouse and later as Burness. It was Robert Burns and his brother Gilbert who decided to change their name, in April 1786, from Burness to Burns, which was closer to the pronunciation of Burness in Ayrshire where they were then living. Robbie Burns' subsequent fame inspired many others to make the same change.

The Dumfriesshire surname of McBurney is well known in Counties Down and Antrim. It was in Gaelic *Mac Biorna*, meaning 'son of Bjarnie', which was a Norse personal name. In Dumfriesshire many McBurneys anglicised their name to Burns.

The defeat of the old Gaelic order in the Nine Years War, 1594-1603 and the escape of the most prominent Gaelic Lords of Ulster in 'the Flight of the Earls' in 1607 from Lough Swilly, County Donegal were ultimately responsible for the settlement of many Scottish families in the northern counties of Ireland.

Movement of Scottish settlers to Ulster began in earnest from 1605 in a private enterprise colonisation of counties Antrim and Down when Sir Hugh Montgomery and Sir James Hamilton acquired title to large estates in north Down and Sir Randall MacDonnell, 1st Earl of Antrim, to large tracts of land in north Antrim.

In 1609 the Earl of Salisbury, Lord High Treasurer, suggested to James I a deliberate plantation of Scottish and English colonists on the forfeited estates of the Gaelic chiefs in counties Armagh, Cavan, Donegal, Fermanagh, Londonderry (then known as Coleraine) and Tyrone.

Settlers to Ulster came, by and large, in three waves: with the granting of the initial leases in the period 1605 to 1625; after 1652 and Cromwell's crushing of the Irish rebellion; and finally in the fifteen years after 1690 and the Glorious Revolution. It is estimated by 1715, when migration to Ulster had virtually stopped, the Scottish population of Ulster stood at 200,000.

CALDWELL

Caldwell can be of Irish, English or Scottish origin. This surname is found almost exclusively in Ulster where it is most common in Counties Antrim, Londonderry and Tyrone.

Ireland was one of the first countries to adopt a system of hereditary surnames which developed from a more ancient system of clan or sept names. The surname was formed by prefixing either Mac (son of) or O (grandson or descendant of) to the ancestor's name.

A number of Irish septs adopted Caldwell as the anglicised form of their name. Ulster septs such as Horish, in Gaelic *O hUarghuis*, of County Tyrone; Houriskey, in Gaelic *O hUaruisce*, of County Tyrone; and Colavin, in Gaelic *Mac Conluain*, of County Cavan have, by and large, been changed to Caldwell.

It would also appear that, in some instances, families of the *Mac Cathmhaoil* sept of County Tyrone (initially anglicised as McCawell) adopted Callwell as an anglicised form of their surname. McCawell was derived from Gaelic *Mac Cathmhaoil*, the root word being *cathmhaol*, meaning 'battle chief'. At the height of their power in the 12th century, from their base at Clogher, the McCawells controlled a large portion of County Tyrone and had penetrated deep into County Fermanagh. By the mid-14th century their power in Fermanagh had been broken by the Maguires and their influence gradually declined thereafter.

In England and Scotland Caldwell is derived from a number of places of the name such as Caldwell in the North Riding of Yorkshire in England, and Caldwell in Renfrewshire in Scotland. This place name is derived from Old English *cald*, meaning 'cold' and *well*, meaning 'stream'.

In Scotland, Caldwell was recorded as a surname in Renfrewshire in the 14th century, and in Dunfermline, Fifeshire and in Glasgow in the 15th and 16th centuries. This surname was common in Edinburgh in the 17th century. An old Scottish pronunciation of the name was Carwall.

Movement of Scottish settlers to Ulster began in earnest from 1605 in a private enterprise colonisation of counties Antrim and Down when Sir Hugh Montgomery and Sir James Hamilton acquired title to large estates in north Down and Sir Randall MacDonnell, 1st Earl of Antrim, to large tracts of land in north Antrim. Further impetus came in 1609 when James I adopted the policy to encourage English and Scottish settlers to settle on the forfeited estates of the Gaelic chiefs in counties Armagh, Cavan, Donegal, Fermanagh, Londonderry (then known as Coleraine) and Tyrone.

Sir James Caldwell, a successful merchant in Enniskillen, County Fermanagh purchased his Castle Caldwell estate in 1662. Sir James was the son of John Caldwell, a member of an old Ayrshire family from Stratton near Prestwick. During the Williamite Wars of 1689 to 1691 Sir James raised a regiment of foot and two troops of horse which operated from Ballyshannon to Donegal town. Sir James' son, Captain John Caldwell repulsed the Duke of Berwick's attack on Donegal Castle.

CAMPBELL

Campbell is an extremely popular and widespread name in Ulster where it is the fifth most common name. It is the third most numerous name in County Down, fourth in County Armagh, seventh in each of Counties Antrim, Derry and Tyrone and thirteenth in County Donegal. The majority of Ulster Campbells are descendants of 17th century Scottish settlers but there are significant local differences.

Most Ulster Campbells descend from Scottish clan Campbell who rose rapidly to power in Argyll in the western Highlands of Scotland in the 17th century at the expense of the Mac-Donalds, 'Lords of the Isles'. Inveraray Castle on the banks of Loch Fyne became the principal seat of the Campbells, the Dukes of Argyll, in the 15th century. In the 18th century the Campbells were loyal supporters of the English crown in their struggles with the Scottish Jacobites.

Originally known as Clan *O'Duibhne* the first to assume the surname Campbell was Gillespic O'Duibhne who, in 1263, was recorded as Gillespic Cambel. The surname is derived from Scots Gaelic *Caimbeul*, meaning 'crooked mouth'

In 1609 the Earl of Salisbury, Lord High Treasurer, suggested to James I a deliberate plantation of Scottish and English colonists on the forfeited estates of the Gaelic chiefs in counties Armagh, Cavan, Donegal, Fermanagh, Londonderry (then known as Coleraine) and Tyrone. Settlers to Ulster came, by and large, in three waves: with the granting of the initial leases in the period 1605 to 1625; after 1652 and Cromwell's crushing of the Irish rebellion; and finally in the fifteen years after 1690 and the Glorious Revolution. It is estimated by 1715, when migration to Ulster had virtually stopped, the Scottish population of Ulster stood at 200,000.

In Donegal, in particular, many Campbells will have an even earlier connection with Scotland. In the 15th century a branch of Clan Campbell, known as *Mac Ailin,* derived from *ail,* meaning rock, were brought to Donegal by the O'Donnells to fight as galloglasses, i.e. mercenary soldiers. As well as Campbell their name was also anglicised to McCallion.

As well as numerous Scottish immigrants of the name many Campbells, especially in County Tyrone, will have Irish origins. The Campbell sept of County Tyrone trace their lineage to Eogan, son of the 5th century High King of Ireland, Niall of the Nine Hostages, who ruled from the Hill of Tara, County Meath. Eogan and his brother Conall *Gulban* conquered northwest Ireland, ca.425 AD, capturing the great hill-fort of Grianan of Ailech in County Donegal which commanded the entrance to the Inishowen peninsula between Lough Swilly and Lough Foyle.

Campbell, in Gaelic *Mac Cathmhaoil,* is derived from *cathmhaol,* meaning 'battle chief'. This name was initially anglicised as McCawell. The Campbells of Tyrone were the leading sept of Clan Ferady (tracing their descent from Faredach, son of Muireadach (Murdock), son of Eogan). At the height of their power in the 12th century, from their base at Clogher, they controlled a large portion of County Tyrone and had penetrated deep into County Fermanagh. They were one of the seven powerful septs supporting O'Neill.

CANNING

Canning can be an Irish or an English name. This surname is most numerous in County Derry.

Ireland was one of the first countries to adopt a system of hereditary surnames which developed from a more ancient system of clan or sept names. The surname was formed by prefixing either Mac (son of) or O (grandson or descendant of) to the ancestor's name.

In County Donegal Canning has been used interchangeably with Cannon. The County Donegal sept of Cannon is derived from Gaelic *O Cananain*, the root word being *cano*, meaning 'wolf cub'. At one time the chiefs of this sept were called the Kings of Cenel Conaill. The Cenel Conaill (the race of Conall) trace their lineage to Conall *Gulban*, son of the 5th century High King of Ireland, Niall of the Nine Hostages, who ruled from the Hill of Tara, County Meath. Conall and his brother Eogan conquered northwest Ireland, ca.425 AD, capturing the great hill-fort of Grianan of Ailech in County Donegal.

Although the Cannons were overthrown by the powerful O'Donnells in the 13th century, descendants of the sept remained in their ancestral homeland. At the time of the mid-19th century Griffith's Valuation there were 22 Canning households and 202 Cannon households in County Donegal.

In England, Canning is derived from the place name of Cannings in Wiltshire. George Canning, agent for the Ironmongers' Company of London, came to County Derry from Barton in Warwickshire in 1615. The Ironmongers' estate in County Derry consisted of 19,450 acres on the west bank of the River Bann. George Canning was a 'country gentleman of the type most needed to make the Plantation a success. He was conscientious, persevering, and capable, with a real interest in the little colony of which he was the centre.' By 1622, 65 British settlers were resident on the Ironmonger's manor, and the Muster Roll of 1630 records the names of George, Paul, Richard and William Canning in this manor.

The Cannings had a long connection with the town of Garvagh in the parish of Errigal, County Derry, and a descendant was created Lord Garvagh. The 1641 rebellion devastated the manor, and William Canning, son of George Canning, was killed with many others in the defence of Garvagh.

When the rebellion was finally crushed Paul Canning sent a report, in 1654, to the Ironmongers' Company in which he stated that the castle, manor house, and all other buildings, together with the church, the mill, and bridges, had been 'totally demolished and destroyed'. Reconstruction was slow after the rebellion, and further damage was inflicted during the Williamite Wars of 1689-1691.

Despite these reversals, by the end of the 17th century, a self-sustaining settlement of British colonists had established itself in Ulster. Settlers came to Ulster, by and large, in three waves: with the granting of the initial leases in the period 1605 to 1625; after 1652 and Cromwell's crushing of the Irish rebellion; and finally in the fifteen years after 1690 and the Glorious Revolution.

CARLIN

The O'Carlin sept trace their lineage to Eogan, son of the 5th century High King of Ireland, Niall of the Nine Hostages, who ruled from the Hill of Tara, County Meath. Eogan and his brother Conall *Gulban* conquered northwest Ireland, ca.425 AD, capturing the great hill-fort of Grianan of Ailech in County Donegal.

Eogan, styled 'King of Ailech', established his own kingdom in the peninsula in County Donegal still called after him Inishowen (Innis Eoghain or Eogan's Isle). His descendants, known as the Cenel Eoghain (the race of Owen), became the principal branch of the Northern Ui Neill (descendants of Niall of the Nine Hostages). The Cenel Eoghain in the next five centuries expanded to the east and south from their focal point in Inishowen.

Ireland was one of the first countries to adopt a system of hereditary surnames which developed from a more ancient system of clan or sept names. The surname was formed by prefixing either Mac (son of) or O (grandson or descendant of) to the ancestor's name. Carlin and O'Carolan, an earlier anglicized form of the name, are derived from Gaelic *O Caireallain*.

The O'Carlins were the leading sept of *Clann Diarmata*, i.e. Clan Dermot. In County Donegal they were *erenaghs*, i.e. hereditary stewards, of the church lands of Clonleigh in the barony of Raphoe. They also seized a portion of O'Gormley territory around Donaghmore, County Donegal in the late 12th century.

Clan Dermot was, in turn, a branch of Clan Connor *Magh Ithe* (Connor was a direct descendant of Eogan). Magh Ithe is the rich countryside stretching southward from Inishowen, later known as the Laggan district in east Donegal. In the 10th century AD the families of Clan Connor moved out from the cramped territory of Magh Ithe and established themselves in County Derry, in the kingdom of Keenaght, to the north of the Sperrin Mountains, from the Foyle to the Bann rivers. In the process they ousted the Cianachta whose leading sept was the O'Connors of Glengiven in the Roe Valley.

By the 12th century when the process of conquest ends the various septs of Clan Connor were firmly settled in County Derry. Clan Dermot, who gave their name to the parish of Clondermot or Glendermott, and its chief family O'Carrolan were firmly established to the south of the Faughan river.

The O'Carolans were very powerful in the neighbourhood of Derry during the 12th century, and were mentioned frequently in the *Annals of Ireland*. In 1177 Niall O'Gormly, Lord of the men of Magh Ithe, was slain by Donough O'Carellan and the Clandermot in the middle of Derry Columbkille. In the same year a Norman raiding party led by John de Courcy slew Conor O'Carellan, chief of Clandermot. In 1200 Egneghan O'Donnell, Lord of Tirconnell defeated Clan Dermot in a battle at Rosses Bay, a short distance north of Derry.

The surnames Carlin, O'Carlin and O'Carolan have also been anglicised to Carleton. This can cause confusion as the Carletons, also recorded as Charlton, were one of the great riding clans on the English side of the Scottish Borders in Cumbria and Northumberland.

CASSIDY

This name is now numerous in all the provinces except Connaught. This name is most common in its homeland, County Fermanagh, where it is the thirteenth most numerous name. The name is also common, in Ulster, in Counties Donegal, Antrim and Monaghan.

Ireland was one of the first countries to adopt a system of hereditary surnames which developed from a more ancient system of clan or sept names. From the 11th century each family began to adopt its own distinctive family name generally derived from the first name of an ancestor who lived in or about the 10th century. The surname was formed by prefixing either Mac (son of) or O (grandson or descendant of) to the ancestor's name. Surnames in Ireland, therefore, tended to identify membership of a sept. Cassidy is derived from Gaelic *O Caiside.*

The Cassidys were hereditary physicians to the rulers of Fermanagh, the Maguires, between 1300 and 1600. *The Annals of The Kingdom of Ireland by the Four Masters,* records that, in 1322, Fineen O'Cassidy, styled the 'Chief Physician of Fermanagh', died. *The Annals* record the deaths of further O'Cassidy 'Chief Physicians of Fermanagh' in 1335, 1450, 1504 and 1520.

These O'Cassidy physicians were based in the barony of Coole in southeast Fermanagh. *The Annals* describe Pierce O'Cassidy of Coole, Chief Physician to the Maguires, who died in 1504, as 'a man truly learned in literature and medical science'. As their fame spread throughout Ireland and, particularly in Ulster, Cassidys became doctors to many other chiefs.

The Cassidys were also prominent in the fields of literature and religion. The name first appears in the field of literature in the person of Giolla Mochuda Mor O Caiside, died 1143, whose Gaelic poetry is still preserved. It is claimed that Rory O'Cassidy, Archdeacon of Clogher, assisted Cathal Maguire in the compilation of the fifteenth century *Annals of Ulster.*

The O'Cassidys were *erenaghs,* i.e. hereditary stewards, of the church lands of Devenish in County Fermanagh. The stronghold of the chief of the O'Cassidys was at Ballycassidy, i.e. 'the townland of the Cassidys', in the parish of Trory, just north of the town of Enniskillen. After the upheavals of the 17th century plantation of Ulster the O'Cassidys, like many Ulster Gaelic septs, sank into relative obscurity. Although no longer rulers of their homeland their name remained prominent. Cassidys were noted as priests in Fermanagh and Monaghan during the Penal period.

In County Donegal the O'Cassidys were *erenaghs* of church lands in Conwall Parish in the barony of Kilmacrenan. The importance of Cassidy as a surname in Derry city today, where it is among the top thirty names, is perhaps due to this Donegal connection as the top three names in the city, namely Doherty, McLaughlin and Gallagher, have Donegal origins. As Derry developed an industrial base in the 19th century in shirt making, shipbuilding and distilling it attracted much of its workforce from Donegal.

CAVAN

This surname is not derived from the place name of Cavan. Cavan is usually an anglicised form of the surname Keevan or occasionally an abbreviation of Kavanagh.

Ireland was one of the first countries to adopt a system of hereditary surnames which developed from a more ancient system of clan or sept names. From the 11th century each family began to adopt its own distinctive family name generally derived from the first name of an ancestor who lived in or about the 10th century. The surname was formed by prefixing either Mac (son of) or O (grandson or descendant of) to the ancestor's name.

Surnames in Ireland, therefore, tended to identify membership of a sept. The anglicisation of Gaelic names, from the 17th century, resulted in many variant spellings of the same name and, in many cases, the dropping of the O and Mac prefixes.

It would appear that a number of Irish septs have had their name anglicised as Cavan.

Keevan and Cavan can be derived from Gaelic *O Ciabhain*, the root word being *ciabhach*, meaning having long locks of hair. This sept had its origins in southwest Cork.

A further distinct origin of Cavan is *O Caomhain*, the root word being *caomh*, meaning mild. This sept originated in north Mayo and Sligo.

In some instances Cavan can be an abbreviated form of Kavanagh. For example, in Kerry, Keevan has been changed to Kavanagh. The Kavanaghs, derived from Gaelic *Caomhanach*, were a famous branch of the MacMurroughs and are still most numerous in the ancient Mc-Murrough lands in Counties Wexford and Carlow. By tradition the Kavanaghs take their name from an ancestor who had been fostered by a successor of St. Caomhan.

At the time of the mid-19th century Griffith's Valuation, which records the names of all heads of households and landholders in Ireland, there were 47 Cavan households in Ireland; 12 in County Down, 9 in Leix, 5 each in Counties Cork and Derry, 4 in Galway, 3 in Antrim, 2 in Clare and one each in Counties Carlow, Dublin, Kerry, Kildare, Monaghan, Tipperary and Wicklow. This includes variant spellings such as Caven and Cavin.

The same source recorded 33 Keevan households in Ireland which also included variant spellings such as Keavan, Keevane, Keevans and Keevin.

By contrast Kavanagh is among the sixty most numerous names in Ireland. The great majority of those of the name are from Leinster (where half are in Dublin alone) and less than 10% are from Ulster. Some of the Ulster Kavanaghs do not descend from the McMurrough sept. In County Antrim and east Tyrone a sept of McCavanas, derived from *Mac an Mhanaigh* (the root word being *manach*, meaning monk), anglicised to Cavanagh. It is possible, but not recorded, that some Cavanaghs were further shortened to Cavan.

CLARK

Clark can be of Irish, English or Scottish origin. It is among the forty most common names in Ireland and among the top twenty in Ulster, where it is most numerous in Counties Antrim and Cavan.

Ireland was one of the first countries to adopt a system of hereditary surnames which developed from a more ancient system of clan or sept names. The surname was formed by prefixing either Mac (son of) or O (grandson or descendant of) to the ancestor's name.

Clark is derived from Gaelic *O Cleirigh*, the root word being *cleireach*, meaning 'clerk'. This surname, initially anglicised as O'Clery and recorded from the middle of the 10th century, was one of the earliest recorded surnames in Ireland. This sept originated in Kilmacduagh, County Galway. The Anglo-Norman military incursions of the 13th century into Connaught which reduced the power and influence of many septs in that province encouraged descendants of the O'Clerys to disperse.

The most notable branch settled in County Donegal where they were famed as poets and antiquaries. Michael O'Clery, born at Kilbarron, County Donegal in 1575, the son of a chief, was the inspiration behind the compilation of *The Annals of The Kingdom of Ireland by the Four Masters* (a chronicle of Irish history from 'the earliest period to the year 1616'). From the 17th century O'Clery was further anglicised as Clark.

Clark is among the thirty most common names in England where it was derived from an occupational name for a scribe or secretary or for a member of a religious order. Originally Old English *clerc*, meaning 'priest', denoted a member of a religious order. In the Middle Ages it was virtually only members of religious orders who could read or write, so that the term clerk came also to be used of any literate man, scribe or scholar. The Clarks of Maghera House, Largantogher, County Derry trace their descent from John Clark of Lancashire, England who came to Ulster in 1690.

Clark is among the twenty most common names in Scotland. In the Lowlands of Scotland Clark was derived as an occupational name for a cleric or scholar, and after 1400 the name was widely adopted as a surname throughout the Lowlands. In the 15th century this surname was recorded in towns throughout the Lowlands such as Dundee, Edinburgh, Irvine and Leith.

In the Highlands of Scotland Clark was derived from Gaelic *Mac an Chleirich,* meaning 'son of the clerk'. This surname was initially anglicised as McCleary. As many clans had their clerics and clerks it is not surprising that there were Clark septs attached to a number of Scottish clans including Cameron, Clan Chattan, Mackintosh and Macpherson. Throughout the 17th century many Scottish families settled in the northern part of Ireland. It is estimated by 1715, when migration to Ulster had virtually stopped, the Scottish population of Ulster stood at 200,000.

During the famous 105 day Siege of Derry, from 18 April to 31 July 1689, Mathew Clarke; Alderman, George, John and Samuel Clarke of County Armagh; Robert Clarke of County Fermanagh; and Edward Clarke of County Monaghan were recorded as 'defenders' of the city.

CLYDE

This surname is found predominantly in Ulster where it was brought at the time of the 17th century Plantation of Ulster by settlers from Scotland. It is most common in Counties Antrim and Londonderry.

Clyde is a local name, which originated in more than one locality in Scotland, referring to someone who lived on the banks of the river Clyde, which flows through Glasgow. A William Clyde was recorded as Burgess of Dundee in 1580.

The Clyde Valley and the lands along the Firth of Clyde in the old county of Ayrshire were home to many of the Scottish settlers who came to Ulster throughout the 17th century.

The defeat of the old Gaelic order in the Nine Years War, 1594-1603 and the escape of the most prominent Gaelic Lords of Ulster in 'the Flight of the Earls' in 1607 from Lough Swilly, County Donegal were ultimately responsible for the settlement of many Scottish families in the northern counties of Ireland.

Movement of Scottish settlers to Ulster began in earnest from 1605 in a private enterprise colonisation of counties Antrim and Down when Sir Hugh Montgomery and Sir James Hamilton acquired title to large estates in north Down and Sir Randall MacDonnell, 1st Earl of Antrim, to large tracts of land in north Antrim.

Further impetus came in 1609 when James I adopted the policy to encourage English and Scottish settlers to settle on the forfeited estates of the Gaelic chiefs in counties Armagh, Cavan, Donegal, Fermanagh, Londonderry (then known as Coleraine) and Tyrone. Settlers came to Ulster, by and large, in three waves: with the granting of the initial leases in the period 1605 to 1625; after 1652 and Cromwell's crushing of the Irish rebellion; and finally in the fifteen years after 1690 and the Glorious Revolution.

Scottish families entering Ireland through the port of Londonderry settled in the Foyle Valley which includes much of the fertile lands of counties Donegal, Londonderry and Tyrone.

Clydes were recorded in County Londonderry from the mid-17th century, especially in the fertile lands in the west of the county. The Hearth Money Rolls of 1663 record four Clyde households – 3 recorded as Clyde and one as Clide- in this county; one each in Clondermot and Tamlaght Finlagan Parishes and two in Faughanvale Parish.

English settlers were particularly prominent in the early years of the Plantation of County Londonderry. The upheavals of the 1641 rebellion and the Williamite Wars of 1689 to 1691, however, tended to discourage English settlers more than Scottish settlers. When large scale migration to County Londonderry resumed in the years after 1652 and 1690 it was Scottish Presbyterian settlers, such as the Clydes, who were more prominent.

It is estimated by 1715, when migration to Ulster had virtually stopped, the Scottish population of Ulster stood at 200,000.

COCHRANE

This surname is found almost exclusively in Ulster where it is most common in Counties Antrim, Derry, Down and Tyrone. This name was brought to Ulster by settlers from Scotland in the 17th century.

In Scotland, this surname is derived from the lands of Cochrane (originally spelt as Coueran) near Paisley in Renfrewshire. The name means 'red brook'. The earliest reference to the surname is of one Waldeve de Coueran who witnessed a charter in Kintyre in 1262.

The Cochranes were a sept of the powerful Clan Donald. Clan Donald claimed the position of 'The Headship of the Gael'. By the time of his death in 1387, John MacDonald, as Lord of the Isles, controlled the whole of the Hebrides from Lewis to Islay, with the exception of Skye, and the mainland from Kintyre to Knoydart.

In 1669 Sir William Cochrane, Baron Cochrane, was created 1st Earl of Dundonald. Dundonald, Kyle, a castle built by the Stewarts in the 13th century became a Cochrane stronghold in the 17th century.

Movement of Scottish settlers to Ulster began in earnest from 1605 in a private enterprise colonisation of counties Antrim and Down when Sir Hugh Montgomery and Sir James Hamilton acquired title to large estates in north Down and Sir Randall MacDonnell, 1st Earl of Antrim, to large tracts of land in north Antrim. By the mid-19th century the Cochranes were concentrated in the barony of Lower Dunluce, near the Giant's Causeway in north Antrim.

As followers of Clan Donald the Cochranes would have been drawn to north Antrim. Clan Donald had acquired new territories in the north of Ireland ca.1400 when John Mor MacDonald had married Margery Bissett, an heiress in the Glens of Antrim. By the mid-16th century the MacDonalds, known as the MacDonnells of the Glens, had carved out an extensive territory in County Antrim at the expense of the MacQuillans.

Further impetus came in 1609 when James I adopted the policy to encourage English and Scottish settlers to settle on the forfeited estates of the Gaelic chiefs in counties Armagh, Cavan, Donegal, Fermanagh, Londonderry (then known as Coleraine) and Tyrone.

Settlers to Ulster came, by and large, in three waves: with the granting of the initial leases in the period 1605 to 1625; after 1652 and Cromwell's crushing of the Irish rebellion; and finally in the fifteen years after 1690 and the Glorious Revolution. It is estimated by 1715, when migration to Ulster had virtually stopped, the Scottish population of Ulster stood at 200,000.

During the famous 105 day Siege of Derry, from 18 April to 31 July 1689, Captain John Coghran of Belrath, County Armagh, Robert Cochrane, Marmaduke Coghran and Thomas Cochrane were recorded as 'defenders' of the city.

In some instances the County Fermanagh sept of Corcoran, in Gaelic *O Corcrain*, adopted Cochrane as the anglicised form of their name.

COLHOUN

This surname is found almost exclusively in Ulster where it is most common in Counties Tyrone and Derry. This name was brought to Ulster by settlers from Scotland in the 17th century.

In Scotland, this surname is derived from the barony of Colquhoun, from Gaelic *coill*, meaning a 'wood', and *cumhann*, meaning 'narrow', in Dunbartonshire. The founder of Clan Colquhoun was Umfridus de Kilpatrick who received a grant of the lands of Colquhoun c. 1241. Robert de Colechon, who attended an inquest at Dumbarton in 1259, appears to have been the first to take his surname from the lands.

The family became a recognised clan and after acquiring the lands of Luss in Dunbartonshire by marriage in the 14th century they became known as the Colquhouns of Luss.

In 1603, during the chiefship of Alexander, 17th chief of the Colquhouns of Luss, the Colquhouns were attacked by the McGregors, and at the battle of Glenfruin, the 'Glen of Sorrow', the McGregors emerged as victors. As a consequence, by Act of Parliament, Clan Gregor was outlawed, an order was given to disperse them 'by fire and sword', and their name was proscribed. The McGregors now resorted to raiding as a 'broken' clan.

Colquhoun was also the name of a sept of Clan Stewart of Appin in Argyllshire. In the Lowlands of Scotland many Colquohouns, pronounced as Cahoon, assumed the names of Cowan and McCowan.

Movement of Scottish settlers to Ulster began in earnest from 1605 in a private enterprise colonisation of counties Antrim and Down when Sir Hugh Montgomery and Sir James Hamilton acquired title to large estates in north Down and Sir Randall MacDonnell, 1st Earl of Antrim, to large tracts of land in north Antrim.

In 1609 the Earl of Salisbury, Lord High Treasurer, suggested to James I a deliberate plantation of Scottish and English colonists on the forfeited estates of the Gaelic chiefs in counties Armagh, Cavan, Donegal, Fermanagh, Londonderry (then known as Coleraine) and Tyrone.

Settlers to Ulster came, by and large, in three waves: with the granting of the initial leases in the period 1605 to 1625; after 1652 and Cromwell's crushing of the Irish rebellion; and finally in the fifteen years after 1690 and the Glorious Revolution. It is estimated by 1715, when migration to Ulster had virtually stopped, the Scottish population of Ulster stood at 200,000.

Early in the Plantation Sir John Colquhoun of Luss bought 1000 acres in Newtowncunningham, County Donegal from Sir Walter Stewart of Minto in Roxburghshire. He brought over several members of the Colquhoun clan and these were the ancestors of most of the present-day Colhouns in Donegal and in the adjacent counties of Derry and Tyrone. It was a feature of 17th century Scotland for tenants to take on the surname of their chief or landlord.

CONNOR

This name is one of the ten most common names in Ireland. In Ulster it is most common in Counties Antrim and Derry. In the 20th century the prefix O was widely resumed. In the 19th century, however, the prefix O was widely discarded.

Ireland was one of the first countries to adopt a system of hereditary surnames which developed from a more ancient system of clan or sept names. The surname was formed by prefixing either Mac (son of) or O (grandson or descendant of) to the ancestor's name.

Connor is derived from Gaelic *O Conchobhair*, meaning 'descendant of Conor'. There were six distinct and important septs of this name located in different parts of the country. The most illustrious of these septs were the O'Connors of Connaught; the main branches of this sept being O'Conor Don, O'Conor Roe and O'Conor Sligo. Tracing their descent from Conchobhar, King of Connacht (died 971) the O'Connors, with extensive territories in Counties Roscommon and Sligo, ruled the Province of Connaught. They provided the last two High Kings of Ireland, i.e. Turlough O'Connor (1088-1156) and Roderick O'Connor (1116-1198). There were also powerful O'Connor septs with origins in Counties Clare, Galway, Offaly and Kerry.

The majority of Ulster Connors, however, will be descended from the once-powerful sept of the O'Connors of Glengiven, lords of the Keenaght in County Derry. The Keenaght, originally Cianachta, meaning 'the territory of the descendants of Cian', claimed descent from Cian, son of Oilioll Olum, King of Munster in the third century. The O'Connors were the principal family of the Cianachta and their territory later became the barony of Keenaght.

Until the 12th century when they were finally ousted by the O'Kanes the Cianachta were rulers of the Roe Valley, near Dungiven, County Derry. Their exploits are recorded in the *The Annals of The Kingdom of Ireland by the Four Masters* from the 6th century AD. In 563 Eochaidh and Baedan, the joint Kings of Ireland, were 'slain by Cronan, chief of Cianachta-Glinne-Gemhin'. Glinne-Gemhin, anglicised as Glengiven, meaning 'Glen of the skins', is the old name for the valley of the River Roe.

The Annals record, in 679, the burning of Ceannfaeladh, chief of Cianachta-Glinne-Geimhin at the Giant's Sconce, a stone fort, in Dunboe parish, County Derry by Maelduin, Lord of the Cinel Eoghain (the race of Owen). In this period the Cinel Eoghain, which included the powerful O'Kane sept, were expanding to the east and south from their original base in County Donegal. This expansion by the Cinel Eoghain intensified in the 11th century, and, in 1076, they inflicted another defeat on the Cianachta at the battle of Belaith. Meaning 'Mouth of the Ford' it is believed that Belaith was located in the townland of Gorticross, on the east bank of the River Faughan, in Clondermot Parish, County Derry.

Internal squabbles finally broke the power of the O'Connors of Glengiven. In 1104 *the Annals* record that 'Dunchadh Ua Conchobhair, lord of Cianachta-an-Ghleinne, was killed by his own people'. From the mid-12th century the O'Connors were forced into the position of small farmers in the district they previously ruled.

CONVERY

This surname is found almost exclusively in County Derry.

Ireland was one of the first countries to adopt a system of hereditary surnames which developed from a more ancient system of clan or sept names. From the 11th century each family began to adopt its own distinctive family name generally derived from the first name of an ancestor who lived in or about the 10th century. The surname was formed by prefixing either Mac (son of) or O (grandson or descendant of) to the ancestor's name. Surnames in Ireland, therefore, tended to identify membership of a sept.

Convery is believed to be derived from Gaelic *Mac Ainmhire*, meaning 'son of Ainmire', the root word possibly being *mire*, meaning 'levity'. This name belongs to County Derry and, in particular, to the lands around the town of Maghera, in the valley of the Moyola River, in south Derry.

The Hearth Money Rolls of 1663 would suggest that the parishes of Ballynascreen and Maghera in south Derry were the original base of this sept. Seven Convery households were recorded in this source in County Derry; with 3 households in Ballynascreen parish and 4 in Maghera Parish.

In the Derry Hearth Money Rolls six of the seven households were recorded as O'Convery, with one recorded as Convery. Seemingly it was not unusual for Mac names beginning with a vowel to be recorded in 17th century documents as O names, the final C of Mac becoming the initial of the anglicised form.

At the time of the 1831 census there were 149 Convery households in County Derry, and all but seventeen of these households were residing in two parishes in south Derry; with 101 Convery households in Maghera Parish and 31 in the adjoining parish of Killelagh. In other words, in 1831, nearly 70% of the descendants of the Convery sept in County Derry were living in the parish of Maghera.

The escape of the most prominent Gaelic Lords of Ulster in 'the Flight of the Earls' in 1607 from Lough Swilly, County Donegal marked the end of Gaelic power and paved the way for the 17th century Plantation of Ulster with English and Scottish settlers.

In the centuries that followed Gaelic names were anglicised, resulting in many variant spellings of the same name and, in many cases, the dropping of the O and Mac prefixes. In the case of Convery the prefixes were not retained. By the time of the 1831 census neither the Mac nor O prefix was recorded against any of the descendants of the Convery sept in County Derry.

At the time of the 1901 census, 413 Converys were living in County Derry, with all but 49 of them living in the parishes of Killelagh and Maghera. Thus, at the turn of the 20th century, nearly 90% of all Converys in County Derry were residing in these two parishes.

31

CONWAY

This surname is found throughout Ireland. In Ulster, Conway is most common in County Tyrone. Although some Conways in Ulster will be of Welsh or English origin, the vast majority of Conways throughout Ireland, including Ulster, will be of Irish origin.

Ireland was one of the first countries to adopt a system of hereditary surnames which developed from a more ancient system of clan or sept names. From the 11th century each family began to adopt its own distinctive family name generally derived from the first name of an ancestor who lived in or about the 10th century. The surname was formed by prefixing either Mac (son of) or O (grandson or descendant of) to the ancestor's name.

Surnames in Ireland, therefore, tended to identify membership of a sept. The anglicisation of Gaelic names, from the 17th century, resulted in many variant spellings of the same name and, in many cases, the dropping of the O and Mac prefixes.

In Ulster, Conway is derived from Gaelic *Mac Conmidhe*, meaning 'son of the hound of Meath'. This sept originated on the lands straddling the border between Counties Derry and Tyrone. Initially the name was anglicised as McConomy and McConway. Indeed, at the turn of the 20th century Conway was still being used interchangeably with McConomy in Counties Derry and Tyrone. McConway and McConaway are forms of McConomy still found in County Donegal today.

Although Conway is Welsh in origin, derived from the river and town of Conwy in north Wales, the surname Conway is usually of Irish origin. A number of Irish septs adopted Conway as the anglicised form of their name. In addition to the McConomys of Ulster: Irish septs such as Kanavaghan, in Gaelic *O Connmhachain*, of County Mayo; Conboy, in Gaelic *O Conbhuidhe*, of Easky, County Sligo; McNama, in Gaelic *Mac Conmeadha*, of County Leitrim; and Conoo, in Gaelic *Mac Conmhaigh*, of County Clare have, by and large, been changed to Conway.

Most Conways in Ulster will be descended from the County Derry-Tyrone sept of *Mac Conmidhe*.

At the time of the 1831 census, in County Derry, there were 43 Conway households, 14 McConomy households and 4 McConway households. By contrast, in County Donegal, at the time of the mid-19th century Griffith's Valuation there were 17 McConway households, 4 McConomy households and 1 Conway household.

Some Conways in Ulster will be descendants of 17th century English and Welsh settlers. English settlers, who migrated to Ulster at this time, tended to favour settlement along the Lagan Valley, in the east of the Province, on lands straddling the borders of Counties Armagh, Antrim and Down. For example the family of the Barons Conway of Lisburn, County Antrim was founded by an Elizabethan army officer, Sir Foulke Conway (died 1624) who acquired extensive estates in Counties Antrim and Down.

CORR

This name is mainly found in Ulster, where it is most common in Counties Tyrone, Cavan and Monaghan.

Ireland was one of the first countries to adopt a system of hereditary surnames which developed from a more ancient system of clan or sept names. From the 11th century each family began to adopt its own distinctive family name generally derived from the first name of an ancestor who lived in or about the 10th century. The surname was formed by prefixing either Mac (son of) or O (grandson or descendant of) to the ancestor's name. Surnames in Ireland, therefore, tended to identify membership of a sept.

Corr is derived from Gaelic *O Corra*, the root possibly being *corra*, meaning 'spear'. This sept originated on the lands bordering the counties of Tyrone and Fermanagh. In some instances this sept anglicised their name to Corry. In the 17th century Hearth Money Rolls for County Armagh there are references to both O'Cor and McCor.

It is claimed that many of the Corrs of County Tyrone and Derry are, however, descended from the 12th century Gilla Corr. *The Annals of The Kingdom of Ireland by the Four Masters* (a chronicle of Irish history from 'the earliest period to the year 1616') record, in 1186, that 'Gillapatrick Mac Gillacorr, Chief of the Hy-Branain, was slain' by his own people.

In the census of 1659 Corr, in the form of O Corr and O Core, was recorded as one of the principal Irish names in the barony of Loughinsholin in south Derry. This association with south Derry is commemorated in the townland name of Ballymacilcurr, meaning 'the townland of the O'Corrs', in the parish of Maghera.

The 1831 census for County Derry clearly demonstrates that this area of south Derry was the ancestral homeland of the Corrs. At the time of the 1831 census there were 31 Corr households in County Derry, and all but two of these households were residing in the parishes of south Derry, centred on and surrounding the parish of Lissan. There were 16 Corr households recorded in Lissan Parish in the 1831 census.

The Hearth Money Rolls of 1663 recorded eight Corr households in County Derry – 6 households of O'Corr and 2 of Corr; all residing in the southeast corner of the county. This source recorded 3 O'Corr households in Maghera Parish, 2 in Artrea Parish and 1 in Desertlyn; and 1 Corr household in the parishes of Ballyscullion and Magherafelt.

The anglicisation of Gaelic names, from the 17th century, resulted in many variant spellings of the same name and, in many cases, the dropping of the O and Mac prefixes. In the case of Corr the prefix O was not retained. By the time of the 1831 census the O prefix was not recorded against any of the descendants of the Corr sept in County Derry.

Outside Ulster the surnames of Cor and Corre were established in Counties Tipperary and Kilkenny as early as 1270. Richard Corre was Bishop of Lismore from 1279 to 1308. *The Annals* record that Cairbre Ua Corra, who died in 972, was abbot of the monastery at Glendalough, County Wicklow.

COWAN

Cowan can be an Irish or a Scottish name. This surname is found almost exclusively in Ulster where it is most common in Counties Antrim, Down and Armagh.

Ireland was one of the first countries to adopt a system of hereditary surnames which developed from a more ancient system of clan or sept names. The surname was formed by prefixing either Mac (son of) or O (grandson or descendant of) to the ancestor's name.

The County Armagh sept of McCoan, in Gaelic *Mac Comhdhain*, was widely anglicised as Cowan. The County Tyrone sept name of McElhone, in Gaelic *Mac Giolla Comhghain*, was also anglicised, in some cases, as Cowan.

Cowan is a common name throughout the Lowlands of Scotland, in particular in Ayrshire and Dumfriesshire. These two areas were home to many of the Scottish settlers who came to Ulster throughout the 17th century.

It is believed that many of the Lowland Scottish Cowans were originally Colquhouns, pronounced as Cahoon. Colquhoun is derived from the barony of Colquhoun, from Gaelic *coill*, meaning a 'wood', and *cumhann*, meaning 'narrow', in Dunbartonshire. The founder of Clan Colquhoun was Umfridus de Kilpatrick who received a grant of the lands of Colquhoun c. 1241. Robert de Colechon, who attended an inquest at Dumbarton in 1259, appears to have been the first to take his surname from the lands. The family became a recognised clan and after acquiring the lands of Luss in Dunbartonshire by marriage in the 14th century they became known as the Colquhouns of Luss. The Cowans of Corstoun in Fife were the principal family of the name.

In the Highlands of Scotland, especially in Argyllshire, Cowan is derived from Gaelic *Mac Gille Chomhghain*, meaning 'son of the servant of St Comgan'. There were Cowan septs attached to Clans Dougall, Colquhoun and Donald.

Movement of Scottish settlers to Ulster began in earnest from 1605 in a private enterprise colonisation of counties Antrim and Down when Sir Hugh Montgomery and Sir James Hamilton acquired title to large estates in north Down and Sir Randall MacDonnell, 1st Earl of Antrim, to large tracts of land in north Antrim.

Further impetus came in 1609 when James I adopted the policy to encourage English and Scottish settlers to settle on the forfeited estates of the Gaelic chiefs in counties Armagh, Cavan, Donegal, Fermanagh, Londonderry (then known as Coleraine) and Tyrone. Settlers to Ulster came, by and large, in three waves: with the granting of the initial leases in the period 1605 to 1625; after 1652 and Cromwell's crushing of the Irish rebellion; and finally in the fifteen years after 1690 and the Glorious Revolution. It is estimated by 1715, when migration to Ulster had virtually stopped, the Scottish population of Ulster stood at 200,000.

During the famous 105 day Siege of Derry, from 18 April to 31 July 1689, Captain John Cowan of St Johnstown, County Donegal and Robert Cowan were recorded as 'defenders' of the city.

COYLE

This name is most common in Ulster in its homeland, County Donegal and in Counties Derry, Tyrone and Cavan. Coyle is among the top ten names in the city of Derry today. The name illustrates the very close links between the city of Derry and County Donegal. As Derry developed an industrial base in the 19th century in shirt making, shipbuilding and distilling it attracted much of its workforce from Donegal.

Ireland was one of the first countries to adopt a system of hereditary surnames which developed from a more ancient system of clan or sept names. From the 11th century each family began to adopt its own distinctive family name generally derived from the first name of an ancestor who lived in or about the 10th century. The surname was formed by prefixing either Mac (son of) or O (grandson or descendant of) to the ancestor's name. Surnames in Ireland, therefore, tended to identify membership of a sept.

Coyle is derived from Gaelic *Mac Giolla Chomhgaill,* meaning 'son of the devotee of St Comgal'. St Comgal was the patron of Galloon parish in south Fermanagh. This sept was based in the parish of Meevagh in the barony of Kilmacrenan in County Donegal. The name was first anglicised as McIlhoyle, then McCoyle and finally Coyle. One branch of the Coyles were *erenaghs,* i.e. hereditary stewards, of the church lands in Galloon Parish, County Fermanagh.

Owing to the mistaken belief that the Gaelic word *coill,* meaning 'wood', was part of this sept's name, *Mac Giolla Chomhgaill* was often anglicised to Woods.

Coyle has also become confused with McCool. Although the surnames of Coyle and McCool have quite distinct origins their ultimate origins have become confused as a result of anglicisation. In some cases people whose origins are *Mac Giolla Chomhgaill* of Kilmacrenan may be disguised by bearing the surname McCool.

The origins of the name McCool are not certain. It has been suggested that McCool, derived from *Mac Giolla Comhghaill,* meaning 'son of the devotee of St Comghal' or from *Mac Comhghaill,* is a distinct sept from the Raphoe area of County Donegal. The surname McCool is most common in Counties Donegal and Tyrone. This name has also been made Cole, which is a common English surname, in the Glenties area of Donegal.

In Scotland MacCool can be a variant of MacDougall, Gaelic *Mac Dhughaill.* In a few cases, therefore, the name may have come with Scottish immigrants at the time of the Plantation of Ulster in the 17th century.

CRAIG

This surname is found predominantly in Ulster where it is among the fifty most common names. It is most numerous in County Antrim, followed by Counties Derry and Tyrone. This name was brought to Ulster in large numbers by settlers from Scotland in the 17th century.

Craig is derived from Gaelic *Creag*, meaning 'crag' or 'rock'. This surname was adopted throughout Scotland by those who lived near a distinctive rock formation. As this surname occurs in early records in many different parts of Scotland it confirms that the surname originated in more than one locality.

In the 13th century the surnames of Crag, Crage and Cragge were recorded in Edinburgh and Lanarkshire. In the 14th century the surname can be found in Ayrshire, where a James del Crag held land in 1323; and in Aberdeenshire where John de Crag was burgess of Aberdeen in 1358. By the sixteenth century the name was common in Edinburgh and throughout the Lowlands of Scotland.

Movement of Scottish settlers to Ulster began in earnest from 1605 in a private enterprise colonisation of counties Antrim and Down when Sir Hugh Montgomery and Sir James Hamilton acquired title to large estates in north Down and Sir Randall MacDonnell, 1st Earl of Antrim, to large tracts of land in north Antrim. By the mid-17th century the name was already very numerous in County Antrim as Craig was recorded as a 'principal name' in the census of 1659 in that county. By the late 19th century the main concentrations of the name in County Antrim were in the baronies of Upper Toome, Lower Toome and Upper Antrim.

Further impetus came in 1609 when James I adopted the policy to encourage Scottish settlers to settle on the forfeited estates of the Gaelic chiefs in counties Armagh, Cavan, Donegal, Fermanagh, Londonderry (then known as Coleraine) and Tyrone.
Settlers came to Ulster, by and large, in three waves: with the granting of the initial leases in the period 1605 to 1625; after 1652 and Cromwell's crushing of the Irish rebellion; and finally in the fifteen years after 1690 and the Glorious Revolution.

Scottish families entering Ireland through the port of Londonderry settled in the Foyle Valley which includes much of the fertile lands of counties Donegal, Londonderry and Tyrone. The lands along the Firth of Clyde in the county of Ayrshire were home to many of these Scottish settlers. It is estimated by 1715, when migration to Ulster had virtually stopped, the Scottish population of Ulster stood at 200,000.

In the initial granting of leases in Ulster in 1610/1611, Sir James Craig of Edinburgh, one of the principal Scottish planters (sixty-one in total), was granted an estate of 1,000 acres in County Armagh. He later sold it and bought another estate in County Cavan. Many of the settlers farming on these estates were also called Craig as it was a feature of 17th century Scotland for tenants to take on their landlord's surname.

Three Craigs, including Alderman Craig of Londonderry and William Cragg of Glenarm, County Antrim, were recorded as 'defenders' of Derry during the famous Siege of Derry, from 18 April to 31 July 1689.

CRAWFORD

This surname is found predominantly in Ulster where it was brought at the time of the 17th century Plantation of Ulster by settlers from Scotland. Crawford is most common in County Antrim, followed by Counties Down, Derry, Tyrone and Fermanagh.

Crawford is derived from the barony of the name on the Upper Clyde in Lanarkshire, Scotland. Derived from Old English *crawe*, meaning 'crow', the surname Crawford was first recorded in Scotland in the latter half of the 12th century. The Crawfords were a sept of Clan Lindsay whose chiefs are the Earls of Crawford.

Many references to the surname appear at an early date in Ayrshire including that of Reginald de Crauford who was appointed Sheriff of Ayr in 1296. The Loudoun estates on the River Irvine in Ayrshire, before they passed through marriage to the Campbells, originally belonged to the Crawfords.

Movement of Scottish settlers to Ulster began in earnest from 1605 in a private enterprise colonisation of counties Antrim and Down when Sir Hugh Montgomery and Sir James Hamilton acquired title to large estates in north Down and Sir Randall MacDonnell, 1st Earl of Antrim, to large tracts of land in north Antrim. Further impetus came in 1609 when James I adopted the policy to encourage Scottish settlers to settle on the forfeited estates of the Gaelic chiefs in counties Armagh, Cavan, Donegal, Fermanagh, Londonderry (then known as Coleraine) and Tyrone.

These settlers came to Ulster, by and large, in three waves: with the granting of the initial leases in the period 1605 to 1625; after 1652 and Cromwell's crushing of the Irish rebellion; and finally in the fifteen years after 1690 and the Glorious Revolution. Scottish families entering Ireland through the port of Londonderry settled in the Foyle Valley which includes much of the fertile lands of counties Donegal, Londonderry and Tyrone. The lands along the Firth of Clyde in the county of Ayrshire, the Clyde Valley and the Border Lands consisting of the counties of Wigtown, Kirkcudbright and Dumfries were home to many of these Scottish settlers. It is estimated by 1715, when migration to Ulster had virtually stopped, the Scottish population of Ulster stood at 200,000.

By the mid-17th century the name was already very numerous in County Antrim, and in the mid-19th century the Antrim Crawfords were mainly concentrated in the barony of Upper Glenarm, and had given their name to Crawfordsland in the parish of Kilbride. In mid-19th century Down the Crawfords were found mainly in the barony of Upper Castlereagh. The town of Crawfordsburn in County Down is named after them.

In the initial granting of leases in Ulster in 1610/1611, George Crawford, one of the principal Scottish planters (sixty-one in total), was granted an estate of 1,000 acres near Mountjoy, County Tyrone. Many of the settlers farming on this estate in Tyrone were also called Crawford as it was a feature of 17th century Scotland for tenants to take on their landlord's surname.

Four Crawfords, two from Donegal, one from Antrim and one from Fermanagh, were recorded as 'defenders' of Derry during the famous Siege of 1689.

CRILLY

This name is almost exclusively found in Ulster, where it is most common in Counties Antrim and Derry.

Ireland was one of the first countries to adopt a system of hereditary surnames which developed from a more ancient system of clan or sept names. From the 11th century each family began to adopt its own distinctive family name generally derived from the first name of an ancestor who lived in or about the 10th century. The surname was formed by prefixing either Mac (son of) or O (grandson or descendant of) to the ancestor's name. Surnames in Ireland, therefore, tended to identify membership of a sept.

The O'Crillys were *erenaghs*, i.e. hereditary stewards, of the church lands of Tamlaght in south Derry. The location of this County Derry sept is indicated by the parish name of Tamlaght O'Crilly, meaning 'the plague monument of the O'Crillys'. 'On rising ground above the Village of Tamlaght is the sepulchral Cave, or *Taimhleacht*, of the O'Crillys, from which the parish derived its name.' In 1647 Friar O'Mellan records O Crili as the name of a priest in Maghera, County Derry.

It is claimed that the O'Crillys came originally from Connaught where they were a branch of the McDermotts of Moylurg whose territory embraced much of County Roscommon. Tracing his descent from Tadhg O'Connor, King of Connaught the chief of the McDermotts was styled 'Prince of Coolavin'. It is possible that the Anglo-Norman military incursions of the 13th century into Connaught which reduced the power and influence of many septs in that province encouraged descendants of the McDermotts to migrate north at an early date.

The 1831 census for County Derry clearly demonstrates that south Derry became the ancestral homeland of the Crillys. At the time of the 1831 census there were 81 Crilly households in County Derry, and all but one of these households were residing in the parishes of south Derry, centred on and surrounding the parish of Maghera. At the time of the 1831 census there were 28 Crilly households recorded in Maghera Parish and 13 households of the name in Tamlaght O'Crilly Parish.

In King James II's Irish army, raised in 1688, Colonel Cormac O'Neill's regiment included an Ensign James O'Crilly. This regiment was part of the 'Jacobite army' which besieged the city of Derry during the famous 105 day Siege of Derry, from 18 April to 31 July 1689.

The anglicisation of Gaelic names, from the 17th century, resulted in many variant spellings of the same name and, in many cases, the dropping of the O and Mac prefixes. In the case of Crilly the prefix O was not retained. By the time of the 1831 census the O prefix was not recorded against any of the descendants of the Crilly sept in County Derry.

In the ancient Kingdom of Oriel which included Counties Armagh and Monaghan and parts of south Down, Louth and Fermanagh Crilly originated as a Mac name although the prefix Mac is now obsolete. The place names of Ballymacreely occur in the 16th century Fiants for Monaghan and south Down.

CROSSAN

This name is mainly found in County Donegal and in the adjacent counties of Derry and Tyrone.

Ireland was one of the first countries to adopt a system of hereditary surnames which developed from a more ancient system of clan or sept names. From the 11th century each family began to adopt its own distinctive family name generally derived from the first name of an ancestor who lived in or about the 10th century. The surname was formed by prefixing either Mac (son of) or O (grandson or descendant of) to the ancestor's name. Surnames in Ireland, therefore, tended to identify membership of a sept.

Crossan is derived from Gaelic *Mac an Chrosain*, the root word being *cros*, meaning 'cross'. There were two distinct septs of the name. In Leinster, the Crossans of County Leix were hereditary poets to the O'Mores and O'Connors. This link is commemorated in the place name of Ballymacrossan which lies on the border of Leix and Offaly. In this region, however, Crossan was usually anglicised to Crosbie.

Most bearers of the surname today are descended from the Crossan sept of County Donegal. This sept provided two Bishops of Raphoe in the 14th century, namely Henry Mac an Crossan and Richard MacCrossan.

Many County Donegal septs trace their lineage to Conall *Gulban*, son of the 5th century High King of Ireland, Niall of the Nine Hostages, who ruled from the Hill of Tara, County Meath. Conall and his brother Eogan conquered northwest Ireland, ca.425 AD, capturing the great hill-fort of Grianan of Ailech in County Donegal which commanded the entrance to the Inishowen peninsula.

Conall, styled 'King of Tir Conaill', established his own kingdom in County Donegal called after him Tyrconnel, i.e. the 'Land of Conall', which was the ancient name of Donegal. His descendants, known as the Cenel Conaill (the race of Conall), firmly established themselves in County Donegal while those descended from Conal's brother Eogan expanded to the east and south into Counties Derry and Tyrone.

At the time of the mid-19th century Griffith's Valuation 68 Crossan households – 63 of Crossan and 5 of McCrossan - were recorded in County Donegal. This source clearly shows that the name was most concentrated in the valley of the River Swilly around the town of Letterkenny. At this time 17 Crossan households were recorded in Aghanunshin Parish and a further 10 in the adjoining parish of Conwal. In other words 40% of descendants of the Crossan sept in County Donegal were living in these two adjoining parishes.

Crossan is a common name in Derry city today. This name, which spread to Derry city in the 19th century, illustrates the very close links, both historic and economic, between the city of Derry and County Donegal. As Derry developed an industrial base in shirt making, shipbuilding and distilling it attracted much of its workforce from County Donegal. In the 90-year period 1821 to 1911 the population of the city quadrupled to 40,780. In this period Derry stamped her dominance over local rivals and emerged as an important urban centre within Ireland.

39

CRUMLEY

This name belongs to Counties Donegal and Derry.

Ireland was one of the first countries to adopt a system of hereditary surnames which developed from a more ancient system of clan or sept names. From the 11th century each family began to adopt its own distinctive family name generally derived from the first name of an ancestor who lived in or about the 10th century. The surname was formed by prefixing either Mac (son of) or O (grandson or descendant of) to the ancestor's name. Surnames in Ireland, therefore, tended to identify membership of a sept.

The origins of this name are uncertain. Crumley may be derived from Gaelic *O Cromlaoich*, meaning 'descendant of the bent hero'. It would also seem likely that, in some cases, Crumley is a variant of the County Donegal sept name of Crumlish.

Many County Donegal septs trace their lineage to Conall *Gulban*, son of the 5th century High King of Ireland, Niall of the Nine Hostages, who ruled from the Hill of Tara, County Meath. Conall and his brother Eogan conquered northwest Ireland, ca.425 AD, capturing the great hill-fort of Grianan of Ailech in County Donegal.

Conall, styled 'King of Tir Conaill', established his own kingdom in County Donegal called after him Tyrconnel, i.e. the 'Land of Conall', which was the ancient name of Donegal. His descendants, known as the Cenel Conaill (the race of Conall), firmly established themselves in County Donegal while those descended from Conal's brother Eogan expanded to the east and south where they established the kingdom of Tir Eoghain (Tir Owen or Tyrone, the land of Owen) which extended over Counties Derry and Tyrone.

The anglicisation of Gaelic names, from the 17th century, resulted in many variant spellings of the same name and, in many cases, the dropping of the O and Mac prefixes.

At the time of the mid-19th century Griffith's Valuation 26 Crumley households, including variant spellings of the surname, were recorded in Ireland, with 7 Crumley households in County Tyrone, 6 in County Derry, 6 in County Monaghan and 4 in County Donegal. In other words this name was not concentrated in one particular area. This source records that there were 11 households recorded as Crumley, 8 as Crumly, 4 as Crimley and 3 as Cromley.

By contrast the surname Crumlish is very much associated with County Donegal. Of 26 Crumlish households recorded in mid-19th century Ireland all but four of them were residing in County Donegal. In other words 85% of descendants of the Crumlish sept in Ireland were living in County Donegal.

Crumley, furthermore, is a common name in Derry city today. As Derry developed an industrial base in the 19th century in shirt making, shipbuilding and distilling it attracted much of its workforce from County Donegal. In the 90-year period 1821 to 1911 the population of the city quadrupled to 40,780.

CRUMLISH

This surname is associated with County Donegal and the city of Derry.

Ireland was one of the first countries to adopt a system of hereditary surnames which developed from a more ancient system of clan or sept names. From the 11th century each family began to adopt its own distinctive family name generally derived from the first name of an ancestor who lived in or about the 10th century. The surname was formed by prefixing either Mac (son of) or O (grandson or descendant of) to the ancestor's name. Surnames in Ireland, therefore, tended to identify membership of a sept.

Crumlish may be derived from Gaelic *O Cromruisc*, meaning 'descendant of the squint-eyed man'. The homeland of this sept was County Donegal.

Many County Donegal septs trace their lineage to Conall *Gulban*, son of the 5th century High King of Ireland, Niall of the Nine Hostages, who ruled from the Hill of Tara, County Meath. Conall and his brother Eogan conquered northwest Ireland, ca.425 AD, capturing the great hill-fort of Grianan of Ailech in County Donegal which commanded the entrance to the Inishowen peninsula between Lough Swilly and Lough Foyle.

Conall, styled 'King of Tir Conaill', established his own kingdom in County Donegal called after him Tyrconnel, i.e. the 'Land of Conall', which was the ancient name of Donegal. His descendants, known as the Cenel Conaill (the race of Conall), formed one of the principal branches of the Northern Ui Neill (descendants of Niall of the Nine Hostages). The septs of the Cenel Conaill firmly established themselves in County Donegal while those descended from Conal's brother Eogan expanded to the east and south into Counties Derry and Tyrone.

The escape of the most prominent Gaelic Lords of Ulster in 'the Flight of the Earls' in1607 from Lough Swilly, County Donegal marked the end of Gaelic power and paved the way for the 17th century Plantation of Ulster with English and Scottish settlers. In the centuries that followed Gaelic names were anglicised, resulting in many variant spellings of the same name and, in many cases, the dropping of the O and Mac prefixes.

At the time of the mid-19th century Griffith's Valuation 26 Crumlish households, including variant spellings of the surname, were recorded in Ireland, with all but four of these households residing in County Donegal. In other words 85% of descendants of the Crumlish sept in Ireland were living in County Donegal. This source records that there were 15 households recorded as Crimlisk, 4 as Cromlish, 4 as Crumlish, 2 as Crimlish and 1 as Crumlis.

This name, which spread to Derry city in the 19th century, illustrates the very close links, both historic and economic, between the city of Derry and County Donegal. As Derry developed an industrial base in shirt making, shipbuilding and distilling it attracted much of its workforce from County Donegal. In the 90-year period 1821 to 1911 the population of the city quadrupled to 40,780.

CUNNINGHAM

This is among the seventy-five most common names in Ireland with almost half of Cunninghams to be found in Ulster, particularly in Counties Antrim and Down. This name was brought to Ulster by settlers from Scotland in the 17th century, and in Ulster most Cunninghams are of Scottish origin. This name, however, was also widely adopted by descendants of several Irish septs.

Cunningham is derived from the district of the name in Ayrshire, Scotland. Derived from Gaelic *cuinneag*, meaning 'milk pail' and from English *ham*, meaning 'village', the manor of Cunningham was granted to Robert, son of Wernebald in the latter half of the 12th century. Alexander de Cunningham was created 1st Earl of Glencairn in 1488 by James III and Kerelaw Castle, at Stevenston in Ayrshire was part of their 15th century stronghold. The surname became widespread in Ayrshire.

In the 16th century Cunninghams from Ayrshire migrated to Strathblane in Stirlingshire. The name became common throughout Scotland with Cunninghams settling in Caithness, Fife and Edinburgh in the 16th and 17th centuries.

Movement of Scottish settlers to Ulster began in earnest from 1605 in a private enterprise colonisation of counties Antrim and Down when Sir Hugh Montgomery and Sir James Hamilton acquired title to large estates in north Down and Sir Randall MacDonnell, 1st Earl of Antrim, to large tracts of land in north Antrim. Further impetus came in 1609 when James I adopted the policy to encourage Scottish settlers to settle on the forfeited estates of the Gaelic chiefs in counties Armagh, Cavan, Donegal, Fermanagh, Londonderry (then known as Coleraine) and Tyrone.

These settlers came to Ulster, by and large, in three waves: with the granting of the initial leases in the period 1605 to 1625; after 1652 and Cromwell's crushing of the Irish rebellion; and finally in the fifteen years after 1690 and the Glorious Revolution. Scottish families entering Ireland through the port of Londonderry settled in the Foyle Valley which includes much of the fertile lands of counties Donegal, Londonderry and Tyrone. It is estimated by 1715, when migration to Ulster had virtually stopped, the Scottish population of Ulster stood at 200,000.

In the initial granting of leases in Ulster in 1610/1611, five of the principal Scottish planters (sixty-one in total) were Cunninghams, and they acquired extensive estates of land in County Donegal. Many of the settlers farming on these Scottish estates in Ulster would also have been called Cunningham as it was a feature of 17th century Scotland for tenants to take on their landlord's surname.

Fifteen Cunninghams, including Alexander Cunningham who was one of the thirteen apprentice boys who shut the gates of Derry on 7 December 1688, were recorded as 'defenders' of Derry during the famous Siege of 1689.

As well as numerous Scottish immigrants of the name many Cunninghams in Ulster, particularly in Derry and Donegal, will have Irish origins. Irish septs such as McCunnigan, in Gaelic *Mac Cuinneagain*, of Glenties, County Donegal; Coonaghan, in Gaelic *O Cuinneachain*, of County Derry; and Conaghan, in Gaelic *O Connachain*, of west Derry and east Donegal have, by and large, been changed to Cunningham.

CURRAN

This name is common in all the provinces in Ireland but especially Ulster, particularly in County Donegal and in the city of Derry.

This name, which is among the top 40 surnames in the city of Derry today, illustrates the very close links, both historic and economic, between Derry and County Donegal. As Derry developed an industrial base in the 19th century in shirt making, shipbuilding and distilling it attracted much of its workforce from Donegal. Her growing industries attracted workers and families from outside the city and county, and in the 90-year period 1821 to 1911 the population of the city quadrupled to 40,780. In this period Derry stamped her dominance over local rivals and emerged as an important urban centre within Ireland.

Ireland was one of the first countries to adopt a system of hereditary surnames which developed from a more ancient system of clan or sept names. From the 11th century each family began to adopt its own distinctive family name generally derived from the first name of an ancestor who lived in or about the 10th century. The surname was formed by prefixing either Mac (son of) or O (grandson or descendant of) to the ancestor's name. Surnames in Ireland, therefore, tended to identify membership of a sept.

Curran is generally derived from Gaelic *O Corrain*. In the 16th and 17th centuries there were distinct septs of this name located in different parts of the country: in Counties Waterford and Tipperary; in Counties Galway and Leitrim; and in County Kerry. The majority of Ulster Currans, however, will be descended from a County Donegal sept, in Gaelic *O Corraidhin*, which was anglicised as Curran, Curren and Cureen.

The escape of the most prominent Gaelic Lords of Ulster in 'the Flight of the Earls' in 1607 from Lough Swilly, County Donegal marked the end of Gaelic power and paved the way for the 17th century Plantation of Ulster with English and Scottish settlers. In the centuries that followed Gaelic names were anglicised, resulting in many variant spellings of the same name and, in many cases, the dropping of the O and Mac prefixes. In the case of Curran the prefix O was not retained.

Although Curran is a significant name in Donegal very little is known about the origins and history of this sept. *The Annals of The Kingdom of Ireland by the Four Masters* (a history of Ireland from 'the earliest period to the year 1616' which was compiled by monks who were followers of the O'Donnells of Donegal) contain no references to the Currans.

It would seem that this sept originated in the western fringes of Donegal between the towns of Falcarragh in the north and Glencolumbkille in the south. At the time of the mid-19th century Griffith's Valuation the greatest concentration of Currans in County Donegal was in the Gweedore area in the parish of Tullaghobegley, which contained 56 Curran households. In total 146 Curran households were recorded in this survey in County Donegal which was published between 1857 and 1858.

In Scotland Curran, possibly derived from Gaelic Irish *MacCorrain*, meaning 'son of Corran', was recorded in Ayrshire and Wigtownshire.

DARCY

This surname originates from outside the province of Ulster. Darcys in Ireland can either be of Norman origin or of Irish Gaelic descent.

Most Darcy families in Leinster are of Norman origin, being originally *D'Arci*, from the place name of Arci in Normandy. They descend from the Anglo-Norman family of d'Arcy who settled in County Meath in the 14ᵗʰ century. The chief seat of the descendants of Sir John D'Arcy, Chief Justice of Ireland in the 14ᵗʰ century, was Platten, County Meath.

In Connaught and Munster Darcy will be of Irish origin. Ireland was one of the first countries to adopt a system of hereditary surnames which developed from a more ancient system of clan or sept names. From the 11ᵗʰ century each family began to adopt its own distinctive family name generally derived from the first name of an ancestor who lived in or about the 10th century. The surname was formed by prefixing either Mac (son of) or O (grandson or descendant of) to the ancestor's name. Surnames in Ireland, therefore, tended to identify membership of a sept.

Darcy is derived from Gaelic *O Dorchaidhe*, the root word being *dorcha*, meaning 'dark'. Initially anglicised as O'Dorcey descendants of two *O Dorchaidhe* septs, one from around Partry near Lough Mask in County Mayo, the other from eastern Galway, adopted Darcy as their surname.

The Darcys who became one of the 'Tribes of Galway' were of true Irish stock, being descended from the O'Dorceys of Partry near Lough Mask, County Mayo. Darcy, together with Kirwan, were the only members of the 'Tribes of Galway' to be of Gaelic Irish origin. The Lynches and Brownes, two of the most powerful and influential families among the 'Tribes of Galway', were of Norman origin; they came to Ireland at the time of the Anglo-Norman invasion in the 12ᵗʰ century.

In some instances it is believed that the County Leitrim sept of *Mac Dhorchaidh* was anglicised as Darcy in County Fermanagh. In the *Annals of Loch Ce* the name MacDarcy appears as a County Leitrim chieftain in the years 1384 and 1403. *The Annals of The Kingdom of Ireland by the Four Masters* (a chronicle of Irish history from 'the earliest period to the year 1616') record, in 1310, the death of Farrell Mac Dorcy. The *Annals*, in a footnote, state that the homeland of the McDarcy sept was the parish of Oughteragh in east Leitrim.

Even by the middle years of the 19ᵗʰ century Darcy was not a common name in Ulster. The mid-19ᵗʰ century Griffith's Valuation records 9 Darcy households in northwest Ulster: with six families of the surname in County Tyrone; three in County Fermanagh and no Darcy households in either Counties Derry or Donegal.

In 1878 Huntly D'Arcy-Irvine of Castle Irvine, Irvinestown, County Fermanagh held estates of 1108 acres in County Fermanagh and 1,669 acres in County Tyrone. The Irvines of Irvinestown, County Fermanagh (which lies close to the border with County Tyrone) claim descent from the Irvings of Bonshaw, Dumfriesshire, Scotland.

DEENEY

In Ulster this name is very much associated with east Donegal and west Derry.

Ireland was one of the first countries to adopt a system of hereditary surnames which developed from a more ancient system of clan or sept names. From the 11th century each family began to adopt its own distinctive family name generally derived from the first name of an ancestor who lived in or about the 10th century. The surname was formed by prefixing either Mac (son of) or O (grandson or descendant of) to the ancestor's name. Surnames in Ireland, therefore, tended to identify membership of a sept.

Deeney is derived from Gaelic *O Duibhne*, the root word being *duibhne* meaning 'disagreeable'. Originating in County Donegal this sept was strongly represented in the priesthood in the Diocese of Raphoe from the 15th century. In many cases the name was further anglicised, through mistranslation, to Peoples. This arose from the similarity of the sound of Gaelic *Daoine*, meaning 'people' and Gaelic *duibhne*. Thus *O Duibhne* was anglicised to Deeney and mistranslated to Peoples.

It would seem that the homeland of this sept was the Fanad Peninsula in north Donegal. At the time of the mid-19th century Griffith's Valuation the greatest concentration of Deeneys in County Donegal were in the parishes of Killygarvan, which contained 29 Deeney households and Clondavaddog with 19 households of the name. In total 60 Deeney households were recorded in this survey in County Donegal which was published between 1857 and 1858. In other words 80% of the descendants of the O'Deeney sept in Donegal lived in these two parishes situated on the Fanad Peninsula.

At the time of the mid-19th century Griffith's Valuation there were 47 Peoples households recorded in County Donegal. Eleven Peoples households were recorded in both the parishes of Conwal and Kilmacrenan which are located to the south of the Fanad Peninsula. In other words over 45% of the Peoples households in County Donegal resided in these 2 parishes to the north and west of the town of Letterkenny.

Both Deeney and Peoples are common names in Derry city today. It would seem, however, that the movement into Derry city began after 1831 as only three Deeney households and three Peoples households were recorded in Derry city in the 1831 census. These names illustrate the very close links, both historic and economic, between the city of Derry and County Donegal. As Derry developed an industrial base in the 19th century in shirt making, shipbuilding and distilling it attracted much of its workforce from Donegal. In the 90-year period 1821 to 1911 the population of the city quadrupled to 40,780.

Peoples is also recorded as a surname in England where it is regarded as a variant of Pepys. It is possible that some Peoples in Ulster may be descendants of 17th century English settlers. Peoples, however, is not a common name in England.

In 1631 Hugh Peoples acquired the lands of Bellehebestocke, County Antrim. The Hearth Money Rolls of 1669 for County Antrim record the surnames of Peoples, Peables, Pebbles, Pebles and Pheables.

DEERY

In Ulster, this surname is found almost exclusively in Counties Derry and Donegal. It would seem that the distinct surname of Derry has now been absorbed into Deery.

Deery is derived from Gaelic *O Daighre*. They were *erenaghs*, i.e. hereditary stewards, of the church in the monastic settlement of Derry. They were a notable ecclesiastical family in Ulster. Strictly speaking this sept should be distinguished from, though it is confused with, O'Derry.

The sept name of O'Derry is derived from Gaelic *O Doireidh*. They were *erenaghs*, i.e. hereditary stewards, of the church lands of Donaghmore in County Donegal. Maeliosa O Doireidh was Bishop of Derry in the 13th century. The Derry Visitation of 1609 records O Doireidh as erenagh of Columbkil in the Diocese of Derry.

Although closely associated with County Derry, the surnames of Derry and Deery have no connection with the place name of Derry. The city of Derry, where St Columcille (also known as St Columba) founded a monastery in 546 AD, is derived from Gaelic *Daire*, meaning 'an oak grove'.

The 1831 census for County Derry clearly demonstrates that the lands along the Faughan Valley in west Derry were the ancestral homeland of the Deerys in County Derry. At the time of the 1831 census there were 23 Deery households and 3 Derry households in County Derry, and 17 of these households, i.e. 65% of the total, were residing in the three parishes of Cumber Lower, Cumber Upper and Clondermot.

At the time of the mid-19th century Griffith's Valuation there were 48 Deery households and 1 Derry household in County Donegal. This source records that in County Donegal Deerys were concentrated in two parishes which were located at opposite ends of the county. Eighteen Deery households were recorded in this survey in Drumhome Parish, at the southern end of the county, and 11 households in Clonca Parish in Inishowen, at the northern end. In other words nearly 60% of Deery households in County Donegal were located in these 2 parishes.

Deery is a common name in Derry city today. It would seem, however, that the movement into Derry city began after 1831 as only 2 Deery households were recorded in Derry city in the 1831 census. As the city of Derry developed an industrial base in the 19th century in shirt making, shipbuilding and distilling it attracted much of its workforce from the surrounding countryside and, in particular, from the Inishowen district of Donegal. In the 90-year period 1821 to 1911 the population of the city quadrupled to 40,780.

The anglicisation of Gaelic names, from the 17th century, resulted in many variant spellings of the same name and, in many cases, the dropping of the O and Mac prefixes. In the case of Deery the prefix O was not retained. By the time of the 1831 Census for County Derry and of the mid-19th century Griffith's Valuation for County Donegal the O prefix was not recorded against any of the descendants of the Deery or Derry septs in northwest Ireland.

DEVENNEY

This name is mainly found in County Donegal and in the adjacent counties of Mayo and Leitrim in Connaught.

Ireland was one of the first countries to adopt a system of hereditary surnames which developed from a more ancient system of clan or sept names. From the 11th century each family began to adopt its own distinctive family name generally derived from the first name of an ancestor who lived in or about the 10th century. The surname was formed by prefixing either Mac (son of) or O (grandson or descendant of) to the ancestor's name. Surnames in Ireland, therefore, tended to identify membership of a sept.

There were two distinct septs of this name with origins in Ulster. The Devenney sept of County Down is derived from Gaelic O Duibheamhna, the root word being dubh, meaning 'black'. This sept's territory was near Lough Neagh. They may also have been the ancient chiefs of Ui Breasail, i.e. the race of Breasal, on the south side of Lough Neagh in County Armagh. Conor O'Devany, the Irish Catholic martyr who was hanged for high treason in Dublin, was Bishop of Down and Connor from 1582 to 1612.

The County Donegal sept of Devenney is derived from Gaelic O Duibheannaigh, the root word being dubh, meaning 'black'. The O'Devannys were followers of the O'Donnells, the pre-eminent family in Donegal from the thirteenth to the seventeenth century. They fought alongside the O'Donnells in resisting English attempts to pacify Ireland during the Nine Years War (1594-1603). The O'Devannys were pardoned with Rory O'Donnell and his followers in 1602.

The Devenneys have had a long association with Donegal. The O'Devenys were recorded in Inishowen, County Donegal in the census of 1659, and their name appears frequently in the records of the Diocese of Raphoe.

This name is now very numerous in Mayo and Leitrim as descendants of the Devenney sept of Donegal settled there. Many Donegal names are found in Mayo today as a result of considerable migration in the early seventeenth century.

The escape of the most prominent Gaelic Lords of Ulster in 'the Flight of the Earls' in 1607 from Lough Swilly, County Donegal marked the end of Gaelic power and paved the way for the 17th century Plantation of Ulster with English and Scottish settlers. In the centuries that followed Gaelic names were anglicised, resulting in many variant spellings of the same name and, in many cases, the dropping of the O and Mac prefixes. In the case of Devenney the prefix O was not retained.

At the time of the mid-19th century Griffith's Valuation there were 90 Devenney households spread throughout County Donegal: with 55 households recorded as Devany; 28 as Devanny; 5 as Deveny; and 2 as Devenny. The O prefix was not recorded against any of the descendants of the Devenney sept in Donegal.

DEVINE

The name Devine, with origins in County Fermanagh, is chiefly found today in Counties Derry and Tyrone.

Ireland was one of the first countries to adopt a system of hereditary surnames which developed from a more ancient system of clan or sept names. From the 11th century each family began to adopt its own distinctive family name generally derived from the first name of an ancestor who lived in or about the 10th century. The surname was formed by prefixing either Mac (son of) or O (grandson or descendant of) to the ancestor's name. Surnames in Ireland, therefore, tended to identify membership of a sept.

The Devine sept trace their lineage to *Daimhin*, who died in 966, and were thus in Gaelic *O Daimhin*, i.e. descendant of Devine. Daimhin, derived from *damh*, meaning 'ox', was the son of Cairbre Dam Argait, King of Oriel. The ancient Kingdom of Oriel covered most of Counties Armagh and Monaghan.

The O'Devines, as Lords of Tirkennedy, a barony in the east of County Fermanagh, were a leading sept in that county up until and including the 15th century. They were for a time the most powerful sept in Fermanagh. In 1278, at the time of his death, Flaherty O'Davine was styled 'Lord of Fermanagh'. In 1427, when Brian O'Devine died, he was styled 'Chief of Tir-Kennedy'.

From the mid-15th century the power of the O'Devines was reduced by pressure from the O'Neills in the north and the Maguires in the south. In 1447 the O'Devines sided with Philip Maguire in his dispute with Donnell Ballagh Maguire, which resulted in the latter's death, over the chieftainship of the Maguires.

The Devines had strong associations with Derry from an early period. *The Annals of The Kingdom of Ireland by the Four Masters* mention, in 1066, one O'Devine, namely Dunchadh Ua Daimhene, as 'coarb' of Derry, i.e. abbot of the monastery at Derry. The abbot was regarded as the 'heir' of the saintly founder, which in the case of Derry was St Columcille (also known as St Columba). In 1212 'Donnell O'Devine was slain by the sons of Mac Loughlin in the doorway of the abbey-church of Derry'.

In County Tyrone the Devines gave Clogher its original name, *Clochar Mac nDaimhin.*

Variants of this name include Divine, Devin, Diven and Divin. In Counties Derry and Tyrone the sept name of *O Duibhin* was anglicised to Divine and Diveen but it is now indistinguishable from *O Daimhin*, i.e. Devine.

DEVLIN

Devlin is most common in County Tyrone where it is the fifth most numerous name, and in the adjacent counties of Antrim, Derry and Armagh. Over 80% of Irish Devlins are from Ulster.

The Devlin sept trace their lineage to Eogan, son of the 5th century High King of Ireland, Niall of the Nine Hostages, who ruled from the Hill of Tara, County Meath. Eogan and his brother Conall *Gulban* conquered northwest Ireland, ca.425 AD, capturing the great hill-fort of Grianan of Ailech in County Donegal which commanded the entrance to the Inishowen peninsula between Lough Swilly and Lough Foyle.

Eogan, styled 'King of Ailech', established his own kingdom in the peninsula still called after him Inishowen (Innis Eoghain or Eogan's Isle). Eogan was converted to Christianity by St Patrick, when he travelled to Ailech, ca. 442 AD. His descendants, known as the Cenel Eoghain (the race of Owen), became the principal branch of the Northern Ui Neill (descendants of Niall of the Nine Hostages). The Cenel Eoghain in the next five centuries expanded to the east and south from their focal point in Inishowen.

Ireland was one of the first countries to adopt a system of hereditary surnames which developed from a more ancient system of clan or sept names. From the 11th century each family began to adopt its own distinctive family name generally derived from the first name of an ancestor who lived in or about the 10th century. The surname was formed by prefixing either Mac (son of) or O (grandson or descendant of) to the ancestor's name. Surnames in Ireland, therefore, tended to identify membership of a sept. O'Devlin is derived from Gaelic *O Doibhilin*, i.e. descendant of Develin.

The O'Devlins were an important Tyrone sept, tracing their descent from Murdock Mac Earca, son of Muireadach (Murdock), son of Eogan. They ruled a territory called *Muintir Dhoiblin* or Munterdevlin on the west shore of Lough Neagh in what the English called 'O'Neill's own country'. The chief of the *Muintir Dhoiblin*, 'people of Develin', was hereditary sword-bearer to O'Neill and the O'Devlins were part of his cavalry.

The 17th century Plantation of Ulster with English and Scottish settlers marked the end of O'Devlin power, but the name remained. Today, Devlins are very common around the County Tyrone towns of Cookstown, Dungannon, Coalisland and Donaghmore.

There was once an important sept of *O Doibhilin* in the barony of Corran, County Sligo. As early as 1031 *The Annals of The Kingdom of Ireland by the Four Masters* record a reference to the County Sligo Devlins. In that year *Cusleibhe Ua Dobhailen* (anglicised Devlin) was slain. As late as 1316 the O'Devlins of Sligo were standard bearers to the O'Connors. Devlin, however, is now an uncommon name in Sligo. It is believed that families of the *O Doibhilin* sept of County Sligo widely changed their name to Dolan.

DIAMOND

This name is associated with County Mayo in north Connaught and with Counties Derry and Donegal in northwest Ulster.

Ireland was one of the first countries to adopt a system of hereditary surnames which developed from a more ancient system of clan or sept names. From the 11th century each family began to adopt its own distinctive family name generally derived from the first name of an ancestor who lived in or about the 10th century. The surname was formed by prefixing either Mac (son of) or O (grandson or descendant of) to the ancestor's name. Surnames in Ireland, therefore, tended to identify membership of a sept.

Diamond is derived from a County Derry sept, in Gaelic *O Diamain.* In the census of 1659 Diamond, in the form of O Dyman, was recorded as one of the principal Irish names in the barony of Loughinsholin in south Derry. The Diamonds were *erenaghs,* i.e. hereditary stewards, of church lands in east Derry.

The 1831 census for County Derry clearly demonstrates that east Derry was the ancestral homeland of the Diamonds. At the time of the 1831 census there were 196 Diamond households in County Derry, with the main concentration in those parishes situated along the western banks of the River Bann and Lough Neagh. At the time of the 1831 census there were 38 Diamond households recorded in Ballyscullion Parish, 34 households of the name in Tamlaght O'Crilly Parish, 22 in Kilrea, 20 in Desertoghill and 19 in Artrea.

The Hearth Money Rolls of 1663 would suggest that the land, in the parishes of Killelagh and Maghera, immediately surrounding the village of Swatragh was the original base of this sept. Seven Diamond households were recorded in this source in County Derry - 6 households of O'Diamond and 1 of Deamon; and they were all residing in the townlands just to the south and east of Swatragh.

The escape of the most prominent Gaelic Lords of Ulster in 'the Flight of the Earls' in 1607 from Lough Swilly, County Donegal marked the end of Gaelic power and paved the way for the 17th century Plantation of Ulster with English and Scottish settlers. In the centuries that followed Gaelic names were anglicised, resulting in many variant spellings of the same name and, in many cases, the dropping of the O and Mac prefixes.

In the case of Diamond the prefix O was not retained. The sept's name was still being recorded as O'Diamond in the Protestant Householders Lists of 1740. By the time of the 1831 census, however, the O prefix was not recorded against any of the descendants of the Diamond sept in County Derry.

The name is now found also in Donegal and Mayo. It would seem likely that the name first spread to Donegal and from there to County Mayo. In the early seventeenth century there was considerable migration of families from County Donegal to Mayo.

DIVER

In Ulster, this surname is found almost exclusively in County Donegal and the city of Derry.

Ireland was one of the first countries to adopt a system of hereditary surnames which developed from a more ancient system of clan or sept names. From the 11th century each family began to adopt its own distinctive family name generally derived from the first name of an ancestor who lived in or about the 10th century. The surname was formed by prefixing either Mac (son of) or O (grandson or descendant of) to the ancestor's name. Surnames in Ireland, therefore, tended to identify membership of a sept.

Diver is derived from Gaelic *O Duibhidhir*, the root word being *dubh,* meaning 'black'. The second part of this name was probably a Gaelic forename which is now obsolete. The Divers were an important sept in County Donegal where they gained some prominence in the medieval period. *The Annals of The Kingdom of Ireland by the Four Masters* (a chronicle of Irish history from 'the earliest period to the year 1616') record, in 1093, that Trenfhear O'Kelly, Lord of Breagh, County Meath 'was killed by Ua Duibhidhir' in Duleek, County Meath.

Many County Donegal septs trace their lineage to Conall *Gulban,* son of the 5th century High King of Ireland, Niall of the Nine Hostages, who ruled from the Hill of Tara, County Meath. Conall and his brother Eogan conquered northwest Ireland, ca.425 AD, capturing the great hill-fort of Grianan of Ailech in County Donegal which commanded the entrance to the Inishowen peninsula between Lough Swilly and Lough Foyle.

Conall, styled 'King of Tir Conaill', established his own kingdom in County Donegal called after him Tyrconnel, i.e. the 'Land of Conall', which was the ancient name of Donegal. His descendants, known as the Cenel Conaill (the race of Conall), formed one of the principal branches of the Northern Ui Neill (descendants of Niall of the Nine Hostages). The septs of the Cenel Conaill firmly established themselves in County Donegal while those descended from Conal's brother Eogan expanded to the east and south into Counties Derry and Tyrone.

At the time of the mid-19th century Griffith's Valuation 222 Diver households, including variant spellings of the surname, were recorded in County Donegal. This source records that in County Donegal in 1857/1858 there were 100 households recorded as Dever, 76 as Devir and 46 as Diver. Fifty-six of these households, i.e. 25% of the total, were recorded in the Inishowen district of Donegal. A further one-quarter, i.e. 53 households, were living in the three parishes of Clondahorky, Kilmacrenan and Tullaghobegley in west Donegal. Of all the parishes in County Donegal the one with the most descendants of the Diver sept was Tullaghobegley Parish which had 24 households of the name.

The name has now spread to Derry city and to County Mayo. As Derry developed an industrial base in the 19th century in shirt making, shipbuilding and distilling it attracted much of its workforce from Donegal. Many Donegal names are also found in Mayo as a result of considerable migration in the early seventeenth century.

DOHERTY

This name, which is by far the most popular name in the city of Derry and the Inishowen peninsula, County Donegal, illustrates the very close links between these two areas. As Derry developed an industrial base in the 19th century in shirt making, shipbuilding and distilling it attracted much of its workforce from Inishowen.

The Doherty sept trace their lineage to Conall *Gulban*, son of the 5th century High King of Ireland, Niall of the Nine Hostages, who ruled from the Hill of Tara, County Meath. Conall and his brother Eogan conquered northwest Ireland, ca.425 AD, capturing the great hill-fort of Grianan of Ailech which commanded the entrance to Inishowen between Lough Swilly and Lough Foyle.

Ireland was one of the first countries to adopt a system of hereditary surnames which developed from a more ancient system of clan or sept names. The surname was formed by prefixing either Mac (son of) or O (grandson or descendant of) to the ancestor's name.

The Dohertys take their name from *Dochartach*, twelfth in lineal descent from Conall Gulban and were thus in Gaelic *O Dochartaigh*. The word *dochartach* means 'hurtful'. The original seat of the Doherty clan was at Ardmire or *Ard Miodhair*, a district to the west of Ballybofey near Lough Finn, County Donegal. In 1203 Donnell Carragh O'Doherty was styled 'Royal Chieftain of Ardmire'.

As the original homeland of the Cenel Eoghain (the race of Owen) in Inishowen became more and more a northern outpost, as they expanded south and east, the O'Dohertys, a powerful branch of the Cenel Conaill (race of Conall), forced their way into Inishowen. When Conor O'Doherty died in 1413 he was styled 'Chief of Ardmire, and Lord of Inishowen'. The Dohertys remained the chief family of Inishowen until their influence was broken after the rebellion of Sir Cahir O'Doherty in 1608, which included the ransacking of the city of Derry.

The defeat and execution of Sir Cahir O'Doherty marked the end of Doherty power and paved the way for the 17th century Plantation of Ulster with English and Scottish settlers. In the centuries that followed the name was anglicised with many variant spellings and in nearly all cases the O prefix was dropped. By 1890 only 2 per cent were still using it. However, in the 20th century, many resumed it and by 1950 half of the Dohertys in Ireland had become O'Doherty again.

In the 17th and 18th centuries many descendants of the old Gaelic order in Ireland emigrated, as the so-called Wild Geese, to Europe, and, in particular, to Spain and France. Dr Ramon Salvador O'Dogherty of San Fernando, near Cadiz, Spain was inaugurated in July 1990 as the 37th O'Dochartaigh, chief of Inishowen. Ramon O'Dogherty is descended from Sir Cahir's brother John who fled from Inishowen to County Cavan and whose descendants settled in Spain, as nobility, in the 18th century. The inauguration ceremony took place on the original 'crowning stone', which tradition states was carried from Grianan, in the grounds of Belmont School in Derry, using the ancient ceremonial ritual of the clan: The claimant to the title of 'The O'Doherty' standing barefoot on the stone, holding a white wand of hazel wood.

DONAGHY

Donaghy can be an Irish or a Scottish name. In Ulster this name is most common in Counties Antrim, Derry and Tyrone.

Ireland was one of the first countries to adopt a system of hereditary surnames which developed from a more ancient system of clan or sept names. The surname was formed by prefixing either Mac (son of) or O (grandson or descendant of) to the ancestor's name.

In western Ulster, especially in Counties Derry and Tyrone, Donaghy is a variant of McDonagh, in Gaelic *Mac Donnchaidh*, meaning 'son of Donagh'. *Donnchadh*, meaning 'brown warrior', was a popular personal name in Ireland.

Four distinct septs of McDonagh originated in Ireland. In County Cork the McDonaghs were a branch of the McCarthys. They held the castle of Kanturk and were known as Lords of Duhallow. In County Sligo the McDonaghs were lords of Corran. They were a branch of the McDermots who were the dominant family in Counties Sligo and Roscommon. In County Galway a small McDonagh sept was an offshoot of the O'Flahertys of Connemara, and in County Fermanagh it is thought that most Donaghys descend from Donnchadh Ceallach Maguire, a 15th century chief.

In some instances Donaghy has also been used for Donohoe, in Gaelic *O Donnchadha*, meaning 'descendant of Donagh'. Distinct septs of this name became established in Counties Cavan, Galway and Kerry. Donohoe is among the fifteen most common names in County Cavan. At the end of the 19th century Donohoe was being used interchangeably with Donaghy in Inishowen, County Donegal.

Some Donaghys in Ulster, particularly in County Antrim, may have Scottish ancestry. Donnchadh was also a common personal name in Scotland where it was usually anglicised as Duncan. Clan Robertson of Atholl in Perthshire was also known as Clan Donnachaidh. This clan traces its descent from Fat Duncan or Donnachaidh Reamhair who fought alongside Robert the Bruce at the Battle of Bannockburn in 1314. As well as being the name of a sept attached to Clan Robertson many members of Clan Robertson, after the 1745 rebellion, adopted the name Donnachie to conceal their identity.

McConachie, in Gaelic *Mac Dhonnchaidh*, meaning 'son of Duncan', became a common surname in the Highlands of Scotland, especially in Argyllshire. Septs of this name were attached to Clans Robertson, Campbell and Gregor. This name was also anglicised as McConaghy, McConkey and Donaghy.

Confusion arises, in Ulster, when Scottish Donnachie and McConachie were further anglicised as Donaghy which is usually regarded as a variant of Irish McDonagh.

Upheavals such as military incursions, feuds and harvest failures would have encouraged many clan members, including Donnachies and McConachies, to migrate to Ulster as settlers during the 17th century. Owing to the nature of the Scottish clan system once the power and influence of the chief had been weakened and the bond of tribal loyalty broken the clan tended to scatter.

DONNELL

In Ulster Donnell may be a shortened form of either O'Donnell or McDonnell. Thus Donnell can be an Irish or a Scottish surname.

The O'Donnell sept, the most famous family of County Donegal, trace their lineage to Conall *Gulban*, son of the 5th century High King of Ireland, Niall of the Nine Hostages. Conall and his brother Eogan conquered northwest Ireland, ca.425 AD, capturing the great hill-fort of Grianan of Ailech in County Donegal. Conall, styled 'King of Tir Conaill', established his own kingdom in County Donegal called after him Tyrconnel, i.e. the 'Land of Conall', which was the ancient name of Donegal.

Ireland was one of the first countries to adopt a system of hereditary surnames which developed from a more ancient system of clan or sept names. The surname was formed by prefixing either Mac (son of) or O (grandson or descendant of) to the ancestor's name. The O'Donnells take their name from *Domhnall,* who died in 901, and were thus in Gaelic *O Domhnaill*, i.e. descendant of Donal.

Prior to their rise to predominance the O'Donnell sept was located in a comparatively small area around Kilmacrenan, County Donegal. The O'Donnells became the pre-eminent family in Donegal from the thirteenth to the seventeenth century. *The Annals of The Kingdom of Ireland by the Four Masters* are full of references, over three hundred in total, to the exploits of the O'Donnells in northwest Ireland. The family also spread into Counties Derry and Tyrone, particularly north Tyrone where the majority dropped the O prefix.

The O'Donnells have produced many illustrious figures in Irish history. The most famous was Red Hugh O'Donnell (1571-1602) who led Gaelic resistance to English attempts to pacify Ireland during the Nine Years War (1594-1603).

Donnell can also be a variant of Scottish McDonnell. According to Clan Donald genealogical lore the McDonnells can trace their ancestry back to Ireland and to *Conn of the Hundred Battles,* King of Connaught, who was killed in 157 AD at Tara, County Meath.

The MacDonalds, Gaelic Mac Dhomhnuill, meaning son of Donald, take their name from Donald of Islay, grandson of Somerled. Under the leadership of Somerled, who expelled the Norsemen from the western side of Scotland in the 12th century, Clan Donald claimed the position of 'The Headship of the Gael'. By the time of his death in 1387, John MacDonald, as Lord of the Isles, controlled the whole of the Hebrides from Lewis to Islay, with the exception of Skye, and the mainland from Kintyre to Knoydart.

Clan Donald acquired new territories in the north of Ireland ca.1400 when one of John's sons, John Mor, married Margery Bissett, an heiress in the Glens of Antrim. Members of the clan had gained a foothold in the Glens in the 13th century through land grants for military service as galloglasses, i.e. mercenary soldiers. By the mid-16th century the MacDonalds, known as the McDonnells of the Glens, had carved out an extensive territory in County Antrim at the expense of the McQuillans. Movement of Scottish settlers to County Antrim began in earnest from 1605 when Sir Randall MacDonnell, 1st Earl of Antrim, acquired title to large tracts of land in north Antrim.

DONNELLY

Donnelly is one of the seventy most numerous names in Ireland and one of the forty most numerous in Ulster. It is most common in its homeland of County Tyrone where it is the fourth most numerous name, and in the adjoining county of Armagh where it is among the first ten names.

The Donnelly sept trace their lineage to Eogan, son of the 5th century High King of Ireland, Niall of the Nine Hostages, who ruled from the Hill of Tara, County Meath. Eogan and his brother Conall *Gulban* conquered northwest Ireland, ca.425 AD, capturing the great hill-fort of Grianan of Ailech in County Donegal which commanded the entrance to the Inishowen peninsula between Lough Swilly and Lough Foyle.

Eogan, styled 'King of Ailech', established his own kingdom in the peninsula still called after him Inishowen (Innis Eoghain or Eogan's Isle). Eogan was converted to Christianity by St Patrick, when he travelled to Ailech, ca. 442 AD. His descendants, known as the Cenel Eoghain (the race of Owen), became the principal branch of the Northern Ui Neill (descendants of Niall of the Nine Hostages). The Cenel Eoghain in the next five centuries expanded to the east and south from their focal point in Inishowen.

Ireland was one of the first countries to adopt a system of hereditary surnames which developed from a more ancient system of clan or sept names. The surname was formed by prefixing either Mac (son of) or O (grandson or descendant of) to the ancestor's name. The Donnellys take their name from *Donnghaile O'Neill*, died 876, seventeenth in descent from Niall of the Nine Hostages, and were thus in Gaelic *O Donnghaile*. The name comes from *donn*, meaning 'brown' and *gal*, meaning 'warrior'. Thus O'Donnelly literally means 'descendant of the brown-haired warrior'.

Originating in County Donegal, the O'Donnelly sept later moved eastwards to Tyrone and settled in what became Ballydonnelly, *Baile Ui Dhonnghaile*, i.e. Donnelly's town. Their base was at Castlecaufield to the west of the town of Dungannon, County Tyrone.

The chief of the O'Donnellys was hereditary marshal of O'Neills armies and they were noted soldiers. One of the most famous was Donnell O'Donnelly who was killed at the Battle of Kinsale where O'Neill's Irish army and Spanish allies were defeated by an English army in 1601.

In the Irish rebellion of 1641 Patrick Modardha O'Donnelly captured the castle of Ballydonnelly from Lord Caulfield. When the castle was retaken Ballydonnelly was renamed Castle Caulfield.

In the 17th and 18th centuries many descendants of the old Gaelic order in Ireland emigrated, as the so-called Wild Geese, to Europe, and, in particular, to Spain and France. O'Donnellys fought for the Spanish in the Netherlands in 1652 and for the French in the 18th century.

In the Coleraine district of County Derry Donnelly has been used interchangeably with the Scottish name Donaldson.

DOWNEY

Downey is found in all the provinces of Ireland. It is a common name in the province of Connaught, particularly in County Galway, and in the province of Munster, especially in Counties Cork, Kerry and Limerick In Ulster, where it is most common in County Antrim, Downey can be an Irish or a Scottish name

Ireland was one of the first countries to adopt a system of hereditary surnames which developed from a more ancient system of clan or sept names. From the 11th century each family began to adopt its own distinctive family name generally derived from the first name of an ancestor who lived in or about the 10th century. The surname was formed by prefixing either Mac (son of) or O (grandson or descendant of) to the ancestor's name. Surnames in Ireland, therefore, tended to identify membership of a sept.

In Ulster, Downey is a shortened form of McEldowney. McEldowney is derived from Gaelic *Mac Giolla Domhnaigh*, meaning 'son of the devotee of the church'. This sept originated in County Derry. It is possible, in some instances, that McEldowney is another form of Muldowney, in Gaelic *O Maoldomhnaigh*, meaning 'descendant of the servant of the church'.

The Hearth Money Rolls of 1663 would suggest that this sept originated in south Derry. Six households, recorded either as McEldowney or Muldowney, were named in this source in County Derry - two households in Tamlaght Parish and one each in the parishes of Ballynascreen, Derryloran, Killelagh and Maghera. At the time of the 1831 census there were 37 McEldowney households in County Derry, and all but two of these households were residing in three parishes in south Derry; with 20 households of the name in Killelagh Parish, 9 in Ballynascreen and 6 in Maghera.

Outside Ulster, Downey is derived from O'Downey, in Gaelic *O Dunadhaigh*, the root word being *dun*, meaning 'fort'. There were 2 distinct septs of this name: in County Galway the O'Downeys, a branch of the O'Maddens, were 'lords of Sil Anmchadha'; and in County Kerry they were 'lords of Luachair'. Both these septs were of some importance in early medieval times.

Some Downeys in Ulster will be descendants of 17th century Scottish settlers. In Scotland, Downie has two distinct origins. It can be derived from the place name of Duny or Downie in Angus. During the 14th, 15th and 16th centuries references to the surname in Scotland can be found in places as far apart as Aberdeen, Arbroath and Glasgow. Downie is also a shortened form of McIldownie, in Gaelic *Mac Gille Domhnaich*, meaning 'son of the lord's servant'. The earliest record of the name is of a Robert Mackildowny who was made a freeman of Glasgow in 1573.

Movement of Scottish settlers to Ulster began in earnest from 1605 in a private enterprise colonisation of counties Antrim and Down when Sir Hugh Montgomery and Sir James Hamilton acquired title to large estates in north Down and Sir Randall MacDonnell, 1st Earl of Antrim, to large tracts of land in north Antrim. Further impetus came in 1609 when James I adopted the policy to encourage Scottish settlers to settle on the forfeited estates of the Gaelic chiefs in counties Armagh, Cavan, Donegal, Fermanagh, Londonderry (then known as Coleraine) and Tyrone.

DUDDY

The Duddy sept of County Derry trace their lineage to Eogan, son of the 5th century High King of Ireland, Niall of the Nine Hostages, who ruled from the Hill of Tara, County Meath. Eogan and his brother Conall *Gulban* conquered northwest Ireland, ca.425 AD, capturing the great hill-fort of Grianan of Ailech in County Donegal.

Eogan, styled 'King of Ailech', established his own kingdom in the peninsula in County Donegal still called after him Inishowen (Innis Eoghain or Eogan's Isle). His descendants, known as the Cenel Eoghain (the race of Owen), became the principal branch of the Northern Ui Neill (descendants of Niall of the Nine Hostages). The Cenel Eoghain in the next five centuries expanded to the east and south from their focal point in Inishowen.

Ireland was one of the first countries to adopt a system of hereditary surnames which developed from a more ancient system of clan or sept names. From the 11th century each family began to adopt its own distinctive family name generally derived from the first name of an ancestor who lived in or about the 10th century. The surname was formed by prefixing either Mac (son of) or O (grandson or descendant of) to the ancestor's name. Surnames in Ireland, therefore, tended to identify membership of a sept. Duddy is derived from Gaelic *O Dubhda*, the root word being *dubh* meaning black.

The Duddys were one of the septs of Clan Connor *Magh Ithe* (Connor was a direct descendant of Eogan). Magh Ithe is the rich countryside stretching southward from Inishowen, later known as the Laggan district in east Donegal. In the 10th century AD the families of Clan Connor moved out from the cramped territory of Magh Ithe and established themselves in County Derry, in the kingdom of Keenaght, to the north of the Sperrin Mountains, from the Foyle to the Bann rivers. In the process they ousted the Cianachta whose leading sept was the O'Connors of Glengiven in the Roe Valley.

By the 12th century when the process of conquest ends the various septs of Clan Connor, including the Duddys, were firmly settled in County Derry.

An important but distinct sept, also descended from *O Dubhda*, ruled over a wide territory which included the northern portions of Counties Mayo and Sligo. This sept trace their descent from Fiachra, brother of Niall of the Nine Hostages. For centuries they were the leading sept of the northern Ui Fiachrach (descendants of Fiachra). Their power was considerably reduced by the Anglo-Norman incursions into Connaught in the 13th century. This sept's name was anglicised to Dowd and O'Dowd.

DUFFY

Duffy is among the fifty most common names in both Ireland and Ulster. It is the single most popular name in County Monaghan and among the first fifteen in County Donegal.

The Duffy sept of County Donegal trace their lineage to Eogan, son of the 5th century High King of Ireland, Niall of the Nine Hostages, who ruled from the Hill of Tara, County Meath. Eogan and his brother Conall *Gulban* conquered northwest Ireland, ca.425 AD, capturing the great hill-fort of Grianan of Ailech in County Donegal.

Eogan, styled 'King of Ailech', established his own kingdom in the peninsula in County Donegal still called after him Inishowen (Innis Eoghain or Eogan's Isle). His descendants, known as the Cenel Eoghain (the race of Owen), became the principal branch of the Northern Ui Neill (descendants of Niall of the Nine Hostages). The Cenel Eoghain in the next five centuries expanded to the east and south from their focal point in Inishowen.

Ireland was one of the first countries to adopt a system of hereditary surnames which developed from a more ancient system of clan or sept names. The surname was formed by prefixing either Mac (son of) or O (grandson or descendant of) to the ancestor's name. Duffy is derived from Gaelic *O Dubhthaigh*, the root word being *dubh* meaning black. O'Duffy literally means 'descendant of the black one'.

The Duffys were one of the septs of Clan Connor *Magh Ithe* (Connor was a direct descendant of Eogan). Magh Ithe is the rich countryside stretching southward from Inishowen, later known as the Laggan district in east Donegal. In the 10th century AD the families of Clan Connor moved out from the cramped territory of Magh Ithe and established themselves in County Derry, in the kingdom of Keenaght, to the north of the Sperrin Mountains, from the Foyle to the Bann rivers. In the process they ousted the Cianachta whose leading sept was the O'Connors of Glengiven in the Roe Valley.

In County Donegal the Duffys were *erenaghs*, i.e. hereditary stewards, of Templecrone in the diocese of Raphoe for eight hundred years. They were kinsmen of the patron of the church, the seventh century St Dubhthach, or Duffy. The O'Duffys were also *erenaghs* at Culdaff in the barony of Inishowen.

O'Dubhthaigh was also the name of other unrelated Irish septs. As well as the Connaught Duffys who were centred at Lissonuffy, County Roscommon there was a sept of Duffys in County Monaghan who ruled the area around Clontibret. The first of the name on record is Patrick O'Duffy, Chief of *Teallach Gealacain* (an area which equates with the parish of Clontibret) in 1296.

In Scotland the Duffys were a sept of Clan Macfie who trace their descent from Kenneth McAlpine, the 9th century King of Scots. The clan's home was the island of Colonsay in the Inner Hebrides. With the decline of Clan Donald power the Macfies scattered at the beginning of the 17th century.

DUNLOP

This surname is found almost exclusively in Ulster where two-thirds are in County Antrim. This name was brought to Ulster by settlers from Scotland in the 17th century.

In Scotland, this surname is derived from the lands of Dunlop, meaning 'muddy fort', in the district of Cunningham in Ayrshire. Dunlop is a common surname in Ayrshire, and this region was home to many of the Scottish settlers who came to Ulster throughout the 17th century.

The earliest reference to the surname is of one William de Dunlop who was a witness to a deed with the burgesses of Irvine in Ayrshire in 1260. Until the middle of the 19th century this name was usually pronounced, in Ayrshire, as Delap or Dulap. The name became common in Kintyre after Lowlanders were encouraged to settle there in the 17th century. Dunlops from Arran then settled in north Antrim in the early 17th century when a Bryce or Bryan Dunlop obtained a grant of lands between Ballycastle and Ballintoy from Sir Randall MacDonnell.

Clan Donald had acquired new territories in the north of Ireland ca.1400 when John Mor MacDonald had married Margery Bissett, an heiress in the Glens of Antrim. By the mid-16th century the MacDonalds, known as the MacDonnells of the Glens, had carved out an extensive territory in County Antrim at the expense of the MacQuillans.
Movement of Scottish settlers to north Antrim began in earnest in 1605 when Sir Randall MacDonnell, 1st Earl of Antrim, acquired title to large tracts of land in the Glens of Antrim. By the mid-19th century the Dunlops were concentrated in the barony of Upper Dunluce in north Antrim.

Further impetus came in 1609 when James I adopted the policy to encourage English and Scottish settlers to settle on the forfeited estates of the Gaelic chiefs in counties Armagh, Cavan, Donegal, Fermanagh, Londonderry (then known as Coleraine) and Tyrone.

Settlers to Ulster came, by and large, in three waves: with the granting of the initial leases in the period 1605 to 1625; after 1652 and Cromwell's crushing of the Irish rebellion; and finally in the fifteen years after 1690 and the Glorious Revolution. It is estimated by 1715, when migration to Ulster had virtually stopped, the Scottish population of Ulster stood at 200,000.

The Hearth Money Rolls of 1663, in recording 6 Delap households, confirm that Dunlops were settled in County Londonderry from the early years of the Plantation of Ulster.

The Protestant Householders Lists of 1740 also confirm that the settlement of Dunlops in County Londonderry was further strengthened towards the end of the 17th century. This source records 14 Delap households and 33 Dunlop households in County Londonderry; with the name spelt as Delap in the parishes in the west of the county and as Dunlop in the parishes in the east. Dunlops were concentrated in the parishes of Macosquin with 9 households of the name, Desertoghill with 8 and Coleraine with 5, and Delaps, with 8 households of the name, in Templemore Parish.

EDWARDS

This name is found mostly in the provinces of Leinster and Ulster. In Ulster the name is more common in County Antrim than elsewhere. This name was brought to Ulster by settlers from England and Wales in the 17th century.

Edwards, derived from the personal name Edward, simply means 'son of Edward'. It is derived from the Old English first name *Eadweard*, meaning 'prosperous guardian'.
The popularity of the name probably stems from Edward the Confessor, who was the greatest Anglo-Saxon king. Indeed Edward was one of the few names acceptable to both Anglo-Saxon and Norman, and there are numerous references to Edwards in the Domesday Book of 1086.

Edward was a very popular choice as a child's name during the later Middle Ages, and at a time when fixed surnames, based on a father's first name, were being established. Today it is the 20th most popular surname in England and Wales.

Edwards became a very common surname in Wales, particularly in Denbighshire in north Wales. This is partly because the English equated the Welsh personal name *Iorwerth* with Edward.

The defeat of the old Gaelic order in the Nine Years War, 1594-1603 and the escape of the most prominent Gaelic Lords of Ulster in 'the Flight of the Earls' in 1607 from Lough Swilly, County Donegal were ultimately responsible for the settlement of many English, Welsh and Scottish families in the northern counties of Ireland.

In 1609 the Earl of Salisbury, Lord High Treasurer, suggested to James I a deliberate plantation of English, Welsh and Scottish colonists on the forfeited estates of the Gaelic chiefs in counties Armagh, Cavan, Donegal, Fermanagh, Londonderry (then known as Coleraine) and Tyrone.

Settlers came to Ulster, by and large, in three waves: with the granting of the initial leases in the period 1605 to 1625; after 1652 and Cromwell's crushing of the Irish rebellion; and finally in the fifteen years after 1690 and the Glorious Revolution. By the end of the 17th century a self-sustaining settlement of British colonists had established itself in Ulster.

Londonderry, Coleraine, Carrickfergus, Belfast and Donaghadee were the main ports of entry into the province of Ulster for 17th century British settlers with the Lagan, Bann and the Foyle valleys acting as the major arteries along which the colonists travelled into the interior. English settlers, mostly drawn from the northern counties of Cheshire, Cumberland, Lancashire, Northumberland, Yorkshire and Westmorland, and Welsh settlers tended to favour settlement along the Lagan Valley, in the east of the Province, on lands straddling the borders of Counties Armagh, Antrim and Down.

During the famous 105 day Siege of Derry, from 18 April to 31 July 1689, Captain Nicholas Edwards of Kilrea, County Derry was recorded as a 'defender' of the city. The Edwards were recorded as an 'old Ulster Plantation family'.

ELLIOTT

Elliott is common only in Ulster. About 80% of the Elliott families in Ireland are in Ulster where this surname came with numerous Scottish immigrants at the time of the Plantation of Ulster in the 17th century. It has long been associated with County Fermanagh, where it is the fifth most common name, and to a lesser extent with County Cavan.

The Elliotts were one of the largest border clans in Liddesdale in the western and middle Marches of England and Scotland. The valley of the Liddel Water which rises in Scotland, close to the border with England, flows south-westwards to the border and joins the Esk before entering the Solway Firth was home to the Elliotts. Although there were a number of branches of this family the Elliotts of Redheugh in Berwickshire were recognized as the principal family.

From the 14th to the late-17th century, the border between England and Scotland – the Debatable Lands – was a turbulent place. The Border country was ravaged by the lawless Reiver families who stole each other's cattle and possessions. They raided in large numbers, on horseback, and they killed and kidnapped without remorse. This type of life resulted in the growth of large closely-knit family groups with intense clan loyalties and fierce feuds against others. The Elliotts were a feared reiving family.

Prior to the Union of the Crowns of England and Scotland in 1603 the Scottish Border was divided into three districts; the east, west and middle Marches. Each March was presided over by a warden who settled disputes with the warden of the appropriate March in England, as border warfare was rife at this time with frequent cattle raids.

Pacification of the riding families began in earnest from 1603 with the Union of the Crowns of England and Scotland. The Elliotts suffered as King James I set about pacifying the borders in a ruthless campaign which included executions and banishment. In 1603 thirty-two Elliotts, Armstrongs, Johnstons, Beattys and others were hanged, fifteen were banished and one hundred and forty outlawed.

When the power of the riding clans was broken by James I in the decade after 1603 many came to Ulster to escape persecution. This flight to Ulster also suited the needs of the king. James I, from 1610, was determined to implement a deliberate plantation of Scottish and English colonists on the forfeited estates of the Gaelic chiefs in Counties Armagh, Cavan, Donegal, Fermanagh, Londonderry (then known as Coleraine) and Tyrone.

The Elliotts settled particularly in County Fermanagh. These Border families were well suited to life in the frontier of the Plantation of Ulster. They were a resilient people who stayed in County Fermanagh throughout the upheavals of the 17th century. Scottish settlers were hardier than their English counterparts, and the Borderers were even better adapted again to life on a new, insecure frontier.

At the Siege of Derry of 1689 six Elliotts, five of whom were from County Fermanagh, were recorded as 'defenders' of the city.

FARREN

The surname Farren is very much associated with County Donegal. Indeed two distinct septs anglicised their name to Farren in this county.

Ireland was one of the first countries to adopt a system of hereditary surnames which developed from a more ancient system of clan or sept names. From the 11th century each family began to adopt its own distinctive family name generally derived from the first name of an ancestor who lived in or about the 10th century. The surname was formed by prefixing either Mac (son of) or O (grandson or descendant of) to the ancestor's name. Surnames in Ireland, therefore, tended to identify membership of a sept.

The main sept of Farren, in Gaelic *O Farachain*, originated in Donegal. In O'Dugan's Topographical Poem *O Furadhran* (anglicised Farren) is described as Lord of Finross, which is now called the Rosses in County Donegal.

In Donegal, in particular, the surnames of Fearon and Farren have become confused. The Fearon sept, in Gaelic *O Fearain*, of the ancient kingdom of Oriel, which included much of Counties Armagh and Monaghan, trace their lineage to Eogan, son of the 5th century High King of Ireland, Niall of the Nine Hostages, who ruled from the Hill of Tara, County Meath. Eogan and his brother Conall *Gulban* conquered northwest Ireland, ca.425 AD, capturing the great hill-fort of Grianan of Ailech in County Donegal which commanded the entrance to the Inishowen peninsula between Lough Swilly and Lough Foyle.

Eogan, styled 'King of Ailech', established his own kingdom in the peninsula still called after him Inishowen (Innis Eoghain or Eogan's Isle). Eogan was converted to Christianity by St Patrick, when he travelled to Ailech, ca. 442 AD. His descendants, known as the Cenel Eoghain (the race of Owen), became the principal branch of the Northern Ui Neill (descendants of Niall of the Nine Hostages). The Cenel Eoghain in the next five centuries expanded to the east and south from their focal point in Inishowen.

Although *O Fearain* was anglicized to Fearon in County Armagh it tended to be changed to Farran in the case of families of this sept living in County Donegal. Thus in the census of 1659 O'Farran is listed as a 'principal name' in the barony of Inishowen, County Donegal. The prefix O has since then been dropped and rarely resumed.

Today this name illustrates the very close links between the city of Derry and the Inishowen peninsula, County Donegal. As Derry developed an industrial base in the 19th century in shirt making, shipbuilding and distilling it attracted much of its workforce from Inishowen.

FEE

This name originated in County Fermanagh and later spread into the neighbouring counties of Armagh and Cavan.

The Fee sept of County Fermanagh trace their lineage to Eogan, son of the 5th century High King of Ireland, Niall of the Nine Hostages, who ruled from the Hill of Tara, County Meath. Eogan and his brother Conall *Gulban* conquered northwest Ireland, ca.425 AD, capturing the great hill-fort of Grianan of Ailech in County Donegal.

Eogan, styled 'King of Ailech', established his own kingdom in the peninsula in County Donegal still called after him Inishowen (Innis Eoghain or Eogan's Isle). His descendants, known as the Cenel Eoghain (the race of Owen), became the principal branch of the Northern Ui Neill (descendants of Niall of the Nine Hostages). The Cenel Eoghain in the next five centuries expanded to the east and south from their focal point in Inishowen.

Ireland was one of the first countries to adopt a system of hereditary surnames which developed from a more ancient system of clan or sept names. From the 11th century each family began to adopt its own distinctive family name generally derived from the first name of an ancestor who lived in or about the 10th century. The surname was formed by prefixing either Mac (son of) or O (grandson or descendant of) to the ancestor's name. Surnames in Ireland, therefore, tended to identify membership of a sept.

Fee is derived from Gaelic *O Fiaich,* the root word being *fiach,* meaning 'a raven'. The Fees were *erenaghs*, i.e. hereditary stewards, of the church lands of Derrybrusk near Enniskillen, County Fermanagh. The name was also anglicised as O'Fee, Fey, Fie and Foy. In the census of 1659 the O'Fees were recorded as a 'principal name' in the parish of Derrybrusk. Their descendants are now usually called Foy and sometimes Fee.

The escape of the most prominent Gaelic Lords of Ulster in 'the Flight of the Earls' in1607 from Lough Swilly, County Donegal marked the end of Gaelic power and paved the way for the 17th century Plantation of Ulster with English and Scottish settlers. In the centuries that followed Gaelic names were anglicised, resulting in many variant spellings of the same name and, in many cases, the dropping of the O and Mac prefixes.

Fee is occasionally changed to Fay. Fay is derived from Norman *de faie,* meaning 'beech', thus denoting an ancestor who lived near beech trees. An Anglo-Norman family of the name settled in County Westmeath at the end of the 12th century. The family then spread to Counties Cavan and Monaghan.

In some instances the name was anglicised to Hunt in the mistaken notion that it was derived from *fiadhach,* meaning 'hunt'.

Fee is also common in County Antrim and it is possible that some of these were originally Scottish MacFees. Throughout the late sixteenth and early seventeenth centuries many Scottish families settled in County Antrim.

FEENEY

Although this surname originated outside of Ulster and is most common in the province of Connaught, Feeney had become a common name in County Derry by the mid-17th century.

Ireland was one of the first countries to adopt a system of hereditary surnames which developed from a more ancient system of clan or sept names. From the 11th century each family began to adopt its own distinctive family name generally derived from the first name of an ancestor who lived in or about the 10th century. The surname was formed by prefixing either Mac (son of) or O (grandson or descendant of) to the ancestor's name. Surnames in Ireland, therefore, tended to identify membership of a sept.

Feeney is derived from Galiec *O Fiannaidhe*, meaning 'soldier'. The Feeneys were a sept of the northern Ui Fiachrach (descendants of Fiachra). Based in the parish of Easky, County Sligo this sept trace their descent from Fiachra, brother of Niall of the Nine Hostages.

Niall of the Nine Hostages, who ruled from the Hill of Tara, County Meath, was High King of Ireland in the 5th century. Eogan and Conall Gulban, sons of Niall of the Nine Hostages, conquered northwest Ireland, ca.425 AD, capturing the great hill-fort of Grianan of Ailech in County Donegal which commanded the entrance to the Inishowen peninsula between Lough Swilly and Lough Foyle.

At an early date the Feeneys became established in County Derry. In the census of 1659 Feeney, in the form of O Feeny, was recorded as one of the principal Irish names in the barony of Keenaght, County Derry.

The village of Feeny is located in the parish of Banager, County Derry. This place name, however, has no association with the surname Feeney. In this case Feeny is derived from Gaelic *fiodnac* meaning 'the woody place or wilderness'.

It is possible that the Anglo-Norman military incursions of the 13th century into Connaught which reduced the power and influence of many septs in that province encouraged descendants of the Feeneys to migrate north at an early date.

The 1831 census for County Derry clearly demonstrates that the lands in the upper reaches of the Faughan and Roe Valleys were the ancestral homeland of the Feeneys in County Derry. At the time of the 1831 census there were 44 Feeney households in County Derry, and all but three of these households were residing in the parishes of Balteagh, Banagher, Cumber Lower, Cumber Upper, Dungiven and Faughanvale. At the time of the 1831 census there were 11 Feeney households recorded in Cumber Upper Parish, 9 households of the name in Dungiven Parish and 7 in Cumber Lower.

The anglicisation of Gaelic names, from the 17th century, resulted in many variant spellings of the same name and, in many cases, the dropping of the O and Mac prefixes. In the case of Feeney the prefix O was not retained. By the time of the 1831 census the O prefix was not recorded against any of the descendants of the Feeney sept in County Derry.

FEENY

Although this surname originated outside of Ulster and is most common in the province of Connaught, Feeny had become a common name in County Derry by the mid-17th century.

Ireland was one of the first countries to adopt a system of hereditary surnames which developed from a more ancient system of clan or sept names. From the 11th century each family began to adopt its own distinctive family name generally derived from the first name of an ancestor who lived in or about the 10th century. The surname was formed by prefixing either Mac (son of) or O (grandson or descendant of) to the ancestor's name. Surnames in Ireland, therefore, tended to identify membership of a sept.

Feeny is derived from Galiec *O Fiannaidhe*, meaning 'soldier'. The Feenys were a sept of the northern Ui Fiachrach (descendants of Fiachra). Based in the parish of Easky, County Sligo this sept trace their descent from Fiachra, brother of Niall of the Nine Hostages.

Niall of the Nine Hostages, who ruled from the Hill of Tara, County Meath, was High King of Ireland in the 5th century. Eogan and Conall Gulban, sons of Niall of the Nine Hostages, conquered northwest Ireland, ca.425 AD, capturing the great hill-fort of Grianan of Ailech in County Donegal which commanded the entrance to the Inishowen peninsula between Lough Swilly and Lough Foyle.

At an early date the Feenys became established in County Derry. In the census of 1659 Feeny, in the form of O Feeny, was recorded as one of the principal Irish names in the barony of Keenaght, County Derry.

The village of Feeny is located in the parish of Banager, County Derry. This place name, however, has no association with the surname Feeny. In this case Feeny is derived from Gaelic *fiodnac* meaning 'the woody place or wilderness'.

It is possible that the Anglo-Norman military incursions of the 13th century into Connaught which reduced the power and influence of many septs in that province encouraged descendants of the Feenys to migrate north at an early date.

The 1831 census for County Derry clearly demonstrates that the lands in the upper reaches of the Faughan and Roe Valleys were the ancestral homeland of the Feenys in County Derry. At the time of the 1831 census there were 44 Feeny households in County Derry, and all but three of these households were residing in the parishes of Balteagh, Banagher, Cumber Lower, Cumber Upper, Dungiven and Faughanvale. At the time of the 1831 census there were 11 Feeny households recorded in Cumber Upper Parish, 9 households of the name in Dungiven Parish and 7 in Cumber Lower.

The anglicisation of Gaelic names, from the 17th century, resulted in many variant spellings of the same name and, in many cases, the dropping of the O and Mac prefixes. In the case of Feeny the prefix O was not retained. By the time of the 1831 census the O prefix was not recorded against any of the descendants of the Feeny sept in County Derry.

FERGUSON

This name is among the fifty most common names of both Scotland and Ulster. This name was brought to Ulster, where it is most numerous in Counties Antrim, Down and Derry, by settlers from Scotland in the 17th century.

Clan Ferguson claim descent from Fergus Mac Erc, descendant of *Conn of the Hundred Battles,* King of Connaught, who was killed in 157 AD at Tara, County Meath. Fergus Mac Erc, and his brothers Angus and Lorn, conquered Kintyre, Argyll and some of the Inner Isles ca.470 AD. They called their Scottish kingdom Dal Riada, after the kingdom they still held in Ulster.

The clan first settled at Kintyre in Argyllshire. Kilkerran, the seat of the Ferguson chiefs, was later renamed Campbelltown. Kilkerran, meaning 'the church of Ciaran', was named after the 6th century St Ciaran, one of the twelve apostles of Ireland. The Fergusons of Kilkerran were hereditary keepers of the cross of St Ciaran.

In Dumfriesshire the Fergusons of Craigdarroch descend from Fergus, the 12th century Prince of Galloway, who married a daughter of Henry I of England. It is believed that the majority of Fergusons in Ulster are descended from the Fergusons of Galloway in southwest Scotland. There were also Ferguson branches at Atholl and at Balquhidder in Perthshire, and in Aberdeenshire.

Fergus was a popular personal name in medieval Scotland. The popularity of the name stems from Fergus, the grandfather of the famous 6th century saint, St Columcille, also known as St Columba, who founded monasteries at Derry in Ireland in 546 AD and at Iona in Scotland in 563 AD. Thus the surname, McFergus, in Gaelic *Mac Fhearghuis,* meaning 'son of Fergus', sprang up in many different locations, independently of each other, throughout Scotland. This name was further anglicised as Ferguson.

Movement of Scottish settlers to Ulster began in earnest from 1605 in a private enterprise colonisation of counties Antrim and Down when Sir Hugh Montgomery and Sir James Hamilton acquired title to large estates in north Down and Sir Randall MacDonnell, 1st Earl of Antrim, to large tracts of land in north Antrim. By the mid-19th century the Fergusons were mainly concentrated in the barony of Upper Antrim in County Antrim, and in the parish of Newtownards in County Down.

Further impetus came in 1609 when James I adopted the policy to encourage English and Scottish settlers to settle on the forfeited estates of the Gaelic chiefs in counties Armagh, Cavan, Donegal, Fermanagh, Londonderry (then known as Coleraine) and Tyrone. Scottish families entering Ireland through the port of Londonderry settled in the Foyle Valley which includes much of the fertile lands of counties Donegal, Londonderry and Tyrone.

During the famous 105 day Siege of Derry, from 18 April to 31 July 1689, Lieutenant Samuel Ferguson was recorded as one of the 'defenders' of the city. It is believed that Samuel was related to Rev. Andrew Ferguson, who was appointed minister of Burt Presbyterian congregation, County Donegal in 1690. Andrew's great grandson Sir Robert Alexander Ferguson was M.P. for the city of Derry from 1830 until 1860.

FERRY

In Ulster, this surname, also spelt Fairy, is found almost exclusively in County Donegal and the city of Derry.

Ireland was one of the first countries to adopt a system of hereditary surnames which developed from a more ancient system of clan or sept names. From the 11th century each family began to adopt its own distinctive family name generally derived from the first name of an ancestor who lived in or about the 10th century. The surname was formed by prefixing either Mac (son of) or O (grandson or descendant of) to the ancestor's name. Surnames in Ireland, therefore, tended to identify membership of a sept.

Ferry is derived from Gaelic *O Fearadhaigh,* the root word possibly being *fearadhach,* meaning 'manly'. The O'Ferrys were followers of the McSweeneys. This County Donegal sept trace their lineage to Conall *Gulban,* son of the 5th century High King of Ireland, Niall of the Nine Hostages, who ruled from the Hill of Tara, County Meath. Conall and his brother Eogan conquered northwest Ireland, ca.425 AD, capturing the great hill-fort of Grianan of Ailech in County Donegal which commanded the entrance to the Inishowen peninsula between Lough Swilly and Lough Foyle.

Conall, styled 'King of Tir Conaill', established his own kingdom in County Donegal called after him Tyrconnel, i.e. the 'Land of Conall', which was the ancient name of Donegal. His descendants, known as the Cenel Conaill (the race of Conall), formed one of the principal branches of the Northern Ui Neill (descendants of Niall of the Nine Hostages). The septs of the Cenel Conaill firmly established themselves in County Donegal while those descended from Conal's brother Eogan expanded to the east and south into Counties Derry and Tyrone.

It would seem that the homeland of this sept was the rugged west coast of Donegal, stretching from the town of Dunfanaghy in the north to The Rosses in the south. At the time of the mid-19th century Griffith's Valuation the greatest concentration of Ferrys in County Donegal were in the parishes of Tullaghobegley, which contained 82 Ferry households, Clondahorky with 31 households of the name and Raymunterdoney with 20. In total 175 Ferry households were recorded in this survey in County Donegal which was published between 1857 and 1858. In other words over 75% of the descendants of the O'Ferry sept in Donegal lived in these three parishes.

Ferry is a common name in Derry city today. This name illustrates the very close links, both historic and economic, between the city of Derry and County Donegal. As Derry developed an industrial base in the 19th century in shirt making, shipbuilding and distilling it attracted much of its workforce from Donegal. In the 90-year period 1821 to 1911 the population of the city quadrupled to 40,780.

The name is now well known in County Sligo and other parts of Connaught. In the early seventeenth century there was considerable migration of families from County Donegal to Connaught.

FLEMING

Although this name is common throughout Ireland it is most numerous in Ulster, especially in Counties Antrim and Derry. The majority of Ulster Flemings will be of Scottish origin.

Fleming is derived from Norman French *le Fleming*, meaning a 'native of Flanders'. In the Middle Ages there was a considerable wool trade between England and Flanders in the Netherlands, and many Flemish weavers and dyers settled in England. In England the surname is chiefly found in the northern counties of Cumberland and Westmorland. In the Furness district of Cumberland the surname can be traced to a Michael le Fleming who held lands there in the early 12th century.

From the 12th century the Flemings settled in significant numbers in Wales and the Scottish Borders. Fleming was introduced into Ireland at the time of the Anglo-Norman invasion of the 12th century when the De Flemmings from Wales acquired considerable estates in Counties Louth and Meath and were created Barons of Slane.

Fleming is one of the eighty most common names in Scotland. This name appears in Scottish records from the second half of the 12th century. For example, Theobald the Fleming, by 1160, held a grant of land from the abbot of Kelso, and Baldwin the Fleming was sheriff of Lanark in 1150. The Flemings of Boghall Castle held extensive lands in Lanarkshire.

The Flemings were also a sept of Clan Murray. Clan Murray, taking their name from the provincial name of Moray, trace their descent from Freskin de Moravia of Duffus in Moray, who was granted the lands of Strabrock in West Lothian by David I, King of Scotland 1124-1153.

Movement of Scottish settlers to Ulster began in earnest from 1605 in a private enterprise colonisation of counties Antrim and Down when Sir Hugh Montgomery and Sir James Hamilton acquired title to large estates in north Down and Sir Randall MacDonnell, 1st Earl of Antrim, to large tracts of land in north Antrim.

Further impetus came in 1609 when James I adopted the policy to encourage English and Scottish settlers to settle on the forfeited estates of the Gaelic chiefs in counties Armagh, Cavan, Donegal, Fermanagh, Londonderry (then known as Coleraine) and Tyrone.

Settlers to Ulster came, by and large, in three waves: with the granting of the initial leases in the period 1605 to 1625; after 1652 and Cromwell's crushing of the Irish rebellion; and finally in the fifteen years after 1690 and the Glorious Revolution. It is estimated by 1715, when migration to Ulster had virtually stopped, the Scottish population of Ulster stood at 200,000.

Flemings fought on both sides during the famous 105 day Siege of Derry, from 18 April to 31 July 1689. James and Richard Fleming of Ballymagorry, County Tyrone, and John Fleming were recorded as 'defenders' of the city, and Lieutenant Christopher Fleming, 22nd Baron of Slane, County Louth and his brother Henry served with the 'Jacobite Army' which besieged Derry.

FOY

This name originated in County Fermanagh and later spread into the neighbouring counties of Armagh and Cavan. Foy has become confused with Fay of Anglo-Norman origin.

The Foy sept of County Fermanagh trace their lineage to Eogan, son of the 5th century High King of Ireland, Niall of the Nine Hostages, who ruled from the Hill of Tara, County Meath. Eogan and his brother Conall *Gulban* conquered northwest Ireland, ca.425 AD, capturing the great hill-fort of Grianan of Ailech in County Donegal.

Eogan, styled 'King of Ailech', established his own kingdom in the peninsula in County Donegal still called after him Inishowen (Innis Eoghain or Eogan's Isle). His descendants, known as the Cenel Eoghain (the race of Owen), became the principal branch of the Northern Ui Neill (descendants of Niall of the Nine Hostages). The Cenel Eoghain in the next five centuries expanded to the east and south from their focal point in Inishowen.

Ireland was one of the first countries to adopt a system of hereditary surnames which developed from a more ancient system of clan or sept names. From the 11th century each family began to adopt its own distinctive family name generally derived from the first name of an ancestor who lived in or about the 10th century. The surname was formed by prefixing either Mac (son of) or O (grandson or descendant of) to the ancestor's name. Surnames in Ireland, therefore, tended to identify membership of a sept.

Foy is derived from Gaelic *O Fiaich*, the root word being *fiach*, meaning 'a raven'. The Foys were *erenaghs*, i.e. hereditary stewards, of the church lands of Derrybrusk near Enniskillen, County Fermanagh. The name was also anglicised as O'Fee, Fee, Fey and Fie. In the census of 1659 the O'Fees were recorded as a 'principal name' in the parish of Derrybrusk. Their descendants are now usually called Foy and sometimes Fee.

The escape of the most prominent Gaelic Lords of Ulster in 'the Flight of the Earls' in1607 from Lough Swilly, County Donegal marked the end of Gaelic power and paved the way for the 17th century Plantation of Ulster with English and Scottish settlers. In the centuries that followed Gaelic names were anglicised, resulting in many variant spellings of the same name and, in many cases, the dropping of the O and Mac prefixes.

Foy is occasionally changed to Fay. Fay is derived from Norman *de faie*, meaning 'beech', thus denoting an ancestor who lived near beech trees. An Anglo-Norman family of the name settled in County Westmeath at the end of the 12th century. The family then spread to Counties Cavan and Monaghan.

In some instances the name was anglicised to Hunt in the mistaken notion that it was derived from *fiadhach*, meaning 'hunt'.

Fee is also common in County Antrim and it is possible that some of these were originally Scottish MacFees.

FRIEL

The surname Friel is almost exclusive to northwest Ulster, being most common in its home-land, County Donegal, and to a lesser extent in the western parts of Counties Derry and Tyrone. This name illustrates the very close links between the city of Derry and County Donegal. In the mid-19th century nearly 70% of Friels living in County Derry were located in the civil parish of Templemore which contains the city of Derry. As Derry developed an industrial base in the 19th century in shirt making, shipbuilding and distilling it attracted much of its workforce from Donegal.

The O'Friel sept of County Donegal trace their lineage to Conall *Gulban*, son of the 5th centu-ry High King of Ireland, Niall of the Nine Hostages, who ruled from the Hill of Tara, County Meath. Conall and his brother Eogan conquered northwest Ireland, ca.425 AD, capturing the great hill-fort of Grianan of Ailech in County Donegal which commanded the entrance to Inishowen between Lough Swilly and Lough Foyle.

Conall, styled 'King of Tir Conaill', established his own kingdom in County Donegal called after him Tyrconnel, i.e. the 'Land of Conall', which was the ancient name of Donegal. His descendants, known as the Cenel Conaill (the race of Conall), formed one of the principal branches of the Northern Ui Neill (descendants of Niall of the Nine Hostages). The septs of the Cenel Conaill firmly established themselves in County Donegal while those descended from Conal's brother Eogan expanded to the east and south into Counties Derry and Tyrone.

Ireland was one of the first countries to adopt a system of hereditary surnames which devel-oped from a more ancient system of clan or sept names. The surname was formed by prefix-ing either Mac (son of) or O (grandson or descendant of) to the ancestor's name. The O'Friels take their name from *Firghil*, meaning 'man of valour', and were thus in Gaelic *O Firghil*, i.e. descendant of Feargal.

This sept also has the distinction of being descended from Eoghan, brother of St Columcille (their father, Fedelmith, was a grandson of Conall *Gulban*). St Columcille founded a mon-astery at Derry in 546AD and at Iona, Scotland in 563AD. The O'Friels were hereditary 'coarbs' of Kilmacrenan, i.e. abbots of the monastery at Kilmacrenan. The abbot was regard-ed as the 'heir' of the saintly founder, which in the case of Kilmacrenan was St Columcille (also known as Columba).

The O'Friels produced many distinguished clerics, including Feargal O'Friel, Bishop of Ra-phoe, who died in 1299, and Awley O'Friel who became Abbot of Iona in 1203.

The leading position of the O'Friels within the Cenel Conaill is further evidenced by their participation, as an hereditary right, in the inauguration of O'Donnell as lord of Tirconnell. The Chief of the O'Friels had the privilege of offering the O'Donnell his mystic wand, a symbol of his command over his sub-chieftains, during his inauguration at *Carraig a Duin*, i.e. Doon, to the west of the town of Kilmacrenan, County Donegal.

GALLAGHER

Gallagher is the third most common name in Ulster and two-thirds of the Ulster total are in the sept's homeland of County Donegal where it is the most numerous name. Although it is only the thirteenth most common name in County Derry, it is the third most numerous in the city of Derry. This name illustrates the very close links between the city of Derry and County Donegal. As Derry developed an industrial base in the 19th century in shirt making, shipbuilding and distilling it attracted much of its workforce from Donegal.

The Gallagher sept trace their lineage to Conall *Gulban*, son of the 5th century High King of Ireland, Niall of the Nine Hostages, who ruled from the Hill of Tara, County Meath. Conall and his brother Eogan conquered northwest Ireland, ca.425 AD, capturing the great hill-fort of Grianan of Ailech in County Donegal which commanded the entrance to Inishowen between Lough Swilly and Lough Foyle.

Conall, styled 'King of Tir Conaill', established his own kingdom in County Donegal called after him Tyrconnel, i.e. the 'Land of Conall', which was the ancient name of Donegal. His descendants, known as the Cenel Conaill (the race of Conall), formed one of the principal branches of the Northern Ui Neill (descendants of Niall of the Nine Hostages). The septs of the Cenel Conaill firmly established themselves in County Donegal while those descended from Conal's brother Eogan expanded to the east and south into Counties Derry and Tyrone.

Ireland was one of the first countries to adopt a system of hereditary surnames which developed from a more ancient system of clan or sept names. The surname was formed by prefixing either Mac (son of) or O (grandson or descendant of) to the ancestor's name.

The Gallaghers take their name from *Gallchobhair*, and were thus in Gaelic *O Gallchobhair*, i.e. descendant of Gallagher. This name is derived from *gallchobhar*, meaning 'foreign help'.

The O'Gallaghers claim to be the senior and most loyal family of the Cenel Conaill. Their territory extended over a wide area in the baronies of Raphoe and Tirhugh in the east and south of County Donegal. The O'Gallaghers, from their bases at Ballybeit and Ballynaglack, were chief marshals and commanders of O'Donnell's military forces from the 14th to the 16th centuries. The O'Gallaghers also provided many wives for the O'Donnell sept.

As well as being a military family the Gallaghers have produced many churchmen. Six O'Gallaghers were bishops of Raphoe in the 15th and 16th centuries, and Redmond O Gallagher, the 16th century Bishop of Derry, befriended the survivors of the Spanish Armada.

Today the name is found widely in Scotland where it often takes the form Gallacher. It also occurs in the English cities of Liverpool, Manchester and Leeds where it is pronounced 'Gallocher'.

GALLEN

This name originated in County Donegal.

Ireland was one of the first countries to adopt a system of hereditary surnames which developed from a more ancient system of clan or sept names. From the 11th century each family began to adopt its own distinctive family name generally derived from the first name of an ancestor who lived in or about the 10th century. The surname was formed by prefixing either Mac (son of) or O (grandson or descendant of) to the ancestor's name. Surnames in Ireland, therefore, tended to identify membership of a sept.

Gallen is derived from Gaelic *O Gaillin*. This sept trace their lineage to Eogan, son of the 5th century High King of Ireland, Niall of the Nine Hostages, who ruled from the Hill of Tara, County Meath. Eogan and his brother Conall *Gulban* conquered northwest Ireland, ca.425 AD, capturing the great hill-fort of Grianan of Ailech in County Donegal which commanded the entrance to the Inishowen peninsula between Lough Swilly and Lough Foyle.

Eogan, styled 'King of Ailech', established his own kingdom in the peninsula still called after him Inishowen (Innis Eoghain or Eogan's Isle). Eogan was converted to Christianity by St Patrick, when he travelled to Ailech, ca. 442 AD. His descendants, known as the Cenel Eoghain (the race of Owen), became the principal branch of the Northern Ui Neill (descendants of Niall of the Nine Hostages). The Cenel Eoghain in the next five centuries expanded to the east and south, from their focal point in Inishowen, into Counties Derry and Tyrone.

At the time of the mid-19th century Griffith's Valuation 52 Gallen households were recorded in County Donegal. This source clearly shows that the name was most concentrated in the lands between the border with County Tyrone and the River Finn, as 46 Gallen households were residing in the parish of Donaghmore. In other words nearly 90% of descendants of the Gallen sept in County Donegal were living in this parish.

During the famous 105 day Siege of Derry, from 18 April to 31 July 1689, Captain Benjamin Galland and Captain Michael Galland were recorded as 'defenders' of the city. These Gallands, of English origin, had no connection with the Gallens of County Donegal. The surname Galland is derived from a nickname, from Old French *galer*, for a cheerful person.

Benjamin and Michael Galland were the sons of Captain John Galland, an officer in the army of Oliver Cromwell, who obtained a grant of land at the Vow, near Ballymoney, County Antrim in the middle years of the 17th century.

In the period 1649 to 1652 Oliver Cromwell's army of 20,000 men ruthlessly crushed the Irish rebellion. In return for serving in the army, Cromwellian soldiers received grants of land on confiscated estates in Ireland.

John Galland became High Sheriff of County Antrim in 1674 and Benjamin, his son, in 1702.

GILLANDERS

Gillanders can be an Irish or a Scottish name. This surname is found almost exclusively in Ulster, particularly in County Monaghan.

Ireland was one of the first countries to adopt a system of hereditary surnames which developed from a more ancient system of clan or sept names. The surname was formed by prefixing either Mac (son of) or O (grandson or descendant of) to the ancestor's name.

Gillanders is derived from Gaelic *Mac Giolla Aindreis*, meaning 'son of the devotee of St Andrew'. The homeland of this sept was County Monaghan.

In the Highlands of Scotland, Gillanders is derived from Gaelic *Mac Gille Andrais*, meaning 'son of the servant of St Andrew'. This name was also anglicised as Anderson, Andrews and McAndrew.

Andrew was a popular choice as a child's name in medieval Scotland, and at a time when fixed surnames, based on a father's first name, were being established. The popularity of the name stems from the Scottish patron saint, Andrew. Andrew was the first of Jesus Christ's disciples, and according to legend the relics of Andrew were brought to Scotland in the 4th century by St Regulus. In the Highlands the personal name Andrew was gaelicised at an early period as Andreis.

A sept of Mac Gille Andrais, usually anglicised as Anderson, was attached to Clan Donald, and they were numerous in the west of Scotland, particularly on Islay and Kintyre. It is believed that the Andersons of Rathlin Island and of north Antrim are descended from this Clan Donald sept. As followers of Clan Donald they came over to Ulster to settle on their lands. MacLandrish, another anglicisation of the Gaelic name, is also common on Rathlin.

Clan Donald had acquired new territories in the north of Ireland ca.1400 when John Mor MacDonald had married Margery Bissett, an heiress in the Glens of Antrim. By the mid-16th century the MacDonalds, known as the MacDonnells of the Glens, had carved out an extensive territory in County Antrim at the expense of the MacQuillans.

Clan Ross, which derives its name from the district of Ross in north Scotland, was also known as Clan Anrias. The chiefs of Clan Ross trace their descent from one Gille Anrias who was the ancestor of Ferchar Mackinsagart, son of the 'Red Priest of Applecross'. As a reward for assisting Alexander II, King of Scotland, crush a rebellion in Moray, Ferchar Mackinsagart was created Earl of Ross in 1234. A sept of Mac Gille Andrais was attached to Clan Ross, and this Gaelic name was variously anglicised as Anderson, Andrews, Gillanders, McAndrew and Ross.

Settlers to Ulster from Scotland came, by and large, in three waves: with the granting of the initial leases in the period 1605 to 1625; after 1652 and Cromwell's crushing of the Irish rebellion; and finally in the fifteen years after 1690 and the Glorious Revolution. It is estimated by 1715, when migration to Ulster had virtually stopped, the Scottish population of Ulster stood at 200,000.

GILLEN

The surname Gillen or Gillan is mainly found in Counties Sligo, Donegal and Tyrone.

The Gillen sept trace their lineage to Eogan, son of the 5th century High King of Ireland, Niall of the Nine Hostages, who ruled from the Hill of Tara, County Meath. Eogan and his brother Conall *Gulban* conquered northwest Ireland, ca.425 AD, capturing the great hill-fort of Grianan of Ailech which commanded the entrance to the Inishowen peninsula between Lough Swilly and Lough Foyle.

Eogan, styled 'King of Ailech', established his own kingdom in the peninsula still called after him Inishowen (Innis Eoghain or Eogan's Isle). Eogan was converted to Christianity by St Patrick, when he travelled to Ailech, ca. 442 AD. His descendants, known as the Cenel Eoghain (the race of Owen), became the principal branch of the Northern Ui Neill (descendants of Niall of the Nine Hostages). The Cenel Eoghain in the next five centuries expanded to the east and south from their focal point in Inishowen.

Ireland was one of the first countries to adopt a system of hereditary surnames which developed from a more ancient system of clan or sept names. From the 11th century each family began to adopt its own distinctive family name generally derived from the first name of an ancestor who lived in or about the 10th century. The surname was formed by prefixing either Mac (son of) or O (grandson or descendant of) to the ancestor's name. Surnames in Ireland, therefore, tended to identify membership of a sept. Gillen is derived from Gaelic *O Giollain*, the root word being *giolla,* meaning 'lad'.

By the 19th century Gillan was chiefly found in Counties Sligo and Antrim, while Gillen was concentrated in north Ulster.

The McGilligans, who in the 16th century were a leading sept in County Derry and gave their name to the district of Magilligan in north Derry between Lough Foyle and Benevenagh Mountain, sometimes abbreviated their name to Gillan. By the middle of the 17th century the McGilligans, derived from Gaelic *Mac Giollagain*, had already widely discarded the Mac prefix and were commonly known as Gilligan.

Although the surnames of Gilligan and Gillan have quite distinct origins, one being a Mac name and the other an O name, their ultimate origins have become confused with anglicisation and the falling into disuse of these prefixes. Thus people whose origins are *Mac Giollagain* may be disguised by bearing the surname of Gillan or Gillen.

The surname Gilliland, a variant of Scottish McLellan or McClelland, was sometimes shortened to Gillan. This means that some Gillens in Ulster could be Scottish Gillilands and others could be Irish McGilligans.

GILLESPIE

Gillespie can be an Irish or a Scottish name. In Ireland 90% of Gillespies live in Ulster, particularly in Counties Antrim, Donegal, Armagh and Tyrone.

In Ireland Gillespie is derived from Gaelic *Mac Giolla Easpuig,* meaning 'son of the servant of the bishop'. Indeed this name has also been anglicised as Bishop. This sept originated in County Down. At the end of the 12th century Mac Giolla Espcoip was recorded as chief of Aeilabhra in the barony of Iveagh in County Down. A branch of this sept was established, at an early date, in County Donegal. In the later medieval period the Gillespies of Donegal were *erenaghs,* i.e. hereditary stewards, of the church lands of Kilrean in Killybegs Parish in the barony of Boylagh.

This name, which is among the top 50 surnames in the city of Derry today, illustrates the very close links, both historic and economic, between Derry and County Donegal. As Derry developed an industrial base in the 19th century in shirt making, shipbuilding and distilling it attracted much of its workforce from Donegal.

In Scotland the Gillespies, in Gaelic *Gilleasbuig ,* meaning 'the bishop's servant', were a sept of Clan Macpherson. In the mid-14th century Gillies Macpherson became the first chief of the Macphersons of Invershie in Inverness-shire. Many of the Macpherson sept names derive from this Gillies including Gillespie, Gillies and McLeish. Gillespie was most common in Argyllshire and the Isles. In some instances Archibald was also adopted as an anglicisation of Gillespie.

Upheavals such as military incursions, feuds and harvest failures would have encouraged many clan members, including Gillespies, to migrate to Ulster as settlers during the 17th century. Owing to the nature of the Scottish clan system once the power and influence of the chief had been weakened or broken the clan tended to disintegrate. Bearing the surname Gillespie simply indicated that you were a follower of the Clan Macpherson chief. Not every clan member was related by blood. Their bond, however, whether they had a common tribal ancestor or not, was their common rule by a chief with loyalty to one's clan being the primary obligation. Once tribal loyalty was broken clans 'scattered'.

Movement of Scottish settlers to Ulster began in earnest from 1605 in a private enterprise colonisation of counties Antrim and Down when Sir Hugh Montgomery and Sir James Hamilton acquired title to large estates in north Down and Sir Randall MacDonnell, 1st Earl of Antrim, to large tracts of land in north Antrim. Further impetus came in 1609 when James I adopted the policy to encourage Scottish settlers to settle on the forfeited estates of the Gaelic chiefs in counties Armagh, Cavan, Donegal, Fermanagh, Londonderry (then known as Coleraine) and Tyrone.

The Gillespies supported the Jacobite cause in Scotland. After the rebellion of 1715 Hugh Gillespie of the Clan Macpherson, like many other Jacobites, was forced to seek refuge in Ulster.

During the famous 105 day Siege of Derry, from 18 April to 31 July 1689, James Gillespie of Londonderry was recorded as a 'defender' of the city.

GILLIGAN

The surname Gilligan is derived from McGilligan, a County Derry sept which was once very powerful and numerous.

Ireland was one of the first countries to adopt a system of hereditary surnames which developed from a more ancient system of clan or sept names. From the 11th century each family began to adopt its own distinctive family name generally derived from the first name of an ancestor who lived in or about the 10th century. The surname was formed by prefixing either Mac (son of) or O (grandson or descendant of) to the ancestor's name. Surnames in Ireland, therefore, tended to identify membership of a sept.

McGilligan, usually spelt Gilligan today, is derived from Gaelic *Mac Giollagain*, the root word being *giolla*, meaning 'lad'.

The McGilligan sept had come originally from *Breadach* which comprised the parishes of Lower and Upper Moville in Inishowen, County Donegal. The name of the district is still preserved in the river Bredagh which falls into Lough Foyle.

In the centuries before the 17th Plantation of Ulster with English and Scottish settlers the McGilligans migrated eastwards and settled in the lands, across Lough Foyle, beneath Benevenagh Mountain in north Derry. The parish here was church lands and the McGilligans became the *erenaghs*, i.e. hereditary stewards, of these ancient church lands in the parish of Tamlaghtard. St Columbkille (Columba) had founded a monastery in this parish in 584AD.

In the 16th century the McGilligans gave their name to the district, Magilligan, i.e. the land of the McGilligans. In the early 17th century the McGilligans were one of the three chief septs under the O'Cahans. At the time of Sir Cahir O'Doherty's rebellion in 1608 Sir Arthur Chichester reported that the chief septs of County Coleraine (renamed Londonderry in 1613) were the O'Cahans and under them the O'Mullans, the McGilligans and McCloskeys.

At the time of the Plantation, in 1611, the McGilligans were granted a freehold at Ballycarton in Aghanloo Parish. The family took an active part in the 1641 rebellion. Manus Magilligan, who held these lands in 1641, joined Manus O'Cathan, in the rebellion, and his lands at Ballycarton were forfeited, as a consequence, in 1652.

By the middle of the 17th century the Mac had already been widely discarded thus the surname commonly became Gilligan. Furthermore, in many cases, Gilligan has been made Gillan or Gillen. The Gillans, derived from Gaelic *O Giollain*, were a distinct sept, tracing their lineage to Eogan, son of the 5th century High King of Ireland, Niall of the Nine Hostages. Thus people whose origins are *Mac Giollagain* may be disguised by bearing the surname of Gillan or Gillen.

GILLILAND

This surname is most common in Counties Antrim and Down. This name was brought to Ulster by settlers from Scotland in the 17th century.

Gilliland, a variant of McClelland, is derived from Gaelic *Mac Gille Fhaolain*, meaning 'son of the devotee of St Fillan'. The earliest reference to the surname is of one Patrick McLolane who captured the Castle of Dumfries in 1305. The McClellands were numerous in Galloway from the end of the 14th century where the name was initially anglicised as Maclellan. John Maclellan was granted the lands of Balmaclellan in Galloway by James III, King of Scotland, in 1466. The province of Galloway in southwest Scotland was home to many of the Scottish settlers who came to Ulster throughout the 17th century.

The anglicisation of Gaelic names resulted in many variant spellings of the same name and, in many cases, the dropping of the Mac prefix. In this case Gilliland is derived from an early form of the name, McGillelan, with the omission of the Mac prefix.

The defeat of the old Gaelic order in the Nine Years War, 1594-1603 and the escape of the most prominent Gaelic Lords of Ulster in 'the Flight of the Earls' in 1607 from Lough Swilly, County Donegal were ultimately responsible for the settlement of many Scottish families in the northern counties of Ireland.

Movement of Scottish settlers to Ulster began in earnest from 1605 in a private enterprise colonisation of counties Antrim and Down when Sir Hugh Montgomery and Sir James Hamilton acquired title to large estates in north Down and Sir Randall MacDonnell, 1st Earl of Antrim, to large tracts of land in north Antrim.

In 1609 the Earl of Salisbury, Lord High Treasurer, suggested to James I a deliberate plantation of Scottish and English colonists on the forfeited estates of the Gaelic chiefs in counties Armagh, Cavan, Donegal, Fermanagh, Londonderry (then known as Coleraine) and Tyrone.

Settlers to Ulster came, by and large, in three waves: with the granting of the initial leases in the period 1605 to 1625; after 1652 and Cromwell's crushing of the Irish rebellion; and finally in the fifteen years after 1690 and the Glorious Revolution. It is estimated by 1715, when migration to Ulster had virtually stopped, the Scottish population of Ulster stood at 200,000.

Scottish families entering Ireland through the port of Londonderry settled in the Foyle Valley which includes much of the fertile lands of counties Donegal, Londonderry and Tyrone. The lands along the Firth of Clyde in the county of Ayrshire, the Clyde Valley and the Border Lands consisting of the counties of Wigtown, Kirkcudbright and Dumfries were home to many of these Scottish settlers.

The 1831 census clearly demonstrates that, in County Derry, the Gillilands were concentrated in Faughanvale Parish. At the time of the 1831 census there were 13 Gilliland households in County Derry, with 9 households of the name, i.e. nearly 70% of the total, in Faughanvale Parish.

GORMLEY

The Gormley sept of County Derry trace their lineage to Eogan, son of the 5th century High King of Ireland, Niall of the Nine Hostages, who ruled from the Hill of Tara, County Meath. Eogan and his brother Conall *Gulban* conquered northwest Ireland, ca.425 AD, capturing the great hill-fort of Grianan of Ailech in County Donegal which commanded the entrance to the Inishowen peninsula between Lough Swilly and Lough Foyle.

Eogan, styled 'King of Ailech', established his own kingdom in the peninsula still called after him Inishowen (Innis Eoghain or Eogan's Isle). Eogan was converted to Christianity by St Patrick, when he travelled to Ailech, ca. 442 AD. His descendants, known as the Cenel Eoghain (the race of Owen), became the principal branch of the Northern Ui Neill (descendants of Niall of the Nine Hostages). The Cenel Eoghain in the next five centuries expanded to the east and south from their focal point in Inishowen.

Ireland was one of the first countries to adopt a system of hereditary surnames which developed from a more ancient system of clan or sept names. From the 11th century each family began to adopt its own distinctive family name generally derived from the first name of an ancestor who lived in or about the 10th century. The surname was formed by prefixing either Mac (son of) or O (grandson or descendant of) to the ancestor's name. Surnames in Ireland, therefore, tended to identify membership of a sept. O'Gormley is derived from Gaelic *O Goirmleadhaigh.*

The O'Gormleys were the leading sept of Clan Moen (tracing their descent from Moen, son of Muireadach (Murdock), son of Eogan). The O'Gormleys originally ruled what is now the barony of Raphoe, County Donegal. In 1177 Niall O'Gormly, styled 'Lord of the men of *Magh Ithe'*, was slain by Donough O'Carellan and the Clandermot in the middle of Derry Columbkille. Magh Ithe refers to the rich countryside stretching southward from Inishowen, later known as the Laggan district in east Donegal. It would appear that the O'Carolans (Carlin), the leading sept of Clan Dermot, seized a portion of O'Gormley territory around Donaghmore, County Donegal at this time.

The O'Gormleys were driven out of Magh Ithe by the O'Donnells, and, from the 14th century, they settled to the east and northeast of Strabane on the border with Counties Derry and Tyrone. Between 1084 and 1583 there are numerous references to the O'Gormlys in *The Annals of The Kingdom of Ireland by the Four Masters.* They are recorded feuding, at various times, with the O'Donnells and the O'Neills. In 1484 'Melaghlin, son of Conor O'Gormly, and Conor, his brother, were slain by the sons of Owen, son of Niall O'Donnell.' In 1507 'O'Neill plundered Kinel-Moen, and slew Brian, the son of O'Gormly.'

The 17th century Plantation of Ulster with English and Scottish settlers marked the end of O'Gormly power, but the name remained, and Gormley is now most common in County Tyrone.

Confusion is caused by the fact that, in some cases, Gormley has been changed to Gorman, Grimley, Grimes and Graham.

GRAHAM

Graham is among the twenty most numerous names in Ulster, and in Counties Down and Fermanagh it is among the ten most common names. Over three-quarters of the Graham families in Ireland are in Ulster where this surname came with numerous Scottish immigrants at the time of the Plantation of Ulster in the 17th century.

Graham is ultimately derived from Grantham in Lincolnshire, a place name noted in the 11th century Domesday Book. The name was introduced to Scotland by William de Graham, an Anglo-Norman, who settled there in the early-12th century and received, from David I, the lands of Abercorn and Dalkeith in Midlothian. From that time the Grahams played an important part in the affairs of Scotland.

One branch of the family led by Sir John Graham of Kilbride, near Dunblane migrated to the Scottish Borders where they occupied most of the best land in the West March of England and Scotland. The Grahams became one of the great riding or reiving clans of the Borders, and one of the most troublesome to the Crowns of both England and Scotland.

From the 14th to the late-17th century, the border between England and Scotland – the Debatable Lands – was a turbulent place. The Border country was ravaged by the lawless Reiver families who stole each other's cattle and possessions. They raided in large numbers, on horseback, and they killed and kidnapped without remorse. This type of life resulted in the growth of large closely-knit family groups with intense clan loyalties and fierce feuds against others.

Prior to the Union of the Crowns of England and Scotland in 1603 the Scottish Border was divided into three districts; the east, west and middle Marches. Each March was presided over by a warden who settled disputes with the warden of the appropriate March in England, as border warfare was rife at this time with frequent cattle raids.

Pacification of the riding families began in earnest from 1603 with the Union of the Crowns of England and Scotland. The Grahams suffered most as King James I set about pacifying the borders in a ruthless campaign which included executions and banishment. In 1605 and 1606, respectively, attempts were made to transport 150 Grahams to the Low Countries and 124 Grahams to Roscommon, Ireland. Within the space of two years the Grahams were scattered.

When the power of the riding clans was broken by James I in the decade after 1603 many came to Ulster to escape persecution. This flight to Ulster also suited the needs of the king. James I, from 1610, was determined to implement a deliberate plantation of Scottish and English colonists on the forfeited estates of the Gaelic chiefs in Counties Armagh, Cavan, Donegal, Fermanagh, Londonderry (then known as Coleraine) and Tyrone.

The Grahams settled initially in County Fermanagh before moving on to other parts of Ulster. These Border families were well suited to life in the frontier of the Plantation of Ulster. They were a resilient people who survived the upheavals of the 17th century. Scottish settlers were hardier than their English counterparts, and the Borderers were even better adapted again to life on a new, insecure frontier. In 1659, Graham was listed as a 'principal name' in both Counties Antrim and Fermanagh.

GRANT

This common Ulster name is most numerous in Counties Antrim and Donegal. The majority of Grants in Ulster are of Scottish origin.

In Scotland, Clan Grant is one of the main branches of Clan Alpine of which Clan Gregor is chief. Thus they claim descent from Kenneth MacAlpine, the 9th century King of Scotland, and prior to this from one Aodh Urchaidh, ruler of Glenorchy in Argyllshire. The Grants trace their descent from Gregor MacGregor who lived in the 12th century in Strathspey.

However, it would seem that the chiefs of Clan Grant were of Anglo-Norman origin. In this case, Grant derived as a nickname, from Old French *grand,* meaning 'tall'. A Norman family of le Grant, who were neighbours of the Bissetts in Nottinghamshire, England, came to Scotland with the Bissetts in 1242. Sir Lawrence Grant was recorded as Sheriff of Inverness in 1263, and his brother Robert held lands in Nairnshire. Through marriage to a local heiress Sir Lawrence Grant acquired lands at Stratherrick.

Grant was one of the names adopted by the McGregors when they were outlawed and their name was proscribed. The McGregors came into conflict with their powerful neighbours the Campbells, and, as a consequence, their lands were dispossessed and they resorted to raiding. In 1603, by Act of Parliament, the clan was outlawed, an order was given to disperse them 'by fire and sword', and their name was proscribed. As a 'broken' clan the McGregors now adopted a great variety of new names, including colour names such as Black or White, clan names such as Graham and Grant, and the names of septs, formerly attached to the clan, such as Greer and Gregg.

The defeat of the old Gaelic order in the Nine Years War, 1594-1603 and the escape of the most prominent Gaelic Lords of Ulster in 'the Flight of the Earls' in 1607 from Lough Swilly, County Donegal were ultimately responsible for the settlement of many Scottish families in the northern counties of Ireland.

Movement of Scottish settlers to Ulster began in earnest from 1605 in a private enterprise colonisation of counties Antrim and Down when Sir Hugh Montgomery and Sir James Hamilton acquired title to large estates in north Down and Sir Randall MacDonnell, 1st Earl of Antrim, to large tracts of land in north Antrim. Further impetus came in 1609 when James I adopted the policy to encourage English and Scottish settlers to settle on the forfeited estates of the Gaelic chiefs in counties Armagh, Cavan, Donegal, Fermanagh, Londonderry (then known as Coleraine) and Tyrone.

Settlers to Ulster came, by and large, in three waves: with the granting of the initial leases in the period 1605 to 1625; after 1652 and Cromwell's crushing of the Irish rebellion; and finally in the fifteen years after 1690 and the Glorious Revolution. It is estimated by 1715, when migration to Ulster had virtually stopped, the Scottish population of Ulster stood at 200,000.

In Ulster the Irish surname of Granny, in Gaelic *Mag Raighne,* meaning 'son of Raghnall', was sometimes changed to Grant.

80

HAMILL

The name Hamill is most common in Ulster, particularly in counties Antrim and Armagh.

The Hamill sept of County Derry trace their lineage to Eogan, son of the 5th century High King of Ireland, Niall of the Nine Hostages, who ruled from the Hill of Tara, County Meath. Eogan and his brother Conall *Gulban* conquered northwest Ireland, ca.425 AD, capturing the great hill-fort of Grianan of Ailech in County Donegal.

Eogan, styled 'King of Ailech', established his own kingdom in the peninsula in County Donegal still called after him Inishowen (Innis Eoghain or Eogan's Isle). His descendants, known as the Cenel Eoghain (the race of Owen), became the principal branch of the Northern Ui Neill (descendants of Niall of the Nine Hostages). The Cenel Eoghain in the next five centuries expanded to the east and south from their focal point in Inishowen.

Ireland was one of the first countries to adopt a system of hereditary surnames which developed from a more ancient system of clan or sept names. From the 11th century each family began to adopt its own distinctive family name generally derived from the first name of an ancestor who lived in or about the 10th century. The surname was formed by prefixing either Mac (son of) or O (grandson or descendant of) to the ancestor's name. Surnames in Ireland, therefore, tended to identify membership of a sept.

Hamill is derived from Gaelic *O hAghmaill*, the root word possibly being *adhmall* meaning active. In this case O'Hamill would literally mean 'descendant of the active one'.

The O'Hamills were one of the leading septs of Clan Binny (*Eochaid Binnigh* was a son of Eogan) possessing territory on the banks of the River Foyle near Lifford in County Donegal.

The first outward thrust of the Owen clan was that of Clan Binny in the 6th century AD who thrust southeast into County Tyrone, bypassing a hard core of resistance in County Derry of the Cianachta, as far as the river Blackwater on the borders of Tyrone and Armagh. A pocket of O'Hamills at Clonfeacle on the Blackwater may mark the extent of the advance of Clan Binny. Clan Binny eventually ousted the Oriella clans from the district lying west of the river Bann from Coleraine to beside Lough Neagh, and drove them across the river.

In the course of time the O'Hamills ruled a territory in south Tyrone and Armagh and from the 12th century they were poets to the powerful O'Hanlons. By the 17th century the name was most numerous in Armagh and Monaghan. The full form O'Hamill is still used by a few families in County Derry, but elsewhere the prefix O has been dropped. In some cases, in the Derry area, the name has been changed to Hamilton.

A few Hamills in Ulster may be of English or Scottish origin. In England the name derives from the Old English word *Hamel*, meaning scarred. In Scotland the name is derived from the place name Hameville in Dumfriesshire.

HAMILTON

The Scottish surname Hamilton is found in every province of Ireland, but especially in Ulster, where it is among the thirty most common names. The name is well known in counties Antrim, Derry, Down, Fermanagh and Tyrone; and in two of these counties, Down and Tyrone, Hamilton is among the fifteen most common surnames.

The defeat of the old Gaelic order in the Nine Years War, 1594-1603 and the escape of the most prominent Gaelic Lords of Ulster in 'the Flight of the Earls' in 1607 from Lough Swilly, County Donegal were ultimately responsible for the settlement of many English and Scottish families in the northern counties of Ireland.

In 1609 the Earl of Salisbury, Lord High Treasurer, suggested to James I a deliberate plantation of Scottish and English colonists on the forfeited estates of the Gaelic chiefs in counties Armagh, Cavan, Donegal, Fermanagh, Londonderry (then known as Coleraine) and Tyrone.

Settlers to Ulster came, by and large, in three waves: with the granting of the initial leases in the period 1605 to 1625; after 1652 and Cromwell's crushing of the Irish rebellion; and finally in the fifteen years after 1690 and the Glorious Revolution. It is estimated by 1715, when Scottish migration to Ulster had virtually stopped, the Presbyterian population of Ulster, i.e. of essentially Scottish origin, stood at 200,000.

Scottish families entering Ireland through the port of Londonderry settled in the Foyle Valley which includes much of the fertile lands of counties Donegal, Londonderry and Tyrone. The lands along the Firth of Clyde in the county of Ayrshire, the Clyde Valley and the Border Lands consisting of the counties of Wigtown, Kirkcudbright and Dumfries were home to many of these Scottish settlers.

The Hamilton surname, derived from the Yorkshire placename of Hambleton, meaning crooked hill, was introduced to Scotland in the 13th century by a Norman family from Leicestershire, namely one Sir Walter Fitzgilbert of Hambledone. After the Battle of Bannockburn in 1314, when Robert the Bruce established himself as king of a united Scotland, Sir Walter Hamilton was granted the lands of Cadzow in Lanarkshire. In the centuries that followed the family was ranked among the nobility of Scotland; they became Earls of Arran and Dukes of Hamilton.

In the initial granting of leases in Ulster in 1610/1611, eight of the principal Scottish planters (sixty-one in total) were Hamiltons, and they acquired extensive estates of land in Counties Armagh, Cavan, Fermanagh and Tyrone. The Dukes of Abercorn, with their family seat at Baronscourt, County Tyrone, trace their descent from Lord Claud Hamilton, the 3rd son of the second Earl of Arran, who had been created Baron Paisley in 1587.

Many of the settlers farming on these Scottish estates in Ulster would also have been called Hamilton as it was a feature of 17th century Scotland for tenants to take on their landlord's surname.

Hamiltons fought on both sides during the Siege of Derry of 1689. Forty-three Hamiltons were recorded as 'defenders' of Derry and six Hamiltons served with the 'Jacobite Army', including Claud Hamilton, Baron Strabane and 4th Earl of Abercorn.

HAMPSEY

Hampsey, and variants such as Hampson, Hanson and Hansen, originated in County Derry.

Ireland was one of the first countries to adopt a system of hereditary surnames which developed from a more ancient system of clan or sept names. From the 11th century each family began to adopt its own distinctive family name generally derived from the first name of an ancestor who lived in or about the 10th century. The surname was formed by prefixing either Mac (son of) or O (grandson or descendant of) to the ancestor's name. Surnames in Ireland, therefore, tended to identify membership of a sept.

Hampsey is derived from Gaelic *O hAmhsaigh*. They were a small sept in County Derry. By the 18th century the name was usually recorded as either Hanson or Hampson. Confusion can occur as Hampson is also recorded as a surname in England where it is regarded as a variant of Hammond.

In the census of 1659 Hampsey, in the form of O Hamson, was recorded as one of the principal Irish names in the barony of Keenaght, County Derry. The Hearth Money Rolls of 1663 record 5 Hampsey households in County Derry: recorded as O'Hampson in Tamlaghtard Parish; O'Hampen in Desertoghill Parish; O'Hanson in Faughanvale Parish; Hanson in Macosquin Parish; and Handson in Tamlaght Parish.

By the time of the 1831 census the O prefix was not recorded against any of the descendants of the Hampsey sept in County Derry. At the time of the 1831 census 27 Hampsey households, including variant spellings of the surname, were recorded in County Derry. This source records that in County Derry in 1831 there were 12 households recorded as Hanson, 5 as Hampson, 4 as Hampsey, 3 as Hamsie, 2 as Hamsay and 1 as Hamson. Nineteen of these households, i.e. 70% of the total, were recorded in the northeast Derry parishes of Aghadowey, Desertoghill, Errigal, Killowen and Macosquin.

In the graveyard of the old parish church in Tamlaghtard Parish (also known as Magilligan), County Derry is the grave of Denis Hempson, also known as Denis O'Hempsey, the celebrated Irish harper. His grave is located beside that of St Aidan, the founder of the monastery at Lindisfarne in Northumberland, England in 635 AD.

Denis O'Hempsey was renowned as a harp player throughout Ireland and Scotland. Born at Craigmore near Garvagh, County Derry, ca.1695, he became blind at the age of three. He was taught to play the harp by Bridget O'Cahan when he was twelve, and many of Ireland's old harp tunes are attributed to him. He lived in the townland of Ballymaclary in Magilligan in a house presented to him by Frederick Harvey, 4th earl of Bristol and Bishop of Derry. Denis O'Hempsey was reputed to have been 112 years old when he died in 1807.

In 1835 Denis O'Hempsey's harp, which was then 270 years old, was kept in Downhill House, the former home of his patron Frederick Hervey who had died in 1803. His harp (made ca.1565) was made out of white willow with a back of fir which had been dug out of a bog.

HAMPSON

Hampson, and variants such as Hampsey, Hanson and Hansen, originated in County Derry.

Ireland was one of the first countries to adopt a system of hereditary surnames which developed from a more ancient system of clan or sept names. From the 11th century each family began to adopt its own distinctive family name generally derived from the first name of an ancestor who lived in or about the 10th century. The surname was formed by prefixing either Mac (son of) or O (grandson or descendant of) to the ancestor's name. Surnames in Ireland, therefore, tended to identify membership of a sept.

Hampson is derived from Gaelic *O hAmhsaigh*. They were a small sept in County Derry. By the 18th century the name was usually recorded as either Hanson or Hampson. Confusion can occur as Hampson is also recorded as a surname in England where it is regarded as a variant of Hammond.

In the census of 1659 Hampson, in the form of O Hamson, was recorded as one of the principal Irish names in the barony of Keenaght, County Derry. The Hearth Money Rolls of 1663 record 5 Hampson households in County Derry: recorded as O'Hampson in Tamlaghtard Parish; O'Hampen in Desertoghill Parish; O'Hanson in Faughanvale Parish; Hanson in Macosquin Parish; and Handson in Tamlaght Parish.

By the time of the 1831 census the O prefix was not recorded against any of the descendants of the Hampson sept in County Derry. At the time of the 1831 census 27 Hampson households, including variant spellings of the surname, were recorded in County Derry. This source records that in County Derry in 1831 there were 12 households recorded as Hanson, 5 as Hampson, 4 as Hampsey, 3 as Hamsie, 2 as Hamsay and 1 as Hamson. Nineteen of these households, i.e. 70% of the total, were recorded in the northeast Derry parishes of Aghadowey, Desertoghill, Errigal, Killowen and Macosquin.

In the graveyard of the old parish church in Tamlaghtard Parish (also known as Magilligan), County Derry is the grave of Denis Hempson, also known as Denis O'Hempsey, the celebrated Irish harper. His grave is located beside that of St Aidan, the founder of the monastery at Lindisfarne in Northumberland, England in 635 AD.

Denis Hempson was renowned as a harp player throughout Ireland and Scotland. Born at Craigmore near Garvagh, County Derry, ca.1695, he became blind at the age of three. He was taught to play the harp by Bridget O'Cahan when he was twelve, and many of Ireland's old harp tunes are attributed to him. He lived in the townland of Ballymaclary in Magilligan in a house presented to him by Frederick Harvey, 4th earl of Bristol and Bishop of Derry. Denis Hempson was reputed to have been 112 years old when he died in 1807.

In 1835 Denis Hempson's harp, which was then 270 years old, was kept in Downhill House, the former home of his patron Frederick Hervey who had died in 1803. His harp (made ca.1565) was made out of white willow with a back of fir which had been dug out of a bog.

HANNA

This surname is found almost exclusively in Ulster where it is most common in Counties Antrim, Down and Armagh. This name was brought to Ulster by settlers from Scotland in the 17th century.

It is believed that Hanna is derived from Gaelic *ap Sheanaigh*, meaning 'son of Senach'. This family, also spelt as Hannay and Hannah, originated in the province of Galloway in southwest Scotland. It is known that migration from Argyll, and in particular from Kintyre, into Galloway began in the mid-eighth century. The earliest reference to the surname is of one Gilbert de Hannethe of Wigtownshire in 1296.

As supporters of John Balliol, who represented the old Celtic Lords of Galloway, the Hannas were forced to submit to Edward Bruce when he conquered Galloway in 1308. The main line were the Hannas of Sorbie in Wigtownshire from which branches settled in Ayrshire, Dumfriesshire, Dunbartonshire, Kirkcudbrightshire and Renfrewshire. The Hannas, at various times, feuded with the Dunbars, Kennedys and Murrays. Soon after 1600 a feud broke out between the Hannas of Sorbie and the Murrays of Broughton in Peebleshire. As a consequence the Hannas of Sorbie were outlawed and their lands confiscated in 1640. The loss of the lands of Sorbie would have encouraged Hannas to migrate to Ulster as settlers during the 17th century.

The defeat of the old Gaelic order in the Nine Years War, 1594-1603 and the escape of the most prominent Gaelic Lords of Ulster in 'the Flight of the Earls' in 1607 from Lough Swilly, County Donegal were ultimately responsible for the settlement of many Scottish families in the northern counties of Ireland.

Movement of Scottish settlers to Ulster began in earnest from 1605 in a private enterprise colonisation of counties Antrim and Down when Sir Hugh Montgomery and Sir James Hamilton acquired title to large estates in north Down and Sir Randall MacDonnell, 1st Earl of Antrim, to large tracts of land in north Antrim.

In 1609 the Earl of Salisbury, Lord High Treasurer, suggested to James I a deliberate plantation of Scottish and English colonists on the forfeited estates of the Gaelic chiefs in counties Armagh, Cavan, Donegal, Fermanagh, Londonderry (then known as Coleraine) and Tyrone.

Settlers to Ulster came, by and large, in three waves: with the granting of the initial leases in the period 1605 to 1625; after 1652 and Cromwell's crushing of the Irish rebellion; and finally in the fifteen years after 1690 and the Glorious Revolution. It is estimated by 1715, when migration to Ulster had virtually stopped, the Scottish population of Ulster stood at 200,000.

During the famous 105 day Siege of Derry, from 18 April to 31 July 1689, Captain Hannah and Lieutenant Andrew Hannagh were recorded as 'defenders' of the city. Indeed the exploits of Captain Hannah in the garrison's sortie against the Jacobite besiegers on 4 June at Windmill Hill are remembered in verse:
And Captain Hannah the foe stoutly fought.

HANSON

Hanson, and variants such as Hampsey, Hampson and Hansen, originated in County Derry.

Ireland was one of the first countries to adopt a system of hereditary surnames which developed from a more ancient system of clan or sept names. From the 11th century each family began to adopt its own distinctive family name generally derived from the first name of an ancestor who lived in or about the 10th century. The surname was formed by prefixing either Mac (son of) or O (grandson or descendant of) to the ancestor's name. Surnames in Ireland, therefore, tended to identify membership of a sept.

Hanson is derived from Gaelic *O hAmhsaigh*. They were a small sept in County Derry. By the 18th century the name was usually recorded as either Hanson or Hampson. Confusion can occur as Hampson is also recorded as a surname in England where it is regarded as a variant of Hammond.

In the census of 1659 Hanson, in the form of O Hamson, was recorded as one of the principal Irish names in the barony of Keenaght, County Derry. The Hearth Money Rolls of 1663 record 5 Hanson households in County Derry: recorded as O'Hampson in Tamlaghtard Parish; O'Hampen in Desertoghill Parish; O'Hanson in Faughanvale Parish; Hanson in Macosquin Parish; and Handson in Tamlaght Parish.

By the time of the 1831 census the O prefix was not recorded against any of the descendants of the Hanson sept in County Derry. At the time of the 1831 census 27 Hanson households, including variant spellings of the surname, were recorded in County Derry. This source records that in County Derry in 1831 there were 12 households recorded as Hanson, 5 as Hampson, 4 as Hampsey, 3 as Hamsie, 2 as Hamsay and 1 as Hamson. Nineteen of these households, i.e. 70% of the total, were recorded in the northeast Derry parishes of Aghadowey, Desertoghill, Errigal, Killowen and Macosquin.

In the graveyard of the old parish church in Tamlaghtard Parish (also known as Magilligan), County Derry is the grave of Denis Hempson, also known as Denis O'Hempsey, the celebrated Irish harper. His grave is located beside that of St Aidan, the founder of the monastery at Lindisfarne in Northumberland, England in 635 AD.

Denis Hempson was renowned as a harp player throughout Ireland and Scotland. Born at Craigmore near Garvagh, County Derry, ca.1695, he became blind at the age of three. He was taught to play the harp by Bridget O'Cahan when he was twelve, and many of Ireland's old harp tunes are attributed to him. He lived in the townland of Ballymaclary in Magilligan in a house presented to him by Frederick Harvey, 4th earl of Bristol and Bishop of Derry. Denis Hempson was reputed to have been 112 years old when he died in 1807.

In 1835 Denis Hempson's harp, which was then 270 years old, was kept in Downhill House, the former home of his patron Frederick Hervey who had died in 1803. His harp (made ca.1565) was made out of white willow with a back of fir which had been dug out of a bog.

HARGAN

This name, with origins in County Cork, is a common name in the city of Derry.

Ireland was one of the first countries to adopt a system of hereditary surnames which developed from a more ancient system of clan or sept names. From the 11th century each family began to adopt its own distinctive family name generally derived from the first name of an ancestor who lived in or about the 10th century. The surname was formed by prefixing either Mac (son of) or O (grandson or descendant of) to the ancestor's name. Surnames in Ireland, therefore, tended to identify membership of a sept.

The origins of this name are uncertain. It would appear that no sept of this name originated in the province of Ulster. There was, however, one sept, with origins outside of Ulster, whose name was anglicised as Hargan.

In Munster the County Cork sept, in Gaelic *O hArgain*, was usually anglicised as Horgan but also as Hargan and Harrigan. Indeed Hargan is recognised as the variant of Horgan that was adopted in Ulster.

It is also possible that Hargan is a variant form of Harrigan. Harrigan is also a common name in Derry city today and, like Hargan, there is no evidence that a sept of this name originated in Ulster. Outside Ulster, however, there were two distinct septs of this name. In Connaught the County Leitrim sept, in Gaelic *O hArchain*, was anglicised as Harraghan and Harrigan, and in Leinster the County Leix sept, in Gaelic O *hArragain*, was also anglicised as Harrigan.

At the time of the mid-19th century Griffith's Valuation 17 Hargan households were recorded in Ireland, with 9 Hargan households in County Derry, 4 in County Donegal, 2 in County Tyrone and one each in Counties Cork and Fermanagh. This clearly shows that Hargan was very much a name associated with northwest Ulster as over 75% of descendants of Hargans in Ireland were living in Counties Derry and Donegal. However it also tends to confirm that this surname didn't originate as a sept within Ulster as the name was not concentrated in one particular area.

In the middle years of the 19th century the surname Harrigan was very much associated with the province of Munster, particularly with Counties Cork and Limerick. The Griffith's Valuation recorded 112 Harrigan households in Ireland, with 59 Harrigan households in County Cork and 25 in County Limerick. In other words 75% of descendants of Harrigans in Ireland were living in Counties Cork and Limerick. At this time only 11 Harrigan households were recorded in Ulster, with 4 in County Antrim, 3 in Derry, 3 in Donegal and 1 in Tyrone.

Hargan is a common name in Derry city today. As Derry developed an industrial base in the 19th century in shirt making, shipbuilding and distilling it attracted much of its workforce from outside of the city and county of Derry. In the 90-year period 1821 to 1911 the population of the city quadrupled to 40,780. In this period Derry stamped her dominance over local rivals and emerged as an important urban centre within Ireland.

HARKIN

Harkins are found only in Ulster where over half are in County Donegal and most of the rest in County Derry. The name is particularly associated with Inishowen, County Donegal. This name, which is among the top ten in the city of Derry, illustrates the very close links between the city of Derry and Inishowen. As Derry developed an industrial base in the 19th century in shirt making, shipbuilding and distilling it attracted much of its workforce from Inishowen.

Ireland was one of the first countries to adopt a system of hereditary surnames which developed from a more ancient system of clan or sept names. From the 11th century each family began to adopt its own distinctive family name generally derived from the first name of an ancestor who lived in or about the 10th century. The surname was formed by prefixing either Mac (son of) or O (grandson or descendant of) to the ancestor's name. Surnames in Ireland, therefore, tended to identify membership of a sept.

Harkin is derived from Gaelic *O hEarcain,* the root word being *earc,* meaning 'red'. In 1659 the Harkins were recorded as a 'principal name' in the barony of Inishowen, County Donegal. This sept's association with Inishowen is recorded long before that, for the O'Harkins were *erenaghs,* i.e. hereditary stewards, of the church lands of Cloncha. One appears as such in Bishop Montgomery's diocesan survey of 1606. Daniel O'Harcan, who died in 1581, was one of the Ulster martyrs defending the Roman Catholic faith.

The Parish of Cloncha, which includes Malin Head, is the most northerly parish in Ireland.

Many Inishowen families trace their lineage to Eogan, son of the 5th century High King of Ireland, Niall of the Nine Hostages, who ruled from the Hill of Tara, County Meath. Eogan and his brother Conall *Gulban* conquered northwest Ireland, ca.425 AD, capturing the great hill-fort of Grianan of Ailech which commanded the entrance to the Inishowen peninsula between Lough Swilly and Lough Foyle.

Eogan, styled 'King of Ailech', established his own kingdom in the peninsula still called after him Inishowen (Innis Eoghain or Eogan's Isle). Eogan was converted to Christianity by St Patrick, when he travelled to Ailech, ca. 442 AD. His descendants, known as the Cenel Eoghain (the race of Owen), became the principal branch of the Northern Ui Neill (descendants of Niall of the Nine Hostages). The Cenel Eoghain in the next five centuries expanded to the east and south from their focal point in Inishowen.

Today there are more Harkins in Derry city than in their original homeland of Inishowen.

HARRIGAN

This name is associated with Counties Mayo and Sligo in north Connaught and with Counties Derry and Donegal in west Ulster.

Ireland was one of the first countries to adopt a system of hereditary surnames which developed from a more ancient system of clan or sept names. From the 11th century each family began to adopt its own distinctive family name generally derived from the first name of an ancestor who lived in or about the 10th century. The surname was formed by prefixing either Mac (son of) or O (grandson or descendant of) to the ancestor's name. Surnames in Ireland, therefore, tended to identify membership of a sept.

The origins of this name are uncertain. It would appear that no sept of this name originated in the province of Ulster. There were, however, three distinct septs, with origins outside of Ulster, whose names were either usually or occasionally anglicised as Harrigan.

In Munster the County Cork sept, in Gaelic *O hArgain*, was usually anglicised as Horgan but also as Hargan and Harrigan. Indeed Hargan is recognised as the variant of Horgan that was adopted in Ulster. Furthermore an examination of the mid-19th century Griffith's Valuation confirms that descendants of this sept were the forebears of most Harrigans in Ireland.

In Connaught the County Leitrim sept, in Gaelic *O hArchain*, was anglicised as Harraghan and Harrigan, and in Leinster the County Leix sept, in Gaelic O *hArragain*, was also anglicised as Harrigan.

At the time of the mid-19th century Griffith's Valuation 112 Harrigan households were recorded in Ireland, with 59 Harrigan households in County Cork and 25 in County Limerick. In other words 75% of descendants of Harrigans in Ireland were living in Counties Cork and Limerick. At this time only 11 Harrigan households were recorded in Ulster, with 4 in County Antrim, 3 in Derry, 3 in Donegal and 1 in Tyrone. This would tend to confirm that this surname didn't originate as a sept within Ulster.

In the middle years of the 19th century the surname Hargan was very much associated with the province of Ulster. The Griffith's Valuation recorded 17 Hargan households in Ireland, with 9 Hargan households in County Derry, 4 in County Donegal, 2 in County Tyrone and one each in Counties Cork and Fermanagh. This clearly shows that Hargan was very much a name associated with northwest Ulster as over 75% of descendants of Hargans in Ireland were living in Counties Derry and Donegal.

Harrigan is a common name in Derry city today. As Derry developed an industrial base in the 19th century in shirt making, shipbuilding and distilling it attracted much of its workforce from outside of the city and county of Derry. In the 90-year period 1821 to 1911 the population of the city quadrupled to 40,780. In this period Derry stamped her dominance over local rivals and emerged as an important urban centre within Ireland.

89

HARRISON

This name is found in all provinces in Ireland. Harrison is most numerous in Ulster especially in Counties Antrim and Down. This name was brought to Ulster by settlers from England in the 17th century.

Harrison, derived from the personal name Henry, simply means 'son of Harry'. Henry was a very popular choice as a child's name during the Middle Ages, and at a time when fixed surnames, based on a father's first name, were being established.

The name rose to national prominence in England during the 16th and 17th centuries through the activities of John Harrison (1579-1656), wool merchant of Leeds and generous philanthropist, and Thomas Harrison (1606-1660), a committed parliamentarian who signed the death warrant of Charles I.

Today Harrison is among the thirty commonest names in England. The name is particularly associated with northern England where it is most common in the counties of Cumberland, Lancashire and Yorkshire.

The defeat of the old Gaelic order in the Nine Years War, 1594-1603 and the escape of the most prominent Gaelic Lords of Ulster in 'the Flight of the Earls' in 1607 from Lough Swilly, County Donegal were ultimately responsible for the settlement of many English, Welsh and Scottish families in the northern counties of Ireland.

In 1609 the Earl of Salisbury, Lord High Treasurer, suggested to James I a deliberate plantation of English, Welsh and Scottish colonists on the forfeited estates of the Gaelic chiefs in counties Armagh, Cavan, Donegal, Fermanagh, Londonderry (then known as Coleraine) and Tyrone.

Settlers came to Ulster, by and large, in three waves: with the granting of the initial leases in the period 1605 to 1625; after 1652 and Cromwell's crushing of the Irish rebellion; and finally in the fifteen years after 1690 and the Glorious Revolution. By the end of the 17th century a self-sustaining settlement of British colonists had established itself in Ulster.

Londonderry, Coleraine, Carrickfergus, Belfast and Donaghadee were the main ports of entry into the province of Ulster for 17th century British settlers with the Lagan, Bann and the Foyle valleys acting as the major arteries along which the colonists travelled into the interior. English settlers, mostly drawn from the northern counties of Cheshire, Cumberland, Lancashire, Northumberland, Yorkshire and Westmorland, tended to favour settlement along the Lagan Valley, in the east of the Province, on lands straddling the borders of Counties Armagh, Antrim and Down.

During the famous 105 day Siege of Derry, from 18 April to 31 July 1689, Captain Edward Harrison of Killultagh, County Antrim and his son Michael were recorded as 'defenders' of the city. Both these men served as High Sheriffs of County Antrim and as Members of Parliament for Lisburn, County Antrim. The first of this 'old family in Ireland' was Captain Edward Harrison's father, 'Sir Michael Harrison, of Ballydargan, Master of the Staple in Charles II's time, who died in 1664.'

HARRON

Harron, and variants such as Heron and Herron, can be an Irish or a Scottish name. This name is mainly found in Ulster, where it is most common in Counties Antrim, Down and Donegal.

Ireland was one of the first countries to adopt a system of hereditary surnames which developed from a more ancient system of clan or sept names. From the 11th century each family began to adopt its own distinctive family name generally derived from the first name of an ancestor who lived in or about the 10th century. The surname was formed by prefixing either Mac (son of) or O (grandson or descendant of) to the ancestor's name. Surnames in Ireland, therefore, tended to identify membership of a sept.

Two distinct Harron septs, in Gaelic *O HEarain*, the root word possibly being *earadh*, meaning 'dread', originated in Ulster: one in County Armagh and the other in County Donegal. In County Fermanagh the Harrons, in Gaelic *O hArain*, were erenaghs, i.e. hereditary stewards, of the church lands of Ballymacataggart in Derryvullan Parish.

In the census of 1659 Harron, in the form of O Haron, was recorded as one of the principal Irish names in the barony of Keenaght, County Derry.

Harron was occasionally used as an abbreviated form of McElheron. MacElheron is derived from Gaelic *Mac Giolla Chiarain*, meaning 'son of the devotee of St Kieran'. St Kieran founded a monastery at Clonmacnois, County Offaly in 548 AD. A small sept of this name originated in east Ulster, where the name was recorded in County Armagh in the 16th century Fiants.

McIlheran, in Gaelic *Mac Gille Chiarain*, meaning 'son of the devotee of St Kieran', is also a Scottish name. The McIlherans, based on the Isle of Bute, were a sept of Clan Donald who took their name from the 7th century St Kieran, the patron saint of Campbeltown in Kintyre.

Movement of Scottish settlers to Ulster began in earnest from 1605 in a private enterprise colonisation of counties Antrim and Down when Sir Hugh Montgomery and Sir James Hamilton acquired title to large estates in north Down and Sir Randall MacDonnell, 1st Earl of Antrim, to large tracts of land in north Antrim. As followers of Clan Donald many Scottish McIlherans would have settled in the Glens of Antrim. In Ulster the name was further anglicised to Heron and Herron.

The Herons were also recorded as one of the lawless riding or reiving families of the Border country between Scotland and England who raided, on horseback, and stole each other's cattle and possessions. They lived in the Middle March on the English side of the border. In England the surname Heron originated as a nickname for a tall, thin person

Tracing their descent from Northumberland in the 11th century, the Herons were also an important family in Kirkcudbrightshire in the province of Galloway. This province of southwest Scotland was home to many of the Scottish settlers who came to Ulster throughout the 17th century.

HASSAN

In Ulster, this name belongs to County Derry.

Ireland was one of the first countries to adopt a system of hereditary surnames which developed from a more ancient system of clan or sept names. From the 11th century each family began to adopt its own distinctive family name generally derived from the first name of an ancestor who lived in or about the 10th century. The surname was formed by prefixing either Mac (son of) or O (grandson or descendant of) to the ancestor's name. Surnames in Ireland, therefore, tended to identify membership of a sept. Hassan is derived from Gaelic *O hOsain*, the root word possibly being *os*, meaning 'deer'. The homeland of this sept was County Derry.

The escape of the most prominent Gaelic Lords of Ulster in 'the Flight of the Earls' in 1607 from Lough Swilly, County Donegal marked the end of Gaelic power and paved the way for the 17th century Plantation of Ulster with English and Scottish settlers. In the centuries that followed Gaelic names were anglicised, resulting in many variant spellings of the same name and, in many cases, the dropping of the O and Mac prefixes.

In the case of Hassan the prefix O was not retained. The name does appear as O'Hassan in the Hearth Money Rolls of 1663 for County Derry and as O'Hessan in the Hearth Money Rolls for County Monaghan. The Hearth Money Rolls of 1663 record 4 O'Hassan households in County Derry; two households of the name in Killelagh Parish and one each in the parishes of Banagher and Drumachose.

By the time of the 1831 census, however, the O prefix was not recorded against any of the descendants of the Hassan sept in County Derry. At the time of the 1831 census 154 Hassan households, including variant spellings of the surname, were recorded in County Derry. This source records that in County Derry in 1831 there were 68 households recorded as Hasson, 31 as Hassin, 26 as Hassan, 6 as Hassen, 5 as Hason, 5 as Hessin, 3 as Hasan, 3 as Hession, 2 as Hassion, 2 as Hesson and one each as Hessan, Hessen and Hessian.

The 1831 census would suggest that the parish of Banagher was the ancestral homeland of the Hassans in County Derry. At this time sixty Hassan households were living in the parish of Banagher. In other words nearly 40% of the descendants of the Hassan sept in County Derry were residing in this one parish. Elizabeth Hassan, the mother of John McCloskey (born in New York on 10 March 1810, who was to become archbishop of New York and, in 1875, the first U.S. cardinal), was born in the townland of Coolnamonan in Banagher Parish.

There was a secondary concentration of Hassans centred on and surrounding the parish of Maghera, County Derry. Fourteen Hassan households were recorded in Maghera Parish in the 1831 census.

Outside Ulster, Hession, which is regarded as being distinct from Hassan, is derived from Gaelic *O hOisin*. The name *O hOisin* occurs in the 11th and 12th centuries in *the Annals* in all the provinces except Ulster. Hession is mainly associated with north Galway and south Mayo.

HEANEY

This surname is most common in Ulster, particularly in Counties Armagh and Derry.

Ireland was one of the first countries to adopt a system of hereditary surnames which developed from a more ancient system of clan or sept names. From the 11th century each family began to adopt its own distinctive family name generally derived from the first name of an ancestor who lived in or about the 10th century. The surname was formed by prefixing either Mac (son of) or O (grandson or descendant of) to the ancestor's name. Surnames in Ireland, therefore, tended to identify membership of a sept.

Heaney is derived from Gaelic *O hEighnigh.* There were at least two distinct septs of the name in Ulster. In the medieval period the O'Heaneys were a powerful sept in Oriel, a territory which included Counties Armagh and Monaghan and parts of south Down, Louth and Fermanagh. Indeed these O'Heaneys were chiefs of Fermanagh before the Maguires took over in 1202.

In County Derry another O'Heaney sept were *erenaghs*, i.e. hereditary stewards, of the church lands in the parish of Banagher in the barony of Keenaght. The ancient church of Banagher in the townland of Magheramore on the south side of the Owenreagh river was founded by St Muriedhach O'Heney who lived in the 11th or 12th century. In 1121 Gilla-Espoig Eoghain O'Hennery, 'lord of Cianachta-Glinne-Geimhin', was slain by his own kinsmen in the grounds of this ancient church.

The Cianachta or Keenaght were rulers of the Roe Valley, near Dungiven, County Derry. Glinne-Geimhin, anglicised as Glengiven, meaning 'Glen of the skins', is the old name for the valley of the River Roe.

The tomb of St Muriedhach O'Heney is located in the graveyard of Banagher Old Church. Beside the tomb of the saint is 'the hole, whence the famous Banagher sand is raised, a sprinkle of which, it is believed, if thrown on a race-horse before starting for a race, insures success.' It is also claimed that St O'Heney appears, at intervals, among the ruins of the ancient Church.

In the census of 1659 Heaney, in the form of O Heany, was recorded as one of the principal Irish names in the barony of Keenaght, County Derry.

The 1831 census for County Derry clearly demonstrates that the lands in the upper reaches of the Roe Valley in County Derry were the ancestral homeland of the Heaneys. At the time of the 1831 census there were 78 Heaney households in County Derry, and all but eleven of these households were residing in an area centred on and surrounding the parishes of Banagher and Dungiven. At the time of the 1831 census there were 26 Heaney households recorded in Banagher Parish and 24 households of the name in Dungiven Parish. Indeed in 1831 there were 17 Heaney households living in the fertile townland of Templemoyle in Banagher parish.

It would also appear that the Heaneys had a connection with south Derry as the parish name of Termoneeny means 'the sanctuary of the O'Heaneys'. At the time of the 1831 census, however, there were no Heaneys living in this parish.

93

HEGARTY

Though the surname Hegarty is now most common in Munster, especially in County Cork, the Hegartys of that province are a branch of an Ulster sept whose homeland lay on the borders of counties Derry and Donegal.

The Hegarty sept trace their lineage to Eogan, son of the 5th century High King of Ireland, Niall of the Nine Hostages, who ruled from the Hill of Tara, County Meath. Eogan and his brother Conall *Gulban* conquered northwest Ireland, ca.425 AD, capturing the great hill-fort of Grianan of Ailech in County Donegal which commanded the entrance to the Inishowen peninsula between Lough Swilly and Lough Foyle.

Eogan, styled 'King of Ailech', established his own kingdom in the peninsula still called after him Inishowen (Innis Eoghain or Eogan's Isle). Eogan was converted to Christianity by St Patrick, when he travelled to Ailech, ca. 442 AD. His descendants, known as the Cenel Eoghain (the race of Owen), became the principal branch of the Northern Ui Neill (descendants of Niall of the Nine Hostages). The Cenel Eoghain in the next five centuries expanded to the east and south from their focal point in Inishowen.

Ireland was one of the first countries to adopt a system of hereditary surnames which developed from a more ancient system of clan or sept names. From the 11th century each family began to adopt its own distinctive family name generally derived from the first name of an ancestor who lived in or about the 10th century. The surname was formed by prefixing either Mac (son of) or O (grandson or descendant of) to the ancestor's name. Surnames in Ireland, therefore, tended to identify membership of a sept. O'Hegarty, in Gaelic *O hEigceartaigh,* is derived from *eigceartach,* meaning 'unjust'.

In the 14th century the homeland of the O'Hegarty sept was the barony of Loughinsholin in south Derry.

By the time of the 17th century Plantation of Ulster by English and Scottish settlers the Hegartys were most numerous in Inishowen, County Donegal and in the barony of Tirkeeran, west of the River Roe, in County Derry. They also had established themselves in the baronies of Barrymore and Carberry West in County Cork.

The Hegartys were sub-lords to the O'Neills. Maolmuire O'Hegarty was killed at the Battle of Kinsale where O'Neill's Irish army and Spanish allies were defeated by an English army in 1601.

In the 17th and 18th centuries many descendants of the old Gaelic order in Ireland emigrated, as the so-called Wild Geese, to Europe, and, in particular, to Spain and France. Hegarty appears frequently in the annals of the Irish Brigades. In the 18th century Lieutenant-Colonel Hegarty, of Lally's Regiment, distinguished himself in the military service of Louis XV of France, while Peter O'Hegarty was made Governor of the Isle of Bourbon.

HENDERSON

This surname is found almost exclusively in Ulster where it is most common in Counties Antrim and Tyrone. This name was brought to Ulster by settlers from Scotland in the 17th century.

Henderson is one of the thirty most common names in Scotland. Henderson, derived from the personal name Henry, simply means 'son of Henry'. The Hendersons were one of the riding or reiving clans of the Scottish Borders. They held lands in Upper Liddesdale on the Scottish side of the Middle March. Prior to the Union of the Crowns of England and Scotland in 1603 the Scottish Border was divided into three districts; the east, west and middle Marches. Each March was presided over by a warden who settled disputes with the warden of the appropriate March in England.

From the 14th to the late-17th century, the border between England and Scotland – the Debatable Lands – was a turbulent place. The Border country was ravaged by the lawless Reiver families who raided, on horseback, and stole each other's cattle and possessions. When the power of the riding clans was broken by James I in the decade after 1603 many came to Ulster to escape persecution.

In the Lowlands of Scotland the chief family of the name were the Hendersons of Fordell in Fifeshire who were descended from the Henrysons of Dumfriesshire.

In the Highlands of Scotland the Hendersons, based in Caithness, were a branch of Clan Gunn, tracing their descent from Henry Gunn, son of George Gunn, the 15th century chief of Clan Gunn. Clan Gunn, in turn, claim descent from the Viking chief Gunni who was killed in Dublin in 1171. By 1594 Clan Gunn was listed as one of the 'broken clans' of the north. . Owing to the nature of the Scottish clan system once the power and influence of the chief had been weakened the clan tended to scatter.

In Glencoe in Argyllshire the Hendersons, in Gaelic *Mac Eanruig*, meaning 'son of Henry', claim descent from 'Big Henry, son of King Nechtan'. Nechtan was an eighth century Pictish king. The Hendersons held Glencoe for three hundred years before Robert the Bruce, King of Scotland, 1306-1329. In the 14th century the McDonalds took over the area and the Hendersons, as hereditary pipers to the McDonalds of Glencoe, became a sept of this clan. As loyal followers of the McDonalds the last chief of the name, Big Henderson of the Chanters, was killed by the Campbells in the Glencoe massacre of 1692.

Movement of Scottish settlers to Ulster began in earnest from 1605 in a private enterprise colonisation of counties Antrim and Down when Sir Hugh Montgomery and Sir James Hamilton acquired title to large estates in north Down and Sir Randall MacDonnell, 1st Earl of Antrim, to large tracts of land in north Antrim. Further impetus came in 1609 when James I adopted the policy to encourage English and Scottish settlers to settle on the forfeited estates of the Gaelic chiefs in counties Armagh, Cavan, Donegal, Fermanagh, Londonderry (then known as Coleraine) and Tyrone.

During the famous 105 day Siege of Derry, from 18 April to 31 July 1689, John Henderson was recorded as one of the 'defenders' of the city.

HENRY

The surname Henry can disguise a number of different origins of the people who bear this name, particularly in north Antrim and Derry owing to the proximity of Gaelic Irish septs, such as McHenry of the Loughan, County Derry and O'Henery of County Tyrone, to Scottish settlers with surnames such as Henry, McHendrie, McKendrick and McKendry.

Ireland was one of the first countries to adopt a system of hereditary surnames which developed from a more ancient system of clan or sept names. The surname was formed by prefixing either Mac (son of) or O (grandson or descendant of) to the ancestor's name.

The McHenrys of the Loughan, in Gaelic *Mac Einri*, were a branch of the O'Cahans (O'Kanes). They trace their descent from Henry O'Cahan, son of Dermot who died 1428, son of Cooey Na Gaal who died in 1385. The McHenrys were based at the Loughan in Kildollagh Parish, to the southeast of the town of Coleraine in County Derry. Thus McHenry literally means son of Henry O'Kane.

In 1609 Mill Loughan was granted to George McHenry O'Cahan from Sir Randal MacDonnell, Earl of Antrim. The McHenrys also obtained adjacent lands in County Antrim in Ballyrashane Parish. Thus from their home near Loughan Island, which divides the River Bann, the McHenry O'Cahans had an outpost across the Bann fronting the Scottish MacDonnells. The family took an active part in the 1641 rebellion and as a consequence the property of the McHenry family of the Loughan was confiscated.

The O'Henery sept, derived from Gaelic *O hInneirghe*, were based at Cullentra, County Tyrone with their territory extending to the valley of Glenconkeine in County Derry.

However, although the surnames of McHenry and O'Henery have quite distinct origins, their ultimate origins are now disguised owing to the widespread discarding of the Mac and O prefixes. Most families descending from these septs now bear the surname Henry.

Henry can also be Scottish in origin as the name came with Scottish immigrants at the time of the Plantation of Ulster in the 17th century. Hendry, MacHendrie and MacKendrick, meaning 'son of Henry', were a branch of the Scottish clan MacNaughton which descends from one Henry MacNaughton. Clan MacNaughton, in Gaelic *Mac Neachdainn*, meaning 'son of Nechtan', claims descent from the eighth-century Pictish king Nechtan.

The MacNaughtons were one of the families brought in by the MacDonnells of the Glens of Antrim in the early 17th century. Shane Dhu, or Black John MacNaghten, became the Earl of Antrim's chief agent. It is believed that the Henry sept based in Argyll and Bute were originally MacKendricks.

Thus in Ulster, and, in particular, in north Antrim and Derry it will be difficult to distinguish Scottish Henrys from Irish Henrys.

HERON

Heron, and variants such as Harron and Herron, can be an Irish or a Scottish name. This name is mainly found in Ulster, where it is most common in Counties Antrim, Down and Donegal.

Ireland was one of the first countries to adopt a system of hereditary surnames which developed from a more ancient system of clan or sept names. From the 11th century each family began to adopt its own distinctive family name generally derived from the first name of an ancestor who lived in or about the 10th century. The surname was formed by prefixing either Mac (son of) or O (grandson or descendant of) to the ancestor's name. Surnames in Ireland, therefore, tended to identify membership of a sept.

Two distinct Heron septs, in Gaelic *O HEarain*, the root word possibly being *earadh*, meaning 'dread', originated in Ulster: one in County Armagh and the other in County Donegal. In County Fermanagh the Herons, in Gaelic *O hArain*, were *erenaghs*, i.e. hereditary stewards, of the church lands of Ballymacataggart in Derryvullan Parish.

In the census of 1659 Heron, in the form of O Haron, was recorded as one of the principal Irish names in the barony of Keenaght, County Derry.

Heron was occasionally used as an abbreviated form of McElheron. MacElheron is derived from Gaelic *Mac Giolla Chiarain*, meaning 'son of the devotee of St Kieran'. St Kieran founded a monastery at Clonmacnois, County Offaly in 548 AD. A small sept of this name originated in east Ulster, where the name was recorded in County Armagh in the 16th century Fiants.

McIlheran, in Gaelic *Mac Gille Chiarain*, meaning 'son of the devotee of St Kieran', is also a Scottish name. The McIlherans, based on the Isle of Bute, were a sept of Clan Donald who took their name from the 7th century St Kieran, the patron saint of Campbeltown in Kintyre.

Movement of Scottish settlers to Ulster began in earnest from 1605 in a private enterprise colonisation of counties Antrim and Down when Sir Hugh Montgomery and Sir James Hamilton acquired title to large estates in north Down and Sir Randall MacDonnell, 1st Earl of Antrim, to large tracts of land in north Antrim. As followers of Clan Donald many Scottish McIlherans would have settled in the Glens of Antrim. In Ulster the name was further anglicised to Heron and Herron.

The Herons were also recorded as one of the lawless riding or reiving families of the Border country between Scotland and England who raided, on horseback, and stole each other's cattle and possessions. They lived in the Middle March on the English side of the border. In England the surname Heron originated as a nickname for a tall, thin person

Tracing their descent from Northumberland in the 11th century, the Herons were also an important family in Kirkcudbrightshire in the province of Galloway. This province of southwest Scotland was home to many of the Scottish settlers who came to Ulster throughout the 17th century.

HOUSTON

This surname is found almost exclusively in Ulster where it is most common in Counties Antrim, Derry, Armagh and Down. This name was brought to Ulster by settlers from Scotland in the 17th century.

In the Lowlands of Scotland this surname is derived from the old barony of Huston, meaning 'Hugh's settlement', located near Glasgow in Lanarkshire. In this case Hugh refers to Hugh de Paduinan, a Saxon lord, who was granted these lands c. 1160. The earliest reference to the surname is of one Finlay of Huwitston who witnessed a charter in Renfrewshire in the late 13th century. During the 15th century references to the surname can be found in Glasgow, Irvine and Paisley. In Ross-shire the Houstons were descended from Reverend Thomas Houston of Inverness, who died in 1605.

It is believed that the Houstons of Craigs' Castle in south Antrim and of Castlestewart in County Tyrone are ultimately descended from the Houstons of Lanarkshire. The ancestors of General Sam Houston are also of this connection. In 1836 the newly founded town of Houston, Texas, was named in honour of Sam Houston whose ancestors had emigrated to Philadelphia from Ulster in the 18th century. As Commander in Chief of the Texan army Sam Houston achieved independence from Mexico.

In the Highlands of Scotland, McCutcheon, in Gaelic *Mac Uisdin*, meaning 'son of Hutcheon', was also anglicised as McQuiston and Houston. The McCutcheons were a branch of Clan Donald. Clan Donald had acquired new territories in the north of Ireland ca.1400 when John Mor MacDonald had married Margery Bissett, an heiress in the Glens of Antrim. By the mid-16th century the MacDonalds, known as the MacDonnells of the Glens, had carved out an extensive territory in County Antrim at the expense of the MacQuillans. It would quite likely that some Houstons, as followers of Clan Donald, settled in County Antrim.

Movement of Scottish settlers to Ulster began in earnest from 1605 in a private enterprise colonisation of counties Antrim and Down when Sir Hugh Montgomery and Sir James Hamilton acquired title to large estates in north Down and Sir Randall MacDonnell, 1st Earl of Antrim, to large tracts of land in north Antrim. Further impetus came in 1609 when James I adopted the policy to encourage Scottish settlers to settle on the forfeited estates of the Gaelic chiefs in counties Armagh, Cavan, Donegal, Fermanagh, Londonderry (then known as Coleraine) and Tyrone. It is estimated by 1715, when migration to Ulster had virtually stopped, the Scottish population of Ulster stood at 200,000.

During the famous 105 day Siege of Derry, from 18 April to 31 July 1689, James Houston of Garveleigh, near Castlederg, County Tyrone, Francis and Colonel Robert Houston of Craigs, County Antrim, Reverend David Houston 'of the old Covenanting spirit of Presbyterian Scotland', and John and Robert Houston were recorded as 'defenders' of the city.

In County Donegal McTaghlin, in Gaelic *Mac Giolla tSeachlainn*, meaning 'son of the devotee of St Seachlainn', was sometimes anglicised as Houston.

98

HUGHES

Hughes can be an Irish or an English name. Hughes is among the forty most common names in Ireland and among the first fifteen in Ulster. It is among the first five names in County Armagh and among the first ten in Counties Tyrone and Monaghan.

Ireland was one of the first countries to adopt a system of hereditary surnames which developed from a more ancient system of clan or sept names. From the 11th century each family began to adopt its own distinctive family name generally derived from the first name of an ancestor who lived in or about the 10th century. The surname was formed by prefixing either Mac (son of) or O (grandson or descendant of) to the ancestor's name. Surnames in Ireland, therefore, tended to identify membership of a sept.

O'Hea, Hayes and Hughes are the anglicised forms of the very common Gaelic surname *O hAodha*, meaning 'descendant of Hugh'. There were at least a dozen different and distinct septs of this name in Ireland. In Ulster the name was usually anglicised as Hughes and in the other provinces it usually became Hayes.

In Ulster there were septs of *O hAodha* located around Tynan in County Armagh; Ballyshannon in County Donegal; Iveagh barony in County Down; Farney in County Monaghan; and Ardstraw in County Tyrone.

The Annals of The Kingdom of Ireland by the Four Masters record the slaying and death, in 1044 and 1069 respectively, of chiefs of the Hughes sept (recorded as *Ua h Aedha*) of Ardstraw, County Tyrone. In 1160 *O hAodha* was described as King of Iveagh, County Down.

Hughes is a well-known name in England and Wales. Hugh, derived from Old German *Hugo*, meaning 'heart' or 'mind', through Old French *Hue*, was a very popular personal name after the Norman Conquest of England in 1066. Hughes was first recorded in the Domesday Book in 1086 and it has now become one of the twenty most common names in England and in Wales. This name was then brought to Ulster by settlers from England and Wales in the 17th century.

The defeat of the old Gaelic order in the Nine Years War, 1594-1603 and the escape of the most prominent Gaelic Lords of Ulster in 'the Flight of the Earls' in 1607 from Lough Swilly, County Donegal were ultimately responsible for the settlement of many English and Welsh families in the northern counties of Ireland. By the end of the 17th century a self-sustaining settlement of British colonists had established itself in Ulster.

Londonderry, Coleraine, Carrickfergus, Belfast and Donaghadee were the main ports of entry into the province of Ulster for 17th century British settlers with the Lagan, Bann and the Foyle valleys acting as the major arteries along which the colonists travelled into the interior. English settlers, mostly drawn from the northern counties of Cheshire, Cumberland, Lancashire, Northumberland, Yorkshire and Westmorland, and Welsh settlers tended to favour settlement along the Lagan Valley, in the east of the Province, on lands straddling the borders of Counties Armagh, Antrim and Down.

HUNTER

This surname is found almost exclusively in Ulster where it is most common in Counties Antrim, Derry and Down. The majority of Ulster Hunters will be of Scottish origin.

Hunter is derived from an occupational name for a hunter. In the Middle Ages the term was used not only to describe hunters on horseback of game such as stags and wild boars, which was restricted to the nobility, but also of bird catchers and poachers seeking food.

Hunter is one of the forty most common names in Scotland. Hunters were established at Hunterston in Ayrshire when a family of Norman descent was granted an estate there in 1271. Hunter became a common surname in Ayrshire, and this region was home to many of the Scottish settlers who came to Ulster throughout the 17th century.

The Hunters were also recorded as one of the lawless riding or reiving families of the Scottish Borders who raided, on horseback, and stole each other's cattle and possessions. They lived in the Middle March of the English side of the frontier where they were followers of the Nixons. When the power of the riding clans was broken by James I in the decade after 1603 many came to Ulster to escape persecution.

Movement of Scottish settlers to Ulster began in earnest from 1605 in a private enterprise colonisation of counties Antrim and Down when Sir Hugh Montgomery and Sir James Hamilton acquired title to large estates in north Down and Sir Randall MacDonnell, 1st Earl of Antrim, to large tracts of land in north Antrim. Further impetus came in 1609 when James I adopted the policy to encourage English and Scottish settlers to settle on the forfeited estates of the Gaelic chiefs in counties Armagh, Cavan, Donegal, Fermanagh, Londonderry (then known as Coleraine) and Tyrone.

Settlers to Ulster came, by and large, in three waves: with the granting of the initial leases in the period 1605 to 1625; after 1652 and Cromwell's crushing of the Irish rebellion; and finally in the fifteen years after 1690 and the Glorious Revolution. It is estimated by 1715, when migration to Ulster had virtually stopped, the Scottish population of Ulster stood at 200,000.

The Hearth Money Rolls of 1663, in recording 10 Hunter households, confirm that Hunters were settled in County Londonderry from the early years of the Plantation of Ulster, and that all but one of these households settled in the Bann valley in the east of the county.

The Protestant Householders Lists of 1740 also confirm that the settlement of Hunters in County Londonderry was further strengthened towards the end of the 17th century. This source records 64 Hunter households in County Londonderry, with the biggest concentrations in the parishes of Macosquin with 9 households of the name, Aghadowey with 8, Templemore with 7 and Desertoghill with 5.

During the famous 105 day Siege of Derry, from 18 April to 31 July 1689, Captain Henry Hunter was recorded as one of the 'defenders' of the city.

HUTCHINSON

This surname is found almost exclusively in Ulster where it is most common in Counties Derry, Antrim, and Down. This name was brought to Ulster by settlers from Scotland in the 17th century.

In the Highlands of Scotland, McCutcheon, in Gaelic *Mac Uisdin*, meaning 'son of Hutcheon', was also anglicised as Hutchinson. The French personal name Huchon, a pet form of Hugh, was made Hutcheon in Scotland. This name in turn was borrowed into Scots Gaelic as Uisdean. The McDonalds of Skye trace their descent from Hugh, a younger son of Alexander MacDonald, Lord of the Isles. This family became known as Clann Uisdin. Thus the McDonalds of Syke were regarded as the offspring of a man called Hutcheon. As early as the 15th century the name was being anglicised as Hutchinson, meaning 'son of Hutcheon'.

The Hutchinsons were, therefore, a branch of Clan Donald. Under the leadership of Somerled, who expelled the Norsemen from the western side of Scotland in the 12th century, Clan Donald claimed the position of 'The Headship of the Gael'. By the time of his death in 1387, John MacDonald, as Lord of the Isles, controlled the whole of the Hebrides from Lewis to Islay, with the exception of Skye, and the mainland from Kintyre to Knoydart.

Clan Donald had acquired new territories in the north of Ireland ca.1400 when John Mor MacDonald had married Margery Bissett, an heiress in the Glens of Antrim. By the mid-16th century the MacDonalds, known as the MacDonnells of the Glens, had carved out an extensive territory in County Antrim at the expense of the MacQuillans. It would quite likely that some Hutchinsons, as followers of Clan Donald, settled in County Antrim. Owing to the nature of the Scottish clan system once the power and influence of the chief had been weakened or broken the clan tended to disintegrate. The MacDonalds finally lost their title as 'Lord of the Isles' in 1493.

The surname Hutchinson was recorded in the Lowlands of Scotland from the 15th century. For example, James Huchonsone held land in Glasgow in 1454, John Huchonson was made burgess of Aberdeen in 1466, and George Huchunson was made burgess of Glasgow in 1471.

Movement of Scottish settlers to Ulster began in earnest from 1605 in a private enterprise colonisation of counties Antrim and Down when Sir Hugh Montgomery and Sir James Hamilton acquired title to large estates in north Down and Sir Randall MacDonnell, 1st Earl of Antrim, to large tracts of land in north Antrim.

Further impetus came in 1609 when James I adopted the policy to encourage Scottish settlers to settle on the forfeited estates of the Gaelic chiefs in counties Armagh, Cavan, Donegal, Fermanagh, Londonderry (then known as Coleraine) and Tyrone.

Settlers to Ulster came, by and large, in three waves: with the granting of the initial leases in the period 1605 to 1625; after 1652 and Cromwell's crushing of the Irish rebellion; and finally in the fifteen years after 1690 and the Glorious Revolution. It is estimated by 1715, when migration to Ulster had virtually stopped, the Scottish population of Ulster stood at 200,000.

INCH

This name, of Scottish origin, belongs to County Londonderry.

In Scotland, this surname is derived from places of this name in Angus and in Perthshire. The earliest reference to the surname is of one John del Inche who was recorded as burgess of Inverkeithing in Fife in 1296. The family of Inches of Perthshire were regarded as a sept of Clan Robertson. In the 15th and 16th centuries references to the surname were also recorded in the town of Montrose in Angus and in the barony of Banff in Banffshire.

The defeat of the old Gaelic order in the Nine Years War, 1594-1603 and the escape of the most prominent Gaelic Lords of Ulster in 'the Flight of the Earls' in 1607 from Lough Swilly, County Donegal were ultimately responsible for the settlement of many Scottish families in the northern counties of Ireland.

Movement of Scottish settlers to Ulster began in earnest from 1605 in a private enterprise colonisation of counties Antrim and Down when Sir Hugh Montgomery and Sir James Hamilton acquired title to large estates in north Down and Sir Randall MacDonnell, 1st Earl of Antrim, to large tracts of land in north Antrim.

In 1609 the Earl of Salisbury, Lord High Treasurer, suggested to James I a deliberate plantation of Scottish and English colonists on the forfeited estates of the Gaelic chiefs in counties Armagh, Cavan, Donegal, Fermanagh, Londonderry (then known as Coleraine) and Tyrone.

Settlers to Ulster came, by and large, in three waves: with the granting of the initial leases in the period 1605 to 1625; after 1652 and Cromwell's crushing of the Irish rebellion; and finally in the fifteen years after 1690 and the Glorious Revolution. It is estimated by 1715, when migration to Ulster had virtually stopped, the Scottish population of Ulster stood at 200,000.

Scottish families entering Ireland through the port of Londonderry settled in the Foyle Valley which includes much of the fertile lands of counties Donegal, Londonderry and Tyrone. The lands along the Firth of Clyde in the county of Ayrshire, the Clyde Valley and the Border Lands consisting of the counties of Wigtown, Kirkcudbright and Dumfries were home to many of these Scottish settlers.

At the time of the mid-19th century Griffith's Valuation 14 Inch households were recorded in Ireland, with 10 Inch households in County Londonderry and one each in Counties Donegal, Dublin, Tyrone and Waterford. This clearly shows that Inch was very much a name associated with northwest Ulster as over 70% of descendants of Inches in Ireland were living in County Londonderry. Indeed this name was very much associated with one particular parish in County Londonderry; seven Inch households (i.e. 50% of the total for all Ireland) were residing in the parish of Faughanvale in the middle years of the 19th century.

It would seem that Inch families first settled in County Londonderry at the end of the 17th century as the Protestant Householders Lists of 1740 record two households headed by John Inch in Faughanvale Parish.

IRVINE

This surname is found predominantly in Ulster, especially in Counties Fermanagh and Antrim, where it was brought at the time of the 17th century Plantation of Ulster by settlers from Scotland.

Irvine is ultimately derived from the Scottish place names of Irving, the name of an old parish in Dumfriesshire, and from the town of Irvine in Ayrshire. The Dumfriesshire Parish, however, was the chief source of the name. The Irvines of Irvinestown, County Fermanagh (which lies close to the border with County Tyrone) claim descent from the Irvings of Bonshaw, Dumfriesshire, Scotland.

Robert de Hirewine, who witnessed a charter in 1226, is the first of the name recorded in Scotland. From William de Irwyne, who was granted the Forest of Drum, Aberdeenshire in 1324, descend the Irvines of Drum. An offshoot of this Aberdeenshire family appears in Shetland in the middle of the sixteenth century.

In Scotland Irvine and Irwin are considered to have a common origin, with Irwin simply being another variant spelling of Irving. Today, in Northern Ireland, Irvine and Irwin are seen as being distinct names. Yet record sources from the very early days of the Scottish settlement in Ulster confirm that these two names have been much confused and were, in effect, interchangeable. Indeed the first of the Irvines of Irvinestown, County Fermanagh, appear in the census of 1659 as William Irwin.

A few Irwins in Ireland may be descended from English Irwyn or Erwyn, derived from Old English *Eoforwine*, meaning 'boar-friend'; or from the County Offaly sept of O'Hirwen, in Gaelic *O hEireamhoin*. However, nearly all Irwins in Ulster are of Scottish Planter stock; in these cases Irwin is ultimately a variant of Irvine.

The Irvines or Irvings were one of the most famous of the lawless riding or reiving families of the Border country between Scotland and England who raided, on horseback, and stole each other's cattle and possessions. They lived in Annandale and Lower Eskdale in the Scottish West March. When the power of the riding clans was broken by James I in the decade after 1603 many came to Ulster, and in particular to County Fermanagh, to escape persecution. Today Irvine is the eleventh most common name in Fermanagh.

The Irvines became a powerful landlord family in Ulster, with eight Irvines in 1878 owning over 12,000 acres in Fermanagh, over 4,000 acres in Tyrone and over 14,000 acres in Donegal.

Movement of Scottish settlers to Ulster began in earnest from 1605 in a private enterprise colonisation of counties Antrim and Down when Sir Hugh Montgomery and Sir James Hamilton acquired title to large estates in north Down and Sir Randall MacDonnell, 1st Earl of Antrim, to large tracts of land in north Antrim. Further impetus came in 1609 when James I adopted the policy to encourage English and Scottish settlers to settle on the forfeited estates of the Gaelic chiefs in counties Armagh, Cavan, Donegal, Fermanagh, Londonderry (then known as Coleraine) and Tyrone. It is estimated by 1715, when migration to Ulster had virtually stopped, the Scottish population of Ulster stood at Fermanagh Fermanagh 200,000.

IRWIN

This surname is found predominantly in Ulster, especially in Counties Armagh, Antrim, Tyrone and Derry, where it was brought at the time of the 17th century Plantation of Ulster by settlers from Scotland.

Irwin is ultimately derived from the Scottish place names of Irving, the name of an old parish in Dumfriesshire, and from the town of Irvine in Ayrshire. The Dumfriesshire Parish, however, was the chief source of the name. Indeed many of the Irwins who came to Ulster in the 17th century came from Dumfriesshire.

This surname is recorded extensively, from the thirteenth century, throughout Scotland. Robert de Hirewine, who witnessed a charter in 1226, is the first of the name recorded. In 1260 Robert de Iruwyn was witness to a charter by the Bishop of St Andrews. In 1324 Robert The Bruce, King of Scotland granted the Forest of Drum in Aberdeenshire to William de Irwyne. An offshoot of this Aberdeenshire family appears in Shetland in the middle of the sixteenth century. In 1332 John de Irwyn was made canon of Dunkeld.

In Scotland Irwin and Irvine are considered to have a common origin, with Irwin simply being another variant spelling of Irving. Today, in Northern Ireland, Irwin and Irvine are seen as being distinct names. Both names are common here with Irwin being more numerous, by a small margin, than Irvine. In 1890 for every two Irvine births registered in Ulster there were three Irwin births.

Record sources from the very early days of the Scottish settlement in Ulster confirm that these two names have been much confused and were, in effect, interchangeable. Indeed the first of the Irvines of Irvinestown, County Fermanagh (which lies close to the border with County Tyrone), appear in the census of 1659 as William Irwin. The Irvines of Irvinestown claim descent from the Irvings of Bonshaw, Dumfriesshire, Scotland. It is only from the 20th century that families, bearing the surnames of Irwin and Irvine, have been consistent in the spelling of their names.

A few Irwins in Ireland may be descended from English Irwyn or Erwyn, derived from Old English *Eoforwine*, meaning 'boar-friend'; or from the County Offaly sept of O'Hirwen, in Gaelic *O hEireamhoin*. However, nearly all Irwins in Ulster are of Scottish Planter stock; in these cases Irwin is ultimately a variant of Irvine.

Movement of Scottish settlers to Ulster began in earnest from 1605 in a private enterprise colonisation of counties Antrim and Down when Sir Hugh Montgomery and Sir James Hamilton acquired title to large estates in north Down and Sir Randall MacDonnell, 1st Earl of Antrim, to large tracts of land in north Antrim. Further impetus came in 1609 when James I adopted the policy to encourage English and Scottish settlers to settle on the forfeited estates of the Gaelic chiefs in counties Armagh, Cavan, Donegal, Fermanagh, Londonderry (then known as Coleraine) and Tyrone.

Eight Irwins, including Alexander Irwin, who was one of the thirteen apprentice boys who shut the gates of Derry on 7 December 1688, were recorded as 'defenders' of Derry during the famous Siege of Derry, from 18 April to 31 July 1689.

JACKSON

Jackson is found throughout Ireland. In Ulster, where it is most common, it is found mainly in Counties Antrim and Armagh.

Jackson is a common name throughout England where it is one of the twenty-five most numerous names. Jackson, derived from the personal names of James and John, simply means 'son of Jack'. Jack was a popular choice as a child's name in the Middle Ages, and at a time when fixed surnames, based on a father's first name, were being established. Thus the surname Jackson sprang up in many different locations, independently of each other, throughout England.

The surname Jackson has been recorded in Scotland from the 15th century. For example, William Jacson was recorded as burgess of Aberdeen in 1409 and William Jaksone as burgess of Glasgow in 1447. However this surname is much less common in Scotland than it is in England as the personal name Jack was never popular in Scotland.

In 1609 the Earl of Salisbury, Lord High Treasurer, suggested to James I a deliberate plantation of English and Scottish colonists on the forfeited estates of the Gaelic chiefs in counties Armagh, Cavan, Donegal, Fermanagh, Londonderry (then known as Coleraine) and Tyrone.

Settlers came to Ulster, by and large, in three waves: with the granting of the initial leases in the period 1605 to 1625; after 1652 and Cromwell's crushing of the Irish rebellion; and finally in the fifteen years after 1690 and the Glorious Revolution. By the end of the 17th century a self-sustaining settlement of British colonists had established itself in Ulster.

Londonderry, Coleraine, Carrickfergus, Belfast and Donaghadee were the main ports of entry into the province of Ulster for 17th century British settlers with the Lagan, Bann and the Foyle valleys acting as the major arteries along which the colonists travelled into the interior. English settlers, mostly drawn from the northern counties of Cheshire, Cumberland, Lancashire, Northumberland, Yorkshire and Westmorland, tended to favour settlement along the Lagan Valley, in the east of the Province, on lands straddling the borders of Counties Armagh, Antrim and Down.

Most of the Jacksons who settled in Armagh and Antrim arrived in the middle of the 17th century. One of the earliest people to spot the commercial potential of Belfast was Rowland Jackson, a merchant of Whitehaven in Cumberland, England, who based himself in the town in 1632.

During the famous 105 day Siege of Derry, from 18 April to 31 July 1689, Ensign Thomas Jackson of Tobermore, County Derry, Ensign Richard Jackson, and Edward Jackson of County Down were recorded as 'defenders' of the city.

Ensign Thomas Jackson of Tobermore was the son of Thomas Jackson of Westmorland, England who settled in Coleraine, County Derry ca. 1639 and built Jackson Hall, overlooking the River Bann. Ensign Thomas Jackson, who survived the Siege of Derry, was killed at the Battle of the Boyne on 1 July 1690.

JAMESON

In Ireland Jameson is almost exclusive to Ulster, where one-half of those of the name are in County Antrim and one-quarter in County Down. This name was brought to Ulster in large numbers by settlers from Scotland in the 17th century.

Jameson, derived from the personal name James, simply means 'son of James'. The Jamesons were the most senior of the septs of Clan Gunn, tracing their descent from James Gunn, the eldest son of the 15th century chief George Gunn the Crowner (i.e. coroner). Clan Gunn, who occupied the northern areas of Caithness and Sutherland, claim descent from the Viking chief Gunni who was killed in Dublin in 1171. By 1594 Clan Gunn was listed as one of the 'broken clans' of the north.

Upheavals such as military incursions, feuds and harvest failures would have encouraged many clan members, including Jamesons, to migrate to Ulster as settlers during the 17th century. Owing to the nature of the Scottish clan system once the power and influence of the chief had been weakened and the bond of tribal loyalty broken the clan tended to scatter.

On the island of Bute the Jamesons, who held the office of hereditary coroners of Bute from the beginning of the 14th century until the 17th century, were a sept of Clan Stuart of Bute. It would seem quite likely that these Jamesons followed the Stuarts of Bute to Ballintoy, County Antrim.

The Stewarts of Ballintoy, a branch of Clan Stuart of Bute, trace their descent from John Stewart, the son of Robert Stewart who was to become Robert II, King of Scotland in 1371. The Stuarts of Bute were the hereditary sheriffs of the island. Two sons of the fifth Sheriff of Bute, Archibald Stuart, settled on the territory of the MacDonnells of the Glens, near Ballintoy on the Antrim coast about 1560. When Sir Randall MacDonnell, 1st Earl of Antrim, acquired title to large tracts of land in north Antrim, from 1605, he sub-leased to Archibald Stewart, grandson of the fifth Sheriff of Bute, the estate of Ballintoy. Movement of Scottish settlers to farm on this estate and other Scottish-owned estates in Ulster now began in earnest. By the mid-19th century the Jamesons were concentrated in the barony of Upper Toome, on the north shore of Lough Neagh, in County Antrim,

The Jamesons were also recorded as one of the lawless riding or reiving families of the Scottish Borders who raided, on horseback, and stole each other's cattle and possessions. These Jamesons lived in the Middle March on the English side of the Border. When the power of the riding clans was broken by James I in the decade after 1603 many came to Ulster to escape persecution.

Further impetus came in 1609 when James I adopted the policy to encourage Scottish settlers to settle on the forfeited estates of the Gaelic chiefs in counties Armagh, Cavan, Donegal, Fermanagh, Londonderry (then known as Coleraine) and Tyrone.
Settlers came to Ulster, by and large, in three waves: with the granting of the initial leases in the period 1605 to 1625; after 1652 and Cromwell's crushing of the Irish rebellion; and finally in the fifteen years after 1690 and the Glorious Revolution. It is estimated by 1715, when migration to Ulster had virtually stopped, the Scottish population of Ulster stood at 200,000.

JOHNSON

Johnson is a common surname in England and Scotland but it has been constantly confused with and used interchangeably with the Scottish surname Johnston. Johnson is among the ten commonest surnames in England, while Johnston is among the twenty commonest in Scotland. Both names were brought to Ulster in large numbers by settlers from England and Scotland in the 17th century. Johnson is five times less common than Johnston in Ireland and is over fifteen times less common in Ulster.

Johnson was established in about equal numbers in Ulster, Munster and Leinster but was rare in Connaught. On the other hand about 80% of the Johnston families in Ireland are in Ulster. Johnston is the fourth most common name in Ulster, and the second most numerous in Counties Antrim and Fermanagh.

Strictly speaking Johnson and Johnston are two distinct names; the former meaning son of John and the latter John's town, pronounced in Scotland John's Toon. In Scotland the two names have become indistinguishable. Even in the Scottish Borders, where the surname Johnston was most common, it was often made Johnson.

The Johnstons were a powerful border clan who occupied the lands of Johnstone, stretching from the border with England northwest to Annandale, in the West March of England and Scotland. Shortly after 1174 John the founder of the family of Johnstone, gave his name to his lands in Annandale, Dumfriesshire. John's son Gilbert then adopted Johnstone as his surname. The Johnstons became one of the great riding or reiving clans of the Borders who raided, on horseback, and stole each other's cattle and possessions.

Prior to the Union of the Crowns of England and Scotland in 1603 the Scottish Border was divided into three districts; the east, west and middle Marches. The Johnstons were intermittently appointed Wardens of the West March, alternating in that role with the Maxwells, with whom they had a deadly feud, which they resolved in 1623.

When the power of the riding clans was broken by James I in the decade after 1603 many came to Ulster to escape persecution. This flight to Ulster also suited the needs of the king. James I, from 1610, was determined to implement a deliberate plantation of Scottish and English colonists on the forfeited estates of the Gaelic chiefs in Counties Armagh, Cavan, Donegal, Fermanagh, Londonderry (then known as Coleraine) and Tyrone. The Johnstons settled principally in County Fermanagh.

Although many Johnsons in Ulster were originally Scottish Johnstons many Johnsons will have English origins. English settlers, mostly drawn from the northern counties of Cheshire, Cumberland, Lancashire, Northumberland, Yorkshire and Westmorland also migrated to Ulster during the 17th century. English settlers tended to favour settlement along the Lagan Valley, in the east of the Province, on lands straddling the borders of Counties Armagh, Antrim and Down.

Further confusion is caused by the fact that a large number of Irish and Scottish septs anglicised their names to Johnston and Johnson. Septs of Clan Gunn in Caithness and of Clan Donald of Glencoe have been anglicised as both Johnson and Johnston. In Ireland a number of septs including McKeown and McShane anglicised their names to Johnson and Johnston.

JOHNSTON

Johnston is among the twenty commonest surnames in Scotland. About 80% of the Johnston families in Ireland are in Ulster where this surname came with numerous Scottish immigrants at the time of the Plantation of Ulster in the 17th century. It is the fourth most common name in Ulster, and the second most numerous in Counties Antrim and Fermanagh.

The Johnstons were a powerful border clan who occupied the lands of Johnstone, stretching from the border with England northwest to Annandale, in the West March of England and Scotland. Shortly after 1174 John the founder of the family of Johnstone, gave his name to his lands in Annandale, Dumfriesshire. John's son Gilbert then adopted Johnstone as his surname. The Johnstons became one of the great riding or reiving clans of the Borders, and one of the most troublesome to the Crowns of both England and Scotland.

Strictly speaking Johnson and Johnston are two distinct names; the former meaning son of John and the latter John's town, pronounced in Scotland John's Toon. The two names, however, are now indistinguishable. Even in the Scottish Borders, where the surname Johnston was most common, it was often made Johnson.

From the 14th to the late-17th century, the border between England and Scotland – the Debatable Lands – was a turbulent place. The Border country was ravaged by the lawless Reiver families who stole each other's cattle and possessions. They raided in large numbers, on horseback, and they killed and kidnapped without remorse. This type of life resulted in the growth of large closely-knit family groups with intense clan loyalties and fierce feuds against others.

Prior to the Union of the Crowns of England and Scotland in 1603 the Scottish Border was divided into three districts; the east, west and middle Marches. The Johnstons were intermittently appointed Wardens of the West March, alternating in that role with the Maxwells, with whom they had a deadly feud, which they resolved in 1623.

Pacification of the riding families began in earnest from 1603 with the Union of the Crowns of England and Scotland. The Johnstons suffered as King James I set about pacifying the borders in a ruthless campaign which included executions and banishment. In 1603 thirty-two Johnstons, Armstrongs, Beattys, Elliotts and others were hanged, fifteen were banished and one hundred and forty outlawed.

When the power of the riding clans was broken by James I in the decade after 1603 many came to Ulster to escape persecution. This flight to Ulster also suited the needs of the king. James I, from 1610, was determined to implement a deliberate plantation of Scottish and English colonists on the forfeited estates of the Gaelic chiefs in Counties Armagh, Cavan, Donegal, Fermanagh, Londonderry (then known as Coleraine) and Tyrone. The Johnstons settled principally in County Fermanagh.

Confusion is caused by the fact that a large number of Irish and Scottish septs anglicised their names to Johnston and Johnson. Septs of Clan Gunn in Caithness and of Clan Donald of Glencoe have been anglicised as both Johnson and Johnston. In Ireland a number of septs including McKeown and McShane anglicised their names to Johnson and Johnston.

JOHNSTONE

Johnston, also spelt Johnstone, is among the twenty commonest surnames in Scotland. About 80% of the Johnston families in Ireland are in Ulster where this surname came with numerous Scottish immigrants at the time of the Plantation of Ulster in the 17th century. It is the fourth most common name in Ulster, and the second most numerous in Counties Antrim and Fermanagh. The Johnstone spelling is most common in Counties Derry and Cavan.

The Johnstons were a powerful border clan who occupied the lands of Johnstone, stretching from the border with England northwest to Annandale, in the West March of England and Scotland. Shortly after 1174 John the founder of the family of Johnstone, gave his name to his lands in Annandale, Dumfriesshire. John's son Gilbert then adopted Johnstone as his surname. The Johnstons became one of the great riding or reiving clans of the Borders, and one of the most troublesome to the Crowns of both England and Scotland.

Strictly speaking Johnson and Johnston are two distinct names; the former meaning son of John and the latter John's town, pronounced in Scotland John's Toon. The two names, however, are now indistinguishable. Even in the Scottish Borders, where the surname Johnston was most common, it was often made Johnson.

From the 14th to the late-17th century, the border between England and Scotland – the Debatable Lands – was a turbulent place. The Border country was ravaged by the lawless Reiver families who stole each other's cattle and possessions. They raided in large numbers, on horseback, and they killed and kidnapped without remorse. This type of life resulted in the growth of large closely-knit family groups with intense clan loyalties and fierce feuds against others.

Prior to the Union of the Crowns of England and Scotland in 1603 the Scottish Border was divided into three districts; the east, west and middle Marches. The Johnstons were intermittently appointed Wardens of the West March, alternating in that role with the Maxwells, with whom they had a deadly feud, which they resolved in 1623.

Pacification of the riding families began in earnest from 1603 with the Union of the Crowns of England and Scotland. The Johnstons suffered as King James I set about pacifying the borders in a ruthless campaign which included executions and banishment. In 1603 thirty-two Johnstons, Armstrongs, Beattys, Elliotts and others were hanged, fifteen were banished and one hundred and forty outlawed.

When the power of the riding clans was broken by James I in the decade after 1603 many came to Ulster to escape persecution. This flight to Ulster also suited the needs of the king. James I, from 1610, was determined to implement a deliberate plantation of Scottish and English colonists on the forfeited estates of the Gaelic chiefs in Counties Armagh, Cavan, Donegal, Fermanagh, Londonderry (then known as Coleraine) and Tyrone. The Johnstons settled principally in County Fermanagh.

Confusion is caused by the fact that a large number of Irish and Scottish septs anglicised their names to Johnston and Johnson. Septs of Clan Gunn in Caithness and of Clan Donald of Glencoe have been anglicised as both Johnson and Johnston. In Ireland a number of septs including McKeown and McShane anglicised their names to Johnson and Johnston.

109

JONES

Jones is the second most common name in England and Wales behind Smith. In Ireland Jones is not even among the top one hundred names. It is, however, found in nearly every county in Ireland, with the heaviest distribution in Leinster. This name was brought to Ulster in large numbers by settlers from England and Wales in the 17th century.

Jones, derived from the personal name John, simply means 'son of John'. By the 14th century John was second only to William in popularity as a forename in England. Although Jones is now regarded as a distinctively Welsh surname it spread to Wales from the adjoining English counties of Gloucestershire, Herefordshire, Shropshire and Worcestershire. This name's unrivalled popularity in Wales stems from the form *Ioan* being adopted for John in the Welsh Authorised Version of the Bible in 1567. Many families in Wales didn't adopt fixed surnames until the first half of the 19th century, and when they did, Jones, meaning 'son of Ioan', became extremely popular. By 1890 ten percent of the rural population in Wales bore the surname Jones.

The defeat of the old Gaelic order in the Nine Years War, 1594-1603 and the escape of the most prominent Gaelic Lords of Ulster in 'the Flight of the Earls' in 1607 from Lough Swilly, County Donegal were ultimately responsible for the settlement of many English and Welsh families in the northern counties of Ireland.

In 1609 the Earl of Salisbury, Lord High Treasurer, suggested to James I a deliberate plantation of English, Welsh and Scottish colonists on the forfeited estates of the Gaelic chiefs in counties Armagh, Cavan, Donegal, Fermanagh, Londonderry (then known as Coleraine) and Tyrone. Settlers came to Ulster, by and large, in three waves: with the granting of the initial leases in the period 1605 to 1625; after 1652 and Cromwell's crushing of the Irish rebellion; and finally in the fifteen years after 1690 and the Glorious Revolution. By the end of the 17th century a self-sustaining settlement of British colonists had established itself in Ulster.

Londonderry, Coleraine, Carrickfergus, Belfast and Donaghadee were the main ports of entry into the province of Ulster for 17th century British settlers with the Lagan, Bann and the Foyle valleys acting as the major arteries along which the colonists travelled into the interior. English settlers, mostly drawn from the northern counties of Cheshire, Cumberland, Lancashire, Northumberland, Yorkshire and Westmorland, and Welsh settlers tended to favour settlement along the Lagan Valley, in the east of the Province, on lands straddling the borders of Counties Armagh, Antrim and Down. As a consequence the surname Jones is now found mainly in Counties Antrim and Armagh and in northwest Down.

English settlers were particularly prominent in the early years of the Plantation of Ulster. The upheavals of the 1641 rebellion and the Williamite Wars of 1689 to 1691 tended to discourage English settlers more than Scottish settlers. When large scale migration to Ulster resumed in the years after 1652 and 1690 it was Scottish Presbyterian settlers who were more prominent.

During the famous 105 day Siege of Derry, from 18 April to 31 July 1689, John Jones of County Armagh and Thomas Jones were recorded as 'defenders' of the city.

KANE

The name Kane, with its many variants including O'Kane, Keane and O'Cahan, is among the seventy-five most common names in Ireland and is most numerous in Ulster. It is among the fifteen most common names in its homeland in County Derry.

The Kane sept trace their lineage to Eogan, son of the 5th century High King of Ireland, Niall of the Nine Hostages, who ruled from the Hill of Tara, County Meath. Eogan and his brother Conall *Gulban* conquered northwest Ireland, ca.425 AD, capturing the great hill-fort of Grianan of Ailech in County Donegal.

Eogan, styled 'King of Ailech', established his own kingdom in the peninsula in County Donegal still called after him Inishowen (Innis Eoghain or Eogan's Isle). His descendants, known as the Cenel Eoghain (the race of Owen), expanded to the east and south from their focal point in Inishowen over the next five centuries.

Ireland was one of the first countries to adopt a system of hereditary surnames which developed from a more ancient system of clan or sept names. The surname was formed by prefixing either Mac (son of) or O (grandson or descendant of) to the ancestor's name. Kane and O'Cahan, an earlier anglicized form of the name, are derived from Gaelic *O Cathain.*

The Kanes were the leading sept of Clan Connor *Magh Ithe* (Connor was a direct descendant of Eogan). Magh Ithe is the rich countryside stretching southward from Inishowen, later known as the Laggan district in east Donegal. In the 10th century AD the families of Clan Connor moved out from the cramped territory of Magh Ithe and established themselves in County Derry, in the kingdom of Keenaght, to the north of the Sperrin Mountains, from the Foyle to the Bann rivers. In the process they ousted the Cianachta whose leading sept was the O'Connors of Glengiven in the Roe Valley.

By the 12th century, when the process of conquest ends the Kanes had assumed pre-eminence inside Clan Connor, and they were overlords and all-powerful in County Derry. The Kanes became the mainstay of power behind the O'Neills and possessed the privilege of inaugurating the chief of the O'Neills at Tullaghoge (near Cookstown, County Tyrone). Hugh O'Neill, Earl of Tyrone acknowledged his reliance on the Kanes saying that 'as long as he had O'Cahan and his country sure behind him, he little cared for anything that they could do to him before.'

The Kanes founded an Augustinian priory at Dungiven in ca.1140. For centuries the Kane chiefs were buried in Dungiven Priory. Today in the ruins of this old priory stands the altar tomb of Cooey-na-Gall, a celebrated Kane chief, who died in 1385. Kane is represented in armour with one hand resting on his sword, and on the front of the tomb are figures of six galloglass warriors in kilts. By the 14th century the Kane chieftains were employing Scottish mercenary soldiers, known as galloglass, in their feuds with local rivals. In the 15th century the Kanes conducted a long-running feud of raid and counter-raid with the McQuillans of the Route, County Antrim. The last chief, Donnell Ballagh O'Cahan, was inaugurated in 1598 and joined O'Neill against the English in the Nine Years War, 1594-1603. He spent the last years of his life imprisoned in the Tower of London. He died in 1617.

KEE

Kee is an abbreviated form of McKee. In Ireland this name is almost exclusive to Ulster, where it is found chiefly in Counties Antrim, Armagh and Down. This name was brought to Ulster by settlers from Scotland in the 17th century.

McKee is derived from Gaelic *Mac Aoidh*, meaning 'son of Hugh'. This name was also anglicised as Mackay, Mackie, McCay, McCoy and McKay. Clan Mackay, claiming descent from Morgund of Pluscarden, originated in Moray. This clan came to prominence in Sutherland in the 13th century and by 1427 the chief, Angus Dow MacKay, could muster an army of 4000 men. In Inverness-shire the Mackays were a sept of Clan Davidson, and in Kintyre and Galloway the MacKays, MacKies and Mackies were followers of Clan Donald. The surname Mackie was recorded in Stirlingshire from the 15th century.

The first McKees in Ireland, also known as McCoys, were Clan Donald galloglasses, i.e. mercenary soldiers. As followers of Clan Donald they came over to Ulster from Kintyre and the southern isles of Scotland such as Islay to fight for the McDonnells of the Glens of Antrim.

Movement of Scottish settlers to Ulster began in earnest from 1605 in a private enterprise colonisation of counties Antrim and Down when Sir Hugh Montgomery and Sir James Hamilton acquired title to large estates in north Down and Sir Randall MacDonnell, 1st Earl of Antrim, to large tracts of land in north Antrim.

Further impetus came in 1609 when James I adopted the policy to encourage Scottish settlers to settle on the forfeited estates of the Gaelic chiefs in counties Armagh, Cavan, Donegal, Fermanagh, Londonderry (then known as Coleraine) and Tyrone. Settlers to Ulster came, by and large, in three waves: with the granting of the initial leases in the period 1605 to 1625; after 1652 and Cromwell's crushing of the Irish rebellion; and finally in the fifteen years after 1690 and the Glorious Revolution. Sir Patrick MacKee of Largs, Ayrshire, was one of the principal Scottish planters (sixty-one in total) of the Ulster Plantation, and in 1610 he was granted an estate of 1000 acres near the town of Donegal.

It has been claimed, however, that the Kees of Donegal and Fermanagh are a branch of the Maguires, the pre-eminent family in Fermanagh from the thirteenth to the seventeenth century. They trace their descent from Aodh, a grandson of Donn Carrach Maguire. Donn Carrach Maguire, who died in 1302, was the first Maguire chief of all Fermanagh.

In this case Kee is derived from Gaelic *Mac Aodha*, meaning 'son of Hugh'. In Ulster, particularly in Counties Donegal and Fermanagh, Gaelic *Mac Aodha* was usually anglicised as McHugh and McCue but also as McCoy, McKee and Kee.

Confusion, therefore, arises as the Gaelic surnames of *Mac Aodha* in Ireland and of *Mac Aoidh* in Scotland have acquired in the process of anglicisation a great number of variants, some of which overlap. Thus in west Ulster, in particular, a surname such as McKee (which was further anglicised to Kee) can be a name of either Irish or Scottish origin.

KELLY

Kelly is the second commonest family name in Ireland, after Murphy, and part of the reason is that, at least seven and possibly as many as ten distinct septs of the same name arose in different parts of the country. Kelly is the sixth most common name in Ulster, and the third most numerous in Counties Derry and Tyrone.

The Kelly sept of County Derry trace their lineage to Eogan, son of the 5th century High King of Ireland, Niall of the Nine Hostages, who ruled from the Hill of Tara, County Meath. Eogan and his brother Conall *Gulban* conquered northwest Ireland, ca.425 AD, capturing the great hill-fort of Grianan of Ailech in County Donegal.

Eogan, styled 'King of Ailech', established his own kingdom in the peninsula in County Donegal still called after him Inishowen (Innis Eoghain or Eogan's Isle). His descendants, known as the Cenel Eoghain (the race of Owen), became the principal branch of the Northern Ui Neill (descendants of Niall of the Nine Hostages). The Cenel Eoghain in the next five centuries expanded to the east and south from their focal point in Inishowen.

Ireland was one of the first countries to adopt a system of hereditary surnames which developed from a more ancient system of clan or sept names. The surname was formed by prefixing either Mac (son of) or O (grandson or descendant of) to the ancestor's name. Kelly is derived from Gaelic *O Ceallaigh*, the root word possibly being *ceallach* meaning strife.

The O'Kellys were one of the leading septs of Clan Binny (*Eochaid Binnigh* was a son of Eogan) possessing territory on the banks of the River Foyle near Lifford in County Donegal.

The first outward thrust of the Owen clan was that of Clan Binny in the 6th century AD who thrust southeast into County Tyrone, bypassing a hard core of resistance in County Derry of the Cianachta, as far as the river Blackwater on the borders of Tyrone and Armagh. Clan Binny eventually ousted the Oriella clans from the district lying west of the river Bann from Coleraine to beside Lough Neagh, and drove them across the river.

In the course of time the O'Kellys moved eastwards into County Derry and were based in the barony of Loughinsholin in south Derry.

The most powerful Kelly sept was that of Ui Maine, often called Hy Many, who ruled O'Kelly's Country in Counties Galway and Roscommon. This sept claims descent from the 4th century *Colla da Crioch*, King of Ulster and first King of Oriel. Other O'Kelly septs originated in Counties Kilkenny, Leix, Meath, Sligo and Wicklow.

Kelly was known as a surname in Scotland long before 19th century Irish immigration really established the name there. There was, for example, a Kelly sept attached to Clan Donald.

KENNEDY

In Ulster Kennedy can be an Irish or a Scottish name. The name is among the twenty most common in Ireland and the fifty most common in Ulster, where it is most numerous in County Antrim.

Ireland was one of the first countries to adopt a system of hereditary surnames which developed from a more ancient system of clan or sept names. The surname was formed by prefixing either Mac (son of) or O (grandson or descendant of) to the ancestor's name.

Kennedy is derived from Gaelic *O Cinneide*, from *ceann*, meaning 'head', and *eidigh*, meaning 'ugly'. Tracing their descent from Cennedig, a nephew of Brian Boru (941-1014), High King of Ireland, the Kennedys were Lords of Ormond from the eleventh to the sixteenth century. Originating in east Clare they later settled in north Tipperary and from there spread as far south as Wexford. A branch of the Tipperary Kennedys migrated north about the year 1600 and established itself in County Antrim.

There was also a small O'Kennedy sept, a minor branch of the Ui Maine (descendants of Maine), often called Hy Many, in Connaught. The County Tyrone name of Minnagh, in Gaelic *Muimhneach*, meaning 'the Munster man', was sometimes anglicised as Kennedy in County Donegal.

In the 17th and 18th centuries many descendants of the old Gaelic order in Ireland emigrated, as the so-called Wild Geese, to Europe. Matthew Kennedy (1652-1735), who went to France in 1691, was a notable literary figure in Paris. The Kennedys supported the Jacobite cause in Ireland and several Kennedys were officers in James II's Irish army which was raised in 1688 to fight the army of William III.

In Ulster many Kennedys will be of Scottish origin. Scottish Kennedys, originally McKennedy, were an offshoot, in remote times, of Irish O'Kennedy. The Kennedys of Lochaber in Inverness-shire, a sept of Clan Cameron, trace their descent from Ualrig Kennedy in Dunure in Ayrshire. Kennedy became a very common name in Galloway and Ayrshire. In the area 'Twixt Wigton and the toun of Air, Portpatrick and the Cruives of Cree', the Kennedys, as Earls of Cassilis, were all-powerful.

Movement of Scottish settlers to Ulster began in earnest from 1605 in a private enterprise colonisation of counties Antrim and Down when Sir Hugh Montgomery and Sir James Hamilton acquired title to large estates in north Down and Sir Randall MacDonnell, 1st Earl of Antrim, to large tracts of land in north Antrim. Further impetus came in 1609 when James I adopted the policy to encourage Scottish settlers to settle on the forfeited estates of the Gaelic chiefs in counties Armagh, Cavan, Donegal, Fermanagh, Londonderry (then known as Coleraine) and Tyrone.

Three Kennedys, including Horace Kennedy, Sheriff of the city, were recorded as 'defenders' of Derry during the famous 105 day Siege of Derry, from 18 April to 31 July 1689. Horace Kennedy, who was appointed Mayor of Derry in 1698, was further commemorated in the memorial window unveiled in St Columb's Cathedral, Londonderry in 1913. The Kennedys of Clogher, County Tyrone descend from one Cornet John Kennedy of Ayrshire who came here with the Scottish army in 1641.

KERR

Kerr is among the fifty most common names in Ulster. In County Antrim, where about one-half of the Ulster Kerrs live, Kerr is among the twenty most common names. It is also very common in Counties Down and Tyrone. Although Kerr is regarded as a surname of Scottish origin it has become confused with Carr which is seen as a surname of Irish origin.

Kerr is among the forty most common names in Scotland. In its homeland on the Scottish Borders this name was variously recorded as Kerr, Ker, Carr and Carre. This name derived as a local name, from Old Norse *Kjarr*, for someone who lived by a marsh. In the 15th and 16th centuries, in particular, the name was frequently spelled Carr.

The Kerrs were one of the great riding or reiving clans of the Scottish Borders, who settled there in the 14th century. They were second only to the Scott family in the Middle March and were strongest in Liddesdale and east Teviotdale.

From the 14th to the late-17th century, the border between England and Scotland – the Debatable Lands – was a turbulent place. The Border country was ravaged by the lawless Reiver families who stole each other's cattle and possessions. They raided in large numbers, on horseback, and they killed and kidnapped without remorse. This type of life resulted in the growth of large closely-knit family groups with intense clan loyalties and fierce feuds against others.

Prior to the Union of the Crowns of England and Scotland in 1603 the Scottish Border was divided into three districts; the east, west and middle Marches. Each March was presided over by a warden who settled disputes with the warden of the appropriate March in England, as border warfare was rife at this time with frequent cattle raids. Kerr of Cessford was appointed Warden of the Middle March, which included the Sheriffdom of Selkirk, in 1515.

When the power of the riding clans was broken by James I in the decade after 1603 many came to Ulster to escape persecution. This flight to Ulster also suited the needs of the king. James I, from 1610, was determined to implement a deliberate plantation of Scottish and English colonists on the forfeited estates of the Gaelic chiefs in Counties Armagh, Cavan, Donegal, Fermanagh, Londonderry (then known as Coleraine) and Tyrone. The Kerrs settled initially in County Fermanagh. However, by the mid-19th century the Kerrs were concentrated in the barony of Upper Dunluce in County Antrim, and in Dromara Parish in County Down.

Carr has become confused with Kerr and indeed the two names were still being used interchangeably in Counties Antrim and Derry at the end of the 19th century. The surname Carr was widely adopted by descendants of several Irish septs. For example Ulster septs such as Kilcarr, in Gaelic *Mac Giolla Chathair*, of County Donegal and Carry, in Gaelic *O Cairre*, of County Armagh have also been anglicised as Carr.

During the famous 105 day Siege of Derry, from 18 April to 31 July 1689, Lieutenant James Kerr, John Kerr of County Fermanagh and Robert and Thomas Kerr of Omagh, County Tyrone were recorded as 'defenders' of the city.

KEYES

Although this name is found in Leinster and Munster it is most common in Ulster, particularly in Counties Fermanagh and Antrim. Although some Keyes in Ulster will be of English origin, the majority of Keyes will be of Irish origin.

In England the surname Keyes may have a number of origins: as a name for someone who lived by a wharf; as an occupational name for a maker of keys; and as an Old Welsh personal name. Some Keyes in Ulster will be descendants of 17th century English settlers. English settlers, who migrated to Ulster at this time, tended to favour settlement along the Lagan Valley, in the east of the Province, on lands straddling the borders of Counties Armagh, Antrim and Down.

The majority of Keyes in Ulster, however, will be originally McKees. In this case Keyes is derived from Gaelic *Mac Aodha*, meaning 'son of Hugh'. In Ulster, particularly in Counties Donegal and Fermanagh, Gaelic *Mac Aodha* was usually anglicised as McHugh and McCue but also as McCoy, McKee and Kee. McKee and Kee were, in turn, further anglicised to Keys and Keyes.

It has been claimed that the Keyes of Donegal and Fermanagh are a branch of the Maguires, the pre-eminent family in Fermanagh from the thirteenth to the seventeenth century. They trace their descent from Aodh, a grandson of Donn Carrach Maguire. Donn Carrach Maguire, who died in 1302, was the first Maguire chief of all Fermanagh.

In Scotland Gaelic *Mac Aoidh*, meaning 'son of Hugh', was anglicised as Mackay and also as Mackie, McCay, McCoy, McKay and McKee. Clan Mackay, claiming descent from Morgund of Pluscarden, originated in Moray. This clan came to prominence in Sutherland in the 13th century and by 1427 the chief, Angus Dow MacKay, could muster an army of 4000 men. In Inverness-shire the Mackays were a sept of Clan Davidson, and in Kintyre and Galloway the MacKays, MacKies and Mackies were followers of Clan Donald.

Confusion, therefore, arises as the Gaelic surnames of *Mac Aodha* in Ireland and of *Mac Aoidh* in Scotland have acquired in the process of anglicisation a great number of variants, some of which overlap. Thus in west Ulster, in particular, a surname such as McKee (which was further anglicised to Keyes) can be a name of either Irish or Scottish origin. Throughout the 17th century many Scottish families migrated to Ireland through the port of Londonderry and settled in the Foyle Valley which includes much of the fertile lands of counties Donegal, Londonderry and Tyrone. It is, therefore, possible that some Scottish McKees adopted Keyes as their surname.

During the famous 105 day Siege of Derry, from 18 April to 31 July 1689, Captain Thomas Keys and his brother Frederick Keys of Cavanacor, County Donegal were recorded as 'defenders' of the city. Local tradition claims that King James II dined at Cavanacor House on his way to Derry, and for that reason the residence was spared when the defeated army burnt many Protestant properties on their withdrawal to Dublin in August 1689.

KEYS

Although this name is found in Leinster and Munster it is most common in Ulster, particularly in Counties Fermanagh and Antrim. Although some Keys in Ulster will be of English origin, the majority of Keys will be of Irish origin.

In England the surname Keys may have a number of origins: as a name for someone who lived by a wharf; as an occupational name for a maker of keys; and as an Old Welsh personal name. Some Keys in Ulster will be descendants of 17th century English settlers. English settlers, who migrated to Ulster at this time, tended to favour settlement along the Lagan Valley, in the east of the Province, on lands straddling the borders of Counties Armagh, Antrim and Down.

The majority of Keys in Ulster, however, will be originally McKees. In this case Keys is derived from Gaelic *Mac Aodha*, meaning 'son of Hugh'. In Ulster, particularly in Counties Donegal and Fermanagh, Gaelic *Mac Aodha* was usually anglicised as McHugh and McCue but also as McCoy, McKee and Kee. McKee and Kee were, in turn, further anglicised to Keys.

It has been claimed that the Keys of Donegal and Fermanagh are a branch of the Maguires, the pre-eminent family in Fermanagh from the thirteenth to the seventeenth century. They trace their descent from Aodh, a grandson of Donn Carrach Maguire. Donn Carrach Maguire, who died in 1302, was the first Maguire chief of all Fermanagh.

In Scotland Gaelic *Mac Aoidh*, meaning 'son of Hugh', was anglicised as Mackay and also as Mackie, McCay, McCoy, McKay and McKee. Clan Mackay, claiming descent from Morgund of Pluscarden, originated in Moray. This clan came to prominence in Sutherland in the 13th century and by 1427 the chief, Angus Dow MacKay, could muster an army of 4000 men. In Inverness-shire the Mackays were a sept of Clan Davidson, and in Kintyre and Galloway the MacKays, MacKies and Mackies were followers of Clan Donald.

Confusion, therefore, arises as the Gaelic surnames of *Mac Aodha* in Ireland and of *Mac Aoidh* in Scotland have acquired in the process of anglicisation a great number of variants, some of which overlap. Thus in west Ulster, in particular, a surname such as McKee (which was further anglicised to Keys) can be a name of either Irish or Scottish origin. Throughout the 17th century many Scottish families migrated to Ireland through the port of Londonderry and settled in the Foyle Valley which includes much of the fertile lands of counties Donegal, Londonderry and Tyrone. It is, therefore, possible that some Scottish McKees adopted Keys as their surname.

During the famous 105 day Siege of Derry, from 18 April to 31 July 1689, Captain Thomas Keys and his brother Frederick Keys of Cavanacor, County Donegal were recorded as 'defenders' of the city. Local tradition claims that King James II dined at Cavanacor House on his way to Derry, and for that reason the residence was spared when the defeated army burnt many Protestant properties on their withdrawal to Dublin in August 1689.

KILLEN

The surname Killen, which is derived from McKillen, is most common in Counties Antrim and Down. McKillen itself is almost exclusive to County Antrim. Names such as Killen, McKillen, McCallion and McAllen represent descendants of Clan Campbell in Argyllshire, Scotland who from the 15th century came to Ulster to fight as galloglasses, i.e. mercenary soldiers, for the O'Donnells of Donegal. Derived from Gaelic *galloglach,* galloglass refers to a paid soldier, often brought over from Scotland, to fight on behalf of an Irish chief.

Although the names of McKillen, McCallion and McAllen represent distinct septs within Clan Campbell there are no septs of Clan Campbell registered with these names today. Anglicisation has disguised the ultimate origins of these names. Furthermore, in many cases, the families in these septs were recorded simply as Campbell. Strictly speaking McKillen, and its abbreviated form Killen, is derived from Gaelic *Mac Coilin,* meaning 'son of Colin'; McAllen stems from Gaelic *Mac Ailin,* meaning 'son of Allen'; and McCallion is derived from *Mac Cailin,* meaning 'son of Cailin'.

Killen and McKillen are most common in Counties Antrim and Down. McCallion, on the other hand, is found almost exclusively in Counties Donegal and Derry. In Derry and Donegal Killen, McAllen, and McCallion are indistinguishable; as many people whose origins may be *Mac Ailin* or *Mac Coilin* bear the surname McCallion. Ballymacallion, meaning 'the townland of the McCallions', is located in Dungiven Parish, County Derry.

As well as providing detailed and graphic descriptions of the activities of the Clan Campbell galloglasses *The Annals of The Kingdom of Ireland by the Four Masters* record the distinct spellings of their associated surnames. In 1555, the *Annals* record that 'the son of O'Donnell, i.e. Calvagh, went to Scotland, attended by a few select persons, and obtained auxiliary forces from Mac Calin (Gillaspick Don), under the command of Master Arsibel. He afterwards came back, with a great body of Scots, to desolate and ravage Tirconnell.' In the same year the O'Donnells, and their Scottish galloglasses, stormed and demolished the castles at Greencastle, Inishowen, County Donegal and the O'Cahan stronghold on the island in Enagh Lough, County Derry.

The *Annals* of 1557 describes in great detail the role of the galloglass in the camp of the O'Neills who were on a raiding expedition into O'Donnell territory in Donegal. It states that 'sixty grim and redoubtable gallowglasses, with sharp, keen axes, terrible and ready for action, and sixty stern and terrific Scots, with massive, broad, and heavy-striking swords in their hands, ready to strike and parry, were watching and guarding the son of O'Neill.'

Scottish galloglasses, led by Donnell and Dowell Mac Allen, raided into Counties Sligo and Mayo in 1558. They were defeated in a fierce battle, during which both Donnell and Dowell Mac Allen were slain, by the Earl of Clanrickard.

In 1586 'a Scotch fleet landed in Inishowen, O'Doherty's country'. One of its leaders was Gillespick Mac Ailin. After this raid the *Annals* record 'that there was nothing of value in Inishowen, whether corn or cattle, which they did not carry off'.

KITSON

In Ulster Kitson and Kitchen are recorded variants of Scottish McCutcheon.

In the Highlands of Scotland, McCutcheon is derived from Gaelic *Mac Uisdin*, meaning 'son of Hutcheon'. The French personal name Huchon, a pet form of Hugh, was made Hutcheon in Scotland. This name in turn was borrowed into Scots Gaelic as Uisdean. The McDonalds of Skye trace their descent from Hugh, a younger son of Alexander MacDonald, Lord of the Isles. This family became known as Clann Uisdin. Thus the McDonalds of Syke were regarded as the offspring of a man called Hutcheon. As early as the 15th century the name was being anglicised as McHutcheon, hence McCutcheon. For example John Roy Makhuchone 'committed slaughter in Ross, 1494-5', and Adam MacHutchoun was recorded in Murthlac in 1550.

The McCutcheons were, therefore, a branch of Clan Donald. Under the leadership of Somerled, who expelled the Norsemen from the western side of Scotland in the 12th century, Clan Donald claimed the position of 'The Headship of the Gael'. By the time of his death in 1387, John MacDonald, as Lord of the Isles, controlled the whole of the Hebrides from Lewis to Islay, with the exception of Skye, and the mainland from Kintyre to Knoydart.

Clan Donald had acquired new territories in the north of Ireland ca.1400 when John Mor MacDonald had married Margery Bissett, an heiress in the Glens of Antrim. By the mid-16th century the MacDonalds, known as the MacDonnells of the Glens, had carved out an extensive territory in County Antrim at the expense of the MacQuillans. It would quite likely that some McCutcheons, as followers of Clan Donald, settled in County Antrim. Owing to the nature of the Scottish clan system once the power and influence of the chief had been weakened or broken the clan tended to disintegrate. The MacDonalds finally lost their title as 'Lord of the Isles' in 1493.

In England Kitchen derived as an occupational name for a cook or someone who worked in a kitchen while Kitson, meaning 'son of Kitt', was derived from the personal name Christopher. Kitson was recorded as a surname in Scotland as early as 1359 by one John Ketyson, bailie (i.e. municipal magistrate) of Stirling. It is also possible that Kitson may be a variant of Kidston which was derived from the lands of Kidston in the parish of Peebles in the Scottish Borders.

Movement of Scottish settlers to Ulster began in earnest from 1605 in a private enterprise colonisation of counties Antrim and Down when Sir Hugh Montgomery and Sir James Hamilton acquired title to large estates in north Down and Sir Randall MacDonnell, 1st Earl of Antrim, to large tracts of land in north Antrim.

Further impetus came in 1609 when James I adopted the policy to encourage Scottish settlers to settle on the forfeited estates of the Gaelic chiefs in counties Armagh, Cavan, Donegal, Fermanagh, Londonderry (then known as Coleraine) and Tyrone.
Settlers to Ulster came, by and large, in three waves: with the granting of the initial leases in the period 1605 to 1625; after 1652 and Cromwell's crushing of the Irish rebellion; and finally in the fifteen years after 1690 and the Glorious Revolution. It is estimated by 1715, when migration to Ulster had virtually stopped, the Scottish population of Ulster stood at 200,000.

LAFFERTY

Lafferty can be an Irish or a Scottish name. This name is almost exclusively found in Ulster, where it is most common in Counties Donegal, Derry and Tyrone. Most Laffertys were originally Irish O'Laffertys, although some may be descendants of Scottish McLavertys. In Ulster Lafferty and Laherty are recorded variants of Laverty. Laverty is also an exclusively Ulster name but is found mainly in County Antrim.

Ireland was one of the first countries to adopt a system of hereditary surnames which developed from a more ancient system of clan or sept names. The surname was formed by prefixing either Mac (son of) or O (grandson or descendant of) to the ancestor's name.

The County Donegal sept of Lafferty is derived from Gaelic *O Laithhbheartaigh*, meaning 'bright ruler'. The Chief of this sept was Lord of Aileach, County Donegal. The great hill-fort of Grianan of Ailech commanded the entrance to the Inishowen peninsula between Lough Swilly and Lough Foyle. *The Annals of The Kingdom of Ireland by the Four Masters* (a chronicle of Irish history from 'the earliest period to the year 1616') record, in 972, the death in battle of Murchadh Ua Flaithbheartaigh, Lord of Aileach, at Dunglady fort in the parish of Maghera, County Derry.

The Laffertys were a powerful sept. *The Annals* record that at the time of his death in 1197 Magrath O Laverty was styled 'Tanist of Tyrone'. This means that the chief of the Laffertys was 'heir presumptive to the chiefly title' of King of Tir Eoghain (Tir Owen or Tyrone, the land of Owen), a territory which then extended over the present counties of Tyrone and Derry. The O'Laffertys were driven from Donegal in the 13th century and settled near Ardstraw in County Tyrone.

The anglicisation of Gaelic names, from the 17th century, resulted in many variant spellings of the same name and, in many cases, the dropping of the O and Mac prefixes.

Some Laffertys in Ulster may have been originally Scottish McLavertys, in Gaelic *Mac Fhlaithbheartaich*. The McLavertys, also spelt as McLafferty, were a sept of Clan Donald. Claiming descent from the Kintyre branch of the MacDonalds the McLavertys, based on Islay, were hereditary heralds of the Lords of the Isles. The name also became common on Arran.

Upheavals such as military incursions, feuds and harvest failures would have encouraged many clan members, including McLavertys, to migrate to Ulster as settlers during the 17th century. Owing to the nature of the Scottish clan system once the power and influence of the chief had been weakened and the bond of tribal loyalty broken the clan tended to scatter.

Movement of Scottish settlers to Ulster began in earnest from 1605 in a private enterprise colonisation of counties Antrim and Down when Sir Hugh Montgomery and Sir James Hamilton acquired title to large estates in north Down and Sir Randall MacDonnell, 1st Earl of Antrim, to large tracts of land in north Antrim. The McLavertys settled in north Antrim. By the mid-19th century the Lavertys in County Antrim were found almost exclusively in the barony of Upper Dunluce.

120

LAVERTY

Laverty can be an Irish or a Scottish name. This name is almost exclusively found in Ulster, where it is most common in County Antrim. Lavertys in Ulster may be descendants of either Scottish McLavertys or of Irish O'Laffertys. Lafferty and Laherty are recorded variants of Laverty. Lafferty is also an exclusively Ulster name but is found mainly in Counties Donegal, Derry and Tyrone.

Many Lavertys in Ulster will have been originally Scottish McLavertys, in Gaelic *Mac Fhlaithbheartaich*, meaning 'bright ruler'. The McLavertys, also spelt as McLafferty, were a sept of Clan Donald. Claiming descent from the Kintyre branch of the MacDonalds the McLavertys, based on Islay, were hereditary heralds of the Lords of the Isles. The name also became common on Arran. The MacDonalds gained a foothold in the Glens of Antrim in the 13th century through land grants for military service as galloglasses, i.e. mercenary soldiers. By the mid-16th century the MacDonalds, known as the MacDonnells of the Glens, had carved out an extensive territory in County Antrim at the expense of the MacQuillans.

Upheavals such as military incursions, feuds and harvest failures would have encouraged many clan members, including McLavertys, to migrate to Ulster as settlers during the 17th century. Owing to the nature of the Scottish clan system once the power and influence of the chief had been weakened and the bond of tribal loyalty broken the clan tended to scatter.

Movement of Scottish settlers to Ulster began in earnest from 1605 in a private enterprise colonisation of counties Antrim and Down when Sir Hugh Montgomery and Sir James Hamilton acquired title to large estates in north Down and Sir Randall MacDonnell, 1st Earl of Antrim, to large tracts of land in north Antrim. The McLavertys, as followers of the MacDonalds, settled in north Antrim.

The anglicisation of Gaelic names, from the 17th century, resulted in many variant spellings of the same name and, in many cases, the dropping of the O and Mac prefixes. By the mid-19th century Lavertys were most numerous in the barony of Upper Dunluce, County Antrim.

Some Lavertys in Ulster will be descendants of the County Donegal sept of O'Lafferty, in Gaelic *O Laithhbheartaigh*. The Chief of this sept was Lord of Aileach, County Donegal. The great hill-fort of Grianan of Ailech commanded the entrance to the Inishowen peninsula between Lough Swilly and Lough Foyle. *The Annals of The Kingdom of Ireland by the Four Masters* (a chronicle of Irish history from 'the earliest period to the year 1616') record, in 972, the death in battle of Murchadh Ua Flaithbheartaigh, Lord of Aileach, at Dunglady fort in the parish of Maghera, County Derry.

The Laffertys were a powerful sept. *The Annals* record that at the time of his death in 1197 Magrath O Laverty was styled 'Tanist of Tyrone'. This means that the chief of the Laffertys was 'heir presumptive to the chiefly title' of King of Tir Eoghain (Tir Owen or Tyrone, the land of Owen), a territory which then extended over the present counties of Tyrone and Derry. The O'Laffertys were driven from Donegal in the 13th century and settled near Ardstraw in County Tyrone.

121

LITTLE

Little can be of Irish, English or Scottish origin. This name is common in Ulster, especially in Counties Antrim and Fermanagh.

This name is found all over England but chiefly in the northern counties of Cumberland, Westmorland and Northumberland. This name derived as a nickname, from Old English *lytel*, denoting a small person.

In Scotland the Littles were one of the riding or reiving clans of the Scottish Borders. They were based in Eskdale and Ewesdale in Dumfriesshire and were recorded as one of the unruly clans of the West March in 1587. Prior to the Union of the Crowns of England and Scotland in 1603 the Scottish Border was divided into three districts; the east, west and middle Marches. Each March was presided over by a warden who settled disputes with the warden of the appropriate March in England.

From the 14th to the late-17th century, the border between England and Scotland – the Debatable Lands – was a turbulent place. The Border country was ravaged by the lawless Reiver families who stole each other's cattle and possessions. They raided in large numbers, on horseback, and they killed and kidnapped without remorse. This type of life resulted in the growth of large closely-knit family groups with intense clan loyalties and fierce feuds against others.

When the power of the riding clans was broken by James I in the decade after 1603 many came to Ulster to escape persecution. This flight to Ulster also suited the needs of the king. James I, from 1610, was determined to implement a deliberate plantation of Scottish and English colonists on the forfeited estates of the Gaelic chiefs in Counties Armagh, Cavan, Donegal, Fermanagh, Londonderry (then known as Coleraine) and Tyrone.

The Littles settled particularly in County Fermanagh. These Border families were well suited to life in the frontier of the Plantation of Ulster. They were a resilient people who stayed in County Fermanagh throughout the upheavals of the 17th century. Scottish settlers were hardier than their English counterparts, and the Borderers were even better adapted again to life on a new, insecure frontier.

Little can also be a variant of Liddell which is derived from the place name of Liddel in Roxburghshire. Indeed these two names were being used interchangeably in County Armagh at the end of the 19th century.

During the famous 105 day Siege of Derry, from 18 April to 31 July 1689, William Little of Drumenagh, County Fermanagh was recorded as one of the 'defenders' of the city.

Little was also widely adopted by descendants of the County Monaghan sept of Beggan, in Gaelic *O Beagain*, the root word being *beag*, meaning 'little'. The homeland of the Beggans was on the lands straddling the borders of Counties Fermanagh and Monaghan. Thus in south Fermanagh, in particular, bearers of the surname Little may either be descendants of Scottish reivers or of an Irish sept.

122

LOGUE

This name is rare outside of Ulster, where over half are in County Donegal and most of the rest in County Derry.

Ireland was one of the first countries to adopt a system of hereditary surnames which developed from a more ancient system of clan or sept names. From the 11th century each family began to adopt its own distinctive family name generally derived from the first name of an ancestor who lived in or about the 10th century. The surname was formed by prefixing either Mac (son of) or O (grandson or descendant of) to the ancestor's name. Surnames in Ireland, therefore, tended to identify membership of a sept.

Logue is derived from Gaelic *O Maolmhaodhog*, meaning 'descendant of the devotee of St Maodhog'. This name became Logue through the anglicised form Mulvogue.

Originating in County Galway in the Ui Maine (descendants of Maine) country, often called Hy Many, this sept is first recorded as chiefs of the district between Athenry and Athlone. In Galway and adjacent areas of Clare and Roscommon this sept's name was anglicised, not as Logue, but as Leech and, in some cases, Lee.

Though originating in County Galway the sept migrated, at an early date, to Donegal-Derry where it took the anglicised form Logue.

By the time of the early-19th century tithe assessment Logues were to be found throughout County Donegal from Clonca parish in the north; to Donegal parish in the south; and to Inishkeel parish in the west. In the same period Logues were well-established in west Derry, especially in the parishes of Clondermot and Faughanvale, and in the northwest tip of Tyrone in the parishes of Donaghedy and Leckpatrick.

No references to the earlier form Mulvogue in either Derry or Donegal are recorded in the early-19th century tithe surveys. The Hearth Money Rolls of 1663, however, for County Derry does record one Donnell O Mulloge in the townland of Barr Cregg in Cumber Upper Parish.

Logue, which is among the top 50 surnames in the city of Derry today, illustrates the very close links, both historic and economic, between Derry and County Donegal. As Derry developed an industrial base in the 19th century in shirt making, shipbuilding and distilling it attracted much of its workforce from Donegal. Her growing industries attracted workers and families from outside the city and county, and in the 90-year period 1821 to 1911 the population of the city quadrupled to 40,780. In this period Derry stamped her dominance over local rivals and emerged as an important urban centre within Ireland.

In County Donegal Molloy was, in some instances, used interchangeably with Logue. It is, therefore, possible that some people whose origins are *O Maolmhaodhog* are disguised by bearing the surname Molloy. Molloy was widely adopted by descendants of two distinct septs with origins in Counties Offaly and Roscommon.

LONG

Long can be of Irish, English or Scottish origin. This name is common in every province in Ireland, especially Munster. In Ulster the name is most common in County Donegal.

Ireland was one of the first countries to adopt a system of hereditary surnames which developed from a more ancient system of clan or sept names. From the 11th century each family began to adopt its own distinctive family name generally derived from the first name of an ancestor who lived in or about the 10th century. The surname was formed by prefixing either Mac (son of) or O (grandson or descendant of) to the ancestor's name. Surnames in Ireland, therefore, tended to identify membership of a sept. The County Armagh sept of Longan, in Gaelic *O Longain*, the root word being *long*, meaning 'tall', was also anglicised as Long.

In England and Scotland, Long derived as a nickname, from Old English *lang*, for a tall person. Long is a common name in England, and families of le long came to Ireland very soon after the Anglo-Norman invasion of 1172.

This surname was recorded in Scotland at an early date. Adam Long appears in Dumfriesshire in 1259, and Gregory le long was a burgess of Dundee in 1268.

The defeat of the old Gaelic order in the Nine Years War, 1594-1603 and the escape of the most prominent Gaelic Lords of Ulster in 'the Flight of the Earls' in 1607 from Lough Swilly, County Donegal were ultimately responsible for the settlement of many English and Scottish families in the northern counties of Ireland.

Movement of Scottish settlers to Ulster began in earnest from 1605 in a private enterprise colonisation of counties Antrim and Down when Sir Hugh Montgomery and Sir James Hamilton acquired title to large estates in north Down and Sir Randall MacDonnell, 1st Earl of Antrim, to large tracts of land in north Antrim.

Further impetus came in 1609 when James I adopted the policy to encourage English and Scottish settlers to settle on the forfeited estates of the Gaelic chiefs in counties Armagh, Cavan, Donegal, Fermanagh, Londonderry (then known as Coleraine) and Tyrone.

Settlers came to Ulster, by and large, in three waves: with the granting of the initial leases in the period 1605 to 1625; after 1652 and Cromwell's crushing of the Irish rebellion; and finally in the fifteen years after 1690 and the Glorious Revolution. By the end of the 17th century a self-sustaining settlement of British colonists had established itself in Ulster.

During the famous 105 day Siege of Derry, from 18 April to 31 July 1689, Lieutenant Henry Long was recorded as one of the 'defenders' of the city. Prior to the Siege Henry Long was one of the leading burgesses of the city corporation, and he was appointed second in command of one of the six companies which were raised on 11 December 1688 to defend Derry's walls.

LYLE

This surname is found almost exclusively in Ulster where it is most common in Counties Antrim and Londonderry. This name was brought to Ulster by settlers from Scotland in the 17th century.

Lyle is ultimately derived from Old French l'*isle,* denoting someone who lived on an island. This name would have been introduced to England when the Normans invaded in 1066. Lyle was then introduced to Scotland by Anglo-Norman settlers.

A family of Lyles were barons of Duchal in Renfrewshire, Scotland as early as the beginning of the 13th century. The first of the name in Scotland appears to be Ralph de Lisle, of Norman descent from Northumberland, England. The Lyles were followers of Walter Fitz Alan, who was granted lands in Renfrew and in Paisley in Ayrshire, and made High Steward of Scotland in the reign of David I (1124 to 1153). In Scotland the title of 'Steward' of the royal household was applied to the person responsible for the collection of taxes and administration of justice. This person was second only in importance to the King of Scotland.

Walter Fitz Alan's grandson, Walter, was the first to adopt the title 'Steward' as a surname. Indeed the royal line of Clan Stewart traces their descent from Walter Fitz Alan, High Steward of Scotland. Robert Stewart, later Robert II, became the first King of Scotland, from 1371-1389, who belonged to the House of Stewart.

In 1296 John del Ille of Berwickshire and Richard del Ilse of Edinburghshire paid homage to Edward I of England.

The defeat of the old Gaelic order in the Nine Years War, 1594-1603 and the escape of the most prominent Gaelic Lords of Ulster in 'the Flight of the Earls' in 1607 from Lough Swilly, County Donegal were ultimately responsible for the settlement of many Scottish families in the northern counties of Ireland.

Movement of Scottish settlers to Ulster began in earnest from 1605 in a private enterprise colonisation of counties Antrim and Down when Sir Hugh Montgomery and Sir James Hamilton acquired title to large estates in north Down and Sir Randall MacDonnell, 1st Earl of Antrim, to large tracts of land in north Antrim. Further impetus came in 1609 when James I adopted the policy to encourage Scottish settlers to settle on the forfeited estates of the Gaelic chiefs in counties Armagh, Cavan, Donegal, Fermanagh, Londonderry (then known as Coleraine) and Tyrone.

Settlers came to Ulster, by and large, in three waves: with the granting of the initial leases in the period 1605 to 1625; after 1652 and Cromwell's crushing of the Irish rebellion; and finally in the fifteen years after 1690 and the Glorious Revolution. It is estimated by 1715, when migration to Ulster had virtually stopped, the Scottish population of Ulster stood at 200,000.

It would seem that Lyle families first settled in County Londonderry at the end of the 17th century as the Protestant Householders Lists of 1740 record ten Lyle households in the county at that time. No Lyle households, however, were recorded in County Londonderry at the time of the Hearth Money Rolls of 1663.

LYNCH

Lynch is among the hundred most common names in Ireland. In Ulster the name is most numerous in County Cavan, where it is among the first five, and in County Derry. Although Lynch in Ireland can be of Norman origin most in Ulster will be of Irish Gaelic descent.

The Norman family of *de Lench*, anglicised Lynch, were very powerful and prominent in the affairs of Galway city. The Lynches were the most influential of the 'Tribes of Galway', providing that city with eighty-four mayors between 1484 and 1654. This Norman family first settled in County Meath before a branch of the family migrated to Galway in the early 15th century.

In the rest of Ireland a number of quite distinct and small independent septs adopted the surname Lynch. Septs of this name established themselves in Antrim, Cavan, Clare, Cork, Sligo and Tipperary. Most of these septs declined in importance with the Anglo-Norman invasion but their descendants are still to found in their several places of origin.

Ireland was one of the first countries to adopt a system of hereditary surnames which developed from a more ancient system of clan or sept names. From the 11th century each family began to adopt its own distinctive family name generally derived from the first name of an ancestor who lived in or about the 10th century. The surname was formed by prefixing either Mac (son of) or O (grandson or descendant of) to the ancestor's name. Surnames in Ireland, therefore, tended to identify membership of a sept.

Lynch is derived from Gaelic *O Loingsigh*, the root word being *loingseach*, meaning 'mariner'. Two septs of this name were located in Ulster. One of these was based in central County Cavan. The other was based in north Antrim and Derry, and their chief was lord of the ancient kingdom of Dalriada. In the 6th century when the Irish Celts, known as the Scots, established themselves in Kintyre, Argyll and some of the Inner Isles they called their kingdom Dal Riata, after the kingdom they still held in north Antrim.

Furthermore the County Donegal sept of Lynchehan, in Gaelic *Mac Loingseachain*, was usually abbreviated to Lynch. The importance of Lynch as a surname in Derry city today, where it is among the top twelve names, is perhaps due to this sept as the top three names in the city, namely Doherty, McLaughlin and Gallagher, have Donegal origins. As Derry developed an industrial base in the 19th century in shirt making, shipbuilding and distilling it attracted much of its workforce from Donegal.

By contrast surnames from the city's eastern hinterlands in County Derry and to the south from Tyrone are not as prominent in Derry city today as those names with Donegal origins.

In some instances, especially where Lynch was anglicised as Lynchey, the name has become Lindsay.

MACKAY

In Ireland this name is almost exclusive to Ulster, where it is found chiefly in Counties Antrim and Derry. This name was brought to Ulster by settlers from Scotland in the 17th century.

Mackay is derived from Gaelic *Mac Aoidh*, meaning 'son of Hugh'. This name was also anglicised as Mackie, McCay, McCoy, McKay and McKee. Clan Mackay, claiming descent from Morgund of Pluscarden, originated in Moray. This clan came to prominence in Sutherland in the 13th century and by 1427 the chief, Angus Dow MacKay, could muster an army of 4000 men. In Inverness-shire the Mackays were a sept of Clan Davidson, and in Kintyre and Galloway the MacKays, MacKies and Mackies were followers of Clan Donald.

The first Mackays in Ireland, also known as McCoys, were Clan Donald galloglasses, i.e. mercenary soldiers. As followers of Clan Donald they came over to Ulster from Kintyre and the southern isles of Scotland such as Islay to fight for the McDonnells of the Glens of Antrim.

Clan Donald had acquired new territories in the north of Ireland ca.1400 when John Mor MacDonald had married Margery Bissett, an heiress in the Glens of Antrim. By the mid-16th century the MacDonalds, known as the MacDonnells of the Glens, had carved out an extensive territory in County Antrim at the expense of the MacQuillans.

Movement of Scottish settlers to Ulster began in earnest from 1605 in a private enterprise colonisation of counties Antrim and Down when Sir Hugh Montgomery and Sir James Hamilton acquired title to large estates in north Down and Sir Randall MacDonnell, 1st Earl of Antrim, to large tracts of land in north Antrim. Further impetus came in 1609 when James I adopted the policy to encourage Scottish settlers to settle on the forfeited estates of the Gaelic chiefs in counties Armagh, Cavan, Donegal, Fermanagh, Londonderry (then known as Coleraine) and Tyrone.

Confusion arises as the Gaelic surname *Mac Aoidh* has acquired in the process of anglicisation a great number of variants. Thus the McKay family of Drumard in Tamlaght O'Crilly Parish, County Londonderry were recorded as McCoy in the 1831 census, as McCay in the tithe book of 1833 and as McKay in the Griffith's Valuation of 1859.

In Ireland, particularly in Counties Donegal and Fermanagh, Gaelic *Mac Aodha*, meaning 'son of Hugh', was usually anglicised as McHugh and McCue but also as McCoy and McKee. Thus in west Ulster Irish McHugh can become indistinguishable from Scottish Mackay.

During the famous 105 day Siege of Derry, from 18 April to 31 July 1689, General Andrew Mackay, Ensign William Mackie, Lieutenant William Mackey, Lieutenant Mackie, Lieutenant Mackay, John Mackay, Josiah Macky and Jannett Mackee were recorded as 'defenders' of the city. On the opposing side Lieutenant Daniel McKay and Ensign Hugh McKay were officers in the 'Jacobite army' which besieged the city of Derry.

MACKEY

In Ireland this name is almost exclusive to Ulster, where it is found chiefly in Counties Antrim, Armagh and Down. This name was brought to Ulster by settlers from Scotland in the 17th century.

Mackey is derived from Gaelic *Mac Aoidh*, meaning 'son of Hugh'. This name was also anglicised as Mackay, Mackie, McCay, McCoy, McKay and McKee. Clan Mackay, claiming descent from Morgund of Pluscarden, originated in Moray. This clan came to prominence in Sutherland in the 13th century and by 1427 the chief, Angus Dow MacKay, could muster an army of 4000 men. In Inverness-shire the Mackays were a sept of Clan Davidson, and in Kintyre and Galloway the MacKays, MacKies and Mackies were followers of Clan Donald. The surname Mackie was recorded in Stirlingshire from the 15th century.

The first Mackeys in Ireland, also known as McCoys, were Clan Donald galloglasses, i.e. mercenary soldiers. As followers of Clan Donald they came over to Ulster from Kintyre and the southern isles of Scotland such as Islay to fight for the McDonnells of the Glens of Antrim.

Clan Donald had acquired new territories in the north of Ireland ca.1400 when John Mor MacDonald had married Margery Bissett, an heiress in the Glens of Antrim. By the mid-16th century the MacDonalds, known as the MacDonnells of the Glens, had carved out an extensive territory in County Antrim at the expense of the MacQuillans.

Movement of Scottish settlers to Ulster began in earnest from 1605 in a private enterprise colonisation of counties Antrim and Down when Sir Hugh Montgomery and Sir James Hamilton acquired title to large estates in north Down and Sir Randall MacDonnell, 1st Earl of Antrim, to large tracts of land in north Antrim. Further impetus came in 1609 when James I adopted the policy to encourage Scottish settlers to settle on the forfeited estates of the Gaelic chiefs in counties Armagh, Cavan, Donegal, Fermanagh, Londonderry (then known as Coleraine) and Tyrone.

Confusion arises as the Gaelic surname *Mac Aoidh* has acquired in the process of anglicisation a great number of variants. Thus the McKay family of Drumard in Tamlaght O'Crilly Parish, County Londonderry were recorded as McCoy in the 1831 census, as McCay in the tithe book of 1833 and as McKay in the Griffith's Valuation of 1859.

In Ireland, particularly in Counties Donegal and Fermanagh, Gaelic *Mac Aodha*, meaning 'son of Hugh', was usually anglicised as McHugh and McCue but also as McCoy and McKee. Thus in west Ulster Irish McHugh can become indistinguishable from Scottish Mackey.

During the famous 105 day Siege of Derry, from 18 April to 31 July 1689, General Andrew Mackay, Ensign William Mackie, Lieutenant William Mackey, Lieutenant Mackie, Lieutenant Mackay, John Mackay, Josiah Macky and Jannett Mackee were recorded as 'defenders' of the city. On the opposing side Lieutenant Daniel McKay and Ensign Hugh McKay were officers in the 'Jacobite army' which besieged the city of Derry.

128

MACKIE

In Ireland this name is almost exclusive to Ulster, where it is found chiefly in Counties Antrim, Armagh and Down. This name was brought to Ulster by settlers from Scotland in the 17th century.

Mackie is derived from Gaelic *Mac Aoidh*, meaning 'son of Hugh'. This name was also anglicised as Mackay, McCay, McCoy, McKay and McKee. Clan Mackay, claiming descent from Morgund of Pluscarden, originated in Moray. This clan came to prominence in Sutherland in the 13th century and by 1427 the chief, Angus Dow MacKay, could muster an army of 4000 men. In Inverness-shire the Mackays were a sept of Clan Davidson, and in Kintyre and Galloway the MacKays, MacKies and Mackies were followers of Clan Donald. The surname Mackie was recorded in Stirlingshire from the 15th century.

The first Mackies in Ireland, also known as McCoys, were Clan Donald galloglasses, i.e. mercenary soldiers. As followers of Clan Donald they came over to Ulster from Kintyre and the southern isles of Scotland such as Islay to fight for the McDonnells of the Glens of Antrim.

Clan Donald had acquired new territories in the north of Ireland ca.1400 when John Mor MacDonald had married Margery Bissett, an heiress in the Glens of Antrim. By the mid-16th century the MacDonalds, known as the MacDonnells of the Glens, had carved out an extensive territory in County Antrim at the expense of the MacQuillans.

Movement of Scottish settlers to Ulster began in earnest from 1605 in a private enterprise colonisation of counties Antrim and Down when Sir Hugh Montgomery and Sir James Hamilton acquired title to large estates in north Down and Sir Randall MacDonnell, 1st Earl of Antrim, to large tracts of land in north Antrim. Further impetus came in 1609 when James I adopted the policy to encourage Scottish settlers to settle on the forfeited estates of the Gaelic chiefs in counties Armagh, Cavan, Donegal, Fermanagh, Londonderry (then known as Coleraine) and Tyrone.

Confusion arises as the Gaelic surname *Mac Aoidh* has acquired in the process of anglicisation a great number of variants. Thus the McKay family of Drumard in Tamlaght O'Crilly Parish, County Londonderry were recorded as McCoy in the 1831 census, as McCay in the tithe book of 1833 and as McKay in the Griffith's Valuation of 1859.

In Ireland, particularly in Counties Donegal and Fermanagh, Gaelic *Mac Aodha*, meaning 'son of Hugh', was usually anglicised as McHugh and McCue but also as McCoy and McKee. Thus in west Ulster Irish McHugh can become indistinguishable from Scottish Mackie.

During the famous 105 day Siege of Derry, from 18 April to 31 July 1689, General Andrew Mackay, Ensign William Mackie, Lieutenant William Mackey, Lieutenant Mackie, Lieutenant Mackay, John Mackay, Josiah Macky and Jannett Mackee were recorded as 'defenders' of the city. On the opposing side Lieutenant Daniel McKay and Ensign Hugh McKay were officers in the 'Jacobite army' which besieged the city of Derry.

MAGEE

Magee, an alternative form of McGee, can be an Irish or a Scottish name. These names are among the 100 most common names in Ireland and among the twenty-five most common in Ulster. Magee is found mainly in Counties Antrim, Armagh and Down, and McGee in Counties Donegal and Tyrone.

Ireland was one of the first countries to adopt a system of hereditary surnames which developed from a more ancient system of clan or sept names. From the 11th century each family began to adopt its own distinctive family name generally derived from the first name of an ancestor who lived in or about the 10th century. The surname was formed by prefixing either Mac (son of) or O (grandson or descendant of) to the ancestor's name. Surnames in Ireland, therefore, tended to identify membership of a sept.

Magee is derived from Gaelic *Mag Aoidh,* meaning 'son of Hugh'. As a general rule the Mag form of the name is more common in east Ulster and the Mac form in the west. There were three distinct Magee septs in Ulster: in County Antrim the seat of the Magees was Islandmagee; in County Fermanagh the Magees were a branch of the Maguires, tracing their descent from Aodh, the great-grandson of Donn Carrach Maguire; and in County Donegal the Magees, an important sept in medieval times, were *erenaghs,* i.e. hereditary stewards, of the church lands of Clondahorky in the barony of Kilmacrenan.

The Magee sept of Donegal trace their lineage to Conall *Gulban,* son of the 5th century High King of Ireland, Niall of the Nine Hostages, who ruled from the Hill of Tara, County Meath. Conall and his brother Eogan conquered northwest Ireland, ca.425 AD, capturing the great hill-fort of Grianan of Ailech in County Donegal which commanded the entrance to Inishowen between Lough Swilly and Lough Foyle.

Magee is a common name in Derry city today. This name illustrates the very close links, both historic and economic, between the city of Derry and County Donegal. As Derry developed an industrial base in the 19th century in shirt making, shipbuilding and distilling it attracted much of its workforce from Donegal. In the 90-year period 1821 to 1911 the population of the city quadrupled to 40,780.

Many Magees in Ulster, especially in Counties Antrim and Down, will be of Scottish origin. In Scotland McGhie and variants such as McGee and Magee are also derived from Gaelic *Mag Aoidh,* meaning 'son of Hugh'. The first reference to the name is of a Gilmighel Mac Ethe in Dumfries in 1296. The name became most common in Ayrshire and in Dumfries and Galloway. These regions were home to many of the Scottish settlers who came to Ulster throughout the 17th century.

Movement of Scottish settlers to Ulster began in earnest from 1605 in a private enterprise colonisation of counties Antrim and Down when Sir Hugh Montgomery and Sir James Hamilton acquired title to large estates in north Down and Sir Randall MacDonnell, 1st Earl of Antrim, to large tracts of land in north Antrim. In County Antrim the Magees are most concentrated around Crumlin, and in County Down in the baronies of Lecale and Upper Ards.

MAGUIRE

Maguire is among the forty most common names in Ireland and among the top twenty-five in Ulster. Maguire is the single most common name in its homeland of County Fermanagh.

Ireland was one of the first countries to adopt a system of hereditary surnames which developed from a more ancient system of clan or sept names. From the 11th century each family began to adopt its own distinctive family name generally derived from the first name of an ancestor who lived in or about the 10th century. The surname was formed by prefixing either Mac (son of) or O (grandson or descendant of) to the ancestor's name. Surnames in Ireland, therefore, tended to identify membership of a sept.

Maguire is derived from Gaelic *Mag Uidhir*, meaning 'son of Odhar', the root word being *uidhire*, meaning 'dun-coloured'. The Maguires became the leading sept in Fermanagh. The first reference to the Maguires in *The Annals of The Kingdom of Ireland by the Four Masters* (a chronicle of Irish history from 'the earliest period to the year 1616') is in the year 956. In that year Tanaidhe Maguire was killed by the Vikings.

The Maguires became prominent around 1200 when Donn Mor Maguire established the sept around Lisnaskea. Donn Carrach Maguire, who died in 1302, was the first Maguire chief of all Fermanagh. For the next three centuries the Maguires were one of the most powerful and important families in Ulster, with their chief residence at Enniskillen Castle.

The Maguires were to the forefront in Gaelic resistance to English attempts to pacify Ireland during the Nine Years War (1594-1603). Hugh Maguire commanded the cavalry at the battle of Yellow Ford in 1598 which inflicted a heavy defeat on the English army.

Cuconnacht Maguire, Lord of Fermanagh, brought a ship to Lough Swilly in 1607 which 'took with them from Ireland the Earl Hugh O'Neill, and the Earl Rury O'Donnell, with a great number of the chieftains of the province of Ulster.' This event known as the 'Flight of the Earls' marked the end of Gaelic power. Cuconnacht Maguire died in exile in Genoa in 1608.

The Maguires continued their resistance to English rule in the 17th century. Conor Maguire, 2nd Baron of Enniskillen, was executed for his part in the 1641 Rising. Colonel Cuconnaught Maguire raised a regiment in Fermanagh which was part of King James II's army which besieged the city of Derry during the famous 105 day Siege, from 18 April to 31 July 1689. Descendants of Colonel Cuconnaught Maguire were in possession of the Tempo estate, County Fermanagh in the 18th century. After the final defeat of James' army in 1691 the Maguires are found prominent among the Wild Geese, serving with distinction in the Irish Brigade in France.

Some Maguires in Ulster may be of Scottish descent as the MacGuires were a sept of Clan Macquarrie of the island of Ulva.

131

MARTIN

Martin can be of Irish, English or Scottish origin. It is among the forty most common names in Ireland and among the top twenty in Ulster, where it is among the first ten in County Down and the first twenty n Counties Antrim, Monaghan and Cavan.

Ireland was one of the first countries to adopt a system of hereditary surnames which developed from a more ancient system of clan or sept names. The surname was formed by prefixing either Mac (son of) or O (grandson or descendant of) to the ancestor's name.

In Monaghan and Cavan most Martins will be originally Gilmartin. The County Tyrone sept of Gilmartin is derived from Gaelic *Mac Giolla Mhartain,* meaning 'son of the devotee of St Martin'. The Gilmartins were a branch of the O'Neills in Fermanagh and Tyrone. Furthermore Martin can be derived from McMartin, in Gaelic *Mac Mairtin.* This sept also originated in Tyrone where they were another branch of the O'Neills.

Martin is among the forty most common names in England where the name is most concentrated in Cornwall and Sussex. The personal name Martin, ultimately derived from Mars, the Roman god of fertility and war, became extremely popular throughout Europe in the Middle Ages. The popularity of the name stems from the famous 4th century saint, Martin of Tours in France. There were twenty-five places named Saint Martin in Normandy and St Martin was a common name among the Normans when they invaded England in 1066. Thus Martin was a popular choice as a child's name at a time when fixed surnames, based on a father's first name, were being established. Martin was recorded as a surname in England from the 12th century.

Martin is among the fifty most common names in Scotland. As in England Martin became a popular personal name which was later adopted as a fixed surname. A Norman family of de St Martin, later shortened to Martin, settled in East Lothian.
St Martin of Tours, the teacher of St Ninian of Whithorn in Galloway, was widely revered in Scotland. Thus Gilmartin, in Gaelic *Mac Gille Mhartainn,* meaning 'son of the devotee of St Martin', was recorded as a surname in Scotland as early as 1185. Gilmartin was further anglicised to McMartin and Martin. The McMartins of Letterfinlay in Inverness-shire were one of the three main branches of Clan Cameron. Their name was also shortened to Martin. The Martins were also a sept of Clan Donald based in Kilmuir in Skye.

Movement of Scottish settlers to Ulster began in earnest from 1605 in a private enterprise colonisation of counties Antrim and Down when Sir Hugh Montgomery and Sir James Hamilton acquired title to large estates in north Down and Sir Randall MacDonnell, 1st Earl of Antrim, to large tracts of land in north Antrim. By the mid-19th century Martin was a common name throughout Counties Antrim and Down.

Further impetus came in 1609 when James I adopted the policy to encourage English and Scottish settlers to settle on the forfeited estates of the Gaelic chiefs in counties Armagh, Cavan, Donegal, Fermanagh, Londonderry (then known as Coleraine) and Tyrone. By the end of the 17th century a self-sustaining settlement of British colonists had established itself in Ulster.

MAXWELL

In Ireland this name is common only in Ulster where it is most numerous in Counties Antrim and Down. This surname was brought to Ulster by settlers from Scotland in the 17th century.

Maxwell is derived from a place near Melrose in Roxburghshire in the Borders of Scotland. Maccus, a Saxon lord, obtained a grant of land, in 1144, on the River Tweed, and from the salmon fishery attached to it, called Maccus's Wiel or Maxwheel, meaning 'Maccus's pool', the lands obtained their name. The first on record to use the surname seems to be Sir John Maxwell, Chamberlain of Scotland in the 13th century.

The Maxwells held lands in Annandale in Dumfriesshire and became Lords of Maxwell and Earls of Nithsdale. The Maxwells were the strongest of the riding or reiving clans of the West March of the Scottish Borders until they were eclipsed by the Johnstones in the 16th century, with whom they had conducted a long and bitter feud. Caerlaverock Castle, south of Dumfries, was the 13th century stronghold of the Maxwells which was besieged by Edward I of England. Prominent branches of the Maxwell family were also established at Pollok, near Glasgow and at Monreith in Wigtownshire.

From the 14th to the late-17th century, the border between England and Scotland – the Debatable Lands – was a turbulent place. The Border country was ravaged by the lawless Reiver families who stole each other's cattle and possessions. They raided in large numbers, on horseback, and they killed and kidnapped without remorse. This type of life resulted in the growth of large closely-knit family groups with intense clan loyalties and fierce feuds against others.

Prior to the Union of the Crowns of England and Scotland in 1603 the Scottish Border was divided into three districts; the east, west and middle Marches. Each March was presided over by a warden who settled disputes with the warden of the appropriate March in England, as border warfare was rife at this time with frequent cattle raids. For many years the Maxwells were Wardens of the West March, and Stewards of Annandale and Kirkcudbright.

When the power of the riding clans was broken by James I in the decade after 1603 many came to Ulster to escape persecution. This flight to Ulster also suited the needs of the king. James I, from 1610, was determined to implement a deliberate plantation of Scottish and English colonists in Ulster. Although many of their neighbours in the Borders such as the Armstrongs and Johnstones migrated to County Fermanagh the Maxwells preferred to settle in Counties Down and Antrim. It is estimated by 1715, when migration to Ulster had virtually stopped, the Scottish population of Ulster stood at 200,000.

During the famous 105 day Siege of Derry, from 18 April to 31 July 1689, sixteen Maxwells, including Sir George Maxwell of Killyleagh Castle, County Down, John and Robert Maxwell of Farnham, County Cavan, Henry and James Maxwell of Glenarb, County Tyrone, and Captain, Thomas and William Maxwell of Derry were recorded as 'defenders' of the city.

133

McAFEE

This name represents the descendants of Scottish Clan MacFie. The name was brought to Ulster at the time of the 17th century Plantation of Ulster by settlers from Scotland. The name is particularly associated with County Donegal.

Clan MacFie, originally Clan MacDuffy, is derived from Gaelic *Mac Dhuibhshithe*, meaning 'son of the black-haired man of peace'. The name was also anglicised as McAfee, McHaffy, Mahaffy and Mehaffy.

Clan MacFie trace their descent from Kenneth McAlpine, the 9th century King of Scotland. The clan's home was the island of Colonsay in the Inner Hebrides where they were hereditary keepers of the records of Clan Donald, Lords of the Isles. They were followers of the Mac-Donalds of Islay. A banch of Clan MacFie, who were followers of the Camerons of Lochiel, established themselves at Lochaber.

Upheavals such as military incursions, feuds and harvest failures would have encouraged many clan members, including McAfees, to migrate to Ulster as settlers during the 17th century. With the decline of Clan Donald power Clan MacFie scattered at the beginning of the 17th century. The loss of clan lands in Colonsay in the mid-17th century provided further encouragement to Clan MacFie members to migrate.

Owing to the nature of the Scottish clan system once the power and influence of the chief had been weakened or broken the clan tended to disintegrate. Bearing the surname McAfee simply indicated that you were a follower of the Clan MacFie chief. Not every clan member was related by blood: people who were not of direct descent might also identify with a particular clan. They may have been granted land in return for services, or simply have lived on clan territories. Their bond, however, whether they had a common tribal ancestor or not, was their common rule by a chief with loyalty to one's clan being the primary obligation. Once tribal loyalty was broken clans 'scattered'.

Movement of Scottish settlers to Ulster began in earnest from 1605 in a private enterprise colonisation of counties Antrim and Down when Sir Hugh Montgomery and Sir James Hamilton acquired title to large estates in north Down and Sir Randall MacDonnell, 1st Earl of Antrim, to large tracts of land in north Antrim.

Further impetus came in 1609 when James I adopted the policy to encourage Scottish settlers to settle on the forfeited estates of the Gaelic chiefs in counties Armagh, Cavan, Donegal, Fermanagh, Londonderry (then known as Coleraine) and Tyrone.

Scottish families entering Ireland through the port of Londonderry settled in the Foyle Valley which includes much of the fertile lands of counties Donegal, Londonderry and Tyrone. It is estimated by 1715, when migration to Ulster had virtually stopped, the Scottish population of Ulster stood at 200,000.

The name was also recorded in Wigtownshire in the province of Galloway from the 16th century. This region was home to many of the Scottish settlers who came to Ulster throughout the 17th century.

McALLISTER

McAllister is a distinctively Ulster name with the great majority being in County Antrim. This name represents the descendants of Clan MacAllister in Scotland who from the 14th century came to Ulster to fight as galloglasses, i.e. mercenary soldiers, for the McDonnells of the Glens of Antrim. Derived from Gaelic *galloglach*, galloglass refers to a paid soldier, often brought over from Scotland, to fight on behalf of an Irish chief.

The Annals of The Kingdom of Ireland by the Four Masters provide detailed and graphic descriptions of the Scottish galloglasses. In one account dated 1557 the *Annals* describe the galloglass in the camp of the O'Neills who were on a raiding expedition into O'Donnell territory in Donegal. It states that 'sixty grim and redoubtable gallowglasses, with sharp, keen axes, terrible and ready for action, and sixty stern and terrific Scots, with massive, broad, and heavy-striking swords in their hands, ready to strike and parry, were watching and guarding the son of O'Neill.'

With the assistance of his McAllister galloglasses the McDonnells were a serious military threat to both the O'Neills and the English Crown in County Antrim in the 16th century. In 1555 the *Annals* record that Hugh O'Neill, Lord of Clannaboy, was killed by the Scots. In the same year an English army, led by the Earl of Sussex, was raised 'to expel the sons of Mac Donnell and the Scots, who were making conquests in the Route and Clannaboy'. The *Annals* record that the Earl's army 'slew one or two hundred of these Scots'.

Clan MacAllister is one of the principal branches of Clan Donald. According to Clan Donald genealogical lore the MacAllisters can trace their ancestry back to Ireland and to *Conn of the Hundred Battles,* King of Connaught, who was killed in 157 AD at Tara, County Meath. Clan MacAllister, derived from Gaelic *Mac Alasdair,* meaning 'son of Alexander', trace their descent from the 13th century Alexander, a great-grandson of Somerled. Under the leadership of Somerled, who expelled the Norsemen from the western side of Scotland in the 12th century, Clan Donald claimed the position of 'The Headship of the Gael'.

The territory of Clan MacAllister was in Kintyre, with their seat on the northwest side of West Loch Tarbert, and they were also numerous on Arran and Bute. The Clan held these lands until the early 19th century. From this region the MacAllisters were brought to Antrim by the McDonnells in the 14th century. They are recognised as one of the great galloglass families of Ireland.

The McAllisters quickly settled in Antrim and they became established as an Irish sept in their own right. By the time of the census of 1659 McAllister was recorded as a 'principal name' in both Counties Antrim and Derry. By the mid-19th century the name was most heavily concentrated in north Antrim in the baronies of Cary and Kilconway.

The name was also brought to Ulster at the time of the 17th century Plantation of Ulster by settlers from Scotland. It is estimated by 1715, when migration to Ulster had virtually stopped, the Scottish population of Ulster stood at 200,000.

135

McATEER

McAteer is virtually exclusive to Ulster, where it is mainly found in Counties Antrim, Donegal and Armagh. McAteer is an Irish surname but it has become confused with Scottish McIntyre.

Ireland was one of the first countries to adopt a system of hereditary surnames which developed from a more ancient system of clan or sept names. From the 11th century each family began to adopt its own distinctive family name generally derived from the first name of an ancestor who lived in or about the 10th century. The surname was formed by prefixing either Mac (son of) or O (grandson or descendant of) to the ancestor's name. Surnames in Ireland, therefore, tended to identify membership of a sept.

The County Armagh sept of McAteer is derived from Gaelic *Mac an tSaoir*, meaning 'son of the craftsman'. The occupation of craftsman referred to a number of trades such as carpenter, mason and wright. The homeland of this sept was Ballymacateer near Lurgan.

The Annals of The Kingdom of Ireland by the Four Masters (a history of Ireland from 'the earliest period to the year 1616') state that, in 762AD, 'Mac an-tsair, Abbot of Eanach-dubh, died'. Gaelic *Eanach-dubh*, meaning 'the Black Marsh', refers to Annaduff, a townland and parish near Drumsna in south Leitrim. *The Annals* also record, in 1288, the death of Michael Mac-an-t-Sair, Bishop of Clogher. Michael McAteer was Bishop of Clogher from 1268-1288.

McIntyre is a Scottish surname but it has become confused with Irish McAteer. McIntyre is found in Leinster and Connaught but is most common in Ulster, particularly in Counties Derry and Antrim. This name was brought to Ulster in large numbers by settlers from Scotland in the 17th century.

As McAteer was often changed to McIntyre it means that some families bearing the surname McIntyre are of Irish, not Scottish, descent.

In Scotland the McIntyres, in Gaelic *Mac an tSaoir*, meaning 'son of the craftsman' were a recognised clan in their own right. 'Glenoe, near Bunawe, Nether Lorn' in Argyllshire was their territory. It is claimed that they came to Lorn from the Hebrides and settled at Glenoe around 1380. The McIntyres were followers of the Stewarts of Appin. The McIntyres supported the Jacobite cause in Scotland. Five McIntyres in Appin's regiment were killed and five were wounded in the 1745 uprising.

Upheavals such as military incursions, feuds and harvest failures would have encouraged many clan members, including McIntyres, to migrate to Ulster as settlers during the 17th century. Owing to the nature of the Scottish clan system once the power and influence of the chief had been weakened and the bond of tribal loyalty broken the clan tended to scatter.

McAteer origins are further disguised as the name was also anglicised as Wright, particularly in County Fermanagh; as Carpenter, especially in the Dublin area; and as Freeman by translation of Gaelic *soar*, meaning 'free'.

136

McBREARTY

This surname is found exclusively in Ulster where it is most common in Counties Donegal and Tyrone.

Ireland was one of the first countries to adopt a system of hereditary surnames which developed from a more ancient system of clan or sept names. From the 11th century each family began to adopt its own distinctive family name generally derived from the first name of an ancestor who lived in or about the 10th century. The surname was formed by prefixing either Mac (son of) or O (grandson or descendant of) to the ancestor's name. Surnames in Ireland, therefore, tended to identify membership of a sept.

McBrearty is derived from Gaelic *Mac Muircheartaigh*, meaning 'son of Murtagh', a personal name, meaning 'sea ruler'. The homeland of this sept was west Donegal.

Many County Donegal septs trace their lineage to Conall *Gulban*, son of the 5th century High King of Ireland, Niall of the Nine Hostages, who ruled from the Hill of Tara, County Meath. Conall and his brother Eogan conquered northwest Ireland, ca.425 AD, capturing the great hill-fort of Grianan of Ailech in County Donegal which commanded the entrance to the Inishowen peninsula between Lough Swilly and Lough Foyle.

Conall, styled 'King of Tir Conaill', established his own kingdom in County Donegal called after him Tyrconnel, i.e. the 'Land of Conall', which was the ancient name of Donegal. His descendants, known as the Cenel Conaill (the race of Conall), formed one of the principal branches of the Northern Ui Neill (descendants of Niall of the Nine Hostages). The septs of the Cenel Conaill firmly established themselves in County Donegal while those descended from Conal's brother Eogan expanded to the east and south into Counties Derry and Tyrone.

At the time of the mid-19th century Griffith's Valuation 105 McBrearty households were recorded in County Donegal. This source clearly shows that the name was most concentrated in west Donegal in the lands around the town of Killybegs, as 43 McBrearty households were residing in the parish of Killybegs Upper, 15 in Killaghtee Parish and a further 14 in Kilcar Parish. In other words nearly 70% of descendants of the McBrearty sept in County Donegal were living in these three adjoining parishes.

McBrearty is a common name in Derry city today. This name, which spread to Derry city in the 19th century, illustrates the very close links, both historic and economic, between the city of Derry and County Donegal. As Derry developed an industrial base in shirt making, shipbuilding and distilling it attracted much of its workforce from County Donegal. In the 90-year period 1821 to 1911 the population of the city quadrupled to 40,780.

In Scotland *Mac Muircheartaigh* was anglicised as McCurdy. McCurdy is a common name on the islands of Arran and Bute where they were a sept of Clan Stuart of Bute. During the 17th century Plantation of Ulster many McCurdys settled in Rathlin Island, the Glens of Antrim and on the north coast of Antrim.

137

McBRIDE

McBride can be an Irish or a Scottish name. McBride is much more common in Ulster then in the rest of Ireland. The name is most numerous in Counties Donegal and Down and is also common in County Antrim.

Ireland was one of the first countries to adopt a system of hereditary surnames which developed from a more ancient system of clan or sept names. The surname was formed by prefixing either Mac (son of) or O (grandson or descendant of) to the ancestor's name. The McBride sept of County Donegal is derived from Gaelic *Mac Giolla Bhrighde*, meaning 'son of the devotee of St Brigid'. The Gaelic name gave rise to variants such as Gilbride, Kilbride and Mucklebreed.

St Brigid, one of the three patrons of Ireland, was abbess of Kildare and died in 525.
In Donegal it appears that there was another St Brigid based at Ray, near Falcarragh. The McBrides were *erenaghs*, i.e. hereditary stewards, of these church lands in the parish of Raymunterdoney in the barony of Kilmacrenan in west Donegal. It is unlikely that St Brigid of Donegal could have competed with St Columkille (also known as Columba) of Derry were it not for the esteem of the Kildare Saint's name. In the 17th century McBrides settled at Gweedore in the same county. Today the name McBride, which has spread throughout northwest Donegal from Carrigart to Dungloe, attests to the strong following for St Brigid of Donegal in the medieval period.

A branch of the sept was also established in County Down as in the census of 1659 McBride was recorded as a 'principal Irish name' in that county. However, some of these must have been Scottish as the cult of St Brigid was active in both Ireland and Scotland from the 9th century.

McBride is also a well known name in Scotland. The McBrides were a sept of Clan Donald, and they were common in the Scottish Isles, particularly Arran. They take their name from Gillebride, the father of Somerled of Argyll. Under the leadership of Somerled, who expelled the Norsemen from the western side of Scotland in the 12th century, Clan Donald claimed the position of 'The Headship of the Gael'.

Upheavals such as military incursions, feuds and harvest failures would have encouraged many Scottish families, including McBrides, to migrate to Ulster as settlers during the 17th century.

Movement of Scottish settlers to Ulster began in earnest from 1605 in a private enterprise colonisation of counties Antrim and Down when Sir Hugh Montgomery and Sir James Hamilton acquired title to large estates in north Down and Sir Randall MacDonnell, 1st Earl of Antrim, to large tracts of land in north Antrim. Further impetus came in 1609 when James I adopted the policy to encourage Scottish settlers to settle on the forfeited estates of the Gaelic chiefs in counties Armagh, Cavan, Donegal, Fermanagh, Londonderry (then known as Coleraine) and Tyrone.

Scottish McBrides settled in large numbers in Counties Antrim and Down. By the mid-19th century McBride was concentrated in the barony of Lower Dunluce, around the Giant's Causeway, in County Antrim and in the barony of Upper Iveagh, around Rathfriland, in County Down.

McCAFFERTY

The surname McCafferty is exclusive to Ulster, where over half are in County Donegal, a third in County Derry and most of the rest in County Antrim. This name illustrates the very close links between the city of Derry and County Donegal. As Derry developed an industrial base in the 19th century in shirt making, shipbuilding and distilling it attracted much of its workforce from Donegal.

The McCafferty sept of County Donegal trace their lineage to Conall *Gulban*, son of the 5th century High King of Ireland, Niall of the Nine Hostages, who ruled from the Hill of Tara, County Meath. Conall and his brother Eogan conquered northwest Ireland, ca.425 AD, capturing the great hill-fort of Grianan of Ailech in County Donegal which commanded the entrance to Inishowen between Lough Swilly and Lough Foyle.

Conall, styled 'King of Tir Conaill', established his own kingdom in County Donegal called after him Tyrconnel, i.e. the 'Land of Conall', which was the ancient name of Donegal. His descendants, known as the Cenel Conaill (the race of Conall), formed one of the principal branches of the Northern Ui Neill (descendants of Niall of the Nine Hostages). The septs of the Cenel Conaill firmly established themselves in County Donegal while those descended from Conal's brother Eogan expanded to the east and south into Counties Derry and Tyrone.

Ireland was one of the first countries to adopt a system of hereditary surnames which developed from a more ancient system of clan or sept names. The surname was formed by prefixing either Mac (son of) or O (grandson or descendant of) to the ancestor's name.

McCafferty is derived from Gaelic *Mac Eachmharcaigh*, from *each*, meaning 'horse', and *marcach*, meaning 'rider'. The McCaffertys were a branch of the O'Donnells, among whom the personal name Eachmarcach was popular. The name was anglicised to McCafferky in County Mayo.

McCafferty has also become confused with McCaffrey. Although the surnames of McCafferty and McCaffrey have quite distinct origins their ultimate origins have become confused as a result of anglicisation. In some cases people whose origins are *Mac Eachmharcaigh* may be disguised by bearing the surname McCaffrey.

McCaffrey, derived from Gaelic *Mac Gafraidh*, i.e. son of Godfrey, is a distinct sept from County Fermanagh. They were a branch of the Maguires tracing their descent from Donn Carrach Maguire, who died in 1302. Located around Rossmacaffry the McCaffreys, by 1580, were considered among the five most powerful families in Fermanagh.

McCaffrey is now the sixth most common name in County Fermanagh. McCaffrey was also shortened to Caffrey particularly in Counties Cavan and Meath. Some McCaffreys in County Fermanagh became Beattys. This can be a source of confusion as Beatty was well known in the Scottish Borders where they were one of the riding clans broken by James I after 1603. Many families from the Borders of Scotland settled in Fermanagh during the 17th century Plantation of Ulster.

McCAFFREY

The surname McCaffrey is almost exclusive to Ulster. It is the sixth most numerous name in its homeland, County Fermanagh, and is common too in County Tyrone and, to a lesser extent, in County Monaghan.

Ireland was one of the first countries to adopt a system of hereditary surnames which developed from a more ancient system of clan or sept names. The surname was formed by prefixing either Mac (son of) or O (grandson or descendant of) to the ancestor's name.

McCaffrey, derived from Gaelic *Mac Gafraidh*, i.e. son of Godfrey, was an important sept in County Fermanagh. Godfrey is a Norse name which was early gaelicised in both Ireland and Scotland. The McCaffreys were a branch of the Maguires tracing their descent from Donn Carrach Maguire, who died in 1302. Located around Rossmacaffry the McCaffreys, by 1580, were considered among the five most powerful families in Fermanagh.

McCaffrey was sometimes shortened to Caffrey particularly in Counties Cavan and Meath. Some McCaffreys in County Fermanagh became Beattys. This can be a source of confusion as Beatty was well known in the Scottish Borders where they were one of the riding clans broken by James I after 1603. Many families from the Borders of Scotland settled in Fermanagh during the 17th century Plantation of Ulster.

McCaffrey has also become confused with McCafferty. Although the surnames of McCaffrey and McCafferty have quite distinct origins their ultimate origins have become confused as a result of anglicisation. In some cases people whose origins are *Mac Gafraidh* may be disguised by bearing the surname McCafferty.

McCafferty, derived from Gaelic *Mac Eachmharcaigh*, from *each*, meaning 'horse', and *marcach*, meaning 'rider', is a distinct sept from County Donegal. The McCaffertys were a branch of the O'Donnells, among whom the personal name Eachmarcach was popular. The name was anglicised to McCafferky in County Mayo.

Like McCaffrey the surname McCafferty is also exclusive to Ulster, where over half are in County Donegal, a third in County Derry and most of the rest in County Antrim.

The McCafferty sept of County Donegal trace their lineage to Conall *Gulban*, son of the 5th century High King of Ireland, Niall of the Nine Hostages, who ruled from the Hill of Tara, County Meath. Conall and his brother Eogan conquered northwest Ireland, ca.425 AD, capturing the great hill-fort of Grianan of Ailech in County Donegal which commanded the entrance to Inishowen between Lough Swilly and Lough Foyle. Conall, styled 'King of Tir Conaill', established his own kingdom in County Donegal called after him Tyrconnel, i.e. the 'Land of Conall', which was the ancient name of Donegal.

McCALLION

McCallion is an exclusively Ulster name found mainly in Counties Donegal and Derry. Names such as McCallion, McAllen, McKillen and Killen represent descendants of Clan Campbell in Argyllshire, Scotland who from the 15th century came to Ulster to fight as galloglasses, i.e. mercenary soldiers, for the O'Donnells of Donegal. Derived from Gaelic *galloglach*, galloglass refers to a paid soldier, often brought over from Scotland, to fight on behalf of an Irish chief.

Although the names of McCallion, McAllen and McKillen represent distinct septs within Clan Campbell there are no septs of Clan Campbell registered with these names today. Anglicisation has disguised the ultimate origins of these names. Furthermore, in many cases, the families in these septs were recorded simply as Campbell. Strictly speaking McKillen, and its abbreviated from Killen, is derived from Gaelic *Mac Coilin*, meaning 'son of Colin'; McAllen stems from Gaelic *Mac Ailin*, meaning 'son of Allen'; and McCallion is derived from *Mac Cailin*, meaning 'son of Cailin'.

McKillen and Killen chiefly belong to County Antrim. McCallion, on the other hand, is found almost exclusively in Counties Donegal and Derry. In Derry and Donegal McAllen and McCallion are indistinguishable; as many people whose origins are *Mac Ailin* will bear the surname McCallion. Ballymacallion, meaning 'the townland of the McCallions', is located in Dungiven Parish, County Derry.

As well as providing detailed and graphic descriptions of the activities of the Clan Campbell galloglasses *The Annals of The Kingdom of Ireland by the Four Masters* record the distinct spellings of their associated surnames. In 1555, the *Annals* record that 'the son of O'Donnell, i.e. Calvagh, went to Scotland, attended by a few select persons, and obtained auxiliary forces from Mac Calin (Gillaspick Don), under the command of Master Arsibel. He afterwards came back, with a great body of Scots, to desolate and ravage Tirconnell.' In the same year the O'Donnells, and their Scottish galloglasses, stormed and demolished the castles at Greencastle, Inishowen, County Donegal and the O'Cahan stronghold on the island in Enagh Lough, County Derry.

The *Annals* of 1557 describes in great detail the role of the galloglass in the camp of the O'Neills who were on a raiding expedition into O'Donnell territory in Donegal. It states that 'sixty grim and redoubtable gallowglasses, with sharp, keen axes, terrible and ready for action, and sixty stern and terrific Scots, with massive, broad, and heavy-striking swords in their hands, ready to strike and parry, were watching and guarding the son of O'Neill.'

Scottish galloglasses, led by Donnell and Dowell Mac Allen, raided into Counties Sligo and Mayo in 1558. They were defeated in a fierce battle, during which both Donnell and Dowell Mac Allen were slain, by the Earl of Clanrickard.

In 1586 'a Scotch fleet landed in Inishowen, O'Doherty's country'. One of its leaders was Gillespick Mac Ailin. After this raid the *Annals* record 'that there was nothing of value in Inishowen, whether corn or cattle, which they did not carry off'.

McCANN

McCann is common in Leinster and Connaught but it is most numerous in Ulster, where it is among the fifty most common names. In Ulster it is most numerous in Counties Armagh, Antrim and Down. It is among the ten most numerous names in its homeland of County Armagh.

Ireland was one of the first countries to adopt a system of hereditary surnames which developed from a more ancient system of clan or sept names. From the 11th century each family began to adopt its own distinctive family name generally derived from the first name of an ancestor who lived in or about the 10th century. The surname was formed by prefixing either Mac (son of) or O (grandson or descendant of) to the ancestor's name. Surnames in Ireland, therefore, tended to identify membership of a sept.

McCann is derived from *Mac Cana*, the root word being *cano*, meaning 'wolf cub'. The McCanns were Lords of Clanbrassil, a district on the southern shores of Lough Neagh and comprising the baronies of Oneilland East and Oneilland West in County Armagh and part of the barony of Dungannon Middle in County Tyrone.

The McCanns were an important sept in County Armagh from the 12th century. They became lords of Clanbrassil on the decline of the O'Garveys. *The Annals of The Kingdom of Ireland by the Four Masters* (a chronicle of Irish history from 'the earliest period to the year 1616') record, in 1155, that 'Amhlaeibh Mac Cana, lord of Cinel-Aenghusa, pillar of the chivalry and vigour of all Cinel-Eoghain, died, and was interred at Ard-Macha.' For the next four centuries the McCanns were one of the leading septs in County Armagh. Donnell McCann was still styled Chief of Clanbrassil as late as 1598.

The McCann sept trace their lineage to Eogan, son of the 5th century High King of Ireland, Niall of the Nine Hostages, who ruled from the Hill of Tara, County Meath. Eogan and his brother Conall *Gulban* conquered northwest Ireland, ca.425 AD, capturing the great hill-fort of Grianan of Ailech in County Donegal which commanded the entrance to the Inishowen peninsula between Lough Swilly and Lough Foyle.

Eogan, styled 'King of Ailech', established his own kingdom in the peninsula still called after him Inishowen (Innis Eoghain or Eogan's Isle). Eogan was converted to Christianity by St Patrick, when he travelled to Ailech, ca. 442 AD. His descendants, known as the Cenel Eoghain (the race of Owen), became the principal branch of the Northern Ui Neill (descendants of Niall of the Nine Hostages). The Cenel Eoghain in the next five centuries expanded to the east and south from their focal point in Inishowen.

In 1688 Colonel Cormac O'Neill of Kilmacevet, near Crumlin, County Antrim raised a regiment in support of King James II. Lieutenant Brian McCann and Ensign Cormac McCann were officers in this regiment, and they were part of the 'Jacobite army' which besieged the city of Derry during the famous 105 day Siege of Derry, from 18 April to 31 July 1689.

McCARRON

In Ireland this name is almost exclusive to Ulster, associated mainly with Counties Donegal and Derry and with north Monaghan.

The McCarron sept of County Donegal trace their lineage to Eogan, son of the 5th century High King of Ireland, Niall of the Nine Hostages, who ruled from the Hill of Tara, County Meath. Eogan and his brother Conall *Gulban* conquered northwest Ireland, ca.425 AD, capturing the great hill-fort of Grianan of Ailech, which commanded the entrance to the Inishowen peninsula, County Donegal.

Eogan, styled 'King of Ailech', established his own kingdom in the peninsula still called after him Inishowen (Innis Eoghain or Eogan's Isle). His descendants, known as the Cenel Eoghain (the race of Owen), became the principal branch of the Northern Ui Neill (descendants of Niall of the Nine Hostages).

Ireland was one of the first countries to adopt a system of hereditary surnames which developed from a more ancient system of clan or sept names. The surname was formed by prefixing either Mac (son of) or O (grandson or descendant of) to the ancestor's name. In its homeland, in County Donegal, McCarron is derived from Gaelic *Mac Cearain*. McCarn was also a variant form of the name.

It would seem that the homeland of the McCarron sept was Inishowen in County Donegal. At the time of the mid-19th century Griffith's Valuation there were 39 McCarn households and 39 McCarron households in County Donegal. Of this total all McCarn households were recorded in the parishes of Inishowen and 23 (nearly two-thirds) of the McCarron households were living in Inishowen. Thus 80% of the descendants of the McCarron sept in County Donegal were living in Inishowen.

McCarron, which is a common name in Derry city today, illustrates the very close links, both historic and economic, between the city of Derry and the Inishowen district of County Donegal. As Derry developed an industrial base in the 19th century in shirt making, shipbuilding and distilling it attracted much of its workforce from Donegal. In the 90-year period 1821 to 1911 the population of the city quadrupled to 40,780.

From 1600 onwards references to the surname McCarron are largely confined to Counties Donegal and Derry. Prior to 1600, however, all references to this surname were outside Ulster as another sept of McCarrons, in Gaelic *Mac Carrghamhna*, were very prominent, from 1100 to 1600, in the barony of Kilkeeny West, County Westmeath. *The Annals of The Kingdom of Ireland by the Four Masters* called the head of this McCarron sept as 'Chief of Muintir-Maoil-t-Sionna', i.e. Chief of the Shannon, their territory lying on the Westmeath side of the River Shannon.

It has been suggested that the McCarrons could also be originally *Mac Caerthain*, the name of a sept who originated along the Foyle in County Derry and gave their name to the barony of Tirkeeran, in Gaelic *Tir Caerthain*, meaning ' the territory of the MacCaerthain'. As Lords of the Faughan Valley, County Derry, prior to the 12th century, this sept claimed descent from Colla Uais, who according to legend was the 121st Monarch of Ireland, from 322 to 326 AD. Colla Uais was banished to Scotland in 326 AD. It is claimed that this McCarron sept later moved to County Monaghan.

143

McCARTNEY

In Ireland this name is almost exclusive to Ulster where two-thirds of those of the name are in County Antrim. This name was brought to Ulster by settlers from Scotland in the 17th century, and in Ulster most McCartneys are of Scottish origin. This name, however, was also adopted by descendants of several Irish septs.

In Scotland, McCartney is derived from Gaelic *Mac Cartaine*, meaning 'son of Artan'. There were McCardney septs attached to Clan Farquharson of Invercauld and to Clan Mackintosh of Moray. Upheavals such as military incursions, feuds and harvest failures would have encouraged clan members, including McCardneys, to migrate to Ulster as settlers during the 17th century. Owing to the nature of the Scottish clan system once the power and influence of the chief had been weakened and the bond of tribal loyalty broken the clan tended to scatter.

However, the majority of Scottish McCartneys who migrated to Ulster in the 17th century originated in Ayrshire, Dumfriesshire and Galloway in the southwest corner of Scotland. McCartney was a common name in these areas from the early sixteenth century.

Movement of Scottish settlers to Ulster began in earnest from 1605 in a private enterprise colonisation of counties Antrim and Down when Sir Hugh Montgomery and Sir James Hamilton acquired title to large estates in north Down and Sir Randall MacDonnell, 1st Earl of Antrim, to large tracts of land in north Antrim. Further impetus came in 1609 when James I adopted the policy to encourage Scottish settlers to settle on the forfeited estates of the Gaelic chiefs in counties Armagh, Cavan, Donegal, Fermanagh, Londonderry (then known as Coleraine) and Tyrone.

These settlers came to Ulster, by and large, in three waves: with the granting of the initial leases in the period 1605 to 1625; after 1652 and Cromwell's crushing of the Irish rebellion; and finally in the fifteen years after 1690 and the Glorious Revolution. It is estimated by 1715, when migration to Ulster had virtually stopped, the Scottish population of Ulster stood at 200,000.

During the famous 105 day Siege of Derry, from 18 April to 31 July 1689, Captain George Macartney of Belfast, County Antrim was recorded as one of the 'defenders' of the city. Captain George Macartney, descended from the Macartneys of Auchinleck in Ayrshire, Scotland, settled in County Antrim in 1649. It was George Macartney's son, also called George, who purchased the castle and 12,000 acre estate of Lissanoure in north Antrim in 1733. The great-grandson of Captain George Macartney, also called George, became a distinguished diplomat as ambassador to the Emperor of China and was created 1st Earl Macartney of Lissanoure.

As well as numerous Scottish immigrants of the name some McCartneys in Ulster will have Irish origins. Irish septs such as Mulhartagh, in Gaelic *O Maolfhathartaigh*, of County Tyrone; McCartan, in Gaelic *Mac Artain*, of County Down; and McCaugherty, in Gaelic *Mac Eachmharcaigh*, of County Down have, in some instances, been changed to McCartney.

McCAULEY

McCauley can be an Irish or a Scottish name. Though found in Leinster and Connaught this name is most common in Ulster, particularly in Counties Antrim and Donegal. It is a widespread name in the Glens of Antrim along the coast from Cushendun to Glenarm.

Ireland was one of the first countries to adopt a system of hereditary surnames which developed from a more ancient system of clan or sept names. From the 11th century each family began to adopt its own distinctive family name generally derived from the first name of an ancestor who lived in or about the 10th century. The surname was formed by prefixing either Mac (son of) or O (grandson or descendant of) to the ancestor's name. Surnames in Ireland, therefore, tended to identify membership of a sept.

The McCauley sept of County Fermanagh is derived from Gaelic *Mac Amhlaoibh*, meaning 'son of Amlaib'. This personal name, pronounced Auley, was the Gaelic form of the Norse name Olaf. The McCauleys were a branch of the Maguires as they were descended from Auley, the son of Donn Carrach Maguire, the first Maguire King of Fermanagh who died in 1302. It is thought that it was this Auley and his sons who first crossed the Erne and won south Fermanagh for the Maguires. This sept gave their name to the barony of Clanawley in that county.

In County Antrim, by contrast, the majority of Irish born McCauleys are descendants of Scottish settlers. There are two clan MacAulays in Scotland. The MacAulays of Lewis in the Hebrides, in Gaelic *Mac Amhlaoibh*, meaning 'son of Olaf', were of Norse descent. Tracing their descent from Olav the Black, brother of Magnus, last king of Man and the Isles, the MacAulays of Lewis were followers of the MacLeods.

The MacAulays of Ardencaple in Dumbartonshire, in Gaelic *Mac Amhalghaidh*, were a branch of Clan Alpine of whom the McGregors were the senior clan. The obsolete Irish personal name of *Amhalghaidh* was pronounced Auley. A branch of the Dumbartonshire MacAulays came to the Glens of Antrim with the MacDonnells in the early-sixteenth century.

By the mid-16th century the MacDonalds, known as the MacDonnells of the Glens, had carved out an extensive territory in County Antrim at the expense of the MacQuillans. Movement of Scottish settlers to County Antrim began in earnest from 1605 when Sir Randall MacDonnell, 1st Earl of Antrim, acquired title to large tracts of land in north Antrim.

By the mid-nineteenth century McAuley was the most common name in the barony of Lower Glenarm in northeast Antrim and was also very common in the adjoining barony of Cary.

There are a great many variant spellings of this surname such as Cauley, Cawley, Gawley, Macauley, McAuley, McAwley, McGawley and Magawley.

McCAUSLAND

This surname is found almost exclusively in Ulster where it is most common in Counties Antrim, Derry and Tyrone. This name was brought to Ulster by settlers from Scotland in the 17th century.

It is claimed that McCausland is derived from Gaelic *Mac Ausalain*, meaning 'son of Ausalan'. Indeed the original name of Clan Buchanan was Macauslan or McCausland as they trace their descent from Ausalan Buoy O'Kane, a chief of a branch of the O'Kanes of County Derry who settled in Argyll in 1016. The name was changed to Buchanan, from the district of Buchanan in Stirlingshire, by Gilbrid MacAuslan in the 13th century.

From the 12th century until the early 17th century the O'Kanes were overlords and all-powerful in County Derry. The O'Kanes trace their lineage to Eogan, son of the 5th century High King of Ireland, Niall of the Nine Hostages, who ruled from the Hill of Tara, County Meath. Eogan and his brother Conall *Gulban* conquered northwest Ireland, ca.425 AD, capturing the great hill-fort of Grianan of Ailech in County Donegal.

It would seem, however, that McCausland means 'son of Absalon'. The first of the name on record is one Absalon, son of Macbethe, who received a charter of the island of Clarinch in Loch Lomond from the 3rd earl of Lennox in 1225. Clarinch was later to become the gathering place of Clan Buchanan. In 1271 Gilbert, son of Absalon was recorded in Dunbartonshire, and in 1308 Malcolm Macabsolon witnessed a charter by Robert the Bruce, King of Scotland.

McCauslands were recorded as followers of the earl of Argyll in the 16th century. In 1613 McCauslands were fined for aiding the outlawed Clan MacGregor. The McGregors had come into conflict with their powerful neighbours the Campbells, and, as a consequence, their lands were dispossessed and they resorted to raiding. In 1603, by Act of Parliament, the clan was outlawed, an order was given to disperse them 'by fire and sword', and their name was proscribed.

Settlers to Ulster from Scotland came, by and large, in three waves: with the granting of the initial leases in the period 1605 to 1625; after 1652 and Cromwell's crushing of the Irish rebellion; and finally in the fifteen years after 1690 and the Glorious Revolution. It is estimated by 1715, when migration to Ulster had virtually stopped, the Scottish population of Ulster stood at 200,000. It would appear that the McCauslands first settled in County Tyrone in the early 17th century.

During the famous 105 day Siege of Derry, from 18 April to 31 July 1689, Captain Oliver McCausland of Strabane, County Tyrone and Andrew McCausland of Clanaghmore, County Tyrone were recorded as 'defenders' of the city. Colonel Robert McCausland who settled at Drenagh near Limavady, County Londonderry in 1729 was a cousin of Captain Oliver McCausland. William Conolly, speaker of the Irish House of Commons, left some lands on his Limavady estate to his agent, Robert McCausland, and these lands became the Drenagh estate, the main house of which was called Fruithill. These McCauslands of Tyrone and Derry were, in turn, descended from the Macauslans of Dunbartonshire, Scotland.

McCAWELL

Although the surname McCawell is now very rare this County Tyrone sept was once very powerful and numerous.

The McCawell sept of County Tyrone trace their lineage to Eogan, son of the 5th century High King of Ireland, Niall of the Nine Hostages, who ruled from the Hill of Tara, County Meath. Eogan and his brother Conall *Gulban* conquered northwest Ireland, ca.425 AD, capturing the great hill-fort of Grianan of Ailech in County Donegal which commanded the entrance to the Inishowen peninsula between Lough Swilly and Lough Foyle.

Eogan, styled 'King of Ailech', established his own kingdom in the peninsula still called after him Inishowen (Innis Eoghain or Eogan's Isle). Eogan was converted to Christianity by St Patrick, when he travelled to Ailech, ca. 442 AD. His descendants, known as the Cenel Eoghain (the race of Owen), became the principal branch of the Northern Ui Neill (descendants of Niall of the Nine Hostages).

Ireland was one of the first countries to adopt a system of hereditary surnames which developed from a more ancient system of clan or sept names. From the 11th century each family began to adopt its own distinctive family name generally derived from the first name of an ancestor who lived in or about the 10th century. The surname was formed by prefixing either Mac (son of) or O (grandson or descendant of) to the ancestor's name. Surnames in Ireland, therefore, tended to identify membership of a sept. McCawell, in Gaelic *Mac Cathmhaoil*, is derived from *cathmhaol,* meaning 'battle chief'.

The McCawells were the leading sept of Clan Ferady (tracing their descent from Faredach, son of Muireadach (Murdock), son of Eogan). At the height of their power in the 12th century, from their base at Clogher, they controlled a large portion of County Tyrone and had penetrated deep into County Fermanagh. They were one of the seven powerful septs supporting O'Neill. By the mid-14th century their power in Fermanagh had been broken by the Maguires and their influence gradually declined thereafter.

In controlling the seat of power of the Clogher diocese, many McCawells held powerful positions in the church. From the mid-14th to the mid-16th centuries they provided two bishops to Clogher diocese, and numerous abbots, deans and canons to the dioceses of Armagh, Clogher and Derry.

It would seem that many McCawells migrated to Down and Armagh towards the end of the 16th century as the name suddenly becomes common in these counties.

The 17th century Plantation of Ulster with English and Scottish settlers not only marked the end of McCawell power, but also, to a large extent, the disappearance of the name. It would seem that families of the *Mac Cathmhaoil* sept adopted various anglicised surnames such as Campbell, Callwell, Caulfield, McCall and many others. Thus people whose origins are *Mac Cathmhaoil* are disguised by a variety of inappropriate anglicised names.

McCAY

In Ireland this name is almost exclusive to Ulster, where it is found chiefly in Counties Antrim and Derry. This name was brought to Ulster by settlers from Scotland in the 17th century.

McCay is derived from Gaelic *Mac Aoidh*, meaning 'son of Hugh'. This name was also anglicised as Mackay, Mackie, McCoy, McKay and McKee. Clan Mackay, claiming descent from Morgund of Pluscarden, originated in Moray. This clan came to prominence in Sutherland in the 13th century and by 1427 the chief, Angus Dow MacKay, could muster an army of 4000 men. In Inverness-shire the Mackays were a sept of Clan Davidson, and in Kintyre and Galloway the MacKays, MacKies and Mackies were followers of Clan Donald.

The first McCays in Ireland, also known as McCoys, were Clan Donald galloglasses, i.e. mercenary soldiers. As followers of Clan Donald they came over to Ulster from Kintyre and the southern isles of Scotland such as Islay to fight for the McDonnells of the Glens of Antrim.

Clan Donald had acquired new territories in the north of Ireland ca.1400 when John Mor MacDonald had married Margery Bissett, an heiress in the Glens of Antrim. By the mid-16th century the MacDonalds, known as the MacDonnells of the Glens, had carved out an extensive territory in County Antrim at the expense of the MacQuillans.

Movement of Scottish settlers to Ulster began in earnest from 1605 in a private enterprise colonisation of counties Antrim and Down when Sir Hugh Montgomery and Sir James Hamilton acquired title to large estates in north Down and Sir Randall MacDonnell, 1st Earl of Antrim, to large tracts of land in north Antrim. Further impetus came in 1609 when James I adopted the policy to encourage Scottish settlers to settle on the forfeited estates of the Gaelic chiefs in counties Armagh, Cavan, Donegal, Fermanagh, Londonderry (then known as Coleraine) and Tyrone.

Confusion arises as the Gaelic surname *Mac Aoidh* has acquired in the process of anglicisation a great number of variants. Thus the McCay family of Drumard in Tamlaght O'Crilly Parish, County Londonderry were recorded as McCoy in the 1831 census, as McCay in the tithe book of 1833 and as McKay in the Griffith's Valuation of 1859.

In Ireland, particularly in Counties Donegal and Fermanagh, Gaelic *Mac Aodha*, meaning 'son of Hugh', was usually anglicised as McHugh and McCue but also as McCoy and McKee. Thus in west Ulster Irish McHugh can become indistinguishable from Scottish McCay.

During the famous 105 day Siege of Derry, from 18 April to 31 July 1689, General Andrew Mackay, Ensign William Mackie, Lieutenant William Mackey, Lieutenant Mackie, Lieutenant Mackay, John Mackay, Josiah Macky and Jannett Mackee were recorded as 'defenders' of the city. On the opposing side Lieutenant Daniel McKay and Ensign Hugh McKay were officers in the 'Jacobite army' which besieged the city of Derry.

McCLAY

In Ireland this name is almost exclusive to Ulster, where it is most common in Counties Antrim, Londonderry and Donegal. This name was brought to Ulster by settlers from Scotland in the 17th century.

McClay is derived from Gaelic *Mac Dhunnshleibhe,* meaning 'son of Dunsleve'. Dunsleve, meaning 'brown of the hill', was an old personal name among the Gaels of Scotland and Ireland. The anglicisation of Gaelic names resulted in many variant spellings of the same name. In Argyll the 'd' and 's' were omitted in old records to give McOnlea which became McClay.

The McClays were numerous in early times in Easter and Wester Ross and in Argyll. The McClays were recorded as a small sept of Clan Stewart of Appin.

Upheavals such as military incursions, feuds and harvest failures would have encouraged many clan members in the Highlands of Scotland, including McClays, to migrate to Ulster as settlers during the 17th century. Owing to the nature of the Scottish clan system once the power and influence of the chief had been weakened and the bond of tribal loyalty broken the clan tended to scatter.

The defeat of the old Gaelic order in the Nine Years War, 1594-1603 and the escape of the most prominent Gaelic Lords of Ulster in 'the Flight of the Earls' in 1607 from Lough Swilly, County Donegal were ultimately responsible for the settlement of many Scottish families in the northern counties of Ireland.

Movement of Scottish settlers to Ulster began in earnest from 1605 in a private enterprise colonisation of counties Antrim and Down when Sir Hugh Montgomery and Sir James Hamilton acquired title to large estates in north Down and Sir Randall MacDonnell, 1st Earl of Antrim, to large tracts of land in north Antrim.

In 1609 the Earl of Salisbury, Lord High Treasurer, suggested to James I a deliberate plantation of Scottish and English colonists on the forfeited estates of the Gaelic chiefs in counties Armagh, Cavan, Donegal, Fermanagh, Londonderry (then known as Coleraine) and Tyrone.

Settlers to Ulster came, by and large, in three waves: with the granting of the initial leases in the period 1605 to 1625; after 1652 and Cromwell's crushing of the Irish rebellion; and finally in the fifteen years after 1690 and the Glorious Revolution. It is estimated by 1715, when migration to Ulster had virtually stopped, the Scottish population of Ulster stood at 200,000.

Scottish families entering Ireland through the port of Londonderry settled in the Foyle Valley which includes much of the fertile lands of counties Donegal, Londonderry and Tyrone. The lands along the Firth of Clyde in the county of Ayrshire, the Clyde Valley and the Border Lands consisting of the counties of Wigtown, Kirkcudbright and Dumfries were home to many of these Scottish settlers.

This name was also anglicised to Livingstone and Lee. William Livingstone, the Islay bard, always wrote his name in Gaelic *M'Dhunleibhe.*

McCLEAN

This surname, usually spelt either as McClean or McLean, is most numerous in Counties Antrim and Derry. This name represents the descendants of Clan Maclean in Scotland who from the 15th century came to Ulster to fight as galloglasses, i.e. mercenary soldiers, for the McDonnells of the Glens of Antrim. Derived from Gaelic *galloglach,* galloglass refers to a paid soldier, often brought over from Scotland, to fight on behalf of an Irish chief.

The Annals of The Kingdom of Ireland by the Four Masters provide detailed and graphic descriptions of the Scottish galloglasses. In one account dated 1557 the *Annals* describe the galloglass in the camp of the O'Neills who were on a raiding expedition into O'Donnell territory in Donegal. It states that 'sixty grim and redoubtable gallowglasses, with sharp, keen axes, terrible and ready for action, and sixty stern and terrific Scots, with massive, broad, and heavy-striking swords in their hands, ready to strike and parry, were watching and guarding the son of O'Neill.'

With the assistance of his McClean galloglasses the McDonnells were a serious military threat to both the O'Neills and the English Crown in County Antrim in the 16th century. In 1555 the *Annals* record that Hugh O'Neill, Lord of Clannaboy, was killed by the Scots. In the same year an English army, led by the Earl of Sussex, was raised 'to expel the sons of Mac Donnell and the Scots, who were making conquests in the Route and Clannaboy'. The *Annals* record that the Earl's army 'slew one or two hundred of these Scots'.

McClean is derived from Gaelic *Mac Giolla Eain,* meaning 'son of the servant of John'. Clan Maclean, trace their descent from 'Gillean of the Battle-axe' who lived in Moray in the 11th century. The clan moved westwards, settling in Lorn, and became followers of MacDougall, the Lord of Lorn. In the 13th century Clan Maclean changed their allegiance to the MacDonalds, Lords of the Isles, and, in 1376, through marriage of their Chief Lachlan Lubanach to Mary MacDonald, daughter of the Lord of the Isles, acquired extensive territory in Mull.

By the end of the 15th century the Macleans held extensive lands on Mull, Tiree, Islay and Jura, and in Knapdale and Morvern in Argyllshire and Lochaber in Inverness-shire. These lands were divided among the four main branches: Duart, Ardgour, Coll and Lochbuie. The chiefs of the clan had their seat at Duart Castle on Mull.

After 1493 when the MacDonalds finally lost their title as 'Lord of the Isles' the various followers of the MacDonalds, including the Macleans, became independent clans. This loss of power also encouraged more supporters of the MacDonalds to hire themselves out as galloglasses to Irish chiefs. Followers of Clan Maclean of Duart were hired by both the O'Donnells and the O'Neills in the 16th century.

The Macleans, who supported the Jacobite cause, in Scotland were defeated in battle in 1691. With their lands forfeited to the Campbells Clan Maclean now scattered, and many emigrated to Ulster and to North America. In the fifteen year period after 1690 it is estimated that 50,000 people came to Ulster from Scotland.

McCLELLAND

In Ireland this name is common only in Ulster where it is most numerous in Counties Antrim, Down, Armagh, Derry and Monaghan. This name was brought to Ulster by settlers from Scotland in the 17th century.

McClelland is derived from Gaelic *Mac Gille Fhaolain*, meaning 'son of the devotee of St Fillan'. The earliest reference to the surname is of one Patrick McLolane who captured the Castle of Dumfries in 1305. The McClellands were numerous in Galloway from the end of the 14th century where the name was initially anglicised as Maclellan. John Maclellan was granted the lands of Balmaclellan in Galloway by James III, King of Scotland, in 1466. The province of Galloway in southwest Scotland was home to many of the Scottish settlers who came to Ulster throughout the 17th century.

In the Aberfeldy district of Perthshire the Maclellans were regarded as a sept of Clan Mac-Nab. During the 14th and 15th century references to the surname are also found in Forfarshire and Inverness-shire as well as in Dumfriesshire and Galloway.

Movement of Scottish settlers to Ulster began in earnest from 1605 in a private enterprise colonisation of counties Antrim and Down when Sir Hugh Montgomery and Sir James Hamilton acquired title to large estates in north Down and Sir Randall MacDonnell, 1st Earl of Antrim, to large tracts of land in north Antrim. By the mid-19th century the McClellands were concentrated in the barony of Upper Antrim in County Antrim, and in the barony of Upper Iveagh, near Banbridge, in County Down.

In 1609 the Earl of Salisbury, Lord High Treasurer, suggested to James I a deliberate plantation of Scottish and English colonists on the forfeited estates of the Gaelic chiefs in counties Armagh, Cavan, Donegal, Fermanagh, Londonderry (then known as Coleraine) and Tyrone.

Sir Robert McClelland of Kirkcudbrightshire in the province of Galloway was one of the nine chief Scottish planters of the Ulster Plantation, and in 1610 he was granted lands in the baronies of Boylagh and Banagh in County Donegal. He sold his estate in Donegal in 1616 but acquired lands, through marriage in 1614, in the Ards peninsula, County Down, and, by lease in 1616 and 1618 respectively, of the manors of the Haberdashers' and Clothworkers' Companies of London in County Londonderry.

The Clothworkers' manor consisted of 13,450 acres of land to the west of the town of Coleraine and the Haberdashers' Manor of 23,100 acres to the east of the town of Limavady. Sir Robert McClelland built his residence, in the style of a castle inside a bawn with four circular flanking towers, at Ballycastle in the parish of Aghanloo, near Limavady.

Sir Robert McClelland brought many members of his own family and other Scots from Galloway to his lands in County Londonderry. Within ten years, largely through the efforts of Sir Robert, there were about a hundred armed British settlers on the Haberdashers' Manor and 106 British settlers on the Clothworkers' Manor. At the time of the census of 1659 the name McClelland, in the form of MacClellan, was most numerous in the baronies of Keenaght and Coleraine in County Londonderry.

McCLINTOCK

In Ireland the McClintocks are found almost exclusively in Ulster, where it is most common in Counties Antrim and Derry. This name was brought to Ulster by settlers from Scotland in the 17th century.

McClintock is derived from Gaelic *Mac Ghille Fhionndaig*, meaning 'son of the devotee of St Fintan'. The McClintocks stem from Luss in Dunbartonshire and Lorn in Argyllshire, where they were recorded at the beginning of the 16th century.

Upheavals such as military incursions, feuds and harvest failures would have encouraged many clan members in the Highlands of Scotland, including McClintocks, to migrate to Ulster as settlers during the 17th century. Owing to the nature of the Scottish clan system once the power and influence of the chief had been weakened and the bond of tribal loyalty broken the clan tended to scatter.

The defeat of the old Gaelic order in the Nine Years War, 1594-1603 and the escape of the most prominent Gaelic Lords of Ulster in 'the Flight of the Earls' in 1607 from Lough Swilly, County Donegal were ultimately responsible for the settlement of many Scottish families in the northern counties of Ireland.

Movement of Scottish settlers to Ulster began in earnest from 1605 in a private enterprise colonisation of counties Antrim and Down when Sir Hugh Montgomery and Sir James Hamilton acquired title to large estates in north Down and Sir Randall MacDonnell, 1st Earl of Antrim, to large tracts of land in north Antrim.

In 1609 the Earl of Salisbury, Lord High Treasurer, suggested to James I a deliberate plantation of Scottish and English colonists on the forfeited estates of the Gaelic chiefs in counties Armagh, Cavan, Donegal, Fermanagh, Londonderry (then known as Coleraine) and Tyrone.

Settlers to Ulster came, by and large, in three waves: with the granting of the initial leases in the period 1605 to 1625; after 1652 and Cromwell's crushing of the Irish rebellion; and finally in the fifteen years after 1690 and the Glorious Revolution. It is estimated by 1715, when migration to Ulster had virtually stopped, the Scottish population of Ulster stood at 200,000.

Scottish families entering Ireland through the port of Londonderry settled in the Foyle Valley which includes much of the fertile lands of counties Donegal, Londonderry and Tyrone.

The 1831 census clearly demonstrates that, in County Derry, the McClintocks settled in the lands surrounding the city of Derry. At the time of the 1831 census there were 20 McClintock households in County Derry, with 15 McClintock households in Templemore Parish and 5 in Clondermot Parish. The city of Derry which was established, in Templemore Parish, as a monastic settlement in 546 AD, has now expanded into the parish of Clondermot. In 1831 seven of the McClintock households were residing in the city of Derry itself.

In Scotland, as early as 1611, McClintock was being anglicised as Lindsay.

McCLOSKEY

The name McCloskey is found almost exclusively in Ulster, and it is most common in County Derry, where it is among the ten most numerous names.

The McCloskey sept trace their lineage to Eogan, son of the 5th century High King of Ireland, Niall of the Nine Hostages, who ruled from the Hill of Tara, County Meath. Eogan and his brother Conall *Gulban* conquered northwest Ireland, ca.425 AD, capturing the great hill-fort of Grianan of Ailech in County Donegal.

Eogan, styled 'King of Ailech', established his own kingdom in the peninsula in County Donegal still called after him Inishowen (Innis Eoghain or Eogan's Isle). His descendants, known as the Cenel Eoghain (the race of Owen), became the principal branch of the Northern Ui Neill (descendants of Niall of the Nine Hostages). The Cenel Eoghain in the next five centuries expanded to the east and south from their focal point in Inishowen.

Ireland was one of the first countries to adopt a system of hereditary surnames which developed from a more ancient system of clan or sept names. The surname was formed by prefixing either Mac (son of) or O (grandson or descendant of) to the ancestor's name.

The McCloskeys are a branch of the O'Cahans. They derive their surname from *Bloscaidh O'Cathain*, whose son Donough, in 1196, slew Murtagh O'Loughlin, heir to the Irish throne, and were thus in Galeic *Mac Bhloscaidh*, i.e. son of Bloskey O'Kane.

The Annals of The Kingdom of Ireland by the Four Masters records, in 1196, this event: 'Murtough, the son of Murtough O'Loughlin, Lord of Kinel-Owen, presumptive heir to the throne of Ireland, destroyer of the cities and castles of the English, was killed by Donough, the son of Blosky O'Kane, at the instigation of the Kinel-Owen. His body was carried to Derry, and there interred with honour and respect.'

The O'Cahans were the leading sept of Clan Connor *Magh Ithe* (Connor was a direct descendant of Eogan). Magh Ithe is the rich countryside stretching southward from Inishowen, later known as the Laggan district in east Donegal. In the 10th century AD the families of Clan Connor moved out from the cramped territory of Magh Ithe and established themselves in County Derry, in the kingdom of Keenaght, to the north of the Sperrin Mountains, from the Foyle to the Bann rivers. In the process they ousted the Cianachta whose leading sept was the O'Connors of Glengiven in the Roe Valley.

By the 12th century when the process of conquest ends the various septs of Clan Connor were firmly settled in County Derry. The McCloskey homeland was the Benady Glen in the valley of the River Roe to the southeast of the town of Dungiven. At the time of the first Ordnance Survey in the early nineteenth century the McCloskeys constituted nearly two-thirds of the population of the parish of Dungiven.

In Ulster and especially in Tyrone the surnames Glasgow and McGlasgow have been noted as variants of McCloskey.

McCOLGAN

This name is almost exclusively found in Ulster, where it is most common in Counties Donegal and Derry.

Ireland was one of the first countries to adopt a system of hereditary surnames which developed from a more ancient system of clan or sept names. From the 11th century each family began to adopt its own distinctive family name generally derived from the first name of an ancestor who lived in or about the 10th century. The surname was formed by prefixing either Mac (son of) or O (grandson or descendant of) to the ancestor's name. Surnames in Ireland, therefore, tended to identify membership of a sept. McColgan is derived from Gaelic *Mac Colgan.*

There were two distinct McColgan septs: one with origins in County Derry and the other was based at Kilcolgan, County Offaly. *The Annals of The Kingdom of Ireland by the Four Masters* (a chronicle of Irish history from 'the earliest period to the year 1616') record, in 1212, the death in battle of Gilchreest Mac Colgan.

It would seem that in early medieval times the prefix O was found with Colgan as well as Mac. In the course of time O'Colgan became McColgan.

The homeland of the McColgan sept of Ulster was on the east side of the river Foyle, in the barony of Tirkeeran, County Derry. O'Dugan, who died in 1372, mentions O'Colgan as lord of this territory. This sept then spread into Inishowen, County Donegal where they became *erenaghs*, i.e. hereditary stewards, of the church lands of Donaghmore.

Sean O Colgain, better known as John Colgan, was born near Carndonagh in Inishowen, County Donegal ca. 1592. He entered the Franciscan order at Louvain in 1620 where he compiled a history of Irish Saints. He was the first to apply the title *The Annals of the Four Masters* to the work of his contemporary Michael O'Clery.

By the middle years of the 19th century the surname McColgan was very much concentrated in Inishowen, County Donegal. At the time of the mid-19th century Griffith's Valuation there were 12 McColgan households in County Derry and 77 McColgan households in County Donegal. Seventy-two of these McColgan households were living in the parishes of Inishowen. They were most concentrated in the northern Inishowen parishes of Donagh, which contained 17 McColgan households, Culdaff with 14 households of the name and Clonmany with 13. Thus over 90% of the descendants of the McColgan sept in County Donegal were living in Inishowen.

This concentration of the surname in Inishowen goes some way to explaining why McColgan is a common name in Derry city today. This surname illustrates the very close links, both historic and economic, between the city of Derry and the Inishowen district of County Donegal. As Derry developed an industrial base in the 19th century in shirt making, shipbuilding and distilling it attracted much of its workforce from Inishowen. In the 90-year period 1821 to 1911 the population of the city quadrupled to 40,780.

McCONNELL

This name is almost exclusive to Ulster where 90% of McConnells in Ireland live. The name is most numerous in Counties Antrim, Down and Tyrone. This name is ultimately of Scottish origin as McConnell is a variant spelling of McDonald.

McConnell, in Gaelic *Mac Dhomhnaill*, means 'son of Donald'. It does not mean 'son of Connell'. The MacDonalds of Scotland, in Gaelic *Mac Dhomhnuill*, meaning 'son of Donald', take their name from Donald of Islay, grandson of Somerled. Under the leadership of Somerled, who expelled the Norsemen from the western side of Scotland in the 12th century, Clan Donald claimed the position of 'The Headship of the Gael'. By the time of his death in 1387, John MacDonald, as Lord of the Isles, controlled the whole of the Hebrides from Lewis to Islay, with the exception of Skye, and the mainland from Kintyre to Knoydart.

Clan Donald acquired new territories in the north of Ireland ca.1400 when one of John's sons, John Mor, married Margery Bissett, an heiress in the Glens of Antrim. Members of the clan had gained a foothold in the Glens in the 13th century through land grants for military service as galloglasses, i.e. mercenary soldiers. By the mid-16th century the MacDonalds, known as the MacDonnells of the Glens, had carved out an extensive territory in County Antrim at the expense of the MacQuillans.

McDonnell became McConnell as in pronouncing the name the D of Dhomhnaill was silent. In Scotland the surname McConnell was mainly found in Argyllshire, Ayrshire and Wigtownshire.

According to Clan Donald genealogical lore the McConnells can trace their ancestry back to Ireland and to *Conn of the Hundred Battles*, King of Connaught, who was killed in 157 AD at Tara, County Meath. Conn's descendants pushed eastwards and northwards out of Connaught, capturing Tara and taking sword land as far north as Inishowen, County Donegal. This expansion was assigned by genealogists to Niall of the Nine Hostages and his sons. The by-product of this northward expansion was the pushing out of the existing peoples in Ulster across the Irish channel to Scotland. By the beginning of the 6th century these Irish Celts, known as Scots, had established themselves in Kintyre, Argyll and some of the Inner Isles. They called their kingdom Dal Riada, after the kingdom they still held in Ulster.

Movement of Scottish settlers to Ulster began in earnest from 1605 in a private enterprise colonisation of counties Antrim and Down when Sir Hugh Montgomery and Sir James Hamilton acquired title to large estates in north Down and Sir Randall MacDonnell, 1st Earl of Antrim, to large tracts of land in north Antrim. In County Antrim the McConnells are most numerous in the baronies of Upper Antrim and Lower Massereene, and in County Down in the barony of Lower Castlereagh.

During the famous 105 day Siege of Derry, from 18 April to 31 July 1689, Robert McConnell was recorded as a 'defender' of the city.

Some McConnells may be descendants of the County Monaghan sept of McConnon, in Gaelic *Mac Canann*, the root word being *cano*, meaning 'wolf cub'. McConnon was, in some instances, anglicised to McConnell.

McCONNELLOGUE

In Ulster, this surname is found almost exclusively in County Donegal and the city of Derry.

Ireland was one of the first countries to adopt a system of hereditary surnames which developed from a more ancient system of clan or sept names. From the 11th century each family began to adopt its own distinctive family name generally derived from the first name of an ancestor who lived in or about the 10th century. The surname was formed by prefixing either Mac (son of) or O (grandson or descendant of) to the ancestor's name. Surnames in Ireland, therefore, tended to identify membership of a sept.

McConnellogue is derived from Gaelic *Mac Dhomhnaill Oig,* meaning 'son of young Daniel'. The homeland of this sept was County Donegal.

The escape of the most prominent Gaelic Lords of Ulster in 'the Flight of the Earls' in 1607 from Lough Swilly, County Donegal marked the end of Gaelic power and paved the way for the 17th century Plantation of Ulster with English and Scottish settlers. In the centuries that followed Gaelic names were anglicised, resulting in many variant spellings of McConnellogue.

At the time of the Griffith's Valuation, which was published between 1857 and 1858, fifty-three McConnellogue households, including variant spellings of the surname, were recorded in County Donegal. This source records that in County Donegal, in the middle years of the 19th century, there were 31 households recorded as McConologe, 10 as McConaloge, 5 as McConalogue, 2 as McConnelloge, 2 as McConnologe, and 1 each as McConneloge, McConnologue and McConologue.

The Griffith's Valuation survey confirms that this name was associated with 2 distinct areas within Donegal. Twenty-four McConnellogue households (i.e. 45% of the Donegal total) were residing at this time in the northeast portion of the Inishowen peninsula; namely 10 in Culdaff parish, 8 in Moville Parish and 6 in Donagh. The other concentration of the name was in the parish of Conwal, near the town of Letterkenny, with 12 McConnellogue households.

McConnellogue is a common name in Derry city today. This name illustrates the very close links, both historic and economic, between the city of Derry and County Donegal and, in particular, the Inishowen district of that county. As Derry developed an industrial base in the 19th century in shirt making, shipbuilding and distilling it attracted much of its workforce from Donegal. In the 90-year period 1821 to 1911 the population of the city quadrupled to 40,780. In this period Derry stamped her dominance over local rivals and emerged as an important urban centre within Ireland.

This surname doesn't begin to appear in the records of Derry city until the census of 1831. By the time of the 1901 census there were 49 McConnellogues living in the city of Derry.

McCONOMY

This surname is found almost exclusively in Counties Derry and Tyrone. This name was often changed to Conway. Indeed, at the turn of the 20th century Conway was still being used interchangeably with McConomy in Counties Derry and Tyrone. McConway and McConaway are forms of McConomy still found in County Donegal.

Ireland was one of the first countries to adopt a system of hereditary surnames which developed from a more ancient system of clan or sept names. From the 11th century each family began to adopt its own distinctive family name generally derived from the first name of an ancestor who lived in or about the 10th century. The surname was formed by prefixing either Mac (son of) or O (grandson or descendant of) to the ancestor's name. Surnames in Ireland, therefore, tended to identify membership of a sept.

McConomy is derived from Gaelic *Mac Conmidhe*, meaning 'son of the hound of Meath'. This sept originated on the lands straddling the border between Counties Derry and Tyrone.

The anglicisation of Gaelic names, from the 17th century, resulted in many variant spellings of the same name and, in many cases, the dropping of the O and Mac prefixes.

Although Conway is Welsh in origin, derived from the river and town of Conwy in north Wales, the surname Conway is usually of Irish origin. A number of Irish septs adopted Conway as the anglicised form of their name. In addition to the McConomys of Ulster: Irish septs such as Kanavaghan, in Gaelic *O Connmhachain*, of County Mayo; Conboy, in Gaelic *O Conbhuidhe*, of Easky, County Sligo; McNama, in Gaelic *Mac Conmeadha*, of County Leitrim; and Conoo, in Gaelic *Mac Conmhaigh*, of County Clare have, by and large, been changed to Conway.

Most Conways in Ulster will be descended from the County Derry-Tyrone sept of *Mac Conmidhe*.

McConway was a common name in Donegal but there was no sept of McConway in County Donegal. There was, however, one of O'Conway or Conboy in the adjacent County of Sligo. It is possible that the Anglo-Norman military incursions of the 13th century into Connaught which reduced the power and influence of many septs in that province encouraged ancestors of the McConways to migrate north to Donegal.

At the time of the 1831 census, in County Derry, there were 43 Conway households, 14 McConomy households and 4 McConway households. By contrast, in County Donegal, at the time of the mid-19th century Griffith's Valuation there were 17 McConway households, 4 McConomy households and 1 Conway household.

Lieutenant Edward McConway and Ensign Terence McConway were officers in James II's army that besieged the city of Derry during the famous 105 day Siege of Derry, from 18 April to 31 July 1689.

McCONWAY

This surname, which is a variant of McConomy, is found almost exclusively in Counties Derry and Donegal. This name was often changed to Conway. Indeed, at the turn of the 20th century Conway was still being used interchangeably with McConomy in Counties Derry and Tyrone.

Ireland was one of the first countries to adopt a system of hereditary surnames which developed from a more ancient system of clan or sept names. From the 11th century each family began to adopt its own distinctive family name generally derived from the first name of an ancestor who lived in or about the 10th century. The surname was formed by prefixing either Mac (son of) or O (grandson or descendant of) to the ancestor's name. Surnames in Ireland, therefore, tended to identify membership of a sept.

McConway is derived from Gaelic *Mac Conmidhe*, meaning 'son of the hound of Meath'. This sept originated on the lands straddling the border between Counties Derry and Tyrone.

The anglicisation of Gaelic names, from the 17th century, resulted in many variant spellings of the same name and, in many cases, the dropping of the O and Mac prefixes.

Although Conway is Welsh in origin, derived from the river and town of Conwy in north Wales, the surname Conway is usually of Irish origin. A number of Irish septs adopted Conway as the anglicised form of their name. In addition to the McConomys of Ulster: Irish septs such as Kanavaghan, in Gaelic *O Connmhachain*, of County Mayo; Conboy, in Gaelic *O Conbhuidhe*, of Easky, County Sligo; McNama, in Gaelic *Mac Conmeadha*, of County Leitrim; and Conoo, in Gaelic *Mac Conmhaigh*, of County Clare have, by and large, been changed to Conway.

Most Conways in Ulster will be descended from the County Derry-Tyrone sept of *Mac Conmidhe*.

McConway was a common name in Donegal but there was no sept of McConway in County Donegal. There was, however, one of O'Conway or Conboy in the adjacent County of Sligo. It is possible that the Anglo-Norman military incursions of the 13th century into Connaught which reduced the power and influence of many septs in that province encouraged ancestors of the McConways to migrate north to Donegal.

At the time of the 1831 census, in County Derry, there were 43 Conway households, 14 McConomy households and 4 McConway households. By contrast, in County Donegal, at the time of the mid-19th century Griffith's Valuation there were 17 McConway households, 4 McConomy households and 1 Conway household.

Lieutenant Edward McConway and Ensign Terence McConway were officers in James II's army that besieged the city of Derry during the famous 105 day Siege of Derry, from 18 April to 31 July 1689.

McCOOL

This name is most common in Ulster in its homeland, County Donegal and in County Tyrone.

Ireland was one of the first countries to adopt a system of hereditary surnames which developed from a more ancient system of clan or sept names. From the 11th century each family began to adopt its own distinctive family name generally derived from the first name of an ancestor who lived in or about the 10th century. The surname was formed by prefixing either Mac (son of) or O (grandson or descendant of) to the ancestor's name. Surnames in Ireland, therefore, tended to identify membership of a sept.

The origins of the name McCool are not certain. It has been suggested that the McCool sept, derived from *Mac Giolla Comhghaill*, meaning 'son of the devotee of St Comhghal' or from *Mac Comhghaill*, originated in the Raphoe area of County Donegal. This name has also been made Cole, which is a common English surname, in the Glenties area of Donegal.

In Scotland MacCool can be a variant of MacDougall, Gaelic *Mac Dhughaill*. In a few cases, therefore, the name may have come with Scottish immigrants at the time of the Plantation of Ulster in the 17th century.

McCool has also become confused with Coyle. Although the surnames of McCool and Coyle have quite distinct origins their ultimate origins have become confused as a result of anglicisation. Both names originated in Donegal with the Mac prefix. In some cases people bearing the surname McCool may originally have been descended from families that belonged to the Coyle sept.

Coyle is derived from Gaelic *Mac Giolla Chomhgaill*, meaning 'son of the devotee of St Comgal'. St Comgal was the patron of Galloon parish in south Fermanagh. This sept was based in the parish of Meevagh in the barony of Kilmacrenan in County Donegal. The name was first anglicised as McIlhoyle, then McCoyle and finally Coyle. One branch of the Coyles were *erenaghs*, i.e. hereditary stewards, of the church lands in Galloon Parish, County Fermanagh.

Coyle is most numerous in its homeland, County Donegal and in Counties Derry, Tyrone and Cavan. Coyle is among the top ten names in the city of Derry today, illustrating the very close links between the city of Derry and County Donegal. As Derry developed an industrial base in the 19th century in shirt making, shipbuilding and distilling it attracted much of its workforce from Donegal.

Owing to the mistaken belief that the Gaelic word *coill*, meaning 'wood', was part of this sept's name, *Mac Giolla Chomhgaill* was often anglicised to Woods.

McCORKELL

This name, of Scottish origin, belongs to Counties Donegal and Derry.

McCorkell is derived from *Mac Thorcuill*, meaning 'son of Thorcull', an Old Norse Norse personal name, meaning 'Thor's kettle'. The McCorkells were a branch of Clan Gunn, who occupied the northern areas of Caithness and Sutherland. Clan Gunn claim descent from the Viking chief Gunni who was killed in Dublin in 1171. By 1594 Clan Gunn was listed as one of the 'broken clans' of the north.

Upheavals such as military incursions, feuds and harvest failures would have encouraged many clan members, including McCorkells, to migrate to Ulster as settlers during the 17th century. Owing to the nature of the Scottish clan system once the power and influence of the chief had been weakened or broken the clan tended to disintegrate. Bearing the surname McCorkell simply indicated that you were a follower of the Clan Gunn chief. Not every clan member was related by blood. Their bond, however, whether they had a common tribal ancestor or not, was their common rule by a chief with loyalty to one's clan being the primary obligation. Once tribal loyalty was broken clans 'scattered'.

In 1609 James I adopted the policy to encourage Scottish settlers to settle on the forfeited estates of the Gaelic chiefs in counties Armagh, Cavan, Donegal, Fermanagh, Londonderry (then known as Coleraine) and Tyrone. Scottish families entering Ireland through the port of Londonderry settled in the Foyle Valley which includes much of the fertile lands of counties Donegal, Londonderry and Tyrone. It is estimated by 1715, when migration to Ulster had virtually stopped, the Scottish population of Ulster stood at 200,000.

McCorkell can also be a shortened form of McCorquodale. McCorquodale is derived from Gaelic *Mac Corcadail*, meaning 'son of Thorketill', an Old Norse Norse personal name, meaning 'Thor's kettle'. Clan MacCorquodale, claiming descent from the MacLeods of Lewis, held lands on the northern side of Loch Awe which they had been granted by Kenneth MacAlpine, the 9th century King of Scotland.

The McCorkell family of Ballyarnett, Londonderry are descended from William McCorkell who founded the shipping line of William McCorkell & Co. in 1778. This company initially acted as agents for American-owned ships in the passenger trade from Londonderry to North America. In 1815, they bought their first ship, the *Marcus Hill*, for the passenger trade. From 1815 until 1897 when their last vessel, the *Hiawatha*, was sold the McCorkell Line owned 26 ships. In the 1860s William McCorkell & Co. demonstrated that first-class sailing ships, such as the *Minnehaha*, known in its New York, East River berth as "the green yacht from Derry", could compete with steamships on the North American passenger run.

According to family tradition the McCorkells, who supported the Jacobite cause in Scotland, sought refuge in Ulster after the defeat of Bonnie Prince Charlie following the rebellion of 1745. Three brothers named McCorquodale, including William the founder of the shipping firm, who were supporters of the Prince, had to escape and rowed in an open boat from the west coast of Scotland to the Antrim coast. On arriving in Ireland, wishing to cover their tracks, they assumed the name McCorkell.

160

McCORMICK

McCormick can be an Irish or a Scottish name. This name is one of the fifty most common names in Ulster where it is most numerous in Counties Antrim and Down.

Ireland was one of the first countries to adopt a system of hereditary surnames which developed from a more ancient system of clan or sept names. The surname was formed by prefixing either Mac (son of) or O (grandson or descendant of) to the ancestor's name.

McCormick is derived from Gaelic *Mac Cormaic*, meaning 'son of Cormac'. In County Fermanagh the McCormicks were a branch of the Maguires, the pre-eminent family in Fermanagh from the thirteenth to the seventeenth century. The seat of this sept was at Kilmacormick, meaning 'McCormick's wood', in the parish of Trory, County Fermanagh.

However, it is believed that elsewhere in Ulster McCormick was adopted by many unrelated families, quite late on, as a fixed surname, based on the father's first name of Cormac. In some cases, particularly in Counties Down and Derry, some McCormicks were originally O'Cormack or O'Cormacan, in Gaelic *O Cormacain*.

Many of the McCormick families in Ulster will be descendants of 17th century settlers from Scotland. McCormick, recorded as a surname in Scotland as early as 1132, is derived from Gaelic *Mac Cormaic*, meaning 'son of Cormac'. In the Highlands of Scotland the McCormicks were recognised as a sept of Clan MacLaine of Lochbuie on the island of Mull. Clan MacLaine of Lochbuie were followers of the MacDonalds, Lords of the Isles. The MacDonalds gained a foothold in Ulster in the Glens of Antrim in the 13th century through land grants for military service as galloglasses, i.e. mercenary soldiers.

There was also a McCormack sept in Stirlingshire, followers of Clan Buchanan, on the east side of Loch Lomond.

Upheavals such as military incursions, feuds and harvest failures would have encouraged many clan members, including McCormicks, to migrate to Ulster as settlers during the 17th century. Owing to the nature of the Scottish clan system once the power and influence of the chief had been weakened and the bond of tribal loyalty broken the clan tended to scatter.

Movement of Scottish settlers to Ulster began in earnest from 1605 in a private enterprise colonisation of counties Antrim and Down when Sir Hugh Montgomery and Sir James Hamilton acquired title to large estates in north Down and Sir Randall MacDonnell, 1st Earl of Antrim, to large tracts of land in north Antrim. By the mid-19th century the McCormicks were concentrated in the barony of Cary in north Antrim, and in the Ards peninsula in County Down.

During the famous 105 day Siege of Derry, from 18 April to 31 July 1689, Captain James McCormick of Lisburn, County Antrim, William McCormac of County Down and Captain William McCormac of Enniskillen, County Fermanagh were recorded as 'defenders' of the city.

McCOURT

This name is found in all the provinces in Ireland but especially Ulster, particularly in Counties Antrim, Armagh and Monaghan.

Ireland was one of the first countries to adopt a system of hereditary surnames which developed from a more ancient system of clan or sept names. From the 11th century each family began to adopt its own distinctive family name generally derived from the first name of an ancestor who lived in or about the 10th century. The surname was formed by prefixing either Mac (son of) or O (grandson or descendant of) to the ancestor's name. Surnames in Ireland, therefore, tended to identify membership of a sept.

McCourt, in Gaelic *Mac Cuarta* or *Mac Cuairt,* was an Oriel sept, which was based in southwest Armagh. The ancient territory of Oriel included Counties Armagh and Monaghan and parts of south Down, Louth and Fermanagh. The parish of Cappagh, near Dungannon, County Tyrone was originally in Gaelic *Ceapach Mhic Cuarta.*

The escape of the most prominent Gaelic Lords of Ulster in 'the Flight of the Earls' in 1607 from Lough Swilly, County Donegal marked the end of Gaelic power and paved the way for the 17th century Plantation of Ulster with English and Scottish settlers.

In the centuries that followed Gaelic names were anglicised, resulting in many variant spellings of the same name and, in many cases, the dropping of the O and Mac prefixes. In the Hearth Money Rolls of 1664 for County Armagh the name was recorded as MacQuorte. Courtney can also be an anglicised form of McCourt. Seamus Mac Cuarta, 1647-1732, the Gaelic poet was also known as James McCourt or Courtney.

McCord, which is a common name in County Antrim, is a variant of McCourt. McCourt and McCord are old surnames in the parish of Ballantrae in Ayrshire, Scotland. References to this surname are found in Wigtownshire from the 15th century; Nigel McCorde is recorded in this Scottish county in 1471 and Gilbert Makcorde in 1473. This region was home to many of the Scottish settlers who came to Ulster throughout the 17th century.

It is, therefore, possible that some McCourts in Ulster may be descendants of 17th century Scottish settlers. Movement of Scottish settlers to Ulster began in earnest from 1605 in a private enterprise colonisation of counties Antrim and Down when Sir Hugh Montgomery and Sir James Hamilton acquired title to large estates in north Down and Sir Randall MacDonnell, 1st Earl of Antrim, to large tracts of land in north Antrim.

Further impetus came in 1609 when James I adopted the policy to encourage English and Scottish settlers to settle on the forfeited estates of the Gaelic chiefs in counties Armagh, Cavan, Donegal, Fermanagh, Londonderry (then known as Coleraine) and Tyrone. It is estimated by 1715, when migration to Ulster had virtually stopped, the Scottish population of Ulster stood at 200,000.

McCOY

McCoy is found throughout Ireland but it is common only in Ulster, where it is found mainly in Counties Antrim, Armagh and Monaghan. This name is a variant of Scottish Mackay.

McCoy is derived from Gaelic *Mac Aoidh*, meaning 'son of Hugh'. This name was also anglicised as Mackay, Mackie, McCay, McKay and McKee. Clan Mackay, claiming descent from Morgund of Pluscarden, originated in Moray. This clan came to prominence in Sutherland in the 13th century and by 1427 the chief, Angus Dow MacKay, could muster an army of 4000 men. In Inverness-shire the Mackays were a sept of Clan Davidson, and in Kintyre and Galloway the MacKays, MacKies and Mackies were followers of Clan Donald.

The first McCoys in Ireland were Clan Donald galloglasses, i.e. mercenary soldiers. As followers of Clan Donald they came over to Ulster from Kintyre and the southern isles of Scotland such as Islay to fight for the McDonnells of the Glens of Antrim. Like the McDonnells some of the McCoys went south to Munster, hence the families of this name found in Counties Cork and Limerick today.

Clan Donald had acquired new territories in the north of Ireland ca.1400 when John Mor MacDonald had married Margery Bissett, an heiress in the Glens of Antrim. By the mid-16th century the MacDonalds, known as the MacDonnells of the Glens, had carved out an extensive territory in County Antrim at the expense of the MacQuillans.

Movement of Scottish settlers to Ulster began in earnest from 1605 in a private enterprise colonisation of counties Antrim and Down when Sir Hugh Montgomery and Sir James Hamilton acquired title to large estates in north Down and Sir Randall MacDonnell, 1st Earl of Antrim, to large tracts of land in north Antrim. Further impetus came in 1609 when James I adopted the policy to encourage Scottish settlers to settle on the forfeited estates of the Gaelic chiefs in counties Armagh, Cavan, Donegal, Fermanagh, Londonderry (then known as Coleraine) and Tyrone.

Confusion arises as the Gaelic surname *Mac Aoidh* has acquired in the process of anglicisation a great number of variants. Thus the McCoy family of Drumard in Tamlaght O'Crilly Parish, County Londonderry were recorded as McCoy in the 1831 census, as McCay in the tithe book of 1833 and as McKay in the Griffith's Valuation of 1859.

In Ireland, particularly in Counties Donegal and Fermanagh, Gaelic *Mac Aodha*, meaning 'son of Hugh', was usually anglicised as McHugh and McCue but also as McCoy and McKee. Thus in west Ulster Irish McHugh can become indistinguishable from Scottish McCoy.

During the famous 105 day Siege of Derry, from 18 April to 31 July 1689, General Andrew Mackay, Ensign William Mackie, Lieutenant William Mackey, Lieutenant Mackie, Lieutenant Mackay, John Mackay, Josiah Macky and Jannett Mackee were recorded as 'defenders' of the city. On the opposing side Lieutenant Daniel McKay and Ensign Hugh McKay were officers in the 'Jacobite army' which besieged the city of Derry.

163

McCRACKEN

In Ireland McCracken is almost exclusive to Ulster, where one-half of those of the name are in County Antrim and one-quarter in County Down. This name was brought to Ulster in large numbers by settlers from Scotland in the 17th century.

McCracken is regarded as a variant, in the province of Galloway, of the Argyllshire clan name of MacNaughton. Clan MacNaughton, in Gaelic *Mac Neachdainn*, meaning 'son of Nechtan', claims descent from the 8th century Pictish king Nechtan. In the 13th century the clan was found in Lochawe, Glenaray, Glenshire and Loch Fyne in Argyllshire.

In the 14th century Dundarave, on the north shore of Loch Fyne, became the stronghold of Clan MacNaughton. In 1627 Colonel Alexander MacNaughten raised a company of 200 Highland bowmen for service in the expedition to France for the relief of La Rochelle. Clan MacNaughton held their lands at Dundarave until 1700 when the last chief, John MacNaughten lost them to the Campbells of Ardkinglas who held the lands on the southern side of Loch Fyne.

The MacNaughtons were one of the families brought in by the MacDonnells of the Glens of Antrim in the early 17th century. Shane Dhu, or Black John MacNaghten, became the Earl of Antrim's chief agent. John was buried in the family burial ground at Bonamargy Friary near Ballycastle, County Antrim.

It is known that migration from Argyll, and in particular from Kintyre, into Galloway began in the mid-eighth century. By the early years of the sixteenth century McCracken was established as a surname in Galloway, especially in Wigtown, in southwest Scotland. This region, in turn, was home to many of the Scottish settlers who came to Ulster throughout the 17th century.

Movement of Scottish settlers to Ulster began in earnest from 1605 in a private enterprise colonisation of counties Antrim and Down when Sir Hugh Montgomery and Sir James Hamilton acquired title to large estates in north Down and Sir Randall MacDonnell, 1st Earl of Antrim, to large tracts of land in north Antrim. By the mid-19th century the McCrackens were located throughout County Antrim, and concentrated in the central Ards peninsula in County Down.

Further impetus came in 1609 when James I adopted the policy to encourage Scottish settlers to settle on the forfeited estates of the Gaelic chiefs in counties Armagh, Cavan, Donegal, Fermanagh, Londonderry (then known as Coleraine) and Tyrone.
These settlers came to Ulster, by and large, in three waves: with the granting of the initial leases in the period 1605 to 1625; after 1652 and Cromwell's crushing of the Irish rebellion; and finally in the fifteen years after 1690 and the Glorious Revolution.

Scottish families entering Ireland through the port of Londonderry settled in the Foyle Valley which includes much of the fertile lands of counties Donegal, Londonderry and Tyrone

It is estimated by 1715, when migration to Ulster had virtually stopped, the Scottish population of Ulster stood at 200,000.

McCREA

In Ireland this name is almost exclusive to Ulster, where it is most common in Counties Antrim and Tyrone. This name was brought to Ulster by settlers from Scotland in the 17th century.

McCrea is derived from Gaelic *Macrath*, meaning 'son of grace' or 'prosperity'. Clan Mac-Rae are said to have settled in Kintail in Wester Ross in the 14th century, and they became Chamberlains of Kintail under the MacKenzies. Eilean Donan Castle, built in the 13th century, on the Kyle of Lochalsh was held by the MacRaes. As hereditary bodyguards to the chief of Clan MacKenzie the McCreas were known as 'MacKenzie's Shirt of Mail'.

Upheavals such as military incursions, feuds and harvest failures would have encouraged many clan members, including MacRaes, to migrate to Ulster as settlers during the 17th century. Owing to the nature of the Scottish clan system once the power and influence of the chief had been weakened and the bond of tribal loyalty broken the clan tended to scatter.

The surname McCrea also originated independently in other parts of Scotland as the old personal name Macrath was in widespread use before the adoption of fixed surnames. Mc-Crea and McCrae are common names in Ayrshire, and this region was home to many of the Scottish settlers who came to Ulster throughout the 17th century. Makcrie and Makreith were common forms of the name in Ayrshire in the 16th century.

Movement of Scottish settlers to Ulster began in earnest from 1605 in a private enterprise colonisation of counties Antrim and Down when Sir Hugh Montgomery and Sir James Hamilton acquired title to large estates in north Down and Sir Randall MacDonnell, 1st Earl of Antrim, to large tracts of land in north Antrim. Further impetus came in 1609 when James I adopted the policy to encourage Scottish settlers to settle on the forfeited estates of the Gaelic chiefs in counties Armagh, Cavan, Donegal, Fermanagh, Londonderry (then known as Coleraine) and Tyrone.

Settlers to Ulster came, by and large, in three waves: with the granting of the initial leases in the period 1605 to 1625; after 1652 and Cromwell's crushing of the Irish rebellion; and finally in the fifteen years after 1690 and the Glorious Revolution.

Scottish families entering Ireland through the port of Londonderry settled in the Foyle Valley which includes much of the fertile lands of counties Donegal, Londonderry and Tyrone. It is estimated by 1715, when migration to Ulster had virtually stopped, the Scottish population of Ulster stood at 200,000.

During the famous 105 day Siege of Derry, from 18 April to 31 July 1689, Ann McCrea was recorded as one of the 'defenders' of the city.

In Ulster, as in Scotland, this name was often shortened to Rea.

165

McCREADY

This surname is found exclusively in Ulster where it is most common in Counties Down, Derry and Antrim.

Ireland was one of the first countries to adopt a system of hereditary surnames which developed from a more ancient system of clan or sept names. From the 11th century each family began to adopt its own distinctive family name generally derived from the first name of an ancestor who lived in or about the 10th century. The surname was formed by prefixing either Mac (son of) or O (grandson or descendant of) to the ancestor's name. Surnames in Ireland, therefore, tended to identify membership of a sept.

McCready is derived from Gaelic *Mac Riada*. The McCreadys were *erenaghs*, i.e. hereditary stewards, of the church lands of Tullaghobegley, a parish consisting of rugged land between the Rosses and Bloody Foreland in west Donegal. Descended from this sept was 'Father Donogh MacReidy, of Coleraine, Dean of Derry, who in 1608 suffered martyrdom by being pulled asunder by four horses.'

By the time of the mid-19th century Griffith's Valuation, however, there were no McCready households recorded in the parish of Tullaghobegley. Fifty McCready households – 27 as McCready and 23 as McReady - were recorded in County Donegal in this survey, with the biggest concentration in the parish of Kilteevoge which contained 15 McCready households. In other words 30% of descendants of the McCready sept in County Donegal were living in this one parish.

Many County Donegal septs trace their lineage to Conall *Gulban*, son of the 5th century High King of Ireland, Niall of the Nine Hostages, who ruled from the Hill of Tara, County Meath. Conall and his brother Eogan conquered northwest Ireland, ca.425 AD, capturing the great hill-fort of Grianan of Ailech in County Donegal which commanded the entrance to the Inishowen peninsula.

Conall, styled 'King of Tir Conaill', established his own kingdom in County Donegal called after him Tyrconnel, i.e. the 'Land of Conall', which was the ancient name of Donegal. His descendants, known as the Cenel Conaill (the race of Conall), firmly established themselves in County Donegal while those descended from Conal's brother Eogan expanded to the east and south into Counties Derry and Tyrone.

McCready is a common name in Derry city today. The name spread to Derry city in the 19th century. As Derry developed an industrial base in shirt making, shipbuilding and distilling it attracted much of its workforce from County Donegal. In the 90-year period 1821 to 1911 the population of the city quadrupled to 40,780.

In County Derry McCready has been used as an abbreviated form of McConready, in Gaelic *Mac Conriada*.

It is quite likely that some McCreadys in Ulster will be descendants of 17th century Scottish settlers. In Scotland, the surname is recorded as MacRedie in Ayrshire and as MacReadie and MacCreadie in Galloway. These two regions were home to many of the Scottish settlers who came to Ulster throughout the 17th century.

McCRORY

McCrory, and variants such as Macrory, McGrory and McRory, can be an Irish or a Scottish name. This name is virtually exclusive to Ulster, where over one-half are in Tyrone and one-third are in County Antrim.

Ireland was one of the first countries to adopt a system of hereditary surnames which developed from a more ancient system of clan or sept names. The surname was formed by prefixing either Mac (son of) or O (grandson or descendant of) to the ancestor's name.

McCrory is derived from Gaelic *Mac Ruaidhri*, meaning 'son of Rory'. There were two distinct McCrory septs in Ulster. It is claimed that the County Tyrone sept of the name trace their descent from the Three Collas. *Colla Uais*, High King of Ireland from 322 to 326 AD, and his two brothers are reputed to have burnt and destroyed Navan Fort in County Armagh. Navan Fort, built ca.300 BC, was the residence of the warrior kings of Ulster, and of Cuchullain and his legendary Red Branch Knights. The Three Collas were banished to Scotland in 326 AD.

A branch of this County Tyrone sept migrated to County Derry where they became *erenaghs*, i.e. hereditary stewards, of the church lands in the parish of Ballynascreen in the barony of Loughinsholin. Another McCrory sept were *erenaghs* of Machaire Croise in Fermanagh. It is believed that they were a branch of the Maguires.

McCrory in Gaelic *Mac Ruairidh*, meaning 'son of Rory', is also a Scottish name. They were an important sept of Clan Donald. In the 14th century some of these families came to Ulster as galloglasses. Derived from Gaelic *galloglach*, galloglass refers to a paid soldier, often brought over from Scotland, to fight on behalf of an Irish chief.

The Annals of The Kingdom of Ireland by the Four Masters provide detailed and graphic descriptions of the Scottish galloglasses. In one account dated 1557 the *Annals* describe the galloglass in the camp of the O'Neills who were on a raiding expedition into O'Donnell territory in Donegal. It states that 'sixty grim and redoubtable gallowglasses, with sharp, keen axes, terrible and ready for action, and sixty stern and terrific Scots, with massive, broad, and heavy-striking swords in their hands, ready to strike and parry, were watching and guarding the son of O'Neill.'

The majority of Scottish McCrorys in Ulster, however, will be descendants of 17th century settlers. Movement of Scottish settlers to Ulster began in earnest from 1605 in a private enterprise colonisation of counties Antrim and Down when Sir Hugh Montgomery and Sir James Hamilton acquired title to large estates in north Down and Sir Randall MacDonnell, 1st Earl of Antrim, to large tracts of land in north Antrim.

As followers of Clan Donald many Scottish McCrorys settled in the Glens of Antrim. Clan Donald had acquired territory here ca.1400. By the mid-16th century the MacDonalds, known as the MacDonnells of the Glens, had carved out an extensive territory in County Antrim at the expense of the MacQuillans.

In many cases McCrory was further anglicised to Rogers and Rodgers.

McCROSSAN

This name is mainly found in County Donegal and in the adjacent counties of Derry and Tyrone.

Ireland was one of the first countries to adopt a system of hereditary surnames which developed from a more ancient system of clan or sept names. From the 11th century each family began to adopt its own distinctive family name generally derived from the first name of an ancestor who lived in or about the 10th century. The surname was formed by prefixing either Mac (son of) or O (grandson or descendant of) to the ancestor's name. Surnames in Ireland, therefore, tended to identify membership of a sept.

McCrossan is derived from Gaelic *Mac an Chrosain*, the root word being *cros*, meaning 'cross'. There were two distinct septs of the name. In Leinster, the McCrossans of County Leix were hereditary poets to the O'Mores and O'Connors. This link is commemorated in the place name of Ballymacrossan which lies on the border of Leix and Offaly. In this region, however, McCrossan was usually anglicised to Crosbie.

Most bearers of the surname today are descended from the McCrossan sept of County Donegal. This sept provided two Bishops of Raphoe in the 14th century, namely Henry Mac an Crossan and Richard MacCrossan.

Many County Donegal septs trace their lineage to Conall *Gulban*, son of the 5th century High King of Ireland, Niall of the Nine Hostages, who ruled from the Hill of Tara, County Meath. Conall and his brother Eogan conquered northwest Ireland, ca.425 AD, capturing the great hill-fort of Grianan of Ailech in County Donegal which commanded the entrance to the Inishowen peninsula.

Conall, styled 'King of Tir Conaill', established his own kingdom in County Donegal called after him Tyrconnel, i.e. the 'Land of Conall', which was the ancient name of Donegal. His descendants, known as the Cenel Conaill (the race of Conall), firmly established themselves in County Donegal while those descended from Conal's brother Eogan expanded to the east and south into Counties Derry and Tyrone.

At the time of the mid-19th century Griffith's Valuation 68 Crossan households – 63 of Crossan and 5 of McCrossan - were recorded in County Donegal. This source clearly shows that the name was most concentrated in the valley of the River Swilly around the town of Letterkenny. At this time 17 Crossan households were recorded in Aghanunshin Parish and a further 10 in the adjoining parish of Conwal. In other words 40% of descendants of the McCrossan sept in County Donegal were living in these two adjoining parishes.

McCrossan is a common name in Derry city today. This name, which spread to Derry city in the 19th century, illustrates the very close links, both historic and economic, between the city of Derry and County Donegal. As Derry developed an industrial base in shirt making, shipbuilding and distilling it attracted much of its workforce from County Donegal. In the 90-year period 1821 to 1911 the population of the city quadrupled to 40,780.

McCUE

McCue is a form of McHugh which is found in Counties Fermanagh and Donegal. The surname McHugh is very numerous in Counties Galway, Mayo and Leitrim in north Connaught and in Counties Donegal and Fermanagh in west Ulster.

Ireland was one of the first countries to adopt a system of hereditary surnames which developed from a more ancient system of clan or sept names. From the 11th century each family began to adopt its own distinctive family name generally derived from the first name of an ancestor who lived in or about the 10th century. The surname was formed by prefixing either Mac (son of) or O (grandson or descendant of) to the ancestor's name. Surnames in Ireland, therefore, tended to identify membership of a sept.

McCue is derived from Gaelic *Mac Aodha*, meaning 'son of Hugh'. There were two distinct McHugh septs in County Galway: one was located near Tuam and the other, a branch of the O'Flahertys, in Connemara. It is believed that these two County Galway septs were the forebears of most McHugh families in Ireland today.

It has been claimed that the McHughs of Donegal and Fermanagh are a branch of the Maguires, the pre-eminent family in Fermanagh from the thirteenth to the seventeenth century. They trace their descent from Aodh, a grandson of Donn Carrach Maguire. Donn Carrach Maguire, who died in 1302, was the first Maguire chief of all Fermanagh.

Confusion arises as the Gaelic surname *Mac Aodha* has acquired in the process of anglicisation a great number of variants. These include McCoy, McHugh, McKay, McKee and Hughes. McCue is the commonest variant spelling of McHugh.

In Scotland Gaelic *Mac Aoidh*, meaning 'son of Hugh', was anglicised as Mackay and also as Mackie, McCay, McCoy, McKay and McKee. Clan Mackay, claiming descent from Morgund of Pluscarden, originated in Moray. This clan came to prominence in Sutherland in the 13th century and by 1427 the chief, Angus Dow MacKay, could muster an army of 4000 men. In Inverness-shire the Mackays were a sept of Clan Davidson, and in Kintyre and Galloway the MacKays, MacKies and Mackies were followers of Clan Donald.

The first Mackays in Ireland, also known as McCoys, were Clan Donald galloglasses, i.e. mercenary soldiers. As followers of Clan Donald they came over to Ulster from Kintyre and the southern isles of Scotland such as Islay to fight for the McDonnells of the Glens of Antrim.

Although the surname McCue is regarded to be of Irish origin it is known, particularly in Fermanagh and Donegal, that some descendants of the Irish sept *Mac Aodha* now bear surnames such as McCoy and McKee. Thus in west Ulster, in particular, Irish McCue and McHugh can become indistinguishable from Scottish Mackay.

It is also possible that some McHughs in Ulster are descended from the Clan Donald sept of McHugh. However, in most cases, McHugh was anglicised as Houston in Scotland.

McCULLAGH

McCullagh can be an Irish or a Scottish name. This name is one of the fifty most common names in Ulster and it is most concentrated in Counties Antrim, Tyrone and Down. Eighty percent of those of the name in Ireland are located in Ulster.

The Ulster Gaelic names *Mac Cu Uladh* or *Mac Con Uladh*, meaning 'son of the hound of Ulster' were anglicised as McCullagh. These names originated east of the River Bann in the ancient kingdom of Dal Riata. From the 6th century Irish Celts from Dalriada, known as the Scots, established a kingdom in Kintyre and Argyll. This kingdom in Scotland was also called Dal Riata.

In the census of 1659 McCullough was listed as one of the 'principal Irish names' in the baronies of Antrim, Belfast, Carrickfergus and Toome in County Antrim and also in the barony of Iveagh, County Down. However, many of these must have been Scottish.

Many of the Ulster McCullaghs stem originally from Scotland where the name is usually spelt MacCulloch. In Scotland MacCullochs were located in the Highlands in both Easter Ross and Argyllshire, and in Galloway in southwest Scotland.

The MacCullochs of Oban in Argyllshire belonged to Clan Dougall and were originally, in Gaelic, *Mac Lulaich*, meaning the 'son of Lulach'. Lulach succeeded MacBeth as the King of Scots in 1057. The MacCullochs also owned considerable lands beside Dornoch Firth in Easter Ross. Upheavals such as military incursions, feuds and harvest failures would have encouraged many families in the Highlands, including MacCullochs, to migrate to Ulster as settlers during the 17th century.

Movement of Scottish settlers to Ulster began in earnest from 1605 in a private enterprise colonisation of counties Antrim and Down when Sir Hugh Montgomery and Sir James Hamilton acquired title to large estates in north Down and Sir Randall MacDonnell, 1st Earl of Antrim, to large tracts of land in north Antrim. Further impetus came in 1609 when James I adopted the policy to encourage Scottish settlers to settle on the forfeited estates of the Gaelic chiefs in counties Armagh, Cavan, Donegal, Fermanagh, Londonderry (then known as Coleraine) and Tyrone.

At the time of this plantation MacCulloch, possibly derived from Scots Gaelic *Mac Cullaich*, meaning 'son of the boar', was already common in the province of Galloway. The name first appears in 1296 when Thomas Maculagh of Wigtown paid homage to Edward I of England. This region was home to many of the Scottish settlers who came to Ulster throughout the 17th century.

Indeed James MacCulloch of Wigtownshire was one of the principal Scottish planters (sixty-one in total) of the Ulster Plantation, and in 1610 he was granted an estate of 1000 acres in Glenties, County Donegal. Many of the settlers farming on this estate would also have been called McCulloch as it was a feature of 17th century Scotland for tenants to take on their landlord's surname.

It is estimated by 1715, when migration to Ulster had virtually stopped, the Scottish population of Ulster stood at 200,000.

McCULLOCH

McCullagh, McCullough and McCulloch together constitute one of the fifty most common names in Ulster and it is most concentrated in Counties Antrim, Tyrone and Down. These names can be of Irish or Scottish origin. In Scotland the name is usually spelt McCulloch. In Ulster McCullagh or McCullough are the more common forms of the name.

The Ulster Gaelic names *Mac Cu Uladh* or *Mac Con Uladh*, meaning 'son of the hound of Ulster' were anglicised as McCullough. These names originated east of the River Bann in the ancient kingdom of Dal Riata. From the 6th century Irish Celts from Dalriada, known as the Scots, established a kingdom in Kintyre and Argyll. This kingdom in Scotland was also called Dal Riata.

In the census of 1659 McCullough was listed as one of the 'principal Irish names' in the baronies of Antrim, Belfast, Carrickfergus and Toome in County Antrim and also in the barony of Iveagh, County Down. However, many of these must have been Scottish.

In Scotland MacCullochs were located in the Highlands in both Easter Ross and Argyllshire, and in Galloway in southwest Scotland. The MacCullochs of Oban in Argyllshire belonged to Clan Dougall and were originally, in Gaelic, *Mac Lulaich*, meaning the 'son of Lulach'. Lulach succeeded MacBeth as the King of Scots in 1057. The MacCullochs also owned considerable lands beside Dornoch Firth in Easter Ross. Upheavals such as military incursions, feuds and harvest failures would have encouraged many families in the Highlands, including MacCullochs, to migrate to Ulster as settlers during the 17th century.

Movement of Scottish settlers to Ulster began in earnest from 1605 in a private enterprise colonisation of counties Antrim and Down when Sir Hugh Montgomery and Sir James Hamilton acquired title to large estates in north Down and Sir Randall MacDonnell, 1st Earl of Antrim, to large tracts of land in north Antrim. Further impetus came in 1609 when James I adopted the policy to encourage Scottish settlers to settle on the forfeited estates of the Gaelic chiefs in counties Armagh, Cavan, Donegal, Fermanagh, Londonderry (then known as Coleraine) and Tyrone.

At the time of this plantation MacCulloch, possibly derived from Scots Gaelic *Mac Cullaich*, meaning 'son of the boar', was already common in the province of Galloway. The name first appears in 1296 when Thomas Maculagh of Wigtown paid homage to Edward I of England. This region was home to many of the Scottish settlers who came to Ulster throughout the 17th century.

Indeed James MacCulloch of Wigtownshire was one of the principal Scottish planters (sixty-one in total) of the Ulster Plantation, and in 1610 he was granted an estate of 1000 acres in Glenties, County Donegal. Many of the settlers farming on this estate would also have been called MacCulloch as it was a feature of 17th century Scotland for tenants to take on their landlord's surname.

It is estimated by 1715, when migration to Ulster had virtually stopped, the Scottish population of Ulster stood at 200,000.

McCULLOUGH

McCullough can be an Irish or a Scottish name. This name is one of the fifty most common names in Ulster and it is most concentrated in Counties Antrim, Tyrone and Down. Eighty percent of those of the name in Ireland are located in Ulster.

The Ulster Gaelic names *Mac Cu Uladh* or *Mac Con Uladh*, meaning 'son of the hound of Ulster' were anglicised as McCullough. These names originated east of the River Bann in the ancient kingdom of Dal Riata. From the 6th century Irish Celts from Dalriada, known as the Scots, established a kingdom in Kintyre and Argyll. This kingdom in Scotland was also called Dal Riata.

In the census of 1659 McCullough was listed as one of the 'principal Irish names' in the baronies of Antrim, Belfast, Carrickfergus and Toome in County Antrim and also in the barony of Iveagh, County Down. However, many of these must have been Scottish.

Many of the Ulster McCulloughs stem originally from Scotland where the name is usually spelt MacCulloch. In Scotland MacCullochs were located in the Highlands in both Easter Ross and Argyllshire, and in Galloway in southwest Scotland.

The MacCullochs of Oban in Argyllshire belonged to Clan Dougall and were originally, in Gaelic, *Mac Lulaich*, meaning the 'son of Lulach'. Lulach succeeded MacBeth as the King of Scots in 1057. The MacCullochs also owned considerable lands beside Dornoch Firth in Easter Ross. Upheavals such as military incursions, feuds and harvest failures would have encouraged many families in the Highlands, including MacCullochs, to migrate to Ulster as settlers during the 17th century.

Movement of Scottish settlers to Ulster began in earnest from 1605 in a private enterprise colonisation of counties Antrim and Down when Sir Hugh Montgomery and Sir James Hamilton acquired title to large estates in north Down and Sir Randall MacDonnell, 1st Earl of Antrim, to large tracts of land in north Antrim. Further impetus came in 1609 when James I adopted the policy to encourage Scottish settlers to settle on the forfeited estates of the Gaelic chiefs in counties Armagh, Cavan, Donegal, Fermanagh, Londonderry (then known as Coleraine) and Tyrone.

At the time of this plantation MacCulloch, possibly derived from Scots Gaelic *Mac Cullaich*, meaning 'son of the boar', was already common in the province of Galloway. The name first appears in 1296 when Thomas Maculagh of Wigtown paid homage to Edward I of England. This region was home to many of the Scottish settlers who came to Ulster throughout the 17th century.

Indeed James MacCulloch of Wigtownshire was one of the principal Scottish planters (sixty-one in total) of the Ulster Plantation, and in 1610 he was granted an estate of 1000 acres in Glenties, County Donegal. Many of the settlers farming on this estate would also have been called McCulloch as it was a feature of 17th century Scotland for tenants to take on their landlord's surname.

It is estimated by 1715, when migration to Ulster had virtually stopped, the Scottish population of Ulster stood at 200,000.

McCURDY

Apart from a few McCurdys in County Derry this name is found exclusively in County Antrim. This name was brought to County Antrim by settlers from Scotland in the 17th century.

McCurdy is derived from Gaelic *Mac Muircheartaigh*, meaning 'son of Murtagh', a personal name, meaning 'sea ruler'. McCurdy is a common name in the islands of Arran and Bute. They were a sept of Clan Stuart of Bute, and in the 15th century the McCurdys owned most of Bute.

Upheavals such as military incursions, feuds and harvest failures would have encouraged many clan members, including McCurdys, to migrate to Ulster as settlers during the 17th century. Owing to the nature of the Scottish clan system once the power and influence of the chief had been weakened or broken the clan tended to disintegrate. Bearing the surname McCurdy simply indicated that you were a follower of the chief of Clan Stuart of Bute. Not every clan member was related by blood. Their bond, however, whether they had a common tribal ancestor or not, was their common rule by a chief with loyalty to one's clan being the primary obligation. Once tribal loyalty was broken clans 'scattered'.

It would seem quite likely that the McCurdys followed the Stuarts of Bute to Ballintoy, County Antrim. Today McCurdy is the most common name on Rathlin Island, and it is common too in the Glens of Antrim and on the north coast of Antrim.

The Stewarts of Ballintoy, a branch of Clan Stuart of Bute, trace their descent from John Stewart, the son of Robert Stewart who was to become Robert II, King of Scotland in 1371. The Stuarts of Bute were the hereditary sheriffs of the island. Two sons of the fifth Sheriff of Bute, Archibald Stuart, settled on the territory of the MacDonnells of the Glens, near Ballintoy on the Antrim coast about 1560. When Sir Randall MacDonnell, 1st Earl of Antrim, acquired title to large tracts of land in north Antrim, from 1605, he sub-leased to Archibald Stewart, grandson of the fifth Sheriff of Bute, the estate of Ballintoy. Movement of Scottish settlers to farm on this estate and other Scottish-owned estates in Ulster now began in earnest.

Scottish settlers came to Ulster, by and large, in three waves: with the granting of the initial leases in the period 1605 to 1625; after 1652 and Cromwell's crushing of the Irish rebellion; and finally in the fifteen years after 1690 and the Glorious Revolution. It is estimated by 1715, when migration to Ulster had virtually stopped, the Scottish population of Ulster stood at 200,000.

In Ayrshire, Edinburgh and Lanarkshire the name McCurdy, from an early date, took the form of McMurtry. For example one Gilbert Makmurtye was recorded as a witness in Edinburgh in 1508.

In Ireland the County Donegal sept of *Mac Muircheartaigh* was anglicised as McBrearty. The homeland of this sept was west Donegal in the lands around the town of Killybegs. McBrearty is a common name in Derry city today. As Derry developed an industrial base in the 19th century in shirt making, shipbuilding and distilling it attracted much of its workforce from County Donegal.

173

McCUTCHEON

This surname is found almost exclusively in Ulster where it is most common in Counties Tyrone, Antrim, and Down. This name was brought to Ulster by settlers from Scotland in the 17ᵗʰ century.

In the Highlands of Scotland, McCutcheon is derived from Gaelic *Mac Uisdin*, meaning 'son of Hutcheon'. The French personal name Huchon, a pet form of Hugh, was made Hutcheon in Scotland. This name in turn was borrowed into Scots Gaelic as Uisdean. The McDonalds of Skye trace their descent from Hugh, a younger son of Alexander MacDonald, Lord of the Isles. This family became known as Clann Uisdin. Thus the McDonalds of Syke were regarded as the offspring of a man called Hutcheon. As early as the 15ᵗʰ century the name was being anglicised as McHutcheon, hence McCutcheon. For example John Roy Makhuchone 'committed slaughter in Ross, 1494-5', and Adam MacHutchoun was recorded in Murthlac in 1550.

The McCutcheons were, therefore, a branch of Clan Donald. Under the leadership of Somerled, who expelled the Norsemen from the western side of Scotland in the 12ᵗʰ century, Clan Donald claimed the position of 'The Headship of the Gael'. By the time of his death in 1387, John MacDonald, as Lord of the Isles, controlled the whole of the Hebrides from Lewis to Islay, with the exception of Skye, and the mainland from Kintyre to Knoydart.

Clan Donald had acquired new territories in the north of Ireland ca.1400 when John Mor MacDonald had married Margery Bissett, an heiress in the Glens of Antrim. By the mid-16ᵗʰ century the MacDonalds, known as the MacDonnells of the Glens, had carved out an extensive territory in County Antrim at the expense of the MacQuillans. It would quite likely that some McCutcheons, as followers of Clan Donald, settled in County Antrim. Owing to the nature of the Scottish clan system once the power and influence of the chief had been weakened or broken the clan tended to disintegrate. The MacDonalds finally lost their title as 'Lord of the Isles' in 1493.

Movement of Scottish settlers to Ulster began in earnest from 1605 in a private enterprise colonisation of counties Antrim and Down when Sir Hugh Montgomery and Sir James Hamilton acquired title to large estates in north Down and Sir Randall MacDonnell, 1ˢᵗ Earl of Antrim, to large tracts of land in north Antrim.

Further impetus came in 1609 when James I adopted the policy to encourage Scottish settlers to settle on the forfeited estates of the Gaelic chiefs in counties Armagh, Cavan, Donegal, Fermanagh, Londonderry (then known as Coleraine) and Tyrone.

Settlers to Ulster came, by and large, in three waves: with the granting of the initial leases in the period 1605 to 1625; after 1652 and Cromwell's crushing of the Irish rebellion; and finally in the fifteen years after 1690 and the Glorious Revolution. It is estimated by 1715, when migration to Ulster had virtually stopped, the Scottish population of Ulster stood at 200,000.

During the famous 105 day Siege of Derry, from 18 April to 31 July 1689, Dan McCustion and John McCutcheon were recorded as 'defenders' of the city.

McDAID

The surname McDaid is virtually exclusive to northwest Ireland. The name is most numerous in County Donegal where over half the McDaids are located; and most of the rest are divided between the adjacent parts of Derry and Tyrone. The name is particularly associated with Inishowen, County Donegal. This name, which is among the top ten in the city of Derry, illustrates the very close links between the city of Derry and Inishowen. As Derry developed an industrial base in the 19th century in shirt making, shipbuilding and distilling it attracted much of its workforce from Inishowen.

The McDaid sept of County Donegal trace their lineage to Conall *Gulban*, son of the 5th century High King of Ireland, Niall of the Nine Hostages, who ruled from the Hill of Tara, County Meath. Conall and his brother Eogan conquered northwest Ireland, ca.425 AD, capturing the great hill-fort of Grianan of Ailech in County Donegal which commanded the entrance to Inishowen between Lough Swilly and Lough Foyle.

Conall, styled 'King of Tir Conaill', established his own kingdom in County Donegal called after him Tyrconnel, i.e. the 'Land of Conall', which was the ancient name of Donegal. His descendants, known as the Cenel Conaill (the race of Conall), formed one of the principal branches of the Northern Ui Neill (descendants of Niall of the Nine Hostages). The septs of the Cenel Conaill firmly established themselves in County Donegal while those descended from Conal's brother Eogan expanded to the east and south into Counties Derry and Tyrone.

Ireland was one of the first countries to adopt a system of hereditary surnames which developed from a more ancient system of clan or sept names. The surname was formed by prefixing either Mac (son of) or O (grandson or descendant of) to the ancestor's name.

The McDaids, in Gaelic *Mac Daibheid*, are a branch of the O'Dohertys. They derive their surname from *Daibhidh O Dochartaigh* who died, in battle, in 1208 when Hugh O'Neill raided Inishowen. Thus McDaid literally means 'son of David O'Doherty'. The name was further anglicised to McDavitt and McDevitt and sometimes Davison. In Counties Louth, Monaghan and Down the name was anglicised to McKevitt. McDaid, however, is by far the most common rendering of the sept name. In Counties Derry, Donegal and Tyrone three-quarters of the *Mac Daibheid* sept are McDaid and one-quarter McDevitt.

The McDaids were long noted for their loyalty to the O'Dohertys. In 1608 Sir Cahir O'Doherty's second-in-command at the capture and burning of Derry city was Phelim Reagh MacDavitt, whose family henceforth became known as the 'Burn-Derrys'. The McDevitts are now chiefly located in the western parts of Donegal, and it is only in northwest Donegal that McDevitt outnumbers McDaid. There are townlands called Ballydevitt in both Derry and Donegal.

In a few cases in Ulster McDaid may be a variant of the Scottish clan name Davidson. In Scotland the names McDade and McDaid are found mostly in Glasgow.

McDERMOTT

This name is among the hundred most common in Ireland, and in Ulster it is most common in the west of the province, particularly in Counties Donegal and Tyrone. This name is particularly associated with the province of Connaught, and especially with County Roscommon where it is the second most common name.

Ireland was one of the first countries to adopt a system of hereditary surnames which developed from a more ancient system of clan or sept names. The surname was formed by prefixing either Mac (son of) or O (grandson or descendant of) to the ancestor's name.

The powerful McDermott sept of Connaught is derived from Gaelic *Mac Diarmada*, meaning 'son of Dermot'. Tracing their descent from Tadhg O'Connor, King of Connaught the McDermotts divided into three distinct septs. The most important were the McDemotts of Moylurg whose territory embraced much of County Roscommon. The chief of the McDermotts was styled 'Prince of Coolavin'.

It is possible that the Anglo-Norman military incursions of the 13th century into Connaught which reduced the power and influence of many septs in that province encouraged descendants of the McDermott sept to migrate north at an early date. The surname is common today in Counties Donegal and Tyrone.

In the 17th and 18th centuries many descendants of the old Gaelic order in Ireland emigrated, as the so-called Wild Geese, to Europe, and, in particular, to Spain and France. The McDermotts rose to positions of prominence in both the church and the armed services on the continent.

The importance of McDermott as a surname in Derry city today, where it is among the top thirty names, is due to the once numerous sept, in Gaelic, *O Duibhdhiorma*, which was based in Inishowen, County Donegal. This name is another example of the very close links between the city of Derry and Inishowen. As Derry developed an industrial base in the 19th century in shirt making, shipbuilding and distilling it attracted much of its workforce from Inishowen.

In Inishowen, McDermott is derived from Gaelic *O Duibhdhiorma*, the root word being *dubhdhiorma*, meaning 'black troop'. Confusion is caused by the many known variants of this name such as Dermond, Deyermott, Diarmid as well as Dermott. Furthermore the name has been recorded as both O'Dermott and McDermott.
The Annals of The Kingdom of Ireland by the Four Masters records ten references to the *O Duibhdhiorma* sept between 1043 and 1454. The head of the family was chief of *Breadach* which comprised the parishes of Lower and Upper Moville in Inishowen. The name of the district is still preserved in the river Bredagh which falls into Lough Foyle.

A small number of McDermotts in Ulster may be of Scottish origin as McDermott is a sept of Clan Campbell of Breadalbane. Upheavals such as military incursions, feuds and harvest failures would have encouraged many clan members, including McDermotts, to migrate to Ulster as settlers during the 17th century.

McDEVITT

The surname McDevitt, a variant of McDaid, is virtually exclusive to northwest Ireland. The name is most numerous in County Donegal where over half the McDaids are located; and most of the rest are divided between the adjacent parts of Derry and Tyrone. The name is particularly associated with Inishowen, County Donegal. McDaid, which is among the top ten surnames in the city of Derry, illustrates the very close links between the city of Derry and Inishowen. As Derry developed an industrial base in the 19th century in shirt making, shipbuilding and distilling it attracted much of its workforce from Inishowen.

The McDevitt sept of County Donegal trace their lineage to Conall *Gulban*, son of the 5th century High King of Ireland, Niall of the Nine Hostages, who ruled from the Hill of Tara, County Meath. Conall and his brother Eogan conquered northwest Ireland, ca.425 AD, capturing the great hill-fort of Grianan of Ailech in County Donegal which commanded the entrance to Inishowen between Lough Swilly and Lough Foyle.

Conall, styled 'King of Tir Conaill', established his own kingdom in County Donegal called after him Tyrconnel, i.e. the 'Land of Conall', which was the ancient name of Donegal. His descendants, known as the Cenel Conaill (the race of Conall), formed one of the principal branches of the Northern Ui Neill (descendants of Niall of the Nine Hostages). The septs of the Cenel Conaill firmly established themselves in County Donegal while those descended from Conal's brother Eogan expanded to the east and south into Counties Derry and Tyrone.

Ireland was one of the first countries to adopt a system of hereditary surnames which developed from a more ancient system of clan or sept names. The surname was formed by prefixing either Mac (son of) or O (grandson or descendant of) to the ancestor's name.

The McDevitts, in Gaelic *Mac Daibheid*, are a branch of the O'Dohertys. They derive their surname from *Daibhidh O Dochartaigh* who died, in battle, in 1208 when Hugh O'Neill raided Inishowen. Thus McDevitt literally means 'son of David O'Doherty'. *Mac Daibheid* was usually anglicised to McDaid; but it was also anglicised as McDevitt, McDavitt and sometimes Davison. In Counties Louth, Monaghan and Down the name became McKevitt. McDaid, however, is by far the most common rendering of the sept name. In Counties Derry, Donegal and Tyrone three-quarters of the *Mac Daibheid* sept are McDaid and one-quarter McDevitt.

The McDevitts were long noted for their loyalty to the O'Dohertys. In 1608 Sir Cahir O'Doherty's second-in-command at the capture and burning of Derry city was Phelim Reagh MacDavitt, whose family henceforth became known as the 'Burn-Derrys'. The McDevitts are now chiefly located in the western parts of Donegal, and it is only in northwest Donegal that McDevitt outnumbers McDaid. There are townlands called Ballydevitt in both Derry and Donegal.

McDONALD

This Scottish name is one of the 100 most numerous in Ireland. In Ulster the name is most common in County Antrim.

According to Clan Donald genealogical lore the McDonalds can trace their ancestry back to Ireland and to *Conn of the Hundred Battles,* King of Connaught, who was killed in 157 AD at Tara, County Meath. Conn's descendants pushed eastwards and northwards out of Connaught, capturing Tara and taking sword land as far north as Inishowen, County Donegal. This expansion was assigned by genealogists to Niall of the Nine Hostages and his sons. The by-product of this northward expansion was the pushing out of the existing peoples in Ulster across the Irish channel to Scotland. By the beginning of the 6th century these Irish Celts, known as Scots, had established themselves in Kintyre, Argyll and some of the Inner Isles. They called their kingdom Dal Riada, after the kingdom they still held in Ulster.

The McDonalds, Gaelic *Mac Dhomhnuill,* meaning son of Donald, take their name from Donald of Islay, grandson of Somerled. Under the leadership of Somerled, who expelled the Norsemen from the western side of Scotland in the 12th century, Clan Donald claimed the position of 'The Headship of the Gael'. By the time of his death in 1387, John MacDonald, as Lord of the Isles, controlled the whole of the Hebrides from Lewis to Islay, with the exception of Skye, and the mainland from Kintyre to Knoydart.

Clan Donald acquired new territories in the north of Ireland ca.1400 when one of John's sons, John Mor, married Margery Bissett, an heiress in the Glens of Antrim. Members of the clan had gained a foothold in the Glens in the 13th century through land grants for military service as galloglasses, i.e. mercenary soldiers. Some of these Scottish galloglasses later acquired the surname Scott, meaning Scotsman. By the mid-16th century the McDonalds, known as the McDonnells of the Glens, had carved out an extensive territory in County Antrim at the expense of the McQuillans.

In Scotland, Clan Donald's ventures to increase their power brought them into conflict with the Scottish Crown in the 15th century. The McDonalds finally lost their title as 'Lord of the Isles' in 1493.

Movement of Scottish settlers to County Antrim began in earnest from 1605 when Sir Randall MacDonnell, 1st Earl of Antrim, acquired title to large tracts of land in north Antrim. Many of the settlers farming on the Earl of Antrim's estate would also have been called McDonnell owing to the nature of the Scottish clan system. Bearing the surname McDonald or McDonnell could simply indicate that you were a follower of a Clan Donald leader. Not every clan member was related by blood: people who were not of direct descent might also identify with a particular clan. They may have been granted land in return for services, or simply have lived on clan territories. Their bond, however, whether they had a common tribal ancestor or not, was their common rule by a chief with loyalty to one's clan being the primary obligation.

A Gaelic Irish sept, with origins in Clankelly, County Fermanagh, also bear the name McDonnell. Ousted by the Maguires they moved to County Monaghan where they were recorded in 1300 as sub-chiefs to the McMahons. Furthermore, from the 14th century McDonald has been anglicized as Donaldson.

McDONNELL

This Scottish name is one of the 100 most numerous in Ireland. In Ulster the name is most common in County Antrim.

According to Clan Donald genealogical lore the MacDonnells can trace their ancestry back to Ireland and to *Conn of the Hundred Battles*, King of Connaught, who was killed in 157 AD at Tara, County Meath. Conn's descendants pushed eastwards and northwards out of Connaught, capturing Tara and taking sword land as far north as Inishowen, County Donegal. This expansion was assigned by genealogists to Niall of the Nine Hostages and his sons. The by-product of this northward expansion was the pushing out of the existing peoples in Ulster across the Irish channel to Scotland. By the beginning of the 6th century these Irish Celts, known as Scots, had established themselves in Kintyre, Argyll and some of the Inner Isles. They called their kingdom Dal Riada, after the kingdom they still held in Ulster.

The MacDonalds, Gaelic Mac Dhomhnuill, meaning son of Donald, take their name from Donald of Islay, grandson of Somerled. Under the leadership of Somerled, who expelled the Norsemen from the western side of Scotland in the 12th century, Clan Donald claimed the position of 'The Headship of the Gael'. By the time of his death in 1387, John MacDonald, as Lord of the Isles, controlled the whole of the Hebrides from Lewis to Islay, with the exception of Skye, and the mainland from Kintyre to Knoydart.

Clan Donald acquired new territories in the north of Ireland ca.1400 when one of John's sons, John Mor, married Margery Bissett, an heiress in the Glens of Antrim. Members of the clan had gained a foothold in the Glens in the 13th century through land grants for military service as galloglasses, i.e. mercenary soldiers. Some of these Scottish galloglasses later acquired the surname Scott, meaning Scotsman. By the mid-16th century the MacDonalds, known as the MacDonnells of the Glens, had carved out an extensive territory in County Antrim at the expense of the MacQuillans.

In Scotland, Clan Donald's ventures to increase their power brought them into conflict with the Scottish Crown in the 15th century. The MacDonalds finally lost their title as 'Lord of the Isles' in 1493.

Movement of Scottish settlers to County Antrim began in earnest from 1605 when Sir Randall MacDonnell, 1st Earl of Antrim, acquired title to large tracts of land in north Antrim. Many of the settlers farming on the Earl of Antrim's estate would also have been called MacDonnell owing to the nature of the Scottish clan system. Bearing the surname MacDonald or MacDonnell could simply indicate that you were a follower of a Clan Donald leader. Not every clan member was related by blood: people who were not of direct descent might also identify with a particular clan. They may have been granted land in return for services, or simply have lived on clan territories. Their bond, however, whether they had a common tribal ancestor or not, was their common rule by a chief with loyalty to one's clan being the primary obligation.

A Gaelic Irish sept, with origins in Clankelly, County Fermanagh, also bear the name McDonnell. Ousted by the Maguires they moved to County Monaghan where they were recorded in 1300 as sub-chiefs to the McMahons.

McDOWELL

This surname is found mainly in east Ulster in Counties Antrim and Down. McDowell, the Irish form of McDougall, represents the descendants of Scottish Clan MacDougall.

From the mid-14th century the McDowells came from the Hebrides to fight as galloglasses in Ireland, and settled in County Roscommon. Derived from Gaelic *galloglach,* galloglass refers to a paid soldier, often brought over from Scotland, to fight on behalf of an Irish chief.

The Annals of The Kingdom of Ireland by the Four Masters provide detailed and graphic descriptions of the Scottish galloglasses. In one account dated 1557 the *Annals* describe the galloglass in the camp of the O'Neills who were on a raiding expedition into O'Donnell territory in Donegal. It states that 'sixty grim and redoubtable gallowglasses, with sharp, keen axes, terrible and ready for action, and sixty stern and terrific Scots, with massive, broad, and heavy-striking swords in their hands, ready to strike and parry, were watching and guarding the son of O'Neill.'

McDowell is a variant of MacDougal, in Gaelic *Mac Dubhghaill,* meaning 'son of Dougal'. The personal name Dougal is derived from *dubh,* meaning 'black', and *gall,* meaning 'foreigner'. Clan MacDougall of Argyll and Lorn trace their descent from Dougal, son of Somerled of Argyll. Somerled was a descendant of *Godfraidh mac Fergus,* 'Lord of the Hebrides', who died in 853 AD. Under the leadership of Somerled the Norsemen were expelled from the western side of Scotland in the 12th century.

Beyond that the McDowells can trace their ancestry back to Ireland and to *Colla Uais,* High King of Ireland in the 4th century, and to *Conn of the Hundred Battles,* King of Connaught, who was killed in 157 AD at Tara, County Meath.

The majority of McDowells in Ulster are descendants of 17th century settlers from Scotland. In Scotland the surname McDowell was established at an early date in the province of Galloway. The first reference to the name is of a Fergus McDuhile in Wigtown in 1296. In 1312 Sir Duugal McDouwille was recorded as 'sheriff of Dumfries and constable of the castle'. McDowell became a common name in Galloway. This region in southwest Scotland was home to many of the Scottish settlers who came to Ulster throughout the 17th century.

Movement of Scottish settlers to Ulster began in earnest from 1605 in a private enterprise colonisation of counties Antrim and Down when Sir Hugh Montgomery and Sir James Hamilton acquired title to large estates in north Down and Sir Randall MacDonnell, 1st Earl of Antrim, to large tracts of land in north Antrim. By the mid-19th century the McDowells were concentrated in the barony of Lower Belfast in County Antrim, and in the baronies of Lower Castlereagh and Upper and Lower Ards in County Down.

During the famous 105 day Siege of Derry, from 18 April to 31 July 1689, Andrew McDowell was recorded as a 'defender' of the city.

180

McELDOWNEY

This surname is found almost exclusively in County Derry. This name has also been shortened to Downey.

Ireland was one of the first countries to adopt a system of hereditary surnames which developed from a more ancient system of clan or sept names. From the 11th century each family began to adopt its own distinctive family name generally derived from the first name of an ancestor who lived in or about the 10th century. The surname was formed by prefixing either Mac (son of) or O (grandson or descendant of) to the ancestor's name. Surnames in Ireland, therefore, tended to identify membership of a sept.

McEldowney is derived from Gaelic *Mac Giolla Domhnaigh*, meaning 'son of the devotee of the church'. This sept originated in County Derry. It is possible, in some instances, that McEldowney is another form of Muldowney, in Gaelic *O Maoldomhnaigh*, meaning 'descendant of the servant of the church'.

The Hearth Money Rolls of 1663 would suggest that this sept originated in south Derry. Six households, recorded either as McEldowney or Muldowney, were named in this source in County Derry - two households in Tamlaght Parish and one each in the parishes of Ballynascreen, Derryloran, Killelagh and Maghera.

At the time of the 1831 census there were 37 McEldowney households in County Derry, and all but two of these households were residing in three parishes in south Derry; with 20 households of the name in Killelagh Parish, 9 in Ballynascreen Parish and 6 in Maghera Parish. In the 1831 census the descendants of this sept were recorded as McEldowney in the parishes of Killelagh and Maghera, and as McIldowney in Ballynascreen Parish.

The anglicisation of Gaelic names, from the 17th century, resulted in many variant spellings of the same name and, in many cases, the dropping of the O and Mac prefixes. In County Down, in the 19th century, the name was variously recorded as Downey, Muldowney, Gildowney and McGilldowny.

In Scotland McIldownie is derived from Gaelic *Mac Gille Domhnaich*, meaning 'son of the lord's servant'. The earliest record of the name is of a Robert Mackildowny who was made a freeman of Glasgow in 1573. In the 17th century references to the surname can be found in places as far apart as Dumfries, Glasgow and Stirlingshire. It is possible that some McEldowneys in Ulster may be descendants of 17th century Scottish settlers.

Movement of Scottish settlers to Ulster began in earnest from 1605 in a private enterprise colonisation of counties Antrim and Down when Sir Hugh Montgomery and Sir James Hamilton acquired title to large estates in north Down and Sir Randall MacDonnell, 1st Earl of Antrim, to large tracts of land in north Antrim. Further impetus came in 1609 when James I adopted the policy to encourage Scottish settlers to settle on the forfeited estates of the Gaelic chiefs in counties Armagh, Cavan, Donegal, Fermanagh, Londonderry (then known as Coleraine) and Tyrone.

McELHINNEY

McElhinney is an exclusively Ulster name found mainly in Counties Derry and Donegal.

The McElhinney sept trace their lineage to Eogan, son of the 5th century High King of Ireland, Niall of the Nine Hostages, who ruled from the Hill of Tara, County Meath. Eogan and his brother Conall *Gulban* conquered northwest Ireland, ca.425 AD, capturing the great hill-fort of Grianan of Ailech in County Donegal.

Eogan, styled 'King of Ailech', established his own kingdom in the peninsula in County Donegal still called after him Inishowen (Innis Eoghain or Eogan's Isle). His descendants, known as the Cenel Eoghain (the race of Owen), became the principal branch of the Northern Ui Neill (descendants of Niall of the Nine Hostages). The Cenel Eoghain in the next five centuries expanded to the east and south from their focal point in Inishowen into Counties Derry and Tyrone.

Ireland was one of the first countries to adopt a system of hereditary surnames which developed from a more ancient system of clan or sept names. The surname was formed by prefixing either Mac (son of) or O (grandson or descendant of) to the ancestor's name.

McElhinney is derived from Gaelic *Mac Giolla Chainnigh*, meaning 'son of the devotee of Canice'. Canice, styled as 'one of the twelve apostles of Ireland' and 'Saint of the Roe Valley', was one of the major figures of the early Celtic church in Ireland and Scotland.

Known as Cainneach by the Irish and as Kenneth in Scotland, Canice was born ca.516AD at Drumramer, four miles east of the town of Limavady, in the valley of the River Roe, County Derry. St Canice founded monasteries in County Derry at Drumachose, Enagh and Faughanvale. In Scotland Canice accompanied Colmcille (also known as Columba) on his missionary work from their island monastery at Iona.

The 1831 census recorded 38 McElhinney households in County Derry, and all but three of these households were residing in the parishes to the west of the River Roe, with the biggest concentration in the parishes of Clondermot, which contained 12 McElhinney households, and Dungiven with 8 households of the name.

The mid-19th century Griffith's Valuation recorded 156 McElhinney households in County Donegal, and 69 of these households were living in the Inishowen peninsula, with the largest concentration in Clonmany Parish which contained 39 McElhinney households. In other words 25% of descendants of the McElhinney sept in County Donegal were living in the parish of Clonmany in the Inishowen peninsula.

The McElhinney sept scattered at an early date, and in north Connaught, and in particular in Counties Leitrim, Mayo and Roscommon, *Mac Giolla Chainnigh* was anglicised to Kilkenny. This surname has no connection with the town of Kilkenny, in Gaelic *Cill Chainnigh*, which means 'the church of St Canice'. By tradition St Canice founded monasteries at Aghaboe in County Leix, and at Kilkenny in the latter years of the 6th century.

McELHONE

This name belongs to County Tyrone.

Ireland was one of the first countries to adopt a system of hereditary surnames which developed from a more ancient system of clan or sept names. From the 11th century each family began to adopt its own distinctive family name generally derived from the first name of an ancestor who lived in or about the 10th century. The surname was formed by prefixing either Mac (son of) or O (grandson or descendant of) to the ancestor's name. Surnames in Ireland, therefore, tended to identify membership of a sept.

McElhone is derived from Gaelic *Mac Giolla Comhghain,* meaning 'son of the devotee of St Comgan'. *The Annals of The Kingdom of Ireland by the Four Masters* (a chronicle of Irish history from 'the earliest period to the year 1616') record, in 868, the death of 'Comhgan Foda, anchorite of Tamhlacht'. An anchorite refers to a religious person who lived in seclusion.

In some cases McElhone was further anglicised, through mistranslation, to Woods. This arose from the assumption that the Gaelic word *coill,* meaning 'wood', formed an element in the Gaelic name. Thus *Mac Giolla Comhghain* was anglicised to McElhone and mistranslated to Woods.

This sept originated in east Tyrone in the lands between and surrounding the towns of Cookstown, Dungannon and Pomeroy. At the time of the mid-19th century Griffith's Valuation there were 58 McElhone households in County Tyrone, and all but one of these households were located either in parishes in the baronies of Dungannon Middle and Upper or in the parish of Bodoney Lower in the barony of Strabane Upper. At this time 10 McElhone households resided in Kildress Parish, 8 in Desertcreat Parish, 7 in Bodoney Lower, 6 in Drumglass, 6 in Pomeroy and 5 in Derryloran. In other words over 70% of descendants of the McElhone sept in County Tyrone lived in these six parishes.

At the time of the Mid-19th century Griffith's Valuation there were 19 McElhone households in County Derry, and they were all located in the parishes of the barony of Loughinsholin in south Derry; with 7 McElhone households living in Artrea Parish and 4 in Maghera Parish.

The association of this name in County Derry with Artrea Parish was even more pronounced in the early-19th century. The 1831 census records 30 McElhone households in County Derry; with 16 (i.e. over 50% of the total) of these households living in Artrea Parish.

This surname clearly belongs to the lands, which straddle the border of Counties Derry and Tyrone, on the west side of Lough Neagh.

The anglicisation of Gaelic names, from the 17th century, resulted in many variant spellings of the same name and, in many cases, the dropping of the O and Mac prefixes. In the case of McElhone the prefix Mac was retained, and the name was usually recorded as either McElhone or McIlhone.

McELWEE

McElwee is an exclusively Ulster name found mainly in Counties Derry and Donegal. This name, which has many variants, has always been closely associated with its homeland of County Donegal.

Ireland was one of the first countries to adopt a system of hereditary surnames which developed from a more ancient system of clan or sept names. From the 11th century each family began to adopt its own distinctive family name generally derived from the first name of an ancestor who lived in or about the 10th century. The surname was formed by prefixing either Mac (son of) or O (grandson or descendant of) to the ancestor's name. Surnames in Ireland, therefore, tended to identify membership of a sept.

McElwee is derived from Gaelic *Mac Giolla Bhuidhe*, meaning 'son of the yellow-haired youth'. *The Annals of The Kingdom of Ireland by the Four Masters* (a history of Ireland from 'the earliest period to the year 1616' which was compiled by monks who were followers of the O'Donnells of Donegal) record that, in 1181, 'Flaherty O'Muldory, Lord of Tirconnell, defeated the sons of the King of Connaught'. In this battle 'sixteen of the sons of the lords and chieftains of Connaught were slain', including two warriors named *mac giollabuide* (translated as MacGillaboy).

The escape of the most prominent Gaelic Lords of Ulster in 'the Flight of the Earls' in 1607 from Lough Swilly, County Donegal marked the end of Gaelic power. In the centuries that followed Gaelic names were anglicised, resulting in many variant spellings of the same name. The County Donegal sept of McElwee was also anglicised as McGilloway, McIlwee and McKelvey.

By the time of the mid-19th century Griffith's Valuation the surnames associated with this sept were spread throughout Donegal. This source records that in County Donegal, in the middle years of the 19th century, there were 13 households recorded as McElwee; 14 as McGillaway; 41 as McIlwee; 6 as McKelvey; and 27 as McKelvy.

This source also clearly demonstrates that in the Inishowen district of Donegal McGillaway was the dominant spelling of the name, with ten of the fourteen McGillaway households in Donegal residing there. As Inishowen was the home of many people who migrated to the city of Derry in the 19th century this probably explains why McGilloway is among the top 50 surnames in the city of Derry today. As Derry developed an industrial base in the 19th century in shirt making, shipbuilding and distilling it attracted much of its workforce from Inishowen. Her growing industries attracted workers and families from outside the city and county, and in the 90-year period 1821 to 1911 the population of the city quadrupled to 40,780.

McKelvey, in Gaelic *Mac Shealbhaigh*, meaning 'son of Selbach' is also a Scottish name, found in southwest Scotland in the counties of Dumfries, Kirkcudbright and Wigtown. This region was home to many of the Scottish settlers who came to Ulster throughout the 17th century. The McKelveys were also recorded as a sept of Clan Campbell. It is quite likely, therefore, that some McKelveys in Ulster will be descendants of 17th century Scottish settlers. The majority of McKelveys in Ulster, however, are descendants of the County Donegal sept of *Mac Giolla Bhuidhe*.

184

McERLEAN

This surname is found almost exclusively in Counties Antrim and Derry.

Ireland was one of the first countries to adopt a system of hereditary surnames which developed from a more ancient system of clan or sept names. From the 11th century each family began to adopt its own distinctive family name generally derived from the first name of an ancestor who lived in or about the 10th century. The surname was formed by prefixing either Mac (son of) or O (grandson or descendant of) to the ancestor's name. Surnames in Ireland, therefore, tended to identify membership of a sept.

McErlean is derived from Gaelic *Mac Fhirleighinn*, the root word being *fearleighinn*, meaning 'learned man'. This title was applied to the head of a monastic school in both Ireland and Scotland. In Iona in 1164 Ferleighinn Dubside was recorded as one of the officials of the monastery.

Although this sept originated in north Sligo a branch of the family migrated to and settled in County Derry. It is possible that the Anglo-Norman military incursions of the 13th century into Connaught which reduced the power and influence of many septs in that province encouraged descendants of the McErleans to migrate north at an early date.

The Hearth Money Rolls of 1663 would suggest that the parishes of Ballyscullion and Tamlaght O'Crilly in south Derry were the original base of this sept in County Derry. Three McErlean households were recorded in this source in County Derry - 2 households of McErlean in Ballyscullion Parish and 1 of McErlyn in Tamlaght O'Crilly Parish.

At the time of the 1831 census there were 63 McErlean households in County Derry, and all but four of these households were residing in three parishes in south Derry; 33 in Tamlaght O'Crilly Parish and 13 each in the parishes of Artrea and Maghera. In the 1831 census the descendants of this sept were generally recorded as McErlain in Tamlaght O'Crilly Parish, as McErlane in Maghera Parish and as McErlean in Artrea Parish.

In Scotland this name is found in the forms of McNerlin and McErlane. Indeed McErlane is a common name in Ayrshire and Dumbartonshire. As these two regions were home to many of the Scottish settlers who came to Ulster throughout the 17th century, it is possible that some McErleans in Ulster may be descendants of Scottish settlers.

Movement of Scottish settlers to Ulster began in earnest from 1605 in a private enterprise colonisation of counties Antrim and Down when Sir Hugh Montgomery and Sir James Hamilton acquired title to large estates in north Down and Sir Randall MacDonnell, 1st Earl of Antrim, to large tracts of land in north Antrim. Further impetus came in 1609 when James I adopted the policy to encourage Scottish settlers to settle on the forfeited estates of the Gaelic chiefs in counties Armagh, Cavan, Donegal, Fermanagh, Londonderry (then known as Coleraine) and Tyrone.

McFADDEN

McFadden can be an Irish or a Scottish name. In Ireland this name is not common outside Ulster. McFadden is among the first ten names in County Donegal and it is also numerous in Counties Antrim and Derry.

Ireland was one of the first countries to adopt a system of hereditary surnames which developed from a more ancient system of clan or sept names. The surname was formed by prefixing either Mac (son of) or O (grandson or descendant of) to the ancestor's name.

The County Donegal sept of McFadden is derived from Gaelic *Mac Phaidin*, meaning 'son of Patrick'. This name has been long associated with west Donegal. This name has also been confused with McPadden, in Gaelic *Mac Paidin*, also denoting 'son of Patrick'.

McFadden is a common name in Derry city today. This name illustrates the very close links, both historic and economic, between the city of Derry and County Donegal. As Derry developed an industrial base in the 19th century in shirt making, shipbuilding and distilling it attracted much of its workforce from Donegal. In the 90-year period 1821 to 1911 the population of the city quadrupled to 40,780.

Many McFaddens in Ulster are descendants of Scottish MacFadyen, in Gaelic *Macphaidein*, meaning 'son of Patrick'. The MacFadyens were a sept of Clan MacLaine of Lochbuie. The MacLaines, with lands on Mull, were followers of the McDonalds, Lords of the Isles. Indeed it is claimed that the MacFadyens were the original owners of Lochbuie. Dispossessed of their lands they became a sept of wandering goldsmiths on Mull. The MacFadyens are still numerous in Mull and Tiree.

The earliest record of the name is of a Malcolm Macpadene in Kintyre in 1304.
During the 14th and 15th centuries references to the surname in Scotland can be found in places as far apart as Argyll, Edinburgh and Kirkcudbright. McFadden became a common name in Galloway, and this region was home to many of the Scottish settlers who came to Ulster throughout the 17th century.

Movement of Scottish settlers to Ulster began in earnest from 1605 in a private enterprise colonisation of counties Antrim and Down when Sir Hugh Montgomery and Sir James Hamilton acquired title to large estates in north Down and Sir Randall MacDonnell, 1st Earl of Antrim, to large tracts of land in north Antrim.

Further impetus came in 1609 when James I adopted the policy to encourage Scottish settlers to settle on the forfeited estates of the Gaelic chiefs in counties Armagh, Cavan, Donegal, Fermanagh, Londonderry (then known as Coleraine) and Tyrone. It is estimated by 1715, when migration to Ulster had virtually stopped, the Scottish population of Ulster stood at 200,000.

During the famous 105 day Siege of Derry, from 18 April to 31 July 1689, Charles McFadden of Cavan was recorded as a 'defender' of the city and a signatory of the Enniskillen address to King William.

186

McFALL

McFall can be an Irish or a Scottish name. In Ireland this name is almost exclusive to Ulster, where it is most common in Counties Antrim and Derry.

Ireland was one of the first countries to adopt a system of hereditary surnames which developed from a more ancient system of clan or sept names. The surname was formed by prefixing either Mac (son of) or O (grandson or descendant of) to the ancestor's name.

The County Donegal sept of Mulfoyle, in Gaelic *O Maolfhabhail*, was often anglicised to McFall. The Mulfoyle sept trace their lineage to Eogan, son of the 5th century High King of Ireland, Niall of the Nine Hostages, who ruled from the Hill of Tara, County Meath. Eogan and his brother Conall *Gulban* conquered northwest Ireland, ca.425 AD, capturing the great hill-fort of Grianan of Ailech in County Donegal which commanded the entrance to the Inishowen peninsula between Lough Swilly and Lough Foyle.

Eogan, styled 'King of Ailech', established his own kingdom in the peninsula in County Donegal still called after him Inishowen (Innis Eoghain or Eogan's Isle). The Mulfoyles were one of the leading septs of Clan Fergus (Fergus was a son of Eogan). The Mulfoyle sept remained in their homeland around Lough Swilly, County Donegal, while the other Clan Fergus septs pushed southeast into County Tyrone from the 6th century AD. The Mulfoyles were based at Carrickabraghy in Clonmany Parish on the Inishowen peninsula.

In Scotland McFall is derived from Gaelic *Mac Phail*, meaning 'son of Paul'. The earliest reference to the surname is of one Gillemore McPhale who attended an inquest at Inverness in 1414. This name became common throughout the Highlands of Scotland as there were McPhail septs attached to Clans Cameron, Mackay and Mackintosh.

Until their defeat at Culloden Moor on 15 April 1746 the clans of the Highlands of Scotland were a very real threat to Royal authority. Upheavals such as military incursions, feuds and harvest failures would have encouraged many clan members, including McFalls, to migrate to Ulster as settlers during the 17th century. Owing to the nature of the Scottish clan system once the power and influence of the chief had been weakened and the bond of tribal loyalty broken the clan tended to scatter.

Movement of Scottish settlers to Ulster began in earnest from 1605 in a private enterprise colonisation of counties Antrim and Down when Sir Hugh Montgomery and Sir James Hamilton acquired title to large estates in north Down and Sir Randall MacDonnell, 1st Earl of Antrim, to large tracts of land in north Antrim. Further impetus came in 1609 when James I adopted the policy to encourage Scottish settlers to settle on the forfeited estates of the Gaelic chiefs in counties Armagh, Cavan, Donegal, Fermanagh, Londonderry (then known as Coleraine) and Tyrone.

It is estimated by 1715, when migration to Ulster had virtually stopped, the Scottish population of Ulster stood at 200,000.

McFARLAND

McFarland can be an Irish or a Scottish name, as Scottish McFarlane has become much confused with Irish McParland. In Ulster McFarland is most common in Counties Tyrone and Armagh.

Ireland was one of the first countries to adopt a system of hereditary surnames which developed from a more ancient system of clan or sept names. From the 11th century each family began to adopt its own distinctive family name generally derived from the first name of an ancestor who lived in or about the 10th century. The surname was formed by prefixing either Mac (son of) or O (grandson or descendant of) to the ancestor's name. Surnames in Ireland, therefore, tended to identify membership of a sept.

McParland, and its variants of McPartlan and McParlan, are derived from Gaelic *Mac Parthalain*, meaning 'son of Parthalan'. In Irish mythology Parthalan, who came from Sicily, was the first invader of Ireland. The homeland of the McParland sept was south Armagh where they were noted as poets and scribes in the 15th century. In the census of 1659 MacParlan was recorded as one of the principal Irish names in the baronies of Orior and Upper and Lower Fews in County Armagh. Confusion arises because McFarland has been recorded as 'a frequent variant' of McParland in the sept's homeland of County Armagh.

In Scotland McFarland is derived from Gaelic *Mac Pharlain*, meaning 'son of Parlan'. The personal name Parlan was further anglicised as Bartholomew. Clan MacFarlane, claiming descent from the ancient Celtic earldom of Lennox, held lands on the western shores of Loch Lomond in Dunbartonshire. In the 16th century the McFarlanes embarked upon feuds with the Colquhouns and with the Buchanans. Having gained the reputation as a troublesome clan the McFarlanes were eventually 'broken' and dispossessed off their lands in the early 17th century.

Upheavals such as military incursions, feuds and harvest failures would have encouraged many clan members, including McFarlanes, to migrate to Ulster as settlers during the 17th century. Owing to the nature of the Scottish clan system once the power and influence of the chief had been weakened and the bond of tribal loyalty broken the clan tended to scatter.

Movement of Scottish settlers to Ulster began in earnest from 1605 in a private enterprise colonisation of counties Antrim and Down when Sir Hugh Montgomery and Sir James Hamilton acquired title to large estates in north Down and Sir Randall MacDonnell, 1st Earl of Antrim, to large tracts of land in north Antrim. Further impetus came in 1609 when James I adopted the policy to encourage Scottish settlers to settle on the forfeited estates of the Gaelic chiefs in counties Armagh, Cavan, Donegal, Fermanagh, Londonderry (then known as Coleraine) and Tyrone.

Settlers to Ulster came, by and large, in three waves: with the granting of the initial leases in the period 1605 to 1625; after 1652 and Cromwell's crushing of the Irish rebellion; and finally in the fifteen years after 1690 and the Glorious Revolution. It is estimated by 1715, when migration to Ulster had virtually stopped, the Scottish population of Ulster stood at 200,000.

McFEELEY

This name belongs to Counties Derry and Donegal.

Ireland was one of the first countries to adopt a system of hereditary surnames which developed from a more ancient system of clan or sept names. From the 11th century each family began to adopt its own distinctive family name generally derived from the first name of an ancestor who lived in or about the 10th century. The surname was formed by prefixing either Mac (son of) or O (grandson or descendant of) to the ancestor's name. Surnames in Ireland, therefore, tended to identify membership of a sept.

McFeeley is derived from Gaelic *Mac Fithcheallaigh*, the root word being *fithcheallach*, meaning 'chess player'. The name is associated with two distinct areas: the Inishowen district of Donegal, and the lands of west Derry between the Rivers Foyle and Roe.

The 1831 census for County Derry clearly demonstrates that the lands to the west of the Roe Valley were the ancestral homeland of the McFeeleys in County Derry. At the time of the 1831 census there were 31 McFeeley households in County Derry, and all but five of these households were residing in the rural area centred on and surrounding the parish of Bovevagh. At the time of the 1831 census there were 10 McFeeley households, i.e. over 30% of the total, living in the townland of Muldonagh in Bovevagh Parish.

The mid-19th century Griffith's Valuation for County Donegal confirms that the Inishowen peninsula was the homeland of the McFeeleys in Donegal. This source recorded 24 McFeeley households in County Donegal, and all of these households were living in Inishowen. Indeed 17 McFeeley households were recorded in Culdaff Parish. In other words 70% of descendants of the McFeeley sept in County Donegal were living in the parish of Culdaff.

Many Inishowen families trace their lineage to Eogan, son of the 5th century High King of Ireland, Niall of the Nine Hostages, who ruled from the Hill of Tara, County Meath. Eogan and his brother Conall *Gulban* conquered northwest Ireland, ca.425 AD, capturing the great hill-fort of Grianan of Ailech which commanded the entrance to the Inishowen peninsula between Lough Swilly and Lough Foyle.

Eogan, styled 'King of Ailech', established his own kingdom in the peninsula still called after him Inishowen (Innis Eoghain or Eogan's Isle). His descendants, known as the Cenel Eoghain (the race of Owen), became the principal branch of the Northern Ui Neill (descendants of Niall of the Nine Hostages). The septs of the Cenel Eoghain expanded to the east and south, from their focal point in Inishowen, into Counties Derry and Tyrone.

McFeeley is a common name in Derry city today. The name spread to Derry city in the 19th century. As Derry developed an industrial base in the 19th century in shirt making, shipbuilding and distilling it attracted much of its workforce from County Donegal and, in particular, from Inishowen. In the 90-year period 1821 to 1911 the population of the city quadrupled to 40,780.

189

McFETRIDGE

This surname is found predominantly in Ulster where it was brought at the time of the 17th century Plantation of Ulster by settlers from Scotland. It is most common in Counties Antrim and Londonderry.

McFetridge is derived from Gaelic *Mac Phetruis*, meaning 'son of Peter'. This surname is recorded from 1503 in Scotland. McPhedrice was an old form of the name in Galloway, and MacPhedderis in Ballantrae Parish in Ayrshire. The province of Galloway and the lands along the Firth of Clyde in the old county of Ayrshire were home to many of the Scottish settlers who came to Ulster throughout the 17th century.

As this name was also anglicised as Patterson it means that some Pattersons in Ulster may have been originally McFetridge.

Patterson simply means 'son of Patrick'. Patrick was one of the most popular names in the west of Scotland in pre-Reformation times. The popularity of the name stems from St Patrick, the fifth century saint, who is regarded as the greatest and most famous of Ireland's Christian missionaries. In modern Scottish Gaelic the name Patrick is found in four forms: *Padruig*; *Paruig*; *Para*; and *Padair*, the common form of Patrick in Arran and Kintyre.

In the Highlands of Scotland Clan MacPatrick, which was anglicised as Patterson, was derived from Gaelic *Mac Gille Phadruig*, meaning 'son of the devotee of St Patrick'. Gillepatrick was a common Gaelic personal name. This surname was recorded in Moray, as Macgyllepatric, as early as 1236. The territory of this clan was on the north side of Lochfyne.

In Scotland Peter and Patrick were frequently interchangeable as Peter was regarded as an endearing form of Patrick. In fact it was said that 'Patrick is the "Sunday name", Peter the everyday one.' Hence, in some cases, McFetridge became Patterson.

Movement of Scottish settlers to Ulster began in earnest from 1605 in a private enterprise colonisation of counties Antrim and Down when Sir Hugh Montgomery and Sir James Hamilton acquired title to large estates in north Down and Sir Randall MacDonnell, 1st Earl of Antrim, to large tracts of land in north Antrim. Further impetus came in 1609 when James I adopted the policy to encourage Scottish settlers to settle on the forfeited estates of the Gaelic chiefs in counties Armagh, Cavan, Donegal, Fermanagh, Londonderry (then known as Coleraine) and Tyrone.

Scottish families entering Ireland through the port of Londonderry settled in the Foyle Valley which includes much of the fertile lands of counties Donegal, Londonderry and Tyrone. It is estimated by 1715, when migration to Ulster had virtually stopped, the Scottish population of Ulster stood at 200,000.

During the famous 105 day Siege of Derry, from 18 April to 31 July 1689, a Lieutenant McPhedris was recorded as a 'defender' of the city who was killed, on 21 April, during a sortie to Pennyburn Mill by the garrison's forces. William McFetrick of Carnglass, County Antrim was also recorded as one of the defenders.

McGARRIGLE

This surname is associated with County Donegal.

Ireland was one of the first countries to adopt a system of hereditary surnames which developed from a more ancient system of clan or sept names. From the 11th century each family began to adopt its own distinctive family name generally derived from the first name of an ancestor who lived in or about the 10th century. The surname was formed by prefixing either Mac (son of) or O (grandson or descendant of) to the ancestor's name. Surnames in Ireland, therefore, tended to identify membership of a sept.

McGarrigle is derived from Gaelic *Mag Fhearghail,* meaning 'son of the man of valour'. The homeland of this sept was County Donegal. *The Annals of Loch Ce* record that Meg Fergail 'was among the notable men slain by the O'Dohertys in 1196'. At this time the O'Dohertys were chiefs of Ardmire, an ancient territory to the west of Ballybofey near Lough Finn, County Donegal. In the census of 1659 McGarrigle, in the form of MacGargill, was recorded as one of the principal Irish names in the barony of Tirhugh in south Donegal.

Many County Donegal septs trace their lineage to Conall *Gulban,* son of the 5th century High King of Ireland, Niall of the Nine Hostages, who ruled from the Hill of Tara, County Meath. Conall and his brother Eogan conquered northwest Ireland, ca.425 AD, capturing the great hill-fort of Grianan of Ailech in County Donegal which commanded the entrance to the Inishowen peninsula between Lough Swilly and Lough Foyle.

Conall, styled 'King of Tir Conaill', established his own kingdom in County Donegal called after him Tyrconnel, i.e. the 'Land of Conall', which was the ancient name of Donegal. His descendants, known as the Cenel Conaill (the race of Conall), formed one of the principal branches of the Northern Ui Neill (descendants of Niall of the Nine Hostages). The septs of the Cenel Conaill firmly established themselves in County Donegal while those descended from Conal's brother Eogan expanded to the east and south into Counties Derry and Tyrone.

At the time of the mid-19th century Griffith's Valuation 46 McGarrigle households were recorded in County Donegal. This source clearly shows that the name was most concentrated in south Donegal in the lands between the towns of Ballyshannon and Donegal, as 17 McGarrigle households were residing in the parish of Kilbarron and a further 15 in the adjoining parish of Drumhome. In other words 70% of descendants of the McGarrigle sept in County Donegal were living in these two parishes.

McGarrigle is a common name in Derry city today. This name, which spread to Derry city in the 19th century, illustrates the very close links, both historic and economic, between the city of Derry and County Donegal. As Derry developed an industrial base in shirt making, shipbuilding and distilling it attracted much of its workforce from County Donegal. In the 90-year period 1821 to 1911 the population of the city quadrupled to 40,780.

McGARVEY

This name originated in County Donegal.

Ireland was one of the first countries to adopt a system of hereditary surnames which developed from a more ancient system of clan or sept names. From the 11th century each family began to adopt its own distinctive family name generally derived from the first name of an ancestor who lived in or about the 10th century. The surname was formed by prefixing either Mac (son of) or O (grandson or descendant of) to the ancestor's name. Surnames in Ireland, therefore, tended to identify membership of a sept.

McGarvey is derived from Gaelic *Mac Gairbhith*, the root word being *garbh*, meaning 'rough'. The homeland of this sept was northwest Donegal.

Many County Donegal septs trace their lineage to Conall *Gulban*, son of the 5th century High King of Ireland, Niall of the Nine Hostages, who ruled from the Hill of Tara, County Meath. Conall and his brother Eogan conquered northwest Ireland, ca.425 AD, capturing the great hill-fort of Grianan of Ailech in County Donegal which commanded the entrance to the Inishowen peninsula between Lough Swilly and Lough Foyle.

Conall, styled 'King of Tir Conaill', established his own kingdom in County Donegal called after him Tyrconnel, i.e. the 'Land of Conall', which was the ancient name of Donegal. His descendants, known as the Cenel Conaill (the race of Conall), formed one of the principal branches of the Northern Ui Neill (descendants of Niall of the Nine Hostages). The septs of the Cenel Conaill firmly established themselves in County Donegal while those descended from Conal's brother Eogan expanded to the east and south into Counties Derry and Tyrone.

At the time of the mid-19th century Griffith's Valuation 93 McGarvey households were recorded in County Donegal. This source clearly shows that the name was most concentrated in northwest Donegal in the lands between the Fanad peninsula and Gweedore, as 22 McGarvey households were residing in the parish of Tullaghobegley, 17 in Kilmacrenan Parish and a further 14 in Clondavaddog Parish. In other words over 55% of descendants of the McGarvey sept in County Donegal were living in these three parishes.

The name spread to Derry city in the 19th century. This name illustrates the very close links, both historic and economic, between the city of Derry and County Donegal. As Derry developed an industrial base in the 19th century in shirt making, shipbuilding and distilling it attracted much of its workforce from Donegal. In the 90-year period 1821 to 1911 the population of the city quadrupled to 40,780.

In Scotland McGarvey has had a long association with the province of Galloway, where the name was recorded in Wigtown from 1484. This region was home to many of the settlers who came to Ulster throughout the 17th century. It is possible, therefore, that some McGarveys in Ulster will be descendants of 17th century Scottish settlers.

McGEADY

This name originated in County Donegal.

Ireland was one of the first countries to adopt a system of hereditary surnames which developed from a more ancient system of clan or sept names. From the 11th century each family began to adopt its own distinctive family name generally derived from the first name of an ancestor who lived in or about the 10th century. The surname was formed by prefixing either Mac (son of) or O (grandson or descendant of) to the ancestor's name. Surnames in Ireland, therefore, tended to identify membership of a sept.

McGeady is derived either from Gaelic *Mag Geadaigh* or *Mag Eidigh*. The homeland of this sept was northwest Donegal.

Many County Donegal septs trace their lineage to Conall *Gulban*, son of the 5th century High King of Ireland, Niall of the Nine Hostages, who ruled from the Hill of Tara, County Meath. Conall and his brother Eogan conquered northwest Ireland, ca.425 AD, capturing the great hill-fort of Grianan of Ailech in County Donegal which commanded the entrance to the Inishowen peninsula between Lough Swilly and Lough Foyle.

Conall, styled 'King of Tir Conaill', established his own kingdom in County Donegal called after him Tyrconnel, i.e. the 'Land of Conall', which was the ancient name of Donegal. His descendants, known as the Cenel Conaill (the race of Conall), formed one of the principal branches of the Northern Ui Neill (descendants of Niall of the Nine Hostages). The septs of the Cenel Conaill firmly established themselves in County Donegal while those descended from Conal's brother Eogan expanded to the east and south into Counties Derry and Tyrone.

At the time of the mid-19th century Griffith's Valuation 23 McGeady households were recorded in County Donegal, and all but five of these households were recorded in the parish of Tullaghobegley. In other words nearly 80% of descendants of the McGeady sept in County Donegal were living in the parish of Tullaghobegley, a rugged stretch of land between the Rosses and Bloody Foreland, on the northwest coast of Donegal.

McGeady is a common name in Derry city today. This name, which spread to Derry city in the 19th century, illustrates the very close links, both historic and economic, between the city of Derry and County Donegal. As Derry developed an industrial base in shirt making, shipbuilding and distilling it attracted much of its workforce from County Donegal. In the 90-year period 1821 to 1911 the population of the city quadrupled to 40,780.

By the time of the 1831 census there were five McGeady households residing in Derry city. There were no McGeady households recorded anywhere else in County Derry at this time. The same situation still existed at the turn of the 20th century as all McGeady households recorded in the 1901 census for County Derry were living in the city of Derry.

McGEEHAN

This name originated in County Donegal.

Ireland was one of the first countries to adopt a system of hereditary surnames which developed from a more ancient system of clan or sept names. From the 11th century each family began to adopt its own distinctive family name generally derived from the first name of an ancestor who lived in or about the 10th century. The surname was formed by prefixing either Mac (son of) or O (grandson or descendant of) to the ancestor's name. Surnames in Ireland, therefore, tended to identify membership of a sept.

McGeehan is derived from Gaelic *Mac Gaoithin*, the root word being *gaoth*, meaning 'wind'. The homeland of this sept was west Donegal.

Many County Donegal septs trace their lineage to Conall *Gulban*, son of the 5th century High King of Ireland, Niall of the Nine Hostages, who ruled from the Hill of Tara, County Meath. Conall and his brother Eogan conquered northwest Ireland, ca.425 AD, capturing the great hill-fort of Grianan of Ailech in County Donegal which commanded the entrance to the Inishowen peninsula between Lough Swilly and Lough Foyle.

Conall, styled 'King of Tir Conaill', established his own kingdom in County Donegal called after him Tyrconnel, i.e. the 'Land of Conall', which was the ancient name of Donegal. His descendants, known as the Cenel Conaill (the race of Conall), formed one of the principal branches of the Northern Ui Neill (descendants of Niall of the Nine Hostages). The septs of the Cenel Conaill firmly established themselves in County Donegal while those descended from Conal's brother Eogan expanded to the east and south into Counties Derry and Tyrone.

At the time of the mid-19th century Griffith's Valuation 78 McGeehan households were recorded in County Donegal. This source clearly shows that the name was most concentrated in west Donegal around the town of Glenties, as 29 McGeehan households were residing in the parish of Inishkeel and a further 26 in Lettermacaward Parish. In other words 70% of descendants of the McGeehan sept in County Donegal were living in these two adjoining parishes.

The escape of the most prominent Gaelic Lords of Ulster in 'the Flight of the Earls' in 1607 from Lough Swilly, County Donegal marked the end of Gaelic power. In the centuries that followed Gaelic names were anglicised, resulting in many variant spellings of the same name and, in many cases, the dropping of the O and Mac prefixes. In the case of McGeehan the prefix Mac was nearly always retained. The mid-19th century Griffith's Valuation for County Donegal records 2 households named Geehan compared to 78 of McGeehan.

The name spread to Derry city in the 19th century. This name illustrates the very close links, both historic and economic, between the city of Derry and County Donegal. As Derry developed an industrial base in the 19th century in shirt making, shipbuilding and distilling it attracted much of its workforce from Donegal. In the 90-year period 1821 to 1911 the population of the city quadrupled to 40,780.

194

McGETTIGAN

This name is found mainly in Counties Derry and Donegal.

The McGettigan sept trace their lineage to Eogan, son of the 5th century High King of Ireland, Niall of the Nine Hostages, who ruled from the Hill of Tara, County Meath. Eogan and his brother Conall *Gulban* conquered northwest Ireland, ca.425 AD, capturing the great hill-fort of Grianan of Ailech in County Donegal.

Eogan, styled 'King of Ailech', established his own kingdom in the peninsula in County Donegal still called after him Inishowen (Innis Eoghain or Eogan's Isle). His descendants, known as the Cenel Eoghain (the race of Owen), became the principal branch of the Northern Ui Neill (descendants of Niall of the Nine Hostages). The Cenel Eoghain in the next five centuries expanded to the east and south from their focal point in Inishowen.

Ireland was one of the first countries to adopt a system of hereditary surnames which developed from a more ancient system of clan or sept names. From the 11th century each family began to adopt its own distinctive family name generally derived from the first name of an ancestor who lived in or about the 10th century. The surname was formed by prefixing either Mac (son of) or O (grandson or descendant of) to the ancestor's name. Surnames in Ireland, therefore, tended to identify membership of a sept.

McGettigan is derived from Gaelic *Mag Eiteagain*. The McGettigans were a sept of *Clann Diarmata*, i.e. Clan Dermot. The O'Carlins or O'Carolans (the earlier anglicised form of the name) were the leading sept of Clan Dermot. The McGettigans, however, were chiefs of Clan Dermot for a short period as *The Annals of The Kingdom of Ireland by the Four Masters* record, in 1132, that 'Diarmaid Mac Eitigen, chief of Clann-Diarmada, died'.

Clan Dermot was a branch of Clan Connor *Magh Ithe* (Connor was a direct descendant of Eogan). Magh Ithe is the rich countryside stretching southward from Inishowen, later known as the Laggan district in east Donegal. In the 10th century AD the families of Clan Connor moved out from the cramped territory of Magh Ithe and established themselves in County Derry, in the kingdom of Keenaght, to the north of the Sperrin Mountains, from the Foyle to the Bann rivers.

Clan Dermot, who gave their name to the parish of Clondermot or Glendermott, established themselves on the east side of the river Foyle and to the south of the Faughan river, in the barony of Tirkeeran, County Derry. Clan Dermot was very powerful in the neighbourhood of Derry during the 12th century. This prominence, however, was short-lived. In 1200 Egneghan O'Donnell, Lord of Tirconnell defeated Clan Dermot in a battle at Rosses Bay, a short distance north of Derry.

The McGettigans gradually moved westwards into County Donegal where the name is chiefly found today.

McGILLIGAN

Although the surname McGilligan is not very numerous today this County Derry sept was once very powerful and numerous.

Ireland was one of the first countries to adopt a system of hereditary surnames which developed from a more ancient system of clan or sept names. From the 11th century each family began to adopt its own distinctive family name generally derived from the first name of an ancestor who lived in or about the 10th century. The surname was formed by prefixing either Mac (son of) or O (grandson or descendant of) to the ancestor's name. Surnames in Ireland, therefore, tended to identify membership of a sept.

McGilligan, usually spelt Gilligan today, is derived from Gaelic *Mac Giollagain*, the root word being *giolla,* meaning 'lad'.

The McGilligan sept had come originally from *Breadach* which comprised the parishes of Lower and Upper Moville in Inishowen, County Donegal. The name of the district is still preserved in the river Bredagh which falls into Lough Foyle.

In the centuries before the 17th Plantation of Ulster with English and Scottish settlers the McGilligans migrated eastwards and settled in the lands, across Lough Foyle, beneath Benevenagh Mountain in north Derry. The parish here was church lands and the McGilligans became the *erenaghs*, i.e. hereditary stewards, of these ancient church lands in the parish of Tamlaghtard. St Columbkille (Columba) had founded a monastery in this parish in 584AD.

In the 16th century the McGilligans gave their name to the district, Magilligan, i.e. the land of the McGilligans. In the early 17th century the McGilligans were one of the three chief septs under the O'Cahans. At the time of Sir Cahir O'Doherty's rebellion in 1608 Sir Arthur Chichester reported that the chief septs of County Coleraine (renamed Londonderry in 1613) were the O'Cahans and under them the O'Mullans, the McGilligans and McCloskeys.

At the time of the Plantation, in 1611, the McGilligans were granted a freehold at Ballycarton in Aghanloo Parish. The family took an active part in the 1641 rebellion. Manus Magilligan, who held these lands in 1641, joined Manus O'Cathan, in the rebellion, and his lands at Ballycarton were forfeited, as a consequence, in 1652.

By the middle of the 17th century the Mac had already been widely discarded thus the surname commonly became Gilligan. Furthermore, in many cases, Gilligan has been made Gillan or Gillen. The Gillans, derived from Gaelic *O Giollain,* were a distinct sept, tracing their lineage to Eogan, son of the 5th century High King of Ireland, Niall of the Nine Hostages. Thus people whose origins are *Mac Giollagain* may be disguised by bearing the surname of Gillan or Gillen.

McGILLOWAY

McGilloway is an exclusively Ulster name found mainly in Counties Derry and Donegal. This name, which has many variants, has always been closely associated with its homeland of County Donegal.

This name, which is among the top 50 surnames in the city of Derry today, illustrates the very close links, both historic and economic, between Derry and County Donegal and, in particular, the Inishowen peninsula. As Derry developed an industrial base in the 19th century in shirt making, shipbuilding and distilling it attracted much of its workforce from Donegal. Her growing industries attracted workers and families from outside the city and county, and in the 90-year period 1821 to 1911 the population of the city quadrupled to 40,780.

Ireland was one of the first countries to adopt a system of hereditary surnames which developed from a more ancient system of clan or sept names. From the 11th century each family began to adopt its own distinctive family name generally derived from the first name of an ancestor who lived in or about the 10th century. The surname was formed by prefixing either Mac (son of) or O (grandson or descendant of) to the ancestor's name. Surnames in Ireland, therefore, tended to identify membership of a sept.

McGilloway is derived from Gaelic *Mac Giolla Bhuidhe*, meaning 'son of the yellow-haired youth'. *The Annals of The Kingdom of Ireland by the Four Masters* (a history of Ireland from 'the earliest period to the year 1616' which was compiled by monks who were followers of the O'Donnells of Donegal) record that, in 1181, 'Flaherty O'Muldory, Lord of Tirconnell, defeated the sons of the King of Connaught'. In this battle 'sixteen of the sons of the lords and chieftains of Connaught were slain', including two warriors named *mac giollabuide* (translated as MacGillaboy).

The escape of the most prominent Gaelic Lords of Ulster in 'the Flight of the Earls' in 1607 from Lough Swilly, County Donegal marked the end of Gaelic power. In the centuries that followed Gaelic names were anglicised, resulting in many variant spellings of the same name. The County Donegal sept of McGilloway was also anglicised as McElwee, McIlwee and McKelvey.

By the time of the mid-19th century Griffith's Valuation the surnames associated with this sept were spread throughout Donegal. This source records that in County Donegal, in the middle years of the 19th century, there were 14 households recorded as McGillaway; 13 as McElwee; 41 as McIlwee; 6 as McKelvey; and 27 as McKelvy. This source also clearly demonstrates that in the Inishowen district of Donegal McGillaway was the dominant spelling of the name, with ten of the fourteen McGillaway households in Donegal residing there. As Inishowen was the home of many people who migrated to the city of Derry in the 19th century this probably explains the strength of McGilloway in Derry today.

McKelvey, in Gaelic *Mac Shealbhaigh*, meaning 'son of Selbach' is also a Scottish name, found in southwest Scotland in the counties of Dumfries, Kirkcudbright and Wigtown. This region was home to many of the Scottish settlers who came to Ulster throughout the 17th century. The McKelveys were also recorded as a sept of Clan Campbell.

McGINLEY

McGinley is an exclusively Ulster name where 80% of those of the name are in County Donegal, making it among the ten most common names there.

This name, which is among the top 60 surnames in the city of Derry today, illustrates the very close links, both historic and economic, between Derry and County Donegal. As Derry developed an industrial base in the 19ᵗʰ century in shirt making, shipbuilding and distilling it attracted much of its workforce from Donegal. Her growing industries attracted workers and families from outside the city and county, and in the 90-year period 1821 to 1911 the population of the city quadrupled to 40,780.

Ireland was one of the first countries to adopt a system of hereditary surnames which developed from a more ancient system of clan or sept names. From the 11ᵗʰ century each family began to adopt its own distinctive family name generally derived from the first name of an ancestor who lived in or about the 10th century. The surname was formed by prefixing either Mac (son of) or O (grandson or descendant of) to the ancestor's name. Surnames in Ireland, therefore, tended to identify membership of a sept.

The County Donegal sept of McGinley is derived from Gaelic *Mag Fhionnghaile*, the root word being *fionnghaile*, meaning 'fair valour'. This sept is most noted for the number of churchmen it has contributed to the Diocese of Raphoe.

McGinley is sometimes confused with the Scottish name McKinley which is also found in County Donegal. McGinley and McKinley are both numerous names in Ulster, with the former concentrated in County Donegal and the latter spread more widely through the province. In Donegal, in particular, it is possible that a person with the surname McKinley is a descendant of the McGinley sept. It is believed, however, that McGinley and McKinley were not usually interchangeable.

The mid-19ᵗʰ century Griffith's Valuation records 327 McGinley households in County Donegal, with the name most concentrated in the western fringes of Donegal in the parishes of Clondahorky, Glencolumbkille and Tullaghobegley. The same source records 37 McKinley households in County Donegal. In the parish of Clondahorky, in particular, both surnames were to be found in significant numbers, with 45 households recorded as McGinley and 14 as McKinley.

In Scotland McKinley is derived from Gaelic *Mac Fhionnlaoich,* from *fionn,* meaning 'fair', and *laoch,* meaning 'hero'. There were McKinley septs associated with Clans Buchanan, Farquharson, MacFarlane, and Stewart of Appin. McKinley country was the Lennox district of Dumbartonshire and Stirlingshire.

Upheavals such as military incursions, feuds and harvest failures would have encouraged many clan members, including McKinleys, to migrate to Ulster as settlers during the 17ᵗʰ century. Owing to the nature of the Scottish clan system once the power and influence of the chief had been weakened and the bond of tribal loyalty broken the clan tended to scatter.

McGINTY

This name originated in County Donegal. The name, without the prefix Mac, is now numerous both as Ginty or Genty in County Mayo. Many Donegal names are found in Mayo as a result of considerable migration in the early seventeenth century.

Ireland was one of the first countries to adopt a system of hereditary surnames which developed from a more ancient system of clan or sept names. From the 11th century each family began to adopt its own distinctive family name generally derived from the first name of an ancestor who lived in or about the 10th century. The surname was formed by prefixing either Mac (son of) or O (grandson or descendant of) to the ancestor's name. Surnames in Ireland, therefore, tended to identify membership of a sept.

McGinty is derived from Gaelic *Mag Fhinneachta*, the root word being *sneachta,* meaning 'snow'. The homeland of this sept was southeast Donegal close to the border with Counties Fermanagh and Tyrone.

Many County Donegal septs trace their lineage to Conall *Gulban,* son of the 5th century High King of Ireland, Niall of the Nine Hostages, who ruled from the Hill of Tara, County Meath. Conall and his brother Eogan conquered northwest Ireland, ca.425 AD, capturing the great hill-fort of Grianan of Ailech in County Donegal which commanded the entrance to the Inishowen peninsula between Lough Swilly and Lough Foyle.

Conall, styled 'King of Tir Conaill', established his own kingdom in County Donegal called after him Tyrconnel, i.e. the 'Land of Conall', which was the ancient name of Donegal. His descendants, known as the Cenel Conaill (the race of Conall), formed one of the principal branches of the Northern Ui Neill (descendants of Niall of the Nine Hostages). The septs of the Cenel Conaill firmly established themselves in County Donegal while those descended from Conal's brother Eogan expanded to the east and south into Counties Derry and Tyrone.

At the time of the mid-19th century Griffith's Valuation 119 McGinty households were recorded in County Donegal. This source clearly shows that the name was most concentrated in the lands to the north of Donegal town, as 51 McGinty households were residing in the parish of Donegal and a further 28 in Kilteevoge Parish. In other words over 65% of descendants of the McGinty sept in County Donegal were living in these two adjoining parishes. This survey also confirms that in Donegal the prefix Mac was retained as there were no references to either Ginty or Genty.

The name spread to Derry city in the 19th century. This name illustrates the very close links, both historic and economic, between the city of Derry and County Donegal. As Derry developed an industrial base in the 19th century in shirt making, shipbuilding and distilling it attracted much of its workforce from Donegal. In the 90-year period 1821 to 1911 the population of the city quadrupled to 40,780. In this period Derry stamped her dominance over local rivals and emerged as an important urban centre within Ireland.

McGIRR

This name belongs to County Tyrone.

Ireland was one of the first countries to adopt a system of hereditary surnames which developed from a more ancient system of clan or sept names. From the 11th century each family began to adopt its own distinctive family name generally derived from the first name of an ancestor who lived in or about the 10th century. The surname was formed by prefixing either Mac (son of) or O (grandson or descendant of) to the ancestor's name. Surnames in Ireland, therefore, tended to identify membership of a sept.

McGirr is derived from *Mac an Ghirr,* the root word being *giorr,* meaning 'short'. Originating in the Clogher Valley, County Tyrone the McGirrs were a branch of the McCawells, in Gaelic *Mac Cathmhaoil,* the root word being *cathmhaol,* meaning 'battle chief'. Although the surname McCawell is now very rare this County Tyrone sept was once very powerful and numerous.

The McGirrs and the McCawells can trace their lineage to Eogan, son of the 5th century High King of Ireland, Niall of the Nine Hostages, who ruled from the Hill of Tara, County Meath. Eogan and his brother Conall *Gulban* conquered northwest Ireland, ca.425 AD, capturing the great hill-fort of Grianan of Ailech in County Donegal which commanded the entrance to the Inishowen peninsula between Lough Swilly and Lough Foyle.

Eogan, styled 'King of Ailech', established his own kingdom in the peninsula still called after him Inishowen (Innis Eoghain or Eogan's Isle). Eogan was converted to Christianity by St Patrick, when he travelled to Ailech, ca. 442 AD. His descendants, known as the Cenel Eoghain (the race of Owen), became the principal branch of the Northern Ui Neill (descendants of Niall of the Nine Hostages).

The McCawells were the leading sept of Clan Ferady (tracing their descent from Faredach, son of Muireadach (Murdock), son of Eogan). At the height of their power in the 12th century, from their base at Clogher, they controlled a large portion of County Tyrone and had penetrated deep into County Fermanagh. They were one of the seven powerful septs supporting O'Neill. By the mid-14th century their power in Fermanagh had been broken by the Maguires and their influence gradually declined thereafter.

The 17th century Plantation of Ulster with English and Scottish settlers not only marked the end of McCawell power, but also, to a large extent, the disappearance of the name. It would seem that families of the *Mac Cathmhaoil* sept adopted various anglicised surnames such as Campbell, Callwell, Caulfield, McCall and many others. Thus people whose origins are *Mac Cathmhaoil* are disguised by a variety of inappropriate anglicised names.

The McGirr sept trace their descent from the 14th century Maelechlainn mac an ghirr meic Cathmhaoil, which literally means 'Malachy, the son of the short fellow McCawell'.

McGLINCHEY

This surname is found exclusively in Ulster where it is most common in Counties Donegal, Derry and Tyrone.

Ireland was one of the first countries to adopt a system of hereditary surnames which developed from a more ancient system of clan or sept names. From the 11th century each family began to adopt its own distinctive family name generally derived from the first name of an ancestor who lived in or about the 10th century. The surname was formed by prefixing either Mac (son of) or O (grandson or descendant of) to the ancestor's name. Surnames in Ireland, therefore, tended to identify membership of a sept.

McGlinchey is derived from Gaelic *Mag Loingsigh*, the root word being *loingseach*, meaning 'mariner'. The homeland of this sept was County Donegal.

Many County Donegal septs trace their lineage to Conall *Gulban*, son of the 5th century High King of Ireland, Niall of the Nine Hostages, who ruled from the Hill of Tara, County Meath. Conall and his brother Eogan conquered northwest Ireland, ca.425 AD, capturing the great hill-fort of Grianan of Ailech in County Donegal which commanded the entrance to the Inishowen peninsula between Lough Swilly and Lough Foyle.

Conall, styled 'King of Tir Conaill', established his own kingdom in County Donegal called after him Tyrconnel, i.e. the 'Land of Conall', which was the ancient name of Donegal. His descendants, known as the Cenel Conaill (the race of Conall), formed one of the principal branches of the Northern Ui Neill (descendants of Niall of the Nine Hostages). The septs of the Cenel Conaill firmly established themselves in County Donegal while those descended from Conal's brother Eogan expanded to the east and south into Counties Derry and Tyrone.

At the time of the mid-19th century Griffith's Valuation 54 McGlinchey households were recorded in County Donegal. This source clearly shows that the name was most concentrated in the parish of Donaghmore in the lands between the River Finn and the border with County Tyrone. At this time there were 16 McGlinchey households recorded in Donaghmore Parish. In other words 30% of descendants of the McGlinchey sept in County Donegal were living in this parish.

McGlinchey is a common name in Derry city today. This name, which spread to Derry city in the 19th century, illustrates the very close links, both historic and economic, between the city of Derry and County Donegal. As Derry developed an industrial base in shirt making, shipbuilding and distilling it attracted much of its workforce from County Donegal. In the 90-year period 1821 to 1911 the population of the city quadrupled to 40,780. In this period Derry stamped her dominance over local rivals and emerged as an important urban centre within Ireland.

McGOLDRICK

This name, which originated on the Fermanagh-Leitrim border, is most numerous in Ulster, particularly in Counties Donegal, Fermanagh and Tyrone, and in the adjoining part of Connaught, particularly in County Sligo.

Ireland was one of the first countries to adopt a system of hereditary surnames which developed from a more ancient system of clan or sept names. From the 11th century each family began to adopt its own distinctive family name generally derived from the first name of an ancestor who lived in or about the 10th century. The surname was formed by prefixing either Mac (son of) or O (grandson or descendant of) to the ancestor's name. Surnames in Ireland, therefore, tended to identify membership of a sept.

McGoldrick is derived from Gaelic *Mag Ualghairg*, meaning 'son of Ulrick', a personal name meaning 'fierce pride'. The McGoldricks were a branch of the O'Rourkes of Leitrim. The O'Rourkes contested with the O'Reillys for the chieftainship of Breffny, an ancient territory which comprised County Cavan and west Leitrim. In the 10th century Breffny was divided into Breffny-O'Reilly and Breffny-O'Rourke which, in the late-16th century, formed the basis for the creation of Counties Cavan and Leitrim respectively

The McGoldricks trace their descent from Ualgharg O'Rourke, Lord of Breffny, who died in 1231 as a pilgrim on his way to the Holy Land. The McGoldricks were, in the early medieval period, an important sept in Leitrim. *The Annals of The Kingdom of Ireland by the Four Masters* (a chronicle of Irish history from 'the earliest period to the year 1616') record that, in 1054, 'Mac Ualghairg, lord of Cairbre, was killed by treachery'.

By the mid-17th century the name was established in County Fermanagh, particularly in the barony of Lurg in north Fermanagh, and in Donegal, as MacGolrick and MacGoulrigg, as it was recorded in the Hearth Money Rolls of the 1660s in both these counties.

At the time of the mid-19th century Griffith's Valuation 44 McGoldrick households were recorded in County Donegal. This source clearly shows that the name was most concentrated in east Donegal on the lands bordering Counties Fermanagh and Tyrone. The largest concentration, of 15 households, was recorded in the parish of Donaghmore, which is bounded by the River Finn to the north and the border of Tyrone to the south.

McGoldrick was also a common name in County Mayo by the end of the 18th century. Many Donegal names, in particular, are found in Mayo as a result of considerable migration in the early seventeenth century. In recent times, in Mayo, McGoldrick has largely been changed to Golden.

The anglicisation of Gaelic names, from the 17th century, resulted in variant spellings of McGoldrick such as Golden, Goulding, Goodwin and Magorlick. The name is now also found in Scotland as MacGoldrick in Glasgow and as MacGorlick in Galloway.

McGONAGLE

This name is almost exclusively found in Ulster, where it is most common in Counties Donegal and Derry. This name, and its variants such as McGonigle and McGonegal, has always been closely associated with its homeland of County Donegal.

This name illustrates the very close links, both historic and economic, between the city of Derry and County Donegal. As Derry developed an industrial base in the 19th century in shirt making, shipbuilding and distilling it attracted much of its workforce from Donegal. Her growing industries attracted workers and families from outside the city and county, and in the 90-year period 1821 to 1911 the population of the city quadrupled to 40,780. In this period Derry stamped her dominance over local rivals and emerged as an important urban centre within Ireland.

Ireland was one of the first countries to adopt a system of hereditary surnames which developed from a more ancient system of clan or sept names. From the 11th century each family began to adopt its own distinctive family name generally derived from the first name of an ancestor who lived in or about the 10th century. The surname was formed by prefixing either Mac (son of) or O (grandson or descendant of) to the ancestor's name. Surnames in Ireland, therefore, tended to identify membership of a sept. McGonagle is derived from Gaelic *Mac Congail.*

Although the McGonagles were counted among the warlike followers of the O'Donnells, this sept is most noted for the number of distinguished churchmen it has produced. The McGonagles were *erenaghs*, i.e. hereditary stewards, of the church lands of Killybegs in southwest Donegal. They also contributed many priests and two bishops to the Diocese of Raphoe.

The Annals of The Kingdom of Ireland by the Four Masters (a history of Ireland from 'the earliest period to the year 1616' which was compiled by monks who were followers of the O'Donnells of Donegal) record the death of Donnell Mag Congail, Bishop of Raphoe on 29 September 1589 at Killybegs. Appointed Bishop of Raphoe in 1562 Donnell McGonagle 'could write well and spoke Latin and English as well as Irish'. As a leader of the Counter-Reformation he assisted at the Council of Trent in 1563 with the Pope's attempts to reform and revive the Roman Catholic church throughout Europe.

It would seem that the homeland of the McGonagle sept was the Inishowen Peninsula in northeast Donegal. At the time of the mid-19th century Griffith's Valuation the greatest concentration of McGonagles in County Donegal were in the Inishowen parishes of Clonmany, which contained 31 McGonagle households, Culdaff with 30 households of the name, Moville with 27 and Clonca with 21. In total 169 McGonagle households were recorded in this survey in County Donegal.

The escape of the most prominent Gaelic Lords of Ulster in 'the Flight of the Earls' in1607 from Lough Swilly, County Donegal marked the end of Gaelic power and paved the way for the 17th century Plantation of Ulster with English and Scottish settlers. In the centuries that followed Gaelic names were anglicised, resulting in many variant spellings of the same name and, in many cases, the dropping of the O and Mac prefixes. In the case of McGonagle the prefix Mac was usually retained.

McGOWAN

McGowan can be an Irish or a Scottish name. In Ireland McGowan is largely confined to Ulster and the adjacent parts of Connaught in Counties Leitrim and Sligo. In Ulster McGowan is most common in County Donegal, where it is among the fifteen most numerous names.

The McGowan sept of County Cavan, in Gaelic *Mac an Ghabhann*, meaning 'son of the smith', was one of the principal septs of the ancient kingdom of Breffny, which included County Cavan and west Leitrim. Originating in central County Cavan the McGowans were *erenaghs*, i.e. hereditary stewards, of the church lands of Drumully in Dartry, County Monaghan. In its homeland, i.e. County Cavan, the great majority of McGowans anglicised their name to Smith. Today Smith is among the five most numerous names in County Cavan.

On the borders of Breffny in County Leitrim and to the northwest in Counties Sligo and Donegal, the true form in English, McGowan persisted. In southwest Donegal, where Counties Donegal and Leitrim meet, the McGowans were *erenaghs* of the church lands at Inishmacsaint. In County Tyrone another family of McGowan, in Gaelic *Mac In Gabhand*, were *erenaghs* of the church lands at Ballymagowan in Clogher.

In the Highlands of Scotland, especially in Inverness-shire and Perthshire, Clan MacGowan, in Gaelic *Mac Gobha*, meaning 'son of the smith' was also anglicised as Gow. As the maker of arms and armour the blacksmith was an important hereditary position in each clan and there were McGowans found throughout the Highlands. The two most important septs, however, were the MacGowans of Clan Donald and those of Clan Macpherson.

McGowan, in Gaelic *Mac Ghobhainn*, meaning 'son of the smith', was the name of an old Stirling family. McGowan was also common in Dumfriesshire, and in the reign of David II (1329-1371) a Clan McGowan lived beside the River Nith in Dumfriesshire. As is the case with Irish McGowans it can be assumed that many Scottish McGowans further anglicised their name to Smith. Indeed it is believed that the majority of Ulster Smiths were originally McGowan.

Until their defeat at Culloden Moor on 15 April 1746 the clans of the Highlands of Scotland were a very real threat to Royal authority. Upheavals such as military incursions, feuds and harvest failures would have encouraged many clan members, including McGowans, to migrate to Ulster as settlers during the 17th century. In 1609 the Earl of Salisbury, Lord High Treasurer, suggested to James I a deliberate plantation of Scottish and English colonists on the forfeited estates of the Gaelic chiefs in counties Armagh, Cavan, Donegal, Fermanagh, Londonderry (then known as Coleraine) and Tyrone.

These settlers came to Ulster, by and large, in three waves: with the granting of the initial leases in the period 1605 to 1625; after 1652 and Cromwell's crushing of the Irish rebellion; and finally in the fifteen years after 1690 and the Glorious Revolution. It is estimated by 1715, when migration to Ulster had virtually stopped, the Scottish population of Ulster stood at 200,000.

204

McGRATH

McGrath is among the sixty most common names in Ireland. Over one-half of the McGraths are in Munster, particularly in Counties Tipperary, Cork and Waterford. One-quarter of Irish McGraths are in Ulster, where the name is most common in County Tyrone.

Ireland was one of the first countries to adopt a system of hereditary surnames which developed from a more ancient system of clan or sept names. From the 11th century each family began to adopt its own distinctive family name generally derived from the first name of an ancestor who lived in or about the 10th century. The surname was formed by prefixing either Mac (son of) or O (grandson or descendant of) to the ancestor's name. Surnames in Ireland, therefore, tended to identify membership of a sept.

McGrath is derived from Gaelic *Mac Graith*, meaning 'son of Craith'. There were two septs of the name. In Munster, the McGraths of County Clare and Waterford were hereditary poets to the O'Briens.

In Ulster, the McGraths were an important sept of the Donegal-Fermanagh border, based originally at Termonmagrath near Pettigo. They trace their lineage to Eogan, son of the 5th century High King of Ireland, Niall of the Nine Hostages, who ruled from the Hill of Tara, County Meath. Eogan and his brother Conall *Gulban* conquered northwest Ireland, ca.425 AD, capturing the great hill-fort of Grianan of Ailech in County Donegal which commanded the entrance to the Inishowen peninsula between Lough Swilly and Lough Foyle.

Eogan, styled 'King of Ailech', established his own kingdom in the peninsula still called after him Inishowen (Innis Eoghain or Eogan's Isle). His descendants, known as the Cenel Eoghain (the race of Owen), became the principal branch of the Northern Ui Neill (descendants of Niall of the Nine Hostages). The septs of the Cenel Eoghain expanded to the east and south, from their focal point in Inishowen, into Counties Derry and Tyrone.

The McGraths were lords of Clan Moen (tracing their descent from Moen, son of Muireadach (Murdock), son of Eogan). Their territory was known as *Magh Ithe* which referred to the rich countryside stretching southward from Inishowen, later known as the Laggan district in east Donegal. The McGraths were driven out of the Ballybofey area in the barony of Raphoe, County Donegal by the O'Donnells, and, from the 14th century, they settled at Ardstraw in County Tyrone. In County Fermanagh the McGraths of the Sillees were a branch of the Maguires.

The anglicisation of Gaelic names, from the 17th century, resulted in variant spellings of McGrath such as McGragh and McGra in Counties Donegal and Derry, and McGraw and Magraw in County Down.

In 1688 Colonel Alexander McDonnell, 3rd Earl of Antrim raised a regiment in support of King James II. Lieutenant Brian McGrath was an officer in this regiment, and he was part of the 'Jacobite army' which besieged the city of Derry during the famous 105 day Siege of Derry, from 18 April to 31 July 1689.

McGREGOR

This name, of Scottish origin, is most concentrated in County Londonderry. Furthermore there are many descendants of this once powerful Scottish clan in Ulster today who no longer bear the name McGregor. In many instances the McGregor origins of seventeenth century Scottish settlers to Ulster are disguised by a great variety of other surnames, such as Black, Grant, Greer, Gregg and many others.

McGregor is derived from Gaelic *Mac Griogair*, meaning 'son of Gregory', a personal name, meaning 'watchful'. The McGregors claim descent from Griogar, third son of Kenneth MacAlpine, the 9th century King of Scotland. In historical times the chiefs of Clan MacGregor descend from one Aodh Urchaidh, ruler of Glenorchy in Argyllshire. From there they came to control a large territory in Perthshire and Argyllshire including Glenstrae, Glenorchy, Glenlyon and Glengyle. In the 14th century branches of the clan migrated to Dumfriesshire under Gilbrid MacGregor.

The McGregors came into conflict with their powerful neighbours the Campbells, and, as a consequence, their lands were dispossessed and they resorted to raiding. In 1603, by Act of Parliament, the clan was outlawed, an order was given to disperse them 'by fire and sword', and their name was proscribed. As a 'broken' clan the McGregors now adopted a great variety of new names, including colour names such as Black or White, and the names of septs, formerly attached to the clan, such as Grant, Greer, Gregg, Gregor, Gregorson and Gregory.

Movement of Scottish settlers to Ulster began in earnest from 1605 in a private enterprise colonisation of counties Antrim and Down when Sir Hugh Montgomery and Sir James Hamilton acquired title to large estates in north Down and Sir Randall MacDonnell, 1st Earl of Antrim, to large tracts of land in north Antrim. Further impetus came in 1609 when James I adopted the policy to encourage Scottish settlers to settle on the forfeited estates of the Gaelic chiefs in counties Armagh, Cavan, Donegal, Fermanagh, Londonderry (then known as Coleraine) and Tyrone.

These settlers came to Ulster, by and large, in three waves: with the granting of the initial leases in the period 1605 to 1625; after 1652 and Cromwell's crushing of the Irish rebellion; and finally in the fifteen years after 1690 and the Glorious Revolution. Apart from a thirty-year period after 1660, the name McGregor remained proscribed for 170 years until 1775. Thus the great movement of descendants of the McGregors to Ulster came at a time when their name was proscribed.

Reverend James McGregor, the Gaelic-speaking minister of Aghadowey Presbyterian Church, County Londonderry, emigrated to New England with a number of his congregation in the summer of 1718, and established the settlement of Londonderry, New Hampshire. It is said that, in case of Indian attack, Reverend James McGregor always marched into the pulpit of his meeting house in New Hampshire, built of logs in 1722, with his gun primed. As a boy of 12 years old, James McGregor (born at Magilligan, County Londonderry in 1677) was inside the walls of Derry during the famous 105 day Siege of the city in 1689. It is claimed that James discharged from the tower of St Columb's Cathedral the large gun which announced the approach of the ships that brought relief to the city.

McGRORY

McGrory, and variants such as Macrory, McCrory and McRory, can be an Irish or a Scottish name. This name is virtually exclusive to Ulster, where over one-half are in Tyrone and one-third are in County Antrim.

Ireland was one of the first countries to adopt a system of hereditary surnames which developed from a more ancient system of clan or sept names. The surname was formed by prefixing either Mac (son of) or O (grandson or descendant of) to the ancestor's name.

McGrory is derived from Gaelic *Mac Ruaidhri*, meaning 'son of Rory'. There were two distinct McGrory septs in Ulster. It is claimed that the County Tyrone sept of the name trace their descent from the Three Collas. *Colla Uais*, High King of Ireland from 322 to 326 AD, and his two brothers are reputed to have burnt and destroyed Navan Fort in County Armagh. Navan Fort, built ca.300 BC, was the residence of the warrior kings of Ulster, and of Cuchullain and his legendary Red Branch Knights. The Three Collas were banished to Scotland in 326 AD.

A branch of this County Tyrone sept migrated to County Derry where they became *erenaghs*, i.e. hereditary stewards, of the church lands in the parish of Ballynascreen in the barony of Loughinsholin. Another McGrory sept were *erenaghs* of Machaire Croise in Fermanagh. It is believed that they were a branch of the Maguires.

McGrory in Gaelic *Mac Ruairidh*, meaning 'son of Rory', is also a Scottish name. They were an important sept of Clan Donald. In the 14th century some of these families came to Ulster as galloglasses. Derived from Gaelic *galloglach*, galloglass refers to a paid soldier, often brought over from Scotland, to fight on behalf of an Irish chief.

The Annals of The Kingdom of Ireland by the Four Masters provide detailed and graphic descriptions of the Scottish galloglasses. In one account dated 1557 the *Annals* describe the galloglass in the camp of the O'Neills who were on a raiding expedition into O'Donnell territory in Donegal. It states that 'sixty grim and redoubtable gallowglasses, with sharp, keen axes, terrible and ready for action, and sixty stern and terrific Scots, with massive, broad, and heavy-striking swords in their hands, ready to strike and parry, were watching and guarding the son of O'Neill.'

The majority of Scottish McGrorys in Ulster, however, will be descendants of 17th century settlers. Movement of Scottish settlers to Ulster began in earnest from 1605 in a private enterprise colonisation of counties Antrim and Down when Sir Hugh Montgomery and Sir James Hamilton acquired title to large estates in north Down and Sir Randall MacDonnell, 1st Earl of Antrim, to large tracts of land in north Antrim.

As followers of Clan Donald many Scottish McGrorys settled in the Glens of Antrim. Clan Donald had acquired territory here ca.1400. By the mid-16th century the MacDonalds, known as the MacDonnells of the Glens, had carved out an extensive territory in County Antrim at the expense of the MacQuillans.

In many cases McGrory was further anglicised to Rogers and Rodgers.

McGUCKIAN

McGuckian is one of the more commonly recorded variants of the surname McGuigan. This name is almost exclusively found in Ulster, where it is most common in its homeland of County Tyrone. In County Tyrone, in particular, other variants of the name such as Mc-Googan, McGookin, McQuiggan and McWiggin are also found. In some cases the name was further anglicised to Fidgeon, Pidgeon and Goodman in County Monaghan and to Goodwin and even Goodfellow in County Tyrone.

The McGuigan sept trace their lineage to Eogan, son of the 5th century High King of Ireland, Niall of the Nine Hostages, who ruled from the Hill of Tara, County Meath. Eogan and his brother Conall *Gulban* conquered northwest Ireland, ca.425 AD, capturing the great hill-fort of Grianan of Ailech in County Donegal.

Eogan, styled 'King of Ailech', established his own kingdom in the peninsula in County Donegal still called after him Inishowen (Innis Eoghain or Eogan's Isle). His descendants, known as the Cenel Eoghain (the race of Owen), became the principal branch of the Northern Ui Neill (descendants of Niall of the Nine Hostages). The Cenel Eoghain in the next five centuries expanded to the east and south from their focal point in Inishowen.

Ireland was one of the first countries to adopt a system of hereditary surnames which developed from a more ancient system of clan or sept names. From the 11th century each family began to adopt its own distinctive family name generally derived from the first name of an ancestor who lived in or about the 10th century. The surname was formed by prefixing either Mac (son of) or O (grandson or descendant of) to the ancestor's name. Surnames in Ireland, therefore, tended to identify membership of a sept.

It is believed that McGuckian, in Gaelic *Mac Uiginn*, is derived from a Norse personal name. Surnames formed from Norse words or forenames were quite common in the Cenel Eoghain.

In the 9th and 10th centuries, in particular, the Vikings or Norsemen, mostly from Norway, conducted numerous hit-and-run raids in their fast sailing ships on Ireland. In 839 they put a fleet on Lough Neagh and plundered the neighbouring monasteries and the surrounding countryside. They over-wintered on Lough Neagh on 840-1.

The north-western shore of Lough Neagh, which was prone to Viking raids, was very much home to the McGuigan sept. The McGuigans were *erenaghs*, i.e. hereditary stewards, of the church lands of Ballinderry which straddled the borders of Counties Derry and Tyrone on the north-western shore of Lough Neagh. In the parish of Artrea, County Derry, just to the north of Ballinderry, and sitting on the shore of Lough Neagh, the townland of Ballymaguigan, i.e. 'the townland of the McGuigans', is a further reminder of the former prominence of the McGuigan sept in this area.

The name McGuigan, in Gaelic *Mac Guagain*, meaning 'son of Eogan or Ewan' is recorded in Scotland at an early date, and found particularly in Argyllshire and Kintyre. Thus, it is possible, that a few bearers of this name came to Ulster at the time of the 17th century Plantation of Ulster by settlers from Scotland.

McGUIGAN

This name is almost exclusively found in Ulster, where it is most common in its homeland of County Tyrone. In County Tyrone, in particular, variants of this name such as McGoogan, McGookin, McGuckian, McQuiggan and McWiggin are commonly found. In some cases the name was further anglicised to Fidgeon, Pidgeon and Goodman in County Monaghan and to Goodwin and even Goodfellow in County Tyrone.

The McGuigan sept trace their lineage to Eogan, son of the 5th century High King of Ireland, Niall of the Nine Hostages, who ruled from the Hill of Tara, County Meath. Eogan and his brother Conall *Gulban* conquered northwest Ireland, ca.425 AD, capturing the great hill-fort of Grianan of Ailech in County Donegal.

Eogan, styled 'King of Ailech', established his own kingdom in the peninsula in County Donegal still called after him Inishowen (Innis Eoghain or Eogan's Isle). His descendants, known as the Cenel Eoghain (the race of Owen), became the principal branch of the Northern Ui Neill (descendants of Niall of the Nine Hostages). The Cenel Eoghain in the next five centuries expanded to the east and south from their focal point in Inishowen.

Ireland was one of the first countries to adopt a system of hereditary surnames which developed from a more ancient system of clan or sept names. From the 11th century each family began to adopt its own distinctive family name generally derived from the first name of an ancestor who lived in or about the 10th century. The surname was formed by prefixing either Mac (son of) or O (grandson or descendant of) to the ancestor's name. Surnames in Ireland, therefore, tended to identify membership of a sept.

It is believed that McGuigan, in Gaelic *Mac Uiginn*, is derived from a Norse personal name. Surnames formed from Norse words or forenames were quite common in the Cenel Eoghain.

In the 9th and 10th centuries, in particular, the Vikings or Norsemen, mostly from Norway, conducted numerous hit-and-run raids in their fast sailing ships on Ireland. In 839 they put a fleet on Lough Neagh and plundered the neighbouring monasteries and the surrounding countryside. They over-wintered on Lough Neagh on 840-1.

The north-western shore of Lough Neagh, which was prone to Viking raids, was very much home to the McGuigan sept. The McGuigans were *erenaghs*, i.e. hereditary stewards, of the church lands of Ballinderry which straddled the borders of Counties Derry and Tyrone on the north-western shore of Lough Neagh. In the parish of Artrea, County Derry, just to the north of Ballinderry, and sitting on the shore of Lough Neagh, the townland of Ballymaguigan, i.e. 'the townland of the McGuigans', is a further reminder of the former prominence of the McGuigan sept in this area.

The name McGuigan, in Gaelic *Mac Guagain*, meaning 'son of Eogan or Ewan' is recorded in Scotland at an early date, and found particularly in Argyllshire and Kintyre. Thus, it is possible, that a few bearers of this name came to Ulster at the time of the 17th century Plantation of Ulster by settlers from Scotland.

McGUINNESS

McGuinness is a well-known name in Connaught and is numerous in Leinster. But the name is most common in Ulster, where it originates. The McGuinnesses were one of the leading septs of Ulster. The name is now found in over twenty different spellings, including Magennis, McGenis and Guinness. The modern spelling of this name is usually McGuinness but in the historical records in English they are called as a rule Magennis.

Ireland was one of the first countries to adopt a system of hereditary surnames which developed from a more ancient system of clan or sept names. From the 11th century each family began to adopt its own distinctive family name generally derived from the first name of an ancestor who lived in or about the 10th century. The surname was formed by prefixing either Mac (son of) or O (grandson or descendant of) to the ancestor's name. Surnames in Ireland, therefore, tended to identify membership of a sept.

McGuinness is derived from Gaelic *Mag Aonghusa* or *Mag Aonghuis*, meaning 'son of Angus'. They trace their descent from Saran, chief of Dal Araidhe in eastern Ulster, in St Patrick's time in the 5th century. From the 12th century the McGuinnesses were Lords of Iveagh in County Down and from their main stronghold in Rathfriland they controlled most of County Down for the following four hundred years.

In the 16th century many of the McGuinnesses accepted the Reformation and, indeed, provided a number of Protestant bishops of Down and Dromore at that time. In 1598, however, the McGuinnesses sided with the O'Neills, and the other Gaelic lords, in their armed resistance to the extension of English rule in Ulster during the Nine Years War (1594-1603).

In the 17th century the McGuinnesses continued to play an active part in resisting English attempts to pacify Ulster. They were finally dispossessed of their lands in County Down in the years after the Battle of the Boyne of 1690. Many McGuinnesses now emigrated, as the so-called Wild Geese, to Europe where they served with distinction in the armies of Austria, France and Spain.

In Scotland Clan MacInnes would seem to have common origins with the McGuinnesses of County Down. Clan MacInnes, in Gaelic *Mac Aonghuis*, meaning 'son of Angus' trace their origins to the Irish Celts, known as the Scots, of the ancient kingdom of Dalriada in eastern Ulster who established a kingdom in Kintyre, Argyll and some of the Inner Isles in the 6th century. This kingdom in Scotland was also called Dal Riata. The MacInneses were hereditary bowmen to the Chiefs of Clan Mackinnon. In the 17th century a chief of the MacInneses was Keeper of Kinlochaline Castle in Morvern in Argyllshire. In Scotland this surname tends to be recorded as McInnes, McKinnes and McKinness.

Upheavals such as military incursions, feuds and harvest failures would have encouraged many clan members, including MacInneses, to migrate to Ulster as settlers during the 17th century. In Ulster it is quite possible that Scottish McInneses may have adopted the Irish way of spelling the name, i.e. McGuinness.

McGURK

This surname is most common in Ulster, particularly in its homeland in County Tyrone and in County Antrim.

The McGurk sept of County Tyrone trace their lineage to Eogan, son of the 5th century High King of Ireland, Niall of the Nine Hostages, who ruled from the Hill of Tara, County Meath. Eogan and his brother Conall *Gulban* conquered northwest Ireland, ca.425 AD, capturing the great hill-fort of Grianan of Ailech in County Donegal which commanded the entrance to the Inishowen peninsula between Lough Swilly and Lough Foyle.

Eogan, styled 'King of Ailech', established his own kingdom in the peninsula in County Donegal still called after him Inishowen (Innis Eoghain or Eogan's Isle). His descendants, known as the Cenel Eoghain (the race of Owen), became the principal branch of the Northern Ui Neill (descendants of Niall of the Nine Hostages). The Cenel Eoghain in the next five centuries expanded to the east and south from their focal point in Inishowen. They established the kingdom of Tir Eoghain (Tir Owen or Tyrone, the land of Owen) which extended over the present counties of Tyrone and Derry.

Ireland was one of the first countries to adopt a system of hereditary surnames which developed from a more ancient system of clan or sept names. From the 11th century each family began to adopt its own distinctive family name generally derived from the first name of an ancestor who lived in or about the 10th century. The surname was formed by prefixing either Mac (son of) or O (grandson or descendant of) to the ancestor's name. Surnames in Ireland, therefore, tended to identify membership of a sept. McGurk is derived from Gaelic *Mag Oirc*.

The McGurks were one of the leading septs of Clan Binny (*Eochaid Binnigh* was a son of Eogan) possessing territory on the banks of the River Foyle near Lifford in County Donegal. The first outward thrust of the Owen clan was that of Clan Binny in the 6th century AD who thrust southeast into County Tyrone, bypassing a hard core of resistance in County Derry of the Cianachta, as far as the river Blackwater on the borders of Tyrone and Armagh.

The McGurks were *erenaghs*, i.e. hereditary stewards, of the church lands in the parish of Termonmaguirk, meaning 'the sanctuary of the McGurks', in the barony of Omagh, County Tyrone. The McGurks, as tenants of the Archbishop of Armagh, were dispossessed of this property in 1624 following the Plantation of Ulster. The McGurks were hereditary joint keepers of St Colmcille's bell. Colmcille (also known as Columba) founded a monastery at Derry in 546 AD.

The association of this sept with south Derry is commemorated in the townland name of Ballygurk, in Gaelic *Baile Mhic Oirc*, meaning 'the townland of the McGurks'. This townland straddles the boundary between the parishes of Artrea and Tamlaght.

Although the name is now chiefly found in Counties Tyrone and Antrim, McGurk does appear frequently in the 17th century Hearth Money Rolls for Counties Armagh and Monaghan.

McHENRY

The McHenry sept of County Derry trace their lineage to Eogan, son of the 5th century High King of Ireland, Niall of the Nine Hostages, who ruled from the Hill of Tara, County Meath. Eogan and his brother Conall *Gulban* conquered northwest Ireland, ca.425 AD, capturing the great hill-fort of Grianan of Ailech in County Donegal.

Eogan, styled 'King of Ailech', established his own kingdom in the peninsula in County Donegal still called after him Inishowen (Innis Eoghain or Eogan's Isle). His descendants, known as the Cenel Eoghain (the race of Owen), became the principal branch of the Northern Ui Neill (descendants of Niall of the Nine Hostages). The Cenel Eoghain in the next five centuries expanded to the east and south from their focal point in Inishowen.

Ireland was one of the first countries to adopt a system of hereditary surnames which developed from a more ancient system of clan or sept names. The surname was formed by prefixing either Mac (son of) or O (grandson or descendant of) to the ancestor's name.

The McHenrys, in Gaelic *Mac Einri*, were a branch of the O'Cahans (O'Kanes). They trace their descent from Henry O'Cahan, son of Dermot who died 1428, son of Cooey Na Gaal who died in 1385. The McHenrys were based at the Loughan in Kildollagh Parish, to the southeast of the town of Coleraine in County Derry. Thus McHenry literally means son of Henry O'Kane. The name was further anglicised to Henry.

By the time of the 17th century Plantation of Ulster by English and Scottish settlers the McHenry O'Cahans were generally known as McHenry although occasionally O'Cahan was added.

In 1609 Mill Loughan was granted to George McHenry O'Cahan from Sir Randal MacDonnell, Earl of Antrim. The McHenrys also obtained adjacent lands in County Antrim in Ballyrashane Parish. Thus from their home near Loughan Island, which divides the River Bann, the McHenry O'Cahans had an outpost across the Bann fronting the Scottish MacDonnells.

The family took an active part in the 1641 rebellion and as a consequence the property of the McHenry family of the Loughan was confiscated.

Confusion arises when dealing with the names Henry and McHenry because of the proximity of Gaelic Irish septs, such as McHenry of the Loughan and O'Henery of County Tyrone, to Scottish settlers with surnames such as Henry, McHendrie, McKendrick and McKendry, particularly in north Antrim and Derry. In these areas it will be difficult to distinguish Scottish Henrys from Irish Henrys. Henry, Hendry, McHendrie, McKendrick were names of a Scottish sept of Clan MacNaughton which descends from one Henry MacNaughton. These names were further anglicised to Henderson.

McHUGH

This name is very numerous in Counties Galway, Mayo and Leitrim in north Connaught and in Counties Donegal and Fermanagh in west Ulster.

Ireland was one of the first countries to adopt a system of hereditary surnames which developed from a more ancient system of clan or sept names. From the 11th century each family began to adopt its own distinctive family name generally derived from the first name of an ancestor who lived in or about the 10th century. The surname was formed by prefixing either Mac (son of) or O (grandson or descendant of) to the ancestor's name. Surnames in Ireland, therefore, tended to identify membership of a sept.

McHugh is derived from Gaelic *Mac Aodha*, meaning 'son of Hugh'. There were two distinct septs of the name in County Galway: one was located near Tuam and the other, a branch of the O'Flahertys, in Connemara. It is believed that these two County Galway septs were the forebears of most McHugh families in Ireland today.

It has been claimed that the McHughs of Donegal and Fermanagh are a branch of the Maguires, the pre-eminent family in Fermanagh from the thirteenth to the seventeenth century. They trace their descent from Aodh, a grandson of Donn Carrach Maguire. Donn Carrach Maguire, who died in 1302, was the first Maguire chief of all Fermanagh.

Confusion arises as the Gaelic surname *Mac Aodha* has acquired in the process of anglicisation a great number of variants. These include McCoy, McCue, McKay, McKee and Hughes. McCue is the commonest variant spelling of McHugh.

In Scotland Gaelic *Mac Aoidh*, meaning 'son of Hugh', was anglicised as Mackay and also as Mackie, McCay, McCoy, McKay and McKee. Clan Mackay, claiming descent from Morgund of Pluscarden, originated in Moray. This clan came to prominence in Sutherland in the 13th century and by 1427 the chief, Angus Dow MacKay, could muster an army of 4000 men. In Inverness-shire the Mackays were a sept of Clan Davidson, and in Kintyre and Galloway the MacKays, MacKies and Mackies were followers of Clan Donald.

The first Mackays in Ireland, also known as McCoys, were Clan Donald galloglasses, i.e. mercenary soldiers. As followers of Clan Donald they came over to Ulster from Kintyre and the southern isles of Scotland such as Islay to fight for the McDonnells of the Glens of Antrim.

Although the surname McHugh is regarded to be of Irish origin it is known, particularly in Fermanagh and Donegal, that some descendants of the Irish sept *Mac Aodha* now bear surnames such as McCoy and McKee. Thus in west Ulster, in particular, Irish McHugh can become indistinguishable from Scottish Mackay.

It is also possible that some McHughs in Ulster are descended from the Clan Donald sept of McHugh. However, in most cases, McHugh was anglicised as Houston in Scotland.

McILFATRICK

This surname is found predominantly in Ulster where it was brought at the time of the 17th century Plantation of Ulster by settlers from Scotland. It is most common in County Londonderry.

McIlfatrick is an anglicised form of McPatrick. In the Highlands of Scotland Clan Mac-Patrick, which was also anglicised as Patterson, was derived from Gaelic *Mac Gille Phadruig*, meaning 'son of the devotee of St Patrick'. Gillepatrick was a common Gaelic personal name. This surname was recorded in Moray, as Macgyllepatric, as early as 1236. The territory of this clan was on the north side of Lochfyne.

Patrick was one of the most popular names in the west of Scotland in pre-Reformation times. The popularity of the name stems from St Patrick, the fifth century saint, who is regarded as the greatest and most famous of Ireland's Christian missionaries. In modern Scottish Gaelic the name Patrick is found in four forms: *Padruig*; *Paruig*; *Para*; and *Padair*, the common form of Patrick in Arran and Kintyre.

McPatrick was one of the names assumed by the Lamonts after their clan was 'broken' in the 17th century. In this case they took the name of an ancestor, baron MacPatrick. The Mc-Patricks were furthermore a sept of Clan Maclaren, active supporters of the Jacobite cause in Scotland during the Risings of 1715 and 1745.

Upheavals such as military incursions, feuds and harvest failures would have encouraged many clan members, including McIlfatricks, to migrate to Ulster as settlers during the 17th century. Owing to the nature of the Scottish clan system once the power and influence of the chief had been weakened and the bond of tribal loyalty broken the clan tended to scatter.

Movement of Scottish settlers to Ulster began in earnest from 1605 in a private enterprise colonisation of counties Antrim and Down when Sir Hugh Montgomery and Sir James Hamilton acquired title to large estates in north Down and Sir Randall MacDonnell, 1st Earl of Antrim, to large tracts of land in north Antrim.

Further impetus came in 1609 when James I adopted the policy to encourage Scottish settlers to settle on the forfeited estates of the Gaelic chiefs in counties Armagh, Cavan, Donegal, Fermanagh, Londonderry (then known as Coleraine) and Tyrone. Settlers came to Ulster, by and large, in three waves: with the granting of the initial leases in the period 1605 to 1625; after 1652 and Cromwell's crushing of the Irish rebellion; and finally in the fifteen years after 1690 and the Glorious Revolution.

Scottish families entering Ireland through the port of Londonderry settled in the Foyle Valley which includes much of the fertile lands of counties Donegal, Londonderry and Tyrone. In the mid-19th century Griffith's Valuation eight McIlfatrick households were recorded in all of Ireland and seven of these lived in County Londonderry.

It is estimated by 1715, when migration to Ulster had virtually stopped, the Scottish population of Ulster stood at 200,000.

McINTYRE

McIntyre is a Scottish surname but it has become confused with Irish McAteer. McIntyre is found in Leinster and Connaught but is most common in Ulster, particularly in Counties Derry and Antrim. This name was brought to Ulster in large numbers by settlers from Scotland in the 17th century.

In Scotland the McIntyres, in Gaelic *Mac an tSaoir*, meaning 'son of the craftsman' (referring to occupations such as carpenter, mason or wright), were a recognised clan in their own right. 'Glenoe, near Bunawe, Nether Lorn' in Argyllshire was their territory. It is claimed that they came to Lorn from the Hebrides and settled at Glenoe around 1380. The McIntyres were followers of the Stewarts of Appin.

The McIntyres supported the Jacobite cause in Scotland. Five McIntyres in Appin's regiment were killed and five were wounded in the 1745 uprising. The McIntyres were hereditary foresters to the Stewarts of Appin and later to the Campbells of Lorn. They were also famed as pipers.

Upheavals such as military incursions, feuds and harvest failures would have encouraged many clan members, including McIntyres, to migrate to Ulster as settlers during the 17th century. Owing to the nature of the Scottish clan system once the power and influence of the chief had been weakened and the bond of tribal loyalty broken the clan tended to scatter.

Movement of Scottish settlers to Ulster began in earnest from 1605 in a private enterprise colonisation of counties Antrim and Down when Sir Hugh Montgomery and Sir James Hamilton acquired title to large estates in north Down and Sir Randall MacDonnell, 1st Earl of Antrim, to large tracts of land in north Antrim. Further impetus came in 1609 when James I adopted the policy to encourage Scottish settlers to settle on the forfeited estates of the Gaelic chiefs in counties Armagh, Cavan, Donegal, Fermanagh, Londonderry (then known as Coleraine) and Tyrone.

The escape of the most prominent Gaelic Lords of Ulster in 'the Flight of the Earls' in 1607 from Lough Swilly, County Donegal marked the end of Gaelic power. In the centuries that followed Gaelic names were anglicised, resulting in many variant spellings of McIntyre such as McEnteer, McTier, Mateer, Tear and Tier. McIntyre was also anglicised to Wright. Although McIntyre is a common name in north Derry and north Antrim, it is not common in the Glens of Antrim. However, Wright is common there and most of these will be originally McIntyres from west Argyll.

In Ireland the County Armagh sept, in Gaelic *Mac an tSaoir*, meaning 'son of the craftsman' was anglicised as McAteer. The homeland of this sept was Ballymacateer near Lurgan. Michael McAteer was Bishop of Clogher from 1268-1288.

As McAteer was often changed to McIntyre it means that some families bearing the surname McIntyre are of Irish, not Scottish, descent. McAteer is virtually exclusive to Ulster, where it is mainly found in Counties Antrim, Donegal and Armagh. McAteer origins are further disguised as the name was also anglicised as Wright, particularly in County Fermanagh; as Carpenter, especially in the Dublin area; and as Freeman by translation of Gaelic *soar*, meaning 'free'.

McIVOR

McIvor, an alternative form of McKeever, can be an Irish or a Scottish name. In Ireland McIvor and McKeever are uncommon outside Ulster, where McIvor is most numerous in Counties Tyrone and Derry, and McKeever in County Derry. Indeed both McKeever and McIvor are well known names in Counties Monaghan, Tyrone and Derry.

Ireland was one of the first countries to adopt a system of hereditary surnames which developed from a more ancient system of clan or sept names. The surname was formed by prefixing either Mac (son of) or O (grandson or descendant of) to the ancestor's name.

In County Monaghan, in the ancient kingdom of Oriel, the McIvor sept is derived from Gaelic *Mac Eimhir*, meaning 'son of Heber'. These McIvors were a branch of the McMahons, rulers of Monaghan from the early-13th century until the end of the 16rth century. The forename *Eimhear* (Heber) was a favourite with the McMahons.

In the rest of Ulster, however, McIvor, of Irish origin, is derived from Gaelic *Mac Iomhair*, meaning 'son of Ivar', from the Norse personal name *Ivaar*.

Many McIvors in Ulster will have Scottish ancestry. In Scotland McIvor is derived from Scots Gaelic *Mac Iomhair*, meaning 'son of Ivar', from the Norse personal name *Ivaar*. In 870-71 Imhair, a Norse chief, joined with Olaf the White, king of Dublin, in the besieging and sacking of Dumbarton. As Iver became a common forename the surname McIvor spread throughout the Highlands of Scotland. In 1292 the lands of Malcolm McIuyr in Lorn became the sheriffdom of Lorne. It is said that 'the Clan Iver lands were forfeited in the seventeenth century and were restored on condition that the heir should take the name of Campbell.'

In addition to Clan Iver in Argyll there were McIvor septs attached to Clans Campbell, Robertson and Mackenzie. It is claimed, that in some instances, McIvor was anglicised as Orr. The fact that the Orrs were a sept of Clan Campbell and that the surname Orr is prominent in Kintyre supports this view.

Upheavals such as military incursions, feuds and harvest failures would have encouraged many clan members, including McIvors, to migrate to Ulster as settlers during the 17th century. Owing to the nature of the Scottish clan system once the power and influence of the chief had been weakened and the bond of tribal loyalty broken the clan tended to scatter.

Movement of Scottish settlers to Ulster began in earnest from 1605 in a private enterprise colonisation of counties Antrim and Down when Sir Hugh Montgomery and Sir James Hamilton acquired title to large estates in north Down and Sir Randall MacDonnell, 1st Earl of Antrim, to large tracts of land in north Antrim. Further impetus came in 1609 when James I adopted the policy to encourage Scottish settlers to settle on the forfeited estates of the Gaelic chiefs in counties Armagh, Cavan, Donegal, Fermanagh, Londonderry (then known as Coleraine) and Tyrone. It is estimated by 1715, when migration to Ulster had virtually stopped, the Scottish population of Ulster stood at 200,000.

McKAY

In Ireland this name is almost exclusive to Ulster, where it is found chiefly in Counties Antrim and Derry. This name was brought to Ulster by settlers from Scotland in the 17th century.

McKay is derived from Gaelic *Mac Aoidh*, meaning 'son of Hugh'. This name was also anglicised as Mackay, Mackie, McCay, McCoy and McKee. Clan Mackay, claiming descent from Morgund of Pluscarden, originated in Moray. This clan came to prominence in Sutherland in the 13th century and by 1427 the chief, Angus Dow MacKay, could muster an army of 4000 men. In Inverness-shire the Mackays were a sept of Clan Davidson, and in Kintyre and Galloway the MacKays, MacKies and Mackies were followers of Clan Donald.

The first McKays in Ireland, also known as McCoys, were Clan Donald galloglasses, i.e. mercenary soldiers. As followers of Clan Donald they came over to Ulster from Kintyre and the southern isles of Scotland such as Islay to fight for the McDonnells of the Glens of Antrim.

Clan Donald had acquired new territories in the north of Ireland ca.1400 when John Mor MacDonald had married Margery Bissett, an heiress in the Glens of Antrim. By the mid-16th century the MacDonalds, known as the MacDonnells of the Glens, had carved out an extensive territory in County Antrim at the expense of the MacQuillans.

Movement of Scottish settlers to Ulster began in earnest from 1605 in a private enterprise colonisation of counties Antrim and Down when Sir Hugh Montgomery and Sir James Hamilton acquired title to large estates in north Down and Sir Randall MacDonnell, 1st Earl of Antrim, to large tracts of land in north Antrim. Further impetus came in 1609 when James I adopted the policy to encourage Scottish settlers to settle on the forfeited estates of the Gaelic chiefs in counties Armagh, Cavan, Donegal, Fermanagh, Londonderry (then known as Coleraine) and Tyrone.

Confusion arises as the Gaelic surname *Mac Aoidh* has acquired in the process of anglicisation a great number of variants. Thus the McKay family of Drumard in Tamlaght O'Crilly Parish, County Londonderry were recorded as McCoy in the 1831 census, as McCay in the tithe book of 1833 and as McKay in the Griffith's Valuation of 1859.

In Ireland, particularly in Counties Donegal and Fermanagh, Gaelic *Mac Aodha*, meaning 'son of Hugh', was usually anglicised as McHugh and McCue but also as McCoy and McKee. Thus in west Ulster Irish McHugh can become indistinguishable from Scottish McKay.

During the famous 105 day Siege of Derry, from 18 April to 31 July 1689, General Andrew Mackay, Ensign William Mackie, Lieutenant William Mackey, Lieutenant Mackie, Lieutenant Mackay, John Mackay, Josiah Macky and Jannett Mackee were recorded as 'defenders' of the city. On the opposing side Lieutenant Daniel McKay and Ensign Hugh McKay were officers in the 'Jacobite army' which besieged the city of Derry.

McKEE

In Ireland this name is almost exclusive to Ulster, where it is found chiefly in Counties Antrim, Armagh and Down. This name was brought to Ulster by settlers from Scotland in the 17th century.

McKee is derived from Gaelic *Mac Aoidh*, meaning 'son of Hugh'. This name was also anglicised as Mackay, Mackie, McCay, McCoy and McKay. Clan Mackay, claiming descent from Morgund of Pluscarden, originated in Moray. This clan came to prominence in Sutherland in the 13th century and by 1427 the chief, Angus Dow MacKay, could muster an army of 4000 men. In Inverness-shire the Mackays were a sept of Clan Davidson, and in Kintyre and Galloway the MacKays, MacKies and Mackies were followers of Clan Donald. The surname Mackie was recorded in Stirlingshire from the 15th century.

The first McKees in Ireland, also known as McCoys, were Clan Donald galloglasses, i.e. mercenary soldiers. As followers of Clan Donald they came over to Ulster from Kintyre and the southern isles of Scotland such as Islay to fight for the McDonnells of the Glens of Antrim.

Clan Donald had acquired new territories in the north of Ireland ca.1400 when John Mor MacDonald had married Margery Bissett, an heiress in the Glens of Antrim. By the mid-16th century the MacDonalds, known as the MacDonnells of the Glens, had carved out an extensive territory in County Antrim at the expense of the MacQuillans.

Movement of Scottish settlers to Ulster began in earnest from 1605 in a private enterprise colonisation of counties Antrim and Down when Sir Hugh Montgomery and Sir James Hamilton acquired title to large estates in north Down and Sir Randall MacDonnell, 1st Earl of Antrim, to large tracts of land in north Antrim.

Further impetus came in 1609 when James I adopted the policy to encourage Scottish settlers to settle on the forfeited estates of the Gaelic chiefs in counties Armagh, Cavan, Donegal, Fermanagh, Londonderry (then known as Coleraine) and Tyrone.

Sir Patrick MacKee of Largs, Ayrshire, was one of the principal Scottish planters (sixty-one in total) of the Ulster Plantation, and in 1610 he was granted an estate of 1000 acres near the town of Donegal.

In Ireland, particularly in Counties Donegal and Fermanagh, Gaelic *Mac Aodha*, meaning 'son of Hugh', was usually anglicised as McHugh and McCue but also as McCoy and McKee. Thus in west Ulster Irish McHugh can become indistinguishable from Scottish McKee.

During the famous 105 day Siege of Derry, from 18 April to 31 July 1689, General Andrew Mackay, Ensign William Mackie, Lieutenant William Mackey, Lieutenant Mackie, Lieutenant Mackay, John Mackay, Josiah Macky and Jannett Mackee were recorded as 'defenders' of the city. On the opposing side Lieutenant Daniel McKay and Ensign Hugh McKay were officers in the 'Jacobite army' which besieged the city of Derry.

McKEEVER

McKeever, an alternative form of McIvor, can be an Irish or a Scottish name. In Ireland McIvor and McKeever are uncommon outside Ulster, where McIvor is most numerous in Counties Tyrone and Derry, and McKeever in County Derry. Indeed both McKeever and McIvor are well known names in Counties Monaghan, Tyrone and Derry.

Ireland was one of the first countries to adopt a system of hereditary surnames which developed from a more ancient system of clan or sept names. The surname was formed by prefixing either Mac (son of) or O (grandson or descendant of) to the ancestor's name.

In County Monaghan, in the ancient kingdom of Oriel, the McKeever sept is derived from Gaelic *Mac Eimhir*, meaning 'son of Heber'. These McKeevers were a branch of the McMahons, rulers of Monaghan from the early-13th century until the end of the 16rth century. The forename *Eimhear* (Heber) was a favourite with the McMahons.

In the rest of Ulster, however, McKeever, of Irish origin, is derived from Gaelic *Mac Iomhair*, meaning 'son of Ivar', from the Norse personal name *Ivaar*.

Some McKeevers in Ulster will have Scottish ancestry. In Scotland McKeever is recorded as a variant of McIver. McIver is derived from Scots Gaelic *Mac Iomhair*, meaning 'son of Ivar'. In 870-71 Imhair, a Norse chief, joined with Olaf the White, king of Dublin, in the besieging and sacking of Dumbarton. As Iver became a common forename the surname McIver spread throughout the Highlands of Scotland. In 1292 the lands of Malcolm McIuyr in Lorn became the sheriffdom of Lorne. It is said that 'the Clan Iver lands were forfeited in the seventeenth century and were restored on condition that the heir should take the name of Campbell.'

In addition to Clan Iver in Argyll there were McIver septs attached to Clans Campbell, Robertson and Mackenzie. It is claimed, that in some instances, McIver was anglicised as Orr. The fact that the Orrs were a sept of Clan Campbell and that the surname Orr is prominent in Kintyre supports this view.

Upheavals such as military incursions, feuds and harvest failures would have encouraged many clan members, including McIvers, to migrate to Ulster as settlers during the 17th century. Owing to the nature of the Scottish clan system once the power and influence of the chief had been weakened and the bond of tribal loyalty broken the clan tended to scatter.

Movement of Scottish settlers to Ulster began in earnest from 1605 in a private enterprise colonisation of counties Antrim and Down when Sir Hugh Montgomery and Sir James Hamilton acquired title to large estates in north Down and Sir Randall MacDonnell, 1st Earl of Antrim, to large tracts of land in north Antrim. Further impetus came in 1609 when James I adopted the policy to encourage Scottish settlers to settle on the forfeited estates of the Gaelic chiefs in counties Armagh, Cavan, Donegal, Fermanagh, Londonderry (then known as Coleraine) and Tyrone. It is estimated by 1715, when migration to Ulster had virtually stopped, the Scottish population of Ulster stood at 200,000.

McKELVEY

McKelvey can be an Irish or a Scottish name. This name is exclusive to Ulster where it is most common in County Donegal and adjacent parts of County Tyrone. The majority of McKelveys in Ulster are of Irish stock.

Ireland was one of the first countries to adopt a system of hereditary surnames which developed from a more ancient system of clan or sept names. From the 11th century each family began to adopt its own distinctive family name generally derived from the first name of an ancestor who lived in or about the 10th century. The surname was formed by prefixing either Mac (son of) or O (grandson or descendant of) to the ancestor's name. Surnames in Ireland, therefore, tended to identify membership of a sept.

The McKelvey sept of County Donegal is derived from Gaelic *Mac Giolla Bhuidhe*, meaning 'son of the yellow-haired youth'. *The Annals of The Kingdom of Ireland by the Four Masters* (a history of Ireland from 'the earliest period to the year 1616') record that, in 1181, 'Flaherty O'Muldory, Lord of Tirconnell, defeated the sons of the King of Connaught'. In this battle 'sixteen of the sons of the lords and chieftains of Connaught were slain', including two warriors named *mac giollabuide* (translated as MacGillaboy).

The escape of the most prominent Gaelic Lords of Ulster in 'the Flight of the Earls' in 1607 from Lough Swilly, County Donegal marked the end of Gaelic power. In the centuries that followed Gaelic names were anglicised, resulting in many variant spellings of the same name. The McKelvey sept was also anglicised as McElwee, McGilloway and McIlwee.

By the time of the mid-19th century Griffith's Valuation the surnames associated with this sept were spread throughout Donegal. This source records that in County Donegal, in the middle years of the 19th century, there were 33 households recorded as McKelvey; 13 as McElwee; 14 as McGillaway; and 41 as McIlwee.

In Scotland McKelvey is derived from Gaelic *Mac Shealbhaigh*, meaning 'son of Selbach'. This name is associated with southwest Scotland and, in particular, the counties of Dumfries, Kirkcudbright and Wigtown. This region was home to many of the Scottish settlers who came to Ulster throughout the 17th century. The McKelveys were also recorded as a sept of Clan Campbell.

It is quite likely, therefore, that some McKelveys in Ulster will be descendants of 17th century Scottish settlers. Movement of Scottish settlers to Ulster began in earnest from 1605 in a private enterprise colonisation of counties Antrim and Down when Sir Hugh Montgomery and Sir James Hamilton acquired title to large estates in north Down and Sir Randall MacDonnell, 1st Earl of Antrim, to large tracts of land in north Antrim. Further impetus came in 1609 when James I adopted the policy to encourage Scottish settlers to settle on the forfeited estates of the Gaelic chiefs in counties Armagh, Cavan, Donegal, Fermanagh, Londonderry (then known as Coleraine) and Tyrone. It is estimated by 1715, when migration to Ulster had virtually stopped, the Scottish population of Ulster stood at 200,000.

McKENNA

This name is among the 100 most common names in Ireland and in the first forty in Ulster. McKenna is the second most common name in County Monaghan and in the first ten in County Tyrone. The name is also numerous in Counties Armagh and Antrim. McKenna is one of the few names from which the old Gaelic prefix of Mac was not generally dropped during the 18ᵗʰ and 19ᵗʰ centuries.

Ireland was one of the first countries to adopt a system of hereditary surnames which developed from a more ancient system of clan or sept names. From the 11ᵗʰ century each family began to adopt its own distinctive family name generally derived from the first name of an ancestor who lived in or about the 10th century. The surname was formed by prefixing either Mac (son of) or O (grandson or descendant of) to the ancestor's name. Surnames in Ireland, therefore, tended to identify membership of a sept. McKenna is derived from Gaelic *Mac Cionaoith.*

The McKenna sept trace their lineage to Fiacha, son of the 5ᵗʰ century High King of Ireland, Niall of the Nine Hostages, who ruled from the Hill of Tara, County Meath. The territory of the Cenel Fiachach (the race of Fiacha) extended over Counties Offaly and Westmeath.

At the invitation of the Fir Leamha, i.e. 'the men of Lemna', who ruled the Clogher Valley, County Tyrone in the 9ᵗʰ century, the McKennas migrated north, at an early date, from their homeland in Meath to fight as swordsmen in Ulster. They settled in north Monaghan, on the boundary with County Tyrone, where they became 'lords of Truagh' (the modern barony of Trough).

The McKennas were well-established in their new territory by the 14ᵗʰ century as *The Annals of The Kingdom of Ireland by the Four Masters* records, in 1325, the slaying of Donough McKenna, chief of the territory of Trough, in 'Mac Mahon's church'. *The Annals* further record, in 1436, that 'Niall, the son of Owen O'Neill, was slain, together with many of his people, in a contest in his own house, by the Clann-Kenna of Trough'. The last chief of the name was Patrick McKenna who died in 1616.

Dispossessed of their lands a branch of the family removed to the parish of Maghera in County Derry in the middle years of the 17ᵗʰ century. The McKennas became well-established in the Maghera area, and by the middle years of the 19ᵗʰ century McKenna had become the most common surname in Maghera Parish.

In the 17ᵗʰ and 18ᵗʰ centuries many descendants of the old Gaelic order in Ireland emigrated, as the so-called Wild Geese, to Europe. One of the most distinguished was General John or Juan MacKenna, born at Clogher, County Tyrone in 1771, who, after a period of service in the Spanish army, assisted Bernard O'Higgins in the liberation of Chile in South America.

Confusion is caused by the fact that some Irish McKennas became both McKenny and McKinney. In County Monaghan, in particular, Kennys and McKennys were originally McKennas. McKinney is also a recorded variant of McKenna although most McKinneys in Ulster are descended from 17ᵗʰ century Scottish settlers.

McKERR

This name, which is a variant form of McGirr, belongs to County Tyrone.

Ireland was one of the first countries to adopt a system of hereditary surnames which developed from a more ancient system of clan or sept names. From the 11th century each family began to adopt its own distinctive family name generally derived from the first name of an ancestor who lived in or about the 10th century. The surname was formed by prefixing either Mac (son of) or O (grandson or descendant of) to the ancestor's name. Surnames in Ireland, therefore, tended to identify membership of a sept.

McKerr is derived from *Mac an Ghirr,* the root word being *giorr,* meaning 'short'. Originating in the Clogher Valley, County Tyrone the McKerrs were a branch of the McCawells, in Gaelic *Mac Cathmhaoil,* the root word being *cathmhaol,* meaning 'battle chief'. Although the surname McCawell is now very rare this County Tyrone sept was once very powerful and numerous.

The McKerrs and the McCawells can trace their lineage to Eogan, son of the 5th century High King of Ireland, Niall of the Nine Hostages, who ruled from the Hill of Tara, County Meath. Eogan and his brother Conall *Gulban* conquered northwest Ireland, ca.425 AD, capturing the great hill-fort of Grianan of Ailech in County Donegal which commanded the entrance to the Inishowen peninsula between Lough Swilly and Lough Foyle.

Eogan, styled 'King of Ailech', established his own kingdom in the peninsula still called after him Inishowen (Innis Eoghain or Eogan's Isle). Eogan was converted to Christianity by St Patrick, when he travelled to Ailech, ca. 442 AD. His descendants, known as the Cenel Eoghain (the race of Owen), became the principal branch of the Northern Ui Neill (descendants of Niall of the Nine Hostages).

The McCawells were the leading sept of Clan Ferady (tracing their descent from Faredach, son of Muireadach (Murdock), son of Eogan). At the height of their power in the 12th century, from their base at Clogher, they controlled a large portion of County Tyrone and had penetrated deep into County Fermanagh. They were one of the seven powerful septs supporting O'Neill. By the mid-14th century their power in Fermanagh had been broken by the Maguires and their influence gradually declined thereafter.

The 17th century Plantation of Ulster with English and Scottish settlers not only marked the end of McCawell power, but also, to a large extent, the disappearance of the name. It would seem that families of the *Mac Cathmhaoil* sept adopted various anglicised surnames such as Campbell, Callwell, Caulfield, McCall and many others. Thus people whose origins are *Mac Cathmhaoil* are disguised by a variety of inappropriate anglicised names.

The McKerr sept trace their descent from the 14th century Maelechlainn mac an ghirr meic Cathmhaoil, which literally means 'Malachy, the son of the short fellow McCawell'.

McKIE

In Ireland this name is almost exclusive to Ulster, where it is found chiefly in Counties Antrim, Armagh and Down. This name was brought to Ulster by settlers from Scotland in the 17th century.

McKie is derived from Gaelic *Mac Aoidh*, meaning 'son of Hugh'. This name was also anglicised as Mackay, Mackie, McCay, McCoy, McKay and McKee. Clan Mackay, claiming descent from Morgund of Pluscarden, originated in Moray. This clan came to prominence in Sutherland in the 13th century and by 1427 the chief, Angus Dow MacKay, could muster an army of 4000 men. In Inverness-shire the Mackays were a sept of Clan Davidson, and in Kintyre and Galloway the MacKays, MacKies and Mackies were followers of Clan Donald. The surname Mackie was recorded in Stirlingshire from the 15th century.

The first McKies in Ireland, also known as McCoys, were Clan Donald galloglasses, i.e. mercenary soldiers. As followers of Clan Donald they came over to Ulster from Kintyre and the southern isles of Scotland such as Islay to fight for the McDonnells of the Glens of Antrim.

Clan Donald had acquired new territories in the north of Ireland ca.1400 when John Mor MacDonald had married Margery Bissett, an heiress in the Glens of Antrim. By the mid-16th century the MacDonalds, known as the MacDonnells of the Glens, had carved out an extensive territory in County Antrim at the expense of the MacQuillans.

Movement of Scottish settlers to Ulster began in earnest from 1605 in a private enterprise colonisation of counties Antrim and Down when Sir Hugh Montgomery and Sir James Hamilton acquired title to large estates in north Down and Sir Randall MacDonnell, 1st Earl of Antrim, to large tracts of land in north Antrim. Further impetus came in 1609 when James I adopted the policy to encourage Scottish settlers to settle on the forfeited estates of the Gaelic chiefs in counties Armagh, Cavan, Donegal, Fermanagh, Londonderry (then known as Coleraine) and Tyrone.

Confusion arises as the Gaelic surname *Mac Aoidh* has acquired in the process of anglicisation a great number of variants. Thus the McKay family of Drumard in Tamlaght O'Crilly Parish, County Londonderry were recorded as McCoy in the 1831 census, as McCay in the tithe book of 1833 and as McKay in the Griffith's Valuation of 1859.

In Ireland, particularly in Counties Donegal and Fermanagh, Gaelic *Mac Aodha*, meaning 'son of Hugh', was usually anglicised as McHugh and McCue but also as McCoy and McKee. Thus in west Ulster Irish McHugh can become indistinguishable from Scottish McKie.

During the famous 105 day Siege of Derry, from 18 April to 31 July 1689, General Andrew Mackay, Ensign William Mackie, Lieutenant William Mackey, Lieutenant Mackie, Lieutenant Mackay, John Mackay, Josiah Macky and Jannett Mackee were recorded as 'defenders' of the city. On the opposing side Lieutenant Daniel McKay and Ensign Hugh McKay were officers in the 'Jacobite army' which besieged the city of Derry.

223

McKILLEN

McKillen chiefly belongs to County Antrim. Names such as McKillen, McCallion and McAllen represent descendants of Clan Campbell in Argyllshire, Scotland who from the 15th century came to Ulster to fight as galloglasses, i.e. mercenary soldiers, for the O'Donnells of Donegal. Derived from Gaelic *galloglach*, galloglass refers to a paid soldier, often brought over from Scotland, to fight on behalf of an Irish chief.

Although the names of McKillen, McCallion and McAllen represent distinct septs within Clan Campbell there are no septs of Clan Campbell registered with these names today. Anglicisation has disguised the ultimate origins of these names. Furthermore, in many cases, the families in these septs were recorded simply as Campbell. Strictly speaking McKillen, and its abbreviated form Killen, is derived from Gaelic *Mac Coilin*, meaning 'son of Colin'; McAllen stems from Gaelic *Mac Ailin*, meaning 'son of Allen'; and McCallion is derived from *Mac Cailin*, meaning 'son of Cailin'.

McKillen and Killen are most common in Counties Antrim and Down. McCallion, on the other hand, is found almost exclusively in Counties Donegal and Derry. In Derry and Donegal McKillen, McAllen, and McCallion are indistinguishable; as many people whose origins may be *Mac Ailin* or *Mac Coilin* bear the surname McCallion. Ballymacallion, meaning 'the townland of the McCallions', is located in Dungiven Parish, County Derry.

As well as providing detailed and graphic descriptions of the activities of the Clan Campbell galloglasses *The Annals of The Kingdom of Ireland by the Four Masters* record the distinct spellings of their associated surnames. In 1555, the *Annals* record that 'the son of O'Donnell, i.e. Calvagh, went to Scotland, attended by a few select persons, and obtained auxiliary forces from Mac Calin (Gillaspick Don), under the command of Master Arsibel. He afterwards came back, with a great body of Scots, to desolate and ravage Tirconnell.' In the same year the O'Donnells, and their Scottish galloglasses, stormed and demolished the castles at Greencastle, Inishowen, County Donegal and the O'Cahan stronghold on the island in Enagh Lough, County Derry.

The *Annals* of 1557 describes in great detail the role of the galloglass in the camp of the O'Neills who were on a raiding expedition into O'Donnell territory in Donegal. It states that 'sixty grim and redoubtable gallowglasses, with sharp, keen axes, terrible and ready for action, and sixty stern and terrific Scots, with massive, broad, and heavy-striking swords in their hands, ready to strike and parry, were watching and guarding the son of O'Neill.'

Scottish galloglasses, led by Donnell and Dowell Mac Allen, raided into Counties Sligo and Mayo in 1558. They were defeated in a fierce battle, during which both Donnell and Dowell Mac Allen were slain, by the Earl of Clanrickard.

In 1586 'a Scotch fleet landed in Inishowen, O'Doherty's country'. One of its leaders was Gillespick Mac Ailin. After this raid the *Annals* record 'that there was nothing of value in Inishowen, whether corn or cattle, which they did not carry off'.

McKINLEY

McKinley is an exclusively Ulster name which is most common in Counties Antrim and Donegal. This name was brought to Ulster in large numbers by settlers from Scotland in the 17th century.

McKinley is usually regarded as a Scottish name. In Scotland McKinley is derived from Gaelic *Mac Fhionnlaoich*, from *fionn*, meaning 'fair', and *laoch*, meaning 'hero'. There were McKinley septs associated with Clans Buchanan, Farquharson, MacFarlane, and Stewart of Appin. McKinley country was the Lennox district of Dumbartonshire and Stirlingshire.

Upheavals such as military incursions, feuds and harvest failures would have encouraged many clan members, including McKinleys, to migrate to Ulster as settlers during the 17th century. Owing to the nature of the Scottish clan system once the power and influence of the chief had been weakened and the bond of tribal loyalty broken the clan tended to scatter.

Movement of Scottish settlers to Ulster began in earnest from 1605 in a private enterprise colonisation of counties Antrim and Down when Sir Hugh Montgomery and Sir James Hamilton acquired title to large estates in north Down and Sir Randall MacDonnell, 1st Earl of Antrim, to large tracts of land in north Antrim. Further impetus came in 1609 when James I adopted the policy to encourage Scottish settlers to settle on the forfeited estates of the Gaelic chiefs in counties Armagh, Cavan, Donegal, Fermanagh, Londonderry (then known as Coleraine) and Tyrone.

McKinley is a common name in County Antrim, particularly in the Glens of Antrim. Although the majority of McKinleys in Antrim will be of Scottish origin some bearers of the name will be of Irish origin as the County Antrim sept of McAlee or McClay, in Gaelic *Mac an Leagha*, meaning 'son of the physician', was sometimes anglicised as McKinley.

In Donegal McKinley is sometimes confused with the local name McGinley. The County Donegal sept of McGinley is derived from Gaelic *Mag Fhionnghaile*, the root word being *fionnghaile*, meaning 'fair valour'. This sept is most noted for the number of churchmen it has contributed to the Diocese of Raphoe.

McGinley is among the ten most common names in Donegal, with 80% of Ulster McGinleys living in that county. Although it is believed that McGinley and McKinley were not usually interchangeable it is possible that, in some instances, especially in County Donegal, a person with the surname McKinley is a descendant of the McGinley sept.

The mid-19th century Griffith's Valuation records 327 McGinley households in County Donegal, with the name most concentrated in the western fringes of Donegal in the parishes of Clondahorky, Glencolumbkille and Tullaghobegley. The same source records 37 McKinley households in County Donegal. In the parish of Clondahorky, in particular, both surnames were to be found in significant numbers, with 45 households recorded as McGinley and 14 as McKinley.

McKINNEY

McKinney can be an Irish or a Scottish name. In Ireland this name is exclusive to Ulster where it is most common in Counties Antrim and Tyrone. In the former county most McKinneys will be of Scottish origin while in County Tyrone they will be of Irish origin.

In the second half of the 19th century there was a fourfold increase in the numbers of McKinneys in Ulster. This was not as a result of immigration; it was owing to the fact that many MacKenzies of Scottish origin and McKennas of Irish origin adopted McKinney as their surname.

The County Tyrone sept of McKinney, derived from Gaelic *Mac Coinnigh*, were based in lands on the border with Fermanagh.

The McKenna sept, derived from Gaelic *Mac Cionaoith*, established themselves in north Monaghan, on the boundary with County Tyrone, where they became 'lords of Truagh'. Dispossessed of their lands a branch of the family removed to the parish of Maghera in County Derry in the middle years of the 17th century. In the 19th century, in particular, some McKennas adopted McKinney as their surname.

Scottish Clan MacKinnon, in Gaelic *Mac Fhionnghuin*, was also known as MacKinney and there was a specific MacKinney sept of the clan. Tracing their descent from Kenneth MacAlpine, the 9th century King of Scotland, the MacKinneys were followers of the MacDonalds, 'Lords of the Isles'. Clan Mackinnon held lands on Mull and the Isle of Skye. Castle Maoil at Dunakin on the Isle of Skye was a MacKinnon stronghold from the 12th to the 15th century.

Upheavals such as military incursions, feuds and harvest failures would have encouraged many clan members, including McKinneys, to migrate to Ulster as settlers during the 17th century.

Movement of Scottish settlers to Ulster began in earnest from 1605 in a private enterprise colonisation of counties Antrim and Down when Sir Hugh Montgomery and Sir James Hamilton acquired title to large estates in north Down and Sir Randall MacDonnell, 1st Earl of Antrim, to large tracts of land in north Antrim. Further impetus came in 1609 when James I adopted the policy to encourage Scottish settlers to settle on the forfeited estates of the Gaelic chiefs in counties Armagh, Cavan, Donegal, Fermanagh, Londonderry (then known as Coleraine) and Tyrone.

At the time of this plantation McKinney, derived from Scots Gaelic *Mac Cionaodha*, was already common in Galloway in southwest Scotland. In the 16th century references are recorded of this surname in the Galloway counties of Wigtownshire and Kirkcudbrightshire. This region was home to many of the Scottish settlers who came to Ulster throughout the 17th century. It is estimated by 1715, when migration to Ulster had virtually stopped, the Scottish population of Ulster stood at 200,000.

In the 19th century, in Ulster, a growing number of MacKenzies adopted McKinney as their surname. Clan Mackenzie, derived from Gaelic *Mac Coinnich*, were chiefs of Kintail in Wester Ross in the Highlands of Scotland.

McKNIGHT

In Ulster, where the name is most common in Counties Antrim and Down, McKnight is of Scottish origin.

The McKnights were a sept of Clan MacNaughton. Clan MacNaughton, in Gaelic *Mac Neachdainn*, meaning 'son of Nechtan', claims descent from the 8th century Pictish king Nechtan. In the 13th century the clan was found in Lochawe, Glenaray, Glenshire and Loch Fyne in Argyllshire.

In the 14th century Dundarave, on the north shore of Loch Fyne, became the stronghold of Clan MacNaughton. In 1627 Colonel Alexander MacNaughten raised a company of 200 Highland bowmen for service in the expedition to France for the relief of La Rochelle. Clan MacNaughton held their lands at Dundarave until 1700 when the last chief, John MacNaughten lost them to the Campbells of Ardkinglas who held the lands on the southern side of Loch Fyne.

Movement of Scottish settlers to Ulster began in earnest from 1605 in a private enterprise colonisation of counties Antrim and Down when Sir Hugh Montgomery and Sir James Hamilton acquired title to large estates in north Down and Sir Randall MacDonnell, 1st Earl of Antrim, to large tracts of land in north Antrim.

The MacNaughtons were one of the families brought in by the MacDonnells of the Glens of Antrim in the early 17th century. Shane Dhu, or Black John MacNaghten, became the Earl of Antrim's chief agent. John was buried in the family burial ground at Bonamargy Friary near Ballycastle, County Antrim.

In Scotland, McKnight is also regarded as a variant of McNaught. It is said that the McKnights of Ayrshire and Galloway were a branch of the McNaughts of Carrick. McNaught is on record in Dumfriesshire, in the form of Gilbert Makenaght, from 1296, and as Macneight it was recorded as the name of an old family in Ayrshire. McKnight was recorded in the province of Galloway from the 16th century, and this region was home to many of the Scottish settlers who came to Ulster throughout the 17th century.

In 1609 James I adopted the policy to encourage Scottish settlers to settle on the forfeited estates of the Gaelic chiefs in counties Armagh, Cavan, Donegal, Fermanagh, Londonderry (then known as Coleraine) and Tyrone. Scottish families entering Ireland through the port of Londonderry settled in the Foyle Valley which includes much of the fertile lands of counties Donegal, Londonderry and Tyrone. It is estimated by 1715, when migration to Ulster had virtually stopped, the Scottish population of Ulster stood at 200,000.

McNaught is regarded as the County Donegal form of McKnight. At the time of the mid-19th century Griffith's Valuation there were 24 McNaught households in County Donegal compared to 9 McKnight households.

In County Meath, a branch of the Fitzsimons family took the Gaelic name *Mac an Ridire*, meaning 'son of the knight', and, in some instances, this was later made McKnight.

227

McLAUGHLIN

This name, which is second to Doherty in both Derry city and Inishowen, County Donegal, illustrates the very close links between these two areas. As Derry developed an industrial base in the 19th century in shirt making, shipbuilding and distilling it attracted much of its workforce from Inishowen. Today, 80% of Donegal McLaughlins are still concentrated in the Inishowen peninsula.

The McLaughlin sept trace their lineage to Eogan, son of the 5th century High King of Ireland, Niall of the Nine Hostages, who ruled from the Hill of Tara, County Meath. Eogan and his brother Conall *Gulban* conquered northwest Ireland, ca.425 AD, capturing the great hill-fort of Grianan of Ailech which commanded the entrance to the Inishowen peninsula between Lough Swilly and Lough Foyle.

Eogan, styled 'King of Ailech', established his own kingdom in the peninsula still called after him Inishowen (Innis Eoghain or Eogan's Isle). Eogan was converted to Christianity by St Patrick, when he travelled to Ailech, ca. 442 AD. His descendants, known as the Cenel Eoghain (the race of Owen), became the principal branch of the Northern Ui Neill (descendants of Niall of the Nine Hostages). The Cenel Eoghain in the next five centuries expanded to the east and south from their focal point in Inishowen.

Ireland was one of the first countries to adopt a system of hereditary surnames which developed from a more ancient system of clan or sept names. The surname was formed by prefixing either Mac (son of) or O (grandson or descendant of) to the ancestor's name.

The McLaughlins take their name from Lochlainn, which in turn was derived from a Norse personal name, and were thus in Gaelic *Mac Lochlainn*, i.e. son of Lochlainn. The McLaughlins were initially the senior branch of the Northern Ui Neill and their territory was in Inishowen.

In the 12th century the McLaughlins, ruling from their royal palace at Ailech in Inishowen, were High Kings of Ireland and patrons of the monastic settlement in Derry. Domhnall Mac Lochlainn, styled 'King of Ireland', died at Doire-Choluim-Chille (by tradition the monastery at Derry was founded in 546 AD by St Columcille, also known as Columba) in 1121.

After a decisive battle in 1241 at *Caimeirge* (which scholars believe was near Maghera in County Derry) the O'Neills of Tyrone ousted the McLaughlins as the leading power in Ulster. Brian O'Neill was now 'installed in the lordship of the Kinel-Owen'. In the 15th century the Dohertys ousted the McLaughlins as Lords of Inishowen.

Some McLaughlins in Ulster, particularly Antrim, may derive from the Argyllshire clan known in Scotland as MacLachlan. The O'Melaghlins of north Leinster have also changed their name to McLaughlin.

McMAHON

McMahon is among the seventy most common names Ireland. It is most numerous in Munster, particularly in Counties Clare and Limerick. The name is also very common in south Ulster, where it is the fourth most numerous name in County Monaghan and among the top twenty in County Cavan.

Ireland was one of the first countries to adopt a system of hereditary surnames which developed from a more ancient system of clan or sept names. From the 11th century each family began to adopt its own distinctive family name generally derived from the first name of an ancestor who lived in or about the 10th century. The surname was formed by prefixing either Mac (son of) or O (grandson or descendant of) to the ancestor's name. Surnames in Ireland, therefore, tended to identify membership of a sept.

McMahon is derived from Gaelic *Mac Mathghamhna*, the root word being *mathghamhan*, meaning 'bear'. There were two septs of the name. In Munster, the McMahons trace their descent form Mahon O'Brien, grandson of Brian Boru, 941-1014, who became King of Munster and High King of Ireland. Their territory was Corcabaskin in west Clare.

In Ulster, the McMahons became a powerful and important sept in County Monaghan in the early-13th century. They became lords of Oriel, an ancient territory which covered much of Counties Armagh and Monaghan, on the decline of the O'Carrolls.

As well as being a military family the McMahons have produced many churchmen. Three McMahons have held the Primacy as Archbishop of Armagh; and of five bishops who held the diocese of Clogher in the 18th century, three were McMahons.

The escape of the most prominent Gaelic Lords of Ulster in 'the Flight of the Earls' in 1607 from Lough Swilly marked the end of Gaelic power. The McMahons continued to resist English rule in the 17th century. Hugh MacMahon, last chief of the Ulster sept, was hanged at Tyburn, London in 1644 for his part in the attempt to capture Dublin Castle. Colonel Brian MacMahon fought and defeated an English army at Benburb in 1646. Heber MacMahon, Bishop of Clogher, took command of the Ulster army on the death of Owen Roe O'Neill in 1649. Defeated in battle and captured by Cromwell's troops he was executed at Enniskillen in 1650.

In 1688 Colonel Arthur MacMahon raised a regiment in County Monaghan in support of King James II. This event is remembered in verse:

> *From Carrickmacross, and from Monaghan*
> *A regiment was raised by Macmahon*

This regiment, with Lieutenant-Colonel Owen MacMahon as second in command, was part of the 'Jacobite army' which besieged the city of Derry in 1689.

After the final defeat of James' army in 1691 the McMahons are found prominent among the Wild Geese, serving with distinction in the Irish Brigade in France, including Marshal Macmahon, Duke of Magenta and President of the French Republic.

McMANUS

This name is most common in Ulster, where it is the fourth most common name in its homeland of County Fermanagh.

Ireland was one of the first countries to adopt a system of hereditary surnames which developed from a more ancient system of clan or sept names. From the 11th century each family began to adopt its own distinctive family name generally derived from the first name of an ancestor who lived in or about the 10th century. The surname was formed by prefixing either Mac (son of) or O (grandson or descendant of) to the ancestor's name. Surnames in Ireland, therefore, tended to identify membership of a sept.

McManus is derived from Gaelic *Mac Maghnuis,* meaning 'son of Manus', which in turn is derived from the Norse personal name Magnus. It was not unusual when Gaels married women of Norse stock to baptise some of their children with Norse names. There were two septs of the name. In Connaught, the McManuses trace their descent from Maghnus O'Connor, who died in 1181, and they were based at Kilronan parish, County Roscommon.

In Ulster, the McManuses trace their descent from Maghnus Maguire, son of Donn Mor Maguire who, around 1200, established the Maguire sept around Lisnaskea, County Fermanagh. The McManuses were second only to the Maguires in Fermanagh. From their base on the island of Belle Isle, formerly called Ballymacmanus, in Lough Erne they controlled the shipping on the lakes of Fermanagh. They were also hereditary managers of the fisheries under the Maguires.

The Annals of Ulster (a history of Ulster from the year 444) were compiled by Cathal Oge MacManus, 'chief of the name, vicar general of Clogher and dean of Lough Erne' at Ballymacmanus in the late 15th century. *The Annals of The Kingdom of Ireland by the Four Masters* (a chronicle of Irish history from 'the earliest period to the year 1616') record, on the occasion of his death in 1498, that Cathal Oge MacManus had 'collected together many historical books, from which he had compiled the historical book of Baile-Mic-Manus for his own use'.

Five MacManus officers, with County Antrim roots, are recorded as being part of James II's army which besieged the city of Derry in 1689 during the famous 105 day Siege. After the final defeat of James' army in 1691, Lieutenant Bryan MacManus of Ballybeg, Henry MacManus and Thomas MacManus of Cardonaghy, all resident on the O'Neill estate in County Antrim, forfeited their lands.

McManus is also a Scottish name as the MacManuses were a sept of Clan Colquhoun. This clan acquired the lands of Colquhoun in Dunbartonshire in the reign of Alexander II, King of Scotland from 1214 to 1249. It is quite possible that some McManuses in Ulster are descendants of 17th century Scottish settlers.

Movement of Scottish settlers to Ulster began in earnest from 1605 in a private enterprise colonisation of counties Antrim and Down when Sir Hugh Montgomery and Sir James Hamilton acquired title to large estates in north Down and Sir Randall MacDonnell, 1st Earl of Antrim, to large tracts of land in north Antrim.

McMENAMIN

In Ireland this name is virtually exclusive to Ulster, where two-thirds of the name are in County Donegal and most of the rest in west Tyrone.

Ireland was one of the first countries to adopt a system of hereditary surnames which developed from a more ancient system of clan or sept names. From the 11th century each family began to adopt its own distinctive family name generally derived from the first name of an ancestor who lived in or about the 10th century. The surname was formed by prefixing either Mac (son of) or O (grandson or descendant of) to the ancestor's name. Surnames in Ireland, therefore, tended to identify membership of a sept.

McMenamin is derived from Gaelic *Mac Meanman*, the root word being *meanma*, meaning 'high spirits'. In County Tyrone the name took the form of McMenamy. The McMenamins were a County Donegal sept, and the name is now concentrated around the towns of Letterkenny and Ballybofey.

The McMenamins were followers of the O'Donnells, Lords of Tirconnell, the pre-eminent family in Donegal from the thirteenth to the seventeenth century. *The Annals of The Kingdom of Ireland by the Four Masters* (a history of Ireland from 'the earliest period to the year 1616') record the deaths in battle of Donough Mac Menman and Hugh Mac Menman, nephews of O'Donnell, in 1303.

McMenamin is a common name in Derry city today. This name illustrates the very close links, both historic and economic, between the city of Derry and County Donegal. As Derry developed an industrial base in the 19th century in shirt making, shipbuilding and distilling it attracted much of its workforce from Donegal. In the 90-year period 1821 to 1911 the population of the city quadrupled to 40,780.

The escape of the most prominent Gaelic Lords of Ulster in 'the Flight of the Earls' in1607 from Lough Swilly, County Donegal marked the end of Gaelic power and paved the way for the 17th century Plantation of Ulster with English and Scottish settlers. In the centuries that followed Gaelic names were anglicised, resulting in variant spellings of McMenamin such as McMenamy and McMenim in County Tyrone; McManamy, McManaway and McVanamy in County Roscommon; and McManamon in County Mayo. Many Donegal names are found in Mayo as a result of considerable migration in the early seventeenth century.

It would seem that the homeland of the McMenamin sept was the barony of Raphoe in east Donegal. At the time of the mid-19th century Griffith's Valuation the greatest concentration of McMenamins in County Donegal were in the parishes of Donaghmore, which contained 30 McMenamin households, Kilteevoge with 27 households of the name, Conwal with 16 and Stranorlar with 14. In total 125 McMenamin households were recorded in this survey in County Donegal.

In Scotland the surname of McMenamin is recorded in Galloway and that of McMenamy in Glasgow. These names were brought to Scotland by Irish emigrants.

McMENAMY

McMenamy is a form of McMenamin that is most associated with County Tyrone. In Ireland this name is virtually exclusive to Ulster, where two-thirds of the name are in County Donegal and most of the rest in west Tyrone.

Ireland was one of the first countries to adopt a system of hereditary surnames which developed from a more ancient system of clan or sept names. From the 11th century each family began to adopt its own distinctive family name generally derived from the first name of an ancestor who lived in or about the 10th century. The surname was formed by prefixing either Mac (son of) or O (grandson or descendant of) to the ancestor's name. Surnames in Ireland, therefore, tended to identify membership of a sept.

McMenamy is derived from Gaelic *Mac Meanma*, the root word being *meanma*, meaning 'high spirits'. This sept originated in County Donegal where the name was usually anglicised as McMenamin. The name is now concentrated around the towns of Letterkenny and Ballybofey in Donegal.

The McMenamins were followers of the O'Donnells, Lords of Tirconnell, the pre-eminent family in Donegal from the thirteenth to the seventeenth century. *The Annals of The Kingdom of Ireland by the Four Masters* (a history of Ireland from 'the earliest period to the year 1616') record the deaths in battle of Donough Mac Menman and Hugh Mac Menman, nephews of O'Donnell, in 1303.

McMenamin is a common name in Derry city today. This name illustrates the very close links, both historic and economic, between the city of Derry and County Donegal. As Derry developed an industrial base in the 19th century in shirt making, shipbuilding and distilling it attracted much of its workforce from Donegal. In the 90-year period 1821 to 1911 the population of the city quadrupled to 40,780.

The escape of the most prominent Gaelic Lords of Ulster in 'the Flight of the Earls' in 1607 from Lough Swilly, County Donegal marked the end of Gaelic power and paved the way for the 17th century Plantation of Ulster with English and Scottish settlers. In the centuries that followed Gaelic names were anglicised, resulting in variant spellings of McMenamin such as McMenamy and McMenim in County Tyrone; McManamy, McManaway and McVanamy in County Roscommon; and McManamon in County Mayo. Many Donegal names are found in Mayo as a result of considerable migration in the early seventeenth century.

It would seem that the homeland of the McMenamin sept was the barony of Raphoe in east Donegal. At the time of the mid-19th century Griffith's Valuation the greatest concentration of McMenamins in County Donegal were in the parishes of Donaghmore, which contained 30 McMenamin households, Kilteevoge with 27 households of the name, Conwal with 16 and Stranorlar with 14. In total 125 McMenamin households were recorded in this survey in County Donegal.

In Scotland the surname of McMenamin is recorded in Galloway and that of McMenamy in Glasgow. These names were brought to Scotland by Irish emigrants.

McMILLAN

This surname is found almost exclusively in Ulster where it is most common in Counties Antrim and Down. This name was brought to Ulster by settlers from Scotland in the 17th century.

In Scotland, Clan Macmillan derives its name from Gaelic *Mac Mhaolain*, meaning 'son of the bald one', which refers to the tonsure of monks. It is claimed that the McMillans are descended from Airbertach who came to Iona from a monastery in Ireland. St Columcille, also known as St Columba, had founded monasteries at Derry in Ireland in 546 AD and at Iona in Scotland in 563 AD.

Clan Macmillan were seated on Loch Arkaig, and later at Loch Tay in Perthshire. The name, in the form of Gillemor MacMolan, was first recorded in Lanarkshire in 1263. The McMillans became established on the Argyllshire coast when Malcolm Mor Macmillan received Knapdale from the Lord of the Isles in 1360. A great rock, the Craig Mhic Maolain, at Knap Point, was described thus:

> *Macmillan's right to Knap shall be*
> *As long as this rock withstands the sea.*

Although the Macmillans had lost all their lands at Knapdale by the early 17th century they had by then spread south into Kintyre and to Galloway and Kirkcudbrightshire.

Movement of Scottish settlers to Ulster began in earnest from 1605 in a private enterprise colonisation of counties Antrim and Down when Sir Hugh Montgomery and Sir James Hamilton acquired title to large estates in north Down and Sir Randall MacDonnell, 1st Earl of Antrim, to large tracts of land in north Antrim. By the mid-19th century the McMillans were concentrated in the barony of Cary in north Antrim, and in the Upper Ards area of County Down.

Further impetus came in 1609 when James I adopted the policy to encourage Scottish settlers to settle on the forfeited estates of the Gaelic chiefs in counties Armagh, Cavan, Donegal, Fermanagh, Londonderry (then known as Coleraine) and Tyrone.
Settlers to Ulster came, by and large, in three waves: with the granting of the initial leases in the period 1605 to 1625; after 1652 and Cromwell's crushing of the Irish rebellion; and finally in the fifteen years after 1690 and the Glorious Revolution. It is estimated by 1715, when migration to Ulster had virtually stopped, the Scottish population of Ulster stood at 200,000.

Confusion is caused by the fact, especially in north Antrim, that the majority of Scottish MacMillans changed their name to McMullan under the local influence of the neighbouring O'Mullans. The O'Mullans, in Gaelic *O Maolain*, meaning 'descendant of the bald one', were one of the leading septs of north Derry, in the kingdom of Keenaght, to the north of the Sperrin Mountains. The surname O'Mullan was frequently shortened to Mullan.

It is also likely that some O'Mullans may have changed their name to McMullan under the Scottish influence from north Antrim. Further confusion will arise, in those instances, where McMullan was shortened to Mullan.

McMONAGLE

This name is almost exclusively found in Ulster, where it is most common in County Donegal and in the city of Derry. This name, and its variants such as McMonigle and McMonegal, has always been closely associated with its homeland of County Donegal where it is now one of the more numerous surnames.

This name, which is among the top 50 surnames in the city of Derry today, illustrates the very close links, both historic and economic, between Derry and County Donegal. As Derry developed an industrial base in the 19th century in shirt making, shipbuilding and distilling it attracted much of its workforce from Donegal. Her growing industries attracted workers and families from outside the city and county, and in the 90-year period 1821 to 1911 the population of the city quadrupled to 40,780. In this period Derry stamped her dominance over local rivals and emerged as an important urban centre within Ireland.

Ireland was one of the first countries to adopt a system of hereditary surnames which developed from a more ancient system of clan or sept names. From the 11th century each family began to adopt its own distinctive family name generally derived from the first name of an ancestor who lived in or about the 10th century. The surname was formed by prefixing either Mac (son of) or O (grandson or descendant of) to the ancestor's name. Surnames in Ireland, therefore, tended to identify membership of a sept.

McMonagle is derived from Gaelic *Mac Maongail,* the root word meaning 'wealth valour'.

The escape of the most prominent Gaelic Lords of Ulster in 'the Flight of the Earls' in 1607 from Lough Swilly, County Donegal marked the end of Gaelic power and paved the way for the 17th century Plantation of Ulster with English and Scottish settlers. In the centuries that followed Gaelic names were anglicised, resulting in many variant spellings of the same name and, in many cases, the dropping of the O and Mac prefixes. In the case of McMonagle the prefix Mac was usually, but not always, retained. The County Donegal Hearth Money Rolls of 1665 even recorded one instance of O'Monigal.

Although McMonagle is a significant name in Donegal very little is known about the origins and history of this sept. *The Annals of The Kingdom of Ireland by the Four Masters* (a history of Ireland from 'the earliest period to the year 1616' which was compiled by monks who were followers of the O'Donnells of Donegal) contain no references to the McMonagles.

It would seem that this sept originated in central and west Donegal in the mountain valleys of the River Swilly and Lough Finn between the towns of Letterkenny and Glenties. At the time of the mid-19th century Griffith's Valuation the greatest concentration of McMonagles in County Donegal were in the parishes of Conwal, which contained 34 McMonagle households, and Inishkeel in west Donegal, with 22 households of the name. In total 136 McMonagle households were recorded in this survey in County Donegal which was published between 1857 and 1858.

McMULLAN

This surname is found almost exclusively in Ulster where it is most common in Counties Antrim and Down. McMullan and McMillan are forms of the name of the Scottish Clan Macmillan. The surname McMullan, although it is four times more common in Ulster than McMillan, is not found in Scotland.

In Scotland, Clan Macmillan derives its name from Gaelic *Mac Mhaolain*, meaning 'son of the bald one', which refers to the tonsure of monks. It is claimed that the Macmillans are descended from Airbertach who came to Iona from a monastery in Ireland. St Columcille, also known as St Columba, had founded monasteries at Derry in Ireland in 546 AD and at Iona in Scotland in 563 AD.

Clan Macmillan were seated on Loch Arkaig, and later at Loch Tay in Perthshire. The name, in the form of Gillemor MacMolan, was first recorded in Lanarkshire in 1263. The Macmillans became established on the Argyllshire coast when Malcolm Mor Macmillan received Knapdale from the Lord of the Isles in 1360. A great rock, the Craig Mhic Maolain, at Knap Point, was described thus:

Macmillan's right to Knap shall be
As long as this rock withstands the sea.

Although the Macmillans had lost all their lands at Knapdale by the early 17th century they had by then spread south into Kintyre and to Galloway and Kirkcudbrightshire.

Movement of Scottish settlers to Ulster began in earnest from 1605 in a private enterprise colonisation of counties Antrim and Down when Sir Hugh Montgomery and Sir James Hamilton acquired title to large estates in north Down and Sir Randall MacDonnell, 1st Earl of Antrim, to large tracts of land in north Antrim. By the mid-19th century the McMullans were concentrated in the barony of Cary in north Antrim, and in the Upper Ards area of County Down.

Further impetus came in 1609 when James I adopted the policy to encourage Scottish settlers to settle on the forfeited estates of the Gaelic chiefs in counties Armagh, Cavan, Donegal, Fermanagh, Londonderry (then known as Coleraine) and Tyrone.
Settlers to Ulster came, by and large, in three waves: with the granting of the initial leases in the period 1605 to 1625; after 1652 and Cromwell's crushing of the Irish rebellion; and finally in the fifteen years after 1690 and the Glorious Revolution. It is estimated by 1715, when migration to Ulster had virtually stopped, the Scottish population of Ulster stood at 200,000.

Confusion is caused by the fact, especially in north Antrim, that the majority of Scottish Macmillans changed their name to McMullan under the local influence of the neighbouring O'Mullans. The O'Mullans, in Gaelic *O Maolain*, meaning 'descendant of the bald one', were one of the leading septs of north Derry, in the kingdom of Keenaght, to the north of the Sperrin Mountains. The surname O'Mullan was frequently shortened to Mullan.

It is also likely that some O'Mullans may have changed their name to McMullan under the Scottish influence from north Antrim. Further confusion will arise, in those instances, where McMullan was shortened to Mullan.

McMURTRY

Apart from a few McMurtrys in County Derry this name is found exclusively in County Antrim. This name was brought to County Antrim by settlers from Scotland in the 17th century.

McMurtry is derived from Gaelic *Mac Muircheartaigh*, meaning 'son of Murtagh', a personal name, meaning 'sea ruler'. They were a sept of Clan Stuart of Bute. On their home island, however, this name was usually anglicised as McCurdy. In the 15th century the McCurdys owned most of Bute. Today McCurdy is a common surname in the islands of Arran and Bute.

In Ayrshire, Edinburgh and Lanarkshire the name McCurdy, from an early date, took the form of McMurtry. For example one Gilbert Makmurtye was recorded as a witness in Edinburgh in 1508.

Upheavals such as military incursions, feuds and harvest failures would have encouraged many clan members, including McCurdys, to migrate to Ulster as settlers during the 17th century. Owing to the nature of the Scottish clan system once the power and influence of the chief had been weakened or broken the clan tended to disintegrate. Bearing the surname McCurdy simply indicated that you were a follower of the chief of Clan Stuart of Bute. Not every clan member was related by blood. Their bond, however, whether they had a common tribal ancestor or not, was their common rule by a chief with loyalty to one's clan being the primary obligation. Once tribal loyalty was broken clans 'scattered'.

It would seem quite likely that the McCurdys followed the Stuarts of Bute to Ballintoy, County Antrim. Today McCurdy is the most common name on Rathlin Island, and it is common too in the Glens of Antrim and on the north coast of Antrim.

The Stewarts of Ballintoy, a branch of Clan Stuart of Bute, trace their descent from John Stewart, the son of Robert Stewart who was to become Robert II, King of Scotland in 1371. The Stuarts of Bute were the hereditary sheriffs of the island. Two sons of the fifth Sheriff of Bute, Archibald Stuart, settled on the territory of the MacDonnells of the Glens, near Ballintoy on the Antrim coast about 1560. When Sir Randall MacDonnell, 1st Earl of Antrim, acquired title to large tracts of land in north Antrim, from 1605, he sub-leased to Archibald Stewart, grandson of the fifth Sheriff of Bute, the estate of Ballintoy. Movement of Scottish settlers to farm on this estate and other Scottish-owned estates in Ulster now began in earnest.

Scottish settlers came to Ulster, by and large, in three waves: with the granting of the initial leases in the period 1605 to 1625; after 1652 and Cromwell's crushing of the Irish rebellion; and finally in the fifteen years after 1690 and the Glorious Revolution. It is estimated by 1715, when migration to Ulster had virtually stopped, the Scottish population of Ulster stood at 200,000.

In Ireland the County Donegal sept of *Mac Muircheartaigh* was anglicised as McBrearty. The homeland of this sept was west Donegal in the lands around the town of Killybegs.

McNAMEE

This name is found in Leinster but is most common in Ulster, especially in Counties Derry and Tyrone.

Ireland was one of the first countries to adopt a system of hereditary surnames which developed from a more ancient system of clan or sept names. From the 11th century each family began to adopt its own distinctive family name generally derived from the first name of an ancestor who lived in or about the 10th century. The surname was formed by prefixing either Mac (son of) or O (grandson or descendant of) to the ancestor's name. Surnames in Ireland, therefore, tended to identify membership of a sept.

McNamee is derived from Gaelic *Mac Con Midhe*, meaning 'son of the hound of Meath'. The principal sept of this name lived in County Tyrone on its boundary with County Derry. They were hereditary poets to the O'Neills. The poems of at least six of these McNamees, compiled in medieval times, have been preserved on manuscript. The last of these great Gaelic-Irish poets was Brian Mac Angus MacNamee, chief poet to Turlough Luineach O'Neill who died in 1595.

The Annals of The Kingdom of Ireland by the Four Masters record, in 1507, the death of O'Neill's Chief Poet, Solomon McNamee. He was described as 'Ollav to O'Neill, an adept in rhyming, literature, and poetry, and who kept a house of general hospitality'. The footnote against this entry (published in 1856) recorded that direct descendants of this poet lived in the village of Draperstown, County Derry.

A branch of the sept was established in County Derry before the 17th century Plantation of Ulster. In 1606 the McNamees were recorded as *erenaghs*, i.e. hereditary stewards, of the church lands of Cumber parish in west Derry.

In Leinster a McNamee sept was based beside the Shannon, in the barony of Kilkenny West, in County Westmeath on its boundary with County Roscommon. *The Annals* record, in 1095, the slaying of Amhlaeibh Mac Conmeadha, son of the chief of Sil-Ronain. Thus in the 11th century the McNamees were chiefs of Sil-Ronain which was a territory on the east side of Lough Ree in County Westmeath.

In the 17th century McNamee was a common name in County Leitrim. Today, however, this name is very rare in Connaught. It is believed that in this province McNamee was anglicised as Conmee which, in turn, often became Conway.

Further confusion can arise as there was another distinct sept, also in Gaelic *Mac Con Midhe*, in Counties Derry and Tyrone. In this case the sept's name was anglicised as McConamy and McConomy which, in time, was often changed to Conway. Indeed Conway has been used as the anglicised form of at least four distinct Gaelic-Irish surnames. This sept, however, didn't anglicise their name to McNamee.

During the famous 105 day Siege of Derry, from 18 April to 31 July 1689, Myles McNamee, an ensign in Colonel Cormac O'Neill's Regiment, served with the 'Jacobite Army' which was besieging the city.

McNATT

McNatt is a variant of McNaught which, in turn, is regarded as the County Donegal form of McKnight. At the time of the mid-19th century Griffith's Valuation there were 24 McNaught households in County Donegal compared to 9 McKnight households and 1 McNatt household.

In Ulster, where the name is most common in Counties Antrim and Down, McKnight is of Scottish origin. The McKnights were a sept of Clan MacNaughton. Clan MacNaughton, in Gaelic *Mac Neachdainn*, meaning 'son of Nechtan', claims descent from the 8th century Pictish king Nechtan. In the 13th century the clan was found in Lochawe, Glenaray, Glenshire and Loch Fyne in Argyllshire.

In the 14th century Dundarave, on the north shore of Loch Fyne, became the stronghold of Clan MacNaughton. In 1627 Colonel Alexander MacNaughten raised a company of 200 Highland bowmen for service in the expedition to France for the relief of La Rochelle. Clan MacNaughton held their lands at Dundarave until 1700 when the last chief, John MacNaughten lost them to the Campbells of Ardkinglas who held the lands on the southern side of Loch Fyne.

Movement of Scottish settlers to Ulster began in earnest from 1605 in a private enterprise colonisation of counties Antrim and Down when Sir Hugh Montgomery and Sir James Hamilton acquired title to large estates in north Down and Sir Randall MacDonnell, 1st Earl of Antrim, to large tracts of land in north Antrim.

The MacNaughtons were one of the families brought in by the MacDonnells of the Glens of Antrim in the early 17th century. Shane Dhu, or Black John MacNaghten, became the Earl of Antrim's chief agent. John was buried in the family burial ground at Bonamargy Friary near Ballycastle, County Antrim.

The surname McNaught is on record in Dumfriesshire, in the form of Gilbert Makenaght, from 1296, and as Macneight it was recorded as the name of an old family in Ayrshire. In Galloway, where the name was recorded from the 16th century, it became McKnight.

In 1609 James I adopted the policy to encourage Scottish settlers to settle on the forfeited estates of the Gaelic chiefs in counties Armagh, Cavan, Donegal, Fermanagh, Londonderry (then known as Coleraine) and Tyrone. These settlers came to Ulster, by and large, in three waves: with the granting of the initial leases in the period 1605 to 1625; after 1652 and Cromwell's crushing of the Irish rebellion; and finally in the fifteen years after 1690 and the Glorious Revolution.

Scottish families entering Ireland through the port of Londonderry settled in the Foyle Valley which includes much of the fertile lands of counties Donegal, Londonderry and Tyrone. The lands along the Firth of Clyde in the county of Ayrshire, the Clyde Valley and the Border Lands consisting of the counties of Wigtown, Kirkcudbright and Dumfries were home to many of these Scottish settlers.

It is estimated by 1715, when migration to Ulster had virtually stopped, the Scottish population of Ulster stood at 200,000.

McNAUGHT

McNaught is regarded as the County Donegal form of McKnight. At the time of the mid-19th century Griffith's Valuation there were 24 McNaught households in County Donegal compared to 9 McKnight households.

In Ulster, where the name is most common in Counties Antrim and Down, McKnight is of Scottish origin. The McKnights were a sept of Clan MacNaughton. Clan MacNaughton, in Gaelic *Mac Neachdainn*, meaning 'son of Nechtan', claims descent from the 8th century Pictish king Nechtan. In the 13th century the clan was found in Lochawe, Glenaray, Glenshire and Loch Fyne in Argyllshire.

In the 14th century Dundarave, on the north shore of Loch Fyne, became the stronghold of Clan MacNaughton. In 1627 Colonel Alexander MacNaughten raised a company of 200 Highland bowmen for service in the expedition to France for the relief of La Rochelle. Clan MacNaughton held their lands at Dundarave until 1700 when the last chief, John MacNaughten lost them to the Campbells of Ardkinglas who held the lands on the southern side of Loch Fyne.

Movement of Scottish settlers to Ulster began in earnest from 1605 in a private enterprise colonisation of counties Antrim and Down when Sir Hugh Montgomery and Sir James Hamilton acquired title to large estates in north Down and Sir Randall MacDonnell, 1st Earl of Antrim, to large tracts of land in north Antrim.

The MacNaughtons were one of the families brought in by the MacDonnells of the Glens of Antrim in the early 17th century. Shane Dhu, or Black John MacNaghten, became the Earl of Antrim's chief agent. John was buried in the family burial ground at Bonamargy Friary near Ballycastle, County Antrim.

The surname McNaught is on record in Dumfriesshire, in the form of Gilbert Makenaght, from 1296, and as Macneight it was recorded as the name of an old family in Ayrshire. In Galloway, where the name was recorded from the 16th century, it became McKnight.

In 1609 James I adopted the policy to encourage Scottish settlers to settle on the forfeited estates of the Gaelic chiefs in counties Armagh, Cavan, Donegal, Fermanagh, Londonderry (then known as Coleraine) and Tyrone. These settlers came to Ulster, by and large, in three waves: with the granting of the initial leases in the period 1605 to 1625; after 1652 and Cromwell's crushing of the Irish rebellion; and finally in the fifteen years after 1690 and the Glorious Revolution.

Scottish families entering Ireland through the port of Londonderry settled in the Foyle Valley which includes much of the fertile lands of counties Donegal, Londonderry and Tyrone. The lands along the Firth of Clyde in the county of Ayrshire, the Clyde Valley and the Border Lands consisting of the counties of Wigtown, Kirkcudbright and Dumfries were home to many of these Scottish settlers.

It is estimated by 1715, when migration to Ulster had virtually stopped, the Scottish population of Ulster stood at 200,000.

McNAUGHTON

This name, of Scottish origin, belongs to County Antrim.

McNaughton is derived from Gaelic *Mac Neachdainn*, meaning 'son of Nechtan'. Clan Mac-Naughton claims descent from the 8th century Pictish king Nechtan. In the 13th century the clan was found in Lochawe, Glenaray, Glenshire and Loch Fyne in Argyllshire.

In the 14th century Dundarave, on the north shore of Loch Fyne, became the stronghold of Clan MacNaughton. In 1627 Colonel Alexander MacNaughten raised a company of 200 Highland bowmen for service in the expedition to France for the relief of La Rochelle. Clan MacNaughton held their lands at Dundarave until 1700 when the last chief, John MacNaughten lost them to the Campbells of Ardkinglas who held the lands on the southern side of Loch Fyne.

The MacNaughtons were one of the families brought in by the MacDonnells of the Glens of Antrim in the early 17th century. Clan Donald had acquired new territories in the north of Ireland ca.1400 when John Mor MacDonald had married Margery Bissett, an heiress in the Glens of Antrim. Members of the clan had gained a foothold in the Glens in the 13th century through land grants for military service as galloglasses, i.e. mercenary soldiers. By the mid-16th century the MacDonalds, known as the MacDonnells of the Glens, had carved out an extensive territory in County Antrim at the expense of the MacQuillans.

Shane Dhu, or Black John MacNaghten, son of Alexander, Chief of Clan MacNaughton, came to north Antrim with his cousin Randall MacDonnell at the end of the 16th century. When Sir Randall MacDonnell, 1st Earl of Antrim, acquired title to large tracts of land in north Antrim, from 1605, he sub-leased substantial estates at Ballymagarry and Benvarden to Shane Dhu. Movement of Scottish settlers to farm on these estates and other Scottish-owned estates in Ulster now began in earnest.

Shane Dhu MacNaghten died in 1630 and was buried in the family burial ground at Bonamargy Friary near Ballycastle, County Antrim. One of the best known stories connected with the city of Londonderry in the 18th century concerns Shane Dhu's great-great-grandson, John MacNaghten who inherited the Benvarden estate near Bushmills, County Antrim in 1740.

This story is remembered as 'The Tale of Half-Hanged MacNaghten'. John MacNaghten became infatuated with Mary Anne Knox, a wealthy young heiress, of Prehen House, Londonderry. In a tragic ambush on a lonely stretch of road between Londonderry and Strabane, on the night of 10 November 1761, Mary Anne Knox was accidentally shot dead by John MacNaghten. Captured at Portrush, attempting to make his escape to Scotland, John Mac-Naghten was taken to Lifford Jail, tried and sentenced to be hanged.

On the day of his execution, 15 December 1761, John MacNaghten threw himself off the gallows and the rope broke. Declining the crowd's encouragement to escape, saying that he didn't want to be known as the 'half-hanged man', John returned to the gallows and was hanged.

McNEILL

Though found in all provinces of Ireland McNeill is common only in Ulster, where it is most numerous in Counties Derry and Antrim. This name represents the descendants of Clan Mac-Neil in Scotland who from the mid-14th century came to Ireland to fight as galloglasses, i.e. mercenary soldiers. Derived from Gaelic *galloglach,* galloglass refers to a paid soldier, often brought over from Scotland, to fight on behalf of an Irish chief.

The Annals of The Kingdom of Ireland by the Four Masters provide detailed and graphic descriptions of the Scottish galloglasses. In one account dated 1557 the *Annals* describe the galloglass in the camp of the O'Neills who were on a raiding expedition into O'Donnell territory in Donegal. It states that 'sixty grim and redoubtable gallowglasses, with sharp, keen axes, terrible and ready for action, and sixty stern and terrific Scots, with massive, broad, and heavy-striking swords in their hands, ready to strike and parry, were watching and guarding the son of O'Neill.'

With the assistance of his McNeill galloglasses the McDonnells were a serious military threat to both the O'Neills and the English Crown in County Antrim in the 16th century. In 1555 the *Annals* record that Hugh O'Neill, Lord of Clannaboy, was killed by the Scots. In the same year an English army, led by the Earl of Sussex, was raised 'to expel the sons of Mac Donnell and the Scots, who were making conquests in the Route and Clannaboy'. The *Annals* record that the Earl's army 'slew one or two hundred of these Scots'.

McNeill is derived from Gaelic *Mac Neill*, meaning 'son of Niall'. Scottish Clan MacNeil claims descent from Niall, twenty-first in descent from Niall of the Nine Hostages, the 5th century High King of Ireland. This Niall came to the island of Barra in the Outer Hebrides in 1049 and founded the clan. The MacNeils, with their stronghold at Kisimul Castle, received a charter for the island of Barra in 1429 from Alexander MacDonald, Lord of the Isles. The MacNeils of Barra became followers of the Macleans of Duart.

A branch of the clan was established at an early date on the island of Gigha, north of Kintyre. The seat of the MacNeils of Gigha, who were followers of the MacDonalds of Islay and Kintyre, was at Castle Sween in Knapdale.

It was the MacNeils of Barra who came to Ireland as galloglasses as early as the mid-14th century and settled, for the most part, in Counties Antrim and Derry. By the late 15th century the McNeills, along with the McQuillans, were lords of Clandeboy in County Antrim. In 1471 the McNeills submitted to Con O'Neill.

By the mid-16th century the MacDonalds, known as the MacDonnells of the Glens, had carved out an extensive territory in County Antrim at the expense of the MacQuillans. Movement of Scottish settlers to County Antrim began in earnest from 1605 when Sir Randall MacDonnell, 1st Earl of Antrim, acquired title to large tracts of land in north Antrim. Many McNeills, as followers of the McDonnells of the Glens, settled in north Antrim in the late sixteenth and early seventeenth centuries. Hugh MacNeil was granted an estate at Ballycastle at this time.

McNELIS

This name originated in County Donegal. The name tends to be spelt as McNelis in Donegal and as Nelis in the adjoining counties.

Ireland was one of the first countries to adopt a system of hereditary surnames which developed from a more ancient system of clan or sept names. From the 11th century each family began to adopt its own distinctive family name generally derived from the first name of an ancestor who lived in or about the 10th century. The surname was formed by prefixing either Mac (son of) or O (grandson or descendant of) to the ancestor's name. Surnames in Ireland, therefore, tended to identify membership of a sept.

McNelis is derived from Gaelic *Mac Niallghuis*, meaning 'son of vigorous Neill', as *gus* attached to the forename means 'vigour'. MacNeilus and MacNellus were recorded among the principal names of County Donegal in the census of 1659.
The homeland of this sept was Glencolumbkille in west Donegal.

Glencolumbkille, a remote parish exposed to the Atlantic Ocean on the west and cut off from the rest of Donegal by high moors, takes its name from St Columcille, meaning 'Dove of the Church', who founded a monastery here in the 6th century. Glencolumbkille is famed for the turas or pilgrimages that are made to its 15 stations on 9 June, the saint's day (St Columcille, also known as St Columba, died on 9 June 597 at the monastery on the island of Iona, Scotland). The tura begins at the door of the present Church of Ireland church which marks the site of the original monastery. All that survives of the monastery is a souterrain which may have been used as a place of concealment from Viking raids.

In the 16th century the McNelises were recorded as coarbs, i.e. abbots, of Glencolumbkille. In Bishop Montgomery's survey of the Diocese of Raphoe, in 1609, it was said of Bernard MacNellus, curate of Glencolumbkille, that he 'paints cleverly and speaks Irish, Latin and English well'.

At the time of the mid-19th century Griffith's Valuation 34 McNelis households were recorded in County Donegal, and all but six of these households were recorded in the parish of Glencolumbkille. In other words over 80% of descendants of the McNelis sept in County Donegal were living in the parish of Glencolumbkille on the west coast of Donegal.

The name has now spread to Derry city and to County Mayo. This name illustrates the very close links, both historic and economic, between the city of Derry and County Donegal. The name spread to Derry city, where it is usually spelt as Nelis, in the 19th century. As Derry developed an industrial base in shirt making, shipbuilding and distilling it attracted much of its workforce from County Donegal. In the 90-year period 1821 to 1911 the population of the city quadrupled to 40,780.

Many Donegal names are also found in Mayo today as a result of considerable migration in the early seventeenth century.

McNERLIN

In Ulster, McNerlin is a variant of McErlean. This surname is found almost exclusively in Counties Antrim and Derry.

Ireland was one of the first countries to adopt a system of hereditary surnames which developed from a more ancient system of clan or sept names. From the 11th century each family began to adopt its own distinctive family name generally derived from the first name of an ancestor who lived in or about the 10th century. The surname was formed by prefixing either Mac (son of) or O (grandson or descendant of) to the ancestor's name. Surnames in Ireland, therefore, tended to identify membership of a sept.

McNerlin is derived from Gaelic *Mac an Fhirleighinn*, the root word being *fearleighinn*, meaning 'learned man'. This title was applied to the head of a monastic school in both Ireland and Scotland. In Iona in 1164 Ferleighinn Dubside was recorded as one of the officials of the monastery.

Although this sept originated in north Sligo a branch of the family migrated to and settled in County Derry. It is possible that the Anglo-Norman military incursions of the 13th century into Connaught which reduced the power and influence of many septs in that province encouraged descendants of the McErleans to migrate north at an early date.

The Hearth Money Rolls of 1663 would suggest that the parishes of Ballyscullion and Tamlaght O'Crilly in south Derry were the original base of this sept in County Derry. Three McErlean households were recorded in this source in County Derry - 2 households of McErlean in Ballyscullion Parish and 1 of McErlyn in Tamlaght O'Crilly Parish.

At the time of the 1831 census there were 63 McErlean households in County Derry, and all but four of these households were residing in three parishes in south Derry; 33 in Tamlaght O'Crilly Parish and 13 each in the parishes of Artrea and Maghera. In the 1831 census the descendants of this sept were generally recorded as McErlain in Tamlaght O'Crilly Parish, as McErlane in Maghera Parish and as McErlean in Artrea Parish.

In Scotland this name is found in the forms of McNerlin and McErlane. Indeed McErlane is a common name in Ayrshire and Dumbartonshire. As these two regions were home to many of the Scottish settlers who came to Ulster throughout the 17th century, it is possible that some McNerlins in Ulster may be descendants of Scottish settlers.

Movement of Scottish settlers to Ulster began in earnest from 1605 in a private enterprise colonisation of counties Antrim and Down when Sir Hugh Montgomery and Sir James Hamilton acquired title to large estates in north Down and Sir Randall MacDonnell, 1st Earl of Antrim, to large tracts of land in north Antrim. Further impetus came in 1609 when James I adopted the policy to encourage Scottish settlers to settle on the forfeited estates of the Gaelic chiefs in counties Armagh, Cavan, Donegal, Fermanagh, Londonderry (then known as Coleraine) and Tyrone.

McNULTY

This name, which originated in County Donegal, is most numerous today in County Donegal in Ulster and in County Mayo in Connaught. Many Donegal names are found in Mayo as a result of considerable migration in the early seventeenth century.

Ireland was one of the first countries to adopt a system of hereditary surnames which developed from a more ancient system of clan or sept names. From the 11th century each family began to adopt its own distinctive family name generally derived from the first name of an ancestor who lived in or about the 10th century. The surname was formed by prefixing either Mac (son of) or O (grandson or descendant of) to the ancestor's name. Surnames in Ireland, therefore, tended to identify membership of a sept.

McNulty is derived from Gaelic *Mac an Ultaigh*, the root word being *Ultach*, meaning 'Ulsterman'. The homeland of this sept was south Donegal.

Many County Donegal septs trace their lineage to Conall *Gulban*, son of the 5th century High King of Ireland, Niall of the Nine Hostages, who ruled from the Hill of Tara, County Meath. Conall and his brother Eogan conquered northwest Ireland, ca.425 AD, capturing the great hill-fort of Grianan of Ailech in County Donegal which commanded the entrance to the Inishowen peninsula between Lough Swilly and Lough Foyle.

Conall, styled 'King of Tir Conaill', established his own kingdom in County Donegal called after him Tyrconnel, i.e. the 'Land of Conall', which was the ancient name of Donegal. His descendants, known as the Cenel Conaill (the race of Conall), formed one of the principal branches of the Northern Ui Neill (descendants of Niall of the Nine Hostages). The septs of the Cenel Conaill firmly established themselves in County Donegal while those descended from Conal's brother Eogan, i.e. the Cenel Eoghain (the race of Owen), expanded to the east and south into Counties Derry and Tyrone.

The Annals of The Kingdom of Ireland by the Four Masters (a chronicle of Irish history from 'the earliest period to the year 1616') record that, in 1281, at the battle of Desertcreat in County Tyrone the Cenel Conaill were defeated by the Cenel Eoghain. In this battle Donnell Oge O'Donnell, chief of the Cenel Conaill, and many of his 'distinguished' followers including Murtough Macan-Ulty were slain. Donnell Oge O'Donnell was buried in the monastery of Derry.

In 1431 the O'Donnells set out on a predatory expedition against the McNultys of Tirhugh (the barony of Tirhugh is situated in the southeast corner of County Donegal). They were resisted by the O'Gallaghers and McNultys, and *The Annals* record that Connell O'Donnell 'was slain by one shot of a javelin'.

In Donegal, McNulty was one of the names assumed by the Dunleavys, in Gaelic *Mac Duinnshleibhe*, the root words being *donn*, meaning 'brown' and *sliabh*, meaning 'mountain'. The Dunleavys, an ancient royal family of Ulster, were driven out of County Down by John de Courcy's Norman army at the end of the 12th century, and settled in Donegal where they became physicians to the O'Donnells.

244

McNUTT

McNutt, which is fairly numerous in Ulster, can be an Irish or a Scottish name.

Ireland was one of the first countries to adopt a system of hereditary surnames which developed from a more ancient system of clan or sept names. From the 11th century each family began to adopt its own distinctive family name generally derived from the first name of an ancestor who lived in or about the 10th century. The surname was formed by prefixing either Mac (son of) or O (grandson or descendant of) to the ancestor's name. Surnames in Ireland, therefore, tended to identify membership of a sept. McNutt is derived from Gaelic *Mac Nuadhat*. This sept may derive their name from *Nuadha*, an ancient sea-god.

In Scotland, McNutt is a variant of McNaught. McNaught is on record in Dumfriesshire, in the form of Gilbert Makenaght, from 1296, and as Macneight it was recorded as the name of an old family in Ayrshire. In Galloway, where the name was recorded from the 16th century, it became McKnight. These regions were home to many of the Scottish settlers who came to Ulster throughout the 17th century.

McNaught can also be an abbreviated form of McNaughton. Clan MacNaughton, in Gaelic *Mac Neachdainn*, meaning 'son of Nechtan', claims descent from the 8th century Pictish king Nechtan. In the 13th century the clan was found in Lochawe, Glenaray, Glenshire and Loch Fyne in Argyllshire.

In the 14th century Dundarave, on the north shore of Loch Fyne, became the stronghold of Clan MacNaughton. In 1627 Colonel Alexander MacNaughten raised a company of 200 Highland bowmen for service in the expedition to France for the relief of La Rochelle. Clan MacNaughton held their lands at Dundarave until 1700 when the last chief, John MacNaughten lost them to the Campbells of Ardkinglas who held the lands on the southern side of Loch Fyne.

Movement of Scottish settlers to Ulster began in earnest from 1605 in a private enterprise colonisation of counties Antrim and Down when Sir Hugh Montgomery and Sir James Hamilton acquired title to large estates in north Down and Sir Randall MacDonnell, 1st Earl of Antrim, to large tracts of land in north Antrim.

The MacNaughtons were one of the families brought in by the MacDonnells of the Glens of Antrim in the early 17th century. Shane Dhu, or Black John MacNaghten, became the Earl of Antrim's chief agent. John was buried in the family burial ground at Bonamargy Friary near Ballycastle, County Antrim.

In County Donegal, at the time of the mid-19th century Griffith's Valuation, there were 24 McNaught households, 20 McNutt households, 9 McKnight households and 1 McNatt household.

Alexander McNutt, a native of Londonderry, acquired over 800,000 acres of land in the province of Nova Scotia, Canada in 1760, on condition that 600 families were to be settled on the lands within four years. He actively promoted Nova Scotia to intending emigrants in his native Londonderry. In the years 1761 and 1762 he persuaded 500 people to emigrate from Ireland to Nova Scotia.

McPEAKE

This name is almost exclusively found in Ulster, where it is most common in Counties Derry and Tyrone.

Ireland was one of the first countries to adopt a system of hereditary surnames which developed from a more ancient system of clan or sept names. From the 11th century each family began to adopt its own distinctive family name generally derived from the first name of an ancestor who lived in or about the 10th century. The surname was formed by prefixing either Mac (son of) or O (grandson or descendant of) to the ancestor's name. Surnames in Ireland, therefore, tended to identify membership of a sept.

McPeake is derived from Gaelic *Mac Peice*. In this case it is believed that the root word *peic* is derived from an Old English word *peac*, meaning 'a thickset man'.

The McPeakes were followers of the O'Donnells, the pre-eminent family in Donegal from the thirteenth to the seventeenth century. Dermot and Manus MacPeake accompanied Rory O'Donnell to Connaught on a revenge raid against the O'Rourkes of Breffny in 1603. According to the *The Annals of The Kingdom of Ireland by the Four Masters* (a chronicle of Irish history from 'the earliest period to the year 1616') 'they plundered and ravaged Breifny, both its crops and corn, and all the cattle they could seize upon'.

In the census of 1659 McPeake was recorded as one of the principal Irish names in the barony of Loughinsholin in south Derry. This association with south Derry is commemorated in the townland name of Ballymacpeake which straddles the boundary between the parishes of Maghera and Tamlaght O'Crilly.

The 1831 census for County Derry clearly demonstrates that this area of south Derry was the ancestral homeland of the McPeakes. At the time of the 1831 census there were 93 McPeake households in County Derry, and all but three of these households were residing in the parishes of south Derry, centred on and surrounding the townland of Ballymacpeake. At the time of the 1831 census there were 33 McPeake households recorded in Tamlaght O'Crilly Parish and 25 McPeake households in Maghera Parish. Indeed in 1831 there were 15 McPeake households living in the townland of Ballymacpeake.

The escape of the most prominent Gaelic Lords of Ulster in 'the Flight of the Earls' in 1607 from Lough Swilly, County Donegal marked the end of Gaelic power and paved the way for the 17th century Plantation of Ulster with English and Scottish settlers. In the centuries that followed Gaelic names were anglicised, resulting in many variant spellings of the same name and, in many cases, the dropping of the O and Mac prefixes.

In the case of McPeake confusion can arise, in those instances, where the Mac prefix has been dropped. The surname Peake was also recorded in England as early as the 13th century where it derived either as a local name for a 'dweller by the peak or hill', or as a nickname for a stout, thickset man. It is, therefore, possible that some Peakes in Ulster are descendants of 17th century English settlers.

246

McRORY

McRory, and variants such as Macrory, McCrory and McGrory, can be an Irish or a Scottish name. This name is virtually exclusive to Ulster, where over one-half are in Tyrone and one-third are in County Antrim.

Ireland was one of the first countries to adopt a system of hereditary surnames which developed from a more ancient system of clan or sept names. The surname was formed by prefixing either Mac (son of) or O (grandson or descendant of) to the ancestor's name.

McRory is derived from Gaelic *Mac Ruaidhri*, meaning 'son of Rory'. There were two distinct McRory septs in Ulster. It is claimed that the County Tyrone sept of the name trace their descent from the Three Collas. *Colla Uais*, High King of Ireland from 322 to 326 AD, and his two brothers are reputed to have burnt and destroyed Navan Fort in County Armagh. Navan Fort, built ca.300 BC, was the residence of the warrior kings of Ulster, and of Cuchullain and his legendary Red Branch Knights. The Three Collas were banished to Scotland in 326 AD.

A branch of this County Tyrone sept migrated to County Derry where they became *erenaghs*, i.e. hereditary stewards, of the church lands in the parish of Ballynascreen in the barony of Loughinsholin. Another McRory sept were *erenaghs* of Machaire Croise in Fermanagh. It is believed that they were a branch of the Maguires.

McRory in Gaelic *Mac Ruairidh*, meaning 'son of Rory', is also a Scottish name. They were an important sept of Clan Donald. In the 14th century some of these families came to Ulster as galloglasses. Derived from Gaelic *galloglach*, galloglass refers to a paid soldier, often brought over from Scotland, to fight on behalf of an Irish chief.

The Annals of The Kingdom of Ireland by the Four Masters provide detailed and graphic descriptions of the Scottish galloglasses. In one account dated 1557 the *Annals* describe the galloglass in the camp of the O'Neills who were on a raiding expedition into O'Donnell territory in Donegal. It states that 'sixty grim and redoubtable gallowglasses, with sharp, keen axes, terrible and ready for action, and sixty stern and terrific Scots, with massive, broad, and heavy-striking swords in their hands, ready to strike and parry, were watching and guarding the son of O'Neill.'

The majority of Scottish McRorys in Ulster, however, will be descendants of 17th century settlers. Movement of Scottish settlers to Ulster began in earnest from 1605 in a private enterprise colonisation of counties Antrim and Down when Sir Hugh Montgomery and Sir James Hamilton acquired title to large estates in north Down and Sir Randall MacDonnell, 1st Earl of Antrim, to large tracts of land in north Antrim.

As followers of Clan Donald many Scottish McRorys settled in the Glens of Antrim. Clan Donald had acquired territory here ca.1400. By the mid-16th century the MacDonalds, known as the MacDonnells of the Glens, had carved out an extensive territory in County Antrim at the expense of the MacQuillans.

In many cases McRory was further anglicised to Rogers and Rodgers.

McSHANE

McShane is common only in County Louth and in Ulster, particularly in County Donegal.

Ireland was one of the first countries to adopt a system of hereditary surnames which developed from a more ancient system of clan or sept names. From the 11th century each family began to adopt its own distinctive family name generally derived from the first name of an ancestor who lived in or about the 10th century. The surname was formed by prefixing either Mac (son of) or O (grandson or descendant of) to the ancestor's name. Surnames in Ireland, therefore, tended to identify membership of a sept.

The McShane sept is derived from Gaelic *Mac Seain*, meaning 'son of John'. In both County Louth and in Ulster the McShanes, who originated in northeast Tyrone, were a branch of the O'Neills. The O'Neill sept, the most famous family of Ulster, trace their lineage to Eogan, son of the 5th century High King of Ireland, Niall of the Nine Hostages. Eogan and his brother Conall *Gulban* conquered northwest Ireland, ca.425 AD, capturing the great hill-fort of Grianan of Ailech in County Donegal which commanded the entrance to the Inishowen peninsula between Lough Swilly and Lough Foyle.

The senior branch of this sept, the O'Neills of Tyrone, were frequently High Kings of Ireland, and in the 16th and 17th centuries they were the leaders of Gaelic resistance to English attempts to pacify Ireland. A junior branch established themselves in County Antrim in the 14th century and from their seat at Shane's Castle became known as the Clannaboy or Clandeboy O'Neills.

In the census of 1659 McShane was recorded as one of the principal Irish names in the barony of Loughinsholin in south Derry. At the time of the 1831 census there were 71 McShane households in County Derry, and all but eighteen of these households were residing in the parishes of south Derry, centred on and surrounding the parish of Maghera. The 1831 census records 18 McShane households living in Maghera Parish.

The surname McShane is not as common as it formerly was as it was widely anglicised to Johnson and Johnston. Johnson is a common surname in England and Scotland but it has been constantly confused with and used interchangeably with the Scottish surname Johnston. Johnson is among the ten commonest surnames in England, while Johnston is among the twenty commonest in Scotland. Both names were brought to Ulster in large numbers by settlers from England and Scotland in the 17th century. Many Johnsons and Johnstons in Ulster, however, will be descendants of Irish McShanes as opposed to settlers from England and Scotland.

Outside of Ulster the Westmeath family of Shane were a branch of the O'Farrells, and in Kerry the surname McShane was assumed by the Fitzmaurices. However both these families appear to be now extinct.

In Scotland the Aberdeenshire surname of McShand is regarded as a variant of Irish McShane.

McTAGGART

McTaggart can be an Irish or a Scottish name. This name is virtually exclusive to Ulster, where it is most common in County Antrim.

Ireland was one of the first countries to adopt a system of hereditary surnames which developed from a more ancient system of clan or sept names. From the 11th century each family began to adopt its own distinctive family name generally derived from the first name of an ancestor who lived in or about the 10th century. The surname was formed by prefixing either Mac (son of) or O (grandson or descendant of) to the ancestor's name. Surnames in Ireland, therefore, tended to identify membership of a sept.

McTaggart is derived from Gaelic *Mac an tSagairt*, the root word being *sagart*, meaning 'priest'. This County Fermanagh sept was based at Ballymacataggart in Derryvullan Parish where they were *erenaghs*, i.e. hereditary stewards, of the church lands.

The anglicisation of Gaelic names, from the 17th century, resulted in many variant spellings of this name which include McEntaggart, Attegart, Haggart, Taggart, Target and Teggart. Though originating in County Fermanagh, and now chiefly located in County Antrim, this surname, and its many variant forms, was widespread, at an early period, throughout Ulster. The name appears frequently in 16th and 17th century records of Counties Antrim, Armagh, Derry, Donegal and Fermanagh.

In Scotland the McTaggarts, in Gaelic *Mac an tSagairt*, meaning 'son of the priest', were a sept of Clan Ross. They claim descent from Ferchar Mackinsagart, son of the 'Red Priest of Applecross'. As a reward for assisting Alexander II, King of Scotland, crush a rebellion in Moray, Ferchar Mackinsagart was created Earl of Ross in 1234.

Others may be descended from less well-known priests as 'the rule of celibacy was not strictly enforced upon the clergy of the primitive church'. From the 15th century references to the surname are found in Dumfries; in the form of Donald McKyntagart in 1459 and Patrick Taggart in 1544. McTaggart became a common name in Dumfriesshire, and this region was home to many of the Scottish settlers who came to Ulster throughout the 17th century.

Movement of Scottish settlers to Ulster began in earnest from 1605 in a private enterprise colonisation of counties Antrim and Down when Sir Hugh Montgomery and Sir James Hamilton acquired title to large estates in north Down and Sir Randall MacDonnell, 1st Earl of Antrim, to large tracts of land in north Antrim. Further impetus came in 1609 when James I adopted the policy to encourage Scottish settlers to settle on the forfeited estates of the Gaelic chiefs in counties Armagh, Cavan, Donegal, Fermanagh, Londonderry (then known as Coleraine) and Tyrone.

Scottish families entering Ireland through the port of Londonderry settled in the Foyle Valley which includes much of the fertile lands of counties Donegal, Londonderry and Tyrone. It is estimated by 1715, when migration to Ulster had virtually stopped, the Scottish population of Ulster stood at 200,000.

McWILLIAMS

McWilliams is common only in Ulster where it is most numerous in Counties Antrim and Derry. This name was brought to Ulster by settlers from Scotland in the 17th century.

The personal name William, derived from the Old German *Willihelm* and introduced into Britain at the time of the Norman conquest in 1066, was early introduced to the Highlands of Scotland. This resulted in the surname McWilliam, in Gaelic *Mac Uilleim*, meaning 'son of William'. Clan MacWilliam trace their descent from William MacLeod, fifth chief of Clan MacLeod.

The McWilliams also flourished as septs of Clan Gunn in Caithness and Sutherland, tracing their descent through a chief of the clan called William, and of Clan MacFarlane. In Scotland McWilliam is the more common form of the name while in Ulster it is McWilliams. The name was also further anglicised to Williamson.

Movement of Scottish settlers to Ulster began in earnest from 1605 in a private enterprise colonisation of counties Antrim and Down when Sir Hugh Montgomery and Sir James Hamilton acquired title to large estates in north Down and Sir Randall MacDonnell, 1st Earl of Antrim, to large tracts of land in north Antrim.

Further impetus came in 1609 when James I adopted the policy to encourage Scottish settlers to settle on the forfeited estates of the Gaelic chiefs in counties Armagh, Cavan, Donegal, Fermanagh, Londonderry (then known as Coleraine) and Tyrone.
Settlers came to Ulster, by and large, in three waves: with the granting of the initial leases in the period 1605 to 1625; after 1652 and Cromwell's crushing of the Irish rebellion; and finally in the fifteen years after 1690 and the Glorious Revolution.

Scottish families entering Ireland through the port of Londonderry settled in the Foyle Valley which includes much of the fertile lands of counties Donegal, Londonderry and Tyrone. It is estimated by 1715, when migration to Ulster had virtually stopped, the Scottish population of Ulster stood at 200,000.

It is possible that some McWilliams in Ulster were originally McQuillan. In County Down, in particular, McQuillan was changed to McWilliams. McQuillan, in Gaelic *Mac Uighilin*, trace their descent from Hugelin de Mandeville. The de Mandevilles, of Norman-Welsh origin, came to north Antrim at the time of the Anglo-Norman invasion of Ireland in the late 12th century and wrested the territory known as the Route from the O'Kanes. They quickly became established as a powerful Irish sept.

In the 15th century they conducted a long-running feud of raid and counter-raid with the O'Kanes of County Derry. The McQuillans were known as Lords of the Route, with their chief residence at Dunluce Castle, until their defeat by Sorley Boy MacDonnell in 1580. By the mid-16th century the MacDonnells of the Glens had carved out an extensive territory in County Antrim at the expense of the McQuillans.

Captain Ross MacQuillan, Lieutenant Cormac MacQuillan and Ensign Theodore MacQuillan were officers in James II's army that besieged the city of Derry during the famous 105 day Siege of Derry, from 18 April to 31 July 1689.

MEHAFFEY

This name represents the descendants of Scottish Clan MacFie. The name was brought to Ulster at the time of the 17th century Plantation of Ulster by settlers from Scotland. The name is particularly associated with County Donegal.

Clan MacFie, originally Clan MacDuffy, is derived from Gaelic *Mac Dhuibhshithe*, meaning 'son of the black-haired man of peace'. The name was also anglicised as McAfee, McHaffy, Mahaffy and Mehaffey.

Clan MacFie trace their descent from Kenneth McAlpine, the 9th century King of Scotland. The clan's home was the island of Colonsay in the Inner Hebrides where they were hereditary keepers of the records of Clan Donald, Lords of the Isles. They were followers of the Mac-Donalds of Islay. A banch of Clan MacFie, who were followers of the Camerons of Lochiel, established themselves at Lochaber.

Upheavals such as military incursions, feuds and harvest failures would have encouraged many clan members, including Mehaffeys, to migrate to Ulster as settlers during the 17th century. With the decline of Clan Donald power Clan MacFie scattered at the beginning of the 17th century. The loss of clan lands in Colonsay in the mid-17th century provided further encouragement to Clan MacFie members to migrate.

Owing to the nature of the Scottish clan system once the power and influence of the chief had been weakened or broken the clan tended to disintegrate. Bearing the surname Mehaffey simply indicated that you were a follower of the Clan MacFie chief. Not every clan member was related by blood: people who were not of direct descent might also identify with a particular clan. They may have been granted land in return for services, or simply have lived on clan territories. Their bond, however, whether they had a common tribal ancestor or not, was their common rule by a chief with loyalty to one's clan being the primary obligation. Once tribal loyalty was broken clans 'scattered'.

Movement of Scottish settlers to Ulster began in earnest from 1605 in a private enterprise colonisation of counties Antrim and Down when Sir Hugh Montgomery and Sir James Hamilton acquired title to large estates in north Down and Sir Randall MacDonnell, 1st Earl of Antrim, to large tracts of land in north Antrim.

Further impetus came in 1609 when James I adopted the policy to encourage Scottish settlers to settle on the forfeited estates of the Gaelic chiefs in counties Armagh, Cavan, Donegal, Fermanagh, Londonderry (then known as Coleraine) and Tyrone.

Scottish families entering Ireland through the port of Londonderry settled in the Foyle Valley which includes much of the fertile lands of counties Donegal, Londonderry and Tyrone. It is estimated by 1715, when migration to Ulster had virtually stopped, the Scottish population of Ulster stood at 200,000.

The name was also recorded in Wigtownshire in the province of Galloway from the 16th century. This region was home to many of the Scottish settlers who came to Ulster throughout the 17th century.

MELLON

The name Mellon, and its variants Mellan and Mallon, are common only in Ulster, particularly in Counties Tyrone and Armagh.

The O'Mellan sept trace their lineage to Eogan, son of the 5th century High King of Ireland, Niall of the Nine Hostages, who ruled from the Hill of Tara, County Meath. Eogan and his brother Conall *Gulban* conquered northwest Ireland, ca.425 AD, capturing the great hill-fort of Grianan of Ailech in County Donegal.

Eogan, styled 'King of Ailech', established his own kingdom in the peninsula in County Donegal still called after him Inishowen (Innis Eoghain or Eogan's Isle). His descendants, known as the Cenel Eoghain (the race of Owen), became the principal branch of the Northern Ui Neill (descendants of Niall of the Nine Hostages). The Cenel Eoghain in the next five centuries expanded to the east and south from their focal point in Inishowen.

Ireland was one of the first countries to adopt a system of hereditary surnames which developed from a more ancient system of clan or sept names. The surname was formed by prefixing either Mac (son of) or O (grandson or descendant of) to the ancestor's name. O'Mellan, in Gaelic *O Meallain*, is derived from *meall*, meaning 'pleasant'.

The O'Mellans were one of the leading septs of Clan Fergus (Fergus was a son of Eogan) who, from their homeland around Lough Swilly, County Donegal, from the 6th century AD, pushed southeast into County Tyrone, bypassing a hard core of resistance in County Derry of the Cianachta. The septs of Clan Fergus have been described as the 'fighting vanguard of McLoughlin and O'Neill, as these clans battled their way towards Tullyhog and Armagh to become masters of Tyrone'.

The septs of Clan Fergus acquired extensive lands to the south of the Sperrin Mountains at the very heart of the kingdom of Tir Eoghain (Tir Owen or Tyrone, the land of Owen) around Tullaghoge (near Cookstown, County Tyrone).

The O'Mellans centred in south Derry and north Tyrone, held a large and well-defined territory which included Slieve Gallion to the north and what is now Cookstown to the south, the whole being known as the *Meallanacht*, 'O'Mellan's Country'. As their influence in ecclesiastical affairs grew the O'Mellans came into considerable church lands. They played an important part in the religious history of Ulster, and were noteworthy as the hereditary keepers of the bell of St Patrick which they kept in a beautiful shrine. They also had a recognised and important position and office within the Owen clans. At the inauguration ceremony of the O'Neill chiefs on the flagstone of the kings at Tullaghoge, the O'Mellans held the privilege of administering the oath on St Patrick's bell.

The name has become much confused with Mullan although the O'Mullans were a distinct sept in County Derry to the north of the Sperrin Mountians. Over time many O'Mellans allowed their names to be changed to O'Mullan.

MILLAR

The great majority of Millars in Ireland are in Ulster. It is among the forty most common names in Ulster, where it is most numerous in Counties Antrim, Down and Derry. Indeed two-thirds of Millars are located in County Antrim where it was first noted as a 'principal name' in the census of 1659. This name was brought to Ulster in large numbers by settlers from England and Scotland in the 17th century.

Millar is regarded as the Scottish form of Miller. In England, Miller is derived from Milner, an occupational name for a miller. This name was most common in the northern and eastern counties of England where it derived from Old Norse *mylnari*, meaning a 'miller'. With the establishment of fixed surnames, from the Middle Ages, the surname Miller became extremely common and widespread throughout England. The surname in its original form of Milner is commonest in Yorkshire.

Millar is among the top fifteen surnames in Scotland. This surname appears in all parts of the country as every district had its miller at whose mill the corn was ground. Millar, which is the more common Scottish form of the name, and Miller appear as hereditary surnames in Scotland from the 15th century, and the surname was recorded in Glasgow and Irvine in the 16th century.

The Millars were also recognised as a sept of Clan MacFarlane. In the 16th century the Mc-Farlanes embarked upon feuds with the Colquhouns and with the Buchanans. Having gained the reputation as a troublesome clan the McFarlanes were eventually 'broken' and dispossessed off their lands in the early 17th century. Owing to the nature of the Scottish clan system once the power and influence of the chief had been weakened and the bond of tribal loyalty broken the clan tended to scatter.

Movement of Scottish settlers to Ulster began in earnest from 1605 in a private enterprise colonisation of counties Antrim and Down when Sir Hugh Montgomery and Sir James Hamilton acquired title to large estates in north Down and Sir Randall MacDonnell, 1st Earl of Antrim, to large tracts of land in north Antrim. By the mid-19th century the Millars were concentrated in the barony of Kilconway in County Antrim, and in the Ards peninsula in County Down.

Further impetus came in 1609 when James I adopted the policy to encourage English and Scottish settlers to settle on the forfeited estates of the Gaelic chiefs in counties Armagh, Cavan, Donegal, Fermanagh, Londonderry (then known as Coleraine) and Tyrone. John Millar was an early Plantation tenant in Magheraboy in Fermanagh.

English settlers, mostly drawn from the northern counties of Cheshire, Cumberland, Lancashire, Northumberland, Yorkshire and Westmorland also migrated to Ulster during the 17th century. English settlers tended to favour settlement along the Lagan Valley, in the east of the Province, on lands straddling the borders of Counties Armagh, Antrim and Down.

During the famous 105 day Siege of Derry, from 18 April to 31 July 1689, Captain Stephen Miller of Kilrea, County Londonderry was recorded as one of the 'defenders' of the city.

MILLIGAN

Milligan can be an Irish or a Scottish name. In Ireland Milligan, and its variant form Milliken, are virtually exclusive to Ulster where half are in County Antrim and most of the rest in Counties Down and Derry.

Ireland was one of the first countries to adopt a system of hereditary surnames which developed from a more ancient system of clan or sept names. From the 11th century each family began to adopt its own distinctive family name generally derived from the first name of an ancestor who lived in or about the 10th century. The surname was formed by prefixing either Mac (son of) or O (grandson or descendant of) to the ancestor's name. Surnames in Ireland, therefore, tended to identify membership of a sept.

In Ulster, Milligan in Gaelic *O Maoileagain*, which originated in south Derry, is said to be a variant form of Mulligan in Gaelic *O Maolagain*. The root word is believed to be *maol*, meaning 'bald', which refers to the tonsure of Irish monks, in which the front of the head was shaven from ear to ear.

The Mulligans were a distinguished sept, its chiefs being lords of a territory called Tir MacCarthain in the baronies of Boylagh and Raphoe in central Donegal. They were *erenaghs*, i.e. hereditary stewards, of the church lands of Tullyfern Parish. At the time of the 17th century Plantation of Ulster by English and Scottish settlers they were dispossessed of their territory, and they migrated to lands straddling the border between Counties Fermanagh and Monaghan and to County Mayo in Connaught.

Confusion can arise as Milligan is a recorded variant of Mulligan. In parts of Counties Armagh and Down, at the turn of the 20th century, Milligan was being used interchangeably with Mulligan.

In Scotland, Milligan is derived from Gaelic *Maolagan*, meaning 'the little bald or shaven one'. Milligan and Milliken are common names in the province of Galloway, where the name was recorded in Wigtown as early as 1296. During the 15th and 16th centuries references to the surname in Scotland were recorded in Dumfries, Perth and Wigtown.

Movement of Scottish settlers to Ulster began in earnest from 1605 in a private enterprise colonisation of counties Antrim and Down when Sir Hugh Montgomery and Sir James Hamilton acquired title to large estates in north Down and Sir Randall MacDonnell, 1st Earl of Antrim, to large tracts of land in north Antrim. Further impetus came in 1609 when James I adopted the policy to encourage Scottish settlers to settle on the forfeited estates of the Gaelic chiefs in counties Armagh, Cavan, Donegal, Fermanagh, Londonderry (then known as Coleraine) and Tyrone.

Scottish families entering Ireland through the port of Londonderry settled in the Foyle Valley which includes much of the fertile lands of counties Donegal, Londonderry and Tyrone. It is estimated by 1715, when migration to Ulster had virtually stopped, the Scottish population of Ulster stood at 200,000.

MILLIKEN

Milliken can be an Irish or a Scottish name. In Ireland Milliken, and its variant form Milligan, are virtually exclusive to Ulster where half are in County Antrim and most of the rest in Counties Down and Derry.

Ireland was one of the first countries to adopt a system of hereditary surnames which developed from a more ancient system of clan or sept names. From the 11th century each family began to adopt its own distinctive family name generally derived from the first name of an ancestor who lived in or about the 10th century. The surname was formed by prefixing either Mac (son of) or O (grandson or descendant of) to the ancestor's name. Surnames in Ireland, therefore, tended to identify membership of a sept.

In Ulster, Milliken in Gaelic *O Maoileagain,* which originated in south Derry, is said to be a variant form of Mulligan in Gaelic *O Maolagain.* The root word is believed to be *maol,* meaning 'bald', which refers to the tonsure of Irish monks, in which the front of the head was shaven from ear to ear.

The Mulligans were a distinguished sept, its chiefs being lords of a territory called Tir Mac-Carthain in the baronies of Boylagh and Raphoe in central Donegal. They were *erenaghs,* i.e. hereditary stewards, of the church lands of Tullyfern Parish. At the time of the 17th century Plantation of Ulster by English and Scottish settlers they were dispossessed of their territory, and they migrated to lands straddling the border between Counties Fermanagh and Monaghan and to County Mayo in Connaught.

In Scotland, Milliken is derived from Gaelic *Maolagan,* meaning 'the little bald or shaven one'. Milligan and Milliken are common names in the province of Galloway, where the name was recorded in Wigtown as early as 1296. During the 15th and 16th centuries references to the surname in Scotland were recorded in Dumfries, Perth and Wigtown.

Movement of Scottish settlers to Ulster began in earnest from 1605 in a private enterprise colonisation of counties Antrim and Down when Sir Hugh Montgomery and Sir James Hamilton acquired title to large estates in north Down and Sir Randall MacDonnell, 1st Earl of Antrim, to large tracts of land in north Antrim.

Further impetus came in 1609 when James I adopted the policy to encourage Scottish settlers to settle on the forfeited estates of the Gaelic chiefs in counties Armagh, Cavan, Donegal, Fermanagh, Londonderry (then known as Coleraine) and Tyrone. These settlers came to Ulster, by and large, in three waves: with the granting of the initial leases in the period 1605 to 1625; after 1652 and Cromwell's crushing of the Irish rebellion; and finally in the fifteen years after 1690 and the Glorious Revolution.

Scottish families entering Ireland through the port of Londonderry settled in the Foyle Valley which includes much of the fertile lands of counties Donegal, Londonderry and Tyrone. It is estimated by 1715, when migration to Ulster had virtually stopped, the Scottish population of Ulster stood at 200,000.

MITCHELL

Mitchell is common in every province except Munster, and found in nearly every county of Ireland. About half of all Mitchells in Ireland are in Ulster. The majority of Ulster Mitchells are descendants of 17th century English and Scottish settlers but there are significant local differences.

Mitchell derives from the Hebrew name Michael, which means 'who is like God', through the French form Michel. In England the name can also derive from Middle English *michel*, meaning 'big'. The name is common in England but is among the thirty most numerous in Scotland where it is found in many parts of the country. From the 15th century references to the surname can be found in places as far apart as Aberdeen, Dumbarton and Glasgow. In Orkney the forename Michael is pronounced Mitchell. In northeast Scotland, in Moray and Banff, the Mitchells were a sept of Clan Innes.

Movement of Scottish settlers to Ulster began in earnest from 1605 in a private enterprise colonisation of counties Antrim and Down when Sir Hugh Montgomery and Sir James Hamilton acquired title to large estates in north Down and Sir Randall MacDonnell, 1st Earl of Antrim, to large tracts of land in north Antrim. Further impetus came in 1609 when James I adopted the policy to encourage English and Scottish settlers to settle on the forfeited estates of the Gaelic chiefs in counties Armagh, Cavan, Donegal, Fermanagh, Londonderry (then known as Coleraine) and Tyrone.

Settlers came to Ulster, by and large, in three waves: with the granting of the initial leases in the period 1605 to 1625; after 1652 and Cromwell's crushing of the Irish rebellion; and finally in the fifteen years after 1690 and the Glorious Revolution. Scottish families entering Ireland through the port of Londonderry settled in the Foyle Valley which includes much of the fertile lands of counties Donegal, Londonderry and Tyrone. It is estimated by 1715, when migration to Ulster had virtually stopped, the Scottish population of Ulster stood at 200,000.

English settlers, mostly drawn from the northern counties of Cheshire, Cumberland, Lancashire, Northumberland, Yorkshire and Westmorland tended to favour settlement along the Lagan Valley, in the east of the Province, on lands straddling the borders of Counties Armagh, Antrim and Down.

During the famous 105 day Siege of Derry, from 18 April to 31 July 1689, Alexander Mitchell, Lieutenant David Mitchell, James Mitchell and John Mitchell were recorded as 'defenders' of the city.

In County Donegal, in particular, Mitchell may be of Irish origin. The Mulvihil sept, in Gaelic *O Maoilmhichil*, meaning 'descendant of the devotee of St Michael', was once an important sept in County Roscommon. The Mulvihils, however, declined in importance from the late-12th century and the sept scattered widely. In the census of 1659 the O'Mulvihils were recorded as a 'principal name' in County Longford. In Ulster, especially in County Donegal, the name Mulvihil has been anglicised to Mitchell. In Counties Clare and Galway the name was changed to Mulville and Melville.

256

MONTGOMERY

The great majority of Montgomerys in Ireland are in Ulster and more than half are in Counties Antrim and Down. This surname was brought to Ulster by settlers from Scotland in the 17th century.

This surname is ultimately of Norman origin where it was derived from the ancient castle of Sainte Foi de Montgomery in the diocese of Lisieux in Normandy in France. Roger de Montgomery, who died in 1094, was a Norman nobleman who assisted in planning the invasion of England in 1066. As a reward for his services by a grateful William the Conqueror he later received the earldoms of Arundel and Shrewsbury.

The name was introduced to Scotland by Robert de Mundegumri (died c.1177) who was granted the manor of Eaglesham in Renfrewshire. The Montgomeries of Braidstane in Ayrshire were a branch of the Montgomerys of Eaglesham. The various offshoots of the Montgomery families on the Ayrshire coast had established by the early part of the 17th century trading connections, on their own ships, with the coastal areas of Ulster. For example the Montgomerys, who were to purchase the Benvarden estate near Bushmills, County Antrim in 1798, had made the harbour at Glenarm their port of entry from Ayrshire to County Antrim in the early 17th century.

Movement of Scottish settlers to Ulster began in earnest from 1605 in a private enterprise colonisation of County Down when Sir Hugh Montgomerie, 6th Laird of Braidstane and Sir James Hamilton acquired title to large estates in north Down. Sir Hugh Montgomery brought to Ulster a great number of his kinsmen from Ayrshire, including members of his own family. Branches of the Montgomery family were established at an early date in Counties Down, Donegal, Fermanagh, Leitrim and Monaghan. Many of the settlers farming on these Scottish estates in Ulster would also have been called Montgomery as it was a feature of 17th century Scotland for tenants to take on their landlord's surname.

Sir Hugh's brother Reverend George Montgomery was appointed Bishop of Derry, Raphoe and Clogher in 1605. This created resentment as these three dioceses, with vast amounts of Church Lands in Counties Derry, Donegal, Fermanagh and Tyrone, were 'now united for one man's benefit'. George Montgomery, however, did settle several of his kinsmen from Braidstane on these church lands.

The Donegal Montgomerys made a fortune from the wine trade in the city of Londonderry and bought a large estate at Moville, County Donegal which they called New Park. Descendants of the Montgomerys of Moville included the Indian administrator Sir Robert Montgomery, Governor of the Punjab, and Field Marshall Bernard Law Montgomery, Commander of the British Eighth Army, who defeated the German army at El Alamein in Egypt in 1942.

When Lord John Lawrence, Viceroy of India from 1863 to 1869, visited Lahore in 1865 he was greeted by his old school friend from Foyle College, Londonderry, Sir Robert Montgomery, Commissioner at Lahore. In his speech Lord Lawrence stated: "It is quite true we were at school together forty years ago at a place very famous in history, Londonderry, celebrated for defending itself against great odds." This speech refers to the famous 105 day Siege of Derry, from 18 April to 31 July 1689.

MOORE

This name, which can be of English, Irish or Scottish origin, is among the twenty most common in Ireland and has the distinction of being found in every county. A quarter of all Moores in Ireland are in County Antrim alone and the name is common too in Counties Derry and Tyrone.

In Northern Ireland most Moores are of Scottish origin. This name, which is the seventh most common in the city of Derry, is regarded as the most numerous name in the city for which a gaelic origin is unlikely. Nowadays Moore is quite common in the lowland hinterland to the east, west and south of Derry, but not in Inishowen.

Although Moore is one of the forty most numerous names in England, deriving from residence in or near a moor or heath, it also comes from that area in the south and west lowlands of Scotland which provided so many of the seventeenth century settlers in Ulster. The surname was first noted there in a variety of places, including Ayrshire and Lanarkshire, in the thirteenth century. In Scotland the name often took the form 'Muir'. There were Mores, a sept of Clan Leslie, and Muirs, a sept of Clan Campbell.

The defeat of the old Gaelic order in the Nine Years War, 1594-1603 and the escape of the most prominent Gaelic Lords of Ulster in 'the Flight of the Earls' in 1607 from Lough Swilly, County Donegal were ultimately responsible for the settlement of many Scottish families in the northern counties of Ireland.

In 1609 the Earl of Salisbury, Lord High Treasurer, suggested to James I a deliberate plantation of Scottish and English colonists on the forfeited estates of the Gaelic chiefs in counties Armagh, Cavan, Donegal, Fermanagh, Londonderry (then known as Coleraine) and Tyrone. Settlers to Ulster came, by and large, in three waves: with the granting of the initial leases in the period 1605 to 1625; after 1652 and Cromwell's crushing of the Irish rebellion; and finally in the fifteen years after 1690 and the Glorious Revolution. It is estimated by 1715, when Scottish migration to Ulster had virtually stopped, the Presbyterian population of Ulster, i.e. of essentially Scottish origin, stood at 200,000.

Scottish families entering Ireland through the port of Londonderry settled in the Foyle Valley which includes much of the fertile lands of counties Donegal, Londonderry and Tyrone. The lands along the Firth of Clyde in the county of Ayrshire, the Clyde Valley and the Border Lands consisting of the counties of Wigtown, Kirkcudbright and Dumfries were home to many of these Scottish settlers.

Confusion arises because the Irish sept name of O'More was invariably changed to Moore. The O'Mores, derived from Gaelic *O Mordha*, meaning 'majestic', were the leading sept of the 'Seven Septs of Leix'. They were based at Dunamanse, near Portlaoise, County Laois (also known as Leix) in central Ireland. The ancestor who gave the O'Mores their name, i.e. Mordha, was twenty-first in descent from Conall Cearnach, the legendary hero of the Red Branch Knights of Ulster.

MORAN

This surname ranks among the sixty commonest in Ireland with over half of the families of this name in the province of Connaught, particularly in Counties Mayo, Galway, Roscommon and Leitrim. This name is less common in Ulster than it is in the other three provinces of Ireland. Moran, however, does rank among the top 50 surnames in the city of Derry today.

Ireland was one of the first countries to adopt a system of hereditary surnames which developed from a more ancient system of clan or sept names. From the 11th century each family began to adopt its own distinctive family name generally derived from the first name of an ancestor who lived in or about the 10th century. The surname was formed by prefixing either Mac (son of) or O (grandson or descendant of) to the ancestor's name. Surnames in Ireland, therefore, tended to identify membership of a sept.

Two quite distinct septs, in Gaelic *O Morain* and *O Moghrain*, now both anglicised as Moran, held their territory in the province of Connaught. The *O Morain* sept, possibly derived from the word *mor*, meaning 'big', was located near Ballina, County Mayo.

The *O Moghrain* sept, a minor branch of the Ui Maine (descendants of Maine), were chiefs of Criffon in County Galway. This sept trace their descent from the 4th century *Colla da Crioch*, King of Ulster and first King of Oriel. The O'Kellys were chiefs of Ui Maine, often called Hy Many, who ruled O'Kelly's Country in Counties Galway and Roscommon.

Another powerful *O Moghrain* sept, a branch of the O'Connors, was seated near Ballintobber in County Roscommon. They trace their descent from Conchobhar, King of Connacht (died 971).

Moran and Morrin are also recorded variants of Morahan, in Gaelic *O Murchain*, the root word being *murchadh*, meaning 'sea warrior'. There were two distinct septs of this name, one originating in east Offaly and the other in County Leitrim.

The County Fermanagh sept of McMorran, in Gaelic *Mac Moruinn*, has also been changed to Moran.

Morrin is usually a variant of either Moran or Morahan. In Ulster, however, Morrin can be a Huguenot name. Many Huguenots, i.e. French Protestants, fled to Ireland from France in the late-17th century in the face of persecution by Louis XIV. The main body of Huguenots came to Ireland from La Rochelle in the fifteen years after the revocation of the Edict of Nantes, which had granted French Protestants freedom of worship, in 1685. In Ulster they settled in Lisburn, County Antrim.

In the 17th and 18th centuries many descendants of the old Gaelic order in Ireland emigrated, as the so-called Wild Geese, to Europe, and, in particular, to Spain and France. General James O'Moran (1739-1794) served with distinction in Dillon's Irish regiment in the army of France.

MORRIN

Morrin is usually a variant of either Moran or Morahan. In Ulster, however, Morrin can be a Huguenot name. Moran ranks among the sixty commonest in Ireland with over half of the families of this name in the province of Connaught, particularly in Counties Mayo, Galway, Roscommon and Leitrim. This name is less common in Ulster than it is in the other three provinces of Ireland. Moran, however, does rank among the top 50 surnames in the city of Derry today.

Ireland was one of the first countries to adopt a system of hereditary surnames which developed from a more ancient system of clan or sept names. From the 11th century each family began to adopt its own distinctive family name generally derived from the first name of an ancestor who lived in or about the 10th century. The surname was formed by prefixing either Mac (son of) or O (grandson or descendant of) to the ancestor's name. Surnames in Ireland, therefore, tended to identify membership of a sept.

Two quite distinct septs, in Gaelic *O Morain* and *O Moghrain*, now both anglicised as Moran, held their territory in the province of Connaught. The *O Morain* sept, possibly derived from the word *mor*, meaning 'big', was located near Ballina, County Mayo.

The *O Moghrain* sept, a minor branch of the Ui Maine (descendants of Maine), were chiefs of Criffon in County Galway. This sept trace their descent from the 4th century *Colla da Crioch*, King of Ulster and first King of Oriel. The O'Kellys were chiefs of Ui Maine, often called Hy Many, who ruled O'Kelly's Country in Counties Galway and Roscommon.

Another powerful *O Moghrain* sept, a branch of the O'Connors, was seated near Ballintobber in County Roscommon. They trace their descent from Conchobhar, King of Connacht (died 971).

Moran and Morrin are also recorded variants of Morahan, in Gaelic *O Murchain*, the root word being *murchadh,* meaning 'sea warrior'. There were two distinct septs of this name, one originating in east Offaly and the other in County Leitrim.

The County Fermanagh sept of McMorran, in Gaelic *Mac Moruinn*, has also been changed to Moran.

In Ulster, Morrin can be a Huguenot name. Many Huguenots, i.e. French Protestants, fled to Ireland from France in the late-17th century in the face of persecution by Louis XIV. The main body of Huguenots came to Ireland from La Rochelle in the fifteen years after the revocation of the Edict of Nantes, which had granted French Protestants freedom of worship, in 1685. In Ulster they settled in Lisburn, County Antrim.

In the 17th and 18th centuries many descendants of the old Gaelic order in Ireland emigrated, as the so-called Wild Geese, to Europe, and, in particular, to Spain and France. General James O'Moran (1739-1794) served with distinction in Dillon's Irish regiment in the army of France.

MORRISON

Morrison is found in all provinces of Ireland but is common only in Ulster, particularly in Counties Antrim, Down and Fermanagh. It is the twenty-first most common name in Fermanagh. Morrison can be an Irish or a Scottish name. This name was brought to Ulster by settlers from Scotland in the 17th century, and it was also adopted by descendants of a County Donegal sept. The majority of Ulster Morrisons are of Scottish origin.

The O'Morison sept of County Donegal is derived from Gaelic *O Muirgheasain*, the root word being *Muirgheas*, meaning 'sea valour'. This sept's association with Inishowen, County Donegal is long-standing as they were *erenaghs*, i.e. hereditary stewards, of the church lands of Clonmany. For generations the O'Morisons were hereditary keepers of the Clonmany relic of St Columcille, the 'Miosach'. St Columcille was the 6th century founder of the monastery at Derry and at Iona in Scotland.

Morrison is one of the thirty most common names in Scotland. A branch of the Donegal O'Morisons migrated at an early date to Lewis and Harris in the Scottish Isles, and they established their stronghold at Habost Ness in Lewis. They became bards to the MacLeods of Dunvegan. In time they became known as Clan Morrison and they conducted a bitter feud with the MacAulays of Lewis.

In addition to their origin as a clan in the West Highlands, Morrison, meaning 'son of Maurice', also originated as a surname elsewhere in Scotland and in England. In the 15th and 16th centuries references to the surname in Scotland can be found in places as far apart as Aberdeen, Glasgow and St Andrews. There were, furthermore, Morrisons in Dunbartonshire, Perthshire and Stirlingshire who had no family connection with the Morrisons of Lewis. For example there were two septs of Clan Buchanan called MacMaurice, anglicised to Morrison, in Stirlingshire.

Movement of Scottish settlers to Ulster began in earnest from 1605 in a private enterprise colonisation of counties Antrim and Down when Sir Hugh Montgomery and Sir James Hamilton acquired title to large estates in north Down and Sir Randall MacDonnell, 1st Earl of Antrim, to large tracts of land in north Antrim. Further impetus came in 1609 when James I adopted the policy to encourage English and Scottish settlers to settle on the forfeited estates of the Gaelic chiefs in counties Armagh, Cavan, Donegal, Fermanagh, Londonderry (then known as Coleraine) and Tyrone.

Settlers came to Ulster, by and large, in three waves: with the granting of the initial leases in the period 1605 to 1625; after 1652 and Cromwell's crushing of the Irish rebellion; and finally in the fifteen years after 1690 and the Glorious Revolution. It is estimated by 1715, when migration to Ulster had virtually stopped, the Scottish population of Ulster stood at 200,000. Morrisons of Scottish origin became particularly prevalent in the eastern Ulster counties of Antrim and Down.

Ten Morrisons, including Robert Morrison who was one of the thirteen apprentice boys who shut the gates of Derry on 7 December 1688, were recorded as 'defenders' of Derry during the famous Siege of 1689.

MULHOLLAND

This name is almost exclusive to Ulster where 90% of Mulhollands in Ireland live. The name is most common in Counties Antrim, Down and Derry.

Ireland was one of the first countries to adopt a system of hereditary surnames which developed from a more ancient system of clan or sept names. The surname was formed by prefixing either Mac (son of) or O (grandson or descendant of) to the ancestor's name.

Mulholland is derived from Gaelic *O Maolchalann*, meaning 'son of the devotee of St Calann'. There were four distinct septs of this name. Although the name is now rare outside of Ulster two of the Mulholland septs had origins outside this province. These septs, one based in Limerick and the other in Meath, were important in early medieval times. *The Annals of The Kingdom of Ireland by the Four Masters* (a chronicle of Irish history from 'the earliest period to the year 1616') record, in 1012, the death in battle of Dubhtaichligh Ua Maelchallann, lord of Demifore in northwest Meath.

In Ulster there was a sept of Mulhollands in County Donegal. However most of the name descend from the Mulhollands of Loughinsholin in south Derry. The Mulhollands of County Derry played an important part in the religious history of Ulster, and were noteworthy as hereditary keepers of the bell of St Patrick.

Legend states that St Columba had found the Bell of the Testament, in Gaelic *Clocc-ind-edechta*, in St Patrick's tomb in 552 AD. Domhnall MacLoughlin, High King of Ireland from 1094-1121, had a beautiful shrine made, ca.1100, to house the bell of St Patrick. In 1100 Cathalan Ua Maelchallain was the 'keeper of the bell', a position his family, the Mulhollands, retained for at least 7 centuries. It would seem that the guardians of this bell fluctuated between the O'Mellans and the Mulhollands. In 1441 the Primate of Armagh removed the custody of the bell from John O'Mellan to Patrick Mulholland.

In the first years of the 19th century the Shrine of St Patrick's Bell, lost to sight for generations, reappeared. On his deathbed an old schoolmaster called Henry Mulholland bequeathed to a former pupil, Adam MacClean of Belfast, a box which had been buried in his garden. This box contained the Shrine of St Patrick's Bell. Today the Shrine is exhibited in the National Museum of Ireland in Dublin.

The Mulhollands were followers of the O'Neills. In a raid by the O'Neills into 'O'Kane's Country', County Derry in 1432 the *Annals* record that 'Patrick O'Mulholland, and the son of O'Mellain' were slain by the O'Kanes.

From the 14th century the family spread from south Derry into the western and southern part of the barony of Massereene in County Antrim.

The anglicisation of Gaelic names, from the 17th century, resulted in many variant spellings of the same name and, in many cases, the dropping of the O and Mac prefixes. Twelve Mulholland households were recorded in the parishes of south Derry in the Hearth Money Rolls of 1663. The name was variously spelt as Mulhallan, Mulhallon, Mulhalane, O'Mulhallen and O'Mulhalan in this source.

MULLEN

The name O'Mullen, with its many variants, is among the seventy most numerous names in Ireland and among the first forty in Ulster. It is one of the first ten names in County Derry, and one of the first five in County Tyrone.

The Mullen sept trace their lineage to Eogan, son of the 5th century High King of Ireland, Niall of the Nine Hostages, who ruled from the Hill of Tara, County Meath. Eogan and his brother Conall *Gulban* conquered northwest Ireland, ca.425 AD, capturing the great hill-fort of Grianan of Ailech in County Donegal.

Eogan, styled 'King of Ailech', established his own kingdom in the peninsula in County Donegal still called after him Inishowen (Innis Eoghain or Eogan's Isle). His descendants, known as the Cenel Eoghain (the race of Owen), became the principal branch of the Northern Ui Neill (descendants of Niall of the Nine Hostages). The Cenel Eoghain in the next five centuries expanded to the east and south from their focal point in Inishowen.

Ireland was one of the first countries to adopt a system of hereditary surnames which developed from a more ancient system of clan or sept names. The surname was formed by prefixing either Mac (son of) or O (grandson or descendant of) to the ancestor's name.

O'Mullen, in Gaelic *O Maolain*, meaning descendant of the bald one, refers to the tonsure of Irish monks, in which the front of the head was shaven from ear to ear. At this time monasteries were an integral part of a Gaelic ruler's prestige, and they frequently became targets for attack during feuds between local kings.

The O'Mullens were one of the leading septs of Clan Connor *Magh Ithe* (Connor was a direct descendant of Eogan). Magh Ithe is the rich countryside stretching southward from Inishowen, later known as the Laggan district in east Donegal. In the 10th century AD the families of Clan Connor moved out from the cramped territory of Magh Ithe and established themselves in County Derry, in the kingdom of Keenaght, to the north of the Sperrin Mountains, from the Foyle to the Bann rivers. In the process they ousted the Cianachta whose leading sept was the O'Connors of Glengiven in the Roe Valley.

Confusion is caused by the fact that the majority of Scottish MacMillans adopted the surname McMullen in Ulster which, like O'Mullen, was frequently shortened to Mullen. Some O'Mullens may have changed their name to MacMullen under the Scottish influence from North Antrim. Furthermore the O'Mellans, a distinct sept with extensive territory to the south of the Sperrin Mountains, have also become confused with the O'Mullens because many allowed their names to be changed to O'Mullen. Hence, in many cases, Mullen is indistinguishable from O'Mullen, MacMillan, McMullen and Mellon.

MULLIGAN

This name originated in County Donegal but it is now most common in Counties Monaghan, Fermanagh and Mayo.

Ireland was one of the first countries to adopt a system of hereditary surnames which developed from a more ancient system of clan or sept names. From the 11th century each family began to adopt its own distinctive family name generally derived from the first name of an ancestor who lived in or about the 10th century. The surname was formed by prefixing either Mac (son of) or O (grandson or descendant of) to the ancestor's name. Surnames in Ireland, therefore, tended to identify membership of a sept.

Mulligan is derived from Gaelic *O Maolagain*, the root word probably being *maol*, meaning 'bald'. *Maol* refers to the tonsure of Irish monks, in which the front of the head was shaven from ear to ear.

The Mulligans were a distinguished sept, its chiefs being lords of a territory called Tir Mac-Carthain in the baronies of Boylagh and Raphoe in central Donegal. They were *erenaghs*, i.e. hereditary stewards, of the church lands of Tullyfern Parish. At the time of the 17th century Plantation of Ulster by English and Scottish settlers they were dispossessed of their territory, and they migrated to lands straddling the border between Counties Fermanagh and Monaghan and to County Mayo in Connaught.

In Fermanagh the Mulligans settled in the baronies of Magherastephana and Clankelly, and in Monaghan, in the northwest and centre of the county. By 1659 the Mulligans were found in considerable numbers in both Fermanagh and Monaghan. Many Donegal names, including Mulligan, are found in Mayo today as a result of considerable migration in the early seventeenth century.

The name spread to Derry city in the 19th century. As Derry developed an industrial base in the 19th century in shirt making, shipbuilding and distilling it attracted much of its workforce from Donegal.

Confusion can arise as Milligan is a recorded variant of Mulligan. In parts of Counties Armagh and Down, at the turn of the 20th century, Milligan was being used interchangeably with Mulligan. In Ireland Milligan, and its variant form Milliken, are virtually exclusive to Ulster where half are in County Antrim and most of the rest in Counties Down and Derry.

Milligan can be an Irish or a Scottish name. In Ulster, Milligan in Gaelic *O Maoileagain*, which originated in south Derry, is said to be a variant form of Mulligan in Gaelic *O Maolagain*.

In Scotland, Milligan is derived from Gaelic *Maolagan*, meaning 'the little bald or shaven one'. Milligan and Milliken are common names in the province of Galloway, where the name was recorded in Wigtown as early as 1296. During the 15th and 16th centuries references to the surname in Scotland were recorded in Dumfries, Perth and Wigtown. Dumfries and Galloway were home to many of the Scottish settlers who came to Ulster throughout the 17th century.

264

MURPHY

Murphy is the most numerous name in Ireland and one of the fifteen most common in Ulster. Murphy is the single most numerous name in County Armagh and it is among the first ten names in Counties Fermanagh and Monaghan.

Ireland was one of the first countries to adopt a system of hereditary surnames which developed from a more ancient system of clan or sept names. From the 11th century each family began to adopt its own distinctive family name generally derived from the first name of an ancestor who lived in or about the 10th century. The surname was formed by prefixing either Mac (son of) or O (grandson or descendant of) to the ancestor's name. Surnames in Ireland, therefore, tended to identify membership of a sept.

Outside of Ulster the great majority of Murphys in Ireland are derived from Gaelic *O Murchadha*, meaning 'descendant of Murchadh', a personal name meaning 'sea warrior'. There were three distinct septs of this name in Counties Cork, Wexford and Roscommon.

The majority of Ulster Murphys, however, will be originally McMurphys, Gaelic *Mac Murchadha*. This Murphy sept trace their lineage to Eogan, son of the 5th century High King of Ireland, Niall of the Nine Hostages, who ruled from the Hill of Tara, County Meath. Eogan and his brother Conall *Gulban* conquered northwest Ireland, ca.425 AD, capturing the great hill-fort of Grianan of Ailech in County Donegal which commanded the entrance to the Inishowen peninsula between Lough Swilly and Lough Foyle.

Eogan, styled 'King of Ailech', established his own kingdom in the peninsula still called after him Inishowen (Innis Eoghain or Eogan's Isle). Eogan was converted to Christianity by St Patrick, when he travelled to Ailech, ca. 442 AD. His descendants, known as the Cenel Eoghain (the race of Owen), became the principal branch of the Northern Ui Neill (descendants of Niall of the Nine Hostages). The Cenel Eoghain in the next five centuries expanded to the east and south from their focal point in Inishowen.

The McMurphys controlled the rich lands of Muintir Birn in south Tyrone, and were chiefs of Siol Aodha, 'the race of Hugh'. Their territory was bounded by the barony of Trough in County Monaghan. However they were driven out of this region by the O'Neills and settled in the highlands of south Armagh under O'Neill of the Fews. There are now fewer Murphys in their homeland of Tyrone than in almost any other Irish county.

It is believed that the Murphys of Fermanagh, in Gaelic *Mac Murchu*, were descendants of Murchadh, a brother of Donn Mor Maguire. These McMurphys were *erenaghs*, i.e. hereditary stewards, of the church lands of Farnamullan and of Tullynagaorthainn, and anglicised their name to both Murphy and Morrow.

In Scotland the Clan Donald sept of MacMurchie was anglicised as McMurphy and Murphy in Arran. Thus, it is possible, that a few bearers of this name came to Ulster at the time of the 17th century Plantation of Ulster by settlers from Scotland.

MURRAY

Murray can be an Irish or a Scottish name. This name is among the twenty most common names in Ireland. It is one of the twenty-five most numerous names in Ulster, among the top ten in County Down, the top twenty in County Monaghan and is numerous too in County Antrim.

Many of the Ulster Murrays stem originally from Scotland. Murray is among the twenty most common names in Scotland where it is derived from the provincial name of Moray in northeast Scotland. Clan Murray trace their descent from Freskin de Moravia of Duffus in Moray, who was granted the lands of Strabrock in West Lothian by David I, King of Scotland 1124-1153. The Murrays of Tullibardine in Perthshire, ancestors of the Dukes of Atholl, trace their descent from Freskin's grandson William who married the heiress of Bothwell and Drumsagard in Lanarkshire and Smailholm in Berwickshire. The seat of the Dukes of Atholl is Blair Castle, Blair Atholl which dates back to 1269.

Movement of Scottish settlers to Ulster began in earnest from 1605 in a private enterprise colonisation of counties Antrim and Down when Sir Hugh Montgomery and Sir James Hamilton acquired title to large estates in north Down and Sir Randall MacDonnell, 1st Earl of Antrim, to large tracts of land in north Antrim. Further impetus came in 1609 when James I adopted the policy to encourage Scottish settlers to settle on the forfeited estates of the Gaelic chiefs in counties Armagh, Cavan, Donegal, Fermanagh, Londonderry (then known as Coleraine) and Tyrone.

At the time of this plantation MacMurray, derived from Gaelic *Mac Muireadhaigh*, meaning 'son of Muireadhach', was already common in the province of Galloway. This region was home to many of the Scottish settlers who came to Ulster throughout the 17th century. Indeed George Murray of Wigtownshire was one of the principal Scottish planters (sixty-one in total) of the Ulster Plantation, and in 1610 he was granted an estate of 1500 acres in west Donegal.

During the famous 105 day Siege of Derry, from 18 April to 31 July 1689, Colonel Adam Murray of Ling, County Donegal commanded the forces defending the city. 'He was the heart and soul of the defence, while he was the leader, and driving force in all the garrison's sorties.'

The surname Murray was also widely adopted by descendants of several Irish septs. Irish septs such as O'Murry, in Gaelic *O Muireadhaigh*, of Counties Cork and Roscommon; McElmurray, in Gaelic *Mac Giolla Mhuire,* of Counties Fermanagh and Tyrone; and Mc-Murray in Gaelic *Mac Muireadhaigh*, of Counties Donegal, Down and Leitrim, have been anglicised to Murray. Muireadhach, a common Irish personal name, means 'a mariner'. The surname McMurray in Ireland is exclusive to Ulster and is most common in Counties Antrim, Armagh and Donegal.

In Ulster, particularly in County Donegal and north Down, many Murrays will be of Gaelic Irish origin. Murray is the tenth most common name in Upper Ards in County Down. In 1034 a Cathalan Mac Muiredaig was ruler of the Ards.

266

NEILL

Neill is common in Ulster but is even more so in Leinster and Munster. In Ulster Neill can be a shortened form of either O'Neill or McNeill. Thus Neill can be an Irish or a Scottish surname.

The O'Neill sept, the most famous family of Ulster, trace their lineage to Eogan, son of the 5th century High King of Ireland, Niall of the Nine Hostages. Eogan and his brother Conall *Gulban* conquered northwest Ireland, ca.425 AD, capturing the great hill-fort of Grianan of Ailech in County Donegal.

Ireland was one of the first countries to adopt a system of hereditary surnames which developed from a more ancient system of clan or sept names. The surname was formed by prefixing either Mac (son of) or O (grandson or descendant of) to the ancestor's name.

The first to take O'Neill as their surname was Domhnall who took the name of his grandfather, Niall, Black Knee, High King of Ireland who was killed in a battle with the Vikings in 919 AD. The O'Neills were thus in Gaelic *O Neill* i.e. grandson of Niall. In the middle years of the 11th century the O'Neills moved their capital from Ailech to Tullaghoge (near Cookstown, County Tyrone).

The senior branch of this sept, the O'Neills of Tyrone, were frequently High Kings of Ireland, and in the 16th and 17th centuries they were the leaders of Gaelic resistance to English attempts to pacify Ireland. A junior branch established themselves in County Antrim in the 14th century and from their seat at Shane's Castle became known as the Clannaboy or Clandeboy O'Neills.

Neill can also be a variant of Scottish McNeill. As early as the mid-14th century descendants of Clan MacNeil migrated from Scotland to Ireland to fight as galloglasses, i.e. mercenary soldiers.

McNeill is derived from Gaelic *Mac Neill*, meaning 'son of Niall'. Scottish Clan MacNeil claims descent from Niall, twenty-first in descent from Niall of the Nine Hostages, the 5th century High King of Ireland. This Niall came to the island of Barra in the Outer Hebrides in 1049 and founded the clan. The MacNeils, with their stronghold at Kisimul Castle, received a charter for the island of Barra in 1429 from Alexander MacDonald, Lord of the Isles. The MacNeils of Barra became followers of the Macleans of Duart.

A branch of the clan was established at an early date on the island of Gigha, north of Kintyre. The seat of the MacNeils of Gigha, who were followers of the MacDonalds of Islay and Kintyre, was at Castle Sween in Knapdale.

It was the MacNeils of Barra who came to Ireland as galloglasses as early as the mid-14th century and settled, for the most part, in Counties Antrim and Derry. By the late 15th century the McNeills, along with the McQuillans, were lords of Clandeboy in County Antrim. Many McNeills, as followers of the McDonnells of the Glens, settled in north Antrim in the late sixteenth and early seventeenth centuries.

NELIS

This name originated in County Donegal. The name tends to be spelt as McNelis in Donegal and as Nelis in the adjoining counties.

Ireland was one of the first countries to adopt a system of hereditary surnames which developed from a more ancient system of clan or sept names. From the 11th century each family began to adopt its own distinctive family name generally derived from the first name of an ancestor who lived in or about the 10th century. The surname was formed by prefixing either Mac (son of) or O (grandson or descendant of) to the ancestor's name. Surnames in Ireland, therefore, tended to identify membership of a sept.

McNelis is derived from Gaelic *Mac Niallghuis*, meaning 'son of vigorous Neill', as *gus* attached to the forename means 'vigour'. MacNeilus and MacNellus were recorded among the principal names of County Donegal in the census of 1659.
The homeland of this sept was Glencolumbkille in west Donegal.

Glencolumbkille, a remote parish exposed to the Atlantic Ocean on the west and cut off from the rest of Donegal by high moors, takes its name from St Columcille, meaning 'Dove of the Church', who founded a monastery here in the 6th century. Glencolumbkille is famed for the turas or pilgrimages that are made to its 15 stations on 9 June, the saint's day (St Columcille, also known as St Columba, died on 9 June 597 at the monastery on the island of Iona, Scotland). The tura begins at the door of the present Church of Ireland church which marks the site of the original monastery. All that survives of the monastery is a souterrain which may have been used as a place of concealment from Viking raids.

In the 16th century the McNelises were recorded as coarbs, i.e. abbots, of Glencolumbkille. In Bishop Montgomery's survey of the Diocese of Raphoe, in 1609, it was said of Bernard MacNellus, curate of Glencolumbkille, that he 'paints cleverly and speaks Irish, Latin and English well'.

At the time of the mid-19th century Griffith's Valuation 34 McNelis households were recorded in County Donegal, and all but six of these households were recorded in the parish of Glencolumbkille. In other words over 80% of descendants of the McNelis sept in County Donegal were living in the parish of Glencolumbkille on the west coast of Donegal.

The anglicisation of Gaelic names, from the 17th century, resulted in many variant spellings of the same name and, in many cases, the dropping of the O and Mac prefixes. The name has now spread to Derry city and to County Mayo. The name spread to Derry city, where it is usually spelt as Nelis, in the 19th century. As Derry developed an industrial base in shirt making, shipbuilding and distilling it attracted much of its workforce from County Donegal. In the 90-year period 1821 to 1911 the population of the city quadrupled to 40,780.

Many Donegal names are also found in Mayo today as a result of considerable migration in the early seventeenth century.

NIXON

Nixon is found mainly in Ulster where the surname came with numerous immigrants at the time of the Plantation of Ulster in the 17th century. The name is most associated with Counties Cavan and Fermanagh.

Nixon, derived from the personal name Nicholas, simply means 'son of Nick'. The Nixons were one of the riding or reiving clans of the Scottish Borders and were found on both sides of the frontier, in Upper Liddesdale in Roxburghsire in Scotland and in Bewcastle in England. *The Surnames of Scotland* (by George F Black) notes that 'the name was common on both sides of the Border, perhaps most so in Bewcastle in Cumberland; but as early as 1376 we find a William Nycson occupying lands in the district of Ermyldoune in Liddesdale'.

From the 14th to the late-17th century, the border between England and Scotland – the Debatable Lands – was a turbulent place. The Border country was ravaged by the lawless Reiver families who stole each other's cattle and possessions. They raided in large numbers, on horseback, and they killed and kidnapped without remorse. This type of life resulted in the growth of large closely-knit family groups, such as the Nixons, with intense clan loyalties and fierce feuds against others. The Nixons were also part of the powerful Armstrong-Elliott-Nixon-Crozier confederacy.

Prior to the Union of the Crowns of England and Scotland in 1603 the Scottish Border was divided into three districts; the east, west and middle Marches. Each March was presided over by a warden who settled disputes with the warden of the appropriate March in England, as border warfare was rife at this time with frequent cattle raids.

Pacification of the riding families began in earnest from 1603 with the Union of the Crowns of England and Scotland. The Nixons suffered as King James I set about pacifying the borders in a ruthless campaign which included executions and banishment.

When the power of the riding clans was broken by James I in the decade after 1603 many came to Ulster to escape persecution. This flight to Ulster also suited the needs of the king. James I, from 1610, was determined to implement a deliberate plantation of Scottish and English colonists on the forfeited estates of the Gaelic chiefs in Counties Armagh, Cavan, Donegal, Fermanagh, Londonderry (then known as Coleraine) and Tyrone.

Nixons settled in County Fermanagh in the very early years of the plantation. The Nixons of Nixon Hall, descend from an Adam Nixon, who had settled in Fermanagh before 1625. By the time of the census of 1659 Nixon was recorded as a 'principal name' in that county. From Fermanagh the Nixons quickly spread into County Cavan.

These Border families were well suited to life in the frontier of the Plantation of Ulster. They were a resilient people who stayed in Cavan and Fermanagh throughout the upheavals of the 17th century. Scottish settlers were hardier than their English counterparts, and the Borderers were even better adapted again to life on a new, insecure frontier.

269

NOBLE

In Ireland, outside of Dublin, this name is common only in Ulster. Nobles in Ireland can be of English or Scottish descent. This name was brought to Ulster, where it is most numerous in County Fermanagh, by settlers from Scotland in the 17th century.

In England the surname Noble was derived from Old French *noble* meaning high-born, distinguished or illustrious; it could refer to someone who was well-known as well as noble. The name was first introduced to Ireland by the Anglo-Normans in the 13th century.

The Nobles were one of the riding or reiving clans who lived on the English side of the West March of the Scottish Borders. From the 14th to the late-17th century, the border between England and Scotland – the Debatable Lands – was a turbulent place. The Border country was ravaged by the lawless Reiver families who stole each other's cattle and possessions. They raided in large numbers, on horseback, and they killed and kidnapped without remorse. This type of life resulted in the growth of large closely-knit family groups with intense clan loyalties and fierce feuds against others.

Noble was introduced to Lowland Scotland by an English family of the name who settled in East Lothian at the end of the 12th century.

In the Highlands of Scotland the Nobles of Strathnairn, near Inverness, and Strathdearn in Nairnshire were a sept of Clan Mackintosh. In Ross the once-common name of MacNoble, derived from Gaelic *Mac Nobuill*, was anglicised as Noble. Upheavals such as military incursions, feuds and harvest failures would have encouraged clan members, including Nobles, to migrate to Ulster as settlers during the 17th century.

It was, however, the pacification of the riding families of the Borders which was largely responsible for the introduction of the surname to Ulster. When the power of the riding clans was broken by James I, with the Union of the Crowns of England and Scotland, in the decade after 1603 many came to Ulster to escape persecution. This flight to Ulster also suited the needs of the king. James I, from 1610, was determined to implement a deliberate plantation of Scottish and English colonists on the forfeited estates of the Gaelic chiefs in Counties Armagh, Cavan, Donegal, Fermanagh, Londonderry (then known as Coleraine) and Tyrone.

The Nobles settled initially in County Fermanagh. The families from the Scottish Borders were well suited to life in the frontier of the Plantation of Ulster. They were a resilient people who stayed in Fermanagh throughout the upheavals of the 17th century. Scottish settlers were hardier than their English counterparts, and the Borderers were even better adapted again to life on a new, insecure frontier. By the time of the 1659 census Noble was recorded as a principal surname in County Fermanagh.

During the famous 105 day Siege of Derry, from 18 April to 31 July 1689, Major Arthur Noble of Derryree, Lisnaskea, County Fermanagh was recorded as one of the 'defenders' of the city. He received "frequent mention for daring venture and gallant achievement in the sorties of the garrison".

270

O'BRIEN

O'Brien is the sixth most common name in Ireland. Three-fifths of the O'Briens are in Munster, one-fifth in Leinster and the rest divided equally between Ulster and Connaught.

Ireland was one of the first countries to adopt a system of hereditary surnames which developed from a more ancient system of clan or sept names. The surname was formed by prefixing either Mac (son of) or O (grandson or descendant of) to the ancestor's name.

O'Brien is derived from Gaelic *O Briain,* meaning 'descendant of Brian Boru', i.e. 'Brian of the tributes'. The O'Briens derive their name and historical importance from the rapid rise to power of Brian Boru. Brian Boru, born in 941, was a member of the Dal gCais tribal grouping based in the Clare/Limerick area. By 978 Brian Boru, who had secured control of the Dal gCais, was King of Munster. In waging war with the other provincial kings, and securing their submissions in the form of tributes, Brian Boru was recognised as High King of Ireland in 1002. He died, in battle, at Clontarf in 1014 after securing victory over the Leinstermen and the Vikings.

Donagh Cairbre, 1194-1242, was the first to take the surname O'Brien. Donagh Cairbre was the son of Domhnall Mor, King of Munster, who submitted to Henry II near Cashel in 1172. The O'Briens of Munster split into a number of branches, including the O'Briens of Aherlow, the O'Briens of Waterford, the O'Briens of Ara in north Tipperary, and the O'Briens of Limerick.

The exploits of the O'Briens are chronicled in over 300 references, from 1055 to 1616, in *The Annals of The Kingdom of Ireland by the Four Masters* (a chronicle of Irish history from 'the earliest period to the year 1616'). Throughout this period the O'Briens of Munster vied with the O'Neills of Ulster and O'Connors of Connaught for the High Kingship of Ireland.

In 1101 Muircheartach O'Brien led a great army consisting of the men of Leinster, Munster and Connaught into Ulster and plundered Inishowen, County Donegal. He destroyed the great hill-fort of Grianan of Ailech which commanded the entrance to the Inishowen peninsula. At this time Domhnall MacLoughlin, ruling from his royal palace at Ailech, was High King of Ireland. *The Annals* record that Muircheartach O'Brien 'commanded his army to carry with them, from Ailech to Limerick, a stone of the demolished building for every sack of provisions which they had'.

In the 17th and 18th centuries many descendants of the old Gaelic order in Ireland emigrated, as the so-called Wild Geese, to Europe. Daniel O'Brien, 3rd Viscount Clare, raised the famous Irish Brigade regiment known as Clare's Dragoons which fought in many battles, under the flag of France, in the 17th and 18th centuries.

Little is known of the history of the O'Briens in Ulster. It is thought that the O'Briens of Counties Cavan and Leitrim were a branch of the Munster O'Briens who migrated there in the 16th century. Although doubt has been expressed over a connection between the O'Briens of Ulster and the O'Briens of Munster no evidence has been identified to suggest that a distinct O'Brien sept originated independently in Ulster.

O'CONNOR

This name is one of the ten most common names in Ireland and although it is very common in Ulster, it is more common in the other three provinces. In Ulster it is most common in Counties Antrim and Derry.

Ireland was one of the first countries to adopt a system of hereditary surnames which developed from a more ancient system of clan or sept names. The surname was formed by prefixing either Mac (son of) or O (grandson or descendant of) to the ancestor's name.

O'Connor is derived from Gaelic *O Conchobhair*, meaning 'descendant of Conor'. There were six distinct and important septs of this name located in different parts of the country. The most illustrious of these septs were the O'Connors of Connaught; the main branches of this sept being O'Conor Don, O'Conor Roe and O'Conor Sligo. Tracing their descent from Conchobhar, King of Connacht (died 971) the O'Connors, with extensive territories in Counties Roscommon and Sligo, ruled the Province of Connaught. They provided the last two High Kings of Ireland, i.e. Turlough O'Connor (1088-1156) and Roderick O'Connor (1116-1198). There were also powerful O'Connor septs with origins in Counties Clare, Galway, Offaly and Kerry.

The majority of Ulster O'Connors, however, will be descended from the once-powerful sept of the O'Connors of Glengiven, lords of the Keenaght in County Derry. The Keenaght, originally Cianachta, meaning 'the territory of the descendants of Cian', claimed descent from Cian, son of Oilioll Olum, King of Munster in the third century. The O'Connors were the principal family of the Cianachta and their territory later became the barony of Keenaght.

Until the 12th century when they were finally ousted by the O'Kanes the Cianachta were rulers of the Roe Valley, near Dungiven, County Derry. Their exploits are recorded in the *The Annals of The Kingdom of Ireland by the Four Masters* from the 6th century AD. In 563 Eochaidh and Baedan, the joint Kings of Ireland, were 'slain by Cronan, chief of Cianachta-Glinne-Gemhin'. Glinne-Gemhin, anglicised as Glengiven, meaning 'Glen of the skins', is the old name for the valley of the River Roe.

The Annals record, in 679, the burning of Ceannfaeladh, chief of Cianachta-Glinne-Geimhin at the Giant's Sconce, a stone fort, in Dunboe parish, County Derry by Maelduin, Lord of the Cinel Eoghain (the race of Owen). In this period the Cinel Eoghain, which included the powerful O'Kane sept, were expanding to the east and south from their original base in County Donegal. This expansion by the Cinel Eoghain intensified in the 11th century, and, in 1076, they inflicted another defeat on the Cianachta at the battle of Belaith. Meaning 'Mouth of the Ford' it is believed that Belaith was located in the townland of Gorticross, on the east bank of the River Faughan, in Clondermot Parish, County Derry.

Internal squabbles finally broke the power of the O'Connors of Glengiven. In 1104 *the Annals* record that 'Dunchadh Ua Conchobhair, lord of Cianachta-an-Ghleinne, was killed by his own people'. From the mid-12th century the O'Connors were forced into the position of small farmers in the district they previously ruled.

272

O'DOHERTY

This name, which is by far the most popular name in the city of Derry and the Inishowen peninsula, County Donegal, illustrates the very close links between these two areas. As Derry developed an industrial base in the 19th century in shirt making, shipbuilding and distilling it attracted much of its workforce from Inishowen.

The O'Doherty sept trace their lineage to Conall *Gulban*, son of the 5th century High King of Ireland, Niall of the Nine Hostages, who ruled from the Hill of Tara, County Meath. Conall and his brother Eogan conquered northwest Ireland, ca.425 AD, capturing the great hill-fort of Grianan of Ailech which commanded the entrance to Inishowen between Lough Swilly and Lough Foyle.

Ireland was one of the first countries to adopt a system of hereditary surnames which developed from a more ancient system of clan or sept names. The surname was formed by prefixing either Mac (son of) or O (grandson or descendant of) to the ancestor's name.

The O'Dohertys take their name from *Dochartach*, twelfth in lineal descent from Conall Gulban and were thus in Gaelic *O Dochartaigh*. The word *dochartach* means 'hurtful'. The original seat of the O'Doherty clan was at Ardmire or *Ard Miodhair*, a district to the west of Ballybofey near Lough Finn, County Donegal. In 1203 Donnell Carragh O'Doherty was styled 'Royal Chieftain of Ardmire'.

As the original homeland of the Cenel Eoghain (the race of Owen) in Inishowen became more and more a northern outpost, as they expanded south and east, the O'Dohertys, a powerful branch of the Cenel Conaill (race of Conall), forced their way into Inishowen. When Conor O'Doherty died in 1413 he was styled 'Chief of Ardmire, and Lord of Inishowen'. The O'Dohertys remained the chief family of Inishowen until their influence was broken after the rebellion of Sir Cahir O'Doherty in 1608, which included the ransacking of the city of Derry.

The defeat and execution of Sir Cahir O'Doherty marked the end of O'Doherty power and paved the way for the 17th century Plantation of Ulster with English and Scottish settlers. In the centuries that followed the name was anglicised with many variant spellings and in nearly all cases the O prefix was dropped. By 1890 only 2 per cent were still using it. However, in the 20th century, many resumed it and by 1950 half of the Dohertys in Ireland had become O'Doherty again.

In the 17th and 18th centuries many descendants of the old Gaelic order in Ireland emigrated, as the so-called Wild Geese, to Europe, and, in particular, to Spain and France. Dr Ramon Salvador O'Dogherty of San Fernando, near Cadiz, Spain was inaugurated in July 1990 as the 37th O'Dochartaigh, chief of Inishowen.
Ramon O'Dogherty is descended from Sir Cahir's brother John who fled from Inishowen to County Cavan and whose descendants settled in Spain, as nobility, in the 18th century. The inauguration ceremony took place on the original 'crowning stone', which tradition states was carried from Grianan, in the grounds of Belmont School in Derry, using the ancient ceremonial ritual of the clan: The claimant to the title of 'The O'Doherty' standing barefoot on the stone, holding a white wand of hazel wood.

273

O'DONNELL

O'Donnell is one of the fifty most common names in Ireland and one of the forty most common in Ulster. Although there are other families of the name from Clare and Galway the O'Donnells of northwest Ireland are related to the great family of County Donegal. This name illustrates the very close links between the city of Derry and County Donegal. As Derry developed an industrial base in the 19th century in shirt making, shipbuilding and distilling it attracted much of its workforce from Donegal.

The O'Donnell sept of County Donegal trace their lineage to Conall *Gulban*, son of the 5th century High King of Ireland, Niall of the Nine Hostages, who ruled from the Hill of Tara, County Meath. Conall and his brother Eogan conquered northwest Ireland, ca.425 AD, capturing the great hill-fort of Grianan of Ailech in County Donegal which commanded the entrance to Inishowen between Lough Swilly and Lough Foyle.

Conall, styled 'King of Tir Conaill', established his own kingdom in County Donegal called after him Tyrconnel, i.e. the 'Land of Conall', which was the ancient name of Donegal. His descendants, known as the Cenel Conaill (the race of Conall), formed one of the principal branches of the Northern Ui Neill (descendants of Niall of the Nine Hostages). The septs of the Cenel Conaill firmly established themselves in County Donegal while those descended from Conal's brother Eogan expanded to the east and south into Counties Derry and Tyrone.

Ireland was one of the first countries to adopt a system of hereditary surnames which developed from a more ancient system of clan or sept names. The surname was formed by prefixing either Mac (son of) or O (grandson or descendant of) to the ancestor's name. The O'Donnells take their name from *Domhnall,* who died in 901, and were thus in Gaelic *O Domhnaill,* i.e. descendant of Donal.

Prior to their rise to predominance the O'Donnell sept was located in a comparatively small area around Kilmacrenan, County Donegal. The O'Donnells became the pre-eminent family in Donegal from the thirteenth to the seventeenth century. *The Annals of The Kingdom of Ireland by the Four Masters* are full of references, over three hundred in total, to the exploits of the O'Donnells in northwest Ireland.

The O'Donnells have produced many illustrious figures in Irish history. The most famous was Red Hugh O'Donnell (1571-1602) who led Gaelic resistance to English attempts to pacify Ireland during the Nine Years War (1594-1603).

The escape of the most prominent Gaelic Lords of Ulster, including Rory O'Donnell, first Earl of Tyrconnell, (1575-1608), in 'the Flight of the Earls' in 1607 from Lough Swilly marked the end of Gaelic power and paved the way for the 17th century Plantation of Ulster with English and Scottish settlers. In the 17th and 18th centuries many descendants of the old Gaelic order in Ireland emigrated, as the so-called Wild Geese, to Europe, and, in particular, to Spain and France. Many O'Donnells became outstanding soldiers in the armies of the continent.

The name is now well spread throughout Donegal, with many in the Gaelic speaking west. The family has also spread into Counties Derry and Tyrone, particularly north Tyrone where the majority have dropped the O prefix.

O'HAGAN

The name O'Hagan, including Hagan, is common in Ulster, and in particular in Counties Armagh and Down.

The O'Hagan sept trace their lineage to Eogan, son of the 5th century High King of Ireland, Niall of the Nine Hostages, who ruled from the Hill of Tara, County Meath. Eogan and his brother Conall *Gulban* conquered northwest Ireland, ca.425 AD, capturing the great hill-fort of Grianan of Ailech in County Donegal.

Eogan, styled 'King of Ailech', established his own kingdom in the peninsula in County Donegal still called after him Inishowen (Innis Eoghain or Eogan's Isle). His descendants, known as the Cenel Eoghain (the race of Owen), became the principal branch of the Northern Ui Neill (descendants of Niall of the Nine Hostages). The Cenel Eoghain in the next five centuries expanded to the east and south from their focal point in Inishowen.

Ireland was one of the first countries to adopt a system of hereditary surnames which developed from a more ancient system of clan or sept names. The surname was formed by prefixing either Mac (son of) or O (grandson or descendant of) to the ancestor's name. O'Hagan, in Gaelic *O hOgain*, is derived from *og*, meaning 'young'.

The O'Hagans were one of the leading septs of Clan Fergus (Fergus was a son of Eogan) who, from their homeland around Lough Swilly, County Donegal, from the 6th century AD, pushed southeast into County Tyrone, bypassing a hard core of resistance in County Derry of the Cianachta. The septs of Clan Fergus have been described as the 'fighting vanguard of McLoughlin and O'Neill, as these clans battled their way towards Tullyhog and Armagh to become masters of Tyrone'.

The septs of Clan Fergus acquired extensive lands to the south of the Sperrin Mountains at the very heart of the kingdom of Tir Eoghain (Tir Owen or Tyrone, the land of Owen) around Tullaghoge (near Cookstown, County Tyrone). Based at Tullaghogue, the territory of the O'Hagans lay just to the south of the lands belonging to their fellow Clan Fergus sept of the O'Mellans.

The O'Hagans were the hereditary custodians of Tullaghoge, the hill where the Ulster kings were inaugurated from the 11th century. In 1081 the O'Hagans were the chief family of Clan Fergus as Magrath O'Hagan was styled 'Lord of Cinel Fergus'. As well as being chief stewards to the O'Neills, the O'Hagans were also hereditary brehons (lawyers) to the O'Neills. At the inauguration ceremony of the O'Neill chiefs on the flagstone of the kings at Tullaghoge, the O'Hagans held the privilege of escorting the king to the inaugural stone and of reading the law during the inaugural ceremony. Many O'Hagans fought with O'Neill at the Battle of Kinsale in 1603 and, as a consequence, suffered much in the land dispossessions that followed.

The County Armagh sept of *O hAodhagain* was also anglicised to O'Hagan. Owing to the proximity of Counties Tyrone and Armagh it is not possible today to distinguish between these two O'Hagan septs.

O'HARA

This name is equally common in Ulster, Leinster and Connaught, its main centres being Dublin, County Sligo and County Antrim.

Ireland was one of the first countries to adopt a system of hereditary surnames which developed from a more ancient system of clan or sept names. From the 11ᵗʰ century each family began to adopt its own distinctive family name generally derived from the first name of an ancestor who lived in or about the 10th century. The surname was formed by prefixing either Mac (son of) or O (grandson or descendant of) to the ancestor's name. Surnames in Ireland, therefore, tended to identify membership of a sept.

O'Hara is derived from Gaelic *O hEaghra*, meaning 'descendant of Eaghra'. Eaghra was chief of Luighne (the modern barony of Leyny) in County Sligo. *The Annals of The Kingdom of Ireland by the Four Masters* record, in 1059, that 'Duarcan Ua hEaghra, lord of the Three Tribes of Luighne, was killed'. *The Annals* further record, in 1183, that Bec O'Hara, styled 'Lord of Leyny in Connaught' was 'treacherously slain by Conor, the grandson of Dermot, who was the son of Roderic, in his own house, on Lough Mac Farry'.

In 1490, *the Annals* state 'there was an earthquake at Sliabh Gamh, by which a hundred persons were destroyed, among whom was the son of Manus Crossagh O'Hara'. Sliabh Gamh refers to the chain of mountains in west Sligo known today as Slieve Gamph or Ox Mountains. The townland in which this eruption took place is called Moymlough, meaning 'the erupted lake', in the parish of Killoran in the barony of Leyny. This townland also contains the ruins of a castle built by the O'Haras.

About 1350 the O'Hara sept formed two divisions, with the chiefs being O'Hara Boy (i.e. *buidhe*, meaning tawny) and O'Hara Reagh (i.e. *riabhach*, meaning grizzled). In the 16ᵗʰ century the stronghold of O'Hara Boy was at Collooney and of O'Hara Reagh at Ballyharry. A full record of the chiefs of the O'Haras survives in a manuscript known as *The Book of O'Hara*.

The O'Haras remained prominent in County Sligo after the upheavals of the 17ᵗʰ century. In the 19ᵗʰ century the O'Haras of Cooper's Hill possessed an estate of 21,000 acres. In 1706 another branch of the Sligo O'Haras were rewarded with a title, Baron Tyrawley.

A branch of the O'Haras migrated to Ulster and the Glens of Antrim in the 14ᵗʰ century and settled at Crebilly, in the parish of Ballyclug, near the town of Ballymena. The O'Haras became an important sept in Antrim and entered into several marriages and alliances with the great families of Antrim. In the middle years of the 19ᵗʰ century O'Haras were still found concentrated in the barony of Lower Glenarm on the coast of northeast Antrim.

It is believed that some O'Haras in County Fermanagh were originally O'Harens. The O'Haren sept, in Gaelic *O hArain*, were *erenaghs*, i.e. hereditary stewards, of the church lands of Ballymacataggart in Derryvullan Parish, County Fermanagh.

O'KANE

The name O'Kane, with its many variants including Kane, Keane and O'Cahan, is among the seventy-five most common names in Ireland and is most numerous in Ulster. It is among the fifteen most common names in its homeland in County Derry.

The O'Kane sept trace their lineage to Eogan, son of the 5th century High King of Ireland, Niall of the Nine Hostages, who ruled from the Hill of Tara, County Meath. Eogan and his brother Conall *Gulban* conquered northwest Ireland, ca.425 AD, capturing the great hill-fort of Grianan of Ailech in County Donegal.

Eogan, styled 'King of Ailech', established his own kingdom in the peninsula in County Donegal still called after him Inishowen (Innis Eoghain or Eogan's Isle). His descendants, known as the Cenel Eoghain (the race of Owen), expanded to the east and south from their focal point in Inishowen over the next five centuries.

Ireland was one of the first countries to adopt a system of hereditary surnames which developed from a more ancient system of clan or sept names. The surname was formed by prefixing either Mac (son of) or O (grandson or descendant of) to the ancestor's name. O'Kane and O'Cahan, an earlier anglicized form of the name, are derived from Gaelic *O Cathain*.

The O'Kanes were the leading sept of Clan Connor *Magh Ithe* (Connor was a direct descendant of Eogan). Magh Ithe is the rich countryside stretching southward from Inishowen, later known as the Laggan district in east Donegal. In the 10th century AD the families of Clan Connor moved out from the cramped territory of Magh Ithe and established themselves in County Derry, in the kingdom of Keenaght, to the north of the Sperrin Mountains, from the Foyle to the Bann rivers. In the process they ousted the Cianachta whose leading sept was the O'Connors of Glengiven in the Roe Valley.

By the 12th century, when the process of conquest ends the O'Kanes had assumed pre-eminence inside Clan Connor, and they were overlords and all-powerful in County Derry. The O'Kanes became the mainstay of power behind the O'Neills and possessed the privilege of inaugurating the chief of the O'Neills at Tullaghoge (near Cookstown, County Tyrone). Hugh O'Neill, Earl of Tyrone acknowledged his reliance on the O'Kanes saying that 'as long as he had O'Cahan and his country sure behind him, he little cared for anything that they could do to him before.'

The O'Kanes founded an Augustinian priory at Dungiven in ca.1140. For centuries the O'Kane chiefs were buried in Dungiven Priory. Today in the ruins of this old priory stands the altar tomb of Cooey-na-Gall, a celebrated O'Kane chief, who died in 1385. O'Kane is represented in armour with one hand resting on his sword, and on the front of the tomb are figures of six galloglass warriors in kilts. By the 14th century the O'Kane chieftains were employing Scottish mercenary soldiers, known as galloglass, in their feuds with local rivals. In the 15th century the O'Kanes conducted a long-running feud of raid and counter-raid with the McQuillans of the Route, County Antrim. The last chief, Donnell Ballagh O'Cahan, was inaugurated in 1598 and joined O'Neill against the English in the Nine Years War, 1594-1603. He spent the last years of his life imprisoned in the Tower of London. He died in 1617.

O'NEILL

This surname, which is one of the very few to have retained not only the O prefix but also the Gaelic spelling, is among the ten most numerous in Ireland, and one of the most famous and prominent in the history of Ireland. It is among the first ten names in Counties Antrim, Derry and Tyrone.

The O'Neill sept trace their lineage to Eogan, son of the 5th century High King of Ireland, Niall of the Nine Hostages, who ruled from the Hill of Tara, County Meath. Eogan and his brother Conall *Gulban* conquered northwest Ireland, ca.425 AD, capturing the great hill-fort of Grianan of Ailech in County Donegal.

Eogan, styled 'King of Ailech', established his own kingdom in the peninsula in County Donegal still called after him Inishowen (Innis Eoghain or Eogan's Isle). His descendants, known as the Cenel Eoghain (the race of Owen), became the principal branch of the Northern Ui Neill (descendants of Niall of the Nine Hostages). The Cenel Eoghain in the next five centuries expanded to the east and south from their focal point in Inishowen.

Ireland was one of the first countries to adopt a system of hereditary surnames which developed from a more ancient system of clan or sept names. The surname was formed by prefixing either Mac (son of) or O (grandson or descendant of) to the ancestor's name.

The first to take O'Neill as their surname was Domhnall who took the name of his grandfather, Niall, Black Knee, High King of Ireland who was killed in a battle with the Vikings in 919 AD. The O'Neills were thus in Gaelic *O Neill* i.e. grandson of Niall. In the middle years of the 11th century the O'Neills moved their capital from Ailech to Tullaghoge (near Cookstown, County Tyrone).

After a decisive battle in 1241 at *Caimeirge* (which scholars believe was near Maghera in County Derry) the O'Neills ousted the McLaughlins as the senior branch of the Northern Ui Neill. Brian O'Neill was now 'installed in the lordship of the Kinel-Owen', his territory being Tir Eoghain (Tir Owen or Tyrone, the land of Owen) which extended over the present counties of Tyrone and Derry.

The senior branch of this sept, the O'Neills of Tyrone, were frequently High Kings of Ireland, and in the 16th and 17th centuries they were the leaders of Gaelic resistance to English attempts to pacify Ireland. A junior branch established themselves in County Antrim in the 14th century and from their seat at Shane's Castle became known as the Clannaboy or Clandeboy O'Neills.

The escape of the most prominent Gaelic Lords of Ulster, including Hugh O'Neill who was styled the 'Prince of Ireland', in 'the Flight of the Earls' in 1607 from Lough Swilly marked the end of Gaelic power and paved the way for the 17th century Plantation of Ulster with English and Scottish settlers.

In the 17th and 18th centuries many descendants of the old Gaelic order in Ireland emigrated, as the so-called Wild Geese, to Europe, and, in particular, to Spain and France. The European branches of the O'Neills distinguished themselves in the military of France, Spain and Portugal.

278

O'REILLY

O'Reilly is among the first fifteen names in both Ulster and all of Ireland. In Ulster it is the single most numerous name in its homeland of County Cavan, seventh in County Fermanagh and thirteenth in County Monaghan. In the 19th century this name was much more commonly found without the prefix O. In the 20th century, however, the prefix O was widely resumed.

Ireland was one of the first countries to adopt a system of hereditary surnames which developed from a more ancient system of clan or sept names. From the 11th century each family began to adopt its own distinctive family name generally derived from the first name of an ancestor who lived in or about the 10th century. The surname was formed by prefixing either Mac (son of) or O (grandson or descendant of) to the ancestor's name. Surnames in Ireland, therefore, tended to identify membership of a sept.

O'Reilly is derived from Gaelic *O Raghallaigh*, meaning 'descendant of Raghallach'. This powerful sept were chiefs of the ancient territory of Breffny which comprised County Cavan and west Leitrim. The O'Reillys contested with the O'Rourkes for the chieftainship of Breffny. In the 10th century Breffny was divided into Breffny-O'Reilly and Breffny-O'Rourke which, in the late-16th century, formed the basis for the creation of Counties Cavan and Leitrim respectively. At the height of their power in the 13th and 14th centuries O'Reilly territory extended from County Cavan into Counties Meath and Westmeath.

As well as being a military family the O'Reillys have produced many churchmen. Five O'Reillys have held the Primacy as Archbishop of Armagh; and five were Bishops of Kilmore, two of Clogher and one of Derry. The family was widely involved in trade in medieval Ireland and at one time 'reilly' was a term for Irish money. It has also been suggested that they lived well, as the phrase 'the life of Reilly' indicates.

The escape of the most prominent Gaelic Lords of Ulster in 'the Flight of the Earls' in1607 from Lough Swilly marked the end of Gaelic power and paved the way for the 17th century Plantation of Ulster with English and Scottish settlers. Philip MacHugh O'Reilly (died 1657) led the Irish rising of 1641 in County Cavan. In King James II's Irish army, raised in 1688, Colonel Edmund O'Reilly's regiment of infantry included thrity-three officers called Reilly or O'Reilly. This regiment was part of the 'Jacobite army' which besieged the city of Derry during the famous 105 day Siege of Derry, from 18 April to 31 July 1689.

In the 17th and 18th centuries many descendants of the old Gaelic order in Ireland emigrated, as the so-called Wild Geese, to Europe, and, in particular, to Spain and France. Many O'Reillys became outstanding soldiers in the armies of the continent including Count Don Alexander O'Reilly (died 1797) who ended his days as Governor of Louisiana in North America after a distinguished military career in the French, Austrian and Spanish service.

In a few cases the County Kerry sept name of O'Rahilly, in Gaelic *O Raithile*, was anglicised as O'Reilly.

ORR

In Ireland this name is common only in Ulster, where it is chiefly found in Counties Antrim, Down, Derry and Tyrone. This name was brought to Ulster by settlers from Scotland in the 17th century.

Orr is derived from the parish name of Orr in Kirkcudbrightshire in the province of Galloway in southwest Scotland. Orr was recorded as a surname in Scotland as early as 1296; it became a common name in Scotland, particularly in the western part of Renfrewshire. In the 16th century references to the surname were recorded in Paisley and Glasgow. There were also Orrs in Campbelltown in Kintyre, Argyllshire, as early as 1640. Indeed these Orrs were recognised as a sept of Clan Campbell.

It is also possible that Orr originated as a nickname for someone with a sallow complexion. In this case Orr is derived from Gaelic *odhar*, meaning 'pale'.

It has also been claimed that Orr is an anglicised form of Scots Gaelic *Mac Iomhair*, meaning 'son of Ivar', from the Norse personal name *Ivaar*. In 870-71 Imhair, a Norse chief, joined with Olaf the White, king of Dublin, in the besieging and sacking of Dumbarton. As Iver became a common forename the surname McIver spread throughout the Highlands of Scotland. In 1292 the lands of Malcolm McIuyr in Lorn became the sheriffdom of Lorne. It is said that 'the Clan Iver lands were forfeited in the seventeenth century and were restored on condition that the heir should take the name of Campbell.'

Although *Mac Iomhair* was usually anglicised as McIver it is possible that McIver was further anglicised to Orr. The fact that the Orrs were a sept of Clan Campbell and that the surname Orr is prominent in Kintyre, the stronghold of Clan Iver, supports this view.

Movement of Scottish settlers to Ulster began in earnest from 1605 in a private enterprise colonisation of counties Antrim and Down when Sir Hugh Montgomery and Sir James Hamilton acquired title to large estates in north Down and Sir Randall MacDonnell, 1st Earl of Antrim, to large tracts of land in north Antrim.

Further impetus came in 1609 when James I adopted the policy to encourage English and Scottish settlers to settle on the forfeited estates of the Gaelic chiefs in counties Armagh, Cavan, Donegal, Fermanagh, Londonderry (then known as Coleraine) and Tyrone. Settlers to Ulster came, by and large, in three waves: with the granting of the initial leases in the period 1605 to 1625; after 1652 and Cromwell's crushing of the Irish rebellion; and finally in the fifteen years after 1690 and the Glorious Revolution.

Scottish families entering Ireland through the port of Londonderry settled in the Foyle Valley which includes much of the fertile lands of counties Donegal, Londonderry and Tyrone. Orr families were recorded in County Tyrone as early as 1655, and within ten years many others were recorded in Derry and adjacent areas.

During the famous 105 day Siege of Derry, from 18 April to 31 July 1689, John Orr and James Orr, both of Letterkenny, County Donegal, were recorded as 'defenders' of the city.

PARKHILL

This name, of Scottish origin, belongs to Counties Antrim and Londonderry.

In Scotland, this surname is derived from the lands of Parkhill in the barony of Torboltoun in Ayrshire. This region was home to many of the Scottish settlers who came to Ulster throughout the 17th century. The name was also established in Glasgow by the early years of the 17th century as a Robert Parkhill was recorded as a merchant in the city of Glasgow in 1605.

The defeat of the old Gaelic order in the Nine Years War, 1594-1603 and the escape of the most prominent Gaelic Lords of Ulster in 'the Flight of the Earls' in 1607 from Lough Swilly, County Donegal were ultimately responsible for the settlement of many Scottish families in the northern counties of Ireland.

Movement of Scottish settlers to Ulster began in earnest from 1605 in a private enterprise colonisation of counties Antrim and Down when Sir Hugh Montgomery and Sir James Hamilton acquired title to large estates in north Down and Sir Randall MacDonnell, 1st Earl of Antrim, to large tracts of land in north Antrim.

In 1609 the Earl of Salisbury, Lord High Treasurer, suggested to James I a deliberate plantation of Scottish and English colonists on the forfeited estates of the Gaelic chiefs in counties Armagh, Cavan, Donegal, Fermanagh, Londonderry (then known as Coleraine) and Tyrone.

Settlers to Ulster came, by and large, in three waves: with the granting of the initial leases in the period 1605 to 1625; after 1652 and Cromwell's crushing of the Irish rebellion; and finally in the fifteen years after 1690 and the Glorious Revolution. It is estimated by 1715, when migration to Ulster had virtually stopped, the Scottish population of Ulster stood at 200,000.

Scottish families entering Ireland through the port of Londonderry settled in the Foyle Valley which includes much of the fertile lands of counties Donegal, Londonderry and Tyrone. The lands along the Firth of Clyde in the county of Ayrshire, the Clyde Valley and the Border Lands consisting of the counties of Wigtown, Kirkcudbright and Dumfries were home to many of these Scottish settlers.

At the time of the mid-19th century Griffith's Valuation 39 Parkhill households were recorded in Ireland. This source clearly shows that the name was most concentrated in north Ulster, as 21 Parkhill households were residing in County Londonderry and a further 15 in the adjoining county of Antrim. In other words over 90% of descendants of Parkhills in Ireland were living in Counties Antrim and Londonderry.

Parkhill is a common name in the city of Londonderry today. As Derry developed an industrial base in the 19th century in shirt making, shipbuilding and distilling it attracted much of its workforce from outside of the city. In the 90-year period 1821 to 1911 the population of the city quadrupled to 40,780.

PATRICK

In the province of Ulster this surname is found predominantly in Counties Antrim and Tyrone. This name was brought to Ulster by settlers from Scotland in the 17th century.

Patrick was one of the most popular names in the west of Scotland in pre-Reformation times. The popularity of the name stems from St Patrick, the fifth century saint, who is regarded as the greatest and most famous of Ireland's Christian missionaries. In modern Scottish Gaelic the name Patrick is found in four forms: *Padruig; Paruig; Para;* and *Padair*, the common form of Patrick in Arran and Kintyre.

In the Highlands Clan MacPatrick, which was anglicised as McIlfatrick and Patterson, was derived from Gaelic *Mac Gille Phadruig*, meaning 'son of the devotee of St Patrick'. Gillepatrick was a common Gaelic personal name. This surname was recorded in Moray, as Macgyllepatric, as early as 1236. The territory of this clan was on the north side of Lochfyne.

Patrick only became a popular forename in Ireland after 1600, due probably to its introduction by the Scots settlers in Ulster.

As a surname, in Scotland, Patrick is common in Ayrshire, and the old family of that name appear to have been connected with Kilwinning Abbey. In 1201, Patrick became abbot of Dunfermline. The lands along the Firth of Clyde in the old county of Ayrshire were home to many of the Scottish settlers who came to Ulster throughout the 17th century.

Movement of Scottish settlers to Ulster began in earnest from 1605 in a private enterprise colonisation of counties Antrim and Down when Sir Hugh Montgomery and Sir James Hamilton acquired title to large estates in north Down and Sir Randall MacDonnell, 1st Earl of Antrim, to large tracts of land in north Antrim. In County Antrim the Patricks of Dunminning trace their descent from Ayrshire.

Further impetus came in 1609 when James I adopted the policy to encourage Scottish settlers to settle on the forfeited estates of the Gaelic chiefs in counties Armagh, Cavan, Donegal, Fermanagh, Londonderry (then known as Coleraine) and Tyrone.
Settlers came to Ulster, by and large, in three waves: with the granting of the initial leases in the period 1605 to 1625; after 1652 and Cromwell's crushing of the Irish rebellion; and finally in the fifteen years after 1690 and the Glorious Revolution.

Scottish families entering Ireland through the port of Londonderry settled in the Foyle Valley which includes much of the fertile lands of counties Donegal, Londonderry and Tyrone.

Patricks were recorded in County Londonderry from the mid-17th century, especially in the fertile lands in the north of the county. The Hearth Money Rolls of 1663 record four Patrick households in this county; one each in Coleraine and Drumachose Parishes and two in Tamlaght Finlagan Parish.

It is estimated by 1715, when migration to Ulster had virtually stopped, the Scottish population of Ulster stood at 200,000.

PATTERSON

Though found in all the provinces of Ireland this name is common only in Ulster where it is one of the forty most numerous names. It is among the first five in County Down and is very common too in Counties Antrim, Armagh, Derry and Tyrone. This name was brought to Ulster in large numbers by settlers from Scotland in the 17th century. This name is among the twenty most common in Scotland.

Patterson simply means 'son of Patrick'. Patrick was one of the most popular names in the west of Scotland in pre-Reformation times. The popularity of the name stems from St Patrick, the fifth century saint, who is regarded as the greatest and most famous of Ireland's Christian missionaries. In modern Scottish Gaelic the name Patrick is found in four forms: *Padruig*; *Paruig*; *Para*; and *Padair*, the common form of Patrick in Arran and Kintyre.

Patterson is the anglicised form of McPatrick. In the Highlands Clan MacPatrick, which was also anglicised as McIlfatrick, was derived from Gaelic *Mac Gille Phadruig*, meaning 'son of the devotee of St Patrick'. Gillepatrick was a common Gaelic personal name. This surname was recorded in Moray, as Macgyllepatric, as early as 1236. The territory of this clan was on the north side of Lochfyne.

McPatrick was one of the names assumed by the Lamonts after their clan was 'broken' in the 17th century. In this case they took the name of an ancestor, baron MacPatrick. The Pattersons were furthermore a sept of Clan Maclaren, active supporters of the Jacobite cause in Scotland during the Risings of 1715 and 1745. It is also claimed that Pattersons were an offshoot of Clan Farquharson of Invercauld.

The Galloway name McFetridge, in Gaelic *Mac Phetruis*, meaning 'son of Peter' was also anglicised as Patterson. During the famous 105 day Siege of Derry, from 18 April to 31 July 1689, a Lieutenant McPhedris was recorded as a 'defender' of the city who was killed, on 21 April, during a sortie to Pennyburn Mill by the garrison's forces. William McFetrick of Carnglass, County Antrim was also recorded as one of the defenders.

The surname Patterson spread throughout Scotland. During the 15th and 16th centuries references to the surname in Scotland can be found in places as far apart as Aberdeen, Cupar, Dundee, Glasgow and North Berwick.

Movement of Scottish settlers to Ulster began in earnest from 1605 in a private enterprise colonisation of counties Antrim and Down when Sir Hugh Montgomery and Sir James Hamilton acquired title to large estates in north Down and Sir Randall MacDonnell, 1st Earl of Antrim, to large tracts of land in north Antrim. By the mid-19th century Patterson was found in twelve out of the fourteen baronies of Antrim, and in Down was most common in the barony of Upper Castlereagh.

Further impetus came in 1609 when James I adopted the policy to encourage Scottish settlers to settle on the forfeited estates of the Gaelic chiefs in counties Armagh, Cavan, Donegal, Fermanagh, Londonderry (then known as Coleraine) and Tyrone. It is estimated by 1715, when migration to Ulster had virtually stopped, the Scottish population of Ulster stood at 200,000.

PATTON

Patton can be of Irish, English or Scottish origin. This name is common in Ulster, where it is most numerous in Counties Antrim, Down and Donegal.

Ireland was one of the first countries to adopt a system of hereditary surnames which developed from a more ancient system of clan or sept names. The surname was formed by prefixing either Mac (son of) or O (grandson or descendant of) to the ancestor's name.

The County Donegal sept of Patton is derived from Gaelic *O Peatain*, meaning 'descendant of Patrick'. They trace their lineage to Eogan, son of the 5th century High King of Ireland, Niall of the Nine Hostages. The Pattons were a sept of Clan Moen (tracing their descent from Moen, son of Muireadach (Murdock), son of Eogan). Their place of origin was near Ballybofey in the barony of Raphoe, County Donegal. *The Annals of The Kingdom of Ireland by the Four Masters* record, that in 1178, Murtough O'Petan, a leading member of Clan Moen, was slain by the O'Kanes.

Many Pattons in Ulster will have Scottish ancestry. In Scotland Patton is derived as a pet form of the given name Patrick. Patrick was one of the most popular names in the west of Scotland in pre-Reformation times, and the personal name Paton spread throughout the western counties. In the 16th century references to the surname were also recorded in Aberdeen and Dundee.

In Scotland McFadden, in Gaelic *Macphaidein*, meaning 'son of Patrick', was also anglicised as Patton. The MacFaddens were a sept of Clan MacLaine of Lochbuie.

Movement of Scottish settlers to Ulster began in earnest from 1605 in a private enterprise colonisation of counties Antrim and Down when Sir Hugh Montgomery and Sir James Hamilton acquired title to large estates in north Down and Sir Randall MacDonnell, 1st Earl of Antrim, to large tracts of land in north Antrim.

Further impetus came in 1609 when James I adopted the policy to encourage Scottish settlers to settle on the forfeited estates of the Gaelic chiefs in counties Armagh, Cavan, Donegal, Fermanagh, Londonderry (then known as Coleraine) and Tyrone.
The Pattons of Springfield in Clondavaddog Parish, County Donegal descend from one William Patton of Fifeshire who settled there in 1630.

A small number of Pattons in Ulster will have English ancestry. In England the surname Patton may have a number of origins: from the place names of Patton in Shropshire and Westmorland; as an occupational name for a maker of clogs (a patten was a wooden clog); and as a pet form of the given name Patrick. English settlers, mostly drawn from the northern counties of Cheshire, Cumberland, Lancashire, Northumberland, Yorkshire and Westmorland also migrated to Ulster during the 17th century. English settlers tended to favour settlement along the Lagan Valley, in the east of the Province, on lands straddling the borders of Counties Armagh, Antrim and Down.

During the famous 105 day Siege of Derry, from 18 April to 31 July 1689, Henry Paton of Ramelton, County Donegal was recorded as a 'defender' of the city.

PEOPLES

In Ulster this name is very much associated with east Donegal and west Derry.

Ireland was one of the first countries to adopt a system of hereditary surnames which developed from a more ancient system of clan or sept names. From the 11th century each family began to adopt its own distinctive family name generally derived from the first name of an ancestor who lived in or about the 10th century. The surname was formed by prefixing either Mac (son of) or O (grandson or descendant of) to the ancestor's name. Surnames in Ireland, therefore, tended to identify membership of a sept.

Peoples is derived from Gaelic *O Duibhne*, the root word being *duibhne* meaning 'disagreeable'. This sept's name was also anglicised as Deeney. This arose from the similarity of the sound of Gaelic *Daoine*, meaning 'people' and Gaelic *duibhne*. Thus *O Duibhne* was anglicised to Deeney and mistranslated to Peoples. Originating in County Donegal this sept was strongly represented in the priesthood in the Diocese of Raphoe from the 15th century.

It would seem that the homeland of this sept was the Fanad Peninsula in north Donegal. At the time of the mid-19th century Griffith's Valuation the greatest concentration of Deeneys in County Donegal were in the parishes of Killygarvan, which contained 29 Deeney households and Clondavaddog with 19 households of the name. In total 60 Deeney households were recorded in this survey in County Donegal which was published between 1857 and 1858. In other words 80% of the descendants of the O'Deeney sept in Donegal lived in these two parishes situated on the Fanad Peninsula.

At the time of the mid-19th century Griffith's Valuation there were 47 Peoples households recorded in County Donegal. Eleven Peoples households were recorded in both the parishes of Conwal and Kilmacrenan which are located to the south of the Fanad Peninsula. In other words over 45% of the Peoples households in County Donegal resided in these 2 parishes to the north and west of the town of Letterkenny.

Both Deeney and Peoples are common names in Derry city today. It would seem, however, that the movement into Derry city began after 1831 as only three Deeney households and three Peoples households were recorded in Derry city in the 1831 census. These names illustrate the very close links, both historic and economic, between the city of Derry and County Donegal. As Derry developed an industrial base in the 19th century in shirt making, shipbuilding and distilling it attracted much of its workforce from Donegal. In the 90-year period 1821 to 1911 the population of the city quadrupled to 40,780.

Peoples is also recorded as a surname in England where it is regarded as a variant of Pepys. It is possible that some Peoples in Ulster may be descendants of 17th century English settlers. Peoples, however, is not a common name in England.

In 1631 Hugh Peoples acquired the lands of Bellehebestocke, County Antrim. The Hearth Money Rolls of 1669 for County Antrim record the surnames of Peoples, Peables, Pebbles, Pebles and Pheables.

PORTER

In Ireland Porter is almost exclusive to Ulster, where it is most common in Counties Antrim, Down, Derry and Armagh. This name was brought to Ulster by settlers from England and Scotland in the 17th century. The majority of Ulster Porters will be of Scottish origin.

The surname Porter sprung up in many different locations, independently of each other, throughout England and Scotland as it was derived from an occupational name for the office of porter or gatekeeper of a castle or monastery. The porter, who kept the keys and had the power to grant or refuse admission, was one of the most important officials connected with the castle or monastery in medieval times. Lands and privileges were often attached to the office. For example, in Scotland, the descendants of 'John the Porter' inherited the lands associated with the office of porter at the monastery at Paisley in Renfrewshire. In Scotland, Porter, in Gaelic *portair*, also had the additional meaning of 'ferryman'.

Movement of Scottish settlers to Ulster began in earnest from 1605 in a private enterprise colonisation of counties Antrim and Down when Sir Hugh Montgomery and Sir James Hamilton acquired title to large estates in north Down and Sir Randall MacDonnell, 1st Earl of Antrim, to large tracts of land in north Antrim.

Further impetus came in 1609 when James I adopted the policy to encourage English and Scottish settlers to settle on the forfeited estates of the Gaelic chiefs in counties Armagh, Cavan, Donegal, Fermanagh, Londonderry (then known as Coleraine) and Tyrone. Settlers to Ulster came, by and large, in three waves: with the granting of the initial leases in the period 1605 to 1625; after 1652 and Cromwell's crushing of the Irish rebellion; and finally in the fifteen years after 1690 and the Glorious Revolution. By the end of the 17th century a self-sustaining settlement of British colonists had established itself in Ulster.

Scottish families entering Ireland through the port of Londonderry settled in the Foyle Valley which includes much of the fertile lands of counties Donegal, Londonderry and Tyrone. English settlers, mostly drawn from the northern counties of Cheshire, Cumberland, Lancashire, Northumberland, Yorkshire and Westmorland also migrated to Ulster during the 17th century. English settlers tended to favour settlement along the Lagan Valley, in the east of the Province, on lands straddling the borders of Counties Armagh, Antrim and Down.

English settlers were particularly prominent in the early years of the Plantation of Ulster. The upheavals of the 1641 rebellion and the Williamite Wars of 1689 to 1691 tended to discourage English settlers more than Scottish settlers. When large scale migration to Ulster resumed in the years after 1652 and 1690 it was Scottish Presbyterian settlers who were more prominent.

During the famous 105 day Siege of Derry, from 18 April to 31 July 1689, the exploits of Robert Porter of Burt, County Donegal in the garrison's sortie against the Jacobite besiegers on 4 June at Windmill Hill are remembered in verse:

Brave Robert Porter his pike away he threw
And with round stones nine Irish soldiers slew.

QUIGG

Quigg belongs mainly to County Derry but it is also found in County Monaghan.

Ireland was one of the first countries to adopt a system of hereditary surnames which developed from a more ancient system of clan or sept names. From the 11th century each family began to adopt its own distinctive family name generally derived from the first name of an ancestor who lived in or about the 10th century. The surname was formed by prefixing either Mac (son of) or O (grandson or descendant of) to the ancestor's name. Surnames in Ireland, therefore, tended to identify membership of a sept.

The County Derry sept of O'Quigg is derived from Gaelic *O Cuaig*. The Bann Valley in east Derry seems to have been their homeland. Quigg and O'Quigg occur quite frequently in the 17th century Hearth Money Rolls for Counties Derry and Antrim. In the Hearth Money Rolls of 1663 O'Quiggs and O'Quigges were recorded in the County Derry parishes of Balteagh, Desertoghill, Macosquin and Tamlaght O'Crilly. In the census of 1659 O'Quig was listed as a 'principal name' in the barony of Coleraine, County Derry.

Quigg is also a recognised variant of Quigley even though Quigley, in Gaelic *O Coigligh*, was the name of a number of distinct septs. Quigley is derived from Gaelic *O Coigligh*, meaning 'descendant of Coigleach', the root word possibly being *coigeal*, denoting a person with unkempt hair.

The major Quigley sept belonged to the Northern Ui Fiachrach, i.e. descendants of Fiachra. Fiachra was the brother of the 5th century High King of Ireland, Niall of the Nine Hostages, who ruled from the Hill of Tara, County Meath. The septs belonging to the Ui Fiachrach were located in North Mayo and Sligo.

The homeland of this Quigley sept was the barony of Carra in County Mayo. This sept, however, had become widely dispersed by the end of the 16th century as they migrated north to Sligo, Derry and Donegal, south to Galway and east to Louth. The upheavals of the 13th century contributed to this dispersal as the power of Gaelic septs in Connaught was much reduced by the Anglo-Norman military incursions of that period.

The importance of Quigley as a surname in Derry city today, where it is among the top twenty names, is explained by the fact that there was an Ulster sept of the name in the Inishowen Peninsula, County Donegal. In the census of 1659 Quigley was recorded as the fifth most numerous name in Inishowen.

The name is also well known in Fermanagh and Monaghan as a sept of O'Quigley were *erenaghs*, i.e. hereditary stewards, of the church lands of Clontivrin in the parish of Clones which straddled the borders of Counties Fermanagh and Monaghan.

Owing to the mistaken notion that the Gaelic for 'five', *cuig*, was an element in their construction both Quigley and Quigg, especially in County Down, have also been anglicised as Fivey. Those who adopted this spelling of the name in the 18th century appear to have been well-to-do.

QUIGLEY

Quigley is common in all four provinces of Ireland but is most numerous in Ulster, particularly in Counties Derry and Donegal.

Ireland was one of the first countries to adopt a system of hereditary surnames which developed from a more ancient system of clan or sept names. From the 11th century each family began to adopt its own distinctive family name generally derived from the first name of an ancestor who lived in or about the 10th century. The surname was formed by prefixing either Mac (son of) or O (grandson or descendant of) to the ancestor's name. Surnames in Ireland, therefore, tended to identify membership of a sept.

Quigley is derived from Gaelic *O Coigligh*, meaning 'descendant of Coigleach', the root word possibly being *coigeal*, denoting a person with unkempt hair. A number of Irish septs adopted Quigley as their family name.

The major Quigley sept belonged to the Northern Ui Fiachrach, i.e. descendants of Fiachra. Fiachra was the brother of the 5th century High King of Ireland, Niall of the Nine Hostages, who ruled from the Hill of Tara, County Meath. The septs belonging to the Ui Fiachrach were located in North Mayo and Sligo.

The homeland of this Quigley sept was the barony of Carra in County Mayo. This sept, however, had become widely dispersed by the end of the 16th century as they migrated north to Sligo, Derry and Donegal, south to Galway and east to Louth. The upheavals of the 13th century contributed to this dispersal as the power of Gaelic septs in Connaught was much reduced by the Anglo-Norman military incursions of that period.

The importance of Quigley as a surname in Derry city today, where it is among the top twenty names, is explained by the fact that there was an Ulster sept of the name in the Inishowen Peninsula, County Donegal. In the census of 1659 Quigley was recorded as the fifth most numerous name in Inishowen.

Today this name illustrates the very close links between the city of Derry and Inishowen, County Donegal. As Derry developed an industrial base in the 19th century in shirt making, shipbuilding and distilling it attracted much of its workforce from Inishowen.

The name is also well known in Fermanagh and Monaghan as a sept of O'Quigley were *erenaghs*, i.e. hereditary stewards, of the church lands of Clontivrin in the parish of Clones which straddled the borders of Counties Fermanagh and Monaghan.

Quigley is the most recognised form of the sept name of *O Coigligh* but it was also anglicised as Cogley, Kegley and Twigley.

In some instances Quigley was abbreviated to Quigg which is also the name of a distinct County Derry sept of, in Gaelic, *O Cuaig*.

QUINN

The name Quinn, including Quin, is among the twenty most common names in Ireland. It is among the twenty-five most numerous names in Ulster, where it is the single most common name in County Tyrone and one of the first ten in County Armagh. There were four distinct septs of this name with territory in Counties Antrim, Clare, Longford and Tyrone.

The O'Quinn sept of Tyrone trace their lineage to Eogan, son of the 5th century High King of Ireland, Niall of the Nine Hostages, who ruled from the Hill of Tara, County Meath. Eogan and his brother Conall *Gulban* conquered northwest Ireland, ca.425 AD, capturing the great hill-fort of Grianan of Ailech in County Donegal.

Eogan, styled 'King of Ailech', established his own kingdom in the peninsula in County Donegal still called after him Inishowen (Innis Eoghain or Eogan's Isle). His descendants, known as the Cenel Eoghain (the race of Owen), became the principal branch of the Northern Ui Neill (descendants of Niall of the Nine Hostages). The Cenel Eoghain in the next five centuries expanded to the east and south from their focal point in Inishowen.

Ireland was one of the first countries to adopt a system of hereditary surnames which developed from a more ancient system of clan or sept names. The surname was formed by prefixing either Mac (son of) or O (grandson or descendant of) to the ancestor's name. The O'Quinns take their name from *Coinne*, a grandson of Fergus, son of Eogan and were thus in Gaelic *O Coinne*, i.e. descendant of Coinne.

The O'Quinns were one of the leading septs of Clan Fergus (Fergus was a son of Eogan) who, from their homeland around Lough Swilly, County Donegal, from the 6th century AD, pushed southeast into County Tyrone, bypassing a hard core of resistance in County Derry of the Cianachta. The septs of Clan Fergus have been described as the 'fighting vanguard of McLoughlin and O'Neill, as these clans battled their way towards Tullyhog and Armagh to become masters of Tyrone'.

The septs of Clan Fergus acquired extensive lands to the south of the Sperrin Mountains at the very heart of the kingdom of Tir Eoghain (Tir Owen or Tyrone, the land of Owen) around Tullaghoge (near Cookstown, County Tyrone). The territory of the O'Quinns, in the vicinity of Lissan on the border of Counties Derry and Tyrone, lay just to the southwest of the lands belonging to their fellow Clan Fergus sept of the O'Mellans. The O'Quinns acted as quartermasters to the O'Neills, being responsible for supplying arms and provisions.

A distinct sept of O'Quinns, Gaelic *O Cuinn*, meaning descendant of Conn, had their origins in north Antrim in the Glens of Antrim.

There has grown up a custom that Catholic families use the spelling Quinn and Protestant ones use Quin. However, there will always be exceptions to this rule. The surname, furthermore, has also been anglicised to Conney, Cunnea and Quinney.

Families of O'Quinn settled in France and became leading citizens in Bordeaux.

RANKIN

This surname is found almost exclusively in Ulster where it is most common in Counties Derry and Donegal. This name was brought to Ulster by settlers from Scotland in the 17th century.

In the Lowlands of Scotland, this surname was derived from the medieval personal name of Rankin. It would seem that Ayrshire was the early home of the Rankins. In the 15th and 16th centuries references to the surname can also be found in places as far apart as Aberdeen, Ayr, Glasgow, Irvine, Kilmarnock and Prestwick. McRankin, meaning 'son of Rankin', was recorded as a common name in Ayrshire from the 16th century.

In the Highlands of Scotland the name McRankin was common in the Glencoe district where it was derived from Gaelic *Mac Fhraing*, meaning 'son of Francis'. The Rankins or McRankins of Coll were hereditary pipers to the Macleans of Duart and later to the Macleans of Coll. Originally known as the Clann Duille the Rankins of Coll trace their descent from Cuduilligh. It is claimed that Cuduilligh, at the invitation of the Macleans, accompanied the McFaddens of Donegal to Argyll.

The Rankins of Coll were a sept of Clan Maclean. The Macleans, with lands on Mull, were followers of the McDonalds, Lords of the Isles. After 1493 when the MacDonalds finally lost their title as 'Lord of the Isles' the various followers of the MacDonalds, including the Macleans, became independent clans. This loss of power also encouraged more supporters of the MacDonalds to hire themselves out as galloglasses, i.e. mercenary soldiers, to Irish chiefs. Followers of Clan Maclean of Duart were hired by both the O'Donnells and the O'Neills in the 16th century. It is quite possible that Rankins were among these galloglasses.

The Annals of The Kingdom of Ireland by the Four Masters provide detailed and graphic descriptions of the Scottish galloglasses. In one account dated 1557 the *Annals* describe the galloglass in the camp of the O'Neills who were on a raiding expedition into O'Donnell territory in Donegal. It states that 'sixty grim and redoubtable gallowglasses, with sharp, keen axes, terrible and ready for action, and sixty stern and terrific Scots, with massive, broad, and heavy-striking swords in their hands, ready to strike and parry, were watching and guarding the son of O'Neill.'

Upheavals such as military incursions, feuds and harvest failures would have encouraged many clan members, including Rankins, to migrate to Ulster as settlers during the 17th century. Owing to the nature of the Scottish clan system once the power and influence of the chief had been weakened or broken the clan tended to disintegrate. In Counties Derry and Donegal the Rankins are thought to be of the Coll McRankin origin.

During the famous 105 day Siege of Derry, from 18 April to 31 July 1689, Lieutenant Rankin, Alick Rankin, John Rankin and Martha Rankin were recorded as 'defenders' of the city. Indeed the exploits of Lieutenant Rankin in the garrison's sortie against the Jacobite besiegers on 21 April at Pennyburn are remembered in verse:

Lieutenant Rankin hewed the Irish down
And in that battle gained much renown

REILLY

Reilly is among the first fifteen names in both Ulster and all of Ireland. In Ulster it is the single most numerous name in its homeland of County Cavan, seventh in County Fermanagh and thirteenth in County Monaghan. In the 20th century the prefix O was widely resumed. In the 19th century, however, the name was much more commonly found without the prefix O.

Ireland was one of the first countries to adopt a system of hereditary surnames which developed from a more ancient system of clan or sept names. From the 11th century each family began to adopt its own distinctive family name generally derived from the first name of an ancestor who lived in or about the 10th century. The surname was formed by prefixing either Mac (son of) or O (grandson or descendant of) to the ancestor's name. Surnames in Ireland, therefore, tended to identify membership of a sept.

Reilly is derived from Gaelic *O Raghallaigh*, meaning 'descendant of Raghallach'. This powerful sept were chiefs of the ancient territory of Breffny which comprised County Cavan and west Leitrim. The O'Reillys contested with the O'Rourkes for the chieftainship of Breffny. In the 10th century Breffny was divided into Breffny-O'Reilly and Breffny-O'Rourke which, in the late-16th century, formed the basis for the creation of Counties Cavan and Leitrim respectively. At the height of their power in the 13th and 14th centuries O'Reilly territory extended from County Cavan into Counties Meath and Westmeath.

As well as being a military family the Reillys have produced many churchmen. Five O'Reillys have held the Primacy as Archbishop of Armagh; and five were Bishops of Kilmore, two of Clogher and one of Derry. The family was widely involved in trade in medieval Ireland and at one time 'reilly' was a term for Irish money. It has also been suggested that they lived well, as the phrase 'the life of Reilly' indicates.

The escape of the most prominent Gaelic Lords of Ulster in 'the Flight of the Earls' in 1607 from Lough Swilly marked the end of Gaelic power and paved the way for the 17th century Plantation of Ulster with English and Scottish settlers. Philip MacHugh O'Reilly (died 1657) led the Irish rising of 1641 in County Cavan. In King James II's Irish army, raised in 1688, Colonel Edmund O'Reilly's regiment of infantry included thrity-three officers called Reilly or O'Reilly. This regiment was part of the 'Jacobite army' which besieged the city of Derry during the famous 105 day Siege of Derry, from 18 April to 31 July 1689.

In the 17th and 18th centuries many descendants of the old Gaelic order in Ireland emigrated, as the so-called Wild Geese, to Europe, and, in particular, to Spain and France. Many Reillys became outstanding soldiers in the armies of the continent including Count Don Alexander O'Reilly (died 1797) who ended his days as Governor of Louisiana in North America after a distinguished military career in the French, Austrian and Spanish service.

In a few cases the County Kerry sept name of O'Rahilly, in Gaelic *O Raithile*, was anglicised as O'Reilly.

ROBERTS

Roberts is a common surname in Ireland in the provinces of Leinster, Munster and Ulster. It is believed that most Roberts will be of either English or Welsh origin. Roberts is among the ten most common names in England and Wales, and it is especially common in North Wales. Roberts was not common in Scotland which retained the longer form of Robertson.

Roberts, derived from the personal name Robert, simply means 'son of Robert'. The personal name Robert, derived from a German personal name meaning 'bright fame', was widely introduced into England at the time of the Norman conquest in 1066. Robert became a popular choice as a child's name in the Middle Ages, and at a time when fixed surnames, based on a father's first name, were being established. Thus the surname Roberts sprang up in many different locations, independently of each other, throughout England and Wales.

The defeat of the old Gaelic order in the Nine Years War, 1594-1603 and the escape of the most prominent Gaelic Lords of Ulster in 'the Flight of the Earls' in 1607 from Lough Swilly, County Donegal were ultimately responsible for the settlement of many English, Welsh and Scottish families in the northern counties of Ireland.

In 1609 the Earl of Salisbury, Lord High Treasurer, suggested to James I a deliberate plantation of English, Welsh and Scottish colonists on the forfeited estates of the Gaelic chiefs in counties Armagh, Cavan, Donegal, Fermanagh, Londonderry (then known as Coleraine) and Tyrone.

Settlers came to Ulster, by and large, in three waves: with the granting of the initial leases in the period 1605 to 1625; after 1652 and Cromwell's crushing of the Irish rebellion; and finally in the fifteen years after 1690 and the Glorious Revolution. By the end of the 17th century a self-sustaining settlement of British colonists had established itself in Ulster.

Londonderry, Coleraine, Carrickfergus, Belfast and Donaghadee were the main ports of entry into the province of Ulster for 17th century British settlers with the Lagan, Bann and the Foyle valleys acting as the major arteries along which the colonists travelled into the interior. English and Welsh settlers tended to favour settlement along the Lagan Valley, in the east of the Province, on lands straddling the borders of Counties Armagh, Antrim and Down.

English settlers were particularly prominent in the early years of the Plantation of Ulster. The upheavals of the 1641 rebellion and the Williamite Wars of 1689 to 1691 tended to discourage English settlers more than Scottish settlers. When large scale migration to Ulster resumed in the years after 1652 and 1690 it was Scottish Presbyterian settlers who were more prominent.

In the Highlands of Scotland, McRobert, in Gaelic *Mac Roibeirt*, meaning 'son of Robert', may, in some instances, have been anglicised as Roberts.

During the famous 105 day Siege of Derry, from 18 April to 31 July 1689, John Roberts was recorded as one of the 'defenders' of the city.

ROBERTSON

Half the Robertsons in Ireland are found in Ulster. This surname was brought to Ulster by settlers from Scotland in the 17th century.

Although Robertson is regarded as a surname of Scottish origin it has become confused with Robinson which is seen as a surname of English origin. Robertson is among the ten most common names in Scotland while Robinson is among the top twenty surnames in England. In Ulster, however, the surnames Robertson and Robinson were frequently interchangeable.

Robinson, derived from the personal name Robert, simply means 'son of Robin'. The personal name Robert, derived from a German personal name meaning 'bright fame', was widely introduced into England at the time of the Norman conquest in 1066. Robert became a popular choice as a child's name in the Middle Ages, and at a time when fixed surnames, based on a father's first name, were being established. Thus the surname Robinson sprang up in many different locations, independently of each other, throughout England.

In addition Robinson was recorded as a surname in Scotland, in the form of John Robynson in Irvine in Ayrshire, as early as 1426. By the 16th century Robinson was a common name in Glasgow.

Robertson, derived from the personal name Robert, simply means 'son of Robert'. In Scotland, Clan Robertson of Atholl in Perthshire was also known as Clan Donnachaidh. This clan traces its descent from Fat Duncan or Donnachaidh Reamhair who fought alongside Robert the Bruce at the Battle of Bannockburn in 1314. It is claimed that they acquired the family name of Robertson as a result of their support of Robert the Bruce, King of Scotland from 1306 to 1329. The Robertsons were ultimately descended from Crinan, the Celtic Lord of Atholl, who died ca. 975.

As well as being the name of a sept attached to Clan Robertson many members of Clan Robertson, after the 1745 rebellion, adopted the name Donnachie, which was further anglicised to Duncan, to conceal their identity.

In the Highlands of Scotland the personal name Robert was gaelicised at an early period as Raibert, and this resulted in the surname McRobert, in Gaelic *Mac Roibeirt*, meaning 'son of Robert'. In some instances this name may have been further anglicised as Roberts and Robertson.

Movement of Scottish settlers to Ulster began in earnest from 1605 in a private enterprise colonisation of counties Antrim and Down when Sir Hugh Montgomery and Sir James Hamilton acquired title to large estates in north Down and Sir Randall MacDonnell, 1st Earl of Antrim, to large tracts of land in north Antrim.

Further impetus came in 1609 when James I adopted the policy to encourage Scottish settlers to settle on the forfeited estates of the Gaelic chiefs in counties Armagh, Cavan, Donegal, Fermanagh, Londonderry (then known as Coleraine) and Tyrone. It is estimated by 1715, when migration to Ulster had virtually stopped, the Scottish population of Ulster stood at 200,000.

ROBINSON

This name is found in all the provinces of Ireland but it is only really common in Ulster. It is among the eighty most common names in Ireland and among the first twenty in Ulster. It is very common in Counties Antrim and Down and is numerous in Counties Armagh, Tyrone and Fermanagh. This surname was brought to Ulster in large numbers by settlers from England and Scotland in the 17th century.

Robinson, derived from the personal name Robert, simply means 'son of Robin'. The personal name Robert, derived from a German personal name meaning 'bright fame', was widely introduced into England at the time of the Norman conquest in 1066. Robert became a popular choice as a child's name in the Middle Ages, and at a time when fixed surnames, based on a father's first name, were being established. Thus the surname Robinson sprang up in many different locations, independently of each other, throughout England.

Although Robinson is regarded as a surname of English origin it has become confused with Robertson which is seen as a surname of Scottish origin. Robinson is among the twenty most common names in England while Robertson is among the top ten surnames in Scotland. In Ulster, however, the surnames Robinson and Robertson were frequently interchangeable.

In addition Robinson was recorded as a surname in Scotland, in the form of John Robynson in Irvine in Ayrshire, as early as 1426. By the 16th century Robinson was a common name in Glasgow. Thus not only did the surname Robinson originate in both England and Scotland it was also used interchangeably with the surname Robertson.

The defeat of the old Gaelic order in the Nine Years War, 1594-1603 and the escape of the most prominent Gaelic Lords of Ulster in 'the Flight of the Earls' in 1607 from Lough Swilly, County Donegal were ultimately responsible for the settlement of many English and Scottish families in the northern counties of Ireland.

Movement of Scottish settlers to Ulster began in earnest from 1605 in a private enterprise colonisation of counties Antrim and Down when Sir Hugh Montgomery and Sir James Hamilton acquired title to large estates in north Down and Sir Randall MacDonnell, 1st Earl of Antrim, to large tracts of land in north Antrim.

Further impetus came in 1609 when James I adopted the policy to encourage English and Scottish settlers to settle on the forfeited estates of the Gaelic chiefs in counties Armagh, Cavan, Donegal, Fermanagh, Londonderry (then known as Coleraine) and Tyrone. Settlers came to Ulster, by and large, in three waves: with the granting of the initial leases in the period 1605 to 1625; after 1652 and Cromwell's crushing of the Irish rebellion; and finally in the fifteen years after 1690 and the Glorious Revolution.

During the famous 105 day Siege of Derry, from 18 April to 31 July 1689, George, Henry and William Robinson of County Monaghan; George and Henry Robinson of County Fermanagh; George Robinson of County Down; John Robinson of County Tyrone; and Mark and Joseph Robinson of County Cavan were recorded as 'defenders' of the city.

ROSS

In Ireland this name is common only in Ulster, where the majority live in Counties Antrim, Derry and Down. This name was brought to Ulster in large numbers by settlers from Scotland in the 17th century.

In England the surname Ross may have a number of origins: as a nickname, derived from Old French *rous*, meaning 'red-haired'; and as a place name derived from a number of places such as Ross in Herefordahire and Northumberland, Roos in the East Riding of Yorkshire and Roose in Lancashire.

In the Highlands of Scotland Clan Ross derives its name from the district of Ross. They claim descent from Ferchar Mackinsagart, son of the 'Red Priest of Applecross'. As a reward for assisting Alexander II, King of Scotland, crush a rebellion in Moray, Ferchar Mackinsagart was created Earl of Ross in 1234. The parish of Tain in Ross was famed in the 19th century for the occurrence of only two surnames – Ross and Munro - among its population.

The earliest reference to the surname, however, was in the Lowlands of Scotland in Ayrshire as in the 12th century the northern portion of this county was held by the Ros or Ross family, a Norman family from Yorkshire. Godfrey de Ros had obtained from his lord, Richard de Moreville, the lands of Stewarton in Cunningham in north Ayrshire. Ross became a common surname in Ayrshire, and this region was home to many of the Scottish settlers who came to Ulster throughout the 17th century.

Movement of Scottish settlers to Ulster began in earnest from 1605 in a private enterprise colonisation of counties Antrim and Down when Sir Hugh Montgomery and Sir James Hamilton acquired title to large estates in north Down and Sir Randall MacDonnell, 1st Earl of Antrim, to large tracts of land in north Antrim. A branch of the Ayrshire de Ros family was one of the more important settler families in 17th century County Down.

Further impetus came in 1609 when James I adopted the policy to encourage Scottish settlers to settle on the forfeited estates of the Gaelic chiefs in counties Armagh, Cavan, Donegal, Fermanagh, Londonderry (then known as Coleraine) and Tyrone.
Settlers came to Ulster, by and large, in three waves: with the granting of the initial leases in the period 1605 to 1625; after 1652 and Cromwell's crushing of the Irish rebellion; and finally in the fifteen years after 1690 and the Glorious Revolution.

Scottish families entering Ireland through the port of Londonderry settled in the Foyle Valley which includes much of the fertile lands of counties Donegal, Londonderry and Tyrone. In 1841, it was noted of the 'ancient and highly respectable' Ross family of County Londonderry, who were described as 'true as the dial to the sun', that they were chiefly settled near the town of Limavady.

During the famous 105 day Siege of Derry, from 18 April to 31 July 1689, Captain David Ross, Andrew Ross, James Ross, Francis Ross of County Monaghan, Robert Ross of County Down, James Ross of County Down, Hugh Ross of County Tyrone and Reverend Robert Ross of County Leitrim were recorded as 'defenders' of the city.

SCOBIE

This name, of Scottish origin, belongs to Counties Antrim and Londonderry.

In Scotland, this surname is derived from the lands of Scobie in Perthshire. The earliest reference to the surname is of one Andrew Scobie who was recorded as bailie (i.e. municipal magistrate) of Perth in 1369. The name was also variously spelt as Schobey, Scoby, Scobey and Scobbie.

The defeat of the old Gaelic order in the Nine Years War, 1594-1603 and the escape of the most prominent Gaelic Lords of Ulster in 'the Flight of the Earls' in 1607 from Lough Swilly, County Donegal were ultimately responsible for the settlement of many Scottish families in the northern counties of Ireland.

Movement of Scottish settlers to Ulster began in earnest from 1605 in a private enterprise colonisation of counties Antrim and Down when Sir Hugh Montgomery and Sir James Hamilton acquired title to large estates in north Down and Sir Randall MacDonnell, 1st Earl of Antrim, to large tracts of land in north Antrim.

In 1609 the Earl of Salisbury, Lord High Treasurer, suggested to James I a deliberate plantation of Scottish and English colonists on the forfeited estates of the Gaelic chiefs in counties Armagh, Cavan, Donegal, Fermanagh, Londonderry (then known as Coleraine) and Tyrone.

Settlers to Ulster came, by and large, in three waves: with the granting of the initial leases in the period 1605 to 1625; after 1652 and Cromwell's crushing of the Irish rebellion; and finally in the fifteen years after 1690 and the Glorious Revolution. It is estimated by 1715, when migration to Ulster had virtually stopped, the Scottish population of Ulster stood at 200,000.

Scottish families entering Ireland through the port of Londonderry settled in the Foyle Valley which includes much of the fertile lands of counties Donegal, Londonderry and Tyrone. The lands along the Firth of Clyde in the county of Ayrshire, the Clyde Valley and the Border Lands consisting of the counties of Wigtown, Kirkcudbright and Dumfries were home to many of these Scottish settlers.

At the time of the mid-19th century Griffith's Valuation 6 Scobie households were recorded in Ireland. This source clearly shows that the name was concentrated in north Ulster, as 4 Scobie households were residing in County Londonderry and a further 2 in the adjoining county of Antrim.

Indeed this surname was very much associated with one particular parish in County Londonderry. At the time of the 1831 census 6 Scobie households were recorded in County Londonderry and 5 of them were living in Faughanvale Parish.

It would seem that Scobies first settled in County Londonderry at the end of the 17th century as the Protestant Householders Lists of 1740 record one household headed by James Scoby residing in the townland of Whitehill in Faughanvale Parish.

SCOTT

Scott is the tenth commonest surname in Scotland. About three-quarters of the Scott families in Ireland are in Ulster where this surname came with numerous Scottish immigrants at the time of the Plantation of Ulster in the 17th century.

The term Scot originally referred to the Gaelic colonists from the ancient kingdom of Dal Riada in Ulster who established themselves, by the beginning of the 6th century, in Kintyre, Argyll and some of the Inner Isles of Scotland.

The Scotts were a border clan who trace their descent from Uchtredus filius Scoti, i.e. Uchtred son of a Scot, who lived in the 12th century. His two sons were Richard, the ancestor of the Scotts of Buccleuch, and Sir Michael, the ancestor of the Scotts of Balweary. The Scotts, based in West Teviotdale, Ewesdale and Liddesdale, were one of the most powerful of the riding or reiving clans of the Scottish Borders. The surname was also prominent on the English side of the border in Northumberland. The Scott clan could muster 600 men in battle and they had a stronghold at Branxholm Castle, near Hawick.

From the 14th to the late-17th century, the border between England and Scotland – the Debatable Lands – was a turbulent place. The Border country was ravaged by the lawless Reiver families who stole each other's cattle and possessions. They raided in large numbers, on horseback, and they killed and kidnapped without remorse. This type of life resulted in the growth of large closely-knit family groups with intense clan loyalties and fierce feuds against others.

Prior to the Union of the Crowns of England and Scotland in 1603 the Scottish Border was divided into three districts; the east, west and middle Marches. Each March was presided over by a warden who settled disputes with the warden of the appropriate March in England, as border warfare was rife at this time with frequent cattle raids. The Scotts of Buccleuch were wardens of the Middle March, which included the Sheriffdom of Selkirk. In 1532 when the then warden, Sir Walter Scott, raided England he was at the head of an army 3,000 strong.

When the power of the riding clans was broken by James I in the decade after 1603 many came to Ulster to escape persecution. This flight to Ulster also suited the needs of the king. James I, from 1610, was determined to implement a deliberate plantation of Scottish and English colonists on the forfeited estates of the Gaelic chiefs in Counties Armagh, Cavan, Donegal, Fermanagh, Londonderry (then known as Coleraine) and Tyrone.

The Scotts settled particularly in County Fermanagh. These Border families were well suited to life in the frontier of the Plantation of Ulster. They were a resilient people who stayed in County Fermanagh throughout the upheavals of the 17th century. Scottish settlers were hardier than their English counterparts, and the Borderers were even better adapted again to life on a new, insecure frontier. In 1659, Scott was listed as a 'principal name' in both Counties Antrim and Fermanagh.

At the Siege of Derry of 1689 ten Scotts, including four from County Monaghan and two from County Donegal, were recorded as 'defenders' of the city.

SCROGGIE

This name, of Scottish origin, belongs to Counties Antrim, Armagh and Tyrone.

In Scotland, this surname is derived from the village of Scroggie in Perthshire. The earliest reference to the surname is of one William Scrogy, curate, who was recorded as a witness to a charter in 1464. In the 16th century references to the surname were also recorded in Aberdeen and Edinburgh. In 1533, for example, Alexander Scrogye was recorded as minister in Auld Aberdeen. The name was also variously spelt as Scroagie, Scroggy, Scroghie and Schrogie.

Robert Scroggy and William Scroggie of Aberdeenshire were supporters of the Jacobite cause in Scotland to replace George II, King of England and Scotland, with Bonnie Prince Charlie during the rebellion of 1745.

The defeat of the old Gaelic order in the Nine Years War, 1594-1603 and the escape of the most prominent Gaelic Lords of Ulster in 'the Flight of the Earls' in 1607 from Lough Swilly, County Donegal were ultimately responsible for the settlement of many Scottish families in the northern counties of Ireland.

Movement of Scottish settlers to Ulster began in earnest from 1605 in a private enterprise colonisation of counties Antrim and Down when Sir Hugh Montgomery and Sir James Hamilton acquired title to large estates in north Down and Sir Randall MacDonnell, 1st Earl of Antrim, to large tracts of land in north Antrim.

In 1609 the Earl of Salisbury, Lord High Treasurer, suggested to James I a deliberate plantation of Scottish and English colonists on the forfeited estates of the Gaelic chiefs in counties Armagh, Cavan, Donegal, Fermanagh, Londonderry (then known as Coleraine) and Tyrone.

Settlers to Ulster came, by and large, in three waves: with the granting of the initial leases in the period 1605 to 1625; after 1652 and Cromwell's crushing of the Irish rebellion; and finally in the fifteen years after 1690 and the Glorious Revolution. It is estimated by 1715, when migration to Ulster had virtually stopped, the Scottish population of Ulster stood at 200,000.

Scottish families entering Ireland through the port of Londonderry settled in the Foyle Valley which includes much of the fertile lands of counties Donegal, Londonderry and Tyrone. The lands along the Firth of Clyde in the county of Ayrshire, the Clyde Valley and the Border Lands consisting of the counties of Wigtown, Kirkcudbright and Dumfries were home to many of these Scottish settlers.

At the time of the mid-19th century Griffith's Valuation 10 Scroggie households were recorded in Ireland. This source clearly shows that the name was concentrated in Ulster, as 4 Scroggie households were residing in County Antrim, 4 more in County Tyrone and the remaining 2 in County Armagh.

SCULLION

This name is almost exclusively found in Ulster, where it is most common in Counties Antrim and Derry.

Ireland was one of the first countries to adopt a system of hereditary surnames which developed from a more ancient system of clan or sept names. From the 11th century each family began to adopt its own distinctive family name generally derived from the first name of an ancestor who lived in or about the 10th century. The surname was formed by prefixing either Mac (son of) or O (grandson or descendant of) to the ancestor's name. Surnames in Ireland, therefore, tended to identify membership of a sept.

Scullion is derived from Gaelic *O Scollain*. In the census of 1659 Scullion, in the form of O Scullin and O Scullen, was recorded as one of the principal Irish names in the barony of Loughinsholin in south Derry. This association with south Derry is commemorated in the parish name of Ballyscullion. The Scullions were *erenaghs*, i.e. hereditary stewards, of the church lands, in the townland of Ballyscullion, which lay between the town of Bellaghy and Lough Beg.

At a very early period a monastery was founded on an island in Lough Beg, about two miles from the shore, now called Church Island. The ruins of the ancient parish church are on this island. In 1788 Frederick Hervey, the 4th Earl of Bristol and Bishop of Derry, erected close to these ruins a steeple and spire to improve the view from the mansion he had built in the townland of Ballyscullion. This magnificent mansion, for a short period, housed one of the finest collections of pictures, statues and books in Ireland. On his death in 1803 the mansion was dismantled and the materials sold.

The 1831 census for County Derry clearly demonstrates that this area of south Derry was the ancestral homeland of the Scullions. At the time of the 1831 census there were 107 Scullion households in County Derry, and all but three of these households were residing in the parishes of south Derry, centred on and surrounding the townland of Ballyscullion. At the time of the 1831 census there were 51 Scullion households recorded in Ballyscullion Parish, 18 households of the name in Maghera Parish, 12 in Termoneeny and 10 in Tamlaght O'Crilly. Indeed in 1831 there were 30 Scullion households living in the townland of Ballyscullion itself.

The escape of the most prominent Gaelic Lords of Ulster in 'the Flight of the Earls' in1607 from Lough Swilly, County Donegal marked the end of Gaelic power and paved the way for the 17th century Plantation of Ulster with English and Scottish settlers. In the centuries that followed Gaelic names were anglicised, resulting in many variant spellings of the same name and, in many cases, the dropping of the O and Mac prefixes.

Variants of Scullion now include Scullin, Scullane, Skoolin and, in some instances, Scully. In the case of Scullion the prefix O was not retained. By the time of the 1831 census the O prefix was not recorded against any of the descendants of the Scullion sept in County Derry.

SHEILS

Although the surname Sheils, and variants such as Shiels and Shields, originated in County Donegal, confusion occurs as these names also originated in both England and Scotland. In Ulster, Shields is most common in Counties Antrim and Down, and Shiels and Sheils in Counties Donegal and Derry.

Ireland was one of the first countries to adopt a system of hereditary surnames which developed from a more ancient system of clan or sept names. The surname was formed by prefixing either Mac (son of) or O (grandson or descendant of) to the ancestor's name.

Sheils is derived from Gaelic *O Siadhail,* meaning 'descendant of Siadhal'. This sept's name was usually anglicised as Shiels, Sheils and Shields rather than O'Shiel. The homeland of this sept was Inishowen in County Donegal, and they trace their descent from the 5th century High King of Ireland, Niall of the Nine Hostages, who ruled from the Hill of Tara, County Meath.

The O'Shiels were famed as a medical family. They became physicians to several great chiefs in various parts of the country. The most famous of these was Murtagh O'Shiel, hereditary physician to MacCoughlan. *The Annals of The Kingdom of Ireland by the Four Masters* (a chronicle of Irish history from 'the earliest period to the year 1616') record that, in 1548, a raid into County Offaly resulted in the death of 'the only son of Murtough O'Sheil, the best physician of his years in the neighbourhood'. The seat of the O'Shiel's family in Mac-Coughlan's country was at Ballysheil, near the River Brosna, in the parish of Gallen, County Offaly.

The anglicisation of Gaelic names, from the 17th century, resulted in many variant spellings of the same name and, in many cases, the dropping of the O and Mac prefixes. At the time of the mid-19th century Griffith's Valuation 140 Sheils households, including variant spellings of the surname, were recorded in County Donegal. This source records that in County Donegal in 1857/1858 there were 60 households recorded as Sheil, 39 as Shiel, 20 as Sheils, 20 as Shiels and one as Shields. In not once instance was the O prefix retained.

The name spread to Derry city, where it is now usually spelt as Shields, in the 19th century. As Derry developed an industrial base in shirt making, shipbuilding and distilling it attracted much of its workforce from County Donegal. In the 90-year period 1821 to 1911 the population of the city quadrupled to 40,780.

This surname was also brought to Ulster by settlers from England and Scotland in the 17th century. In Scotland the surname originated in the Borders of Scotland as a local name, derived from Old Norse *skali,* meaning 'shepherd's summer hut'. During the 15th century references to the surname can be found in both Edinburgh and Glasgow. In Scotland the name was variously recorded as Shiel, Shiels, Sheil, Sheils and Shield.

In England the surname Shields may have a number of origins: as an occupational name for a maker of shields; as a name for someone who lived near the shallow part of a river; and as a place name, i.e. North and South Shields in northern England. In England this name takes the form of either Shield or Shields.

SHIELDS

Although the surname Shields, and variants such as Sheils and Shiels, originated in County Donegal, confusion occurs as these names also originated in both England and Scotland. In Ulster, Shields is most common in Counties Antrim and Down, and Shiels and Sheils in Counties Donegal and Derry.

Ireland was one of the first countries to adopt a system of hereditary surnames which developed from a more ancient system of clan or sept names. The surname was formed by prefixing either Mac (son of) or O (grandson or descendant of) to the ancestor's name.

Shields is derived from Gaelic *O Siadhail*, meaning 'descendant of Siadhal'. This sept's name was usually anglicised as Shiels, Sheils and Shields rather than O'Shiel. The homeland of this sept was Inishowen in County Donegal, and they trace their descent from the 5th century High King of Ireland, Niall of the Nine Hostages, who ruled from the Hill of Tara, County Meath.

The O'Shiels were famed as a medical family. They became physicians to several great chiefs in various parts of the country. The most famous of these was Murtagh O'Shiel, hereditary physician to MacCoughlan. *The Annals of The Kingdom of Ireland by the Four Masters* (a chronicle of Irish history from 'the earliest period to the year 1616') record that, in 1548, a raid into County Offaly resulted in the death of 'the only son of Murtough O'Sheil, the best physician of his years in the neighbourhood'. The seat of the O'Shiel's family in Mac-Coughlan's country was at Ballysheil, near the River Brosna, in the parish of Gallen, County Offaly.

The anglicisation of Gaelic names, from the 17th century, resulted in many variant spellings of the same name and, in many cases, the dropping of the O and Mac prefixes. At the time of the mid-19th century Griffith's Valuation 140 Shields households, including variant spellings of the surname, were recorded in County Donegal. This source records that in County Donegal in 1857/1858 there were 60 households recorded as Sheil, 39 as Shiel, 20 as Sheils, 20 as Shiels and one as Shields. In not once instance was the O prefix retained.

The name spread to Derry city, where it is now usually spelt as Shields, in the 19th century. As Derry developed an industrial base in shirt making, shipbuilding and distilling it attracted much of its workforce from County Donegal. In the 90-year period 1821 to 1911 the population of the city quadrupled to 40,780.

This surname was also brought to Ulster by settlers from England and Scotland in the 17th century. In Scotland the surname originated in the Borders of Scotland as a local name, derived from Old Norse *skali*, meaning 'shepherd's summer hut'. During the 15th century references to the surname can be found in both Edinburgh and Glasgow. In Scotland the name was variously recorded as Shiel, Shiels, Sheil, Sheils and Shield.

In England the surname Shields may have a number of origins: as an occupational name for a maker of shields; as a name for someone who lived near the shallow part of a river; and as a place name, i.e. North and South Shields in northern England. In England this name takes the form of either Shield or Shields.

SIMMONS

In Ireland this name tends to be found in the provinces of Leinster and Ulster. This name was brought to Ulster by settlers from England and Scotland in the 17th century.

Simmons, derived from the personal name Simond, simply means 'son of Simond'. Simond is, in turn, derived from the Old Norse personal name *Sigmund*, meaning 'victory protector'. In the English counties of Norfolk and Lincolnshire, in particular, this personal name was introduced by the Vikings. The popularity of this personal name, resulting in the surnames of Simmonds and Simmons, was reinforced at the time of the Norman Conquest of England in 1066 as *Simund* was a common Norman name.

The personal name Simond was also confused, at an early date, with Simon. Simon is derived from the Old Testament Simeon. Simon became a popular choice as a child's name from the Middle Ages onwards, and at a time when fixed surnames, based on a father's first name, were being established. In medieval England Simond was the common form of Simon. Thus it is now impossible to distinguish between the various origins of the surname Simmons.

In Scotland, George F. Black in *The Surnames of Scotland* recorded that Simond is a name associated with Fifeshire.

Movement of Scottish settlers to Ulster began in earnest from 1605 in a private enterprise colonisation of counties Antrim and Down when Sir Hugh Montgomery and Sir James Hamilton acquired title to large estates in north Down and Sir Randall MacDonnell, 1st Earl of Antrim, to large tracts of land in north Antrim.

Further impetus came in 1609 when James I adopted the policy to encourage English and Scottish settlers to settle on the forfeited estates of the Gaelic chiefs in counties Armagh, Cavan, Donegal, Fermanagh, Londonderry (then known as Coleraine) and Tyrone. These settlers came to Ulster, by and large, in three waves: with the granting of the initial leases in the period 1605 to 1625; after 1652 and Cromwell's crushing of the Irish rebellion; and finally in the fifteen years after 1690 and the Glorious Revolution.

Scottish families entering Ireland through the port of Londonderry settled in the Foyle Valley which includes much of the fertile lands of counties Donegal, Londonderry and Tyrone. It is estimated by 1715, when migration to Ulster had virtually stopped, the Scottish population of Ulster stood at 200,000.

A significant number of Simmons in Ulster will have English ancestry. English settlers, mostly drawn from the northern counties of Cheshire, Cumberland, Lancashire, Northumberland, Yorkshire and Westmorland also migrated to Ulster during the 17th century. English settlers tended to favour settlement along the Lagan Valley, in the east of the Province, on lands straddling the borders of Counties Armagh, Antrim and Down.

During the famous 105 day Siege of Derry, from 18 April to 31 July 1689, Gunner Quartermaster Simond was recorded as a 'defender' of the city.

SIMMS

In Ireland this name is common only in Ulster and in particular in County Antrim and east Donegal. This name was brought to Ulster by settlers from England and Scotland in the 17th century.

Simms, derived from the personal name Simon, simply means 'son of Sim'. Simon is, in turn, derived from the Old Testament Simeon. Simon became a popular choice as a child's name from the Middle Ages onwards, and at a time when fixed surnames, based on a father's first name, were being established.

Simms can also be a variant of Simond which is derived either from Simon or from the Old Norse personal name *Sigmund*, meaning 'victory protector'. In England, Sim and Simm are most concentrated in the Lake District (in Cumberland) and Simms in Derbyshire and Cheshire and in the southern counties of Gloucester, Somerset and Wiltshire.

In Scotland, Sim is recognised as a sept name of Clan Fraser of Lovat, among whom the name Simon was popular. Indeed the first chief of Clan Fraser was Simon Fraser who fought for Robert the Bruce in the 14th century. From this Simon the chiefs of Clan Fraser derive their Gaelic name *Mac Shimidh*, meaning 'son of Simon', pronounced MacKimmie. MacKimmie was anglicised as Sim, Simson and Simpson.

Movement of Scottish settlers to Ulster began in earnest from 1605 in a private enterprise colonisation of counties Antrim and Down when Sir Hugh Montgomery and Sir James Hamilton acquired title to large estates in north Down and Sir Randall MacDonnell, 1st Earl of Antrim, to large tracts of land in north Antrim. The surname Simms was recorded in County Antrim from the early seventeenth century.

Further impetus came in 1609 when James I adopted the policy to encourage English and Scottish settlers to settle on the forfeited estates of the Gaelic chiefs in counties Armagh, Cavan, Donegal, Fermanagh, Londonderry (then known as Coleraine) and Tyrone. These settlers came to Ulster, by and large, in three waves: with the granting of the initial leases in the period 1605 to 1625; after 1652 and Cromwell's crushing of the Irish rebellion; and finally in the fifteen years after 1690 and the Glorious Revolution.

Scottish families entering Ireland through the port of Londonderry settled in the Foyle Valley which includes much of the fertile lands of counties Donegal, Londonderry and Tyrone. It is estimated by 1715, when migration to Ulster had virtually stopped, the Scottish population of Ulster stood at 200,000.

A significant number of Simms in Ulster will have English ancestry. English settlers, mostly drawn from the northern counties of Cheshire, Cumberland, Lancashire, Northumberland, Yorkshire and Westmorland also migrated to Ulster during the 17th century. English settlers tended to favour settlement along the Lagan Valley, in the east of the Province, on lands straddling the borders of Counties Armagh, Antrim and Down.

Several of the name were prominent United Irishmen; Robert and William Simms of Belfast were two of the founders of the Society of United Irishmen in 1791.

303

SIMPSON

In Ireland this name is common only in Ulster, where three-quarters of all Simpsons are to be found, and in particular in County Antrim. This name was brought to Ulster in large numbers by settlers from England and Scotland in the 17th century. Simpson is one of the fifty most common names in Scotland.

Simpson, derived from the personal name Simon, simply means 'son of Sim'. Simon is, in turn, derived from the Old Testament Simeon. Simon became a popular choice as a child's name from the Middle Ages onwards, and at a time when fixed surnames, based on a father's first name, were being established. In England Simpson can also be derived from one of three places of that name in Devon, all of which were previously called Siwineston.

The first record of the surname in Scotland was of a William Symsoun, burgess of Edinburgh in 1405. During the 15th century references to the surname in Scotland can be found in places as far apart as Aberdeen, Edinburgh and Lanark.

The Simpsons also flourished as a sept of Clan Fraser of Lovat, among whom the name Simon was popular. Indeed the first chief of Clan Fraser was Simon Fraser who fought for Robert the Bruce in the 14th century. From this Simon the chiefs of Clan Fraser derive their Gaelic name *Mac Shimidh*, meaning 'son of Simon', pronounced MacKimmie. MacKimmie was further anglicised as Simpson.

The Simpsons were also recorded as one of the lawless riding or reiving families of the Border country between Scotland and England who raided, on horseback, and stole each other's cattle and possessions.

Movement of Scottish settlers to Ulster began in earnest from 1605 in a private enterprise colonisation of counties Antrim and Down when Sir Hugh Montgomery and Sir James Hamilton acquired title to large estates in north Down and Sir Randall MacDonnell, 1st Earl of Antrim, to large tracts of land in north Antrim. Simpsons were recorded in County Antrim from the early seventeenth century, and the name was to become most concentrated in the barony of Lower Toome.

Further impetus came in 1609 when James I adopted the policy to encourage English and Scottish settlers to settle on the forfeited estates of the Gaelic chiefs in counties Armagh, Cavan, Donegal, Fermanagh, Londonderry (then known as Coleraine) and Tyrone. These settlers came to Ulster, by and large, in three waves: with the granting of the initial leases in the period 1605 to 1625; after 1652 and Cromwell's crushing of the Irish rebellion; and finally in the fifteen years after 1690 and the Glorious Revolution. It is estimated by 1715, when migration to Ulster had virtually stopped, the Scottish population of Ulster stood at 200,000.

A significant minority of Simpsons in Ulster will have English ancestry. English settlers, mostly drawn from the northern counties of Cheshire, Cumberland, Lancashire, Northumberland, Yorkshire and Westmorland also migrated to Ulster during the 17th century. English settlers tended to favour settlement along the Lagan Valley, in the east of the Province, on lands straddling the borders of Counties Armagh, Antrim and Down.

SMITH

Smith is the most common name in England and Wales, in Scotland and in Ulster, and is fifth in Ireland. It is the single most numerous name in County Antrim and is among the first five in Counties Down and Cavan, among the first ten in Counties Armagh, Derry, Fermanagh and Monaghan and among the first fifteen in County Tyrone. The majority of Ulster Smiths are descendants of 17th century English and Scottish settlers but there are significant local differences. In Ireland the spelling Smyth has been favoured by almost one family in three.

The surname Smith sprung up in many different locations, independently of each other, throughout England and Scotland as it was derived from an occupational name to describe a metal-worker, blacksmith or farrier. Every small community would have had a smith. In Scotland Smith was being used as a surname from the 12th century.

In the Highlands of Scotland, especially in Inverness-shire and Perthshire, Clan Gow, in Gaelic *Mac Gobha*, meaning 'son of the smith' was anglicised as Gow, McGowan and Smith. The smith was a man of importance in most clans. McGowan, in Gaelic *Mac Ghobhainn*, meaning 'son of the smith', was the name of an old Stirling family. McGowan was also common in Dumfriesshire. It can be assumed that many Scottish McGowans further anglicised their name to Smith.

In 1609 the Earl of Salisbury, Lord High Treasurer, suggested to James I a deliberate plantation of Scottish and English colonists on the forfeited estates of the Gaelic chiefs in counties Armagh, Cavan, Donegal, Fermanagh, Londonderry (then known as Coleraine) and Tyrone. Settlers to Ulster came, by and large, in three waves: with the granting of the initial leases in the period 1605 to 1625; after 1652 and Cromwell's crushing of the Irish rebellion; and finally in the fifteen years after 1690 and the Glorious Revolution. It is estimated by 1715, when migration to Ulster had virtually stopped, the Scottish population of Ulster stood at 200,000.

Scottish families entering Ireland through the port of Londonderry settled in the Foyle Valley which includes much of the fertile lands of Counties Donegal, Londonderry and Tyrone. English settlers, mostly drawn from the northern counties of Cheshire, Cumberland, Lancashire, Northumberland, Yorkshire and Westmorland tended to favour settlement along the Lagan Valley in the east of the Province on lands straddling the borders of Counties Armagh, Antrim and Down.

In County Cavan, in particular, most Smiths will be of Irish origin. The McGowan sept, in Gaelic *Mac an Ghabhann*, meaning 'son of the smith', was one of the principal septs of the ancient kingdom of Breffny, and in County Cavan the great majority of McGowans anglicised their name to Smith. In Counties Armagh and Down a distinct sept of O'Gowan, in Gaelic *O Gabhann*, has also become Smith. This sept gave their name to Ballygowan in County Down.

In Ireland the surname Smith is numerically strongest in Counties Antrim and Cavan. In the former county most Smiths will be of English or Scottish origin while in County Cavan they will be of Irish origin.

During the famous 105-day Siege of Derry, from 18 April to 31 July 1689, eighteen Smiths were recorded as 'defenders' of the city.

STARRETT

This surname is found almost exclusively in Ulster where it is most common in Counties Antrim and Londonderry. This name was brought to Ulster by settlers from Scotland in the 17th century.

In Scotland, this surname is derived from the place name of Stairaird (now known as Stirie) near Stair in Ayrshire. Ayrshire was home to many of the Scottish settlers who came to Ulster throughout the 17th century. Starrat and Stirrat were at one time common surnames in the parish of Dalry in Ayrshire. The earliest reference to the surname is of one Andreas Starheved who, in 1341, 'resigned the serjandship of Lanark in reign of David II'.

The defeat of the old Gaelic order in the Nine Years War, 1594-1603 and the escape of the most prominent Gaelic Lords of Ulster in 'the Flight of the Earls' in 1607 from Lough Swilly, County Donegal were ultimately responsible for the settlement of many Scottish families in the northern counties of Ireland.

Movement of Scottish settlers to Ulster began in earnest from 1605 in a private enterprise colonisation of counties Antrim and Down when Sir Hugh Montgomery and Sir James Hamilton acquired title to large estates in north Down and Sir Randall MacDonnell, 1st Earl of Antrim, to large tracts of land in north Antrim.

In 1609 the Earl of Salisbury, Lord High Treasurer, suggested to James I a deliberate plantation of Scottish and English colonists on the forfeited estates of the Gaelic chiefs in counties Armagh, Cavan, Donegal, Fermanagh, Londonderry (then known as Coleraine) and Tyrone.

Settlers to Ulster came, by and large, in three waves: with the granting of the initial leases in the period 1605 to 1625; after 1652 and Cromwell's crushing of the Irish rebellion; and finally in the fifteen years after 1690 and the Glorious Revolution. It is estimated by 1715, when migration to Ulster had virtually stopped, the Scottish population of Ulster stood at 200,000.

Scottish families entering Ireland through the port of Londonderry settled in the Foyle Valley which includes much of the fertile lands of counties Donegal, Londonderry and Tyrone. The lands along the Firth of Clyde in the county of Ayrshire, the Clyde Valley and the Border Lands consisting of the counties of Wigtown, Kirkcudbright and Dumfries were home to many of these Scottish settlers.

It would seem that Starrett families first settled in County Londonderry at the end of the 17th century as the Protestant Householders Lists of 1740 record six households of the name. It would appear that they settled in 2 distinct areas of the county: in south Derry in the parishes of Lissan, Maghera and Tamlaght O'Crilly; and in the farm lands, in the parishes of Clondermot and Templemore, surrounding the city of Derry.

Starrett is a common name in the city of Londonderry today. As Derry developed an industrial base in the 19th century in shirt making, shipbuilding and distilling it attracted much of its workforce from outside of the city. In the 90-year period 1821 to 1911 the population of the city quadrupled to 40,780.

306

STEPHENSON

In Ireland this name is common only in Ulster where it is most numerous in Counties Antrim, Armagh and Down. This surname was brought to Ulster by settlers from England and Scotland in the 17th century.

Although Stephenson is often regarded as a surname of English origin it has become confused with Stevenson which is frequently seen as a surname of Scottish origin. Although Stevenson is among the top seventy surnames in Scotland the surname Stephenson was also recorded there from the 15th century. In England, Stephenson is a common name in the northern counties but it mingles with and becomes less common in the Midlands and Sussex where Stevenson prevails.

Stephenson, derived from the personal name Stephen, simply means 'son of Stephen'. In Scotland Stephen was usually spelt Steven. The personal name Stephen was a popular name throughout Europe in the Middle Ages, having been borne by the first Christian martyr, stoned to death at Jerusalem three years after the death of Jesus Christ. Stephen was widely introduced into England at the time of the Norman conquest in 1066. Stephen was, therefore, a popular choice as a child's name during the period when fixed surnames, based on a father's first name, were being established. Thus the surnames Stephenson and Stevenson sprang up in many different locations, independently of each other, throughout England and Scotland from the 14th century.

Movement of Scottish settlers to Ulster began in earnest from 1605 in a private enterprise colonisation of counties Antrim and Down when Sir Hugh Montgomery and Sir James Hamilton acquired title to large estates in north Down and Sir Randall MacDonnell, 1st Earl of Antrim, to large tracts of land in north Antrim. Further impetus came in 1609 when James I adopted the policy to encourage English and Scottish settlers to settle on the forfeited estates of the Gaelic chiefs in counties Armagh, Cavan, Donegal, Fermanagh, Londonderry (then known as Coleraine) and Tyrone. Settlers to Ulster came, by and large, in three waves: with the granting of the initial leases in the period 1605 to 1625; after 1652 and Cromwell's crushing of the Irish rebellion; and finally in the fifteen years after 1690 and the Glorious Revolution. By the end of the 17th century a self-sustaining settlement of British colonists had established itself in Ulster.

During the famous 105 day Siege of Derry, from 18 April to 31 July 1689, Robert Stevenson was recorded as one of the 'defenders' of the city. Indeed the exploits of Robert Stevenson, an artillery officer, during the siege are remembered in verse:

Robert Stevenson ne'er missed the enemy
But furiously among the troops let fly.

In County Fermanagh, during the Williamite Wars of 1689-1691, another Robert Stevenson raised a company of soldiers for the defence of Enniskillen.

The surnames Steenson, Stinson and Steen, ultimately derived from the personal name Stephen, are common in Counties Antrim and Armagh. Steen and Stein are forms of Steven found principally in Scotland in Ayrshire, Fife, the Lothians and Roxburghshire, while Steenson and Stinson are variants of Stephenson.

STERLING

This surname is found almost exclusively in Ulster where it is most common in County Antrim. This name was brought to Ulster by settlers from Scotland in the 17th century.

In Scotland, this surname is derived from the town of Stirling. Stirling Castle was an important royal stronghold. The earliest reference to the surname is of one Gilbertus de Striuelin who was recorded as a witness of King David's gift of Patrick to the church of Glasgow in 1136. During the 13th century references to the surname can be found in places as far apart as Dunkeld, Glasgow, Inverkeithing, Moray and St Andrews.

The Stirlings of Keir on the outskirts of Stirling were established in the 12th century. In the family papers of the Stirlings of Keir between 1160 and 1677 their surname is spelled in no less than 64 different ways. A family of the name also settled at a very early period at Dunmaglass in Nairnshire

The defeat of the old Gaelic order in the Nine Years War, 1594-1603 and the escape of the most prominent Gaelic Lords of Ulster in 'the Flight of the Earls' in 1607 from Lough Swilly, County Donegal were ultimately responsible for the settlement of many Scottish families in the northern counties of Ireland.

Movement of Scottish settlers to Ulster began in earnest from 1605 in a private enterprise colonisation of counties Antrim and Down when Sir Hugh Montgomery and Sir James Hamilton acquired title to large estates in north Down and Sir Randall MacDonnell, 1st Earl of Antrim, to large tracts of land in north Antrim.

In 1609 the Earl of Salisbury, Lord High Treasurer, suggested to James I a deliberate plantation of Scottish and English colonists on the forfeited estates of the Gaelic chiefs in counties Armagh, Cavan, Donegal, Fermanagh, Londonderry (then known as Coleraine) and Tyrone.

Settlers to Ulster came, by and large, in three waves: with the granting of the initial leases in the period 1605 to 1625; after 1652 and Cromwell's crushing of the Irish rebellion; and finally in the fifteen years after 1690 and the Glorious Revolution. It is estimated by 1715, when migration to Ulster had virtually stopped, the Scottish population of Ulster stood at 200,000.

Sterlings settled at an early date in the parish of Ballyrashane which straddles the boundary between Counties Antrim and Derry. At the time of the Hearth Money Rolls of 1663 two households headed by James and Archibald Sterling were residing in Ballyrashane Parish. Three generations later, at the time of the Protestant Householders Lists of 1740, ten Sterling households were recorded in the parish of Ballyrashane.

During the famous 105 day Siege of Derry, from 18 April to 31 July 1689, Lieutenant Robert Sterling was recorded as one of the 'defenders' of the city.

STEVENSON

In Ireland this name is common only in Ulster where it is most numerous in Counties Antrim, Armagh and Down. This surname was brought to Ulster by settlers from England and Scotland in the 17th century.

Although Stevenson is often regarded as a surname of Scottish origin it has become confused with Stephenson which is frequently seen as a surname of English origin. Although Stevenson is among the top seventy surnames in Scotland the surname Stephenson was also recorded there from the 15th century. In England, Stephenson is a common name in the northern counties but it mingles with and becomes less common in the Midlands and Sussex where Stevenson prevails.

Stevenson, derived from the personal name Stephen, simply means 'son of Steven'. In Scotland Stephen was usually spelt Steven. The personal name Stephen was a popular name throughout Europe in the Middle Ages, having been borne by the first Christian martyr, stoned to death at Jerusalem three years after the death of Jesus Christ. Stephen was widely introduced into England at the time of the Norman conquest in 1066. Stephen was, therefore, a popular choice as a child's name during the period when fixed surnames, based on a father's first name, were being established. Thus the surnames Stevenson and Stephenson sprang up in many different locations, independently of each other, throughout England and Scotland from the 14th century.

Movement of Scottish settlers to Ulster began in earnest from 1605 in a private enterprise colonisation of counties Antrim and Down when Sir Hugh Montgomery and Sir James Hamilton acquired title to large estates in north Down and Sir Randall MacDonnell, 1st Earl of Antrim, to large tracts of land in north Antrim.

Further impetus came in 1609 when James I adopted the policy to encourage English and Scottish settlers to settle on the forfeited estates of the Gaelic chiefs in counties Armagh, Cavan, Donegal, Fermanagh, Londonderry (then known as Coleraine) and Tyrone. Settlers to Ulster came, by and large, in three waves: with the granting of the initial leases in the period 1605 to 1625; after 1652 and Cromwell's crushing of the Irish rebellion; and finally in the fifteen years after 1690 and the Glorious Revolution. By the end of the 17th century a self-sustaining settlement of British colonists had established itself in Ulster.

During the famous 105 day Siege of Derry, from 18 April to 31 July 1689, Robert Stevenson was recorded as one of the 'defenders' of the city. Indeed the exploits of Robert Stevenson, an artillery officer, during the siege are remembered in verse:

Robert Stevenson ne'er missed the enemy
But furiously among the troops let fly.

In County Fermanagh, during the Williamite Wars of 1689-1691, another Robert Stevenson raised a company of soldiers for the defence of Enniskillen.

The surnames Steenson, Stinson and Steen, ultimately derived from the personal name Stephen, are common in Counties Antrim and Armagh. Steen and Stein are forms of Steven found principally in Scotland in Ayrshire, Fife, the Lothians and Roxburghshire, while Steenson and Stinson are variants of Stephenson.

STEWART

This name is one of the sixty most common names in Ireland and one of the ten most common in Ulster. Stewart is among the first five names in County Antrim and the name is common too in Counties Down, Derry, Donegal and Tyrone. This name was brought to Ulster in large numbers by settlers from Scotland in the 17th century. It is estimated that 90 percent of Stewarts are to be found in Ulster.

Stewart is derived from the Old English *stigweard*, meaning a 'steward' or 'keeper of the house'. As every Bishop and Landlord had his 'steward' this surname soon spread throughout Scotland. Furthermore the title of 'Steward' of the royal household was applied to the person responsible for the collection of taxes and administration of justice. This person was second only in importance to the King of Scotland.

Indeed the royal line of Clan Stewart traces their descent from Walter Fitz Alan, who was granted lands in Renfrew and in Paisley in Ayrshire, and made High Steward of Scotland in the reign of David I (1124 to 1153). Walter's grandson, Walter, was the first to adopt the title 'Steward' as a surname. Robert Stewart, later Robert II, became the first King of Scotland, from 1371-1389, who belonged to the House of Stewart. Clan Stewart, based in the Lowlands of Scotland, eventually divided into separate clans: the Stewarts of Appin, of Atholl, of Bute and of Galloway. The French spelt the name as Stuart and through the fame of Mary Queen of Scots, who was brought up in France, this spelling became popular.

Movement of Scottish settlers to Ulster began in earnest from 1605 in a private enterprise colonisation of counties Antrim and Down when Sir Hugh Montgomery and Sir James Hamilton acquired title to large estates in north Down and Sir Randall MacDonnell, 1st Earl of Antrim, to large tracts of land in north Antrim. Stewarts of Bute had settled in MacDonnell territory near Ballintoy on the north Antrim coast from ca.1560.

Further impetus came in 1609 when James I adopted the policy to encourage Scottish settlers to settle on the forfeited estates of the Gaelic chiefs in counties Armagh, Cavan, Donegal, Fermanagh, Londonderry (then known as Coleraine) and Tyrone.
Settlers came to Ulster, by and large, in three waves: with the granting of the initial leases in the period 1605 to 1625; after 1652 and Cromwell's crushing of the Irish rebellion; and finally in the fifteen years after 1690 and the Glorious Revolution. It is estimated by 1715, when migration to Ulster had virtually stopped, the Scottish population of Ulster stood at 200,000.

In the initial granting of leases in Ulster in 1610/1611, ten of the principal Scottish planters (sixty-one in total) were Stewarts, and they acquired extensive estates of land in Counties Cavan, Donegal and Tyrone. Many of the settlers farming on these Scottish estates in Ulster would also have been called Stewart as it was a feature of 17th century Scotland for tenants to take on their landlord's surname.

Stewarts fought on both sides during the Siege of Derry of 1689. Twenty-one Stewarts were recorded as 'defenders' of Derry and two Stewarts served with the 'Jacobite Army'. Indeed descendants of the Stewart family of Ballintoy, County Antrim fought in both armies.

STUART

This is the French spelling of the Scottish surname Stewart. This spelling of the name became popular through the fame of the 16th century Mary Queen of Scots, who had been brought up in France. Stewart is one of the sixty most common names in Ireland and one of the ten most common in Ulster. Stewart is among the first five names in County Antrim and the name is common too in Counties Down, Derry, Donegal and Tyrone. This name was brought to Ulster in large numbers by settlers from Scotland in the 17th century. It is estimated that 90 percent of Stewarts are to be found in Ulster.

Stewart is derived from the Old English *stigweard,* meaning a 'steward' or 'keeper of the house'. As every Bishop and Landlord had his 'steward' this surname soon spread throughout Scotland. Furthermore the title of 'Steward' of the royal household was applied to the person responsible for the collection of taxes and administration of justice. This person was second only in importance to the King of Scotland.

Indeed the royal line of Clan Stewart traces their descent from Walter Fitz Alan, who was granted lands in Renfrew and in Paisley in Ayrshire, and made High Steward of Scotland in the reign of David I (1124 to 1153). Walter's grandson, Walter, was the first to adopt the title 'Steward' as a surname. Robert Stewart, later Robert II, became the first King of Scotland, from 1371-1389, who belonged to the House of Stewart. Clan Stewart, based in the Lowlands of Scotland, eventually divided into separate clans: the Stewarts of Appin, of Atholl, of Bute and of Galloway.

Movement of Scottish settlers to Ulster began in earnest from 1605 in a private enterprise colonisation of counties Antrim and Down when Sir Hugh Montgomery and Sir James Hamilton acquired title to large estates in north Down and Sir Randall MacDonnell, 1st Earl of Antrim, to large tracts of land in north Antrim. Stewarts of Bute had settled in MacDonnell territory near Ballintoy on the north Antrim coast from ca.1560.

Further impetus came in 1609 when James I adopted the policy to encourage Scottish settlers to settle on the forfeited estates of the Gaelic chiefs in counties Armagh, Cavan, Donegal, Fermanagh, Londonderry (then known as Coleraine) and Tyrone.
Settlers came to Ulster, by and large, in three waves: with the granting of the initial leases in the period 1605 to 1625; after 1652 and Cromwell's crushing of the Irish rebellion; and finally in the fifteen years after 1690 and the Glorious Revolution. It is estimated by 1715, when migration to Ulster had virtually stopped, the Scottish population of Ulster stood at 200,000.

In the initial granting of leases in Ulster in 1610/1611, ten of the principal Scottish planters (sixty-one in total) were Stewarts, and they acquired extensive estates of land in Counties Cavan, Donegal and Tyrone. Many of the settlers farming on these Scottish estates in Ulster would also have been called Stewart as it was a feature of 17th century Scotland for tenants to take on their landlord's surname.

Stewarts fought on both sides during the Siege of Derry of 1689. Twenty-one Stewarts were recorded as 'defenders' of Derry and two Stewarts served with the 'Jacobite Army'. Indeed descendants of the Stewart family of Ballintoy, County Antrim fought in both armies.

SWEENEY

Sweeney is among the sixty most common names in Ireland and it is more or less equally distributed between Munster, Connaught and Ulster. McSweeney, also spelt McSweeny and McSwiney, is now regarded as much a Cork-Kerry surname as a Donegal one, for though still common in its original territory in Ulster, it is today more numerous in the south of Ireland.

Sweeney is derived from Gaelic *Mac Suibhne*, the root word being *suibhne*, meaning 'pleasant'. The McSweeneys trace their descent form Suibhne O'Neill, a chieftain in Argyll, Scotland around 1200. The first mention of a McSweeney in the *The Annals of The Kingdom of Ireland by the Four Masters* is the death of Murrough Mac Sweeny in 1267. Murrough Mac Sweeny, grandson of Suibhne, was one of the famous McSweeney galloglasses. Derived from Gaelic *galloglach*, galloglass refers to a paid soldier, often brought over from Scotland, to fight on behalf of an Irish chief.

At the invitation of the O'Donnells the McSweeneys first settled in Fanad, which extended from Lough Swilly to Mulroy Bay, in north Donegal, and they gained territory at the expense of the O'Boyles and O'Breslins. In the 14th century the McSweeneys became established as an Irish sept in Donegal with three great septs of the name: MacSweeny Fanad, MacSweeny Banagh and MacSweeny of the Battleaxes.

From the 14th to the 17th centuries the McSweeneys, as galloglasses to the O'Donnells, were involved in many battles in Ulster. In the 16th century, in particular, the *Annals* make numerous references to the Mac Sweenys. The strongholds of the McSweeneys included Doe Castle, near Creeslough on Sheep Haven Bay and Rathmullan Castle on Lough Swilly.

According to the *Annals* in 1516 'a great war arose between O'Donnell and O'Neill; and each lord hired a great number of men.' In the same year the *Annals* record that 'the castle of Mac Sweeny Fanad, i.e. Rath-Maelain, fell'. This refers to Rathmullan. The castle of Rathmullan was soon after rebuilt by Mac Sweeny Fanad, and in 1618 this castle and a small abbey attached to it were converted into a dwelling house by the Knox family.

A branch of MacSweeny Fanad migrated to Munster, about the year 1500, to soldier for the McCarthys, and acquired territory in Muskerry, County Cork. Thomas William Sweeny (1820-1892), leader of the Fenian raid into Canada, was born in County Cork.

The escape of the most prominent Gaelic Lords of Ulster in 'the Flight of the Earls' in 1607 from Lough Swilly marked the end of Gaelic power. In the 17th and 18th centuries many descendants of the old Gaelic order in Ireland emigrated, as the so-called Wild Geese, to Europe, and, in particular, to Spain and France. Many McSweeneys distinguished themselves as soldiers in the Irish Brigades of the continent. Eleven officers called McSweeny fought in James II's army during his unsuccessful campaign in Ireland in the late-17th century. A Lieutenant Terence McSweeney of County Donegal was a Jacobite officer in James' army that besieged the city of Derry in 1689.

TAGGART

Taggart can be an Irish or a Scottish name. This name is virtually exclusive to Ulster, where it is most common in County Antrim.

Ireland was one of the first countries to adopt a system of hereditary surnames which developed from a more ancient system of clan or sept names. From the 11th century each family began to adopt its own distinctive family name generally derived from the first name of an ancestor who lived in or about the 10th century. The surname was formed by prefixing either Mac (son of) or O (grandson or descendant of) to the ancestor's name. Surnames in Ireland, therefore, tended to identify membership of a sept.

Taggart is derived from Gaelic *Mac an tSagairt*, the root word being *sagart*, meaning 'priest'. This County Fermanagh sept was based at Ballymacataggart in Derryvullan Parish where they were *erenaghs*, i.e. hereditary stewards, of the church lands.

The anglicisation of Gaelic names, from the 17th century, resulted in many variant spellings of this name which include McTaggart, McEntaggart, Attegart, Haggart, Target and Teggart. Though originating in County Fermanagh, and now chiefly located in County Antrim, this surname, and its many variant forms, was widespread, at an early period, throughout Ulster. The name appears frequently in 16th and 17th century records of Counties Antrim, Armagh, Derry, Donegal and Fermanagh.

In Scotland the Taggarts and McTaggarts, in Gaelic *Mac an tSagairt*, meaning 'son of the priest', were a sept of Clan Ross. They claim descent from Ferchar Mackinsagart, son of the 'Red Priest of Applecross'. As a reward for assisting Alexander II, King of Scotland, crush a rebellion in Moray, Ferchar Mackinsagart was created Earl of Ross in 1234.

Others may be descended from less well-known priests as 'the rule of celibacy was not strictly enforced upon the clergy of the primitive church'. From the 15th century references to the surname are found in Dumfries; in the form of Donald McKyntagart in 1459 and Patrick Taggart in 1544. Taggart became a common name in Dumfriesshire, and this region was home to many of the Scottish settlers who came to Ulster throughout the 17th century.

Movement of Scottish settlers to Ulster began in earnest from 1605 in a private enterprise colonisation of counties Antrim and Down when Sir Hugh Montgomery and Sir James Hamilton acquired title to large estates in north Down and Sir Randall MacDonnell, 1st Earl of Antrim, to large tracts of land in north Antrim. Further impetus came in 1609 when James I adopted the policy to encourage Scottish settlers to settle on the forfeited estates of the Gaelic chiefs in counties Armagh, Cavan, Donegal, Fermanagh, Londonderry (then known as Coleraine) and Tyrone.

Scottish families entering Ireland through the port of Londonderry settled in the Foyle Valley which includes much of the fertile lands of counties Donegal, Londonderry and Tyrone. It is estimated by 1715, when migration to Ulster had virtually stopped, the Scottish population of Ulster stood at 200,000.

TAYLOR

This name is common in Ulster, and in particular in Counties Antrim, Down and Derry. This name was brought to Ulster in large numbers by settlers from England and Scotland in the 17ᵗʰ century. Taylor is the fourth most common name in England and ranks among the top twenty in Scotland.

Taylor is derived from an occupational name for a tailor which originally meant a 'cutter'. With the establishment of fixed surnames, from the Middle Ages, the surname Taylor became extremely common and widespread throughout England.

In Lowland Scotland, too, Taylor was a common occupational name in early records and was first noted in 1276 when Alexander le Tayllur was valet to Alexander III, King of Scotland from 1249 to 1286. During the 13th and 14ᵗʰ centuries references to the surname in Scotland can be found in places as far apart as Angus, Dumfries, Edinburgh, Lanark, Roxburgh and Selkirk.

In the Highlands, Gaelic *Mac an tailleir*, meaning 'son of the tailor', which was a common name in Perthshire, was initially anglicised as MacIntaylor and then Taylor. The Taylors of Cowal in Argyllshire were a sept of Clan Cameron. The *Taillear dubh na tuaighe*, meaning 'Black tailor of the battle-axe', was a semi-legendary figure in Clan Cameron folklore. In addition the rare Galloway name of MacTaldrach was, in some instances, changed to Taylor.

The Taylors were also recorded as one of the lawless riding or reiving families of the Scottish Borders, residing on the English side of the frontier in the West March, who raided, on horseback, and stole each other's cattle and possessions.

Movement of Scottish settlers to Ulster began in earnest from 1605 in a private enterprise colonisation of counties Antrim and Down when Sir Hugh Montgomery and Sir James Hamilton acquired title to large estates in north Down and Sir Randall MacDonnell, 1ˢᵗ Earl of Antrim, to large tracts of land in north Antrim.

Further impetus came in 1609 when James I adopted the policy to encourage English and Scottish settlers to settle on the forfeited estates of the Gaelic chiefs in counties Armagh, Cavan, Donegal, Fermanagh, Londonderry (then known as Coleraine) and Tyrone. These settlers came to Ulster, by and large, in three waves: with the granting of the initial leases in the period 1605 to 1625; after 1652 and Cromwell's crushing of the Irish rebellion; and finally in the fifteen years after 1690 and the Glorious Revolution. It is estimated by 1715, when migration to Ulster had virtually stopped, the Scottish population of Ulster stood at 200,000.

A significant number of Taylors in Ulster will have English ancestry. English settlers, mostly drawn from the northern counties of Cheshire, Cumberland, Lancashire, Northumberland, Yorkshire and Westmorland also migrated to Ulster during the 17ᵗʰ century. English settlers tended to favour settlement along the Lagan Valley, in the east of the Province, on lands straddling the borders of Counties Armagh, Antrim and Down.

During the famous 105 day Siege of Derry, from 18 April to 31 July 1689, Captain Taylor and Richard Taylor were recorded as 'defenders' of the city.

THOMPSON

Thompson is among the fifty most common names in Ireland and among the first ten in Ulster. Three-quarters of all Thompsons in Ireland are to be found in Ulster. It is the single most numerous name in County Down, among the first five in County Antrim and among the first twenty in Counties Armagh and Fermanagh. This name was brought to Ulster in large numbers by settlers from England and Scotland in the 17ᵗʰ century.

Thompson is the fourth commonest surname in Scotland, where the more usual spelling is without the 'p', and ranks among the fifteen most common in England. Thompson, derived from the personal name Thomas, simply means 'son of Thom'. The surname Thompson became widespread throughout England, particularly around Northampton, and the Lowlands of Scotland. The first record of the surname in Scotland was of a John Thomson leader of the men of Carrick, Ayrshire in Edward Bruce's invasion of Ireland in 1318.

In the Highlands of Scotland, and particularly in Perthshire and Argyllshire, Scots Gaelic *Mac Thomais*, meaning 'son of Thomas' and *Mac Thomaidh*, meaning 'son of Tommy' were anglicised to McTavish, McThomas and Thomson. Clan MacThomas of Glenshee, a branch of Clan Mackintosh, were recognized as a clan in their own right by the end of the 16ᵗʰ century.

The Thomsons were also recorded as one of the lawless riding or reiving families of the Scottish Borders who raided, on horseback, and stole each other's cattle and possessions. These Thomsons lived in the Middle March on the English side of the Border. When the power of the riding clans was broken by James I in the decade after 1603 many came to Ulster, particularly County Fermanagh, to escape persecution.

Movement of Scottish settlers to Ulster began in earnest from 1605 in a private enterprise colonisation of counties Antrim and Down when Sir Hugh Montgomery and Sir James Hamilton acquired title to large estates in north Down and Sir Randall MacDonnell, 1ˢᵗ Earl of Antrim, to large tracts of land in north Antrim. Further impetus came in 1609 when James I adopted the policy to encourage English and Scottish settlers to settle on the forfeited estates of the Gaelic chiefs in counties Armagh, Cavan, Donegal, Fermanagh, Londonderry (then known as Coleraine) and Tyrone.

These settlers came to Ulster, by and large, in three waves: with the granting of the initial leases in the period 1605 to 1625; after 1652 and Cromwell's crushing of the Irish rebellion; and finally in the fifteen years after 1690 and the Glorious Revolution. Scottish families entering Ireland through the port of Londonderry settled in the Foyle Valley which includes much of the fertile lands of Counties Donegal, Londonderry and Tyrone. English settlers, mostly drawn from the northern counties of Cheshire, Cumberland, Lancashire, Northumberland, Yorkshire and Westmorland tended to favour settlement along the Lagan Valley in the east of the Province on lands straddling the borders of Counties Armagh, Antrim and Down.

Five Thompsons, including descendants of Hugh Thompson who was Sheriff of Derry as early as 1623, were recorded as 'defenders' of Derry during the famous Siege of 1689.

315

TOHILL

This name is almost exclusively found in Ulster, where it is most common in County Derry.

Ireland was one of the first countries to adopt a system of hereditary surnames which developed from a more ancient system of clan or sept names. From the 11th century each family began to adopt its own distinctive family name generally derived from the first name of an ancestor who lived in or about the 10th century. The surname was formed by prefixing either Mac (son of) or O (grandson or descendant of) to the ancestor's name. Surnames in Ireland, therefore, tended to identify membership of a sept.

Tohill is derived from Gaelic *O Tuathail*, the root word *tuathal*, meaning 'people mighty'. The location of this County Derry sept is indicated by the parish name of Desertoghill, meaning 'the hermitage of the O'Tuahills'. At the time of Primate John Colton's *Visitation of the Diocese of Derry* in 1397 the name of the parish was recorded as Tuahill's sanctuary.

O'Tuathghail Buidhe was the last chief who resided here as his lands were forfeited for assisting Sir Phelimy Roe O'Neill in the Rebellion of 1641. Although the power of the sept was now much reduced, descendants did remain in the area.

At the time of the 1831 census there were 31 Tohill households in County Derry, centred on and surrounding the parish of Maghera. The 1831 census records 18 Tohill households in Maghera Parish, 4 households of the name in Ballyscullion Parish, 4 in Tamlaght O'Crilly, 2 in Kilrea, 2 in Magherafelt and 1 in Desertoghill.

The escape of the most prominent Gaelic Lords of Ulster in 'the Flight of the Earls' in 1607 from Lough Swilly, County Donegal marked the end of Gaelic power and paved the way for the 17th century Plantation of Ulster with English and Scottish settlers. In the centuries that followed Gaelic names were anglicised, resulting in many variant spellings of the same name and, in many cases, the dropping of the O and Mac prefixes.

Variant spellings of Tohill recorded in the 1831 census of County Derry included Toaghill, Toghill, Tohal and Toughill. In the case of Tohill the prefix O was not retained. By the time of the 1831 census the O prefix was not recorded against any of the descendants of the Tohill sept in County Derry.

Outside of Ulster Toohill and Twohill are variants of O'Toole, also in Gaelic *O Tuathail*, the root word *tuathal*, meaning 'people mighty'. The O'Tooles were one of the great septs of the province of Leinster. Originating in County Kildare they moved to County Wicklow after the Anglo-Norman invasion of the 12th century. In County Mayo the O'Tooles were a branch of the O'Malleys. The O'Tooles were relentless in their resistance to English attempts to pacify Ireland from the late-12th century until the end of the 17th century.

TOLAN

This name originated in County Donegal. The name is now numerous in County Mayo where the name was formerly spelt as Toolan. Many Donegal names are found in Mayo as a result of considerable migration in the early seventeenth century.

Ireland was one of the first countries to adopt a system of hereditary surnames which developed from a more ancient system of clan or sept names. The surname was formed by prefixing either Mac (son of) or O (grandson or descendant of) to the ancestor's name.

Tolan is derived from Gaelic *O Tuathalain,* the root word being *tuathal,* meaning 'people mighty'. Although the homeland of this sept was the barony of Tirhugh in south Donegal there was an early reference to the name in Connaught. *The Annals of The Kingdom of Ireland by the Four Masters* (a chronicle of Irish history from 'the earliest period to the year 1616') record, in 1306, the death of Petrus O'Tuathalain, Vicar of the ancient church of Killaspugbrone in County Sligo.

Many County Donegal septs trace their lineage to Conall *Gulban,* son of the 5th century High King of Ireland, Niall of the Nine Hostages, who ruled from the Hill of Tara, County Meath. Conall and his brother Eogan conquered northwest Ireland, ca.425 AD, capturing the great hill-fort of Grianan of Ailech in County Donegal which commanded the entrance to the Inishowen peninsula between Lough Swilly and Lough Foyle.

Conall, styled 'King of Tir Conaill', established his own kingdom in County Donegal called after him Tyrconnel, i.e. the 'Land of Conall', which was the ancient name of Donegal. His descendants, known as the Cenel Conaill (the race of Conall), firmly established themselves in County Donegal while those descended from Conal's brother Eogan expanded to the east and south into Counties Derry and Tyrone.

At the time of the mid-19th century Griffith's Valuation 82 Tolan households were recorded in County Donegal. This source clearly shows that, by the middle years of the 19th century, the name was most concentrated in the Inishowen peninsula, as 53 Tolan households were residing in the parishes of the Inishowen district of Donegal. In other words 65% of descendants of the Tolan sept in County Donegal were living in this district. Tolans were most concentrated in the parish of Clonmany which, at this time, was home to 32 households of the name.

Tolan, in the form of Toland, is a common name in the city of Derry today. This name illustrates the very close links, both historic and economic, between the city of Derry and County Donegal and, in particular, the Inishowen peninsula. As Derry developed an industrial base in the 19th century in shirt making, shipbuilding and distilling it attracted much of its workforce from Inishowen. In the 90-year period 1821 to 1911 the population of the city quadrupled to 40,780.

This surname has been established in County Mayo since the early 17th century. The O'Toolans migrated, like many other Donegal families, to Mayo with some of the leading O'Donnells in 1602.

TONER

The name Toner is found almost exclusively in Ulster, particularly in counties Derry and Armagh.

The Toner sept trace their lineage to Eogan, son of the 5th century High King of Ireland, Niall of the Nine Hostages, who ruled from the Hill of Tara, County Meath. Eogan and his brother Conall *Gulban* conquered northwest Ireland, ca.425 AD, capturing the great hill-fort of Grianan of Ailech in County Donegal.

Eogan, styled 'King of Ailech', established his own kingdom in the peninsula in County Donegal still called after him Inishowen (Innis Eoghain or Eogan's Isle). His descendants, known as the Cenel Eoghain (the race of Owen), became the principal branch of the Northern Ui Neill (descendants of Niall of the Nine Hostages). The Cenel Eoghain in the next five centuries expanded to the east and south from their focal point in Inishowen.

Ireland was one of the first countries to adopt a system of hereditary surnames which developed from a more ancient system of clan or sept names. From the 11th century each family began to adopt its own distinctive family name generally derived from the first name of an ancestor who lived in or about the 10th century. The surname was formed by prefixing either Mac (son of) or O (grandson or descendant of) to the ancestor's name. Surnames in Ireland, therefore, tended to identify membership of a sept.

The Toners take their name from Tomar, which in turn was derived from a Norse personal name, and were thus in Gaelic *O Tomhrair*, i.e. descendant of Tomar. It was not unusual when Gaels married women of Norse stock to baptise some of their children with Norse names.

The O'Toners were one of the leading septs of Clan Binny (*Eochaid Binnigh* was a son of Eogan) possessing territory on the banks of the River Foyle near Lifford in County Donegal.

The first outward thrust of the Owen clan was that of Clan Binny in the 6th century AD who thrust southeast into County Tyrone, bypassing a hard core of resistance in County Derry of the Cianachta, as far as the river Blackwater on the borders of Tyrone and Armagh. Clan Binny eventually ousted the Oriella clans from the district lying west of the river Bann from Coleraine to beside Lough Neagh, and drove them across the river.

In the course of time the Toners moved eastwards into County Derry and thence to Armagh, where Toner appears as a 'principal name' in the census of 1659.

A few Toners in Ulster may be of English origin where the surname was derived from le Toner, signifying 'dweller by the farm or village'.

WALKER

This name is common in Ulster, where over half of all Walkers in Ireland are to be found, and in particular in Counties Antrim, Down and Derry. This name was brought to Ulster in large numbers by settlers from England and Scotland in the 17th century. Walker is among the twenty most common names in England and Wales and the thirty most common in Scotland.

Walker is derived from an Old English word for a fuller. In medieval times it was the fuller's job to scour and thicken cloth by 'walking' or trampling upon it in a trough filled with water. With the establishment of fixed surnames, from the Middle Ages, the surname Walker became widespread throughout England, particularly in the north and Midlands. The surname was most concentrated in the counties of Durham, Yorkshire, Derby and Nottingham. In some cases the name is derived from the Northumberland place name of Walker, which means 'marsh by the Roman wall'.

The name was first recorded in the Lowlands of Scotland in 1324. During the 15th and 16th centuries references to the surname in Scotland can be found in places as far apart as Edinburgh, Glasgow and Perth. In the Highlands Walker is derived from Gaelic *Mac an fhucadair*, meaning 'son of the fuller of cloth'. Now anglicised as Walker this name was initially anglicised as MacNucator and, in some cases, as MacKnocker.

Movement of Scottish settlers to Ulster began in earnest from 1605 in a private enterprise colonisation of counties Antrim and Down when Sir Hugh Montgomery and Sir James Hamilton acquired title to large estates in north Down and Sir Randall MacDonnell, 1st Earl of Antrim, to large tracts of land in north Antrim.

Further impetus came in 1609 when James I adopted the policy to encourage English and Scottish settlers to settle on the forfeited estates of the Gaelic chiefs in counties Armagh, Cavan, Donegal, Fermanagh, Londonderry (then known as Coleraine) and Tyrone. These settlers came to Ulster, by and large, in three waves: with the granting of the initial leases in the period 1605 to 1625; after 1652 and Cromwell's crushing of the Irish rebellion; and finally in the fifteen years after 1690 and the Glorious Revolution. It is estimated by 1715, when migration to Ulster had virtually stopped, the Scottish population of Ulster stood at 200,000.

A significant number of Walkers in Ulster will have English ancestry. English settlers, mostly drawn from the northern counties of Cheshire, Cumberland, Lancashire, Northumberland, Yorkshire and Westmorland also migrated to Ulster during the 17th century. English settlers tended to favour settlement along the Lagan Valley, in the east of the Province, on lands straddling the borders of Counties Armagh, Antrim and Down.

The most famous bearer of this name in Ulster history was that of Reverend George Walker, Rector of Donaghmore, County Tyrone, who was Governor of Derry, in 1689, during the famous 105 day Siege of Derry. George Walker's great grandfather was Thomas Walker who was born ca. 1538 at Ruddington in Nottinghamshire, England. Appointed Bishop of Derry by a grateful King William III, George Walker was killed at the Battle of the Boyne on 1 July 1690.

319

WARD

Ward can be an Irish or an English name. This name is common in every province in Ireland but it is most numerous in Ulster, where it is among the ten most common names in County Donegal and among the first twenty in County Monaghan. In Ulster the majority of Wards will be of Irish stock.

Ireland was one of the first countries to adopt a system of hereditary surnames which developed from a more ancient system of clan or sept names. From the 11th century each family began to adopt its own distinctive family name generally derived from the first name of an ancestor who lived in or about the 10th century. The surname was formed by prefixing either Mac (son of) or O (grandson or descendant of) to the ancestor's name. Surnames in Ireland, therefore, tended to identify membership of a sept.

Ward is derived from Gaelic *Mac an Bhaird*, meaning 'son of the bard'. There were two noted poet septs of this name, one in Ulster and the other in Connaught. The County Galway Wards, based near Ballinasloe, were hereditary poets to the O'Kellys.

Ulster Wards will be descended from the County Donegal sept of the name. They were hereditary bards to the O'Donnells, the pre-eminent family in Donegal from the thirteenth to the seventeenth century. This Ward sept was based at Lettermacaward near Glenties. A branch of the sept also became poets to the O'Neills of Tyrone.

The name was initially anglicised as Macanward, then MacAward, then Ward. Eight Macanwards of this Donegal sept were notable poets in the 17th century. Hugh Boy Macanward, who was born at Lettermacaward in 1580, was appointed, in 1616, the first Professor of Theology in the Irish College at Louvain in Belgium.

In the 17th and 18th centuries many descendants of the old Gaelic order in Ireland emigrated, as the so-called Wild Geese, to Europe, and, in particular, to Spain and France. General Thomas Ward (1749-1794) served with distinction in the French army.

Ward is one of the thirty most common names in England where it is derived from an occupational name, from Old English *weard*, meaning 'watchman'. This name was brought to Ulster by settlers from England in the 17th century. English settlers, mostly drawn from the northern counties of Cheshire, Cumberland, Lancashire, Northumberland, Yorkshire and Westmorland tended to settle along the Lagan Valley, in the east of the Province, on lands straddling the borders of Counties Armagh, Antrim and Down.

The Wards of Bangor and of Castleward, County Down, the head of which family is Viscount Bangor, are of English origin. They trace their descent from Sir Thomas Ward of Cheshire, Surveyor-General of Ireland in 1570, who purchased the Castleward estate. Seven Wards, including Bernard Ward of Castleward, grandfather of the first Viscount Bangor, were recorded as 'defenders' of Derry during the famous 105 day Siege of Derry, from 18 April to 31 July 1689.

In Scotland, Gaelic *Mac a Bhaird*, meaning 'son of the bard' was anglicised initially as MacWard and then as Baird. It was not anglicised as Ward.

320

WATSON

In Ireland this name is almost exclusive to Ulster. It is one of the ten most common names in County Armagh and is numerous in Counties Antrim and Down. This name was brought to Ulster in large numbers by settlers from England and Scotland in the 17th century. Most Watsons in Ulster will be of Scottish origin.

Watson is one of the thirty most common names in Scotland and one of the fifty most common in England and Wales. Watson, derived from the personal name Walter, simply means 'son of Wat'. The surname Watson became widespread throughout England, especially in north England, and the Lowlands of Scotland. The first record of the surname in Scotland was of a John Watson who held land in Edinburgh in 1392.

In the 16th and 17th centuries the name was common throughout the Lowlands of Scotland, and it became one of the most common surnames in the northeastern counties of Aberdeenshire and Banffshire. In the Highlands of Scotland Watt, McWatt and Watson have become confused as the McWatt sept attached to Clan Forbes and the McWattie sept attached to Clan Buchanan have anglicised their name to Watson.

The Watsons were also recorded as one of the lawless riding or reiving families of the Border country between Scotland and England who raided, on horseback, and stole each other's cattle and possessions. When the power of the riding clans was broken by James I in the decade after 1603 many came to Ulster to escape persecution.

Movement of Scottish settlers to Ulster began in earnest from 1605 in a private enterprise colonisation of counties Antrim and Down when Sir Hugh Montgomery and Sir James Hamilton acquired title to large estates in north Down and Sir Randall MacDonnell, 1st Earl of Antrim, to large tracts of land in north Antrim. In County Antrim the Watsons were most concentrated in the barony of Upper Massereene. In County Down the name was most concentrated in the baronies of Lower Iveagh and Upper Ards.

Further impetus came in 1609 when James I adopted the policy to encourage English and Scottish settlers to settle on the forfeited estates of the Gaelic chiefs in counties Armagh, Cavan, Donegal, Fermanagh, Londonderry (then known as Coleraine) and Tyrone.

These settlers came to Ulster, by and large, in three waves: with the granting of the initial leases in the period 1605 to 1625; after 1652 and Cromwell's crushing of the Irish rebellion; and finally in the fifteen years after 1690 and the Glorious Revolution. Scottish families entering Ireland through the port of Londonderry settled in the Foyle Valley which includes much of the fertile lands of Counties Donegal, Londonderry and Tyrone. English settlers, mostly drawn from the northern counties of Cheshire, Cumberland, Lancashire, Northumberland, Yorkshire and Westmorland tended to favour settlement along the Lagan Valley in the east of the Province on lands straddling the borders of Counties Armagh, Antrim and Down.

During the famous 105 day Siege of Derry, from 18 April to 31 July 1689, Alexander Watson, Captain of the Artillery, and George Watson were recorded as 'defenders' of the city.

WHITE

White can be of Irish, English or Scottish origin. This name is one of the fifty most common names in Ireland and it is very common in Leinster, Munster, and Ulster, where it is most numerous in Counties Antrim and Down.

Irish names that contain either *ban* or *geal,* which both mean 'white', were often anglicised as White. Thus Irish surnames such as Bawn of County Down; Galligan of County Cavan; and Kilbane of County Sligo were further anglicised as White.

White is one of the twenty-five most common names in England and Wales. In England the surname White may have a number of origins: as a nickname, from Old English *hwit,* denoting a person of fair hair or complexion; as a local name, from Old English *wiht,* for someone who lived by a bend in a river or road; and as a local name, from Old English *wait,* for someone who lived by a look-out post.

White was introduced into Ireland at the time of the Anglo-Norman invasion of the 12th century, and by the 14th century it had become numerous in every province. The Whites who settled in County Down in the 14th century were to become Lords of Dufferin.

White is one of the forty-five most common names in Scotland. In the Lowlands of Scotland the majority of Whites derive their surname from the nickname for a person of fair hair or complexion. In the Highlands of Scotland White is derived from Gaelic *Mac Gille Bhain,* meaning 'son of the fair youth or servant'. White was also one of the names adopted by both the McGregors and Lamonts, in the early 17th century, when they were outlawed and their names were proscribed.

Movement of Scottish settlers to Ulster began in earnest from 1605 in a private enterprise colonisation of counties Antrim and Down when Sir Hugh Montgomery and Sir James Hamilton acquired title to large estates in north Down and Sir Randall MacDonnell, 1st Earl of Antrim, to large tracts of land in north Antrim. By the mid-19th century the Whites were concentrated in the barony of Lower Antrim in County Antrim, and in the Ards peninsula in County Down.

Further impetus came in 1609 when James I adopted the policy to encourage English and Scottish settlers to settle on the forfeited estates of the Gaelic chiefs in counties Armagh, Cavan, Donegal, Fermanagh, Londonderry (then known as Coleraine) and Tyrone.

Settlers came to Ulster, by and large, in three waves: with the granting of the initial leases in the period 1605 to 1625; after 1652 and Cromwell's crushing of the Irish rebellion; and finally in the fifteen years after 1690 and the Glorious Revolution. By the end of the 17th century a self-sustaining settlement of British colonists had established itself in Ulster.

During the famous 105 day Siege of Derry, from 18 April to 31 July 1689, ten Whites, including Reverend Fulke White of Whitehall, County Antrim, Francis and John White of County Tyrone, Thomas White of County Cavan and David White of County Down were recorded as 'defenders' of the city.

WILLIAMS

In Ireland Williams is more common in Leinster and Munster than in Ulster. In Ulster the name is more common in County Antrim than elsewhere. It is believed that most Williams will be of either English or Welsh origin. Williams is the third most common name in England and Wales behind Smith and Jones. Williams was never common in Scotland which retained the longer form of Williamson.

Williams, derived from the personal name William, simply means 'son of William'. The personal name William derives from the Old German *Willihelm* and when introduced into Britain at the time of the Norman conquest in 1066, it became the single most popular personal name in England and remained so until it was superseded by John. The surname Williams became widespread throughout England.
In Wales and on its border with England William was made Gwilym, which became the surname Gwilliams and then Williams. Many families in Wales didn't adopt fixed surnames until the first half of the 19th century, and when they did, Williams, meaning 'son of Gwilym', became popular.

The defeat of the old Gaelic order in the Nine Years War, 1594-1603 and the escape of the most prominent Gaelic Lords of Ulster in 'the Flight of the Earls' in 1607 from Lough Swilly, County Donegal were ultimately responsible for the settlement of many English, Welsh and Scottish families in the northern counties of Ireland.

In 1609 the Earl of Salisbury, Lord High Treasurer, suggested to James I a deliberate plantation of English, Welsh and Scottish colonists on the forfeited estates of the Gaelic chiefs in counties Armagh, Cavan, Donegal, Fermanagh, Londonderry (then known as Coleraine) and Tyrone.

Settlers came to Ulster, by and large, in three waves: with the granting of the initial leases in the period 1605 to 1625; after 1652 and Cromwell's crushing of the Irish rebellion; and finally in the fifteen years after 1690 and the Glorious Revolution. By the end of the 17th century a self-sustaining settlement of British colonists had established itself in Ulster.

Londonderry, Coleraine, Carrickfergus, Belfast and Donaghadee were the main ports of entry into the province of Ulster for 17th century British settlers with the Lagan, Bann and the Foyle valleys acting as the major arteries along which the colonists travelled into the interior. English settlers, mostly drawn from the northern counties of Cheshire, Cumberland, Lancashire, Northumberland, Yorkshire and Westmorland, and Welsh settlers tended to favour settlement along the Lagan Valley, in the east of the Province, on lands straddling the borders of Counties Armagh, Antrim and Down.

English settlers were particularly prominent in the early years of the Plantation of Ulster. The upheavals of the 1641 rebellion and the Williamite Wars of 1689 to 1691 tended to discourage English settlers more than Scottish settlers. When large scale migration to Ulster resumed in the years after 1652 and 1690 it was Scottish Presbyterian settlers who were more prominent.

During the famous 105 day Siege of Derry, from 18 April to 31 July 1689, John Williams of County Tyrone and William Williams were recorded as 'defenders' of the city.

WILLIAMSON

In Ireland Williamson is almost exclusive to Ulster and is most common in Counties Antrim, Derry, Armagh and Tyrone. This name was brought to Ulster in large numbers by settlers from Scotland in the 17th century. Most Williamsons in Ulster will be of Scottish origin.

Williamson, derived from the personal name William, simply means 'son of William'.
The surname Williamson sprang up in many different locations, independently of each other, in Scotland. This name became very common in the Lowlands of Scotland.

The Highland name MacWilliam, in Gaelic *Mac Uilleim*, meaning 'son of William', was also anglicised to Williamson. The McWilliams trace their descent from William MacLeod, fifth chief of Clan MacLeod. MacWilliams or Williamsons also flourished as a sept of Clan Gunn in Caithness and Sutherland, tracing their descent through a chief of the clan called William. There were also Williamsons in Caithness, a sept of Clan Mackay.

Movement of Scottish settlers to Ulster began in earnest from 1605 in a private enterprise colonisation of counties Antrim and Down when Sir Hugh Montgomery and Sir James Hamilton acquired title to large estates in north Down and Sir Randall MacDonnell, 1st Earl of Antrim, to large tracts of land in north Antrim.

Further impetus came in 1609 when James I adopted the policy to encourage Scottish settlers to settle on the forfeited estates of the Gaelic chiefs in counties Armagh, Cavan, Donegal, Fermanagh, Londonderry (then known as Coleraine) and Tyrone.
These settlers came to Ulster, by and large, in three waves: with the granting of the initial leases in the period 1605 to 1625; after 1652 and Cromwell's crushing of the Irish rebellion; and finally in the fifteen years after 1690 and the Glorious Revolution.

Scottish families entering Ireland through the port of Londonderry settled in the Foyle Valley which includes much of the fertile lands of counties Donegal, Londonderry and Tyrone. The lands along the Firth of Clyde in the county of Ayrshire, the Clyde Valley and the Border Lands consisting of the counties of Wigtown, Kirkcudbright and Dumfries were home to many of these Scottish settlers. It is estimated by 1715, when migration to Ulster had virtually stopped, the Scottish population of Ulster stood at 200,000.

Some Williamsons in Ulster may have English ancestry although Williams, rather than Williamson, was the most common form of the name in England. Williams is the third most common name in England. Williams was never common in Scotland which retained the longer Williamson. English settlers, mostly drawn from the northern counties of Cheshire, Cumberland, Lancashire, Northumberland, Yorkshire and Westmorland also migrated to Ulster during the 17th century. English settlers tended to favour settlement along the Lagan Valley, in the east of the Province, on lands straddling the borders of Counties Armagh, Antrim and Down.

During the famous 105 day Siege of Derry, from 18 April to 31 July 1689, one of the 'defenders' of the city was recorded as Joseph Williamson of County Armagh.

324

WILSON

This name is one of the thirty most common names in Ireland and the third most common in Ulster. Wilson is among the first five names in County Antrim and the first ten in Counties Down, Fermanagh and Tyrone. This name was brought to Ulster in large numbers by settlers from Scotland in the 17th century. It is estimated that 80 percent of the Ulster Wilsons are of Scottish origin.

Wilson is among the first ten names in Scotland and the first fifteen in England. The surname Wilson sprang up in many different locations, independently of each other, in both England and Scotland. Wilson, derived from the personal name William, simply means 'son of Will'.

In Scotland, prominent Wilson families were recorded in the 15th century in Irvine and Berwick. Around the same time the Wilsons also flourished as a sept of Clan Gunn in Caithness and Sutherland, tracing their descent through George Gunn's son William. The name became common all over the Lowlands of Scotland, particularly in Glasgow, during the 16th century. Around Banffshire and Edinburgh the Wilsons were a sept of Clan Innes. The Wilsons were also recorded as one of the lawless riding or reiving families of the Border country between Scotland and England who raided, on horseback, and stole each other's cattle and possessions.

Movement of Scottish settlers to Ulster began in earnest from 1605 in a private enterprise colonisation of counties Antrim and Down when Sir Hugh Montgomery and Sir James Hamilton acquired title to large estates in north Down and Sir Randall MacDonnell, 1st Earl of Antrim, to large tracts of land in north Antrim. Further impetus came in 1609 when James I adopted the policy to encourage Scottish settlers to settle on the forfeited estates of the Gaelic chiefs in counties Armagh, Cavan, Donegal, Fermanagh, Londonderry (then known as Coleraine) and Tyrone.

These settlers came to Ulster, by and large, in three waves: with the granting of the initial leases in the period 1605 to 1625; after 1652 and Cromwell's crushing of the Irish rebellion; and finally in the fifteen years after 1690 and the Glorious Revolution. Scottish families entering Ireland through the port of Londonderry settled in the Foyle Valley which includes much of the fertile lands of counties Donegal, Londonderry and Tyrone. The lands along the Firth of Clyde in the county of Ayrshire, the Clyde Valley and the Border Lands consisting of the counties of Wigtown, Kirkcudbright and Dumfries were home to many of these Scottish settlers. It is estimated by 1715, when migration to Ulster had virtually stopped, the Scottish population of Ulster stood at 200,000.

A significant minority of Wilsons in Ulster will have English ancestry. English settlers, mostly drawn from the northern counties of Cheshire, Cumberland, Lancashire, Northumberland, Yorkshire and Westmorland also migrated to Ulster during the 17th century. English settlers tended to favour settlement along the Lagan Valley, in the east of the Province, on lands straddling the borders of Counties Armagh, Antrim and Down.

Nine Wilsons, including Captain Frank Wilson whose name is honoured in the memorial window in St Columb's Cathedral, Londonderry, were recorded as 'defenders' of Derry during the famous Siege of 1689.

YOUNG

This name is common in Leinster and Munster, but two-thirds of the Youngs in Ireland are in Ulster. It is most numerous in Counties Antrim, Tyrone, Down and Derry. This name was brought to Ulster in large numbers by settlers from England and Scotland in the 17th century. The majority of Ulster Youngs are of Scottish origin.

The name in both England and Scotland derives from the Old English *geong*, meaning 'young', and was used to distinguish a father and son of the same Christian name. In England this name was most numerous in County Durham and in the Southwest of the country. The name was first introduced to Ireland, as le Jeune, at the time of the Anglo-Norman invasion in the 12th century.

Young is one of the twenty most common names in Scotland. In the 14th and 15th centuries references to the surname can be found in places as far apart as Aberdeen, Dumbarton, Edinburgh, Fife, Glasgow, Moffat and Orkney. The Youngs were also recorded as one of the lawless riding or reiving families of the Border country between Scotland and England who raided, on horseback, and stole each other's cattle and possessions. These Youngs lived in East Teviotdale in the Scottish Middle March. When the power of the riding clans was broken by James I in the decade after 1603 many came to Ulster, particularly County Fermanagh, to escape persecution.

Movement of Scottish settlers to Ulster began in earnest from 1605 in a private enterprise colonisation of counties Antrim and Down when Sir Hugh Montgomery and Sir James Hamilton acquired title to large estates in north Down and Sir Randall MacDonnell, 1st Earl of Antrim, to large tracts of land in north Antrim. Further impetus came in 1609 when James I adopted the policy to encourage English and Scottish settlers to settle on the forfeited estates of the Gaelic chiefs in counties Armagh, Cavan, Donegal, Fermanagh, Londonderry (then known as Coleraine) and Tyrone.

Settlers came to Ulster, by and large, in three waves: with the granting of the initial leases in the period 1605 to 1625; after 1652 and Cromwell's crushing of the Irish rebellion; and finally in the fifteen years after 1690 and the Glorious Revolution. Scottish families entering Ireland through the port of Londonderry settled in the Foyle Valley which includes much of the fertile lands of counties Donegal, Londonderry and Tyrone. It is estimated by 1715, when migration to Ulster had virtually stopped, the Scottish population of Ulster stood at 200,000.

English settlers, mostly drawn from the northern counties of Cheshire, Cumberland, Lancashire, Northumberland, Yorkshire and Westmorland tended to favour settlement along the Lagan Valley, in the east of the Province, on lands straddling the borders of Counties Armagh, Antrim and Down.

Six Youngs, including descendants of the Scottish Youngs of Coolkeeragh, County Derry and the English (Devonshire) Youngs of Culdaff, County Donegal, were recorded as 'defenders' of Derry during the famous 105 day Siege of 1689.

A few Youngs in Ulster may be of Irish origin as the Gaelic epithet *og*, meaning 'young', occasionally gave rise to Young as a surname.